Hans van Dijk | Dai Hanzhi
A Life with Art in China
1986–2002

By Marianne Brouwer

Ullens Center for Contemporary Art
Witte de With Center for Contemporary Art

Table of Contents

Defne Ayas and Philip Tinari

Foreword

In 2014, Witte de With Center for Contemporary Art in Rotterdam and Ullens Center for Contemporary Art (UCCA) in Beijing, devoted part of their year's program to explore the legacy of the curator, art historian, and gallerist Hans van Dijk, who played a seminal role in the development of Chinese contemporary art during the time he resided there from the mid-1980s until his passing in 2002. When curator Marianne Brouwer approached us with her plans for a research project and exhibition exploring van Dijk's momentous and complex legacy, we immediately agreed to co-commission the exhibition, build a platform around it, and devote the necessary time and space to this important student, mentor, and champion of the Chinese contemporary art scene. Leading up to the show and to this volume, we were delighted the project could be mounted as a collaboration between an institution in van Dijk's native country and another in his adopted home. We set out to make this project a reality, with the hope that it would generate significant interest—the kind that van Dijk deserves—internationally and locally in the Netherlands and China.

Witte de With's goal in working on van Dijk's legacy was urgent and explicit: to introduce him to an international context—and especially to his homeland within the North European context—which had formed him as an artist and a thinker but which he left behind in moving to China. We were convinced of the necessity to show his contribution to audiences in his birthplace, where he had been little recognized. We also hoped to use his practice to give attention to the Chinese artists and related histories with which he was most closely associated, and that are under-recognized outside the country, especially in Europe. UCCA was particularly drawn to van Dijk given he, like the Ullens family, is from the Low Countries and likewise sought to make sense of the art scene he encountered and to connect it to networks beyond China. We also saw this project as a way to move beyond an often monolithic and unidirectional art historical narrative of "Chinese contemporary art" and toward the kind of nodal, contextual research that we believe has become increasingly important and convincing. With these ideas in mind, the two institutions decided to present, under the guidance of Brouwer, an exhibition that would have different manifestations according to the specific context of each city and venue.

Numerous partners, organizations, and stakeholders were invited to join our effort. Apart from Witte de With and UCCA, fundamental support for the project came from Asia Art Archive, Hong Kong, which was then digitizing van Dijk's copious archive and made these materials available to us. Cultural agents including Zhang Wei and Hu Fang of Vitamin Creative Space in Beijing and Guangzhou, and BizArt Art Center founder Davide Quadrio in Shanghai—who had worked in different capacities with and for van Dijk in their early careers—joined us. In van Dijkian spirit, their art spaces combine an adventurous curatorial voice with strong business savvy, bringing attention and resources to some of China's most innovative and rigorous art practices. They each made distinct contributions to this project that convey their affection and respect for van Dijk, even if they were all a bit uncertain whether such homage could ever do him justice. Andreas Schmid, the German artist and curator with whom van Dijk co-curated *China Avant-garde*—the seminal exhibition of new art and culture from China that opened at Berlin's Haus der Kulturen der Welt in 1993 and went on to venues in Rotterdam, Oxford, Odense, and Hildesheim—offered the uniquely valuable perspective of a peer and collaborator.

The exhibition *Hans van Dijk: 5000 Names* at UCCA (24 May–10 August 2014) included works and archival materials from across China, representing many of the artists with whom van Dijk had developed close relationships of mentorship and patronage. Brouwer curated it as an artistic biography, starting with van Dijk's own early works, and moving nimbly first through the period in the mid-1980s when he moved to Nanjing and quickly found his way to the avant-garde work being made at the academy there, and in nearby Hangzhou and Shanghai. It then covered the aftermath of 1989, when Van Dijk, after a brief hiatus, came back to China to work on *China Avant-garde*. Further sections looked at the period of 1994 to 1996, when van Dijk set up his New Amsterdam Art Consultancy and organized exhibitions all over Beijing, as well as in Europe, and the rather sad period between 1996 and 1998, when several major projects fell through for political reasons and many more straightforwardly commercial galleries arrived on the scene. Final sections examined the exhibitions he made with Ai Weiwei at the China Art Archives and Warehouse (established in 1998), and works made in homage and remembrance, direct and indirect, to his work and legacy.

The exhibition *Dai Hanzhi: 5000 Artists* at Witte de With (4 September 2014–4 January 2015) focused on van Dijk's early activities in his home country, but also saw loans gathered from collectors and galleries throughout Europe, allowing the institution to further show works by artists Zheng Guogu, Wang Xingwei, Duan Jianyu, and Ding Yi, which were mostly made in recent years, as the curatorial logic was to show evolution in the individual practices of the artists that van Dijk worked with closely. For the exhibition at Witte de With, Brouwer also located the Ming-inspired Rietveld-style tables and stools that van Dijk designed, along with photographs of his student life in Brabant and his academic writings that were published by Leiden University. A banner traversed Witte de With's four floors that illustrated a multi-colored database interface of van Dijk's own making—a compendium of over 5000 artists' names, dates, exhibitions, and publications that was his magnum opus. Uncovered by Brouwer, this database inspired the exhibition's title. The exhibition included further works by artists Ni Haifeng, Meng Huang, Liu Ding, Huang Yong Ping, and Geng Jianyi. A room curated by Shi Yong and Davide Quadrio showed BizArt's documentation of its experimental exhibitions in Shanghai during the early 2000s, along with a display of its *Dial 62761232* (2006), in which artists contributed works to a parcel delivered from one to the next by a local courier service. All in all, this was an encyclopedic, resourceful, and fulfilling undertaking for Witte de With to share with others in Rotterdam and abroad.

Taking inspiration from, and hopefully expanding upon the two exhibitions, this book illustrates and documents the recent history of contemporary art in China through the lens of van Dijk's extraordinary life and work. Including never before published correspondences between van Dijk and artists such as Ding Yi, Wang Xingwei, and Huang Yong Ping, unique historical photographs and documents, as well as a full-length scholarly essay about the history of Chinese modern and contemporary art written by van Dijk, the publication outlines his seminal role in and influence on a field and an art world that has grown exponentially in the years since his untimely passing.

Above all, we would like to thank Marianne Brouwer, curator of the two exhibitions and author of this publication, for her thorough and sensitive research, her tireless dedication to the project, and her devoted effort to make it a reality, along with all the artists, whose commitment to participate in the project sometimes came at the cost of personal and professional difficulties. We would like to also thank Samuel Saelemakers and Paul van Gennip of Witte de With and May Xue, Joanna Lee, Dong Shuo, Zoe Diao, Kong Lingyi, Patrick Rhine, Winnie Hu, Venus Lau, Robin Peckham, Ray Wang, and the late Yi Zhanpo of UCCA. Zhang Li and Andreas Schmid provided valuable curatorial advice. We extend our gratitude to Claire Hsu, Anthony Yung, Fiona He, and Hammad Nasar of Asia Art Archive who generously shared their research with us, and Pascale Geulleaume, who made van Dijk's physical office and files available for research and display. In addition, the van Dijk family for lending us their wisdom and counsel.

In the end we feel grateful to have completed this project, which, though it may not capture the entire import of van Dijk's contribution to art history, has, through its complexity and nuance, evoked, and expanded upon that contribution.

Defne Ayas
Director Witte de With Center for Contemporary Art, Rotterdam (2012–2017)

Philip Tinari
Director Ullens Center for Contemporary Art, Beijing

Introduction
Marianne Brouwer

A legendary figure in the Chinese art world of the 1990s, Hans van Dijk's role in recent Chinese art history has never before been presented to the public at large, neither in China nor, indeed, in the Netherlands. The exhibitions at Witte de With Center for Contemporary Art in Rotterdam, and at Ullens Center for Contemporary Art in Beijing, attempt to bridge that gap for the first time. While each exhibition has its own character, they come together in this publication to form a single history.

But no exhibition and no amount of scholarly work can describe the love and respect one encounters with those who knew van Dijk. More than a decade after his death, people are sometimes moved to tears at the thought of him. Many of those who knew him lay claim to a piece of van Dijk, hanging on to it with jealous exclusivity. They talk about how he gave up everything to come to China, about the sacrifices he made for art, about his fierce independence in the midst of the Chinese political and artistic landscape. They recount his unassuming attitude and ironic sense of humor, and how he helped artists by making their work known abroad. He was especially active in this respect during years of great hardship following 1989, when it was forbidden to show or sell contemporary art in China, and there was no infrastructure for it—no galleries, no museums, no collectors, no curating. His friends and colleagues remember how he taught them without seeming to do so just by listening, observing, and acting. His life was legendarily frugal, his home reduced to such bare necessities that it looked like a monk's cell; but what little he owned was shaped with unerring taste.

I met him only once, in 1996, at the CIFA Gallery, where he exhibited artist Wang Xingwei's paintings and talked to me passionately about their unique iconography. We spent the afternoon in his apartment near Beijing's second ring road, where he talked about 1989 and showed me photos of the Hangzhou protest banners. The Plexiglas work by Zhao Bandi hung on the wall above his bed. He later wrote me that he had lived in China for so long that at times he thought of himself as "an albino".

Van Dijk, as everyone hastened to tell me, was no businessman. His true strength was his scholarly informed vision. This was first expressed when he set up the New Amsterdam Art Consultancy in Beijing, which organized more than forty exhibitions and activities involving Chinese art in just a few years, and later, in 1999, when he joined with his Maecenas, the Belgian collector Frank Uytterhaegen and artist Ai Weiwei to found the gallery China Art Archives and Warehouse, and the Modern Chinese Art Foundation. In these endeavors he tirelessly championed and archived Chinese art domestically and abroad. The artists he exhibited and wrote about, managed to withstand the test of time almost without exception, and today represent some of the most influential and significant artists in China. This tells us something about van Dijk's principles in art and about his character, too, when he wrote to an old friend a few months before his death:

> Like many people, I'm a bit fed up with the modern art world: too much what's new, what's hot. Writing this, in front of me are those rectangular aluminum food tins from the Nanjing Arts Institute, in which I used to put cards with dates about artists. Now I'm adding the dates on those cards into a database about artists I started in Berlin in 1991, when I bought my first computer. I know I'm good at archiving. It's not new and hot but will be useful. There is a Chinese expression [about] denying short-term success, "xiao congming"—small smart. I believe in that.

Many people have at different times contributed to the Hans van Dijk project. The exhibition and book were first discussed in 2008 between van Dijk's friend and co-curator of the *China Avant-garde* show, Andreas Schmid—who wrote the initial draft for it—Frank Uytterhaegen, Annemarie Montulet, then attached to the Netherlands' Embassy in Beijing, and myself. Many ideas and attempts followed. During those years Ai Weiwei was put in police prison, and Uytterhaegen passed away. By 2012, the project had all but halted when I was invited by another of van Dijk's friends, gallerist Martijn Kielstra, to take it on again.

The research for the project has been conducted through interviews with dozens of Chinese artists and others who knew van Dijk well. The NAAC/CAAW archive in Beijing has been an abundant source of material and information, so has the Asia Art Archive in Hong Kong. My thanks go first of all to the van Dijk family and Pascale Geulleaume, Frank Uytterhaegen's wife, for their support and generosity. For the rediscovery of the lexicon I am indebted to van Dijk's former assistants and his family. Thanks to registrar André Straatman, for beautifully reviving the lexicon files. Invaluable knowledge about van Dijk's life amidst the art scene in China came from his witty letters to his friends in the Netherlands, a correspondence he kept up over many years, and which they faithfully preserved and generously shared with me. My thanks go to Ernst Dinkla and Jeroen Vinken in particular. Many thanks to Andreas Schmid for sharing his knowledge and materials, and for the "Berlin wall" of the exhibition; to Zhang Li for his crucial additions to the exhibition including the map of van Dijk's abodes. Writer and curator Karen Smith has been a great friend: many heartfelt thanks. My thanks to Robert Bernell for being a haven of spiritual and practical sustenance. For very welcome advice I thank Egbert Dommering. I thank all artists with all my heart. Sadly, two wonderful friends and great artists, who both have an important place in this publication, have since passed away: Chen Shaoxiong left us in 2016, and in December 2017 we received the message of Geng Jianyi's passing. Last but not least, I owe Defne Ayas and Philip Tinari a great debt of gratitude for their belief in the project and their support, at times against all odds, from the inception of the exhibitions until the conclusion of this publication. Special thanks to Samuel Saelemakers, to Patrick Rhine, and to the wonderful crews of Witte de With Center for Contemporary Art in Rotterdam, and UCCA in Beijing. I owe everything to others; all errors and omissions are mine.

Marianne Brouwer
Amsterdam, December 2017

Opposite page: Unknown photographer (Zhang Hai'er?), portrait of Hans van Dijk, Guangzhou, 1992, courtesy Lin Yilin

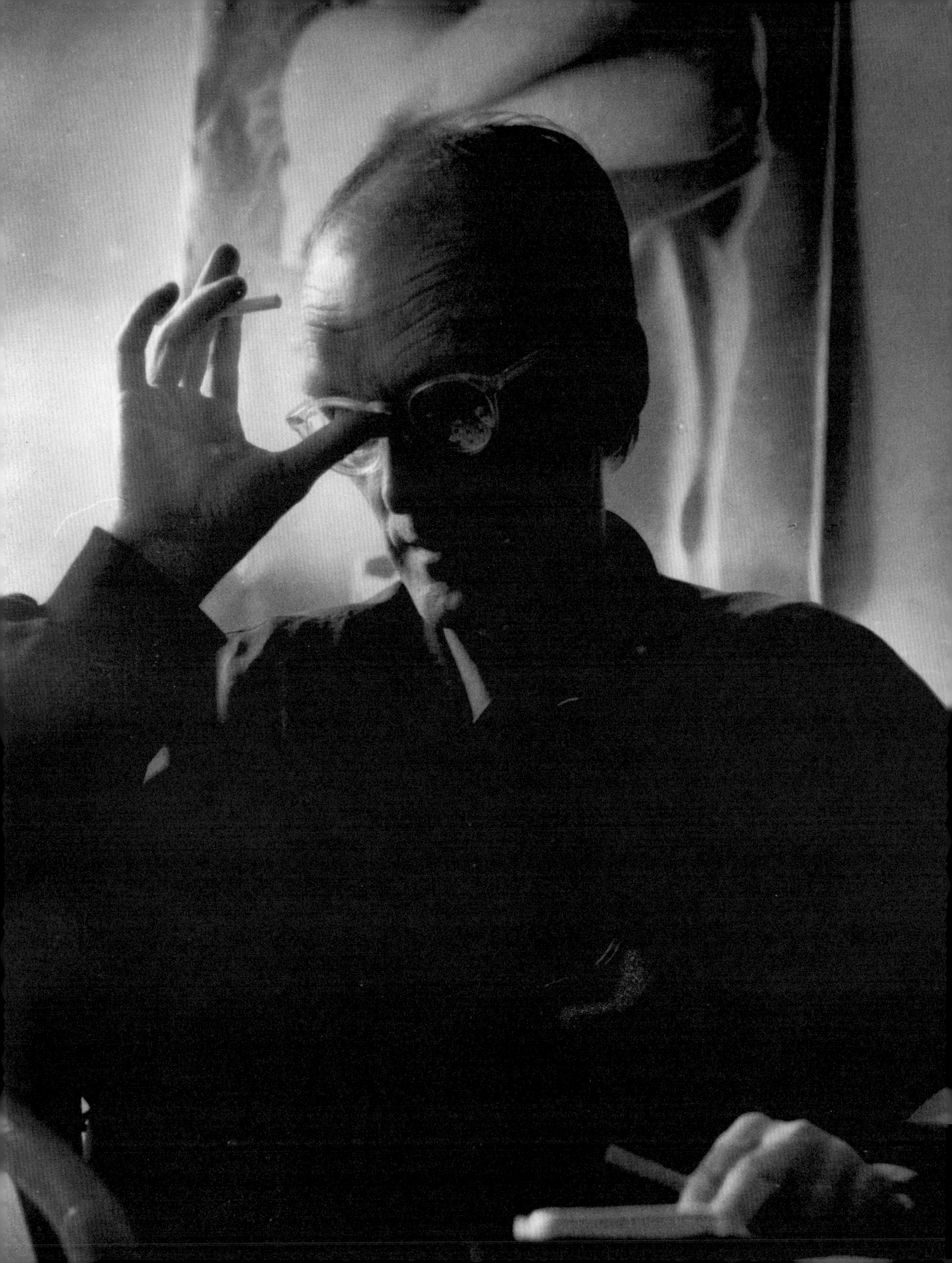

Beginnings
The Netherlands, 1946–1986

Although Hans could at times be difficult, irascible, and extremely obstinate, I never knew anyone who was so erudite and so much fun to talk and be with.

Ernst Dinkla

19 November 1946

Johannes (Hans) Gerardus Adrianus Wilhelmus Cloeck van Dijk is born in the historical town of Deventer in the Netherlands. A thriving Hanseatic city in Medieval times, Deventer is now part of the Dutch Bible Belt.

Van Dijk's father, Jan van Dijk, is a technical engineer and an Elder of the local Reformed Church. His mother, Ada, is Jan's second wife. Jan's first wife, Laura—Ada's older sister—was killed in a World War II air raid. Laura bore him two sons, Pieter in 1942 and Jan in 1944. After Laura's death, Jan Sr. asks Ada to live with the family to take care of the boys. Dreading gossip among the Calvinist community, the grandmother strongly disapproves of the arrangement. Jan and Ada marry in 1945. In 1948, Ronald, the fourth and youngest son, is born. The marriage is a happy one, although the shadow of Laura's death looms over it for many years.

Van Dijk and his brothers grow up in a typical post-war, Dutch middle-class household. Their father, a stern, pious man, raises them in the faith, reading the Bible daily and going to church twice on Sundays. They move in the local Calvinist circles, buying their groceries from the Calvinist grocer, their meat from the Calvinist butcher.
Following the hardship of the post-war years, the 1950s see rapid economic recovery in Europe, thanks to America's Marshall Plan. Germany's *Wirtschaftswunder* is equaled in the Netherlands by the years of *Wederopbouw* (Reconstruction). Like many Dutch families, the van Dijks enjoy life amidst the growing financial ease—they buy their first car, take road trips to the seaside, and the children go to summer camp.

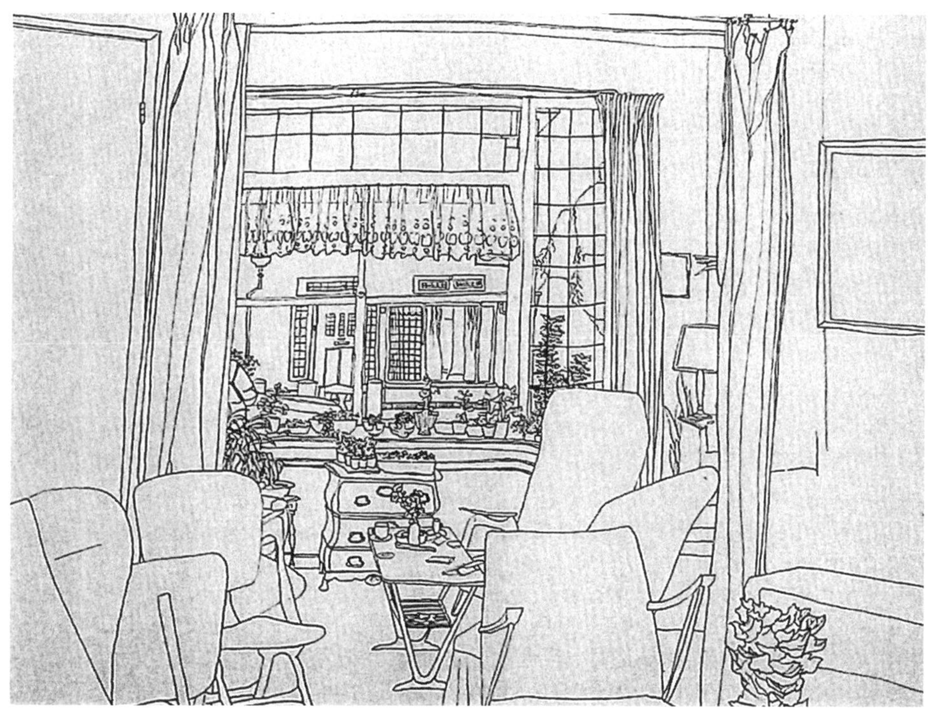

Hans van Dijk, drawing of the interior of his childhood home in Deventer, circa 1960, coll. van Dijk family

When van Dijk is about five years old, he falls prey to a serious illness that keeps him hospitalized for a long time. His family keeps him busy by giving him jigsaw puzzles. It turns out he loves puzzles and is so good at them that he tackles increasingly intricate ones. He even puts them together blank side up.

Growing up, the children learn music and play instruments that suit a hallowed ambiance, such as the harmonium. Van Dijk, who plays both the harmonium and the church's pipe organ, particularly loves playing Bach, whose music will stay with him throughout his life.

1959 Having finished elementary school the two younger van Dijk boys are sent to MULO (extended primary education), one of the lowest types of Dutch middle schools, which virtually precludes them from going to university. It is unclear why; their parents have already sent the two older boys to gymnasium, which prepares them for higher education. Pieter will go on to study theology and Jan, mathematics.
Hans hates his school. There is nothing in the curriculum to prepare him for the life and studies he will later embrace, or the passionate, self-taught scholar he is to become. In 1997, he writes to his niece Olwen van Dijk, Ronald's daughter, who has just started school in Australia and loves it, how happy he is for her. He writes: "I was always sick with stomach cramps. The teachers were dressed terribly and had hair growing from their noses. One couldn't look at them, let alone listen to them," adding that he himself had been extremely glad to be rid of it.

Early on, van Dijk shows a talent for drawing and making things. While in middle school, he amuses himself by folding increasingly complicated polyhedrons from paper, with pleasant rhythms of color in the folded sequences that require highly abstract mathematical thinking. He hangs them from the ceiling of his room in the attic of the family home. Perhaps because nothing else comes to mind, his parents send him to art school.

According to his brother Ronald, van Dijk already knew he was gay in his early teens. His older brothers recall that growing up, they too somehow knew about it. Once they even pretended to be interested in the neighbor's daughter so that van Dijk could approach her brother on whom he had a crush. Overall, however, he has no outlet for his feelings; Calvinism severely condemns homosexuality and believes that homosexuals are destined for hell no matter how pious or irreproachable their lives. This makes it impossible to discuss van Dijk's homosexuality within the family, let alone admit it openly. Jan Sr.'s inner battle between his unforgiving faith and his fatherly love puts a tragic strain on their relationship. They suffer from it acutely up to his father's dying moments, when van Dijk is already well into his forties. It is likely that van Dijk's fierce rejection of all religion grew out of these painful days in his youth. His relationship with his mother, on the contrary, is affectionate; she is not stern at all and exerts a softening influence on the household.

1962–1965 Van Dijk enters the Arnhem Academy of Fine Arts at the age of sixteen. He submits a small sculptural study of an open hand to qualify for admission. He commutes between Arnhem and Deventer by train every day for the next three years. Among his teachers there are two important artists who have a lasting influence on him: Henk Peeters (1925–2013) and Peter Struycken (b. 1939). Peeters, whose works evince a deadpan humor that greatly appeals to van Dijk, is a member of the *zero* international movement, a famous group of radically inventive painters and sculptors from the fifties and sixties that includes Yves Klein and Piero Manzoni. Struycken, who is a great admirer of Mondrian, soon becomes the first Dutch artist to create a systematic, computer-based art.

What exactly happened to terminate van Dijk's career at the Arnhem Academy? There are rumors of rows and love affairs gone wrong, or perhaps he is just miserable because he feels out of place. After three years, on Struycken's advice, he switches to a very different type of academy.

1965–1967 Van Dijk enters the Academy for Industrial Design in Eindhoven (AIVE). It is a progressive, open-minded institute, the only Bauhaus-oriented academy in the Netherlands. Van Dijk is free for the first time: from family obligations at home, from the struggle of commuting, from the repression of Calvinism. He is happy and independent at last. He makes friends with artists and designers, kindred spirits. He begins a lifelong friendship with classmate Ernst Dinkla. He begins avidly reading books by A. J. Ayer, Noam Chomsky, Bertrand Russell, and Ludwig Wittgenstein. He is interested in the life and work of Polish mathematical logician Alfred Tarski and the tragic British computer scientist Alan Turing. A copy of Antonin Artaud's famous selfportrait, his face disfigured by self-inflicted cigarette burns, hangs in his room. He reads prominent gay Dutch writers Gerard Reve and Gerrit Komrij. In his letters from China many years later, he will adopt Reve's carefully mannered, ironic style of writing. Thanks to Dinkla, we know how voraciously and widely he read on science, philosophy, and literature, concentrating on gay authors and thinkers, as if to discover, through their struggles and sufferings, his own existential road toward life as a gay man.

Together with Dinkla, he completes numerous design projects for the Academy. With fellow student friends, he moves to live in "The Wash," an abandoned factory in Eindhoven in 1966. He plays Handel and Bach on the organ of Eindhoven's St. Catherine's Church. He has a part in Alfred Jarry's famous absurdist play *Ubu Roi* (1896), which is staged and directed by one of the teachers at the Academy. The play must have made a lasting impression on him: his own *Ubu Roi Art Research Committee Report* (URARC) of 1994 is based on it. He is the first at the Academy to buy the Beatles' album *Sgt. Pepper's Lonely Hearts Club Band* and play it for everyone at school. But even in Eindhoven, Elders from the Calvinist church show up on his doorstep trying to lure him back into the fold. Half a decade later when living as an artist in the small town of Nuenen, van Dijk takes his creative revenge on Calvinism. He joins two harmoniums to create a single instrument with two keyboards. He attaches the hose of an old vacuum cleaner to the bellows and calls it *The Calvinist Circular See-Saw.*

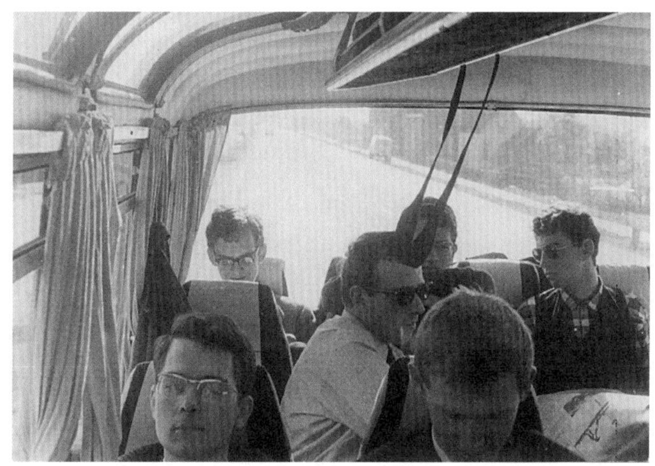

Hans van Dijk (far left) and fellow students from the AIVE on an outing to the Gemeentemuseum, The Hague, 1966, courtesy Ernst Dinkla

It is within the lively and stimulating environment of the Eindhoven Academy that van Dijk matures, becoming the man one later encounters in numerous photographs in China—tall, bony, with an expressive mouth and fine eye betraying an extraordinarily sensitive character. His is a mixture of open-mindedness and a humble, often self-deprecatory, disposition. His impish sense of humor is paired with a fierce need for independence and a dogged, sometimes peevish, obstinacy where his ideals and causes are concerned. And although he has few social graces, he has an amazing gift for friendship.

During the sixties and seventies, the Netherlands enjoys international renown for its anti-authoritarian lifestyle and high artistic standards. A hotbed of experimental art, it is also a haven for museum culture. Van Dijk regularly visits Eindhoven's Van Abbemuseum (he never attends openings), which is internationally famous for its brilliant collection of modern art, and, from the mid-seventies on, its exhibitions of minimal and conceptual art and German neo-expressionist painting. Judging from his gallery shows in China many years later, the best of that Dutch zeitgeist left an indelible imprint on his personal and artistic development. It is uncanny how much his style of exhibition making embodies that of seminal Dutch museums of modern art like the Van Abbemuseum and the Stedelijk Museum in Amsterdam: clarity, balance, and order; rhythmic in space and form, bold in content.

1967–1968

In the fall of 1967, van Dijk is sent to what is then Czechoslovakia. To satisfy his mandatory one-year international internship for the Academy, he works for the design department of the Chirana medical instruments factory in the Slovak village of Stará Turá near the city of Bratislava. In Bratislava, he experiences the impact of the Prague Spring, which begins on 5 January 1968. But when the Soviet Union invades the country on 21 August, the Czech borders are closed, and van Dijk is unable to leave. His friends take him to the mountains, where he hides with a family of farmers for several weeks. From there, he is secretly taken across the border to the free West, smuggling photographs for the Dutch press documenting the bloody end of the Prague Spring. It is unclear where the photos end up or whether they are actually published. But the feeling of witnessing history makes a lasting impression on van Dijk. When the tragic uprisings in China culminate in the Tiananmen Square massacre of 1989, his decision to keep a diary of the events unfolding is based almost on *déjà vu*.

1969

Van Dijk and Dinkla graduate from the Eindhoven Academy with a joint thesis. Their project is a multifunctional, convertible set of wooden furniture for an experimental Jenaplan school. Van Dijk designs a set of hexagonal tables, which, when joined together, convert into a theater podium, as well as a pre-fab wooden chair inspired by Joe Colombo's plywood reclining chair and Gerrit Rietveld's *Red Blue Chair*. After graduation, van Dijk hitchhikes to Lebanon, where his brother Pieter, having abandoned theology, works as an independent academic researcher.

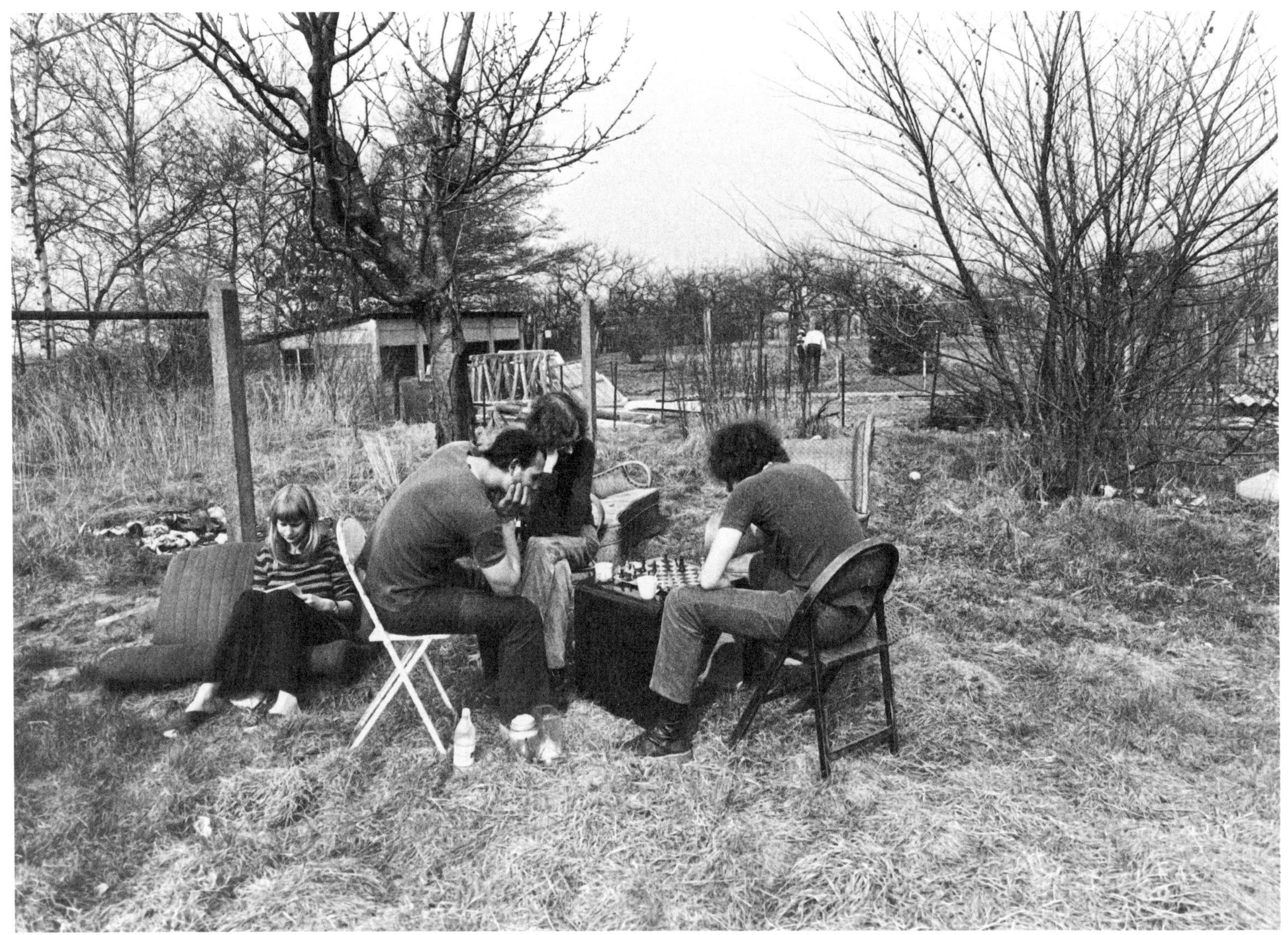

Hans van Dijk (middle), and two friends playing competition chess in the garden in Nuenen, early 1970s, photo Ernst Dinkla

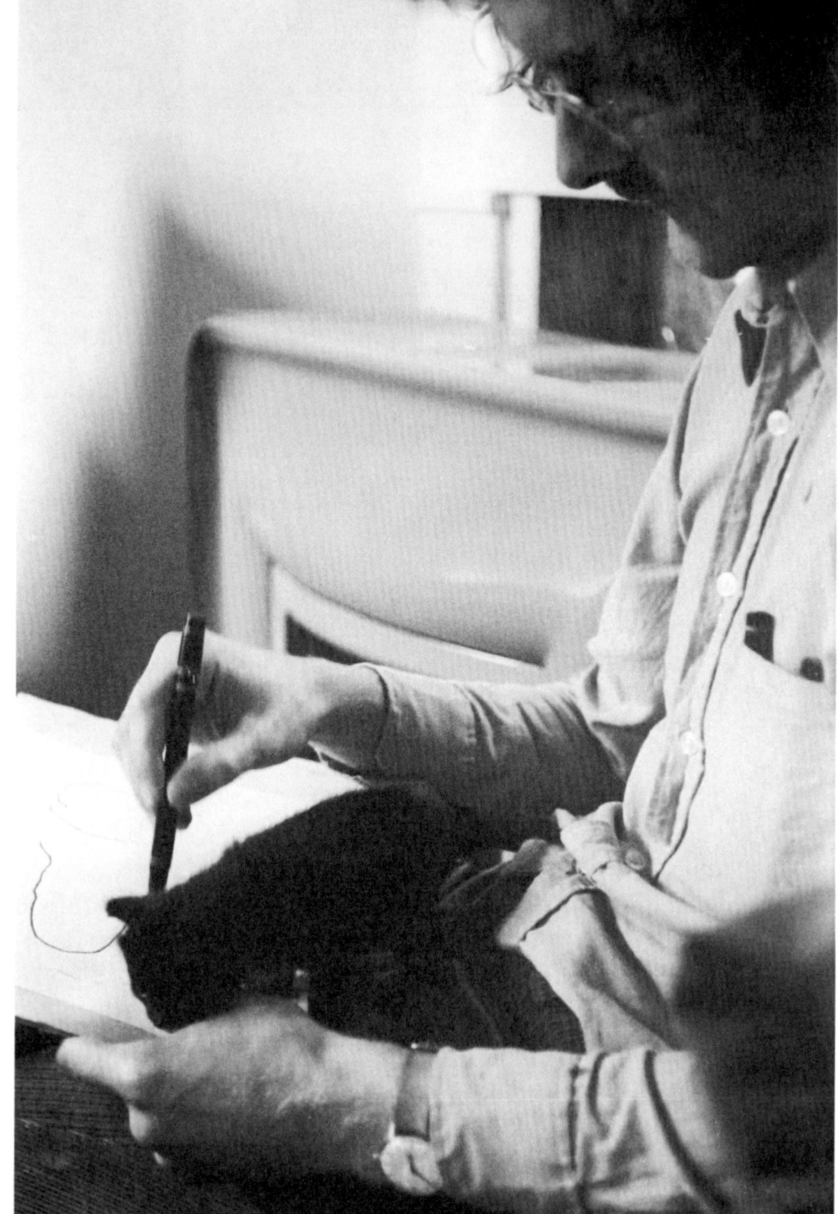

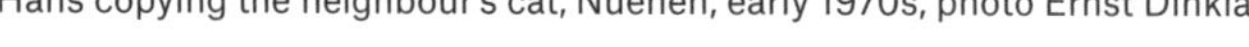

Hans copying the neighbour's cat, Nuenen, early 1970s, photo Ernst Dinkla

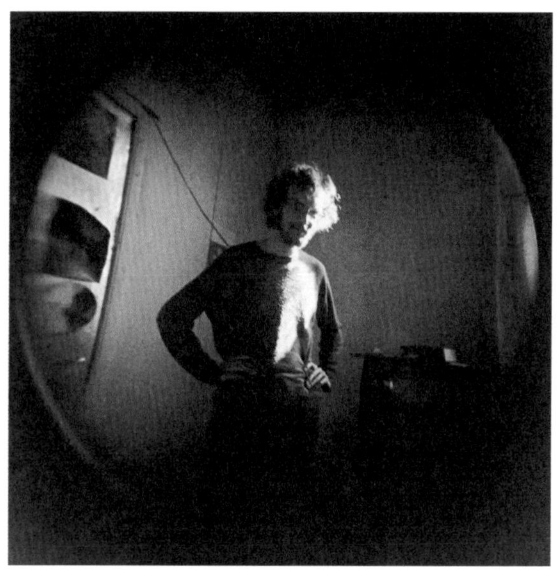

Hans van Dijk, Nuenen, early 1970s, photo Ernst Dinkla

1970

Van Dijk and Dinkla find a condemned house in the small town of Waalre, not far from Eindhoven. Among the circle of friends who already moved to Waalre are comic book designer Joost Swarte and graphic printer Bernhard Ruijgrok, older brother of artist Marc Ruijgrok. While in Waalre, van Dijk continues to play the organ in the local church. When the house is torn down, they move to a derelict building in Nuenen (van Gogh's birthplace), where they have their own studios and a garden. Van Dijk builds a little conservatory, in which he grows cannabis. He is extremely fond of the neighboring black cat. He and his friends take part in chess competitions that sometimes last for days. With his brother Ronald, he rides by motorbike to concerts by Frank Zappa and Thelonious Monk. Van Dijk's brother Jan builds a boat, on which they sail across the IJsselmeer.

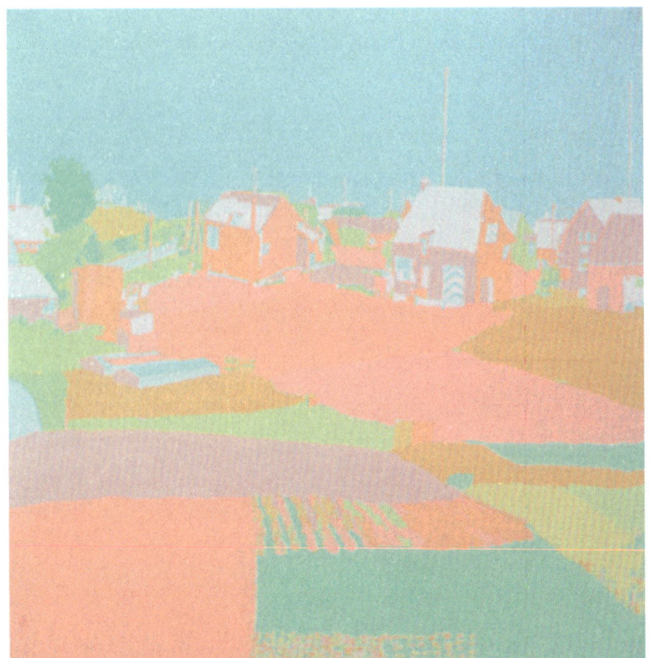

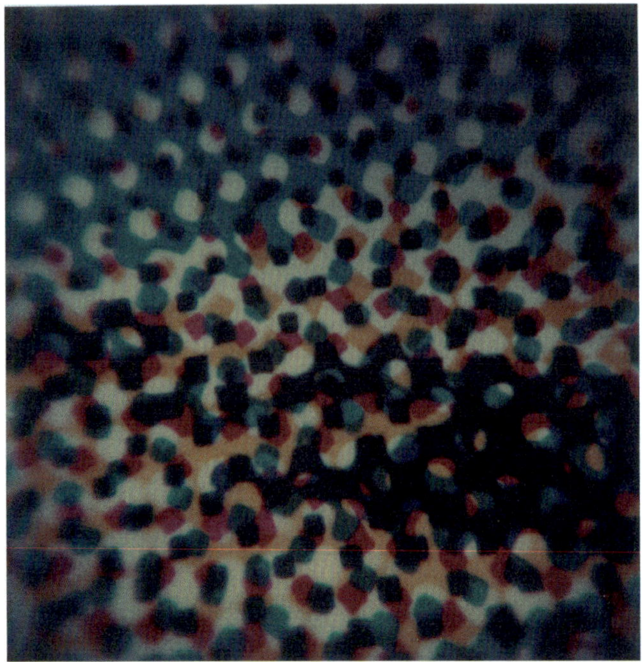

Left: Hans van Dijk, landscape painting based on a systematic color scheme, 1969–70, private coll., photo courtesy Ernst Dinkla; right: Hans van Dijk, Polaroid of random color painting, probably mid-1970s, coll. Ernst Dinkla

While living in Nuenen, van Dijk decides to become an artist. He takes courses at the University of Utrecht on randomness and systems in art. He paints small landscapes at first, with methodical color schemes defined not by nature but by science. He is fascinated with light and darkness and invents a color alphabet, which he calls a *chromatic spectrum*. It consists of an enormous collection of chromatically arranged, hexagonal bits of colored paper. He then chooses random combinations to make patterns, which he glues onto cardboard or Plexiglas. The intended effect of the patterns is for the dots to appear as individual colors up close, but as a uniform gray or white from afar. He photographs the finished works in his Nuenen garden against a backdrop of grass and trees. The effect is not unlike that of an impressionist or pointillist painting. He first uses the *I Ching* (the Chinese *Book of Changes*) to generate random patterns, and later speeds up the aleatory process by throwing dice. His brother Jan, a mathematician and phonologist, helps him to write computer programs simulating randomness until van Dijk can do his own programming.

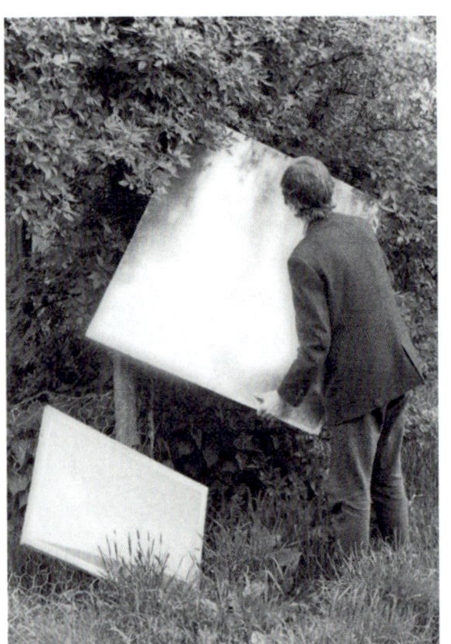

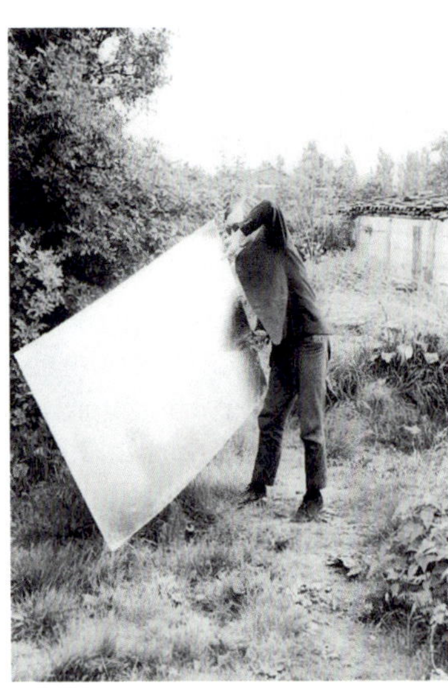

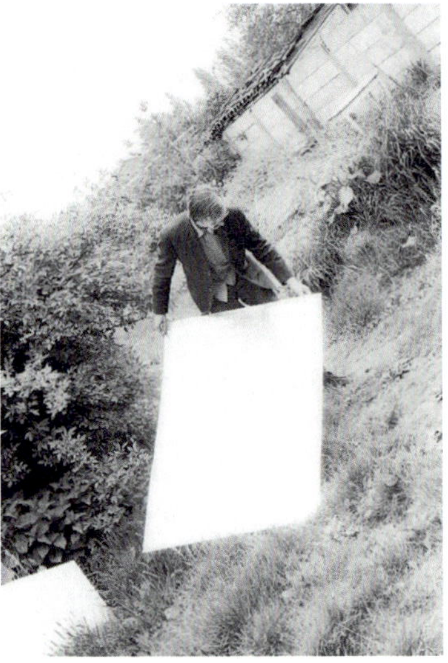

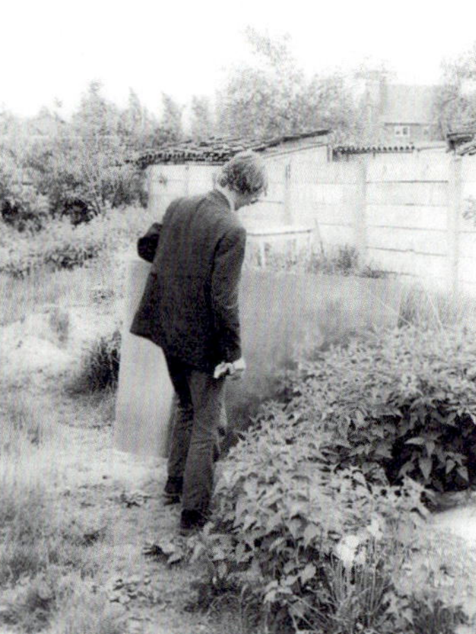

Hans experimenting with mirrors in the garden, Nuenen, early 1970s, photo Ernst Dinkla

1972

Around this time, van Dijk buys his first Polaroid camera. He uses it to photograph his paintings in the Nuenen garden, but his other photos are experiments in ways of looking, using ordinary subjects like houses, a chair, or the neighboring black cat.

In 2003, a year after van Dijk's death, his friend and business partner Ai Weiwei will discover a substantial amount of the early Polaroid photos among van Dijk's personal belongings, and gathers a selection into a little book dedicated to him.

In 1972, van Dijk has his first one-man show at Galerie Swart on the Keizersgracht in Amsterdam. The owner, Riekje Swart, is a highly respected gallerist, famous for her uncompromising taste and vanguard exhibitions of neo-constructivism, geometric abstraction, hard-edge painting, and early conceptual art. She exhibits Dutch artists like Peter Struycken, Herman de Vries, and Ger van Elk, as well as international artists like François Morellet and Agnes Martin early on.

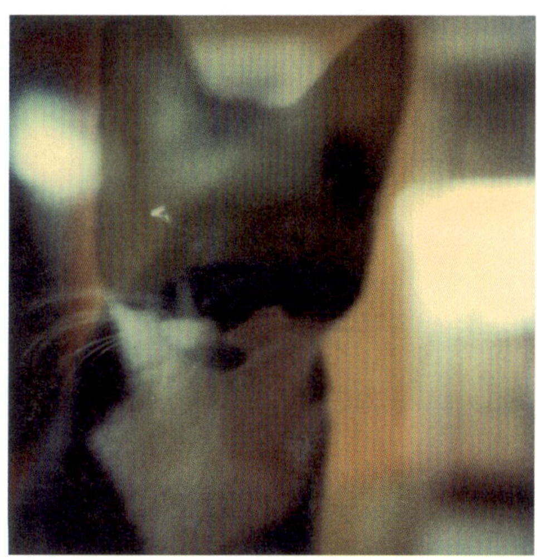

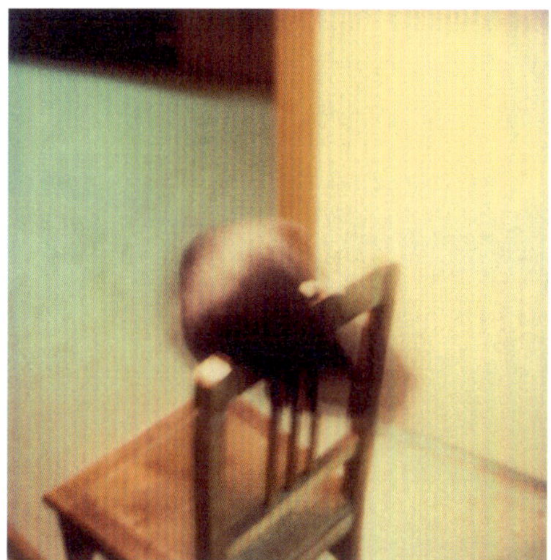

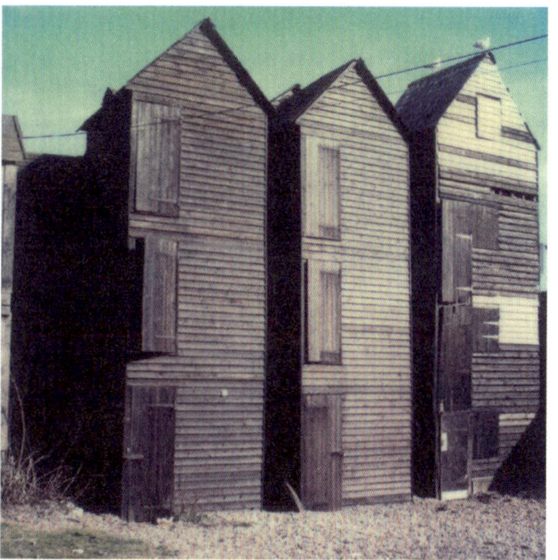

Hans van Dijk, Polaroids probably made between 1972 and 1986, private coll.

1973

To finance his art practice, van Dijk starts working in commercial advertising. As an accomplished graphic designer, he lives off designing billboards and inventing display systems for industrial companies. To provide for his basic needs as an artist, he calculates that he must work two days a week full-time. To save time, he develops an ingenious assembly system that allows him to mount a giant billboard by himself in a single day. He buys a second-hand transportation van. He lives an extremely frugal life but tends to neglect himself. He makes his own furniture, basic but always beautiful, and early on he develops the monk-like lifestyle for which he will be known in China. Around this time, van Dijk gets his teeth knocked out in a carnival brawl. From then on, he wears characteristically ill-fitting dentures.

Van Dijk has his second one-man show at Galerie Swart, where he exhibits *series 1, 2, 3, 4,* and *5*, each a set of twenty-seven numbered paper squares printed in varying diagonal patterns of black and white laid out in three three-by-three grids. "Hans was fascinated by color, meaning 'no color = black' and 'all colors together = white.' He experimented with chance, thickness, and size. Applying these three dimensions systematically, Hans arrived at a series of twenty-seven black-and-white diagonal drawings. These can be laid out in various ways, depending on personal preference. The composition shown here takes 'module size' as its starting point and varies 'chance' horizontally and 'thickness' vertically."[1]

1—Ronald van Dijk on *serie 4*, 2014.

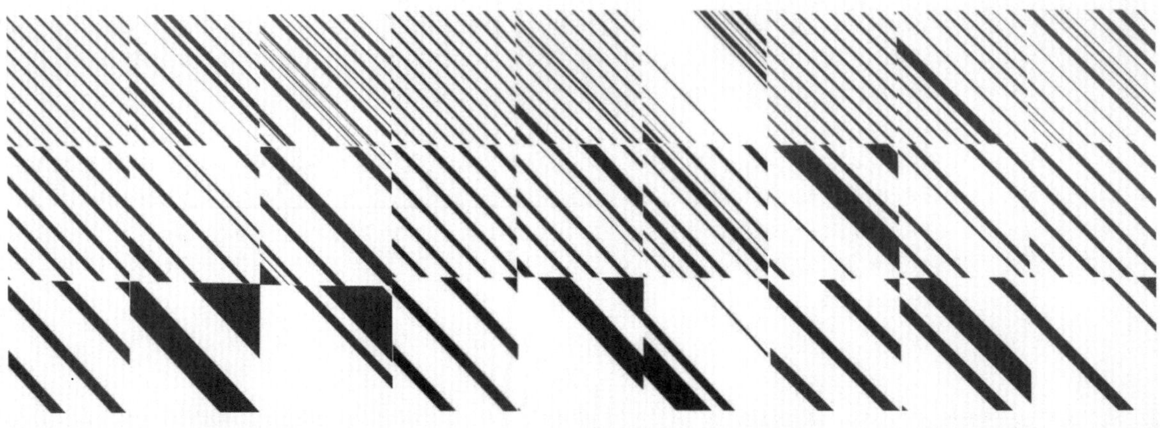

First tableau: randomness from left to right, thickness from top to bottom, and module size one.

111	211	311
121	221	321
131	231	331

Second tableau: randomness from left to right, thickness from top to bottom, and module size two.

112	212	312
122	222	322
132	232	332

Third tableau: randomness from left to right, thickness from top to bottom, and module size three.

113	213	313
123	223	323
133	233	333

Hans van Dijk, *serie 4*, 27 black-and-white drawings, 9 x 9 cm each, printed in an edition of 50, each in a cardboard box with elastic band and cover sheet, printed by Pieter Stapel, Amsterdam, 1973, coll. Ronald van Dijk and Effie Ferdinandus; first shown together with *series 1*, *2*, *3*, and *5* at Galerie Swart, Amsterdam, 1973

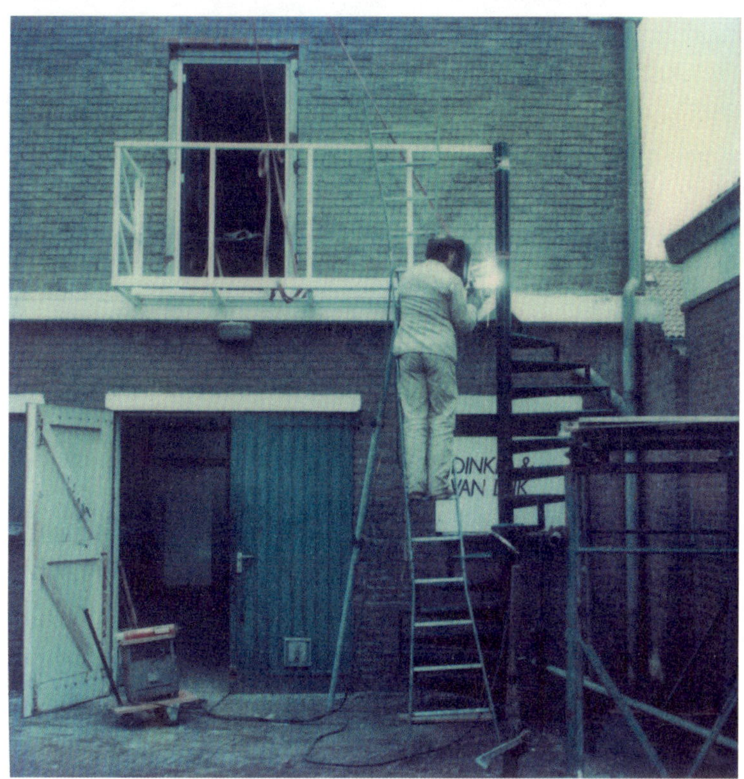

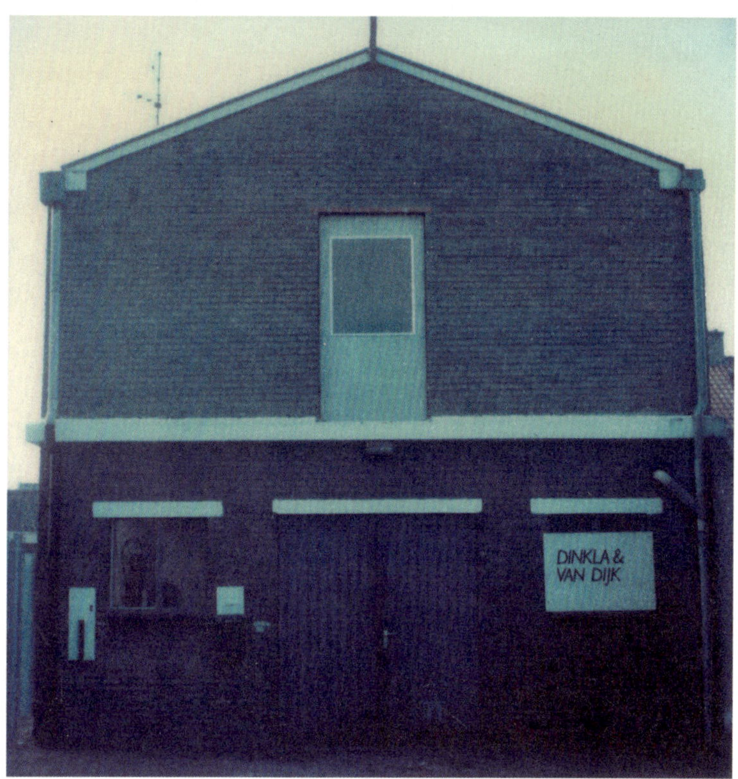

Hans van Dijk, Polaroids of the factory in Eindhoven with the logo for Dinkla & van Dijk, 1975, private coll.

1975 – 1979

The house in Nuenen is torn down, and van Dijk and Dinkla move to Eindhoven, where they rent a small factory at 10 Hessen Kasselstraat. Dinkla establishes his printing business *Dinkla Graphic Techniques* on the ground floor, while van Dijk rents the back part of the top floor, nailing the brand-new logo of his own company, *Van Dijk Display Technique*, above his door. In 1977, van Dijk meets artist and designer Jeroen Vinken, who becomes another life-long friend.

He participates in the group exhibition *Toeval Kunst* (Random Art) in Amsterdam. The show is organized by the Dutch Foundation for the Arts and displays works from the Dutch state collection of contemporary art. Van Dijk's *serie 4* hangs alongside works by well-known Dutch artists such as Stanley Brouwn, Peter Struycken, and Herman de Vries and is included in the catalogue. Van Dijk has his third solo exhibition at Galerie Swart entitled *Arranged Patterns*.

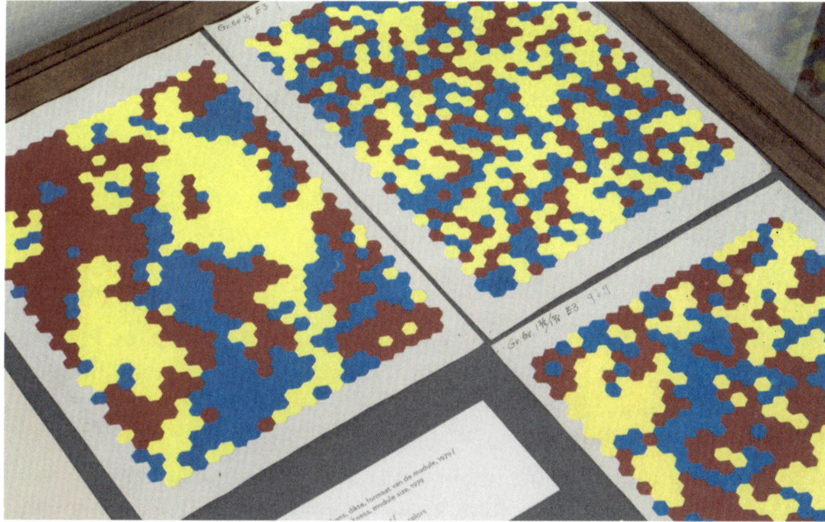

Hans van Dijk, three studies in grid graphics in three colors, based on chance, thickness, and module size, watercolor on A4 paper, 1979, coll. Ronald van Dijk and Effie Ferdinandus

Four panels from Hans van Dijk, *Arranged Patterns, group 2*, digital print on paper on plastic panel, 23 × 32 × 0.6 cm each, 40 panels in wooden box, 1977, coll. Jeroen Vinken; exhibited at Galerie Swart, Amsterdam, 1977, and at Sally East Gallery, London, 1982 (→ p. 26)

1979 – 1982

Van Dijk and a group of close friends (Dick Bakker, Ria van Boekholt, Josien Brenneker, Ernst Dinkla, Gaston Klein, and Jeroen Vinken) decide to found an art magazine. The magazine is published every two months and is a collage of original artists' silk-screen prints, poems, and experimental typeface. Van Dijk comes up with the name *Daglicht* (Daylight). He asks Dutch designer Wim Crouwel to permit *Daglicht* to use his iconic font, New Alphabet. Crouwel, one of the most influential Dutch designers and typographers, invented New Alphabet in 1967 as a purely experimental font based on cathode ray tube technology; each letter is composed of vertical and horizontal lines, making it ideal for computers.

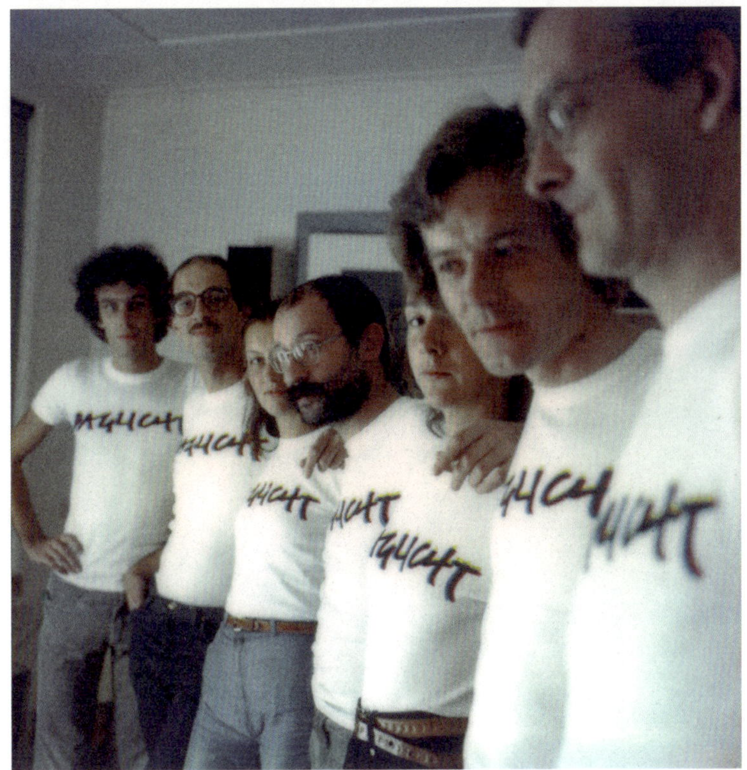

Daglicht editorial team, left to right: Jeroen Vinken, Ernst Dinkla, Ria van Boekholt, Gaston Klein, Josien Brenneker, Dick Bakker, and Hans van Dijk, Polaroid, early 1980s, courtesy Ernst Dinkla

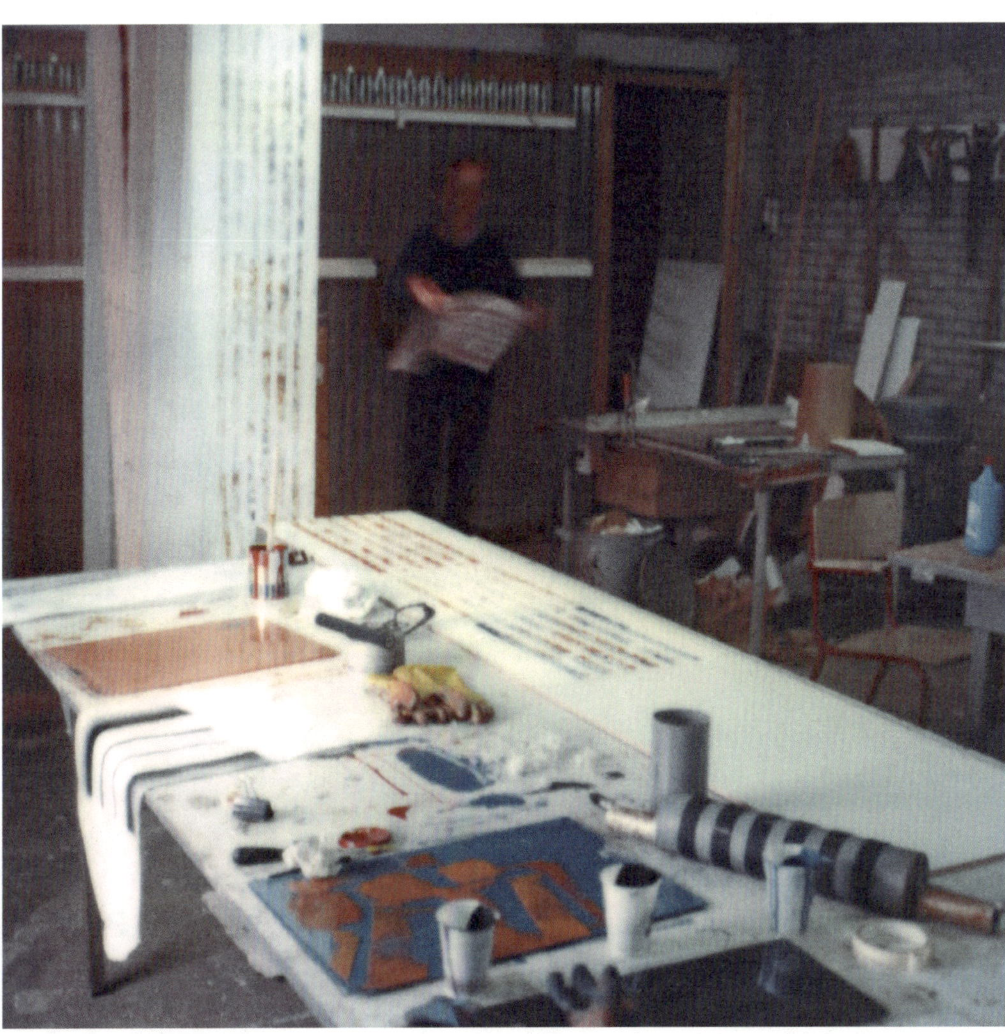

Hans van Dijk producing a page for *Daglicht* magazine in his studio at Hessen Kasselstraat, Eindhoven, Polaroid, 1975–81, courtesy Ernst Dinkla

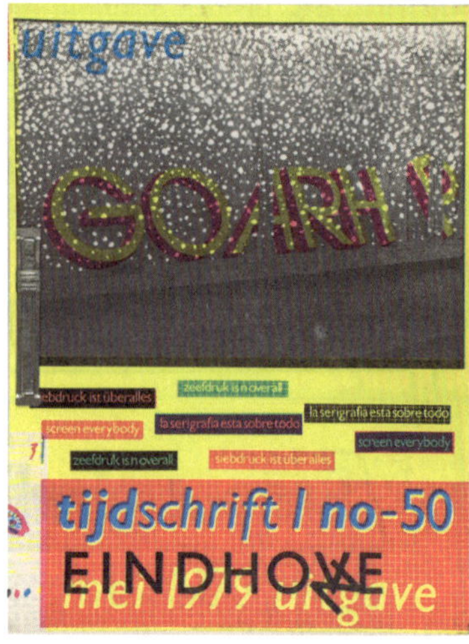

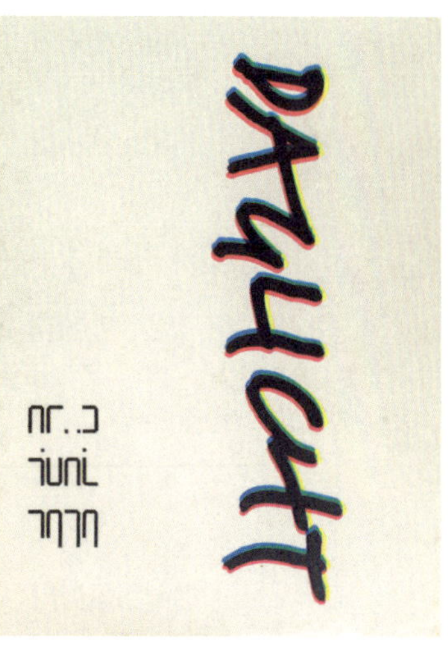

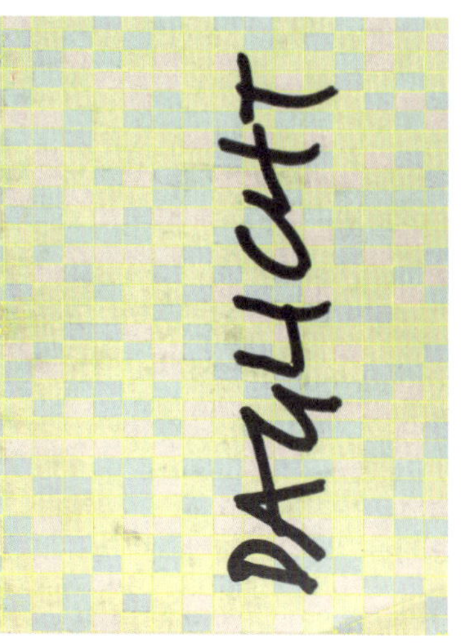

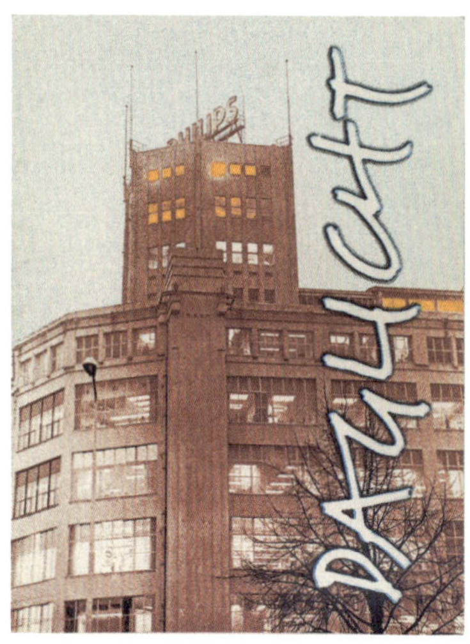

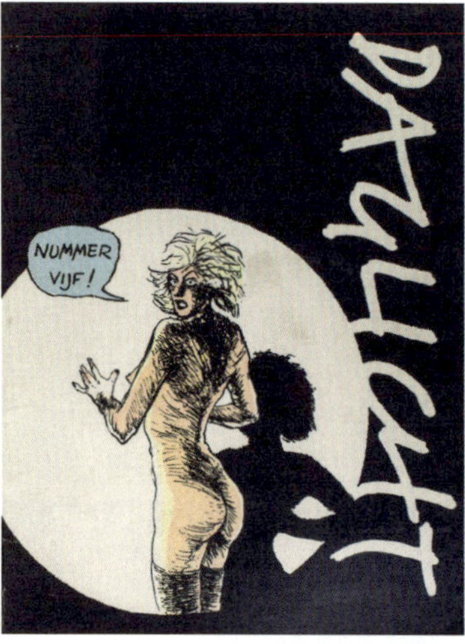

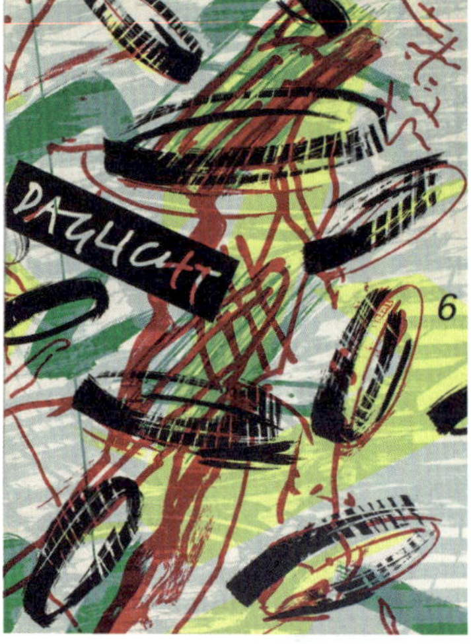

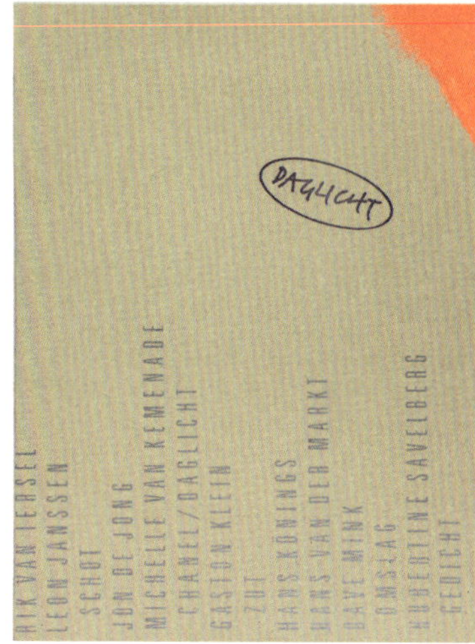

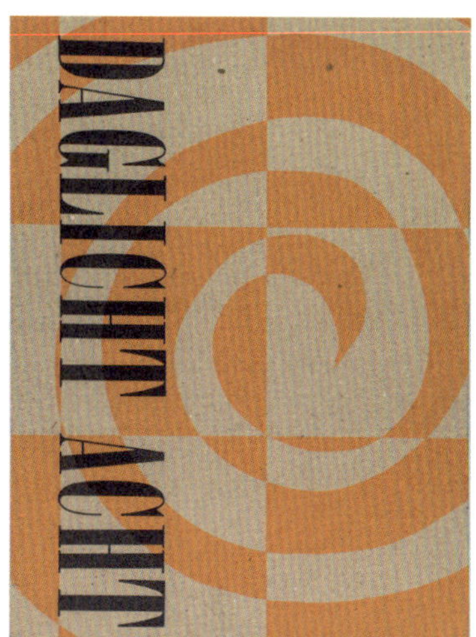

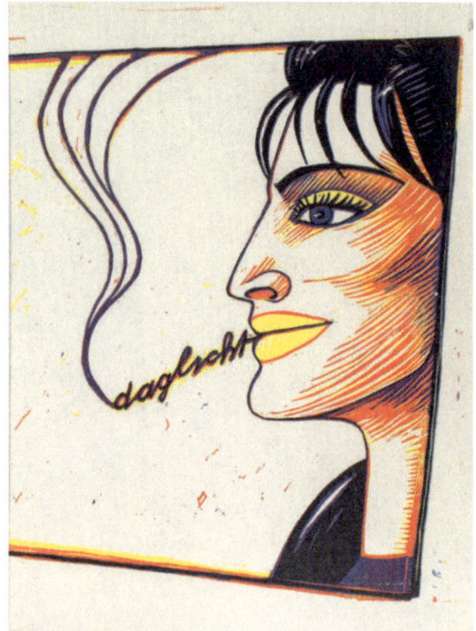

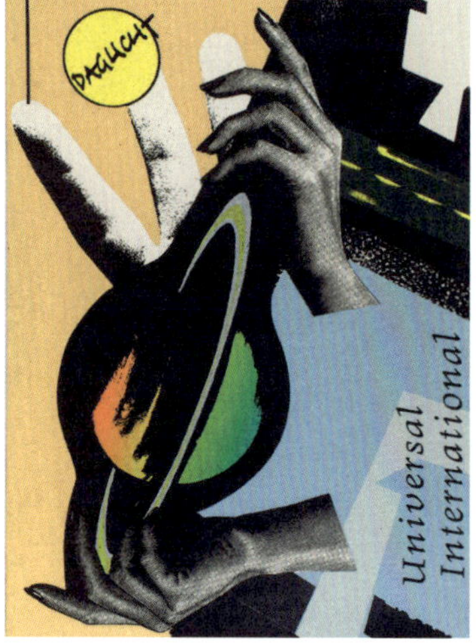

Daglicht magazine covers, silkscreen prints, 32 × 25 cm each, 1979–82, coll. Ernst Dinkla

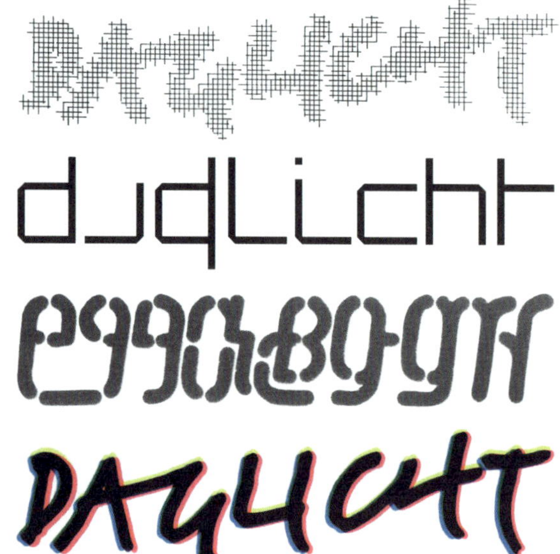

Daglicht typefaces, top to bottom: *Daglicht* logo; *Daglicht* logo in Wim Crouwel, New Alphabet, 1967; Hans van Dijk, *Daglicht* phonetic logo, 1980; *Daglicht* logo

For the fourth issue of *Daglicht,* van Dijk designs a phonetic alphabet consisting of characters both for handwriting and printing. As a reference, he uses the first phonological treatise in Dutch history: *Announcement of a new art, called the Art of Speech, discovered and described by Petrus Montanus of Delft: in which is discussed and brought to light the rights and up until now hidden nature of all pronunciation*, published in 1635. Van Dijk asks his brother Jan, who teaches at the Institute of Phonetic Sciences, University of Amsterdam, to provide design advice once more.

Dinkla buys the factory at Hessen Kasselstraat. Van Dijk continues to rent the back part of the second floor. He has a fourth solo show at Galerie Swart and an exhibition at Galerie Magazijn in Groningen.

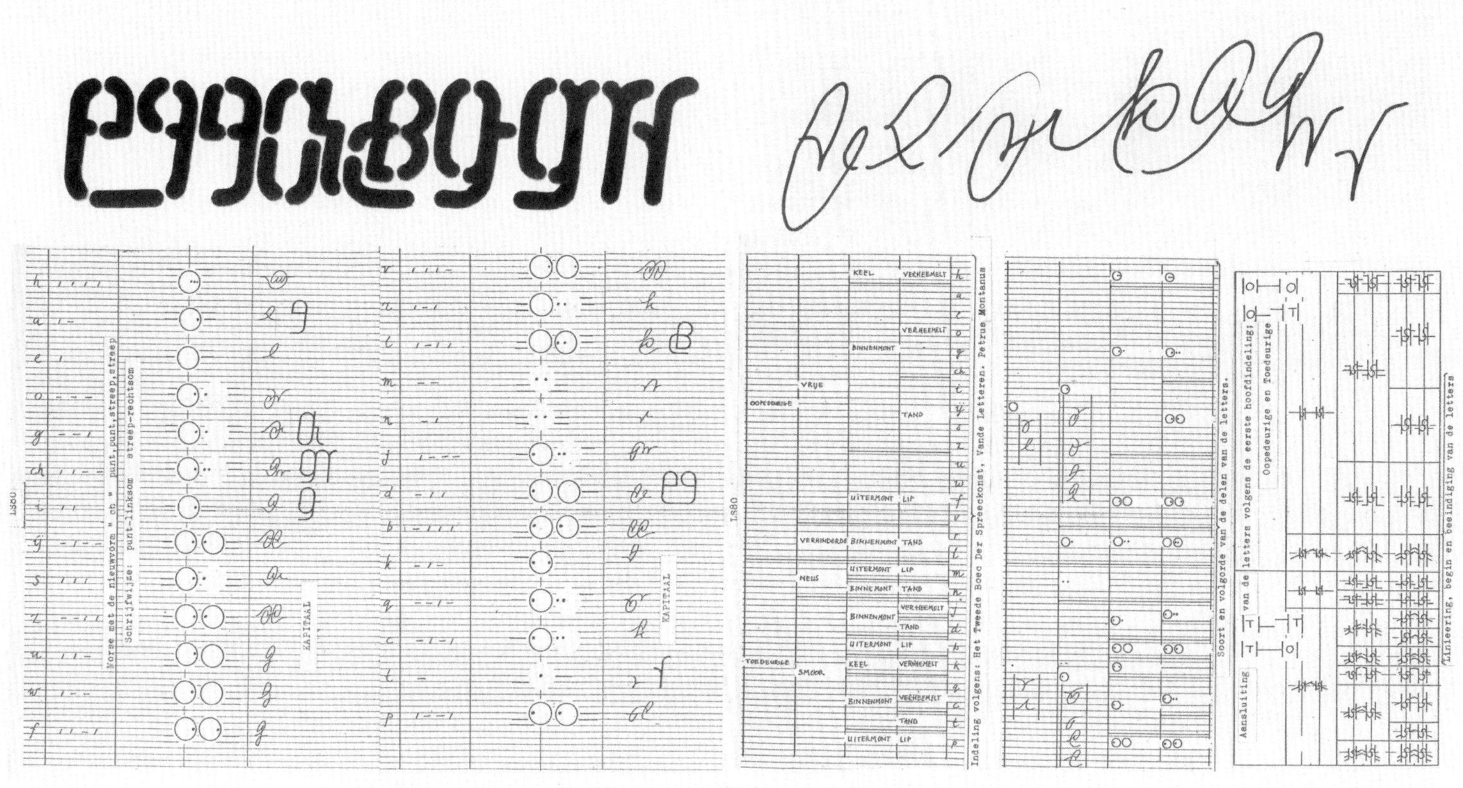

Hans van Dijk, phonetic alphabet, *Daglicht* no. 4, 1980

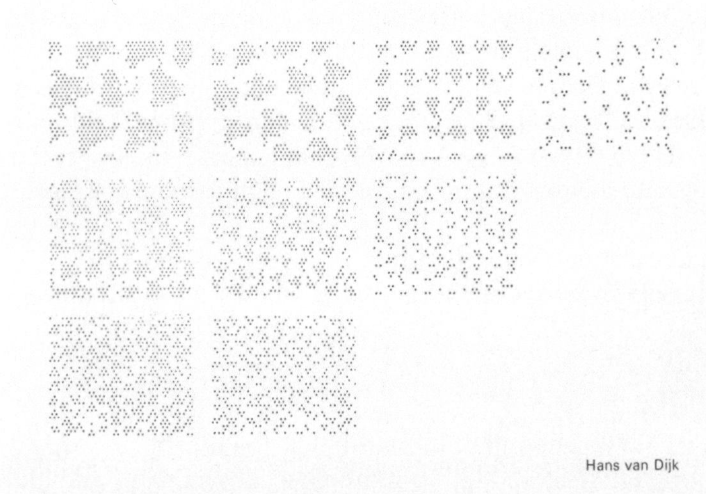

Hans van Dijk

Born November 19 1946, Deventer, Holland

Education
Academy for Art, Arnhem
Academy for Industrial Design, Eindhoven

One-man Exhibitions
1972 Gal. Swart, Amsterdam
1973 Gal. Swart, Amsterdam
1977 Gal. Swart, Amsterdam
1980 Gal. Magazijn, Groningen
1981 Gal. Swart, Amsterdam

Group Exhibition
1976 Gal. Magazijn, Groningen

Opening Sunday, 15th November 4-7 pm
Exhibition continues until 13th December

Sally East Gallery
229 Camberwell New Road
London SE5
01-701 9152
Open Thursday to Sunday 2-7 pm

Invitation card of Hans van Dijk's exhibition at Sally East Gallery, London, 1982, private coll.

1982 – 1984

Van Dijk gets his first international solo show at Sally East Gallery in London. He and Dinkla travel there together to install the show, where he exhibits *Arranged Patterns* and a series of new oil paintings of geometric color variations. They are different from any known works of van Dijk's so far, but it is unknown what led to their making, or whether they were part of a cycle. The paintings themselves have disappeared; only a photograph of a series of color studies remains in van Dijk's personal archive in Beijing.

While in London, they visit *The Great Japan Exhibition: Art of the Edo Period* at the Royal Academy of Arts. To Dinkla's surprise, van Dijk seems well informed on Japanese art. After the opening at Sally East, Dinkla returns to the Netherlands, while van Dijk travels on to Portsmouth to visit British artist Jeffrey Steele, who shows with Riekje Swart and whom van Dijk much admires.

The exhibition at Sally East Gallery is at once the highlight and the end of van Dijk's career as an artist. To this day, not even his closest friends know the precise reason for his decision to stop making art. He certainly would not have made his decision lightly or without fundamentally questioning the future of art, and of his own art practice.

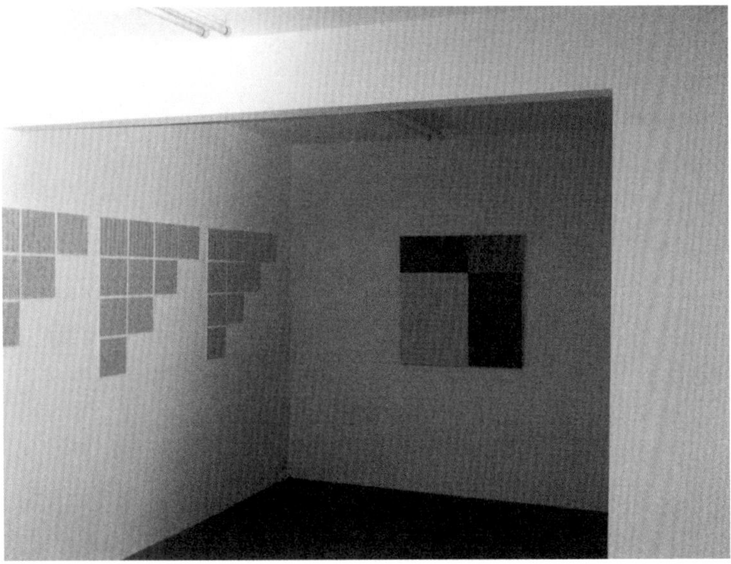

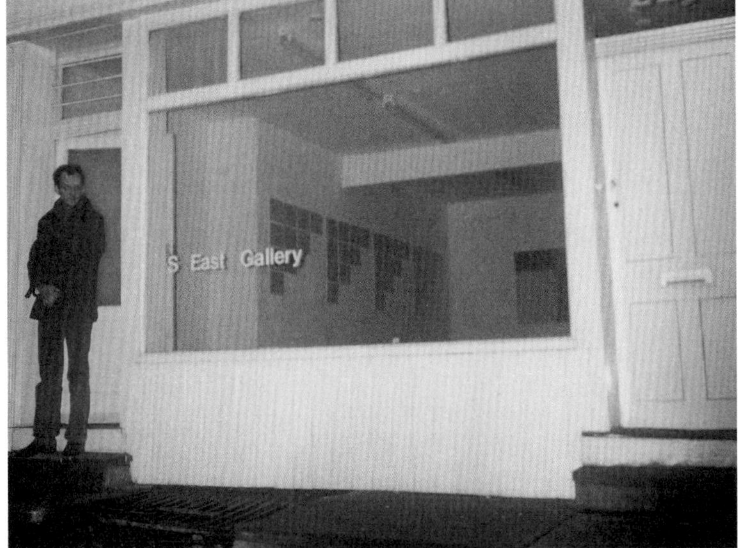

Exhibition view of *Arranged Patterns, group 2*, Sally East Gallery (left); Hans van Dijk in front of Sally East Gallery (right), 1982, photos Ernst Dinkla

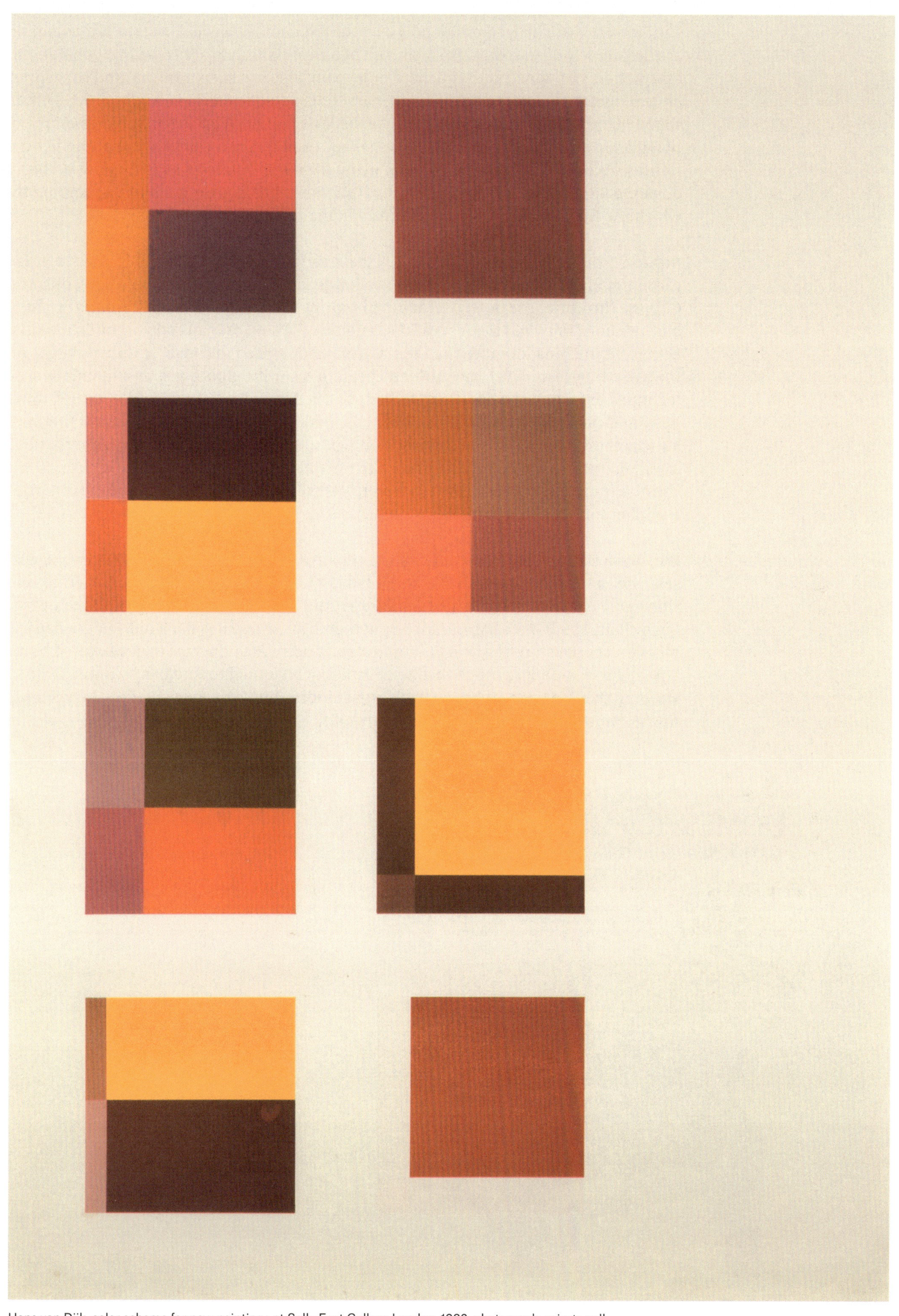

Hans van Dijk, color scheme for new paintings at Sally East Gallery, London, 1982, photograph, private coll.

The art world has changed profoundly over the last decade. The ideals of the sixties and seventies are definitively over. Postmodernism and neo-expressionism are trending; geometrical abstraction, neo-constructivism, hard-edge painting, and even minimal and conceptual art appear outdated. What about computer art? Compared to Struycken, whom van Dijk admires so much, he has always felt himself to be the lesser artist. What are his chances of making a living as an artist? In thirteen years, he has sold half a dozen works at most, and he adamantly refuses, according to Dinkla, to make a living from the Dutch art subsidy system, the much disputed *Beeldende Kunstenaars Regeling* (BKR, Fine Artists Arrangement), a program through which the Dutch state buys artworks from living artists.

Around 1983, van Dijk makes a discovery that changes the course of his life. Always interested in carpentry and the puzzles of its construction techniques, van Dijk buys a book on antique Chinese furniture. The book is a modified reprint of *Chinese Domestic Furniture in Photographs and Measured Drawings* by Gustav Ecke, a German professor in art and architectural history. Ecke lived in China for more than thirty years and wanted to conserve China's heritage before it was entirely lost to war and politics. Through beautiful photographs and uniquely detailed technical drawings, the book shows the construction of traditional tables, chairs, wardrobes, beds, and clothing racks, often made of rosewood. Their designs are timeless, sometimes dating back to the Ming (1368–1644), or even Song (960–1279) dynasties. The chairs in particular are often made to be dismountable, their parts fitting together like pieces of a puzzle without the use of any metal. First published in 1944 by Henri Vetch in Beijing, the book was reprinted in a smaller format by Richard Tuttle in 1962.

When van Dijk tries to make sense of the construction drawings, however, they are not always self-evident, and he cannot, of course, read the Chinese instructions. He travels to Leiden University to ask the department of Chinese studies about the instructions for a dismountable Ming chair, which he thinks cannot be put together the way it is depicted. But the department's scholars, specialists in classical Chinese art and poetry, are reluctant to get involved in carpentry. This angers van Dijk so much that he becomes determined to find out by himself. He starts learning Chinese from exchange students at Eindhoven University of Technology. Soon, he finds himself immersed in full-time Chinese lessons.

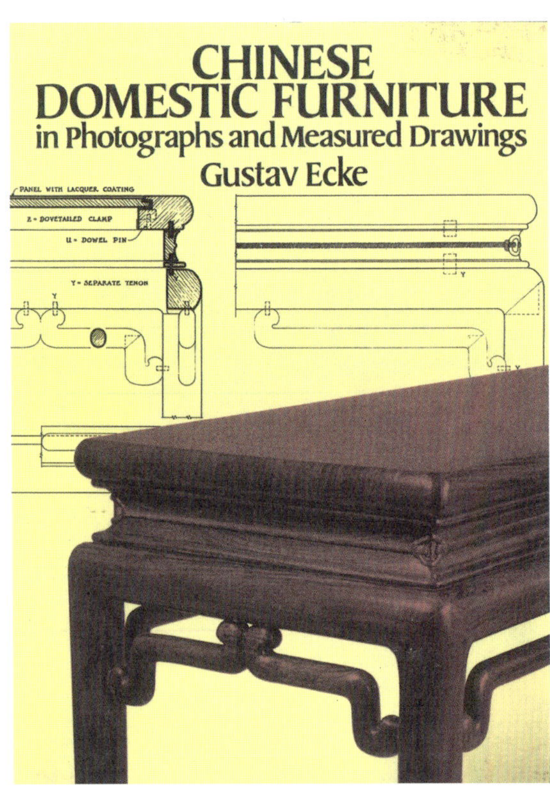

Gustav Ecke, *Chinese Domestic Furniture in Photographs and Measured Drawings*, reprint, Dover Publications Inc., New York, 1986

1984 - 1986

The book by Ecke proves to be a wonderful source of inspiration. Van Dijk designs a series of tables, stools, and screens in a semi-Chinese style, which he dubs "Ming-inspired Rietveld." He makes them for just a few friends and himself. Vinken gets a long table with a dark blue table top and legs, embellished with a light green rim and red accents. Dinkla opts for a granite and vermillion table top with silver legs. Photographer Peter Cox receives two bamboo stools in exchange for professional photos of van Dijk's commercial display systems. For his folding screens, van Dijk invents a system that allows him to connect the frames without the use of metal. For this technical feat, he collaborates with the famed TextielLab, the experimental production laboratory of the TextielMuseum in Tilburg. He makes three folding screens, four tables, and two bamboo stools in all. Sadly, the screens will not survive the ravages of time. As with all his designs, van Dijk refuses to make money from his "Ming-inspired Rietveld" by producing it on a commercial scale.

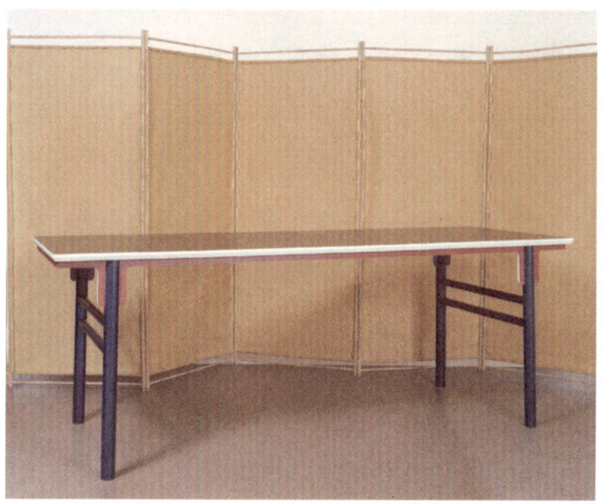

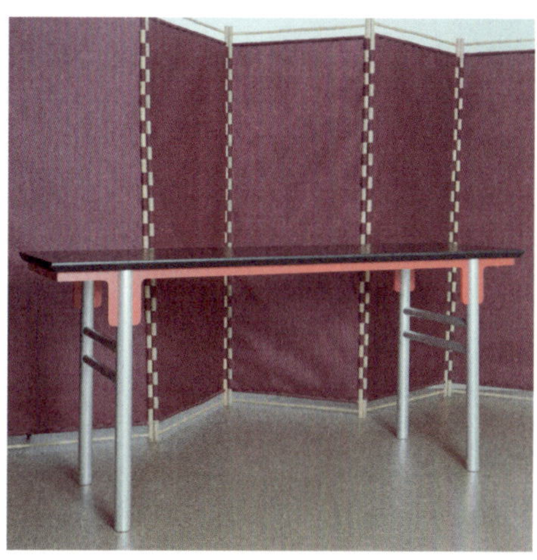

Hans van Dijk, screens and tables, 1983–84, private coll., photographer unknown; the screens have been lost

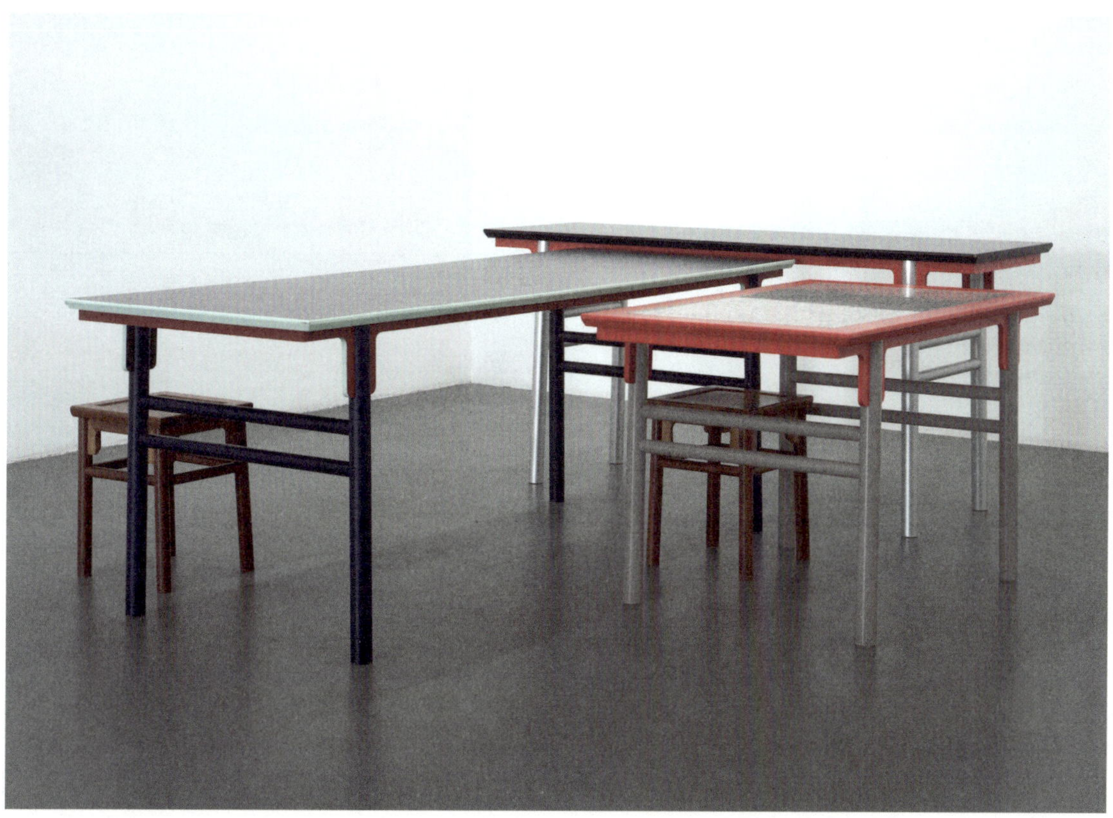

Hans van Dijk, "Ming-inspired Rietveld-style" tables and stools, dimensions variable, 1983-84, coll. Peter Cox, coll. Ernst Dinkla, coll. Monique Kies, coll. Jeroen Vinken, photo Witte de With, Cassander Eeftinck Schatterkerk

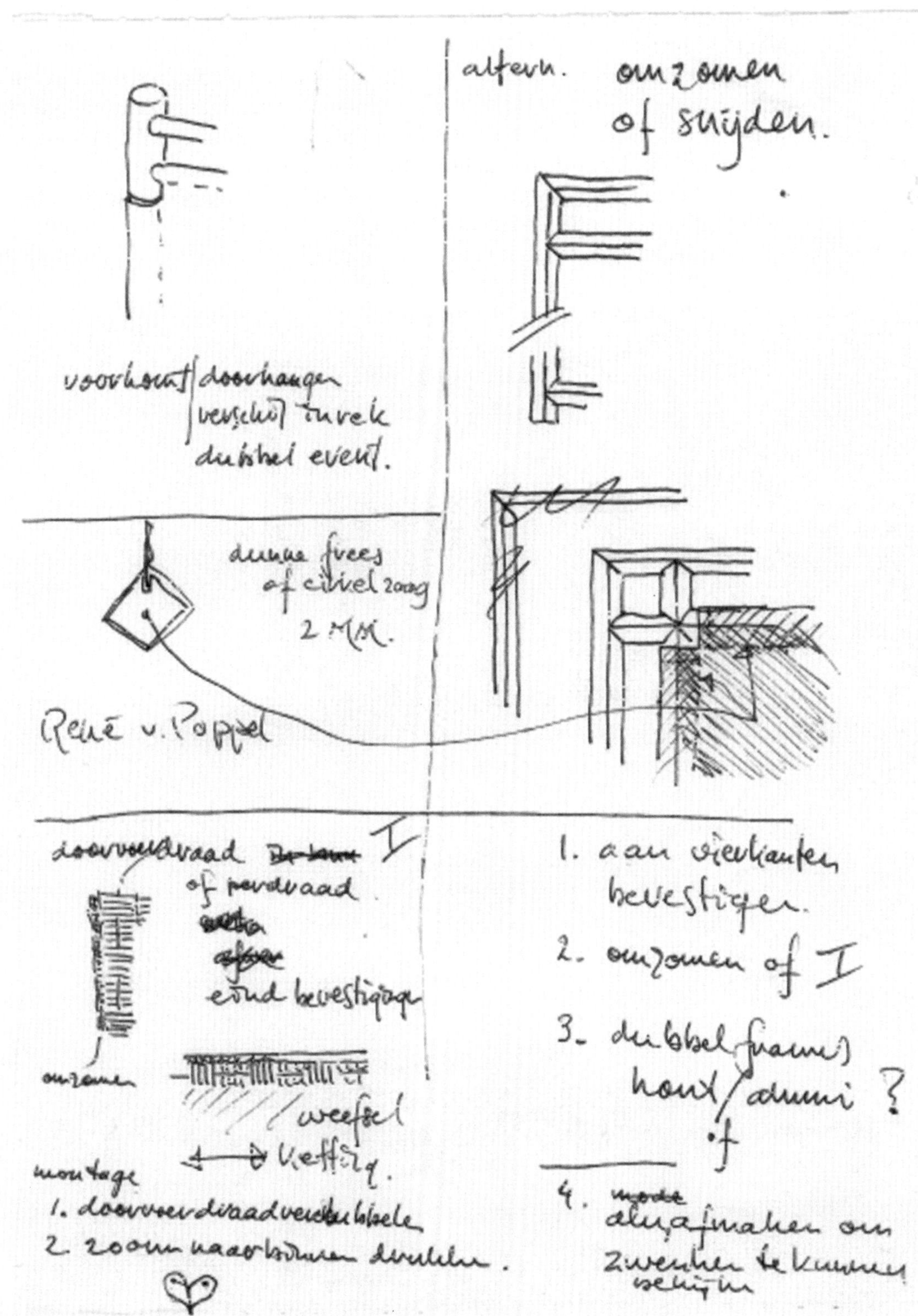

Hans van Dijk, technical drawings of joints and weaving for his screens, pencil on A4 paper, 1983–84, private coll.

For his favorite nephew, nine-year-old Julian, Pieter's son who is sick at home, he creates a funny, rhyming cartoon story. The lead character is a traditional Chinese carpenter who is (just like van Dijk) manufacturing a Ming table and encounters all sorts of adventures along the way. Van Dijk takes his character from a Ming-style ink drawing that is the frontispiece of Ecke's book.

During this period, many of van Dijk's friends begin to marry and settle down. Some move away to start businesses elsewhere. Dinkla marries his long-time girlfriend Ria van Boekholt. When she becomes pregnant, they need the factory to themselves. Van Dijk finds other lodgings in Eindhoven, where he lives in increasing isolation. This, perhaps more than anything else, inspires him to radically change his life and career.

He applies to study Chinese language and calligraphy at Nanjing University for an initial course of two years. He asks the City of Eindhoven for a grant. His parents support him with a one-time gift of fl.1000 (Dutch guilders, approx. € 455 today). A well-wishing aunt donates fl.500, promising to send more when needed. Van Dijk sells or gives away everything he owns. Dinkla supports him with another fl.1000, buying his van. Van Dijk rents out his room and leaves most of his books with Dinkla. While in China, Dinkla takes care of van Dijk's finances, and Vinken acts as his business representative in the Netherlands.

On 28 August 1986, van Dijk's friends throw him a farewell party. Vinken recalls that van Dijk, with a fine sense of the historical moment, asks them to preserve his letters from China "with an eye to the future." Under the assumption that the city will sponsor his trip, the local newspaper *Eindhovens Dagblad* dedicates an article to his departure.

So, at nearly forty years old, van Dijk leaves everything behind and moves to China.

八月二八号晚上
戴汉志的朋友给
汉志和他的朋友
欢送会欢迎你们

DONDERDAG 'S AVONDS
28 AUGUSTUS GEVEN
VRIENDEN VAN HANS
EEN AFSCHEIDSFEEST
VOOR HANS EN VRIENDEN.
ETEN EN DRINKEN IS
TEN DELE INGEVULD,
MAAR KAN NOG WORDEN
AANGEVULD.

HESSEN KASSELSTR. 10A
EINDHOVEN

Invitation to the farewell party thrown by van Dijk's friends before his departure for Nanjing, 1986, coll. Ernst Dinkla;
"Thursday evening 28 August friends of Hans throw a farewell party for Hans and friends. Food and drinks are partially provided for, but additions can be made."

Immersion
Nanjing, 1986–1989

Hans' way of working was like a gardener's: collecting documents, creating an archive.

Zhou Tiehai

1986

Van Dijk arrives in Nanjing via Hong Kong and Guangzhou in the first week of September. His first letter from China is to Ernst Dinkla and his wife. With obvious delight, he describes his first taste of Chinese street life and his ability to communicate:

> I spent the last evening in Guangzhou in the street. I bought two cans of beer at one of the innumerable kiosks, one to drink on the spot and one to go, which, very kindly, went back into the [vendor's] fridge. After some mutual orientating questions, we got into a functioning dialogue. [...] When food arrived for him and his wife, they insisted I eat with them, and from between the rubble they produced a table and three chairs, blocking up the rest of the sidewalk. More and more family members kept showing up.
> **HvD, letter to Ernst Dinkla, Nanjing, 8 September 1986**

Tourists are still a rarity in China; English is hardly spoken. The country is deeply impoverished, the population still numb from the aftermath of the Cultural Revolution. It is almost impossible to imagine that within fifteen years, China's east-coast cities will be well on their way to rivaling Tokyo or Singapore. But to those who want to see them, the signs are there: a vibrant, almost electric, current runs through the country. There is an energy that wants to be set free. And one of its outlets, although barely visible in 1986, is the radical rejuvenation of the arts.

Van Dijk takes to China with a growing sense of having reached his destiny in life. In witty, detailed letters, he reports to his friends back home in the Netherlands on life in China, the progress of his studies, and his gradual discovery of Chinese contemporary art, even as he struggles with the oddities of daily life.

He enrolls at the Nanjing University, where he follows the international course on Chinese language and culture. He is given the former room of fellow student Magnus Nordenhaake, a Swedish sinologist who is the first to introduce van Dijk to a contemporary artist: the young, Nanjing-based painter Zhou Yunxia. Another fellow student, the American Robert Bernell, a sinologist from Stanford University, will become a close friend.

Living quarters at the Institute's dormitory are tiny. Measuring 3.8 by 4.5 meters, he shares his room with two other students. "It's a bit tight, but that's the price you pay for a Chinese roommate," he writes to Dinkla a month after his arrival. "These are normal dimensions in China. Of all eighty rooms with a total of 160 'foreigners,' our room is the most frequented. [...] We—my roommate Chandra and I—applied for, and duly received, a Chinese student with bed, table, and a huge thermos. The idea was that he could practice more, because like all Chinese students he has learned English for some six years but hardly ever spoken a word of it, and doesn't seem to want to do so in the future." In the same letter, van Dijk announces, "I am now certain that I want to stay here for two years or maybe even more."[1]

1—HvD, letter to Ernst Dinkla, Nanjing, 11 October 1986.

As winter approaches, he sometimes falls ill, possibly more often than he likes to admit. The city of Eindhoven has refused the subsidy he applied for. He studies Chinese diligently: writing and grammar, compiling his own Dutch-English-Chinese dictionary. In a playful challenge to himself, he writes down his dreams in Dutch free verse and translates them into Chinese. Communication with Liu, his Chinese roommate, is improving: "Via Futurism we already arrived at Nietzsche. Together with Freud, he was published here in translation in 1984. Both became hugely popular and thus constitute the successors to Sartre and Camus, who were released in '81."[2]

2—HvD, letter to Ernst Dinkla, 21 January 1987. These were the years of China's *culture fever*, when people were avidly trying to catch up with previously forbidden Western literature and philosophy. Phrases like *two hundred years in two days* were coined.

In 1985, the first generation of young Chinese artists—which comes to be known as the '85 Generation, the Heroic Generation, or simply the New Wave—graduates from the art academies, which were closed during the Cultural Revolution (1966–76). Until 1985–86, "experimental" art was not allowed to be shown in public at all. This is slowly changing, however. Intense debates about the future of art are taking place all over China, with Nanjing as one of its most important intellectual centers and the Zhejiang Academy of Fine Arts (now the China Academy of Art) in Hangzhou as its pioneering institute.

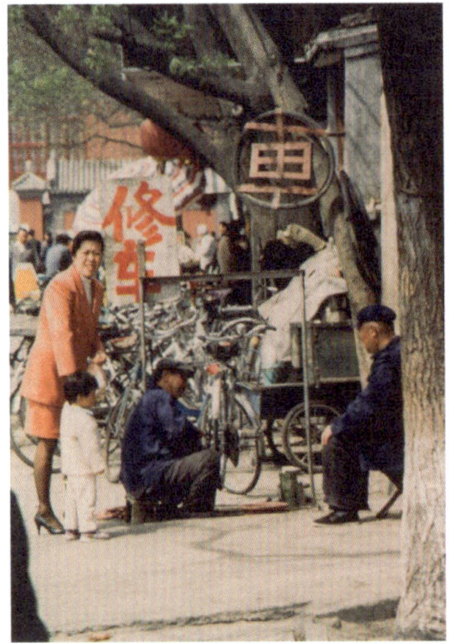

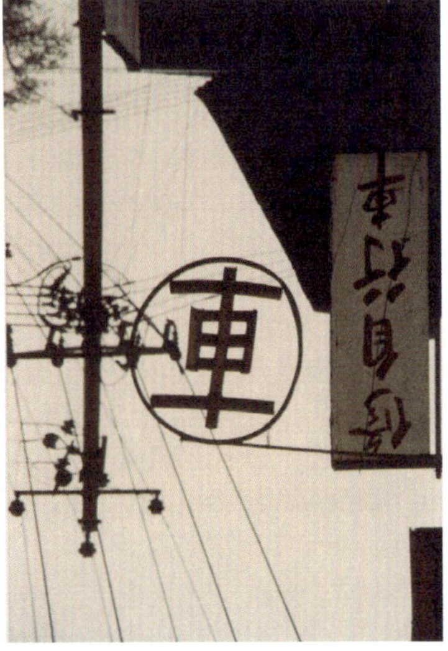

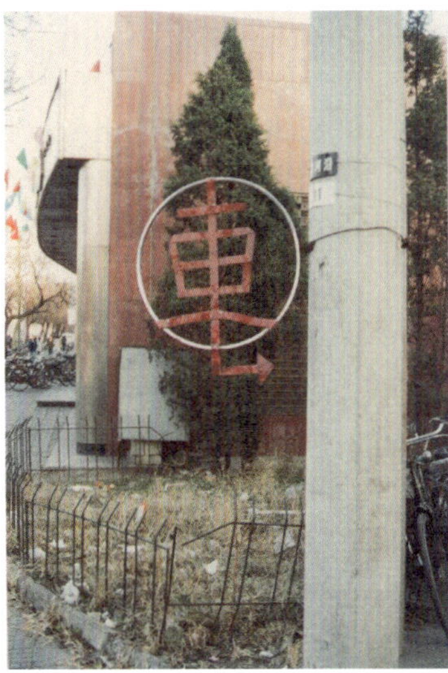

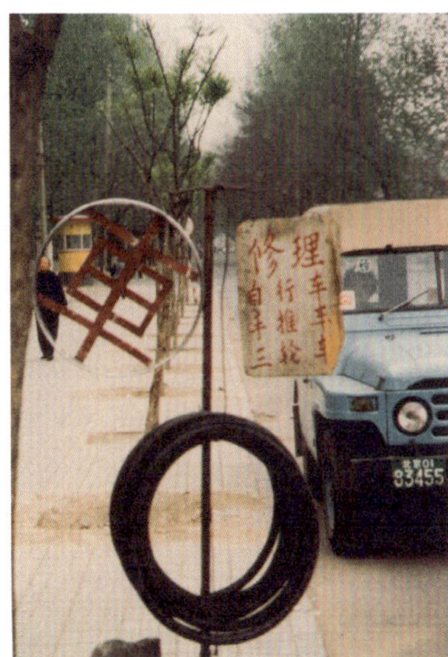

Hans van Dijk, photographs of car and vehicle repair shops, Nanjing, circa 1986, private coll.

In 1985, Li Xiaoshan, a young professor of Chinese ink painting at the Nanjing Arts Institute, publishes one of the most important critical essays of the eighties: "My Opinion on Contemporary Chinese Ink Painting" (Dangdai zhongguohua zhi wojian) in the magazine *Jiangsu Art Monthly* (*Jiangsu Huakan*), issue 7. It is a passionate plea to either abandon or radically transform traditional ink painting, the most venerated of Chinese arts and one of the two official state arts. The article triggers a nation-wide debate, of which Nanjing is the intellectual center.

Although van Dijk initially has no concept of the emerging young art scene in China, it doesn't take him long to recognize that something extraordinary is happening, something he wants to bear witness to: an irresistible current that will determine the course of many lives, including his own, sweeping him into a future very different from what he, or anyone else, anticipated. Seeing Gu Wenda's self-invented, radical calligraphy in *Meishu*, China's leading art magazine, van Dijk discovers for the first time how innovative the '85 New Wave (*xinchao*) is.

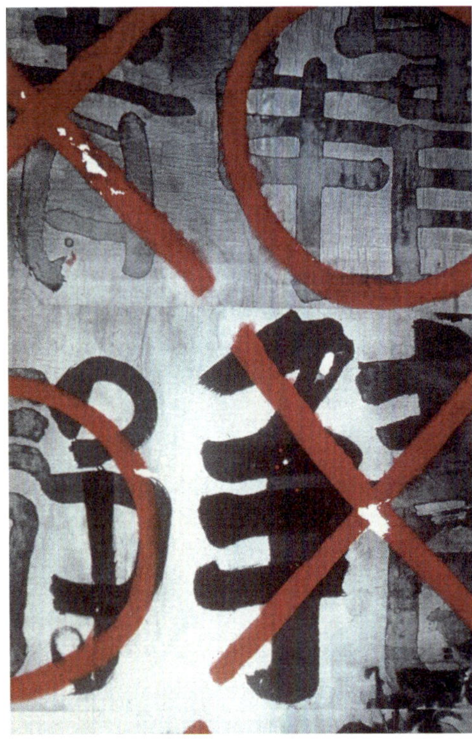

Gu Wenda, *Mythos of Lost Dynasties Series – I Evaluate Characters Written by Three Men and Three Women* (detail), ink on paper, 285 × 178 cm, 1985; featured in *Meishu* 7, 1986

Dear Ernst, Ria, and Sip, happy New Year,
I have subscribed to eight magazines on fine art, folk art, and art history. Suddenly there are articles everywhere on the conflict between traditional and modern art. Until a month ago, modern art was synonymous with oil painting. But recent articles already discuss "action art." Veritable happenings are taking place in the streets of Xiamen. *Meishu*, a magazine published in Beijing and aimed at those with a medium- to high-level education, recently contained a lengthy interview with an artist who totally disowns his former, classical work, and was elaborately praised in another article for his modern, free work. And it looks good: big panels with very un-calligraphic [Chinese] characters with crosses and zeros painted over them. Images of a mouth, sometimes, accompanied by brush strokes and characters, all of it painted over rather randomly, full of symbolism and meaning, yet robust and open. I saw so many exhibitions by now with mountains, waterfalls, and clouds, or grass with bamboo, always paired with calligraphy, that I believed it to be the norm. I am curious whether there is still enough [money to last] for a third year here. I'll walk back if necessary.
HvD, letter to Ernst Dinkla, Nanjing, 21 January 1987

1987

Van Dijk spends Chinese New Year in the countryside with the family of a Chinese fellow student on a farm some thirty kilometers from Nanjing. "I shared a bed with the fourteen-year-old son of the family. As I woke up in the morning, some six people stood staring at me: 'Is that the guy, now, forty years? Doesn't look it, studying at that age is not good.'"[3]

3—HvD, letter to Ernst Dinkla, 9 March 1987.

By the beginning of the year, van Dijk is already translating Li Xiaoshan's essay into Dutch. In addition, he conducts a number of interviews with the protagonists of the Nanjing polemic, translating their art-theoretical contributions to the debate: Dong Xibin, *A Few Words about My Opinion as Well* (1985); Liu Ruli, *A Visit to the Art World* (1986); and Fan Zeng, *An Overview of Chinese Art* (1987).[4]

4—Unfortunately, there are no recordings of the interviews. Van Dijk's transcripts are still in his personal archive in Beijing, however.

His second semester begins in February:

> My weekly schedule consists of a few lessons, three in total, and appointments outside University. Except for the course "newspaper reading," all my attempts at mastering the language are connected to the broad field of the "visual arts." There is an interesting course about the development of Chinese script, [...] I found a booklet about that, including contemporary decorative script for commercial and propaganda purposes. In due course, I hope to send something in translation; it's also about fonts. Other subjects are garden architecture—the traditional environmental art of China—painting, and calligraphy. [...]
> There is a lot of inspection going on here: who is visiting, who enters, and who leaves. It's very normal as well to inquire about others, where they are, where they were, at what time. When I go out for a bite around eleven in the evening, the time I leave gets written down, and when I return half an hour later, the night watch in the gateway interrupts his meal to write a note about what time and in whose company. A nice guy by the way, that night watch, he explained to me: "We Chinese may have little eyes, but we see everything!"
> **HvD, letter to Ernst Dinkla, Nanjing, 9 March 1987**

In May, van Dijk travels to Hangzhou for the first time, visiting a student exhibition at the Zhejiang Academy of Fine Arts. There, he meets with some of the New Wave artists: Yan Lei and Liu Anping, who are still very young, and the somewhat older Tang Song (who at the time goes by Tangselman). He also meets Geng Jianyi and Zhang Peili, who are both teachers and co-founders of the experimental artist collective Pond Society (*Chi She*). Following van Dijk's visit, Geng Jianyi and Zhang Peili send him the "Pond Society Manifesto" (May 1986), and the "Pond Society Bulletin No. 1–2" (June 1986). Strangely, van Dijk doesn't mention anything about these encounters when writing to Jeroen Vinken in a somewhat despondent letter:

It's all true, the superstition, the shitting in the streets, a panicky fear of illness and death, horribly authoritarian: what the master says or what is printed is true […] Happy in China? Don't ask me such a question. It's the biggest island on earth, they don't mind explaining the world to you […] the level of teaching is so low that your grades are not taken seriously by any other country in the world—Africa excepted. […] When I remark this to [Chinese] friends they say: why do you think we are so keen to leave this country? I really like it here, compared to the Netherlands I have interesting work, I am rich, I squatted a room, and I can dispose of my own time.

I have now definitely shaped my program:

I. The development of Chinese writing according to various fonts used in printing until today
II. The discussions in art magazines about the renewal in art
III. Recent art history and the formation of groups '85–86 (since the student demonstrations, forming groups and exhibiting contemporary art has become somewhat dangerous)
IV. To visit artists that are trying out things, exchange of exhibitions in the future.

Much information on Western modern art is used in China as a kind of example for copying, like the obligatory copying of traditional art in art academies. Progressive artists in turn paint on the sly after Cézanne or such in their studios in their spare time. Teaching Western fine arts and crafts here should be done with minimal use of images; it should, in any case, be dominated by content, the reasoning behind our recent art history. How to achieve that, I don't yet know; my language skills are still insufficient, but I continue working at it through II and III. Luckily, I found good friends who help me. Chinese, they say, are intelligent, cowardly, and diligent, this upon further acquaintance.

HvD, letter to Jeroen Vinken, Nanjing, 9 June 1987

Van Dijk is becoming increasingly interested in the history of modernity in China: the beginnings of Western-inspired oil painting at the end of the nineteenth century; printmaking during the New Culture movement; and the avant-garde underground artist groups from the seventies and early eighties, like the No Name Painting Society (*Wuming Huahui*) and the Stars (*Xingxing Huahui*). Throughout the next two years he collects as much material on Chinese modern and contemporary art as he can find, creating an archive of names, images, books, magazines, and articles for reference. He notes his findings in English and Chinese on hundreds of small filing cards that he keeps in aluminum meal trays, while also keeping photos of artists and their works in plastic files.

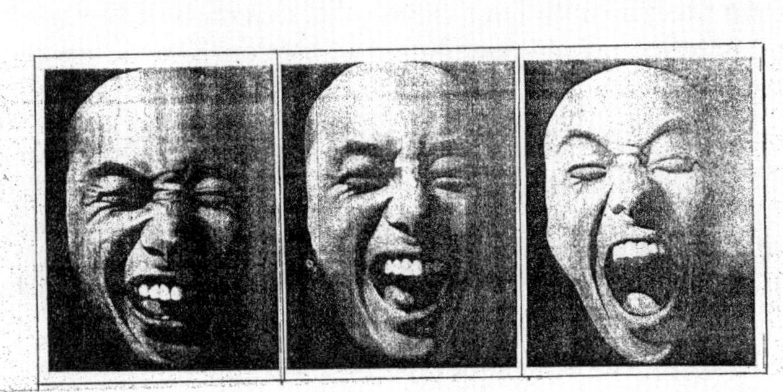

Gelukkig Nieuwjaar Lieve Jeroen,

mijn Japanse kamergenoot was geschokt toen hij de ingesloten lachers zag. Ik ben zo gelukkig geweest met de schilder in mei–'87 kennis te maken. Een koele chinees. Dit werk had hij toen nog niet. Het is een verademing vergeleken met de zachte, gevoelose lacht die tot de omgangsvorm behoort.

Ik heb dus een fanbrief geschreven.

Heb je het boek over de klederdrachten van de minderheids-volken in China ontvangen? Hoe gaat het eigenlijk.

Hans. 31-12-87 Nanjing

Hans van Dijk, letter to Jeroen Vinken, Nanjing, 31 December 1987, including photocopies of three of the four faces from Geng Jianyi's *The Second State*, 1987, coll. Jeroen Vinken

By the end of 1987, Geng Jianyi sends him photocopies of a new series of paintings. This time he does find the words to describe the impression they make on him:

> Happy New Year, dear Jeroen, my Japanese roommate was quite shocked when he saw the laughing faces I've enclosed here. In May '87, I had the good fortune to make the painter's acquaintance, a cool Chinese. He hadn't made this work at the time. It's a relief compared to the soft, emotionless laugh that is part of polite Chinese manners.
> So I sent him a letter of fan mail.
>
> **HvD, letter to Jeroen Vinken, Nanjing, 31 December 1987**

1988

By now, van Dijk is known amongst artists by his Chinese name, Dai Hanzhi: Dai meaning Dijk; Hanzhi, Hans. In February, Zhang Peili sends him the texts of two elaborate conceptual art works, *Project "X?"* and *Art Project No. 2*. Van Dijk immediately starts translating the texts into both Dutch and English, corresponding with Zhang Peili about the precise meaning of phrases and words. He also writes an essay, "The Artists Geng Jianyi and Zhang Peili, Founders of the Pond Society."[5]

5—HvD, *De kunstenaars Zhang Peili en Geng Jianyi, oprichters van de Vijver-gemeenschap,* unpublished article, Nanjing, 1988. Dutch manuscript kept in the CAAW archive, Beijing.

Van Dijk decides to study Chinese art history after he finishes his course at the Nanjing University in September. He applies for a Master in Chinese art history at the prestigious Central Academy of Fine Arts (CAFA) in Beijing. To be on the safe side, he also applies for a similar Master course with professor Liu Ruli at the Nanjing Arts Institute.

As part of his program at the Nanjing University, van Dijk plans to set up a cultural exchange program between the Netherlands and China with the help of Els Boertje, a Dutch artist he met at the Zhejiang Academy: "Something like a foundation called Modern Art in China. She could manage the contacts, and I could keep feeding her interesting things from China."[6] In fall 1987, Boertje returns to the Netherlands with a stash of artworks, Tang Song's among them. As a follow-up, van Dijk sends her his translations and a great amount of illustrative material. Most of the material gets lost in the mail, however. His efforts to establish a link between the printing departments of the art academies in Hangzhou and Nanjing, and the *Daglicht* graphic studio in Eindhoven are equally dogged by bad luck. The Dutch side shows interest, but the phone doesn't work, packages get mislaid.

6—HvD, letter to Jeroen Vinken, Nanjing, 9 June 1988.

Van Dijk starts to feel slightly uprooted as a consequence. On 20 March he writes to Jeroen Vinken, "I am in fact dealing with three different worlds here; I'm starting to slightly lose my grip on the one I come from." The other worlds are the multicultural one within the walls of the college, and the one outside it: China. Van Dijk's repeated observations on cultural differences in his letters, though witty and seemingly anecdotal, are deeply serious: their core subject is the interpretation of contemporary Chinese art. As a foreigner, can he trust his gut reactions to what he sees?[7] These days, his comments on Geng Jianyi's works function like a red thread. Throughout his letters home, they become the yardstick by which he measures his own growing understanding of Chinese art.

7—"World Three: Differences in habit are always small and gradual, but their provenance may be rooted so deeply that you can get used to them and sometimes be able to explain them, but they will never become a part of you." Ibid.

> I met the laughing artist in May last year and sent him a fan letter in reply to those photocopies which I sent you too. Since that time, we have been keeping up a correspondence. He answered my letter using the familiar "you"-mode, which pleased me a lot. At the time, he asked me outright: what are your motives? Geng Jianyi is one of the three more important members of the Pond Society—there is an abundance of art groups here—but I believe he truly stands out. [...] Lately, the Pond Society mainly produces manifestos, which I am diligently translating. [...] Modern art holds an ambiguous position in China. There is an enormous hunger for Western modern art amongst artists under the age of forty. After that, they rightfully start to fear for their job or position and take on a more distant stance, without ceasing their cordial cooperation. In practice, however, this interest in modern art manifests itself in zealously copying a style without paying much attention to theory. The biggest wish of many is to see the works in real

> life; there is a great distrust towards reproductions. I find it difficult to judge a work painted in an impressionist or cubist manner. Most of the time it is technically perfect, which makes it difficult to distinguish any personal traits.
>
> **HvD, letter to Jeroen Vinken, Nanjing, 20 March 1988**

Around March or April 1988, van Dijk visits Hangzhou again to see the trial installation of Geng Jianyi's *Water Factory* at the Silk Institute, where the latter is teaching:

> In Hangzhou, I met with Geng Jianyi once more after a year. This time, we embraced each other. He showed me his latest project, a confrontation with the audience in which the audience is the artwork. I've also seen the paintings with the heads, of which I've sent you copies before. They are harsh, raw, well painted. You could see them as Chinese versions of *The Scream* by Edvard Munch. More friends have confronted me with that shrill ambiguity in which joy and catastrophe come together in one expression [...].
> The second article of the collected works of the Pond Society, page three "The Recent Paintings of the Pond Society," highlights their interest in rituals and more-or-less unplanned activities. The question on page six especially caught my attention: "It's worth wondering whether you can remember images that do not originate from a repeated experience." What's special about both Zhang Peili and Geng Jianyi (they are the driving forces in the group) is their focus on their relation to the audience. Generally, writers in this field evince a psychological insight that sometimes frightens me. At Zhang Peili's home, I came across a large number of paintings with swimming pools or water sports. He lives with his parents, and just like Geng he married last year and has become a father. Above the Zhangs' dining table, there hangs a big painting of a boy basking in the sun. Like his wife, I thought it was an amazing piece, but Zhang thought it was "too sweet."
> Chinese traditional art, which is what the art academies teach, is best described in terms of art practice: subjects and content are a given, the medium—brush, ink, and a special kind of paper—has been laid down in advance, and an artist's personal expression is only accepted after he reaches the age of forty, when he is able to measure up to his teachers and to the classical examples which he used to copy thus far.
> Perhaps the centuries-old stress on the performative aspect of the arts (for instance in calligraphy), has also caused that great sensitivity concerning human behavior and its psychological aspects. The [Dutch] poet Komrij speaks of the artless, the unaffected; in Chinese art, it's about naturalness of expression in spite of the fact that the expression has come about after much travail.
> It is the time of openings; therefore, I'm going to Shanghai tomorrow for a few days.
>
> **HvD, fax to Jeroen Vinken, Nanjing, 24 April 1988**

While in Shanghai, van Dijk meets Ni Haifeng, one of the most radical ink painters of the New Wave. He also goes to see an exhibition of experimental painting at the Shanghai Art Museum. There is one artist in the show whose works he finds truly interesting: Ding Yi. Meanwile, van Dijk is becoming increasingly uneasy; CAFA's permission to enroll in the Master course he applied for keeps being delayed for reasons unknown.

> What is corruption? To express it very mildly, you don't get much done in this country without personal intervention. [...] When I applied for Beijing, I was given the name of a friend of a friend, an artist who had just finished her studies at the Beijing art academy. Each time my trustworthy go-between took my letters to a friendly teacher/civil servant, that person added more conditions: you still need to send us an essay on Chinese art written by you, not a translation, in my opinion you can do with any article in any chosen language, adding that you are the author. After another month: You have to send us a personal recommendation by a foreign teacher at a university who can confirm your capacities in the art historical field, I believe the statement suffices that you have already sent the request to said foreign authority, that the recommendation is certain to be written but, due to postal delays, has not yet arrived.
>
> **HvD, letter to Jeroen Vinken, Nanjing, 16 August 1988**

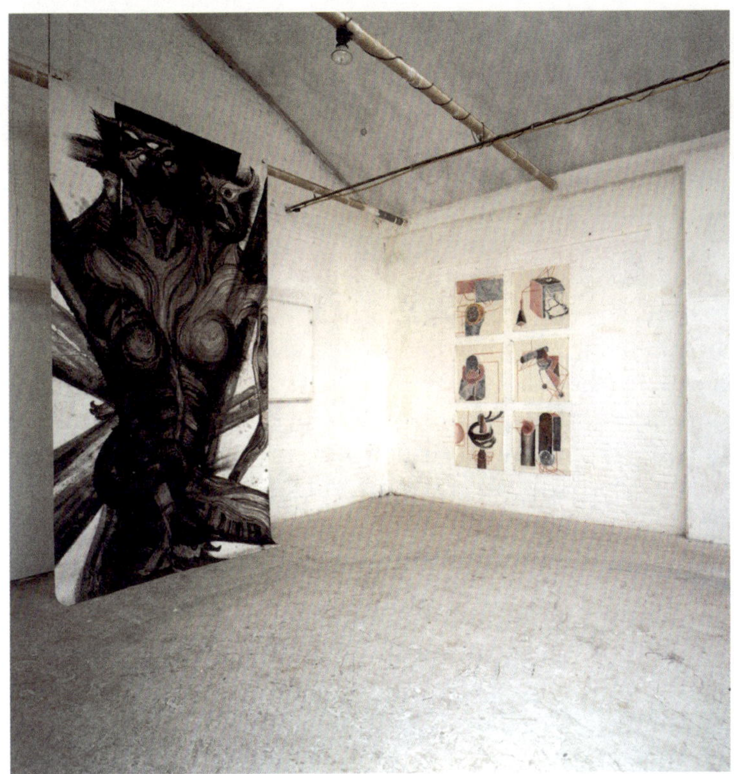
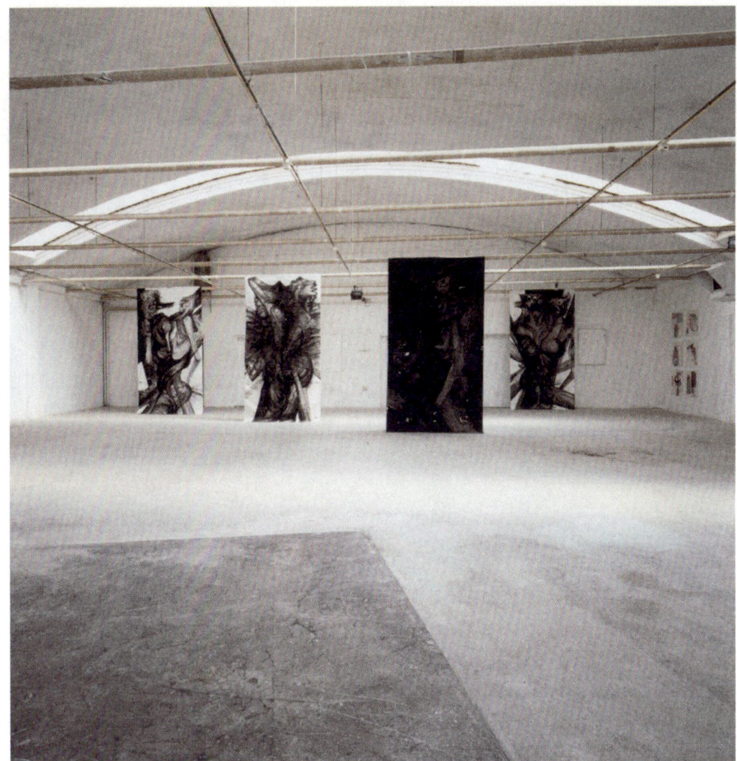

China—Het Westen, De Fabriek, Eindhoven, 1988, exhibition views with large ink paintings by Tangselman (Tang Song), photo Peter Cox

From 8–14 May, Els Boertje organizes the exhibition *China – The West* at De Fabriek (The Factory), an alternative artist exhibition space in Eindhoven founded by the *Daglicht* team. Li Xiaoshan's *My Opinion on Contemporary Chinese Ink Painting* is published in the catalogue in van Dijk's translation. Following the show, Boertje sends van Dijk a letter, declining his invitation to work together further. For the time being, van Dijk abandons his plan to establish a cultural exchange program.

> For the past one and a half years, I have been propagating that there is great curiosity in the Netherlands about the art here. I now believe that I begin to develop a somewhat more realistic view. There is some interest in the Netherlands, and certain expectations regarding contemporary art in China, but many may be severely disappointed when confronted with reality on the ground: first of all, the wish for an interesting modern art, able to play a role in the West, will rarely be satisfied. That may take some time still. Secondly, there is the request for mysticism both in the Netherlands and in other countries. [...] Visitors often feel cheated when they discover how much materialism exists in daily life here. Many artists let themselves be guided by fame and money. Chinese culture has always been very pragmatic. For mysticism, one had perhaps better go to India or Tibet.
>
> HvD, letter to Jeroen Vinken, Nanjing, 9 June 1988

Although he lives extremely frugally, van Dijk needs money to pay for his studies and to ensure his prolonged stay in China. Yet another subsidy application to the City of Eindhoven has been turned down, but he has help: "Ernst has done a lot of good by continuously reassuring my parents, and by putting money in my bank account, the source of which I don't know." Van Dijk's correspondence with CAFA has been dragging on for months, but he finally receives word that he has been accepted:

> Eight letters in total went to and fro... this procedure went on for months on end: the letters go missing, I fall ill, the mail goes missing, the teacher falls ill, et cetera. In July the confirmation arrived: I have been admitted to the most famous academy of the country with the longest cultural tradition in the world, could I transfer the tuition fee

of 2,500 US dollars? I haughtily turned that down clarifying that an application for a Dutch subsidy would be to no avail because this amount is more than four times higher than the tuition fee at Dutch universities. [...] What is offered in Beijing for that kind of money actually doesn't mean so much. In reality, you pay for your residence permit, and that is all it means. Libraries remain inaccessible to foreigners just as much as to the Chinese themselves. Teachers basically don't have much leeway to get anything accomplished. Who exactly is responsible for setting up all these double tariffs here, one for foreigners—according to what one assumes is paid in "foreign countries"—and one for domestic use, is not clear. It's a mixture of stupidity and arrogance.
Most of the time you can negotiate such fees, but I had just received permission anyway to continue in Nanjing for less than half the money. Here, I can get around by bike most of the time. Nanjing is a beautiful city. A lot of it was built when it was the capital of the Kuomintang-republic, all those houses and small palaces rise royally above their surrounding walls, and have been painted yellow. Around the end of the nineteenth century, the French introduced plane trees here, and after the recent heatwave I will forever remain grateful to them for doing so.

HvD, letter to Jeroen Vinken, Nanjing, 16 August 1988

Though his description is idyllic, van Dijk's life in Nanjing is not without its dangers. Homosexuality is still illegal in China, and there is a real risk for foreigners who have been reported on to be deported or have their visa refused. He is constantly heckled by an intrusive, "26-year-old brute" who manages the entrance gate of the campus. "He acts obscenely toward the girls and has it in for the boys. [...] He has his suspicions and provokes me from time to time. He asks my friends whether they amuse themselves in my bed."[8] During his student days in Nanjing, van Dijk is arrested once in a police raid on a cruising area for homosexuals, and he almost has his passport taken away. When he returns to China in 1991 to prepare for the *China Avant-garde* show, this incident in Nanjing still haunts him; even after his visa has been granted, he is still terrified that he may have been given some "black mark" by the city administration, which, when discovered, will bar his access to China.

8—HvD, letter to Jeroen Vinken, Nanjing, 16 August 1988.

By mid-August, van Dijk travels to Beijing for the first time, staying in the city for three weeks: "It came as a recognition of sorts. The Forbidden City, for six centuries the quarters of the emperors and their courts, resembled the arrangement of the university campus quite a bit, lots of walls and gates, everyone knows their place and their function. Gates are also always gate buildings, where the responsible controllers are stationed."[9]

9—HvD, letter to Jeroen Vinken, Nanjing, 20 September 1988.

In September, van Dijk moves to the Nanjing Arts Institute to start his Master in Chinese art history. It is a small fine arts college of only 200 students.

I now live at the art academy in a single room of 3 by 4 meters filled with 14 holdalls and a table. For two weeks, I have been busy applying for cupboards and already started to gather bricks and planks lying around in the yard of the academy. I dismantled a dining table, which I also found amid the junk, and which is perhaps some ten years old. It was an easy task because it had been constructed entirely according to the rules of carpentry from the Ming dynasty.
At the academy I live in a free-standing house that was built for the 92-year-old Liu Haisu six years before, who founded the academy in the thirties after returning from his studies in Paris. He is now director in name only and lives in Shanghai. When in Nanjing, he resides in the grandest tourist hotel. From time to time he donates a painting to that business, which means that the academy is now burdened with an empty "Liu Palace." The building is semi-Western, and everything that's Western about it suffers from shortcomings: the roof leaks and the toilets will be functioning shortly.
The security service, three men strong, has been housed in the erstwhile director's residence, while the two foreign students occupy the room of 3 by 4 meters intended for personnel. I play chess with the members of the security service, and they help me wash the bricks.

HvD, letter to Jeroen Vinken, Nanjing, 20 September 1988

Deborah Nash, an English art student, has just arrived. Together they will attend the student demonstrations in the fatal year of 1989. "She is 27 years old and wants to enrich her art by learning Chinese painting techniques. She doesn't speak Chinese as yet, so I am translating for her."[10]

10—HvD, letter to Jeroen Vinken, Nanjing, 20 September 1988.

Van Dijk studies with art historian Liu Ruli on the condition that he doesn't need to follow classes.

> I met Liu Ruli because of one of his articles. He is seventy years old and writes in a rather classical style. Unfortunately, he speaks a pure Suzhou dialect, which baffles other students too. We agreed that I will present him with a plan for my studies: researching artist collectives in the PRC in the early eighties. That was a new phenomenon to him, but he is open to new things and not afraid of things foreign, nor of internal meddling. Most teachers at the academy are between fifty and sixty years old, and whatever art education they might have had, it would have been one with a lot of Russian socialist realism. Throughout the years this has been watered down to "social" or "progressive realism" and this is what they stick to in their teaching. Professor Liu is above it all; he grumbles about the scant knowledge artists have of their own culture.
>
> **HvD, letter to Jeroen Vinken, Nanjing, 20 September 1988**

In October 1988, together with Chinese friends[11], van Dijk departs on a 6,000-kilometer, 300-dollar journey to west China to see the Buddhist caves in Dunhuang, Gansu province. In postcards and a five-page letter to Dinkla, he describes their journey by train and bus through China's westernmost provinces in a sparse, almost denuded language, as if trying to mirror the vast landscape of mountains and deserts:

11—Including the painter Ge Hui (b. 1961), who also studies at Nanjing Arts Institute.

> Only the color changed from anthracite to salt-white, then the camels appear, wild by the look of them, then marram grass and a few sheep, and you are in Dunhuang. A junction in the silk road: N-S Mongolia-Tibet, E-W Turkey-China, inside-outside the Wall. [...] From Dunhuang to Golmud in the south, it's 520 kilometers and fifteen city buses. A few enormous mountain chains, a single stopping place. Not a blade of green, but green mountains, yellow mountains, grey, and red mountains. [...] Golmud: go left to return to the heart of China, straight on for Tibet. To the right is the desert with re-education camps and ore-mining.
>
> **HvD, letter to Ernst Dinkla, Nanjing, 12 November 1988**

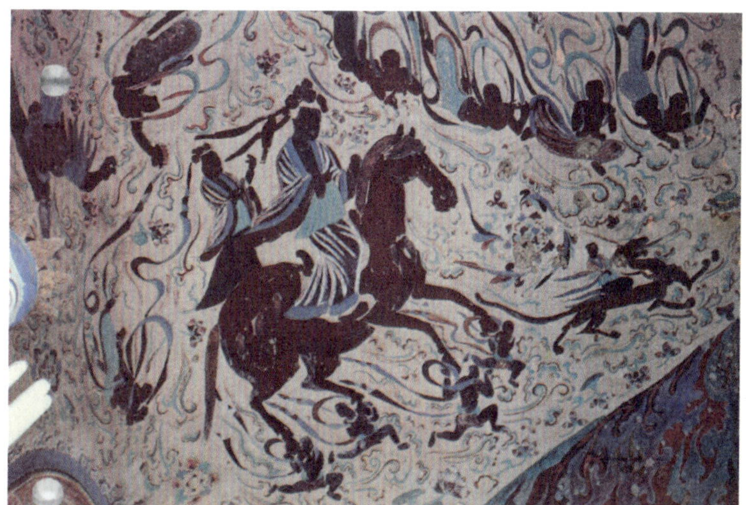

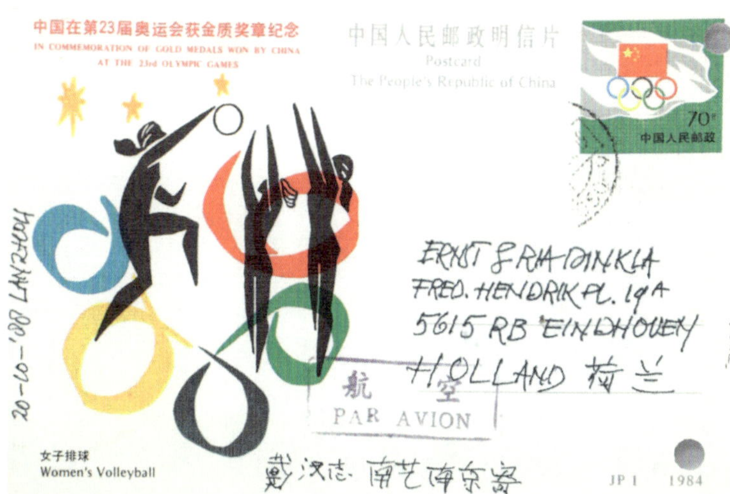

Hans van Dijk, two postcards sent to Ernst Dinkla during his travels in west China, fall 1988, coll. Ernst Dinkla

From Golmud they travel 800 kilometers to Xining on the Tibetan Plateau, and from there another 900 kilometers to Xi'an, the ancient capital of the Tang dynasty. They return to Beijing by the second week of November. By Christmas 1988, student and worker demonstrations are taking place in Nanjing, which van Dijk brushes off rather lightly in a letter to Jeroen Vinken:

> Although the Chinese people as a whole have a very low opinion of African people and look up to everything and anybody coming from the West, one can't call the Christmas demonstrations racist just like that; there also were slogans like "Bash the foreigners," "Democracy," "Higher wages." It was just an occasion for everyone to have loads of fun together, not fanatical. There is always some entertainment to be had, everything is put into perspective, made vague. At the academy, someone shouted "Out with the foreigners" when I passed him by; I put up my fist and shouted "Long live socialism." Everybody happy. Their attitude towards blacks is caused by backwardness and the unfamiliar. It is slowly improving over time.
>
> HvD, letter to Jeroen Vinken, Nanjing, probably early January 1989

January – May 1989

During the first months of the New Year, van Dijk starts a correspondence with Huang Yong Ping, the most prominent member of the radical artist collective Xiamen Dada. He travels to Beijing to visit *China/Avant-Garde* (*zhongguo xiandai yishu zhan*), the much-anticipated, first nation-wide exhibition of contemporary art in China, which runs from 5 to 19 February at the China Art Gallery (now the National Art Museum of China). While staying at the student quarters of CAFA, he falls ill with a bad flu and is nursed back to health by the art students, Hong Hao in particular. In the company of other students, van Dijk goes to visit Li Xianting, a famous art critic and one of the curators of the exhibition. Still ill with the flu, he lies down on a couch and doesn't say much.

China/Avant-Garde is the absolute zenith of half a decade of daring developments in the arts. Hope and optimism carry the exhibition. Van Dijk meets old friends, like Tang Song, Geng Jianyi, and Zhang Peili; he encounters interesting artists like Gu Dexin and the New Measurement Group (*Xin Kedu*), and he starts a correspondence with Wu Shanzhuan, one of the most prominent conceptual artists in the exhibition. After getting his MA in spring, van Dijk applies for another semester at the Nanjing Arts Institute with a view to securing a job in the arts in China as soon as possible.

No one guesses that in less than four months, it will all be over.

Pond Society

One of the many artist collectives to emerge during the eighties, the Pond Society wants to remove art from a narrow academic context, to engage the public in a direct interaction with its artworks. Established in May 1986 by Geng Jianyi, Zhang Peili, and Song Ling, the first activity of the Pond Society, *Work No. 1, Yang Taiji Series*, consists of large newspaper cut-out figures pasted on the wall outside the Zhejiang Academy in Hangzhou.

The Pond Society's attempts to involve the public fail, however. Geng Jianyi deals with this disappointment by denying the possibility of a personal approach to his works, and to the works any individual or subjective content. Zhang Peili punishes the public for its indifference by involving the audience in strange behavioral contracts. His *Art Project No. 2* (1987) and *Brown Leather Book* (1988) are both mailings, "developed as a reaction to public apathy towards the Pond Society activities. They explored social interaction through themes of conformity, manipulation, and the ominous connotations of health and sterility."[12]

12—Eduardo Welsh, *Pond Society* in *Encyclopedia of Contemporary Chinese Culture*, ed. Edward L. Davis, London, Routledge, 2005.

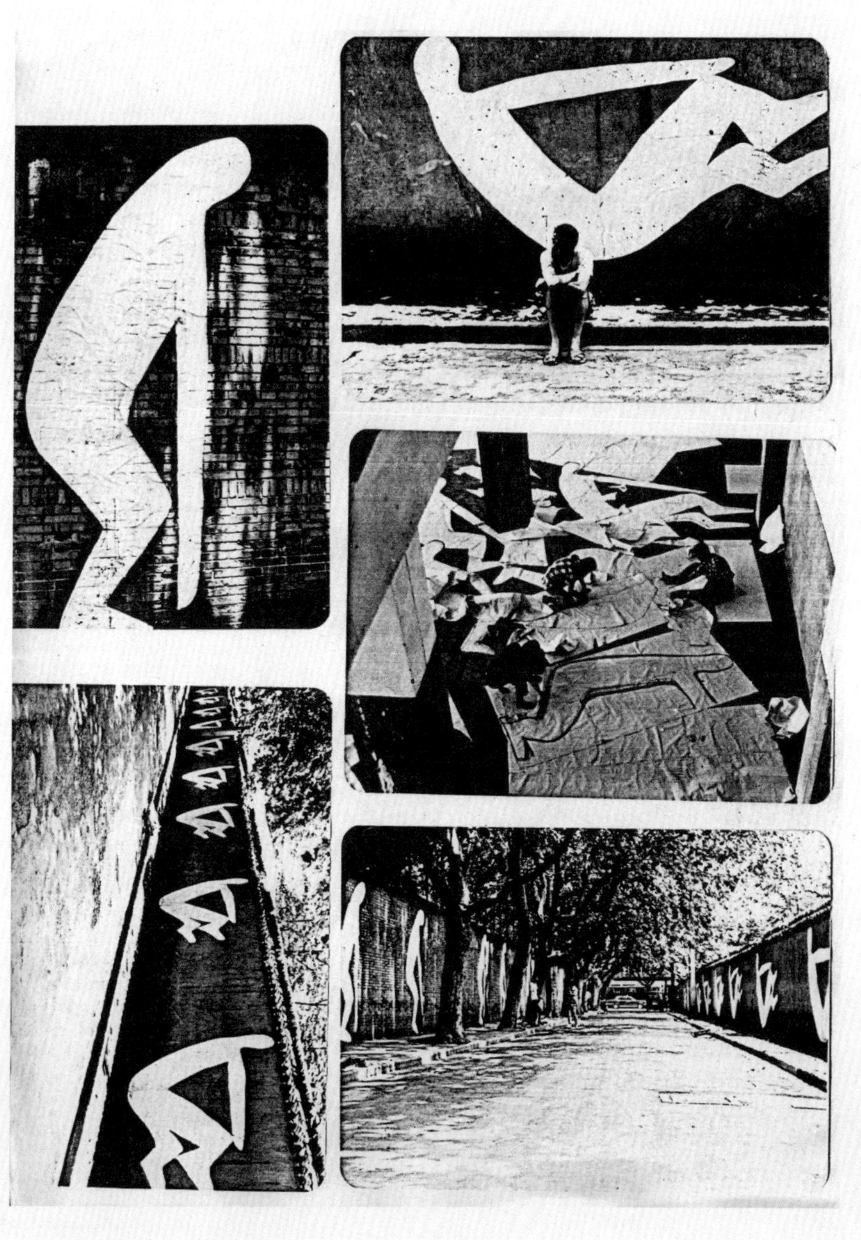

Pond Society, *Work No. 1, Yang Taiji Series*, 1986

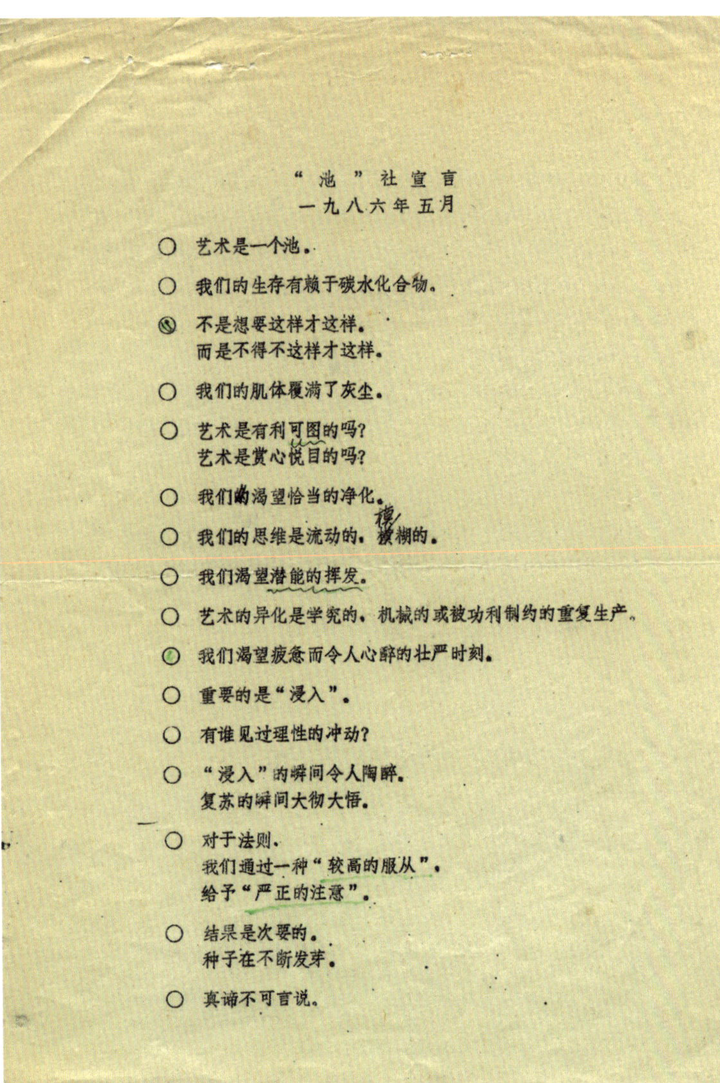

"池"社宣言
一九八六年五月

○ 艺术是一个池。
○ 我们的生存有赖于碳水化合物。
○ 不是想要这样才这样。
而是不得不这样才这样。
○ 我们的肌体覆满了灰尘。
○ 艺术是有利可图的吗？
艺术是赏心悦目的吗？
○ 我们渴望恰当的净化。
○ 我们的思维是流动的，模糊的。
○ 我们渴望潜能的挥发。
○ 艺术的异化是学究的，机械的或被功利制约的重复生产。
○ 我们渴望疲惫而令人心醉的壮严时刻。
○ 重要的是"浸入"。
○ 有谁见过理性的冲动？
○ "浸入"的瞬间令人陶醉。
复苏的瞬间大彻大悟。
○ 对于法则，
我们通过一种"较高的服从"，
给予"严正的注意"。
○ 结果是次要的。
种子在不断发芽。
○ 真谛不可言说。

Pond Society, *Pond Society Declaration*, mimeograph, 1986, private coll.

"池"社简报
○第一号○
○一九八六年六月○

○"池"社于一九八六年五月二十七日成立○
○"池"社成员○王强○包剑斐○关颖○宋陵○张培力○耿建翌
○自举办"85新空间画展"后○我们觉得已有的表现手段不能全面反映我们的观念及愿望○我们渴望最大限度地揭示内在空间○我们寻求更为直接的体验○以达到不可名状的状态○凡能体验冲动的一切手段我们都将尝试○过去的或现在的○单一的或综合的○我们所关心的是具有个性的全体的参与的过程○而非结果○
○"池"社旨在通过艺术这个池中的体验进入这样的一种状态○
○"池"社真诚期待各界人士的支援和协助○
○"池"社联系人○关颖○浙江杭州杭大新村28幢64号○

Pond Society, *Pond Society Bulletin No.1-2*, mimeograph, 1986, private coll.

Pond Society Declaration
May 1986

- art is a pond
- our existence depends on carbohydrates
- this so not because we think it but because we cannot deny it
- our body envelops matter
- is art making images?
  is art heartwarming and visually pleasing?
- we long for an effective cleansing
- our thoughts are agile and elusive
- we want to turn latent energy into gas
- the estrangement of art is caused by pedantry and its mechanization and painting bound by strict production regulations
- we strive towards riveting and exhausting activities
- we emphasize the importance of "immersion"
- who has ever experienced rational impulsiveness
- a sudden "immersion" can make one drunk with joy suddenly coming back to one's senses can lead to relief
- we acknowledge the importance of rules by following them rigorously
- results are of secundary importance seed sprouts continuously
- the truth cannot be spoken

Pond Society Bulletin
No. 1–2

- the Pond Society was founded on 27 May 1987
- the members of Pond Society are • She Chengyuan • Bao Jianfei • Song Ling • Zhang Peili • Geng Jianyi • as participants to the exhibition "New Space '85", in hindsight, we were unsatisfied with the image means we used • they weren't apt to give shape to our ideas and wishes • we wish to express our thoughts and emotions as freely as possible • we strive towards a way of working that directly corresponds with our experiences • we want to take up unnamable positions • we want to try out every idea or impulse stemming from our experience in a visual manner • both recent experiences and those from the past • both singular and assembled
- what we all care for is an individual and total participation in activities
- we care less about the result of an activity
- the Pond Society aspires to realize the goals listed above by means of our art activities*
- the Pond Society truly hopes for support from and collaboration with people from different backgrounds*
- Pond Society contact person* Guan Ying*

In 1993, Hans van Dijk writes on Zhang Peili:

> "Report first, then execute" (*xian zou hou zhan*) was Zhang Peili's motto from a draft for an exhibition, published in *Fine Arts in China*. It is the reverse of a Chinese proverb "execute first, then report," which referred to the political practice of the imperial court and the creation of *fait accompli*. The article contained detailed painting and installation instructions for a series of 41 large paintings, which he called series "X?". The recurring motif was a pair of rubber gloves. The article concluded with instructions and specific rules for visitors to the exhibition, for example "use the marked route and do not go in the opposite direction." It was also prohibited for visitors to initiate discussions within the exhibition hall if two or more visitors were involved, or if two or more visitors were at an exhibition stand. Those dressed in red or yellow clothes or who were shorter than 130 cm or taller than 173 cm were not admitted. Nor were couples. This punitive attitude towards the public was a reaction to the 1986 failed attempt by the Pond Society to involve the public in artistic events.
>
> A draft of *Art Project No. 2* followed, subtitled *Plan for the Realization of a Dialogue and Its Observation*.[13] Zhang wrote a twenty-page-long draft for this event, including behavior instructions for participants—their functions, rights, and obligations, admission procedures, necessary testimonials, identification papers, and guidelines for what the dialogue should include. The Kafkaesque world of bureaucratic formalities evoked in this way were very similar to the examinations of imperial China as well as to the Communist bureaucracy. The draft was published in a limited edition and mailed to friends and art critics. […] All of Zhang's works have something in common—oil paintings, "mail-art-happenings," performances, videos, or conceptual art—a cynical stance and the desire to make an aggressive and deliberately tormenting art in the face of the public.
>
> HvD, *Zhang Peili*, biographical entry in *China Avant-garde*, exhib. cat., Berlin, Edition Braus, 1993

13—Van Dijk incorrectly describes the first line of instruction in *Art Project No. 2* as its subtitle.

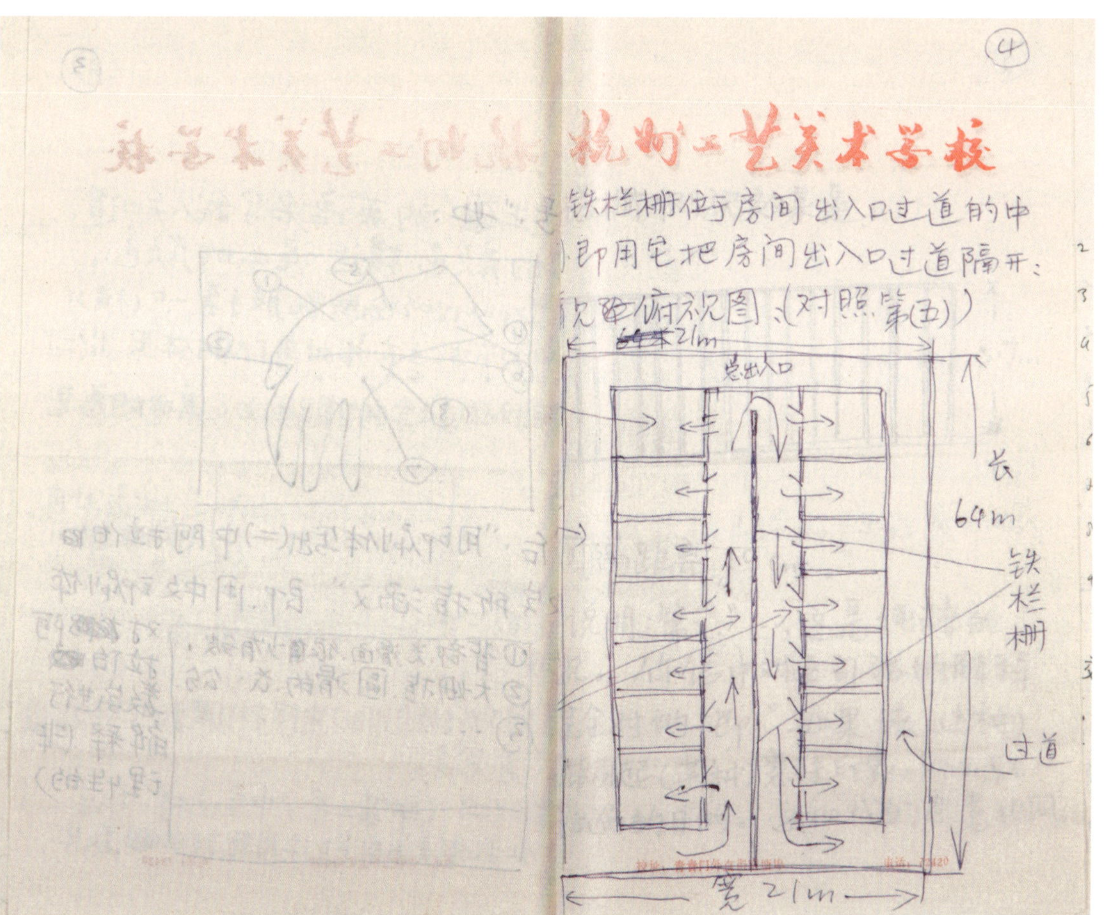

Zhang Peili, notes with drawings of *Project "X?"*, 1987, private coll.

Zhang Peili's *30×30* is known as the first video work in Chinese contemporary art. It was shown for the first time on 22 November 1988 at the Chinese Modern Art Conference (known as the Huangshan, or Yellow Mountain, Conference), organized by art critic Gao Minglu. In a recent interview, Zhang Peili talks about this work: "You can find many reasons for breaking the mirror, putting it together [...] in Chinese proverbs, such as the phrase *po jing chong yuan* [a broken mirror joined together], which is a metaphor for people or things reuniting after a rupture. But for me, the most basic motivation or departure point for making this work is monotony and meaninglessness."[14] Whether van Dijk saw the video—and one likes to assume that he did—or if Zhang told him about it when van Dijk came to Hangzhou one last time before leaving China, he never mentions it in his writings or letters.

14—Zhang Peili interviewed by Barbara Pollack for ArtNews.com, 5 May 2017

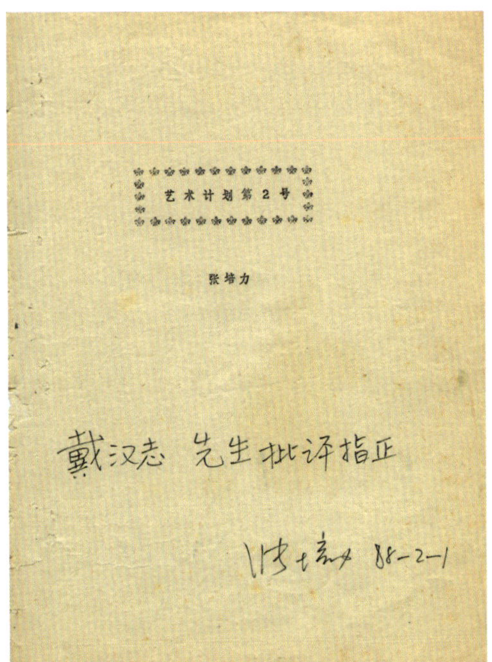

艺术计划第2号

张培力

戴汉志 先生批评指正

88-2-1

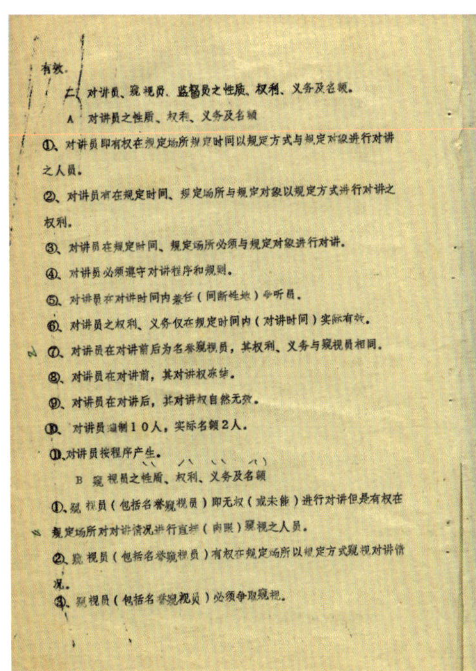

有效。

二、对讲员、窥视员、监督员之性质、权利、义务及名额。

A 对讲员之性质、权利、义务及名额

①、对讲员即有权在规定场所规定时间以规定方式与规定对象进行对讲之人员。

②、对讲员有在规定时间、规定场所与规定对象以规定方式进行对讲之权利。

③、对讲员在规定时间、规定场所必须与规定对象进行对讲。

④、对讲员必须遵守对讲程序和规则。

⑤、对讲员在对讲时间内兼任（间断性地）旁听员。

⑥、对讲员之权利、义务仅在规定时间内（对讲时间）实际有效。

⑦、对讲员在对讲前后为名誉窥视员，其权利、义务与窥视员相同。

⑧、对讲员在对讲前，其对讲权冻结。

⑨、对讲员在对讲后，其对讲权自然无效。

⑩、对讲员编制10人，实际名额2人。

⑪、对讲员按程序产生。

B 窥视员之性质、权利、义务及名额

①、窥视员（包括名誉窥视员）即无权（或未能）进行对讲但是有权在规定场所对对讲情况进行直接（肉眼）窥视之人员。

②、窥视员（包括名誉窥视员）有权在规定场所以规定方式窥视对讲情况。

③、窥视员（包括名誉窥视员）必须争取窥视。

Zhang Peili, *Art Project No. 2*, 3 pages of 21, mimeograph, 1987, private coll.; the cover page shows a handwritten note: "To Mr. Dai Hanzhi for your critical reading, February 1, 1988"; below: English translation by Hans van Dijk of the first two pages of Zhang Peili's *Art Project No. 2*

Art Project No. 2
Zhang Peili

This plan aims to realize a dialogue and the peeping of it.
The whole plan consists of eight parts:

- I The dialogue, the peeping, the right to speak and the right to peep.
- II The qualities, rights and duties, and the appointment of the speakers, peepers and supervisors.
- III The procedures of the appointment of the speakers, peepers and supervisors.
- IV The construction of the space the dialogue takes place and of the space the peeping takes place.
- V The procedure of the dialogue.
- VI The regulations for the dialogue and the peeping.
- VII Taboos.
- VIII Explanation.

I. The dialogue, the peeping, the right to speak and the right to peep.

- The dialogue: a kind of restricted, passive form of dispute, participated by those who obtained "the speakers' right" according to the regulations and who will speak at the assigned place within the fixed time in the described way about the stipulated subjects (also named: talk, discussion, conversation or debate).
- The peeping: a restricted, pure way of looking. An observation of the process of the dialogue at the assigned place within the fixed time.
- The right to speak: the right to participate in the dialogue. The right to speak is only valid within the fixed time (the time the dialogue takes place) at the assigned place (the dialogue hall).
- The right to peep: the right to participate the peeping. The right to peep is only valid within the fixed time (the time the dialogue takes place) at the assigned place (the dialogue hall).

II. The qualities, rights and duties, and the appointment of the speakers, peepers and supervisors.

A. The qualities, rights and duties, and the appointment of the speakers.

1. By speakers are understood those who have the right to speak at the assigned place within the fixed time in the described way about stipulated subjects.
2. Speakers have the right to speak at the assigned place within the fixed time in the described way about the stipulated subjects.
3. Speakers are obliged to speak at the assigned place within the fixed time in the described way about the stipulated subjects.
4. Speakers are obliged to obey the procedure and regulations of the dialogue.
5. Speakers are during the time of the dialogue (by interruptions) fulfilling the part of listener.
6. The rights of speakers are only valid within the fixed time (the time the dialogue takes place).
7. Before and after the duration of the dialogue a speaker is considered to be a honorary peeper and will obtain the same rights and duties as the other peepers.
8. Before the time the dialogue takes place the speakers' rights to speak is guaranteed.
9. After the time the dialogue takes place the speakers' rights will automatically be expired.
10. 10 speakers will be nominated, 2 will actually be appointed.
11. Speakers are appointed according the appointment-regulations.

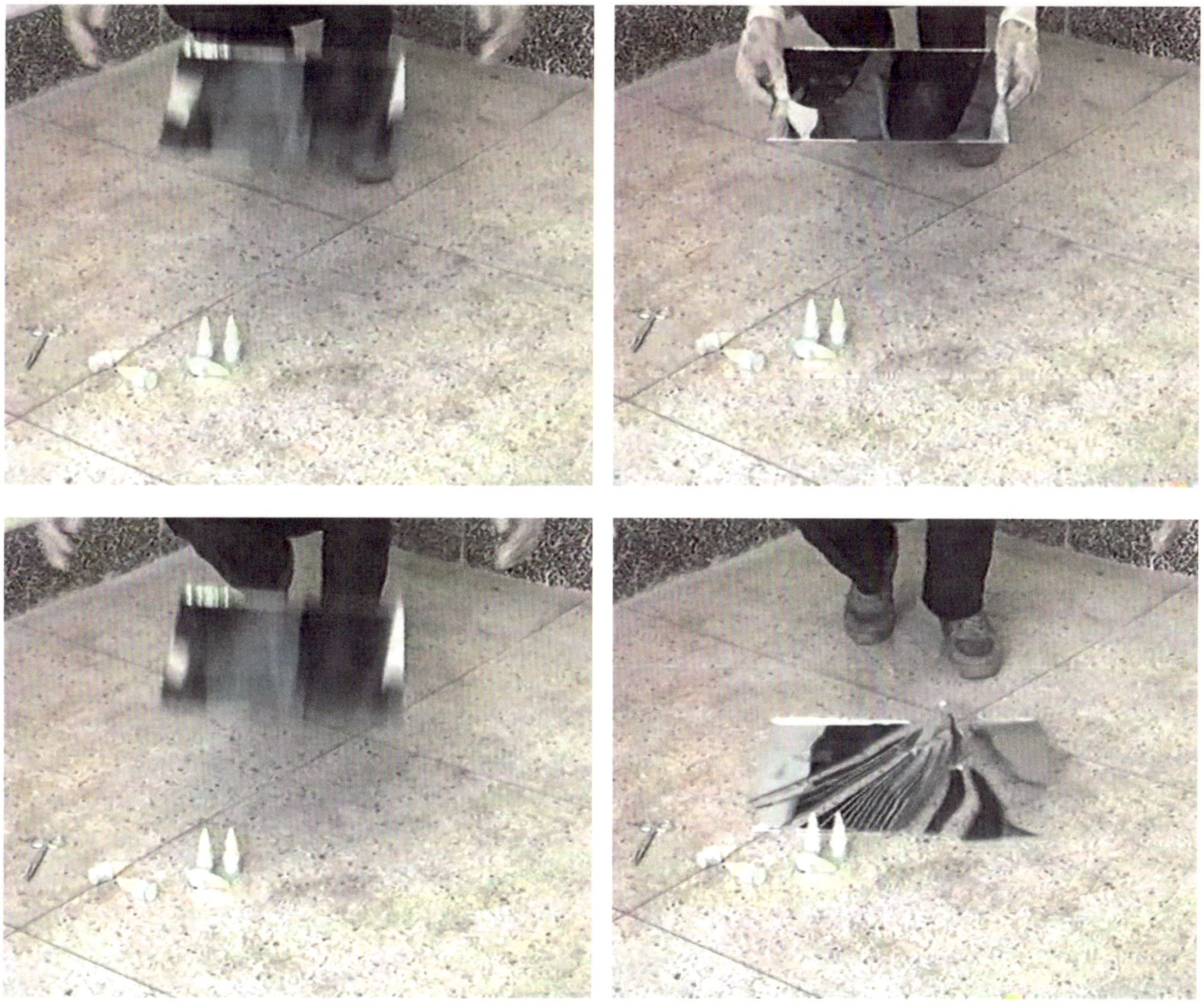

Zhang Peili, *30×30*, video, 32'09", 1988, four stills, courtesy the artist and Boers-Li Gallery, Beijing; considered to be the first video artwork made in China

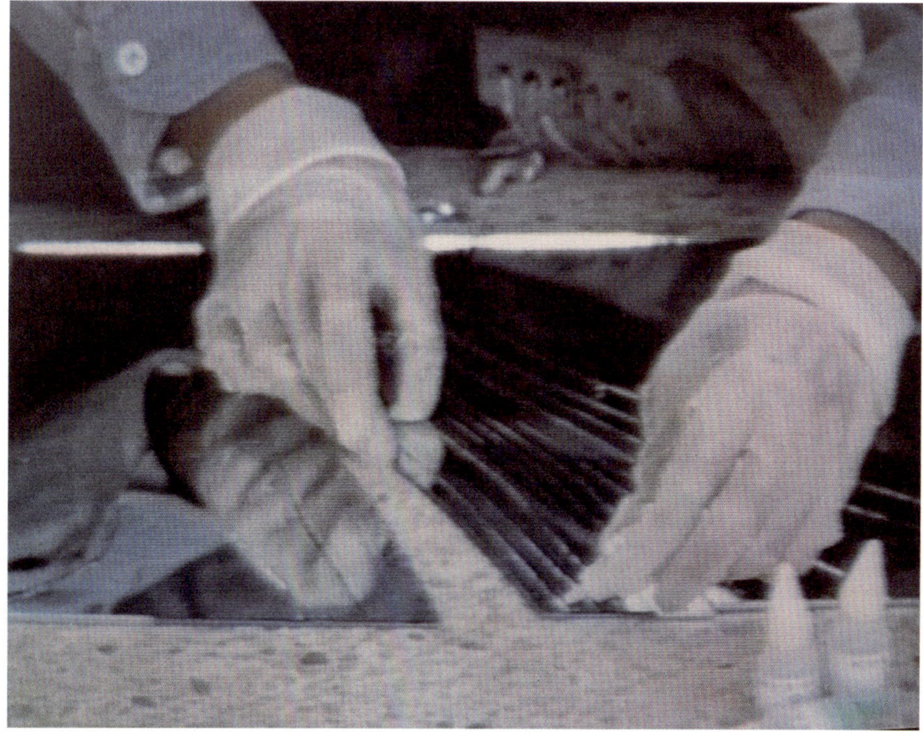

Zhang Peili, *30×30*, video, 32'09", 1988, still, courtesy the artist and Boers-Li Gallery, Beijing

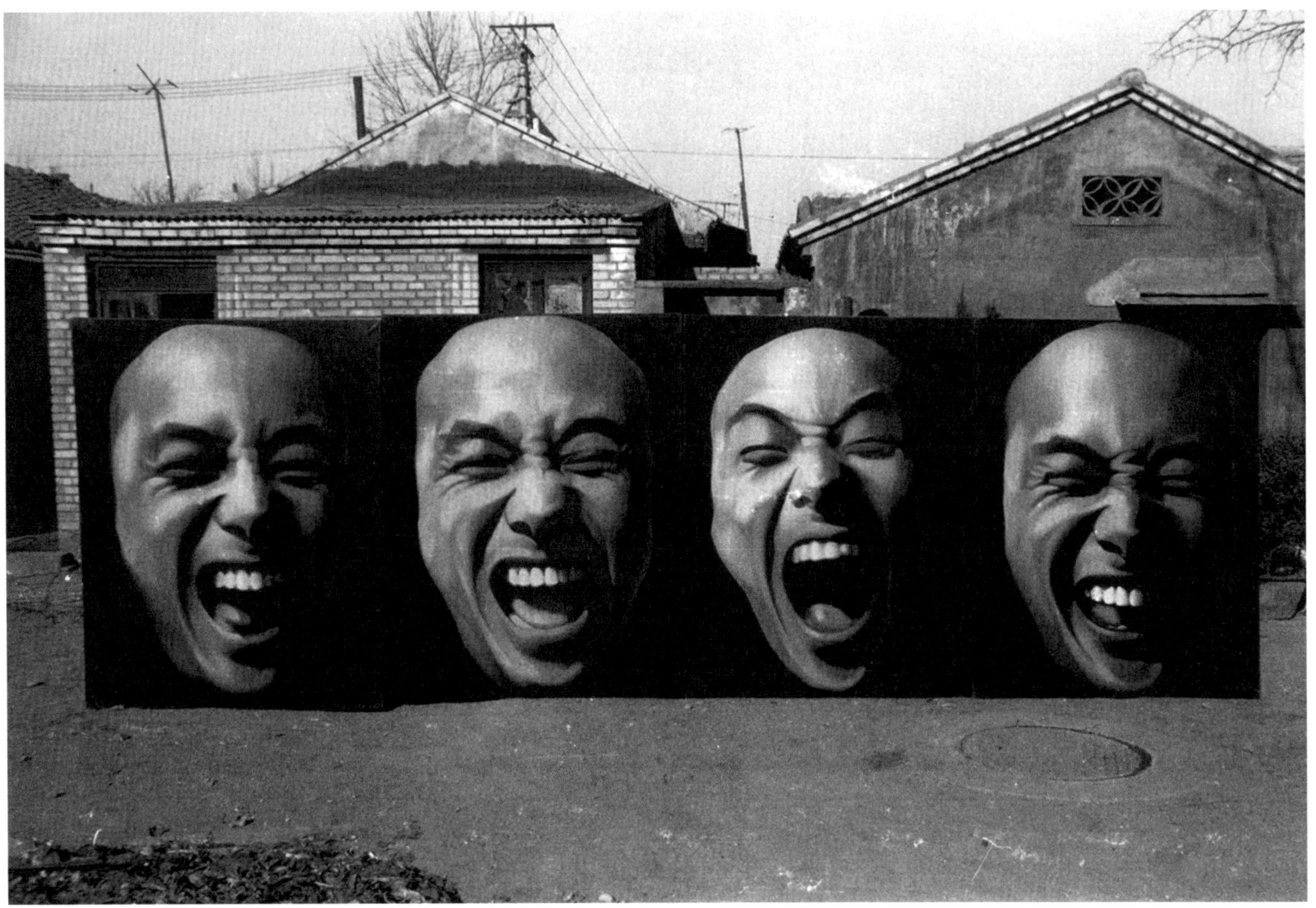

Wang Youshen, *China Avant-Garde No. 3 (The Second State by Geng Jianyi)*, photograph, 37×120 cm, 1989, courtesy the artist and ShanghART Gallery, Shanghai

Geng Jianyi

In 1993, Hans van Dijk writes on Geng Jianyi:

> In his own words, Geng Jianyi's works are an attempt to "demand a reaction" from the "shortsighted" public. Through different media—oil paintings, installations, conceptual works, and collage—he investigates in a very individual manner the ambivalent relationships between an artist, his work, and the public. Two oil paintings of a serious couple, which Geng put forward as his final works at the Zhejiang Academy of Fine Arts in 1985, were met with opposition by the examination board because they showed no "positive" expression. As a reaction to this criticism, he painted two enormous series that he called *The Second State* and *Double Happiness*. Both series depicted hysterically laughing heads in a near photo-realistic style. Since his participation in the performances of the "Pond" group, Geng has no longer restricted himself to painting but also makes collages, conceptual art, and installations. [...] Geng regards his work not only as an expression of the disappearance of established roles and customs in a changing society, but particularly as the questioning of society through the exposure of its conventions within the medium of art.
>
> HvD, *Geng Jianyi*, biographical entry in *China Avant-garde*, exhib. cat., Edition Braus, Berlin, 1993

In 1988, Geng Jianyi published photos and an article in the magazine *Fine Arts in China* issue no. 22 about a test arrangement of his installation *Water Factory*.
The work presents a situation in which the viewers are not confronted by a painting, but by each other. The floor plan of the exhibition shows walls placed in a double spiral constituting two separate corridors, which lead into the center of the space. Within the two-meter-high walls, there are openings at head height. When they leave or arrive, visitors can stare at each other through the openings, some of which are framed by picture frames.

Here, the empty space plays an activating role. Even stronger than in the exhibition Zhang Peili is planning, in which the visitor ends his journey in an empty cabin, the visitor here is confronted with himself and his own expectations. He is given a double role to play, which he acts out in the very moment he enters the space—namely, the role of the artwork as spectator and of the spectator as artwork. Both the visitor's decision to approach another visitor as an artwork and what he expresses as an artwork are entirely his own responsibility.

The sense of uncertainty that Geng Jianyi produces in his public is all the greater because Chinese society attaches much more importance to correct behavior than Western society. As a precondition for attaining anything at all, correct behavior weighs more heavily than personal achievements or capabilities. In the photos Geng Jianyi took of the test arrangement in the school where he teaches, one can see how each person emphatically poses either as an artwork or as a spectator. There are no signs of hesitation on the part of the visitors, nor are there any attempts on their part to give a certain shape or form to their double role.

HvD, *The artists Zhang Peili and Geng Jianyi, Founders of the Pond Society*, unpublished article, Nanjing, 1988

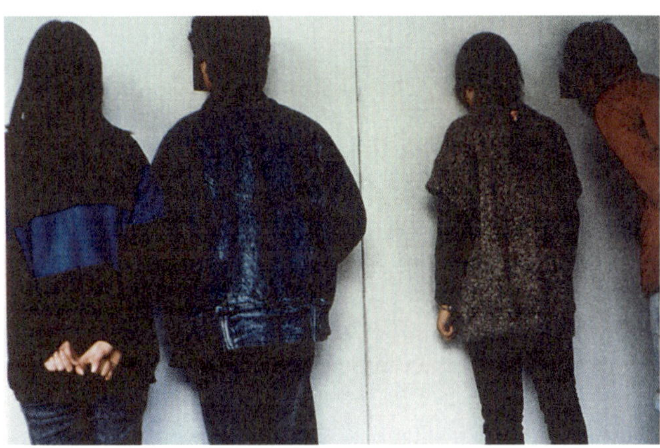

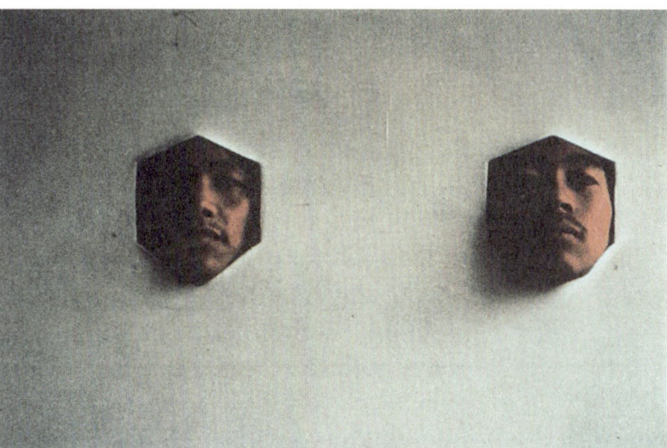

Unknown photographer, two photos of the trial installation of Geng Jianyi's *Water Factory*, Hangzhou Silk Institute, 1988, private coll.; right: Geng Jianyi and Zhang Peili

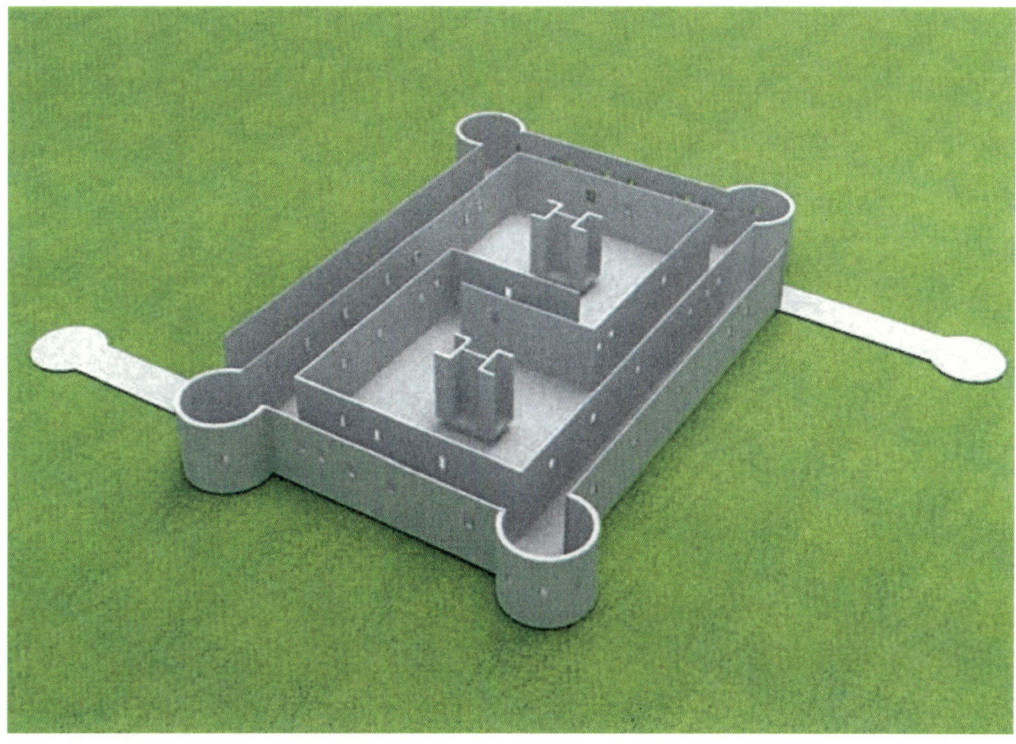

Geng Jianyi, *Water Factory (The owner has the right to (re)construct the work)*, digital drawings and 3D model, 1987/2013, courtesy Geng Jianyi and ShanghART Gallery, Shanghai

GENG JIANYI: I knew Hans when he was still a student in Nanjing. He was very interested in art. He came to Hangzhou and we met at the home of the art historian Fan Shaoming. I remember him smoking his cigarettes. He didn't speak much; he looked like a frail scholar. He spoke slowly, and when he had certain thoughts or concepts, he could explain them in a simple way. He visited Hangzhou several times, mainly because of the Berlin show where I showed *Investigative Form*. I visited Hans several times in Beijing in a tiny apartment, and in a slightly better apartment later on.
Hans once wrote me a letter of about one page, which was very impressive for me because it ended with the word "perseverance." He was very lonely and very poor, and since as artists we were celebrating avant-garde art at the time, these words have stayed with me. Why did he give me the impression of loneliness? Because he lived so frugally and soberly. We had other foreign friends, Italians who also were not rich, but they had at least a few antiques in their apartments. I had the impression that Hans didn't own anything at all. I always had the impression that Hans didn't work for profit. At the time, Western institutions or companies or individuals were all after Chinese art, but the artists were not helped to develop. Hans was the only one to do so in a serious and professional way.
MB, interview with Geng Jianyi, Shanghai, 8 September 2012

Ni Haifeng

Van Dijk and Ni Haifeng meet in Shanghai in May 1988, possibly through Zhao Jianren, also from Zhejiang Academy, at the East China Normal University. Ni shows him slides of his work. They talk all afternoon and have dinner together at the university mess. Van Dijk is very interested in radical ink painting, and Ni is at the forefront of experimental calligraphy. He co-founded "Red Humor" with a group of radical conceptual artists including Wu Shanzhuan who, like Ni, was born on the island of Zhoushan, off the coast of Shanghai. Working with so-called "nonsense characters" and "non-artistic" texts, they focus on the act of writing, re-appropriating, and deconstructing forms of language. Their first exhibition, *75% Red, 20% Black, 5% White*, takes place at the Zhejiang Academy in 1986, though not officially. Back in Zhoushan, Ni paints mysterious numbers and characters over rocks, buildings, windows, doors, and streets, subverting conventional notions of poetry and landscape. As a punishment, he is condemned to work in an electrical supplies factory for two years.

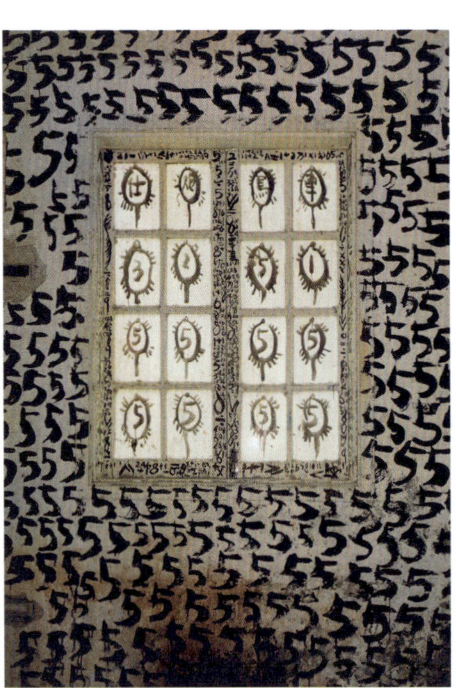

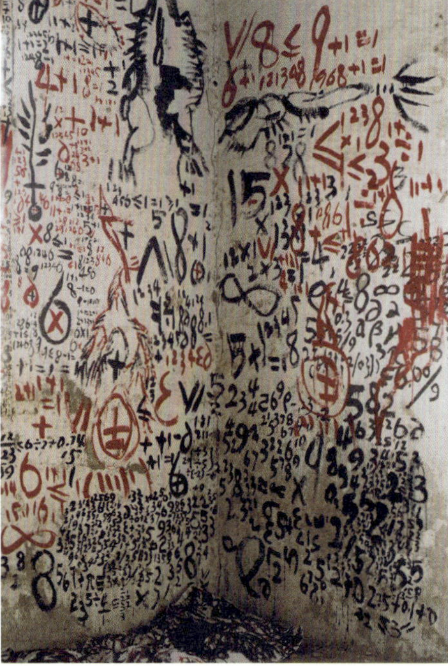

Ni Haifeng, left: *Warehouse No. 10*, photograph, 1988; right: *Untitled*, photograph, 1988, both courtesy the artist
Opposite page: *Warehouse No. 1*, photograph, 1988, courtesy the artist

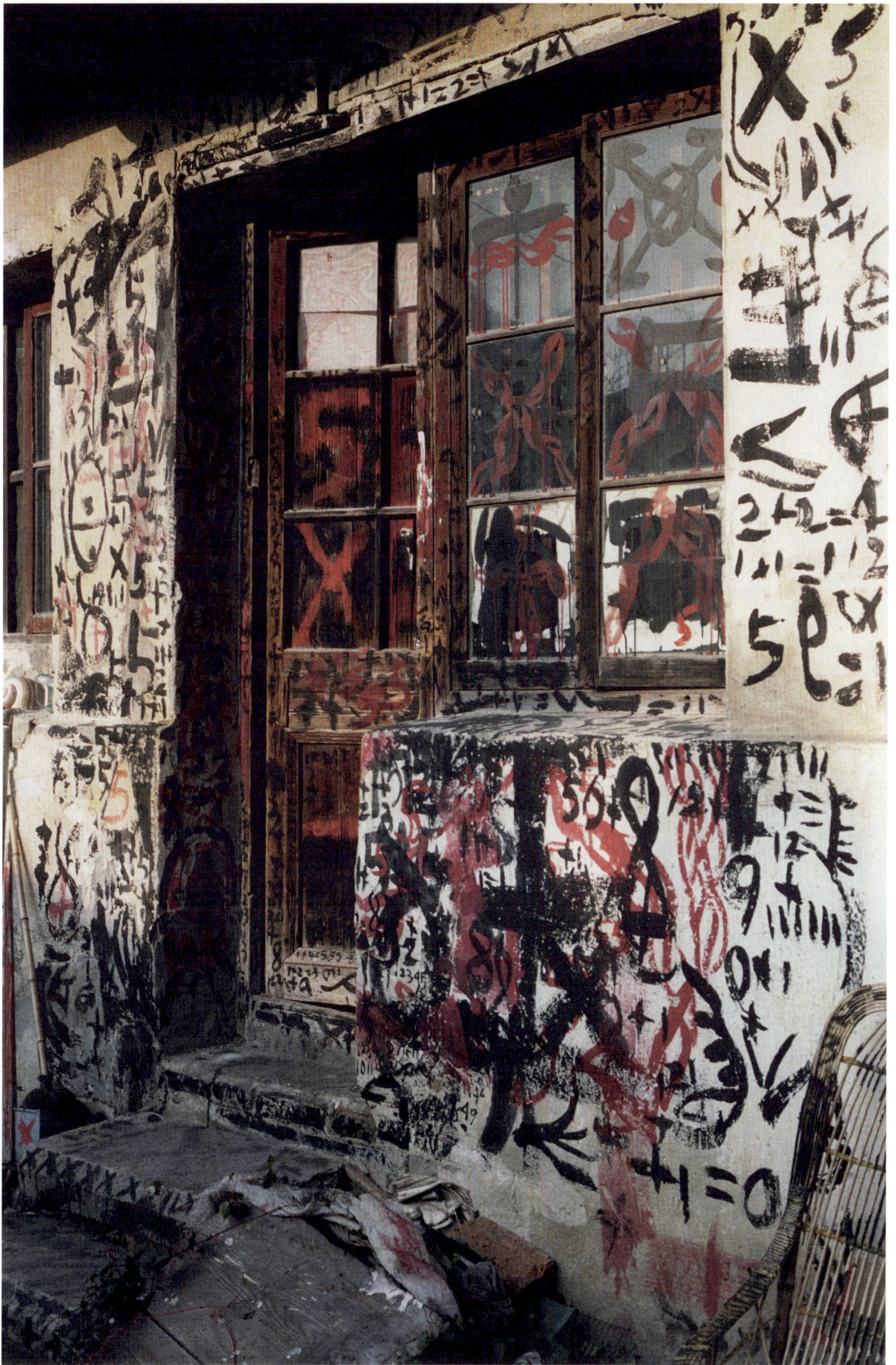

Ding Yi

In the summer of 1988, van Dijk travels to Shanghai to see a group exhibition of "experimental" painting, and there encounters Ding Yi's work for the first time. He immediately pays him a studio visit. They begin a correspondence, and later become life-long friends.

> Dear Hans, I have enlarged and reprinted the photos of my works according to the requirements you made a few days ago when we met in Shanghai, as can be seen in the attachment. Do you think it is ok? Feel free to let me know if you have other requirements.
> As for us young Chinese modern artists, if your efforts can promote the development of Chinese modern art to some extent or can guide people who have no idea about Chinese modern art to obtain a new understanding of it, it will be an exciting and honorable deed.
> Wishing you success in your career. Ding Yi
>
> Ding Yi, letter to Hans van Dijk, Hongqiao, 8 May 1989

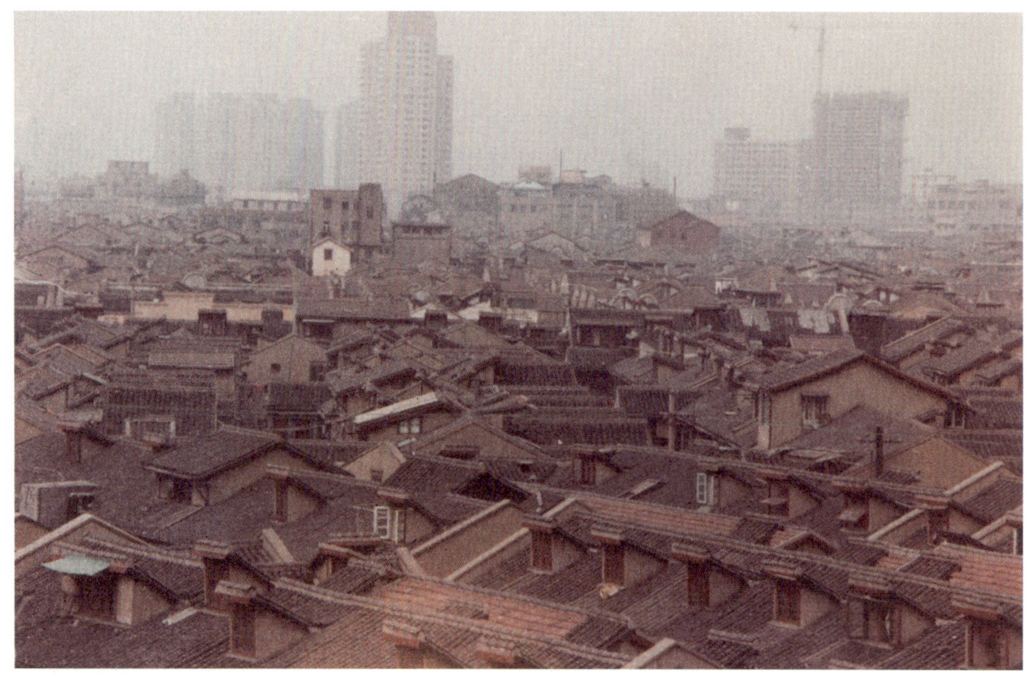

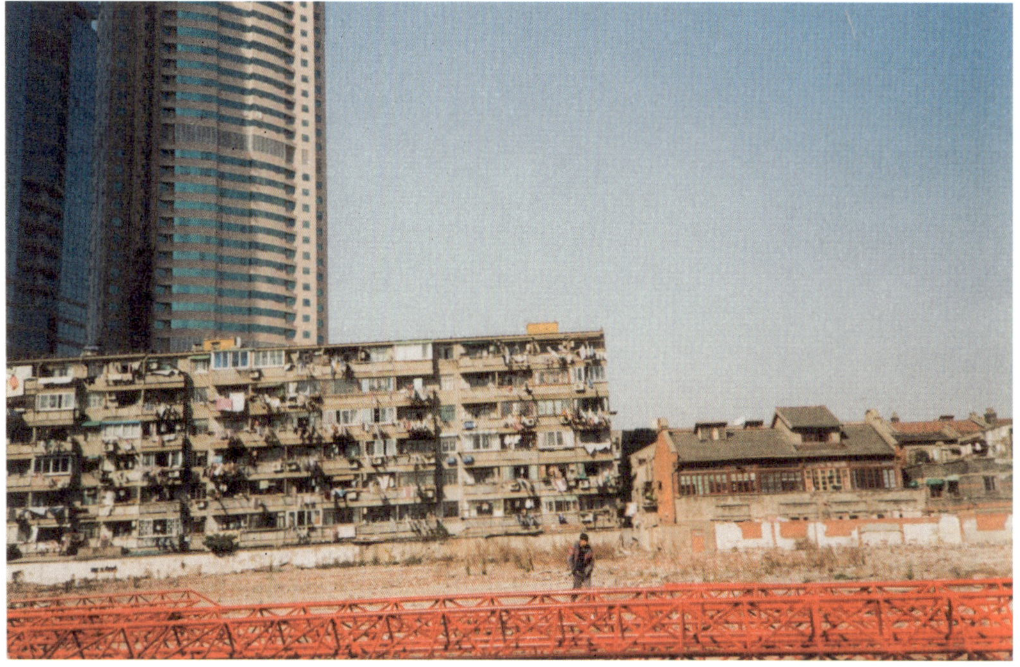

Ding Yi, two photographs of urban landscapes in Shanghai, early 1980s, sent to van Dijk in 1988, private coll.

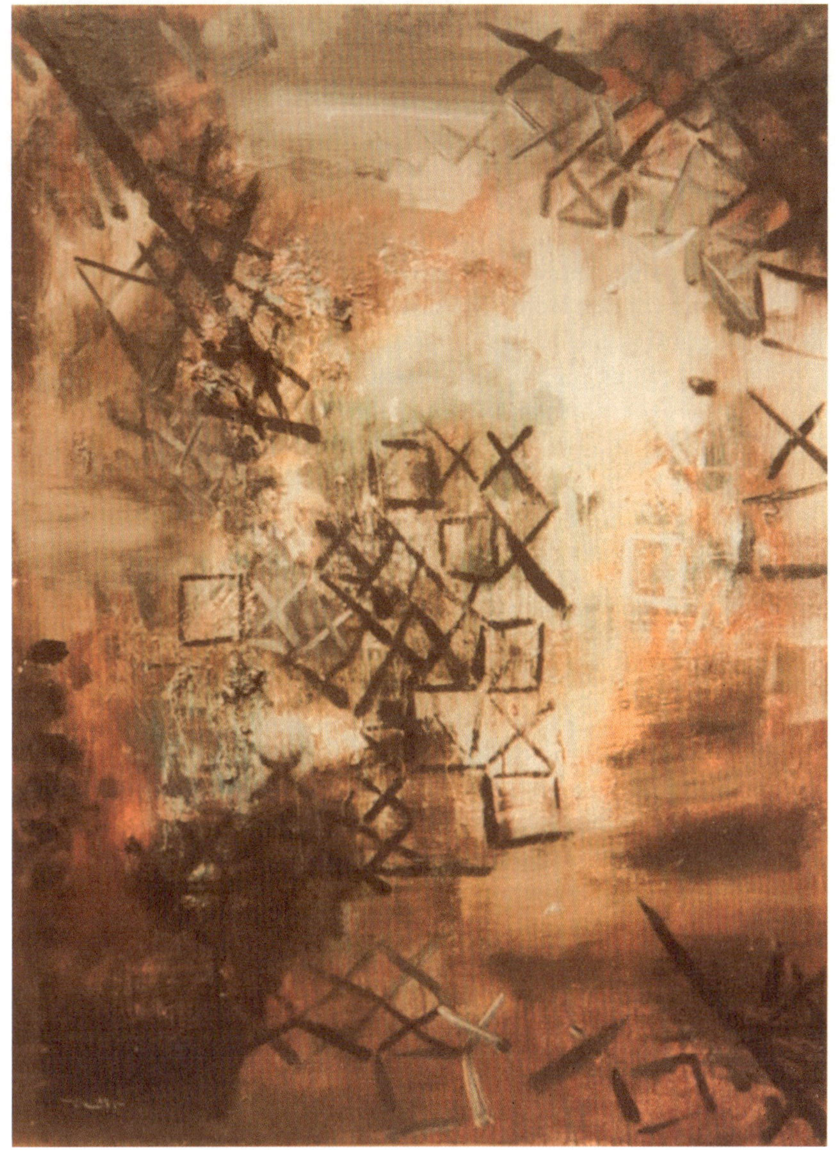
Ding Yi, *Breaking Through the Sacrifice*, 1985, photograph sent to van Dijk in 1988, private coll.

DING YI: I met Hans in May 1988 at the opening of the *Exhibition of Today's Art* at the Shanghai Art Museum. [...] In those days, there were no private phones or mobiles, but soon afterwards I received a page on my beeper from Hans. I had a tiny studio at a farmhouse in Hongqiao[15] at the time, quite far from Shanghai. We agreed to meet at a bus station. I will never forget the number of my bus: it was 57. And there was Hans who arrived on a bike he had rented, cycling all the way from Shanghai through the mud! The '88 exhibition made a deep impression on Hans. It was the first time I showed my new work with crosses. At the time, I was still at university. A lot of people thought I was going the wrong way with my work. But Hans didn't, and I learned through Hans how someone from the West looked at and judged painting. Hans would look at the photos of my works and analyze them for me, pointing out the logical consequences of certain decisions I had been making. Many Chinese artists respected Hans very much. They called him Dr. Bethune, after the Canadian doctor who saved thousands of Chinese lives during the Japanese occupation without regard for his own life. Hans even resembled him physically. With Hans there were lots of firsts: the first time writing condition reports, transporting works from China, even receiving the press clippings after the end of a show. Each time I traveled to Beijing, I would stay in Hans' office.

15—Hongqiao, then a farmer's village 25 km outside Shanghai, now part of Shanghai.

He kept two beds in it, and I would have to leave early in the morning [because overnight stays were not allowed in the office]. When Hans came to Shanghai, he had to sleep in my kitchen. Whenever the police discovered Hans' office, they would close it down and Hans would call me.
Hans did three projects with Siemens, one about photography, one about painting, and one about video. I finished all the works for the show and even went to Berlin to select the paintings with Katharina Grosse, who was my partner for that exhibition, but only the photo exhibition opened.
I feel the best things Hans did were his many shows of Chinese art in Europe. He was also the first person to take Chinese curators under his wing, like Zhang Li and Zhang Wei. Another great thing he did was to document Chinese contemporary art from the beginning. Business with Hans in Beijing was not so good, but I trusted Hans and worked together with him until his death.

MB, interview with Ding Yi, Shanghai, October 2012

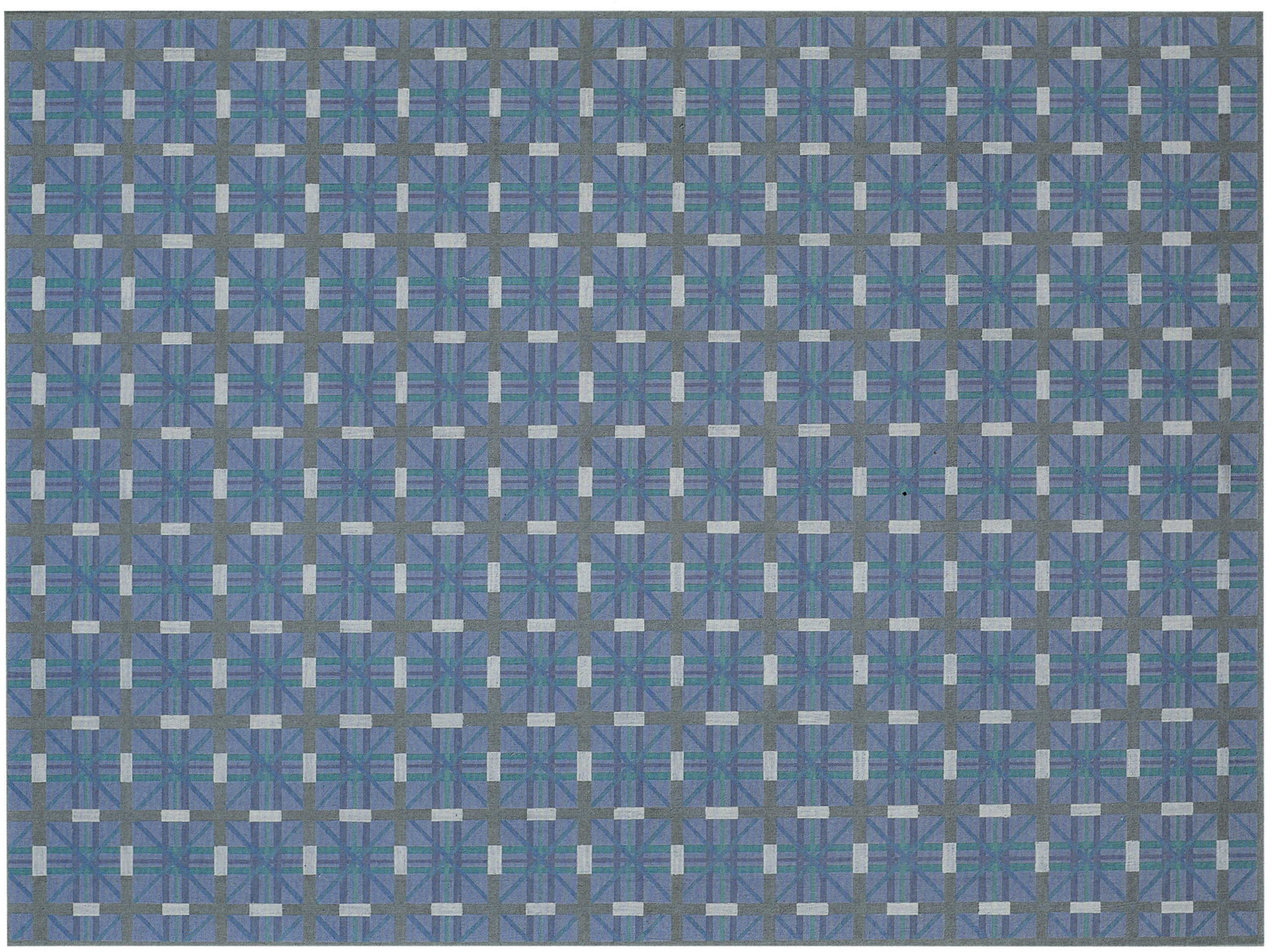

Ding Yi, *Appearance of Crosses 1989-6*, acrylic on canvas, 50×70 cm, 1989, private coll.; this painting hung in van Dijk's NAAC office/apartment for many years

Xiamen Dada

Xiamen Dada (1983–88) is probably the best-known radical artist group in the eighties in China. Based in Xiamen, a harbor city in the southeast, the group embraces absurdity—referencing Dada—as an artistic strategy. One of the most remarkable artists from the group is Huang Yong Ping.

厦门达达 （附）
1983—1988
活动简历

1983.5.9—12"厦门五人现代艺术展"
在厦门市群众艺术馆举办，展出八十四件作品，有各种样式的抽象画、实物拼贴和金属焊接，重点在于探讨艺术的语言和实验的手段，这个展览在当时未能公开展出只能发票内部观展。参加者：林嘉华、焦耀明、俞晓刚、许成斗、黄永砯。

1986.5—6月组成"厦门现代美术研究室"
由厦门市群众艺术馆纪恭然的发起，定期交流和策划展览，参加者有黄永砯、林嘉华、焦耀明、俞晓刚、蔡立雄、林春、陈承宗等。研究室至1987年初便废弃不再活动。

1986.9.28—10.5"厦门达达现代艺术展"
在厦门新艺术馆举办的展览获得公开展出，有14人参加，展出作品八十三件，作品的观念和形式多样，就其中最主要倾向而言，基本上顺"83年五人展览"的路子，但更注重对"艺术性质"的关注，并去纯形式主义，首次在中国直言不讳地提出"达达精神"。"达达"的提出不仅为这次展览命名，更重要的是提供一种思路，并开始作为"厦门达达"的群体而存在。

1986.11.20—23"厦门达达展出作品改装、毁坏和焚烧活动"
有六十多件作品在展出之后进行了改装，毁坏成为意外的，更

1.

加非形式的样式，体验一件作品实际存在着各种变化的可能性，
11月23日下午焚烧活动持续二个多小时，改装后的作品被挑散在馆前广场，用石灰在地上书写大标语，有一百多人观看这一场面。焚烧活动提供了一份声明。

1986.11.29"厦门达达"在厦门大学艺术学院举行座谈会
座谈会是应艺术系和新闻系学生会的邀请与会者对"厦门达达"坚持无意义举动和言谈的相悖不能理解，不是说艺术问题不能讨论，而是说讨论艺术经常会陷入另一种无意义。这次座谈会后来被认为是公然反对艺术院校而引起艺术学院院方的强烈不满。

1986.12.16—19"发生在福建省美术展览馆内的事件展览"
在福州举办的事件展览是把美术馆大院内各种现成的实物移入馆内展览，展出后再移出归回原处。在福建师范大学美术系一些师生的帮助下，把各种废物移入完成布馆并张贴照片、文字和标志，放映厦门达达展览和焚烧的录相。但事件展览与当时的大学学潮被混为一谈，展览开馆一个半小时即被封闭。参加者：焦耀明、林嘉华、黄永砯、俞晓刚。

1987.1—2月"厦门达达之后，关于海洋污染报告"
这个活动历时一个月，制作范围包括海洋实地考察，厦门地区海洋污染现场摄像，国家海洋三所海生物污染实验室的采访，厦门环境保护所的资料收集等等。参加者：陈承宗、蔡立雄、李世雄。

2

1987.3.18"废品仓库活动"
87年要寻找展览场地极度困难，利用美术馆和美术观众就是利用约定俗成去更换艺术概念。但没有观众和非展览场所的活动也是可能的。废品仓库的活动是采用人干预的方式，有时需挪动或无需挪动而成为作品，这些只留下一组照片，最后这些底片也被仓库管理者没收。参加者：林嘉华、黄永砯、林春。

1987.11.9"作品垃圾处理"
这次活动是将"83年5人展览"的十几件作品丢置垃圾堆，等候垃圾车的参与，考察艺术品与观者的非博物馆行为。由于拍摄过往行人动手拆画和拿走的场景，引起争执被扣去相机胶卷，最后递交检讨书。参加者：黄永砯、曾颖宏。

1987.11.12"纠缠—捆绑活动"
参与这次活动的有十几个人，三部录相机参与者赤膊，头套香烟广告袋，40米长的麻绳。活动包括：绳索纠缠，人填入坑内，火烧画册，点燃鞭炮裤子。这些活动都是在干裂的旷地中举行。参加者：林嘉华、黄永砯、吴艺明等。

1988.10.15"进入美术史——幻灯活动"
这是用幻灯将美术史的范例投射在人身上。这种直接了当的投射和拍摄改变了伟大的艺术品（幻灯片）同时也改变了艺术家（制作者）本身。参加者：林嘉华、吴艺明。

3.

焚 烧 声 明

1986.9.28—10.5厦门达达展览的展出作品已经于1986.11.23下午在厦门新艺术馆广场当众焚烧。

这个展览已经不复存在，关于对它的赞扬或支持，怀疑或反对业已失去意义。

由于我们无法确定展出作品就是作品的最终样式，也许它们可能再次变得更好，或者变得更坏，我们也无法确定这些艺术品的最终应该存放在哪里，以避免人工或自然的损坏，于是决定实施一项对已展出的作品进行"改装→毁坏→焚烧"的计划。所有这些活动用照片和录相记录下来。

艺术作品历来被看作是艺术家的心血，一旦创作出来，就积心处虑地保护以避免损坏，艺术家就是靠其作品来显示自己的难度和伟大。人家说看看你的作品，我们说作品已经烧了。

中国没有艺术收藏这可能是件好事，艺术家可以任意处置自己的作品而无须小心翼翼。对待自己作品的态度标志着艺术家自己解放自己的程度，无所谓，甚至进行不合常理的处理。

艺术作品对于艺术家就像照片对于人。

不消灭艺术生活不得安宁。

达达死了。火小心。

厦 门 达 达
1986.11.24

Huang Yong Ping et al., *Xiamen Dada, List of Activities, 1983–88*; mimeograph, 1988, private coll.; bottom right: Huang Yong Ping et al., *Statement on the Burning*, 24 November 1986, mimeograph, 1986, private coll.; both sent to van Dijk in 1988

Xiamen Dada
List of Activities, 1983–1988

9 – 12 May 1983
A Modern Art Exhibition of Five Artists
Organized at the Xiamen People's Art Centre with eighty-four works, including abstract paintings, collage, and welded metal. It focuses on exploring artistic language and ways of experimentation. As it is not possible for the exhibition to open to the public at the time, it is for private viewing only.
Participants: Lin Jiahua, Jiao Yaoming, Yu Xiaogang, Xu Chengdou, and Huang Yong Ping

May – June 1986
Formation of the Xiamen Laboratory of Modern Art
Initiated by Ji Tairan[16] from the Xiamen People's Art Center to exchange ideas and organize exhibitions on a regular basis. The laboratory is abandoned in early 1987 and held no further events.
Participants: Huang Yong Ping, Lin Jiahua, Jiao Yaoming, Yu Xiaogang, Cai Lixiong, Lin Chun, Chen Chengzong, and others

16—Also referred to as Ji Naijin.

28 September – 5 October 1986
Xiamen Modern Art
The exhibition, organized at the Xiamen New Art Center, is permitted to open to the public.[17] Fourteen artists take part in the show with eighty-three works. Concept and format vary greatly, though its overall direction continues on the path of the 1983 five-person exhibition but with more attention to the nature of art and the dismissal of pure formalism. It is the first time the spirit of "Dada" is brought up in China, which not only gives it its title but also, more importantly, a way of thinking. The Xiamen Dada group thus comes into being.

17—It was rare in those years for exhibitions of contemporary art to obtain permission to be open to the public. Underground initiatives flourished as a result. It remains a topic of debate to what extent Chinese authorities condoned the development of experimental art between 1985 and 1989.

20 – 23 November 1986
An event to modify, destroy, and burn the works exhibited by Xiamen Dada
More than sixty artworks are modified and destroyed in order to become accidental and more non-formal following the exhibition, awakening the sense that many transformative possibilities exist in one specific work. On the afternoon of 23 November, the burning lasts for more than two hours. Modified artworks are scattered in the square in front of the Art Center. Big slogans are written on the ground with lime. More than 100 people watch the scene and a statement is provided for the Burning Event.

29 November 1986
Symposium held by Xiamen Dada at the Art College of Xiamen
The symposium is held on invitation from the student unions of the art department and the department of journalism. Attendees cannot understand Xiamen Dada's insistence on meaningless action and contradictory speech. This does not mean that artistic issues cannot be discussed, but such discussions often descend into another kind of meaninglessness. Later this symposium is considered an open critique of art academies, and thus arouses strong resentment from the Art College.

16 – 19 December 1986
Events Exhibition at the Exhibition Hall of the Fujian Art Museum
This *Events Exhibition* in Fuzhou sees various objects from outside the exhibition hall moved into the building, to be returned afterwards to their original positions in the yard outside. With the help of some teachers and students from the fine art department of Fujian Normal University, all sorts of waste materials are relocated and installed in the hall. Photographs, texts, and slogans are put up. Videos of the *Xiamen Modern Art* exhibition and the *Burning Event* are also on display. However, this *Events Exhibition* gets mixed up with the student unrest at the time, forcing it to close after an hour and a half.
Participants: Jiao Yaoming, Lin Jiahua, Huang Yong Ping, Yu Xiaogang

January – February 1987
Post-Xiamen Dada, Report on Ocean Pollution
This activity lasts for an entire month and includes marine field investigations; on-site filming of marine pollution in the Xiamen area; conducting interviews at the Marine Life Pollution Laboratory of the Third Institute of Oceanography, State Oceanic Administration; and collecting material from the Xiamen Environmental Protection Bureau, et cetera.
Participants: Chen Chengzong, Cai Lixiong, and Li Shixiong

18 March 1987
Junk Warehouse Event
In 1987, it is extremely difficult to find venues for exhibitions. Using art museums and art audiences is a way to adopt conventions to renew artistic concepts. But it is also possible to hold events without an audience and in non-exhibition spaces. The *Junk Warehouse Event* is an intervention by which the artists' choice to relocate waste (or to not relocate it) becomes the artwork. Only a few photographs remain from the event. At the end, even the negatives are confiscated by the warehouse administrator.
Participants: Lin Jiahua, Huang Yong Ping, and Lin Chun

9 November 1987
Waste Management
This event involves dumping more than ten artworks from 1983's *A Modern Art Exhibition of Five Artists* into the garbage and waiting for the participation of the garbage truck, in order to investigate the behaviors of artworks and their viewers outside a museum context. Because the artists film passersby dismantling and taking away the artworks, a dispute arises at the site. The film is confiscated and the artists have to write statements of self-criticism.
Participants: Huang Yong Ping and Zeng Yinghong

12 November 1987
Tangling-Binding Event
More than ten people take part in this event, using three video recorders and a forty-meter-long hemp rope. The participants are naked from the waist up, with plastic bags on their heads displaying tobacco advertisements. Actions include tangling the rope, burying a body in the ground, burning exhibition catalogues, and igniting "firework trousers." All actions take place on a piece of barren land.
Participants: Lin Jiahua, Huang Yong Ping, Wu Yiming, and others

15 October 1988
Entering Art History – Slide Show Event
During this event, a slideshow of exemplary art historical images is projected onto human bodies. The straightforward projection alters the great artworks while changing the artists (the makers) themselves.
Participants: Lin Jiahua and Wu Yiming

Xiamen Dada, Statement on the Burning
24 November 1986

The artworks shown at the *Xiamen Dada* exhibition, which was held from 28 September to 5 October 1986, are burned in public on the afternoon of 23 November 1988 in the square of the Xiamen New Art Center. Consequently, this exhibition and the works it gathered no longer exist. At this instant, everything loses its meaning, whether praise or support for the exhibition, or suspicion of and opposition to it.

Because we could not determine whether the artworks in the exhibition had reached their final stages or whether they might yet be worked on for better or for worse, and because we could not determine where or how to store them in order to avoid artificial or natural damage, we decided to put in motion a plan with a view to "modify/destroy/burn" the exhibited works. All activities were recorded by photograph and video. Artworks have been historically perceived as the brainchildren of the artist. Once created, they would be meticulously protected from harm. Artists demonstrate their own apprehension and greatness through their works. People would say to us: show us your works, to which we respond by burning the works to ashes. The fact that art collecting doesn't exist in China might be a good thing. Artists can freely dispose of their own works without being cautious. The attitude towards their own work indicates to what extent artists liberate themselves—if they don't care, or even if they dispose of it unconventionally. Art is to the artist what opium is to man. If we don't destroy the art, life won't be peaceful.

Dada has died. Beware of the fire.

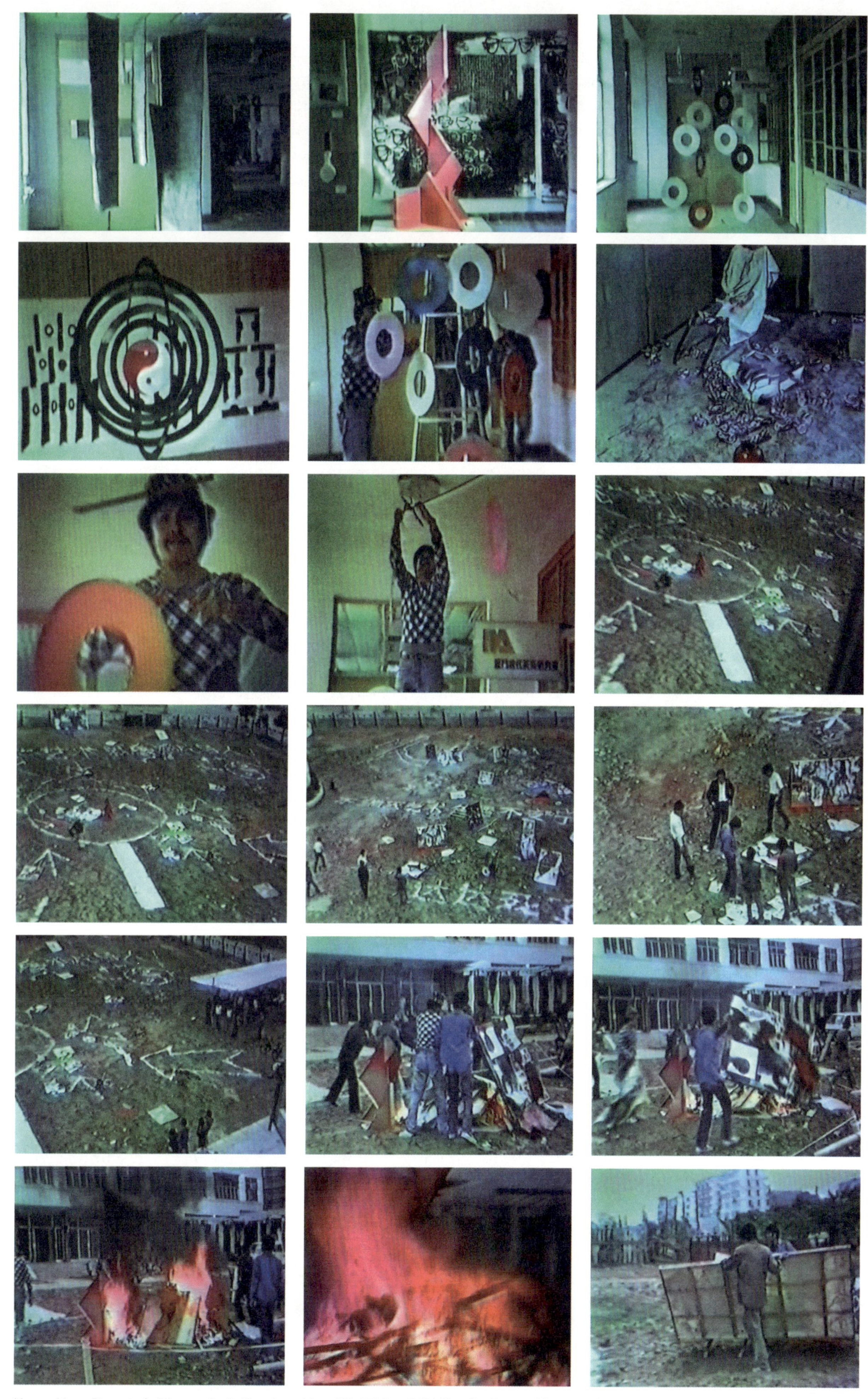

Huang Yong Ping et al., *Xiamen Dada Burning*, video, 23', 1986, coll. Walker Art Center, Minneapolis

In January 1989, van Dijk writes Huang Yong Ping a letter to express his admiration for his work. An interesting correspondence ensues. Huang Yong Ping's final letter is written in March, shortly before he leaves for Paris to participate in the exhibition *Magiciens de la terre* [*Magicians of the Earth*] at the Centre Pompidou. Huang's letter optimistically concludes with, "Of course I'll be back!" But while in Paris, where his work—and all other Chinese entries—are enormously successful, the Tiananmen Square massacre happens. Huang receives political asylum in France, along with two other Chinese participants in the exhibition, art critic Fei Dawei and ink artist Yang Jiechang. Gu Dexin, who also participates, returns to China.

Dear Mr. Huang Yong Ping,
I am from the Netherlands, and it's my third year studying Chinese in Nanjing. I started translating articles about Chinese contemporary art around two years ago, visiting exhibitions and artists at the same time. Now I have a chance to study the '85 Art Movement in 1985 and 1986 in the Nanjing Arts Institute.
I am planning to write a short passage about the connection between the theories, practices, and reality of Chinese contemporary art, because I believe there is a huge difference among these three things. For instance, subversive, passionate, and philosophical words are quite different from those beautiful and sometimes monotonous artworks, and the former two—words and material—are also quite different from everyday life.
I was told by Li Xiaoshan recently that you washed his *History of Modern Chinese Painting* in the washing machine for two hours and turned that thing into an artwork. I guess this work has answered my question about the connection between theories, reality, and art, so I hope this art practice of yours could be included in my article. But I don't know any details, nor did I see any pictures. I would appreciate it very much if you could write to me about your work. With best regards, Hans van Dijk

HvD, letter to Huang Yong Ping, Nanjing, 15 January 1989

Dear Mr. Huang Yong Ping,
I am from the Netherlands, and it's my third year in China. I am studying Chinese contemporary art in the Nanjing Arts Institute. I sent you a letter in January where I raised some questions about your artworks. I have seen some works recently in the Chinese contemporary art exhibition in Beijing, which has answered my questions. I just finished some articles to introduce Chinese contemporary artists. As for your work, I used the following articles for reference:
Arts, 1983, No. 1; 1986, No. 12; 1987, No. 5; 1988, No. 12
Fine Arts in China, 1986, No. 38
Jiangsu Art Monthly, 1986, No. 2; 1988, No. 2
GALLERY, No. 19
ARTIST, 3 issues
Art Monthly, 1987, No. 5; 1986, No. 3; 1985, No. 6; 1987, No. 6
Xiamen Dada, 1986
I plan to send my article to a foreign art association in the Netherlands and a magazine in Britain. My problem is I don't have pictures of your works. Could you send them to me? I would also like to know about your recent art practice. My third question is how to write your name in pinyin, Huang Yong Ping (according to your own pronunciation) or Huang Yong Li (according to *cihai* [a standard Chinese dictionary])?
I would appreciate it very much if you could help me. Thank you very much!

HvD, letter to Huang Yong Ping, Nanjing, 26 February 1989

南京藝術學院

黄永砯先生您好，

我是一个荷兰人，第三年在中国。我现在在南京艺术学院研究中国当代艺术。

1988年12月，我寄给你一封信。在那封信我提了一些关于你的作品的问题。最近在北京的"中国当代艺术展"我已经看过了那个作品，所以那个问题解决了。

我现在写了一些关于当代中国的艺术家的介绍文章。关于你的艺术工作和经历我用了下面的文章：美术83年1期，87年5期，86年12期，88年12期，~~89年3期~~

中国美术报86年38期

江苏画刊86年2期，88年2期，

画廊19期

画家 ~~86年9期~~ 总3期 87年6期

美术思潮87年5期，86年[illegible]期，85年6期，

1986年的厦门达达报

我把我写的介绍文章打算寄给荷兰的一个外国美术协会，和给一个英国的杂志。

我的问题是：我没有你的作品的照片，你能不能寄给我？

南京藝術學院

我也很想知道关于你的最近的艺术运向。

第三个问题是：怎么用拼音写你的夕字：Haung Yong ping 听说了你自己这样发音，或者按照《辞海》：Haung Yong Li？

如果你能给我帮助，我很高兴。在此谢谢你！

Hans van Dijk 戴汉志 南京艺术学院
23楼201号
南京
1989-2-26

Hans van Dijk, letter to Huang Yong Ping, Nanjing, 26 February 1989, private coll.

Dear Mr. Dai Hanzhi,

How are you? I just saw the two letters from you. Please kindly forgive that I didn't write back until now.

Your very well-written letters in Chinese and the depth of your comprehension of Chinese contemporary art much surprised me. During the *China/Avant-Garde* exhibition in Beijing, I was inside the museum the whole time. It was a great pity that we couldn't meet and have a good talk.

1) The contradiction between theory, practice, and reality in Chinese contemporary art that you mentioned is indeed the Chinese "characteristic." Chinese artists and theorists indeed have the problem of "talking too much, doing too little," although I don't think a total consolidation of art theory, practice, and reality is necessary.
2) The book I put in the washing machine is not by Li Xiaoshan. It is the *History of Chinese Painting* written by Wang Bomin and the Chinese translated version of Herbert Read's *A Concise History of Modern Painting*. About this work, my explanation is: their two minutes in the washing machine better realized the combination of "Eastern and Western painting" than 100 years of arguments.
3) I attach with this letter to you a photocopied version of something I wrote in February 1988, together with the *Xiamen Dada List of Activities* and a few photographs of my work. Should you need more materials, please write to me.
4) Lately I have been busy preparing for the exhibition *Magiciens de la terre* at the Centre Pompidou, for which I'm heading to Paris on 15 April. There are also Chinese artists from Beijing and Guangzhou invited. I'll be in France for one month.
5) The pinyin of my name "砯"—I'm used to writing it as Huang Yong Ping. It was perhaps a mistake made by my father, but by now it's kind of been fixed. I don't attempt to change it.
6) Before 25 March I'll be in Xiamen. If you'd like to contact me during this period, please write to Huang Yong Ping, F2, No. 11 Dazhong Road, Xiamen.

Hope all is well with you!

P.S. In the future, if your article is published in Dutch or British magazines, please post a copy to me. I'd be very grateful.

Huang Yong Ping, letter to HvD, Xiamen, 3 March 1989

Dear Mr. Dai Hanzhi,
How are you? I received your letter. Here I send you photographs of the two works you mentioned: (colored) *Les Foins*, (black/white) *Roulette-Oval*, from the series of non-expressive paintings.
Nowadays in China, there are indeed a large group of theorists and artists who always refer to extremely abstract or metaphysical concepts, e.g. transcendence, eternity. These borrowed philosophical terminologies probably have already become totally void signifiers in modern philosophy and linguistics (I have discussed this topic in an article published in the latest issue of *Meishu*—vol. 2 or 3). If I have any anti-art inclination, it'd be anti-those art theorists and artists. There's not much difference between an artist and a cobbler. But cobblers never talk about things as such.
I'm not craving success from the coming trip to Paris. We ought to dissolve any kind of desire: to be guided by the happenings, not the other way around. This trip is roughly "official" (I'm an official passport holder) -> "touring." And of course I'll be back! Until later.

Huang Yong Ping, letter to HvD, Xiamen, 20 March 1989

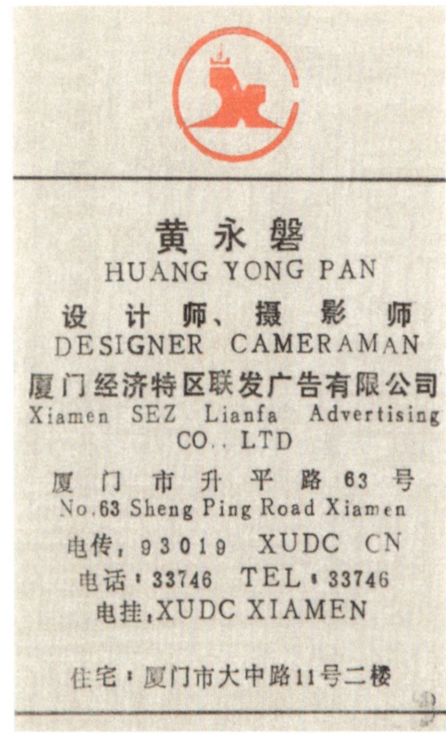

Huang Yong Ping's business card, 1989, private coll.

China/Avant-Garde

On 5 February 1989, *China/Avant-Garde*, the first large-scale manifestation of contemporary art in China, opens at the China Art Gallery in Beijing. The exhibition is carried by optimism and hope and has an enormous impact on the entire Chinese art world. It features 186 contemporary artists from across China, including Tibet and Inner Mongolia. 297 artworks are shown in six exhibition halls occupying the three floors of the building. It is curated by art critics Gao Minglu, Li Xianting, and a dozen others (critic Fei Dawei and a young Hou Hanru among them), and includes performance art, public debates, site-specific installations, conceptual art, rationalist oil painting, Political Pop, and experimental ink painting. The "No U-turn" traffic sign is the exhibition logo, symbolizing the determination never to return to the wasteland of old standards. On the opening day, artists Tang Song and his girlfriend Xiao Lu cause an enormous upheaval by firing a bullet at Xiao Lu's installation, *Dialogue*. The police temporarily shut down the exhibition. Both artists are arrested and put in prison for three days. Nonetheless, authorities allow the exhibition to reopen the next day. After an anonymous bomb threat (a prank call), the exhibition is closed down a second time, but it reopens and remains so until ending as scheduled on 19 February. Four months to the day after the opening of the show, the events of Tiananmen Square put a stop to the development of this new artistic climate.

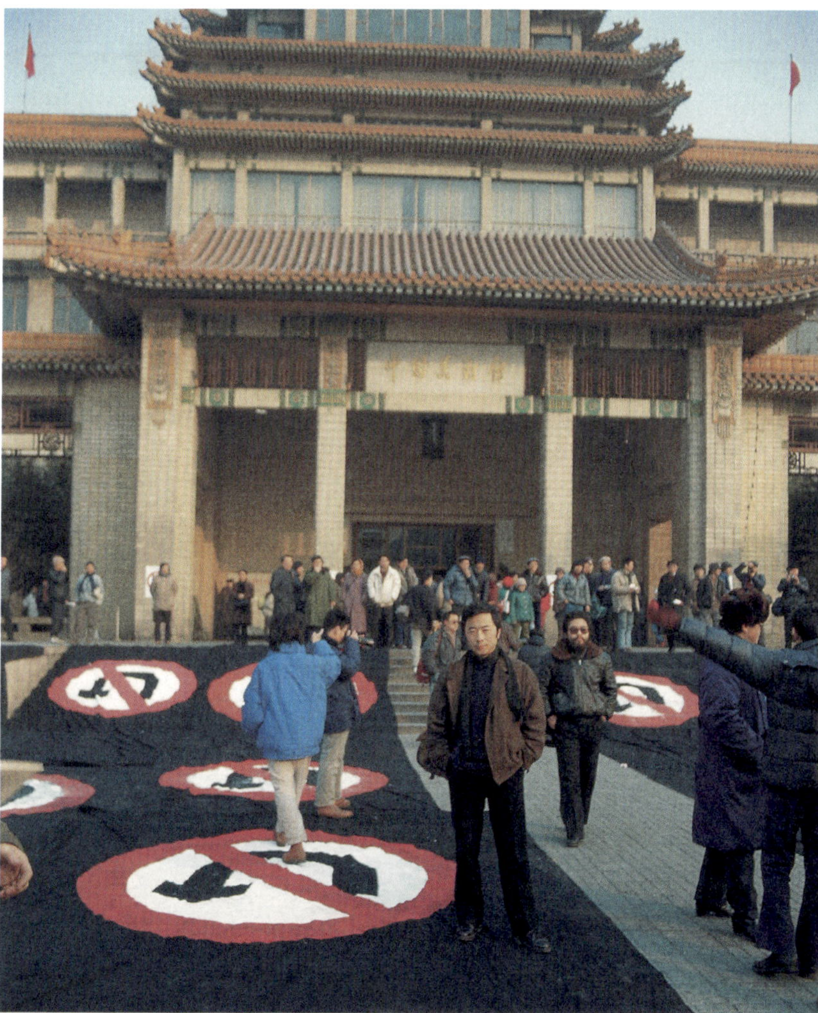

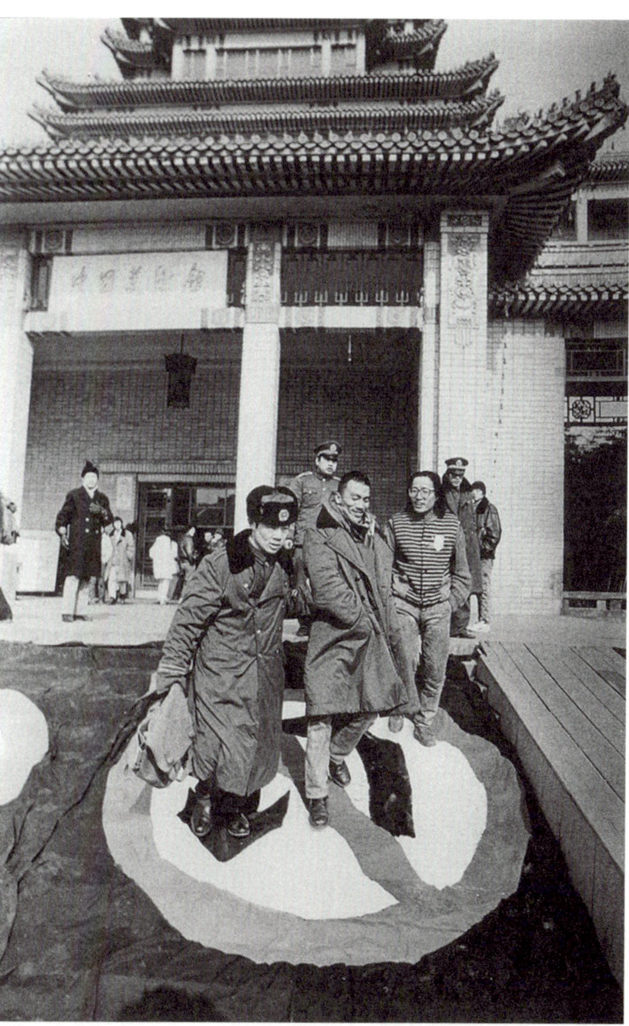

Left: Wang Luyan standing next to No U-Turn signs on the opening day of *China/Avant-Garde*, China Art Gallery, Beijing, 5 February 1989, photo courtesy Xin Kedu; right: Tang Song's arrest during the opening of *China/Avant-Garde*, National Art Gallery, Beijing, 5 February 1989

Hans van Dijk
Beijing Happenings

In a Beijing prison, there is a tortoise with "1989/2/9" (9 February 1989) engraved on its shell. It was on this date that two artists from Hangzhou, Tang Song and Xiao Lu, were released from that prison.

Some days before, at the opening of the first national exhibition of Chinese modern art, *China/Avant-Garde* at the China Art Gallery in Beijing, they were arrested after firing two shots at the exhibited work of Xiao Lu. Xiao Lu's exhibit was an installation piece entitled *Dialogue* and consisted of two telephone kiosks separated by a long mirror. She and Tang Song had prepared this act together with the intention of discovering how well the phenomenon "modern art" was understood and accepted in China: for example, what would be the legal consequences of their act?

With the gunshots, they also hoped to break the isolation of art and project it beyond the gallery walls. There were other artists who shared similar intentions and on the day of the opening also carried out various acts, inside and outside the exhibition building. There was, for instance, Wu Shanzhuan, from the island of Zhoushan near Shanghai, who brought a packet of shrimps from his island and sold them in front of the gate of the exhibition hall. [...] I have known Tang Song for two years. In that time, we corresponded quite frequently, and so I asked him if he could write to me about his contribution to the exhibition.

It was in the beginning of March that he sent me a report about his experiences in jail. [...] He was plied with questions about the phenomenon "modern art." Using a newspaper, playing cards, a pin-up photograph, and such-like, he developed a game. After drawing a square on the newspaper, he spread it over the other things and asked his cellmates to guess what was under the drawn square. The game was elaborated on with variations like "look for the pin-up girl," and so on. Tang Song then took the opportunity to explain—"Well, that's modern art, it's something we developed together and it looks rather like a game. But we, here in this prison, we decide ourselves about the things we play with. We don't need an artist for that. It's not about what is ugly or what is beautiful, but about values which matter to us, here and now."

He continues his letter by examining the concepts of "time" and "space" at great length, looking at them from several art historical and philosophical points of view. Suddenly he interjects with the question: "But Hans, after all, what do you think 'time' and 'space' mean for eight men in a cell of 3.5 by 7.5 meters?" And he tells of how, at the moment of being released, he took a live tortoise out of his pocket and, after engraving the date on its shell, he handed the still young animal over to the cell-mate who was next to be set free with the request that he do the same on the day of his own release.

Such an act may be seen in a broader context: the logo chosen for the *China/Avant-Garde* exhibition and used on posters and on the catalogue was the traffic sign signaling "No U-turn." By acknowledging that the sudden gunshots at the opening could be considered as a work of art, the organizers make a clear decision about what direction Chinese modern art should take. Thus, in contrast, the silent and prolonged existence of the tortoise in the Beijing prison also symbolizes in a living creature the hope that modern art in China will continue its progress forward.

HvD, *Beijing Happenings*, written in Nanjing, English text sent to his friends in the Netherlands, 1989

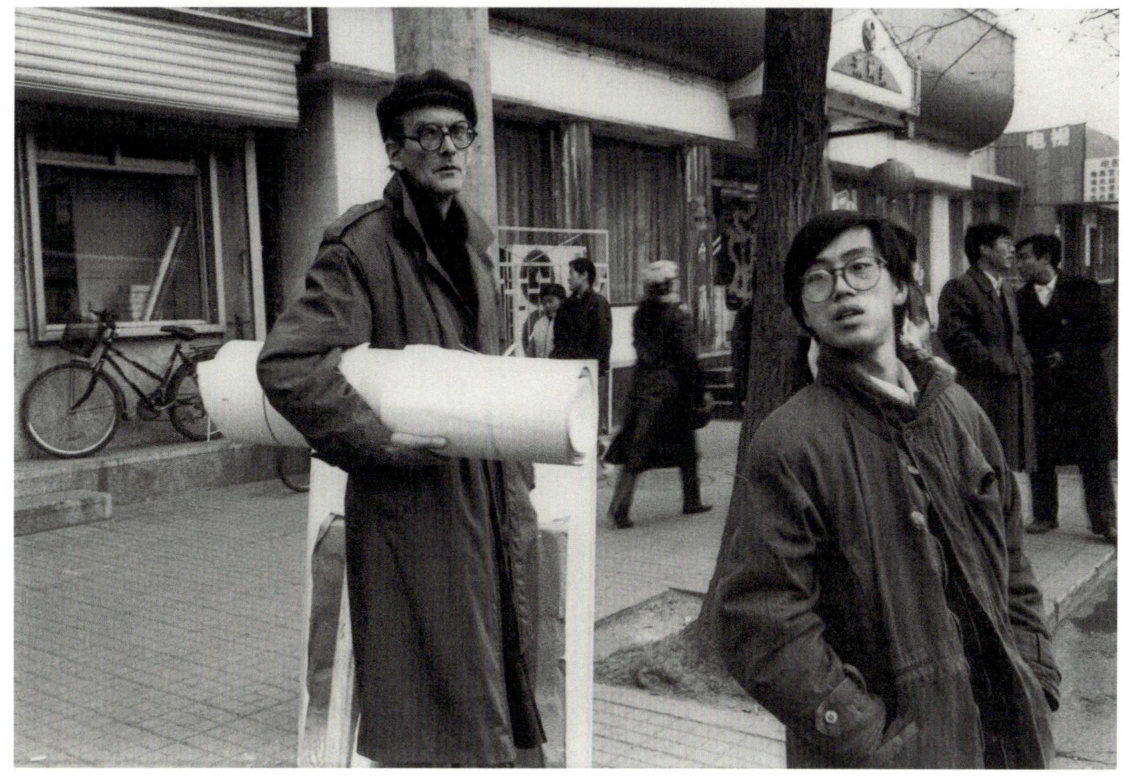

Zhang Hai'er, *Hans with Hong Hao*, Beijing, 1995, coll. Zhang Hai'er

Hong Hao

Van Dijk meets Hong Hao in Beijing in February 1989 when he goes to see *China/Avant-Garde* in Beijing. He stays at the CAFA student dormitory. Hong Hao, already an accomplished printmaker, is one of the students who takes care of him when he falls ill. In future years, van Dijk will work closely with Hong Hao, who becomes one of the most successful artists shown abroad by van Dijk's Beijing gallery, the New Amsterdam Art Consultancy. In 1995 van Dijk and Hong Hao try to set up an artist silkscreen printmaking studio in Beijing because nothing of the sort exists in China.

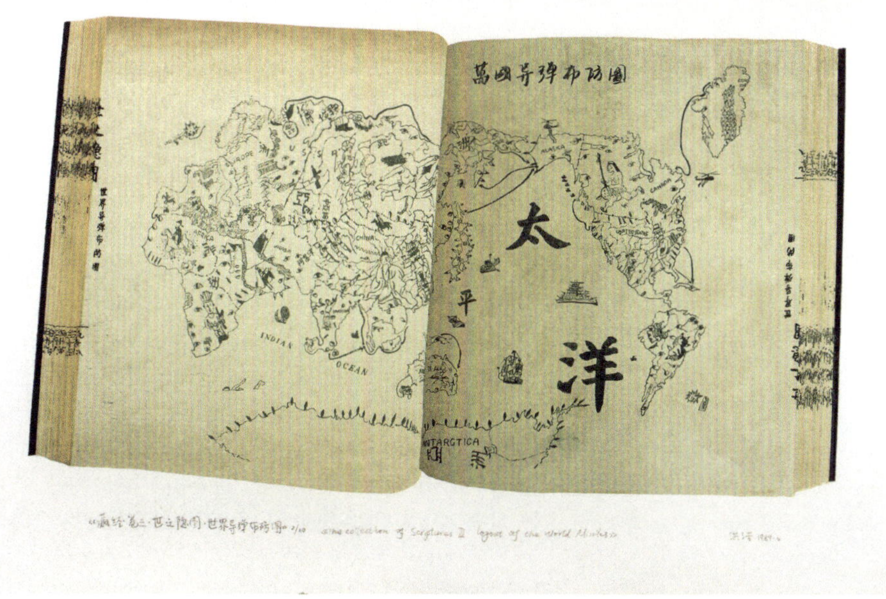

Hong Hao, *The Collection of Scripture. Volume III, Layout of the world Missiles*, silk-screen print, 56 × 78.5 cm, 1989, private coll.; given to van Dijk by the artist in 1995 in memory of their first meeting

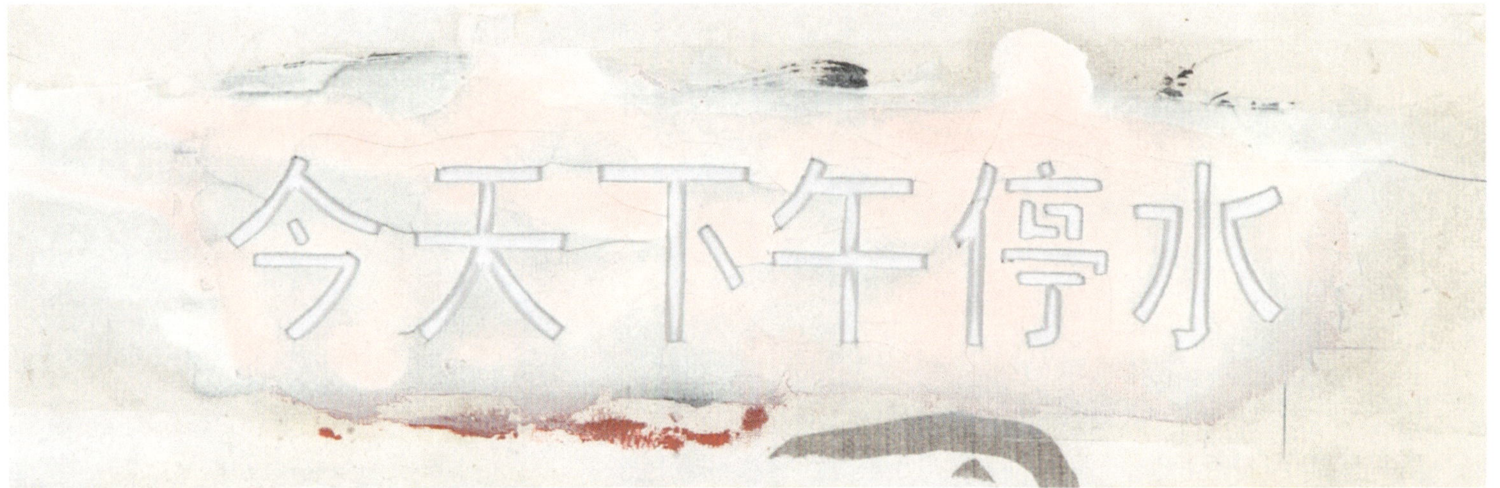

Wu Shanzhuan, *No Water this Afternoon*, stencil for installation at *China / Avant-Garde*, Beijing, 1989, private coll.
Opposite page: Wu Shanzhuan, *Drawings*, 1989, private coll.

Wu Shanzhuan

Wu Shanzhuan is perhaps the most radical conceptual ink artist of the '85 movement. He aspires to rid calligraphy and the written character of all inherent meaning, until only the empty sign remains. In his drawings and installations, he uses a well-known style of writing from the slogan campaigns of the Cultural Revolution. Yet he writes announcements from everyday life instead, like "Cabbage three cents a pound" or "No water today." He calls his characters "Red Signs," and uses only red, black, and white paint. With Ni Haifeng, he is a co-founder of the "Red Humor" movement and a main organizer of the exhibition *75% Red, 20% Black, 5% White*.

At *China/Avant-Garde*, his is probably the most radical installation: for his performance *Big Business*, he has 200 kilograms of fresh shrimp brought in from his native Zhoushan to sell at the entrance steps of the China Art Gallery with a notice saying: "The China Art Gallery is not just a place to display artworks; it also can be a black market. For Chinese New Year, I have brought top-quality shrimp suitable for export from my home village in celebration of the holiday and to enrich people's spiritual and material life in our capital. The unit price: 9.5 yuan. Place of display: China Art Gallery. Urgent for buying." His installation is closed down by the police because he has no business permit.

> Dear Mr. Dai Hanzhi,
> Cabbage is just cabbage. Later I cooked and ate it. The red mark on the cabbage was drawn in chalk. It can be washed away. There are no more problems. The purpose of selling prawns is merely to tell people: anyone can succeed on a business deal. Anyone can become a ten-thousand-yuan household with one sale. One must stand against (the present) art ecology, aka art museums, critics, visitors, artists, art magazines, et cetera. This is because my concerns in art are as follows: you have certain things, but you can't sell them directly; you want certain things, but you can't buy them directly. The guy in the middle, the one with the black handbag, is holding up our tradition of mythologizing. Please come to Zhoushan when you have time. The wind here is very nice; the water here can dissolve salt.
>
> **Wu Shanzhuan, letter to HvD, Zhoushan, 5 March 1989**

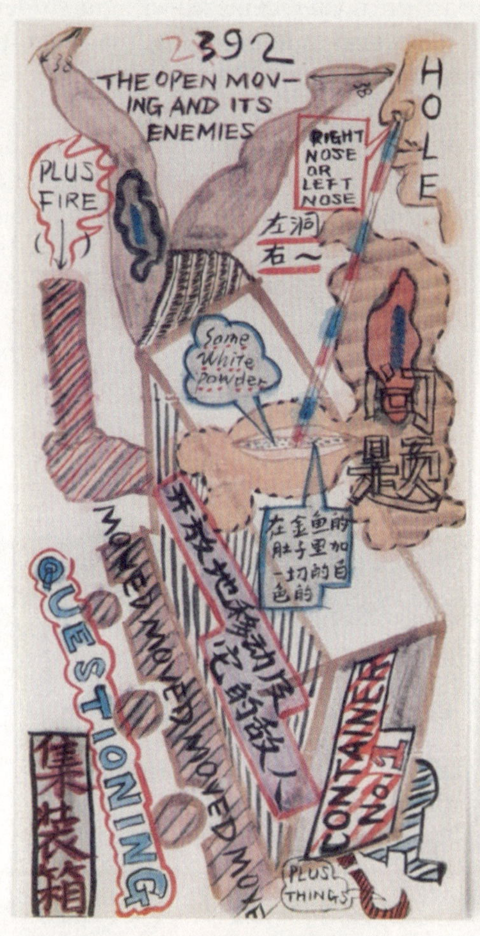

THE OPEN MOVING AND ITS ENEMIES
HOLE
RIGHT NOSE OR LEFT NOSE
PLUS FIRE
左洞
右～
Some White powder
问题
在金鱼的肚子里加一切的白色的
开放地移动及它的敌人
QUESTIONING
MOVED MOVED MOVED MOVED MOVE
CONTAINER No 1
集装箱
PLUS THINGS

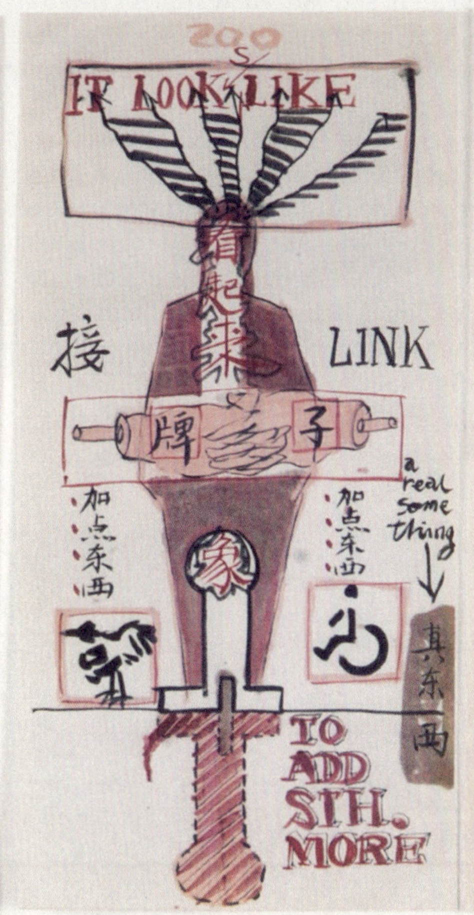

IT LOOK LIKE
看起来
接
LINK
牌
子
加点东西
加点东西
a real some thing
象
TO ADD STH. MORE

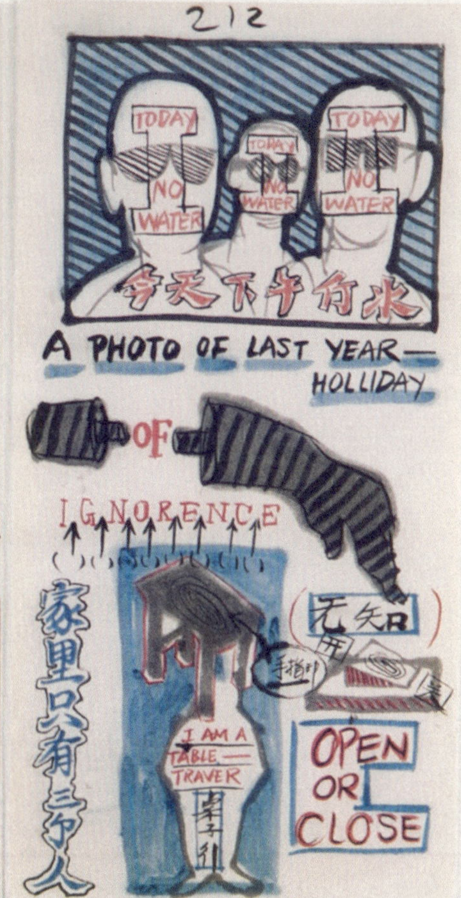

212
TODAY NO WATER
TODAY NO WATER
TODAY NO WATER
A PHOTO OF LAST YEAR— HOLLIDAY
OF
IGNORENCE
家里只有三个人
无知
I AM A TABLE— TRAVER
桌子
OPEN OR CLOSE

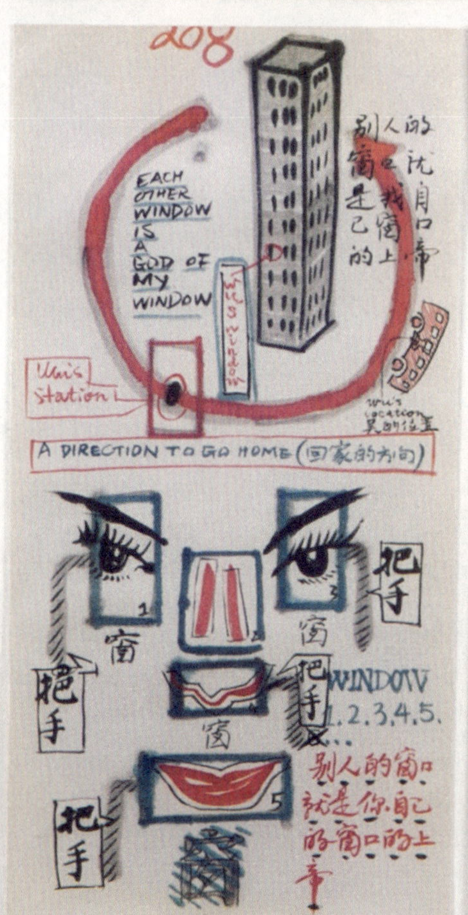

208
EACH OTHER WINDOW IS A GOD OF MY WINDOW
Wu's station
A DIRECTION TO GO HOME (回家的方向)
把手
窗
WINDOW 1.2.3.4.5.
别人的窗口就是你自己的窗口的上

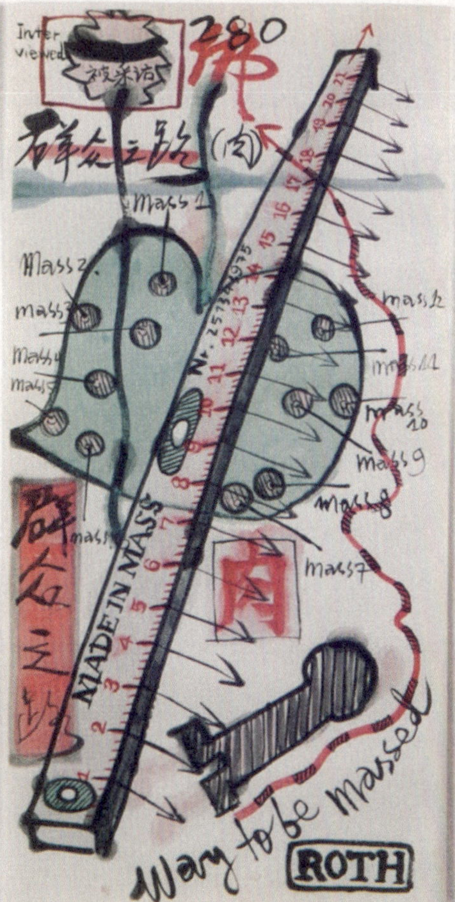

Inter viewed
280
群众之路
MADE IN MASS
肉
Way to be massed
ROTH

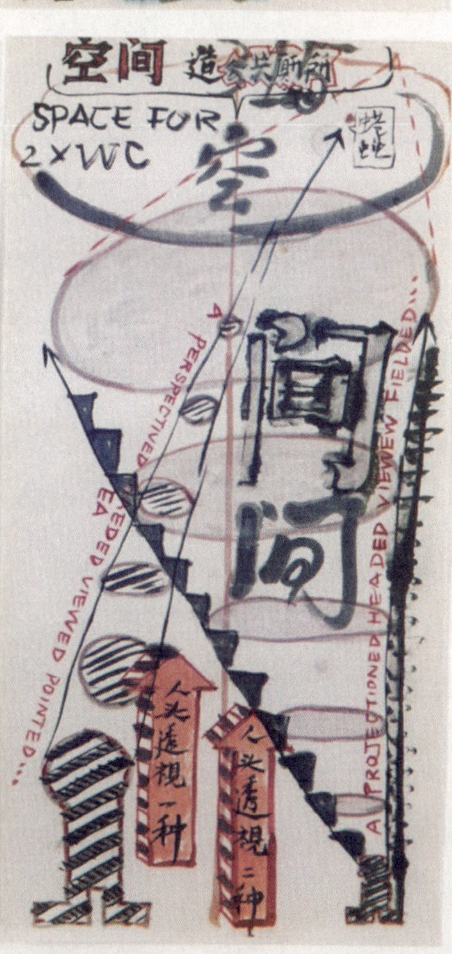

空间
SPACE FOR 2×WC
空
间
PERSPECTIVED
A PROJECTIONED HEADED VIEWED FIELDED...
人头透视一种
人头透视二种

18 May 1989

Van Dijk and his friend and fellow student Deborah Nash are invited to march with the student demonstrations in Nanjing to support the hunger strikers there and in Beijing. They are the only foreigners. He sends Ernst Dinkla photographs of the demonstrations:

> The demonstrations in Nanjing have lasted for four days now. They start at two o'clock, after the midday meal, and continue until the early morning hours. Civil servants and teachers also participate. Today the posters with slogans, in all sizes and colors, have been glued everywhere outside the schools. Groups of demonstrators big and small can be seen and heard throughout the entire city; songs and shouts waft through the air twelve hours out of twenty-four. The smart students in the photo are from the University of Nanjing; banner: "Let history judge," with a clock tower from the Ming dynasty in the background.
>
> HvD, letter to Ernst Dinkla, Nanjing, 18 May 1989

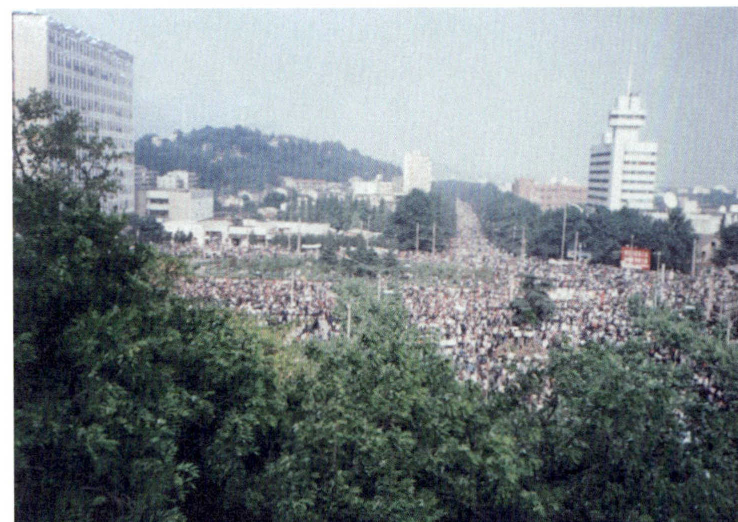

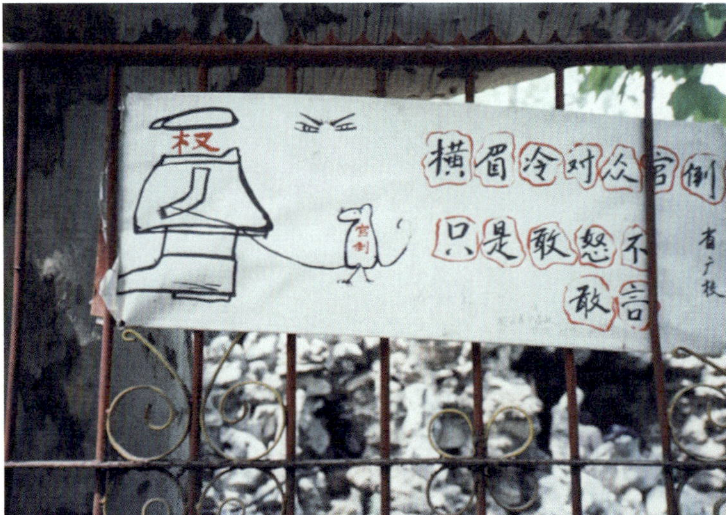

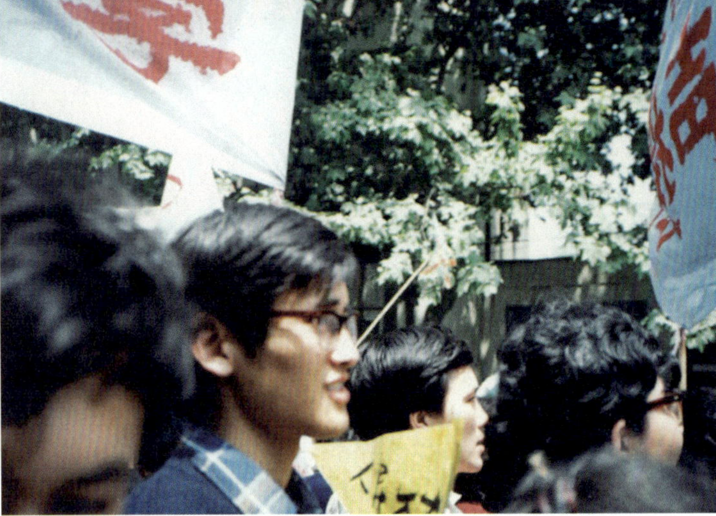

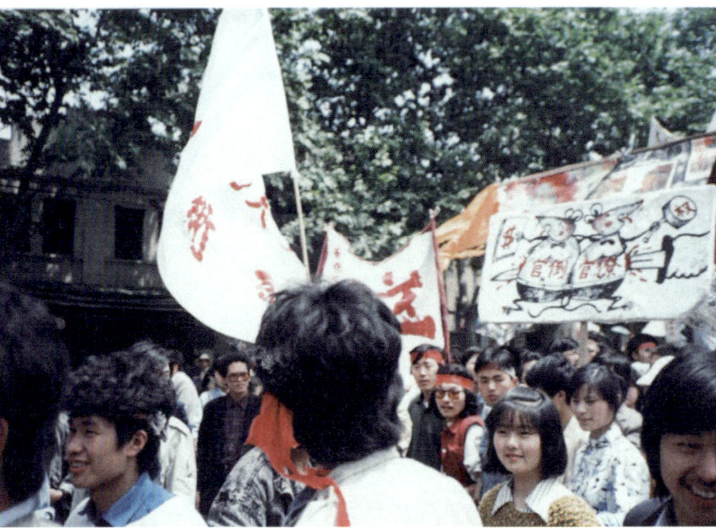

Hans van Dijk, mass demonstrations in Nanjing, May 1989; top left: the square next to the Telecommunication Center; top right: banner of a robot named "Power" leading "Corruption" on a string, with the text: "With frowning eyebrows and a cold approach, I confront massive corruption, but alas I have to keep my indignation to myself."; bottom left: students marching on the street in Nanjing; bottom right: students with banner saying: "Where money and power unite bureaucracy and corruption."; all photos coll. Ernst Dinkla

22 May 1989

Day and night, the avant-garde of the academies sets out, yesterday afternoon following Li Peng's ultimatum stating that tomorrow (Monday morning) Tiananmen Square will be cleared. To return in the evening means to wash, eat, and paint new banners. At one o'clock at night, again lots of commotion; assembling and again marching into town, at three a.m., following the alleged abdication by Li and Deng, fireworks in the dorms, after which a blazing fire breaks out. [...] The uncertainty about the future; a divided (non-functional) government, a divided army command, and student factions at odds with each other. [...] After four days of twenty-four-hour demonstrations, spread out over the entire city, the masses that make the city inaccessible to any traffic from midday on become a bit impatient, not enough sensation. I had to cross them again yesterday evening. The telecommunication center is in the square, which is the center where groups come and go, where news is exchanged between student leaders and groups, and, until yesterday, the location of the 200 local hunger-strikers, most of whom gave up after three hours.

HvD, letter to Ernst Dinkla, Nanjing, 22 May 1989

26 May 1989

Yesterday they came back exhausted after a 25km march: "Strike Li Peng," "Punish Deng Xiaoping." In the evening, a self-assured Li Peng on TV, who declares that the term "Martial Law" changes its meaning in translation, so that the foreign interpretation of the situation, according to which the government is powerless, is unjustified.

In Prague, twenty years ago, they changed the Russian troops after they had been in contact with the civil population in Prague for too long. It seems that at present the same tactics are being applied here.

Only a small part of the intelligentsia seems emancipated. With many, the idea that legal power also represents moral power is deeply embedded. Not ripe for democracy. There is an attitude of indignation about so little reaction from the authorities after all their efforts.

HvD, letter to Ernst Dinkla, Nanjing, 26 May 1989

4 June 1989

Around nine in the morning, following reports via Voice of America about the violent takeover of Tiananmen Square by the 27th army, Nanjing students and teachers march to the city center. At 10 a.m., a demonstration by Nanda and others passes around Gulou and continues to Xinjiekou. At 1 p.m., there are reports of continued violent conflicts, always with injuries and fatalities. The troops shoot, and not out of self-defense. [...] Some people don't want to believe the news, or give no response, or show only the most superficial interest, driven by sensationalism. The events confirm the most negative opinions about the government to which I listened somewhat incredulously for such a long time. [...] By the evening, according to VoA, the death toll has risen to a thousand or many more.

HvD, diary entry, 4 June 1989

6 June 1989

A death toll of 1,400 on the first day, and increasingly strong reactions from abroad. [...] On the way to the demonstrations, the gatekeeper of the Provincial Government forbade me to take pictures of the signs on the pavement written in minium. In other places, too, I see the sign "blood" on the pavement and on blocked crossroads. The latter also with wreaths. All over China, roads and bridges are blocked by protesters. Foreign students are evacuated by their embassies, Chinese students are advised to go home. The situation is extremely tense.

HvD, diary entry, 6 June 1989

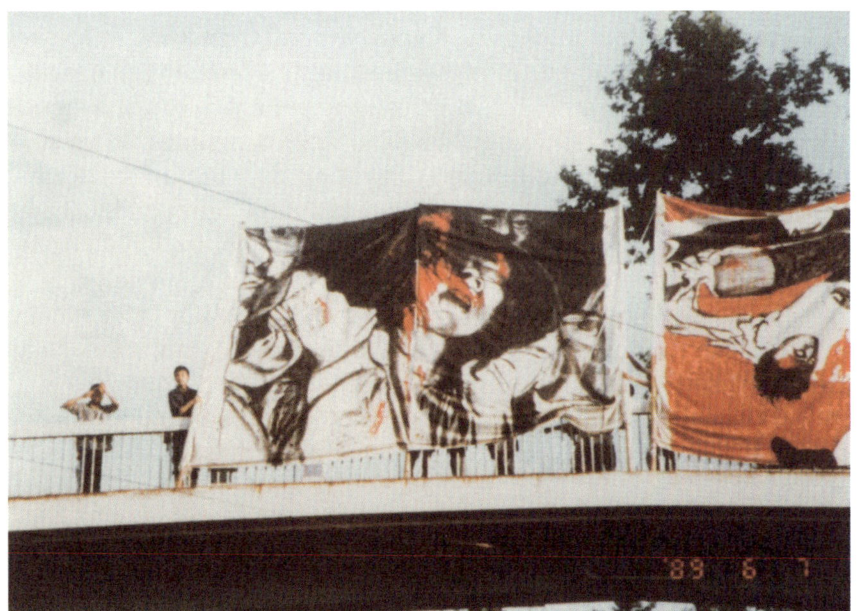

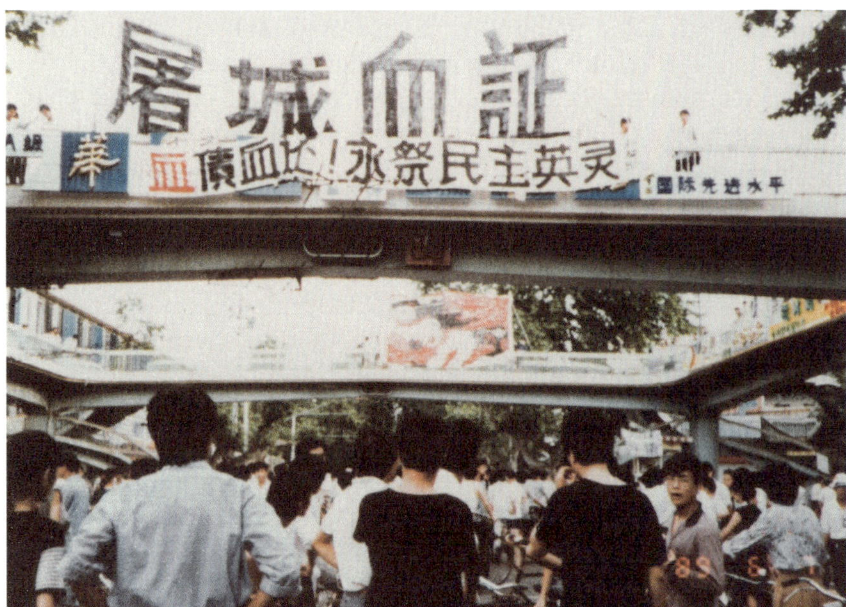

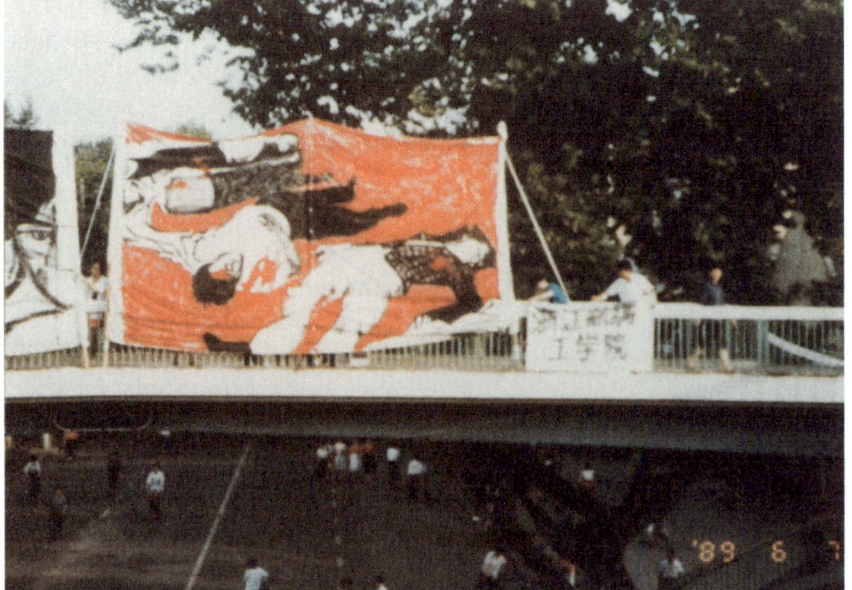

Hangzhou, 7 June 1989, protest banners with paintings based on photos of victims shot in Tiananmen Square on 4 June 1989; the banners hung in the square in front of the Zhejiang Art Academy for three days before anyone dared to take them down; photographs sent to Hans van Dijk by Zhang Peili and Geng Jianyi in 1989, private coll.

8 June 1989

Van Dijk leaves for Lianyungang and Qingdao in the north with three Chinese student friends. He takes his camera, the photo negatives, and his diary with him. They listen to BBC radio and Voice of America for news:

> The last days in Nanjing were filled with listening to and translating from foreign radio stations and the stream of rumors that form the most important source of information here. The director of the academy advised the students to leave because they feared the army which, looking for the centers of agitation, would certainly not omit the academies. When on Wednesday evening rumors arrived that Nanjing hospitals were preparing places for expected victims, one group decided to leave that very night. Because the train track linking Nanjing with the north and with Shanghai was destroyed the day before, and bus traffic had come to a complete standstill, we departed very early in the morning by bike for the ferry over the Yangtze, to fight with a few thousand students at the station across the river for tickets to the countryside. From the ferry, we saw an abandoned, blockaded bridge over the Yangtze. At that instant, the north-south connection was broken over thousands of kilometers: from Shanghai to Wuhan.
>
> HvD, letter to Ernst Dinkla, Lianyungang, 11 June 1989

13 June 1989

Students traveling on a train from Beijing going in the opposite direction confirm the number of victims mentioned by the BBC and VoA, and tell them that martial law may be imminent for Nanjing and other big cities. The contrast with life in the country when they arrive at the home of a fellow student could not be bigger:

> His sixty-year-old father serves in the army, and one may safely call him conservative. The family only watches domestic TV and had no idea of what has happened in Beijing. They distrust foreign broadcasting stations and are happy that order is beginning to be restored, 300 victims amongst the soldiers and just a few students—an image that endless TV broadcasts keep repeating continuously.
>
> Ibid.

> The TV does not mention the bloodbath in the capital, but for ten hours a day shows interviews with relieved citizens who complain of the past unrest in terms taken from the official version of recent history: demonstrations degenerated into an antirevolutionary rebellion to which the army, with great loss of life on their end, put a halt.
> The citizens of Beijing know better, and the same is true for part of the intelligentsia, but everybody keeps silent to save their life. A gigantic propaganda machine—newspapers, TV, radio, loudspeakers in the streets, in the factories, schools, on public billboards, through wanted notices—repeats the above message non-stop, illustrated with images of victims, or of parents who have lost children. For those involved, it is a warning; for the largest part of the population, it is brainwashing. [...] "After a wanted notice was broadcast on TV, the older sister turns in her student leader younger brother to the police!" True or not, doesn't matter much.
>
> HvD, diary entry, 13 June 1989

Among his friends, energy and hope gradually turn into depression and lethargy. They eat and drink instead:

> Took a stroll through a rainy Qingdao feeling blue. They had forgotten almost everything, yet were not cheerful. The first joyous attempts at an escape through cynical jokes had lost their attraction. We did not listen to the loudspeakers in the streets warning about forbidden radio stations, and we did not stop to look at TV programs in shops. There was another feeding frenzy in the evening, in which I hardly took part; I wasn't that hungry, and I was a bit nauseous again from the violence of the eating.
>
> Ibid.

The radio announces increasing arrests and executions of students and workers. Afraid to get caught, van Dijk burns his photos of the Nanjing demonstrations and other incriminating material on the way.

16 June 1989

> What happened and its ending correspond to the most negative, paranoid image of their country that friends would often describe to me, and to which I always reacted with some skepticism. They are also ashamed of their country, of which they would like to be so proud. The past weeks, the four of us have continuously been traveling together, from one city to the next. Foreigners seem to have disappeared from the more remote cities we went to.
>
> HvD, letter to Ernst Dinkla, Qingdao, 16 June 1989

20 June 1989

From Qingdao, van Dijk takes the boat to Shanghai. There, he meets some of his friends and asks their advice about the possibility of staying on in China, finding a job in the arts, perhaps. They all tell him that they expect a very bad future for contemporary art. He continues onto Hangzhou. On his return to Nanjing on 28 June, he hears that his application to spend another semester at the Nanjing Arts Institute has been rejected; on what grounds, he doesn't know. There are still police raids at the university, and the situation is highly uncertain. Most foreign students have already left. By 2 July, he is back in Hangzhou and decides to buy a ticket to the Netherlands. "I am again a foreigner in this country," he writes.

11 July 1989

> Memories of the last days in Prague 1968: short, reticent conversations when people understand you are no accidental tourist; the rumor mill, the broadcasts; the artificial inflation; the occupation of communist centers; brave journalists; the roving channels; the condescending jokes about "farmer-soldiers"; the nationalist sense of fatality. Just like then, I feel a strong sense of unity through knowledge, yet remain an outsider, an observer more than ever.
>
> HvD, diary entry, 11 July 1989

15 July 1989

Van Dijk is back in Nanjing, where police forces raid the student dormitories at night, checking the identities of the sleeping students. Many artists have asked him to help them leave the country. On 27 July, he gathers his belongings in two crates to be shipped to the Netherlands.

29 July 1989

Van Dijk takes the train from Hangzhou to Guangzhou and Shenzhen, then crosses the border to Hong Kong on foot. After staying in Hong Kong for a few days, he returns to the Netherlands.

1989: The Aftermath

The bloody end to the demonstrations in Tiananmen Square on 4 June 1989 reverberates throughout China. For the contemporary art world in China, so fresh and hopeful only a little while before, 1989 will prove disastrous for many years to come. Aside from artists thrown in jail, teachers denied promotions or courses, and artists and critics leaving the country, the very fabric of the art world is undone. Contemporary art, dubbed "experimental," is forbidden. One can make work in the solitude of one's studio, but it is forbidden to exhibit, export, teach, or sell, effectively killing any chance for artists to make a living from their work. For the next two years, there are no exhibitions of contemporary art in all of China.

ZHANG PEILI: In 1989, we artists were in a very bad state. The political environment was really bad. I was thinking about leaving China. Hans, too, was ready to leave China, and he said to me, "I can help you." Hans had a brother working in Paris at the UN. He phoned him and left a message. I gave Hans the phone number of a friend of mine in Britain. Hans left China and wrote me a letter, but he never mentioned any of the things he had been doing for me. He also mailed me an English art magazine that was confiscated by the authorities.

At the time I had no passport, because that was very difficult to get. Hans had left in the summer, and in October, a professor from my academy phoned to say that a French professor wanted to speak to me urgently. I met with this professor from the French national design institute, and they promised to cover my living and study expenses in France if I wanted to go there. They asked me whether I was sure I wanted to leave.

I said it is not possible for me to leave or even to get a passport, as I was watched closely and constantly checked by the academy because of the action Geng Jianyi and I did in the Railway Square in Hangzhou in June.

Everybody was very disappointed about 4 June. But everybody had also given up, and we didn't want it to be like that.

We had received prints of photos of bloody corpses. We painted them very large on a banner that we hung in Hangzhou Square. We knew it wouldn't have any effect, but we still felt compelled to do this. This was the most serious action after 4 June in Hangzhou. After two weeks, the police came and told us they wanted to speak to us. They gave their findings to the academy, so it was impossible for me to leave.

Why do I talk about this? Because I want people to know how much Hans cared for his artist friends. Hans left in 1989 because he had finished his MA in Nanjing, but perhaps his leaving was also related to the happenings in Tiananmen. I actually had a work, which does not exist anymore: I made a silk-screen on Plexiglas of Hans' letter. It's an installation entitled *Private Letters, the Proof of Never Doing Something I Regret*. I made that work in 1990 and exhibited it in 1991.

MB, interview with Zhang Peili, Shanghai, 8 October 2012

Dear Hans,

It has been a long time since we contacted each other.

How are you doing these days? When will you come back to China?

After June, the art circle in China has been far from prosperous. No major artistic activities have been held since *China/Avant-Garde* in Beijing. There was supposed to be an exhibition called the *Chinese Abstract Art Exhibition*, but it was not held because of what happened in June.

I have painted some new works recently, which are still part of *Appearance of Crosses*. My painting style is freer than before, and I am quite relaxed while painting. But in general, it is still about patterns in terms of the style and intention. I have enclosed them with my letter.

I am now on a train, quite close to Xining[18]. I have attended our school's annual sketching course. After reaching Xining, I plan to go to Tibet to sketch, where I will stay for a month before returning to Shanghai.

Ding Yi, letter to HvD, Xining, 7 October 1989

18—Captial of Qinghai, on the Tibetan Plateau.

Introducing China's Avant-Garde in Europe 1990–1993

Hans did not act like a lot of foreign curators who treat Chinese artists like sick people or patients, looking to diagnose the problem and telling them what to do; Hans treated us as friends.

Zhang Peili

While China is closing off after the Tiananmen Square tragedy, the West is about to enter a new era of globalism and post-colonialism. The year is further marked by the fall of the Berlin Wall and the end of the Cold War. The Paris blockbuster show *Magiciens de la terre* becomes the much-disputed hallmark of the time. *Magiciens* is the first exhibition to promote a global art market by bringing together artists and artworks, both contemporary and indigenous, from the remotest corners of all continents.[1] The Chinese art in the show is an instant hit with the public. The Tiananmen tragedy, after which some of the artists are granted political asylum, creates an instant market for "dissident" Chinese art. On the other hand, there is little knowledge or understanding of the art itself. It is unclear whether van Dijk saw the exhibition, but there is no escaping its influence on both the art market and the art discourse.

Upon returning to Eindhoven in the summer of 1989, van Dijk devotes himself to writing about Chinese art. Over the next two years, he publishes a number of articles, including an essay entitled "Traditional Chinese Painting Has Reached Its Dead End," which runs close to Li Xiaoshan's ideas.[2] In the winter of 1991–92, he publishes "Painting in China after the Cultural Revolution: Style Developments and Theoretical Debates," an in-depth scholarly article in two parts written for *China Information*, the quarterly journal of the China Research Center of Leiden University—the same university that refused to help him research Ming carpentry.[3]

Simultaneously, van Dijk starts working on proposals for a major survey exhibition of Chinese contemporary art. The director of the Museum of Ethnology in Rotterdam invites him to develop his ideas. Van Dijk is also in touch with Dragon Bridge (*Drachenbrücke*), the German Society for Cultural Exchange with Asia, which wants to promote young art from China.

1—Curated by Jean-Hubert Martin and Marc Francis, *Magiciens de la terre* was held in Paris from 18 May to 14 August 1989 at the Musée National d'Art Moderne in the Centre Pompidou, and the Parc de la Villette. The Tiananmen Square massacre occurred on 4 June, less than three weeks after the opening. There were three Chinese artists in the exhibition, Huang Yong Ping, Gu Dexin, and Yang Jiechang. Huang Yong Ping, Yang Jiechang, and art critic Fei Dawei obtained political asylum. Gu Dexin returned to China.

2—Hans van Dijk, "Die traditionelle chinesische Malerei ist am Ende ihrer Sackgasse angekommen," and "Huang Yongping," in *Gebrochene Bilder- Junge Kunst aus China; Selbstdarstellungen*, ed. Drachenbrücke (Dragon Bridge), Society for Cultural Exchange with Asia, project group Martina Köppel-Yang, Peter Schneckmann, Eckard Schneider, Horlemann Verlag, Germany, 1991.

3—Hans van Dijk, "Painting in China after the Cultural Revolution: Style Developments and Theoretical Debates" in *China Information: A Quarterly Journal on Contemporary China Studies*, Leiden University, in vol. 6, no. 3 & 4, 1991–92 (→ p. 290).

1990

Scouting for other interested parties, van Dijk visits conferences on China in Frankfurt, and Heidelberg. In the spring of 1990, while attending a China conference organized by the Heinrich Böll Foundation in Bonn, van Dijk meets German artist Andreas Schmid. Schmid studied calligraphy at the Zhejiang Academy from 1983–86. He too is deeply moved by the developments in China and wants the world to know about the new Chinese art. With Jochen Noth, a business consultant and former Maoist who lived in China for many years, Schmid has written an exhibition proposal for the newly rebuilt Haus der Kulturen der Welt (HKW, House of World Cultures) in Berlin. It contains a general overview on urban developments in China, with a part devoted to the changes in the arts.

> JOCHEN NOTH: I worked for Radio Beijing as representative of the German Communist Union. Andreas and I met in Beijing in '83 at the Friendship Hotel, and I introduced Andreas to Beijing. I was very close to the No Name Painting Society around Yang Yushu and Zhao Wenliang. I wanted to make an exhibition about Beijing as a city—historical development, urbanism, architecture, et cetera. The HKW was interested in that.

Andreas Schmid, who closely witnessed the developments in the arts at the Zhejiang Academy, adds the arts' perspective to the show:

> It was my deep belief that there were crucially important developments in contemporary art in China during the early 80s. Contemporary art had been reinvented after the dark years of the Cultural Revolution. I was lucky as a student to be one of the witnesses in China, being in touch with Ma Desheng, Ma Kelu, Gu Wenda, Zheng Chongbin, Zhang Peili, and others. The attitude of many artists and the power of the artworks impressed me very much. Since my return to Berlin in 1986, I had been thinking about a way to show those strong works. Jochen Noth and I presented a first draft in 1990 to "players" within the Berlin contemporary art scene, but all refused due to the tragedy of 4 June 1989. We could not overcome existing prejudices. Jochen Pöhlmann from the HKW Art and Film Department was the first person to be interested. We were asked to come back with more image materials two weeks later, when General Secretary Günter Coenen would be there. The second draft of the project was accepted by Coenen and Pöhlmann. In 1990,

Jochen and I went to Bonn to attend a two-day seminar arranged by the Heinrich Böll Foundation. Fei Dawei and Huang Yong Ping had been invited to give a talk. Huang divined from the *I Ching* instead. During a coffee break, I happened to run into someone looking for partners for a China art project. He had brought various art magazines from China. That was Hans, who was quite frustrated because the Böll Foundation had just rejected his request for support. After we talked for about 30 minutes, I thought that he would be a great addition to our team. He not only knew a lot about the contemporary art situation in China, but also seemed to have true art-theoretical knowledge. Back in Berlin, I proposed to the HKW that Hans should become a member of our team. We both had the same contracts. The final selection of the artists belonged to the HKW, but the first choice was primarily left to the two of us, and secondly to Jochen. Hans and I first spent entire days discussing things in my studio, which was our first office where all the artist applications and materials arrived.

Following that, decisions were made by the whole team, including the HKW. It became clear that we needed exhibition partners to bring the works to a wider audience and also, crucially, to share the costs. Hans did a lot of negotiating with various important people in the Netherlands, and with the Kunsthal in Rotterdam in particular.

MB, interview with Jochen Noth and Andreas Schmid, Berlin, 16–17 December 2012

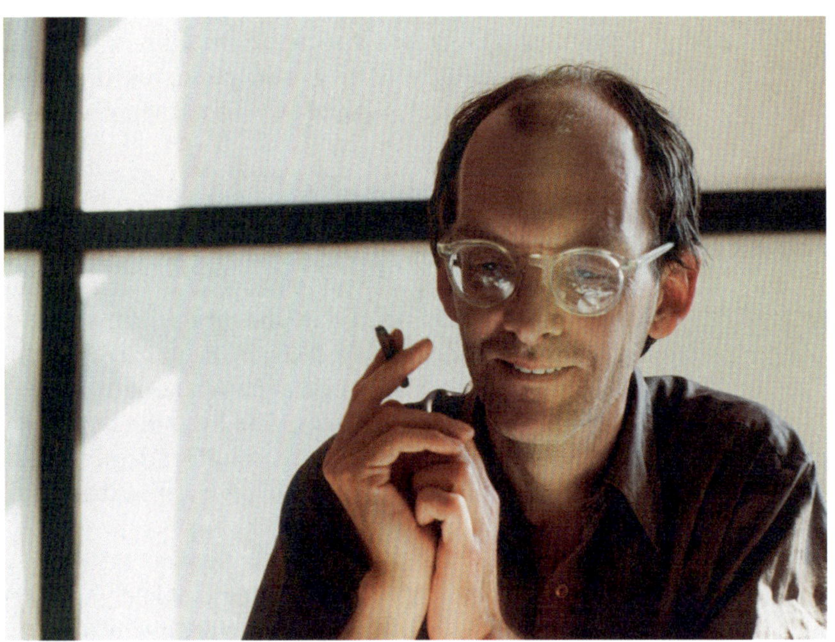

Hans van Dijk in Schmid's studio in Berlin, serving as their first office for *China Avant-garde*, Berlin, 1990, photo Andreas Schmid

1991

Following their meeting, van Dijk keeps Schmid and Noth abreast of developments on his end in a letter dated 16 May 1991:

To date, I have made two plans for an exhibition of Chinese modern art.[4]

The first one is from the end of 1989 with works made by eighteen artists between 1985–89 (fourteen on the mainland, four abroad). I was invited to do this by Hein Reedijk, director of the Museum of Ethnology in Rotterdam. In late 1990, he (finally) asked Albert Roskam of the Foundation for Art Projects in Rotterdam to make a financial plan and look for other art institutions in Europe.

March 1991, Albert Roskam presented the results of his investigations; besides Holland, he found three locations in Europe that were interested in exhibiting (Belgium, Aachen in Germany, and Denmark). The financial side of the plan was even less convincing. [...] Therefore, new hope arose when the Vorsitzende Schneckmann[5] appeared. According to His wishes, I made a new plan, the retrospective one (I showed you in Bonn), which could fit into the plans for the Drachenbrücke. However, Schneckmann, shocked by the

4—Van Dijk is referring to the Chinese title of the exhibition in Beijing, 1989. *China/Avant-Garde* was its English title.

5—Peter Schneckmann, chair of the *Drachenbrücke* project group.

> indecent financial proposals made by Roskam, showed no interest at all in my work when I visited Bonn and Frankfurt. Back in Holland, I informed Roskam, who said it wasn't meant that way, we could negotiate, et cetera.
> I'm writing you this boring story because there are still one or two hundred thousand Dutch guilders floating somewhere in the Dutch sky and a long list with more or less vague contacts of interested art institutions in Europe. Both can only be used if we succeed in realizing a co-production between Rotterdam and Berlin. One of the consequences for you would be to introduce Berlin to the idea of a traveling exhibition.
> For the Rotterdam side, of course, all things are negotiable: exhibition period, selected artists, et cetera, because it is their last hope, not mine.

In the fall of 1991, a renewed proposal with van Dijk as the third curator is accepted by the HKW, and the date of the exhibition is set for January 1993. The HKW also insists that an extensive cultural program, showing China's latest developments in theater, film, poetry, and classical and modern music, be part of the project. Wolfgang Pöhlmann, head of the HKW Art and Film Department, acts as the project manager, reserving the right of final decision on the artworks. Partly in homage to the 1989 Beijing show, they title the exhibition *China Avantgarde*. In subsequent English tranlations, the title is hyphenated.[6]

6—In this publication we follow the English translation.

Andreas Schmid gives an elaborate account of the art-theoretical and art-critical issues at stake:

> In a letter addressed to me dated 30 September 1991, soon after he joined the team of curators for *China Avantgarde*, Hans raised basic issues related to the exhibition. [...] One was that we try to work against a tendency that was especially prevalent in Western media—to equate Chinese experimental artists with political dissidents. In addition, we wanted to put forward a more differentiated and realistic image of what represented contemporary Chinese art at that time. In the same letter, van Dijk also critically addresses the thinking and exhibition concepts of Western theoreticians and exhibition organizers like Michael Sullivan, Jean-Hubert Martin, and David Elliott in a very clear stance. Since Elliott was our exhibition partner in The Museum of Modern Art, Oxford, where he then served as director, the discussion continued in personal conversations. [...] The question of what is "Chinese," of "identity," and of the "contextual" remained with us beyond the opening and led to self-critical reflections.
>
> Andreas Schmid, "Hans van Dijk: Principles and Challenges," in *Yishu: Journal of Contemporary Chinese Art*, Jan/Feb 2015, pp. 35–47

> Dear Andreas, [...] On the participation of Chinese artists living abroad:
> First: Dissident art is present in the exhibition in any case, even without the participation of *huaqiao* [Chinese artists abroad]. These works might be exemplary of the environment for the arts in China (what the PRC allows and what it forbids). We should however avoid the impression that, just because they went abroad, these "foreigners" are necessarily dissidents and for that reason part of the Chinese avant-garde.
> In general, how do we gauge the political impact of the exhibition? I'm not just thinking of some elderly gentlemen in Qingdao, but also of the youthful *geming tongzhimen* [revolutionary comrades] in Beijing and Shanghai.
> Second: The artworks by those fortune hunters abroad can only be of hypothetical significance to the development of Chinese art. What I mean is that these works, especially those that have been created abroad, should not be presented as a logical or inevitable development of Chinese art as a whole. Because if we were to consider it in this way, we would be understanding/using "China" as a race, not as a culture.
> Third: You suggested that the cultural background (education, et cetera) of these artists, when confronted with a new cultural context, is always sure to remain a dominant and important part of their practice. But what about the cultural differences between Japanese, American, and Western-European contexts? With such broad comparisons, what is to become of the most important characteristics, that is, their individual traits—are those to come third and last?

About the exhibition as a whole:
Elliott from Oxford has organized several successful exhibitions from South Africa, the Soviet Union, and other "societies in turbulence." In Heidelberg, he declared that art plays an isolated role in Western society today. He believes that modern art originally developed "from a dialectical process, and played a revolutionary role in society." Capitalism played its final trick with the introduction of Conceptual Art and Minimalism. As a consequence, the revolutionary role of modern art lost its power—this is all Oxford academic nonsense—so Elliott's last hope is a nose-dive into sweet, Third-World Weariness. There have been similar cases of exploiting non-Western modern art in recent years. Curating the exhibition *Magiciens de la terre*, Jean-Hubert Martin, director of the "Collapsing New Building"[7] Centre Pompidou in Paris, wanted to illustrate the concept of the "Global Village": we are all primitives, hence we are all the same. He carelessly exhibited hundreds of artworks next to each other regardless of their original contexts. The selection of works was based entirely on his aesthetic preferences, fashionable to a fault and in keeping with the modern French lifestyle. [...]
In his essay "Selling Nations," published in *Art in America* in September 1991, pp. 85–91, Brian Wallis writes about some recent very large exhibitions in America: *Mexico: A Work of Art* (currently on view in New York), *Turkey: The Continuing Magnificence* (1987–88), and *Festival of Indonesia* (1990–92). "The art exhibitions these festivals embrace in particular demonstrate the drive to reassert nationalism as a sort of decoy. Given the simulated nature of such representations of nationalism, we must ask how the nation is being reconstructed through culture. Whose version of national culture is being shown? What is not shown and why?" Best wishes, Hans

HvD, letter to Andreas Schmid, Eindhoven, 30 September 1991

7—Pun on the German pop group Einstürzende Neubauten (collapsing new buildings), referring to the fact that the Centre Pompidou, due to its architecture, will collapse if the maximum occupancy (indicated at the entrance) is surpassed.

By November 1991, following the final confirmation of all participating institutions—the HKW in Berlin; Kunsthal Rotterdam; MoMA, Oxford; and Kunsthallen Brandts Klædefabrik in Odense, Denmark—van Dijk and Schmid leave for China at last. Around the same time, the first part of van Dijk's essay "Painting in China after the Cultural Revolution: Style Developments and Theoretical Debates" is published.
With his first advance as a curator, van Dijk buys a camera and a computer. He creates a special database to house his growing archive on Chinese artists. Ready to begin their scouting of artists and artworks, Schmid and van Dijk arrive to a slowly reawakening art world in a China that has just heard Chairman Deng Xiaoping declare, "It is glorious to be rich!"

Dear Jeroen and Monique, Having visited five cities in five weeks, I'm back in Beijing [...]. Guangzhou is a superlative example of the booming consumer culture that is terrorizing China. [...] Since making money has become all the rage these past few years, disproportionate economic conditions have emerged that give me the chills. The official monthly salary of a middle management civil servant working at the Ministry of Foreign Affairs is around 60 guilders, barely enough to live off in Beijing. In Shanghai, a taxi driver can easily earn up to 300 guilders in one evening. In Guangzhou, the gate to trading with Hong Kong, the situation is plainly grotesque, as they dodge all trade limitations imposed by Beijing. The government once launched the official, bland slogan "Socialism Is Good." In Guangzhou, the sales people have no problem turning that into "Socialism Is Good; Nike Trainers 30% off!"
Meanwhile the faith in the future of China has dropped to an all-time low, such that none of the newly acquired wealth is invested here. Those who have the money leave the country. Down south, one can order all the necessary papers for 35,000 American dollars: passports, diplomas, official invitations, airplane tickets. They travel via Singapore or Bangkok to their destination: Australia, the U.S., or Europe. Two years ago, that same undertaking would have cost between 15,000 and 20,000 dollars (at least according to the *Hong Kong China Mirror*, December '91). Today, double that amount seems to be no objection to the 50,000 Chinese from the southern provinces of Guangdong and Fujian to go to Bangkok and leave China behind. [...]
This concludes the latest updates on the Yellow Peril. Greetings, Hans

HvD, letter to Jeroen Vinken and Monique Kies, Beijing, December 1991

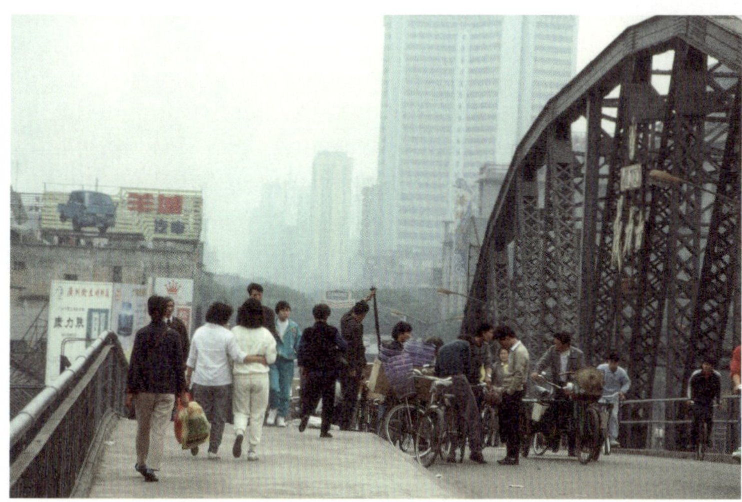

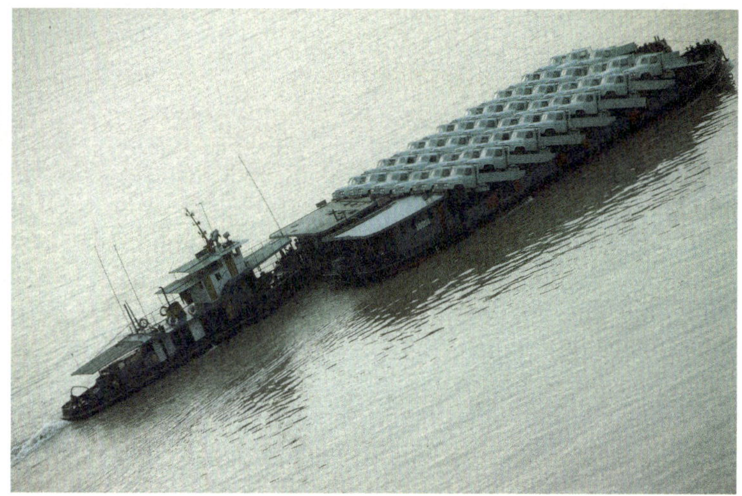

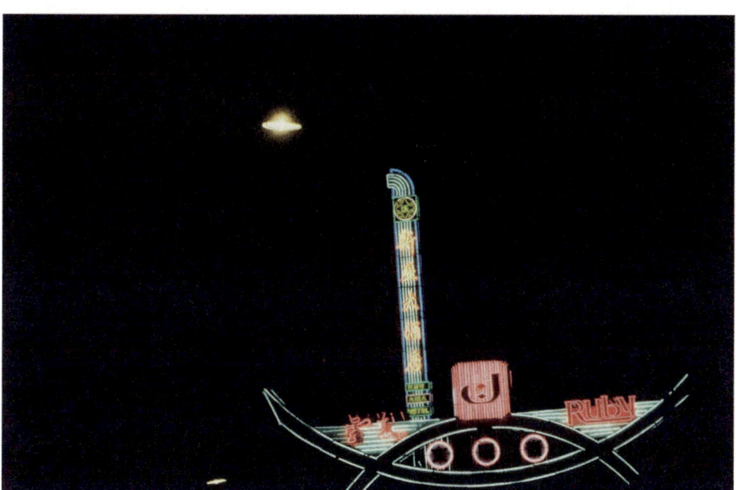

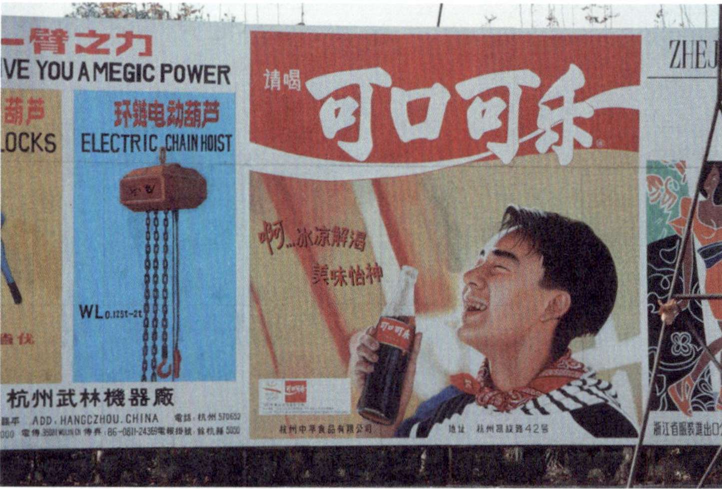

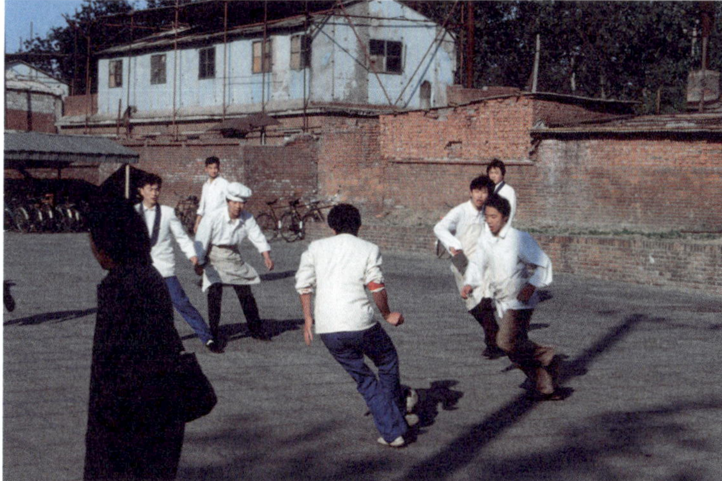

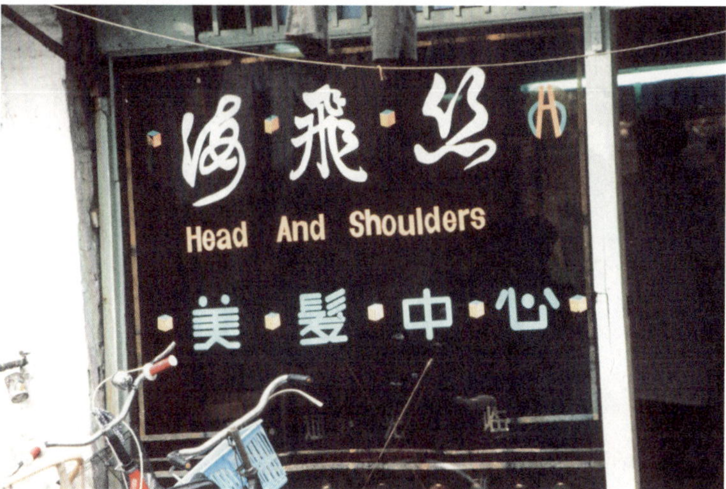

Hans van Dijk, photographs of Beijing, Guangzhou, and Nanjing taken during his travels in preparation for *China Avant-garde*, 1991–92, coll. Andreas Schmid

Garage Show, Shanghai

After two years of silence, exhibitions of contemporary art slowly reemerge in China in the summer of 1991, beginning with the highly original, conceptual traveling show *Modern Chinese Art Research Documents Exhibition*, curated by Wang Lin. Testing the waters, it does not contain actual artworks, only documents. It is presented first in Beijing, then Shenyang, Nanjing, Chongqing, Wuhan, and Guangzhou. This exhibition is followed by *The Actuality of the Experience at the Moment*, the so-called *Garage Show* in Shanghai in November 1991. Finally, the first exhibition by the Big Tail Elephant Working Group, consisting of Lin Yilin, Chen Shaoxiong, and Liang Juhui, takes place in December 1991 in Guangzhou.[8]

8—Xu Tan joins the group in 1992, when their second exhibition, *A Joint Exhibition of Big Tail Elephant Group*, takes place at the Guangdong Broadcasting and Television University in Guangzhou.

Van Dijk and Schmid do not make it to Shanghai in time for the opening of the *Garage Show*, but word has gotten around that van Dijk was coming to China again. During his opening speech, Chen Xiaoxin, editor of the Nanjing-based art magazine *Jiangsu Art Monthly* and one of the organizers of the show, rejoices that after two years of silence, Chinese art is once again gaining momentum in cities across the country. At the end of his address, he adds one more bit of fortuitous news: Hans is coming back.

Shortly afterwards, van Dijk and Schmid appear, scouting artists for the Berlin exhibition. At that time, most artists have never even heard of the possibility of a show of their work happening outside China.

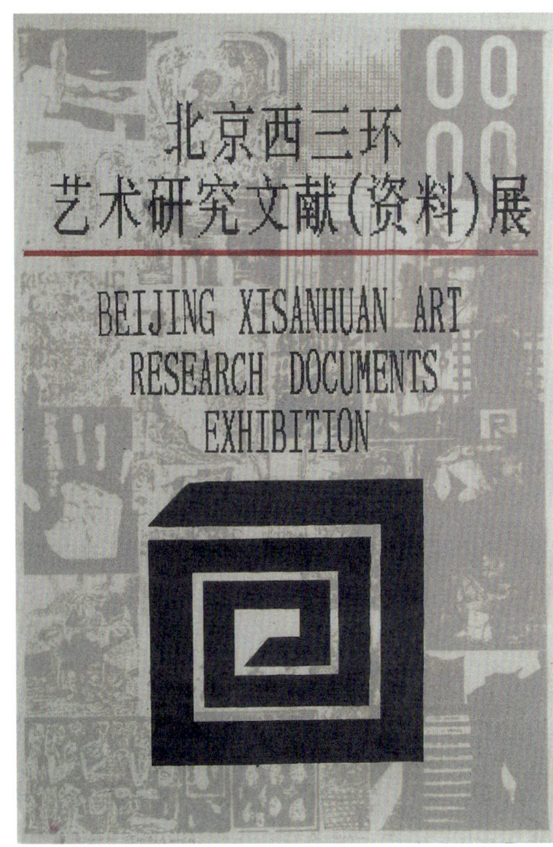

Beijing Xisanhuan Art Research Documents Exhibition, poster, summer–fall 1991, photo courtesy Andreas Schmid

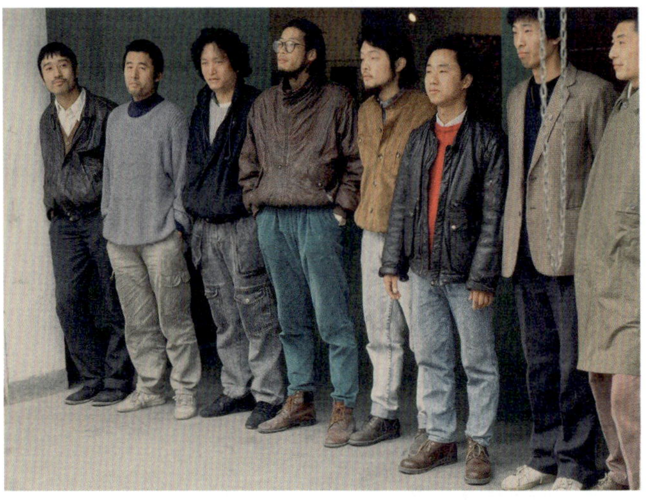

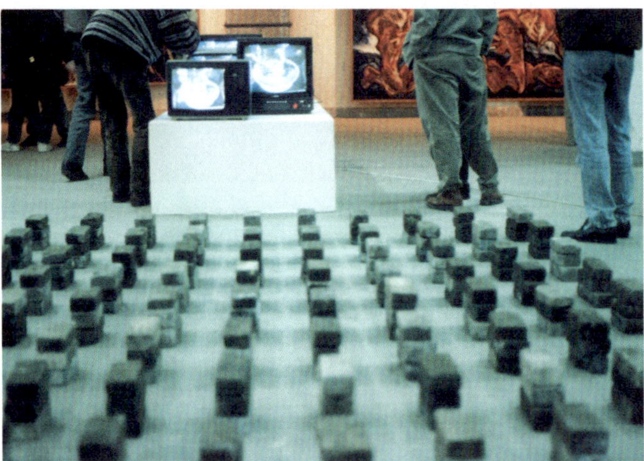

Top: Opening of *Garage Show*, Shanghai Education Hall, Yueyang Road, Shanghai, 1991; participating artists: Song Haidong, Zhang Peili, Sun Liang, Ni Haifeng, He Yang, Gong Jianqing, Hu Jianping, Geng Jianyi (left to right); bottom: exhibition view *Garage Show*, Shanghai Education Hall, Yueyang Road, Shanghai, 1991, with Zhang Peili, video installation (front & center), photos Andreas Schmid

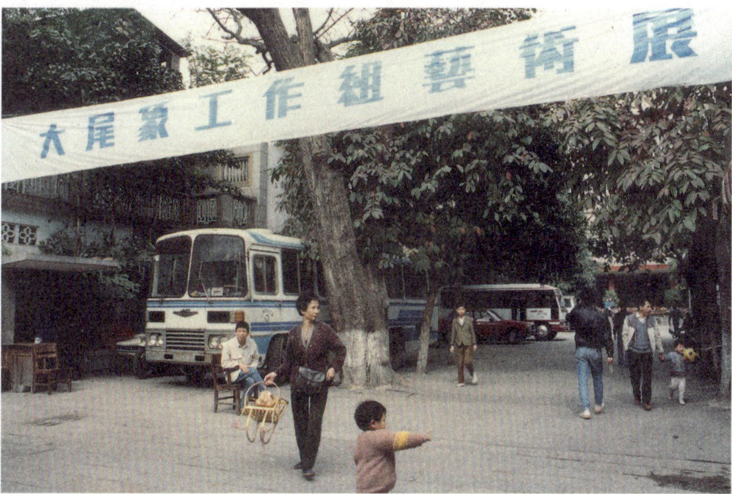

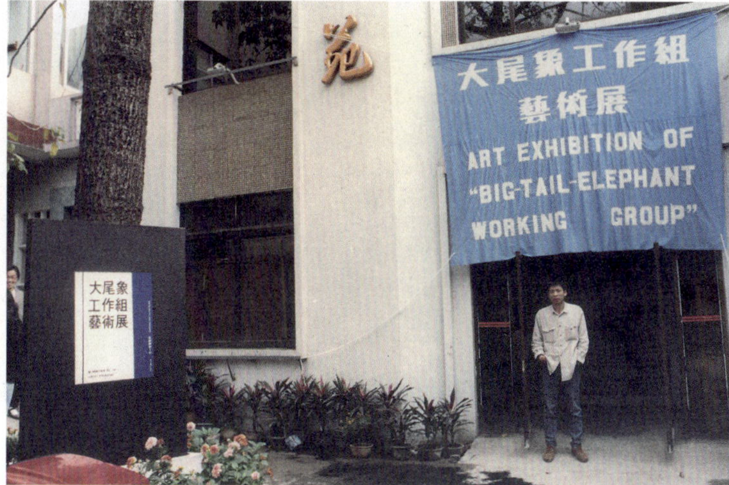

Left: Lin Yilin seated underneath the banner of the *Big Tail Elephant Working Group Exhibition*, No. 1 Workers' Palace, Guangzhou, 1991, private coll.; right: Lin Yilin in front of entrance to *Big Tail Elephant Working Group Exhibition*, No. 1 Workers' Palace, Guangzhou, 1991, private coll.

Works in January 1991

We began to hastily work for the first time.

During this complex and disorderly transition period, we tried to find a way to sort out these issues. It was not the beginning of contemplation; it was due to an excess of accumulated considerations.

We opened our minds to add a bit of clarity. We discovered all these unused tools. Without intending to, we grasped these tools, dismantling an iron-frame bed before devoutly putting it back together. We realized that the head of the bed became the end, the legs became the headboard, and the base became a shoe rack. We were satisfied with this result.

We will also destroy this result. We will tell every Tom, Dick, and Harry to imagine lying on this bed. Originality compels us to work, to work continuously. When these tools are worn out, we will take up others.

Big Tail Elephant Working Group

Lin Yilin, Chen Shaoxiong, and Liang Juhui, introductory wall text for the *Big Tail Elephant Working Group Exhibition*, Guangzhou, 1991

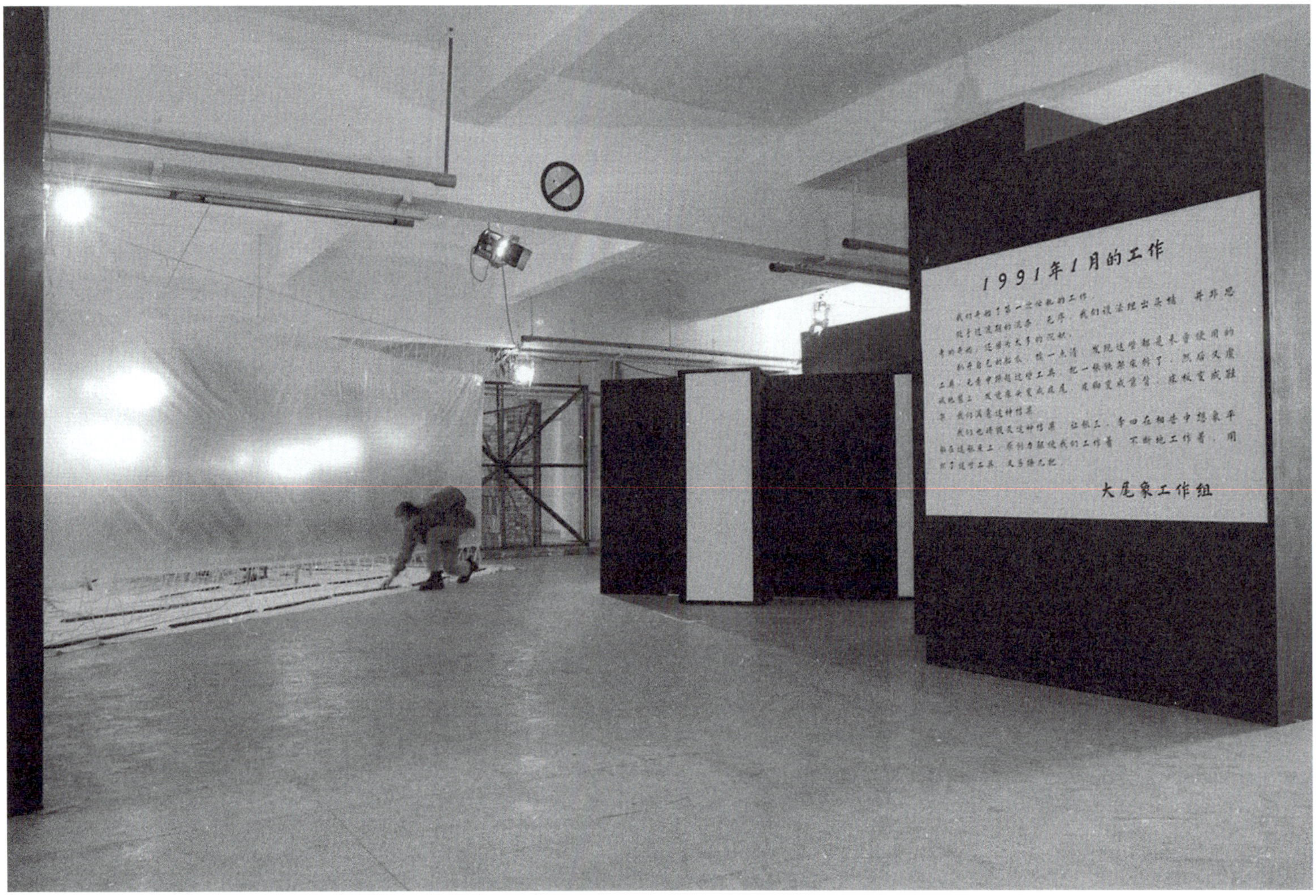

Entrance to the *Big Tail Elephant Working Group Exhibition*, No. 1 Workers' Palace, Guangzhou, 1991, private coll.

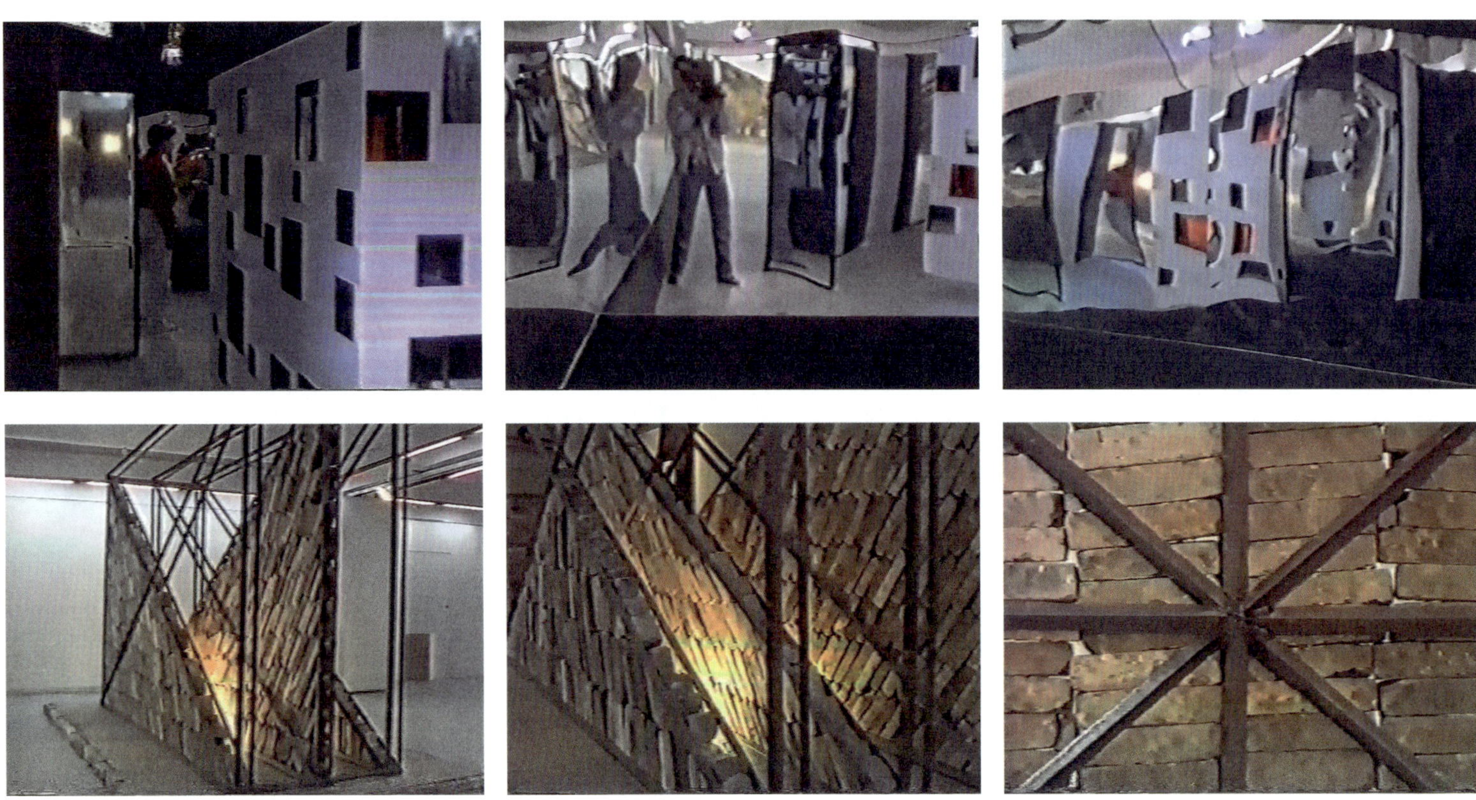

Top row: Liang Juhui, *Entering the Project*, installation for *Big Tail Elephant Working Group Exhibition*, Guangzhou 1991; bottom row: Lin Yilin, *Standard Series of Ideal Residence*, installation for *Big Tail Elephant Working Group Exhibition*, Guangzhou 1991. All stills from the video *Big Tail Elephant Group, 1990–1996*, courtesy Andreas Schmid

XU TAN: At the time of the Berlin show, we were preparing the second *Big Tail Elephant Working Group* show. It was my first, because I became a member of the group in October 1992. Lin Yilin went to Berlin, but the others and I couldn't. After the show, we sent Hans our new files. He said, "What a pity I can't show these because it's too late. I would have loved to." He was critical of the Berlin exhibition; he said it wasn't easy working with certain people at the museum, and he would have preferred to do things by himself. All throughout the nineties, from that winter of 1991 until 2000, he was the most important guest, friend, and teacher, and the closest friend I had in Western art circles. His critique was very important. After my first works, I started to make more conceptual work around 1995. He said, "Before, your work was really nice, but now it's a bit dry and needs to be fleshed out aesthetically."

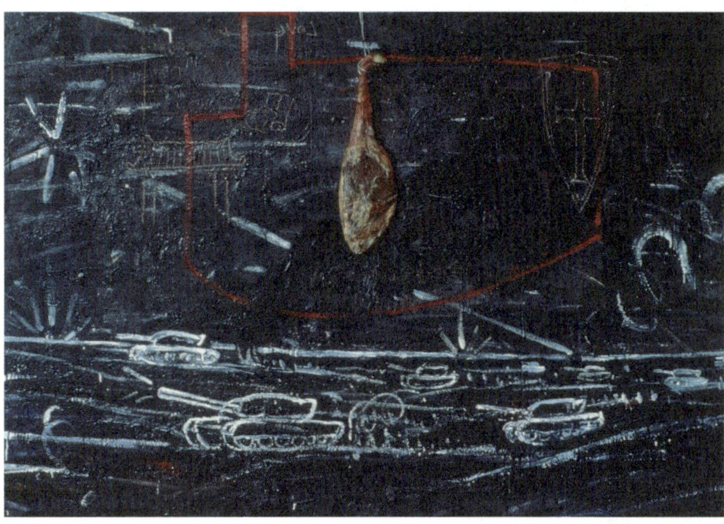

Xu Tan, *The Nineties—Without Title No. 2*, oil on canvas, 1991; shown at *A Joint Exhibition of Big Tail Elephant Group*, Guangdong Broadcast/Television University, Guangzhou, 1992, still from the video *Big Tail Elephant Group, 1990–1996*, courtesy Andreas Schmid

Hans was the first person who came to me to work together on contemporary art. We had long talks about many issues, about society, art. At the time, I still painted. Way back when I began to make contemporary art, I liked Max Beckmann, Expressionism, and De Stijl. I loved the big paintings by Rembrandt and Soutine of the ox carcasses. But unfortunately, cows are rare in Chinese markets. There are lots and lots of pigs, however, so I used to go to the market to draw the hanging pigs. Around when Hans came, I stopped drawing and painting and started making video and installation art. I remember we discussed the meat market. Hans was amazed that you could still see how fresh meat was butchered; he said that wasn't so in Holland any longer. We really talked about everything. I recall that we talked about homosexuality as well. It was still a taboo subject in China, but Hans was quite open about it.

When I stopped painting, he was very interested in discussing the reasons with us. We felt he showed us a very open future. When we met art critics from the West, they seemed to have very fixed ideas. I feel Hans was very Chinese: he always went with the artists, observing, his comments based on the questions you yourself asked.

We really talked about everything. We had a strange relationship. We were very good friends, although we didn't work together much. Certainly in the beginning there were not many chances to do exhibitions. I was a member of Hans' "secret list," because at that time it was forbidden to talk contemporary art. There used to be spies everywhere. I had a job at the Guangzhou Academy of Fine Arts, and the Party Committee warned me; they said maybe you are not our friend. Today it's not a problem anymore to talk about contemporary art.

MB, interview with Xu Tan, Guangzhou, 18 January 2013

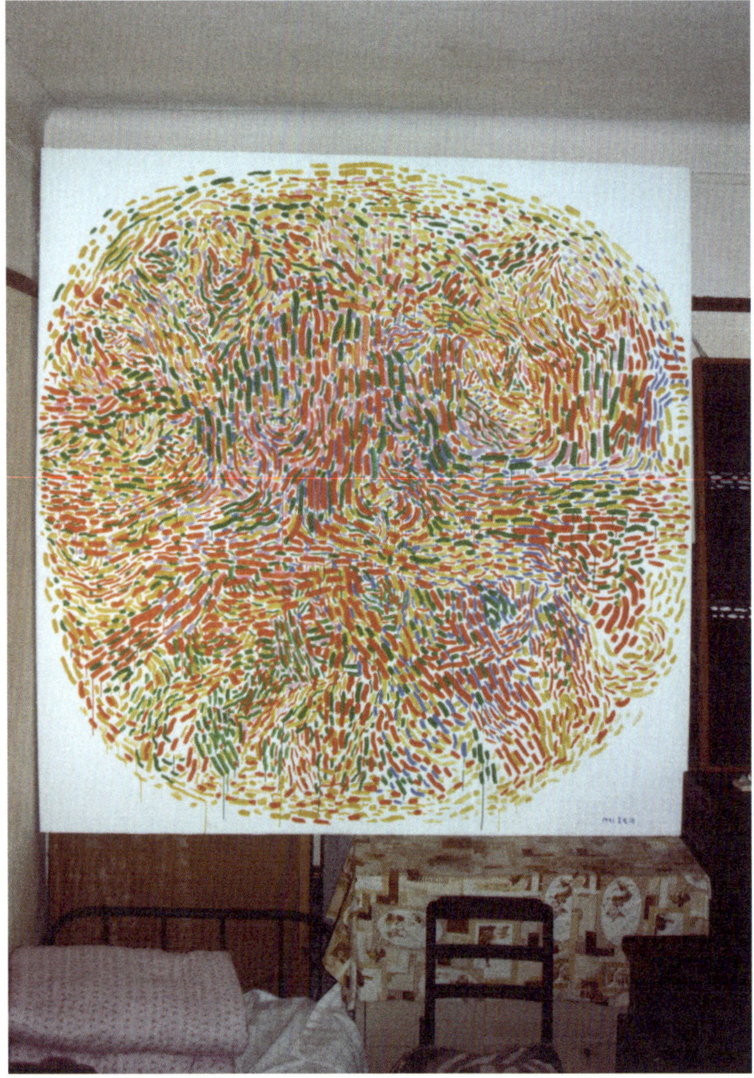

Yu Youhan's bedroom/studio, Shanghai, 1991, courtesy Andreas Schmid

YU YOUHAN: At the time of the 1989 incident, I was teaching at the Shanghai Institute of Industrial Arts, located forty-two kilometers from Shanghai's People's Square. We knew vaguely about Beijing, so some students said: "Let's go to Shanghai, to People's Square." [...] Ten teachers volunteered to come as well to protect the students. I was one of them.

At the time, I made large paintings of renminbi, the people's money. The students wanted to borrow them, because they wanted to say, "The teachers are so poor they have to paint their money instead." But those paintings were Pop Art, using objects from everyday life, so I didn't agree to lend them. After two or three years, the school started to evaluate the teachers for promotion, but because of this story they didn't want to promote me at all. After I explained to them what Pop Art was, my promotion was still delayed for a year. At the time, the student protests were not as fierce as in Beijing. The mayor of Shanghai played it down to not incite the students even more.

I met Hans in 1991. He came to my studio with Andreas [Schmid] for the Berlin show. Almost at the same time, preparations were underway for the exhibition *China's New Art: Post-1989*, at Hanart TZ Gallery in Hong Kong, so I split my paintings between the two shows. I was quite surprised to be invited by Hans because I was not so famous, but after that my reputation grew. I did not work with Hans after that. I didn't know Lorenz[9] at the time. Johnson Chang[10] of Hanart knew about me through Li Xianting. He wanted to buy my paintings even before the show. Initially I said no, but he kept offering more

9—Lorenz Helbling, founder (1994) and director of ShanghART Gallery, Shanghai.

10—Johnson Chang, English name of Chang Tsong-zung, founder and owner of Hanart TZ Gallery, Hong Kong.

money, and even put pressure on me through my school. In the end, I made a contract with them, though it wasn't an official contract. At the time, my studio was so small I had to move my bed out to paint. I gave Hanart five paintings; the best three were sold immediately. I was not told for how much, and they were also not in the show. The other two paintings were never returned to me.
Comparing those two exhibitions in Berlin and Hong Kong, I found Hans to be much more knowledgeable about art. In the late nineties, Hans came to my house for dinner with me and my wife. Other than that, we didn't have much contact, possibly because Hans was much younger. I felt that he was a very nice person though; someone with ideals, not out for profit. That wasn't very common among Chinese dealers at the time, even though Hans was not partial to Pop Art painting.

MB, interview with Yu Youhan, Shanghai, 8 September 2012

Wang Guangyi

WANG GUANGYI: I met Hans in 1991 in a tiny nameless hotel in Beijing where a lot of people were having dinner together. He was introduced to me by an acquaintance as someone who was interested in Chinese art. He looked really shabby in an old, yellow T-shirt—not at all suitable. But you could trust him. In 1992, he came to visit me for the exhibition in Berlin. I met with Andreas after that. It was the first time I exhibited in a foreign country. This was the only time I worked with him, because in 1993 I signed a contract with Johnson Chang of Hanart. I didn't show with Hans after that, but we kept meeting on a regular basis between 1993 and 2002. There were not many people like him. When he came to my studio, he was always calm, quietly discussing my work or other things.
In my conversations with Hans, he didn't emphasize what made Chinese art different; he just considered it art, contemporary art like anywhere else. He treated artists as equals, not by his words alone, but by his attitude. That was the most important thing about him. It explains why so many artists continued seeing him and talking with him, even though they didn't work with him or were no longer working with him.

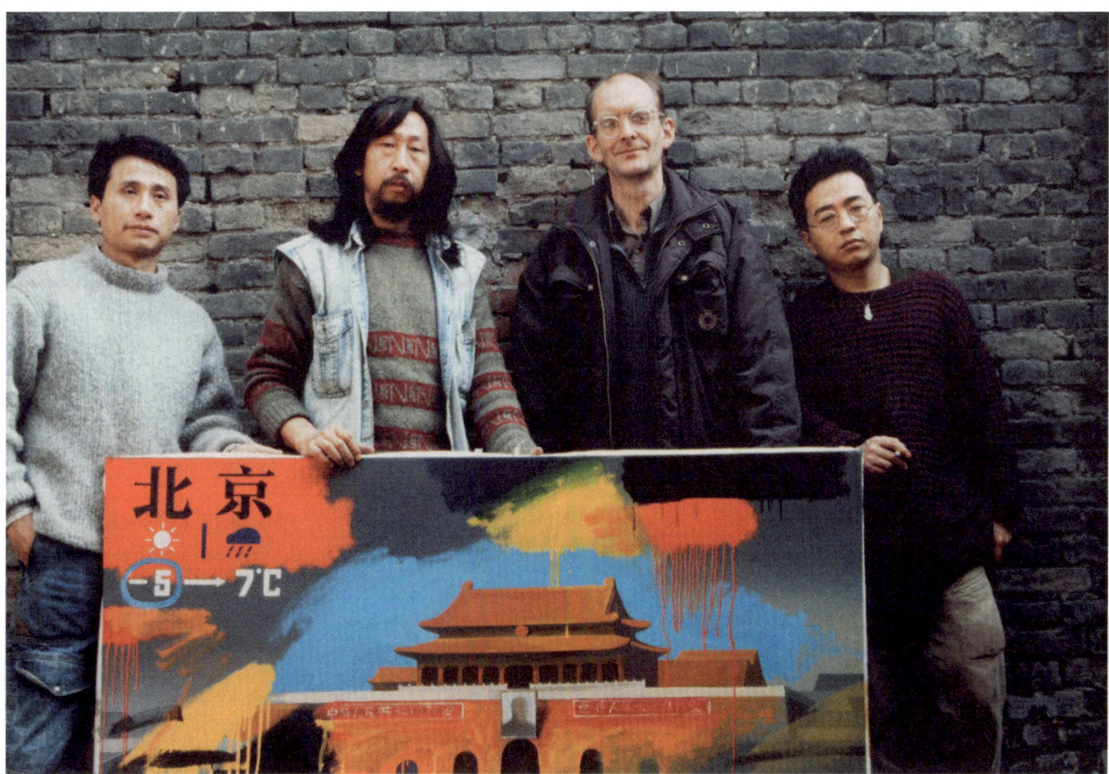

Left ro right: unknown artist, Wang Guanyi, Hans van Dijk, Wei Guangqing, Wuhan, 1991, photo Andreas Schmid

Hans was very important for contemporary art in China for three main reasons: he was the first to introduce Chinese art to the West. That first exhibition in Berlin was very successful. He did documentary research on Chinese art, which was very important as well. And thirdly, he had very good relations with Chinese artists. Chinese artists considered Hans to be one of them—he was like family. Hans was not about power; he was a friend.

After his death, many artists went to the memorial service, and his family was quite touched. His brother talked about that, how only after he came to China did he understand how important Hans was. According to his brother, he didn't have that many friends in Holland. He believed that in China, Hans found the meaning of his life.

If Hans were alive today, his space still running, I think he would be the number one most important figure in contemporary Chinese art. Not as a dealer, no, but as a scholar, able to influence the entire discourse of art.

MB, interview with Wang Guangyi, Beijing, 14–15 September 2012

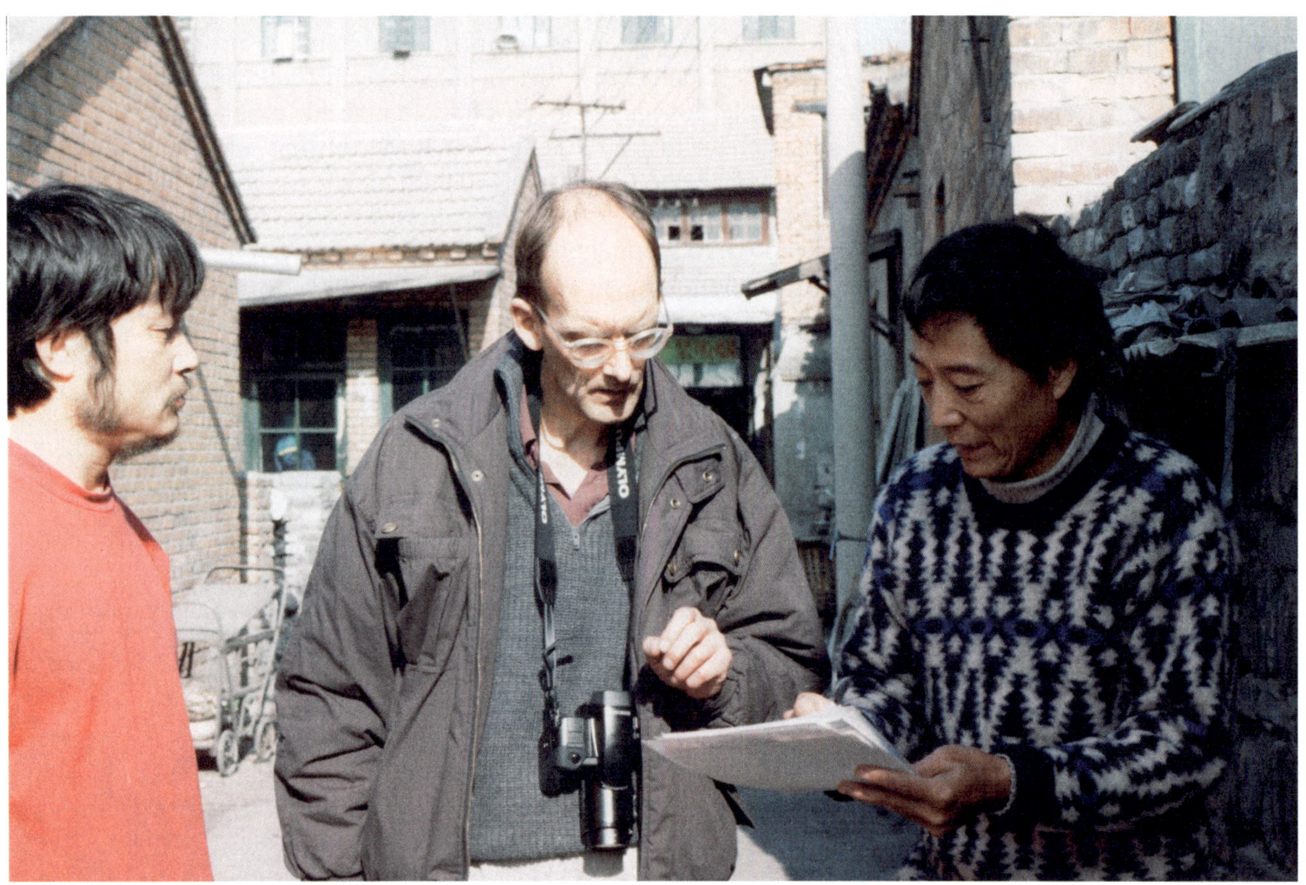

Hans van Dijk with Yang Yushu (left) and Zhao Wenliang (right), members of the No Name Painting Society, Beijing, 1991, photo Andreas Schmid; both artists were important mentors in the underground art scene during the Cultural Revolution, when the art academies were closed

Zhang Peili

ZHANG PEILI: I met Hans around 1987, when he was learning Chinese in Nanjing. The first time we actually worked together was for the show in Berlin in 1993. There I showed one triptych,[11] three paintings placed vertically of the lady who reads the news,[12] and my video *Document on Hygiene No. 3*.[13] I went to the opening in Berlin, and from there to Paris by train. [...] It was the first time I officially showed my work.

There were other times I worked with him: in 1996, Hans invited me to come to Munich where he organized a show, *China – Aktuelles aus 15 Ateliers*. I showed a video I had made that year, *Related Rhythm*, my first multi-channel video work. The Munich show in 1996 was part of the increased cultural activity in Germany of Chinese music, theater, et cetera.

11—*Chinese Body-building According to the Year 1989*, triptych, oil on canvas, 100×100 cm each, 1990.

12—*The Standard Pronunciation of 1989*, triptych, oil on canvas, 100×80 cm each, 1991.

13—*Document on Hygiene No. 3*, video, 36'49", 1991.

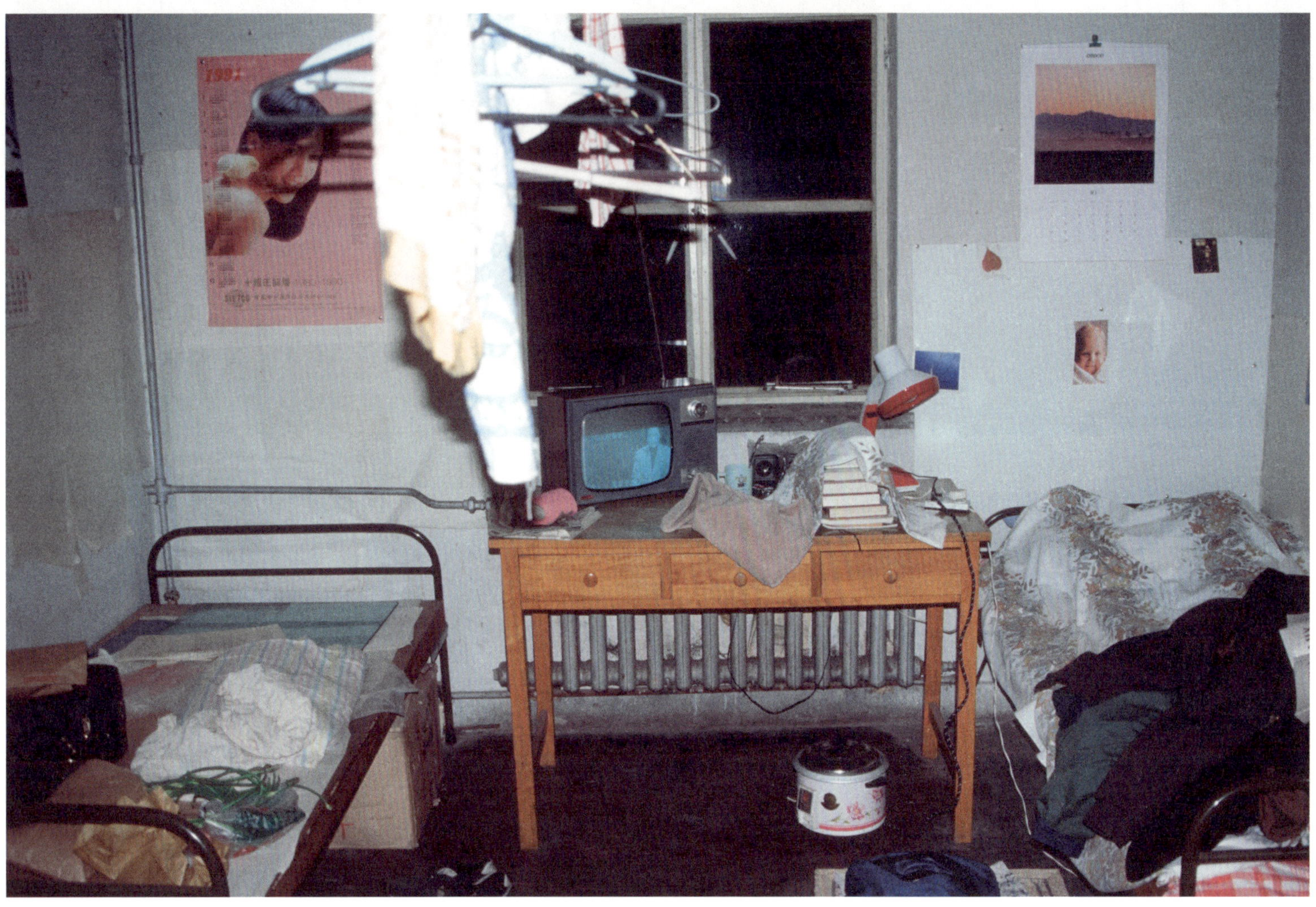

Hans van Dijk, photograph taken during his research trip in preparation for *China Avant-garde*, 1991, courtesy Andreas Schmid; playing on screen is Zhang Peili, *Water – Standard Version from the Cihai Dictionary*, 1991

The Dalai Lama, however, then came to visit Germany. China threatened to cancel all events. We wondered what would happen to our show. But Hans said, "We are only such a small part of the event, the Chinese government might not notice our show." So we went and did it anyway. The local media came to interview us, and all their questions were about politics. Today it's all about Ai Weiwei. Never about art.

In 1996, too, he asked me to write an essay. It was published in a Chinese magazine, "Should We Start a War with the West." Hans asked me because he knew that I had shown overseas and I had thoughts about the situation. The moment was very specific: many Chinese artists were participating in important exhibitions, the Venice Biennale for instance. But China was very nationalistic at the time, and artists were worried about their positions in the art world. Hans didn't like to talk a lot, but we did seriously discuss this. Hans had very specific ideas. Unlike other Western curators and some artists, he didn't like to emphasize "Chineseness"; rather, he wanted to stimulate Chinese artists to be more creative. He didn't show Political Pop, for instance. Hans was enormously respected because he was a very sincere person. He did not act like a lot of foreign curators who treat Chinese artists like sick people or patients, looking to diagnose the problem and telling them what to do; Hans treated us as friends.

You never felt any pressure; he didn't want anything from you. Even when we talked about art it was never anything huge or blown up. He had a very small voice, so you really needed to pay close attention at times, especially when his health deteriorated.

MB, interview with Zhang Peili, Shanghai, 8 September 2012

Van Dijk moves from the Netherlands to Berlin. He has to find his own lodgings, because the HKW, which should have put him up in a hotel or an apartment to prepare for the show, argues that it lacks the funds. Schmid finds him a room in a housing commune or *Wohngemeinschaft* (WG) in Kreuzberg, a Berlin neighborhood popular with artists.

The exhibition runs into unexpected trouble, partly because the HKW did not follow through on loan forms to China in time to secure the artworks. A different curatorial team is now collecting artworks in preparation for a show of contemporary art from China: Hong Kong-based art dealer Johnson Chang has commissioned Li Xianting to curate the show, *China's New Art: Post-1989*. It will open in Hong Kong in January 1993 and travel to Australia.

> Concerning the exhibition, it seems everything is uncertain and unclear, even whether it will actually take place. *Do not tell this to anyone*, so that Rotterdam doesn't freak out and pull back already committed financial contributions. What I'm sure has reached Holland already is the abominable organization of the Haus der Kulturen der Welt. Though there is money in place, the people at the top cause Andreas [Schmid], Jochen [Noth], and me to worry a great deal. They agree to a lot but neglect to follow through on anything. One of the consequences is that I will need to return to China very soon to make sure the competition doesn't make off with all the works we want to show.
> HvD, letter to Jeroen Vinken, 3 February 1992

Van Dijk leaves for China almost immediately to secure the exhibition contracts with the artists and prepare loans and transportation for the artworks. He will be joined by Schmid, Noth, and Pöhlmann later on for the final selection of works. From the minute he arrives in China, his letters show that he is trying his utmost to save the exhibition through damage control and crisis management, talking to as many people as he can and getting anyone who may be of help on his side. Not for a minute, though, does he forget his sense of humor and his principles. Schmid provides a fascinating insight into the difference between the two exhibitions and the resulting competition for the artists' favor:

> Hans proposed a fundamental principle, that in the preparatory phase of the exhibition, we as a team should not buy anything from the artists in order to speculate on the works' future value. [...] This principle was debated initially with some controversy by the entire team (including the officials from the HKW), because some argued that one could help "the poor artists" with some money. However, we quickly agreed with the position that Hans had formulated in this and other letters, a position that I shared from the beginning: you can only be credible in the preparatory phase if you don't act as a gallerist or a dealer. Among the trust-building measures here were, for example, loan contracts.
> Andreas Schmid, "Hans van Dijk: Principles and Challenges," in *Yishu: Journal of Contemporary Chinese Art*, Jan/Feb 2015, pp. 35–47

On 24 February, van Dijk writes to Andreas Schmid from Beijing:

> Greetings in the name of Hermes, god of traders and thieves.
> I visited the four painters we chose in Beijing, and our selection is 80–87% secured.
> Yu Hong[14] will visit Li Xianting again, who still can't be reached. I am seeing Gu Dexin today. Clearly everyone is sympathetic to our exhibition. The feeling is even stronger than before, because the competition game is now in full swing. [...] They all operate with big money. Zhang Songren[15] from Hong Kong wants to buy at least ten works each from forty-five artists, and from some of them he wants to buy all of their paintings. He is taking advantage of Li Xianting, who is gradually discovering this but can no longer back out. Because we have thus far discussed loans exclusively, there is a growing trust in our exhibition. Tell Pöhlmann: Buying is forbidden! That would be extremely dangerous. Good loan contracts are the next step. Without those I cannot continue here.
> I tried to calm down Yu Youhan [...].

14—Yu Hong, famous woman artist who participated in *China/Avant-Garde*, Beijing, 1989.

15—Zhang Songren, Johnson Chang's name in pinyin romanization, which van Dijk uses throughout his letters.

Another letter follows on 26 February:

> I talked to Francesca Dal Lago from the cultural department of the Italian Embassy on the 25th. She was shocked by Zhang Songren. [...] She was convinced by our selection. She has known Li and the other artists for a long time and is upset by the tragedy.
> To buy in advance of an exhibition is a dirty affair. Artists feel obliged to sell (cheaper) because they are afraid they will be excluded from the exhibition if they don't. Secondly, the artists we chose can easily sell their paintings for two to three thousand marks or more. These [artists] are not so pitiful that they need to be helped out with a bit of a discount. There has been an art market in place since '88. Instead of selling indiscriminately (the paintings are out of their hands), today they are more interested in recognition from the international art world. So far, they believe that our exhibition offers that possibility.

On 28 February:

> Dear Andreas, had you been here, I wouldn't have been so upset about everything that is happening. In this sense, I feel like your representative. Fortunately, I recently met with very capable foreigners, Francesca Dal Lago and Misha Raab (who lives with Fang Lijun in the *Youyi Binguan* [Friendship Hotel]). She has worked here for a long time and knows the art circles quite well. What I like about her is that she hardly knows foreigners (as you know I hate foreigners). You also know of my prejudice against men—prejudices which have been confirmed here, mostly with Zhang Songren.
> Only a dealer wants to buy everything from an artist. Only a crook offers 10% of the total sum and says he will pay the rest later. Or gives the artists a worthless slip of paper—without any legal meaning—and tells them he has to donate a few works to promote the exhibition, so please lower your prices a bit. Finally, he asks the artists to confirm in writing that the paintings have been given to him so he won't have problems with customs. Then it's goodbye. Li Xianting does not know where to look and murmurs to Francesca that one has to take risks in life.
> He can no longer back out. Several artists—no one knows how many exactly—for example Pan Dehai and Zhang Xiaogang, have already transported their best work of the past ten years to Beijing. These are now in Hong Kong, *Hanyaxuan Hualang*—stored at the Hanart Gallery. Francesca: "The demise of Li Xianting." Misha: "Here you have an opportunity to look into the abyss." Jochen's reaction to my warning was astounding—please tell Mannpöhl [a pun on Pöhlmann] that buying here is forbidden and taboo. In the second fax, I tried to explain to him that the artists we have selected cannot be placated with a little money, because they can already sell their work for three or four thousand dollars to the many dealers, ambassadors, et cetera, that come to visit them. While all of this was happening here, I suddenly remembered a rather painful visit to Pöhlmann at his home on 10 January of this year, and how he lisped, gasping for air, "Well, Mr. van Dijk, did you buy?" If I remember correctly, he was drooling a bit, but I cannot say so for certain. Anyway, I had a bad night's sleep in Beijing after all.
> So Jochen responded to my first fax that it would have helped the artists if they were paid, [...] and he thought my ideas naïve. In my second fax on 26 February—please Andreas, read it carefully—I once again stress that we need proper loan forms.
> Zhao Bandi committed all four paintings (and promised a bike when I return). He refused to participate in the Hong Kong/Australia exhibition.
> Wang Jinsong: Apart from two paintings reserved by us, Zhang Songren already got ten paintings and also reserved two not-yet-ready. Jinsong was simply robbed; his wife managed to save two for our exhibition. Jinsong felt embarrassed and offered to talk about two paintings which are already promised to Songren. Secondly, he proposed, *non-binding*, to paint two new works which he has worked out in his head already, *Xuexi Leifeng* [Learn from Lei Feng] (working title), and a man and woman playing cards. Ready—dry?—before I leave on 27 April. [...]

Fang Lijun thought it funny how many visits I paid [the artists], taking the bus and the underground across town. At his studio in the artists' colony, rattling taxis are regularly standing around, as many as three at a time. In the beginning of February, he even turned off the phone for a couple of evenings because Songren was calling him frantically, almost panicking—When can you get the money?—randomly promising exhibitions, catalogues, etc. Fang Lijun is not even on Christie's or Sotheby's lists, but was already published in *Flash Art*. Songren is getting stomach cramps. Fang never sold anything before, surprisingly not even to the French ambassador, who has never seen anything like it. Yu Hong has not yet been visited by Li and Songren—she was away on holiday. I chose five paintings with her (one piece of our selection was sold in the beginning of November last year when we were visiting).

There have been several reports in the press these last weeks about extensive economic/ideological liberalization. *China Daily*, *Guangming Daily*, *International Herald Tribune*. It only confirms what we saw three months ago in Beijing, Shanghai, and Guangzhou. [...] There is change, not only in the economic sector. *Jiangsu Art Monthly*,'92–1 published the images of our selection by Yu Hong, Fang Lijun, and others. [...] As you can see, China is on the verge of something; it is a great moment for our exhibition. I hope you will find the time to get to know Fang and Misha better. One afternoon, I ended up drinking beers with Gu Dexin without getting drunk. Like Zhou Yunxia, he is way more mature than many, if not all, academically schooled artists. He was really happy to meet Huang Yong Ping again [in Berlin].

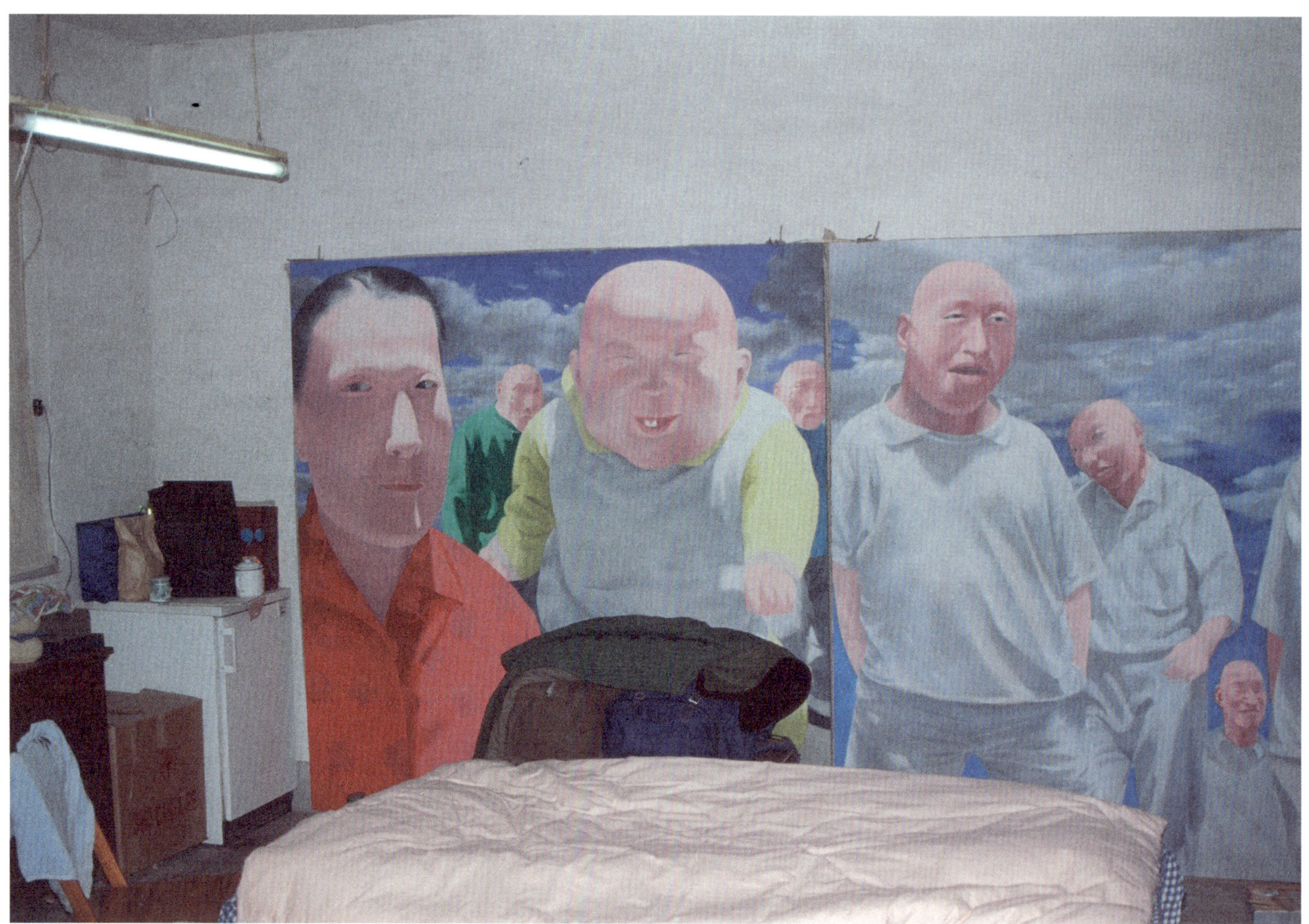

Fang Lijun's bedroom/studio, Beijing, 1991, courtesy Andreas Schmid

In van Dijk's letter from 6 March to Schmid, Noth, and Pöhlmann, the worst seems to be over:

> From Travel Agency van Dijk. Returned from Shanghai yesterday. Talked to the artists about their work/paintings, 90% according to our selection. Made further arrangements for our visit, booked hotel rooms and bought boat tickets, Shanghai–Zhoushan. There, Ni Haifeng is expecting us. Telephone contact with him was established in order to book rooms, et cetera. Jochen, I asked Andreas to send you image materials from our first dossiers. Leiden University asked me to send images and illustrations. This also improves our exhibition and publication in April. In the loan forms, we must include the duration of the lending period, the insurance, and the guaranteed return of the works.

Through Jochen Noth, van Dijk gets in touch with Bao Le'an in Beijing, a big, cheerful man who has his own export company. He agrees to act as art handler for the *China Avant-garde* exhibition. Bao Le'an will be van Dijk's art handler for many years to come; rock solid and trustworthy, he will take care of all international NAAC shipments in the future—not always an easy task. To bypass legal restrictions—in addition to selling and exhibiting "experimental" art, it is also forbidden to export it—artworks need to be labeled theater sets or educational materials, sent off under all sorts of pretenses and titles. Van Dijk creates a Hong Kong art handling company to that purpose, HACT Arts & Design Products, Ltd. Always looking for the off-beat joke, he uses the mystifying Cyrillic abbreviation HACT for NAST, New Amsterdam Shipping & Trade. He designs an ornate logo for the company, using a pompous 19th-century frame.

> I spoke with almost all parties here and went this morning with Bao Le'an to visit his painting storage. Only the paintings of three Beijing painters are not here yet, but we will collect them within the next two days. There are some resolvable problems:
>
> 1) Collector Zhao Huiqun still refuses to deliver Zhao Bandi's paintings. He needs to see either the insurance policy or a note including the titles of the paintings and the prices + confirmation of the insurance. Only then will he agree, Zhao Bandi and Bao Le'an reckon as well. Bao Le'an did not make much progress with the packaging. Together with him, I made a list of 27 cardboard packages + formats which, he says, can be delivered this weekend. Then I can start, probably with one of the artists, to put the paintings in Xuan paper, bubble wrap, and crates. Further, wooden barriers need to be built—I calculated for him, two extra, five overall. One and another will add extra costs.
> 2) After negotiating, he asked me to propose to Berlin an additional $400 packaging charge. He started higher, and also took into consideration the low dollar rate.
> 3) Secondly, he politely asked to transfer $1,000 to HACT. He needs the money for custom fees (now $3,000 in the contract). A detailed invoice will follow.
>
> Artists are not having any troubles getting passports anymore. Zhao Bandi will be coming to Berlin by the end of November. Everything has been going well these last two days.
> Regards, Hans
>
> **HvD, letter to Andreas Schmid and Wolfger Pöhlmann, Beijing Asia Hotel, room no. 1214, undated, 1992**

May – December 1992

On his return to Berlin in mid-May 1992, van Dijk has to vacate his room in the WG and instead moves into a dilapidated garden house with no telephone or street number that Schmid has found.[16] It lies an hour and a half by bicycle and ferry from the HKW.
As preparatory work grows, and van Dijk needs to finish the catalogue, he moves into the HKW for the last weeks before the opening. He installs himself in an office, where he sleeps on a makeshift bed under his desk.

16—HvD, letter to Jeroen Vinken, 23 May 1992: "It took me two days and a lot of sweat to remove a few square meters of rampant weeds. Underneath emerged two ferns, three stunted hollyhocks, and some pale plants, which I address as 'dear lettuce' for lack of botanical knowledge."

29 January – 16 May 1993 *China Avant-garde*
Haus der Kulturen der Welt, Berlin

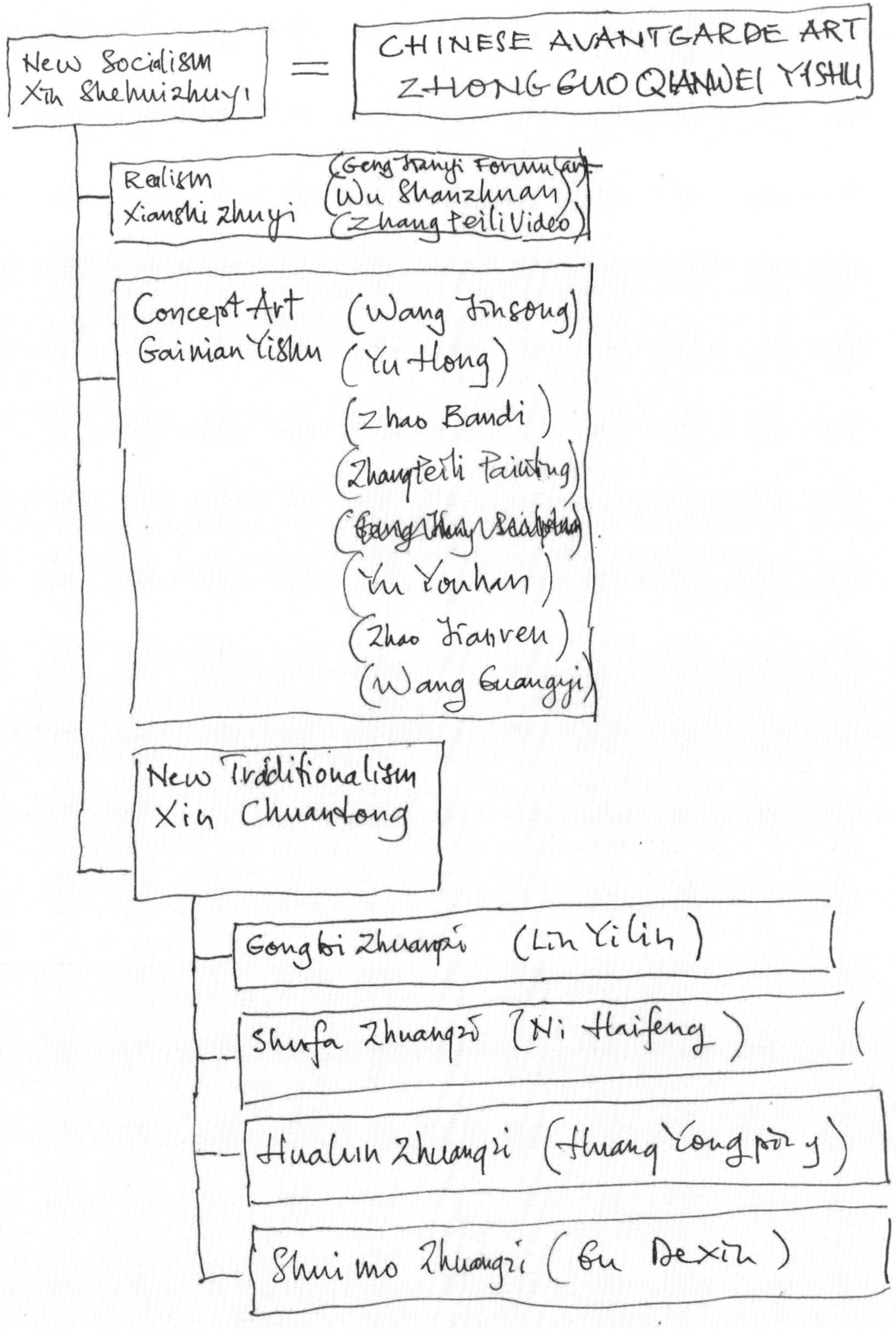

Hans van Dijk, conceptual scheme for *China Avant-garde*, felt pen on A4 paper, 1992, coll. Asia Art Archive, Hong Kong, courtesy Andreas Schmid

Curated by Hans van Dijk, Jochen Noth, and Andreas Schmid, *China Avant-garde* is the first large-scale survey in Europe of Chinese contemporary art. It brings together installations, paintings, prints, videos, conceptual art, and performances by Ding Yi, Fang Lijun, Geng Jianyi, Gu Dexin, Huang Yong Ping, Lin Yilin, Ni Haifeng, Wang Guangyi, Wang Jinsong, Wu Shanzhuan, Yan Peiming, Yu Hong, Yu Youhan, Zhang Peili, Zhao Bandi, and Zhao Jianren.

Through its accompanying program, the exhibition also presents new forms of literature, theater, film, and rock and contemporary music. Van Dijk contributes his own special discovery to the opening's program: *COBRA*, an all-girl rock band from Beijing. Many artists and their friends travel to Berlin; for most of them, it is their first time outside China.

Besides an extensive article by van Dijk, "The Fine Arts after the Cultural Revolution: Stylistic Development and Theoretical Debates," the exhibition catalogue, published in German, English, and Chinese, contains in-depth essays about the history of Chinese contemporary art and its precursors, covering visual art as well as theater, cinema, rock and neoclassical music, photography, poetry, and literature. It also features reproductions of works by all participating artists and an exhaustive glossary of other contemporary Chinese artists from the 1980s and 1990s who are not included in the exhibition.

From Berlin, the show travels to the Kunsthal Rotterdam from 29 May–22 August 1993, where it is hugely successful. David Elliott, director of MoMA, Oxford, curates an additional exhibition entitled *New Art from China, Part I: Silent Energy*, which mainly shows installations by Chinese artists living abroad: Huang Yong Ping, Chen Zhen, Cai Guo-Qiang, Gu Wenda, Yan Pei-Ming, and Yang Jiechang. It runs from 27 June–24 October. From 4 September–24 October 1993, Elliott shows a modified version of *China Avant-garde* under the title *New Art from China, Part II: China Avant-garde*. From 12 November 1993–6 February 1994, it travels to Brandts Klædefabrik in Odense, Denmark. A fifth venue is found at the Römer Museum in Hildesheim, Germany, in 1994. Because van Dijk returns to China in March 1993, the exhibitions in Oxford and Odense, as well as the show in Hildesheim, are curated by Schmid.

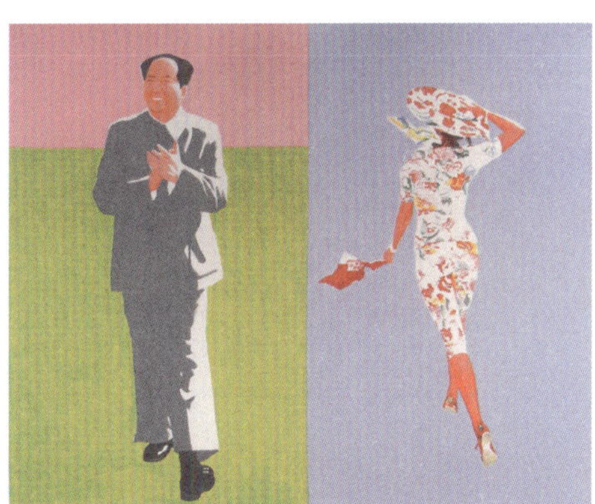

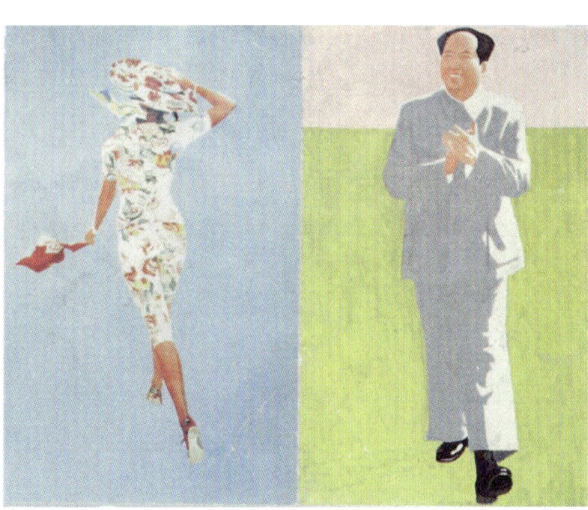

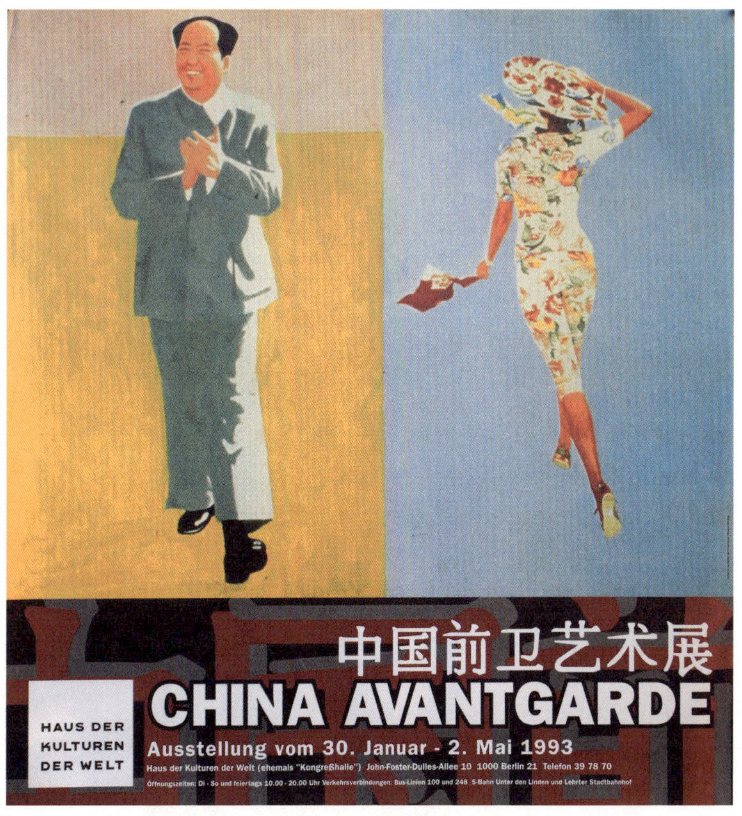

Top left: Yu Youhan, *Girl of Flower*, silk-screen print, 76.7 × 94.2 cm, 2010, coll. the artist; Yu Youhan based this print on his painting *Girl* (1988), which was included in *China Avant-garde*, Berlin, 1993; bottom left: Hans van Dijk, design of invitation card for *China Avant-garde*, based on Yu Youhan's painting *Girl* (1988), but reversing the two figures; the design was rejected, 1992, coll. Ernst Dinkla; right: Hans van Dijk, *China Avantgarde*, poster, 1993, coll. Ernst Dinkla

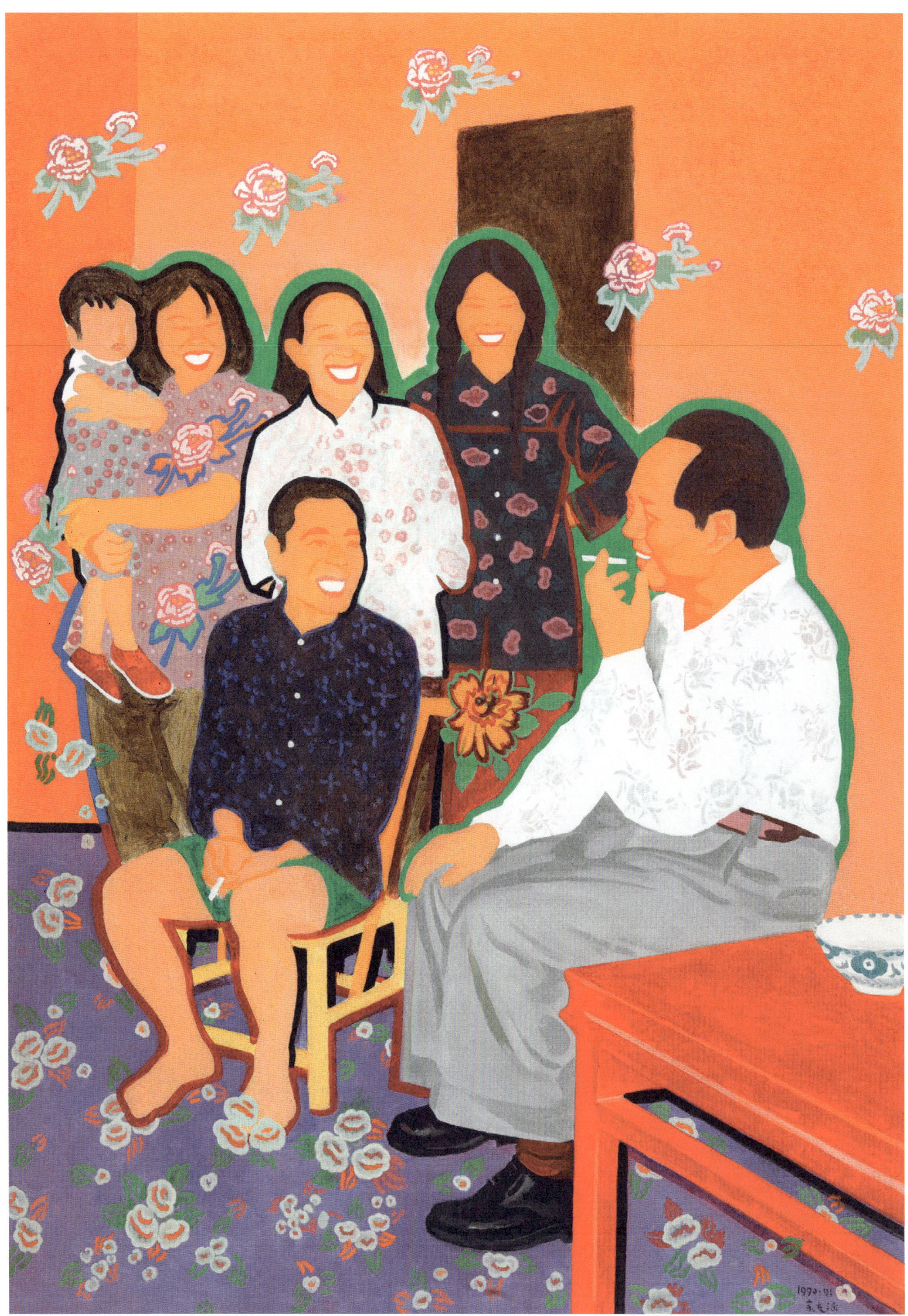
1990-91

Yu Youhan

Drawing Mao Zedong
1992

For me, every painting is a juncture, a juncture of numerous crooked lines. These crooked lines are changes in my aesthetics, changes in how I sense my surrounding environment, and changes in my understanding of our society and history. I am not a scientifically oriented artist; I don't take the new results of a certain visual exploration as the starting point of my work. Even if certain new visual results appear in my paintings, they can only be called byproducts. I am more concerned with humanity's survival and the development of civilization. My art only presents this concern, even though it doesn't clearly tell people anything—this is like the famous Zen method of expression: answering riddles with riddles.

In recent years, my paintings started showing Mao Zedong, this famous figure in Chinese history. A decade or so ago, his image and his words were plastered all over China. For those who lived in this "ocean of red," any changes in Mao's image will form a stark contrast to the image remembered. This is exactly where my interest lies. I hope people can, from my paintings, sense the progress of history and reflect on this whole period.

The progress or regress of history, even though an individual can sometimes have an immense effect, I still think the pace of a country's modernization is, in the end, a learning process for the entire nation. It is the nation's process of complete renewal, starting from culture, economics, and even the thinking of every individual. It is a process full of pain and contradiction. If people have distilled the correct lesson from the experiences of history, then no one can obstruct the tide of modernization.

Previously unpublished text, handwritten for *China Avant-garde* from the collection of Andreas Schmid, revised by Yu Youhan for the exhibition *Hans van Dijk: 5000 Names* at UCCA, Beijing, 2014

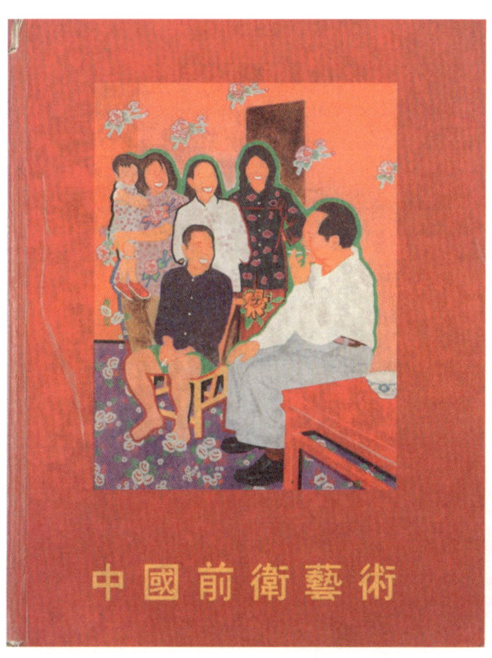

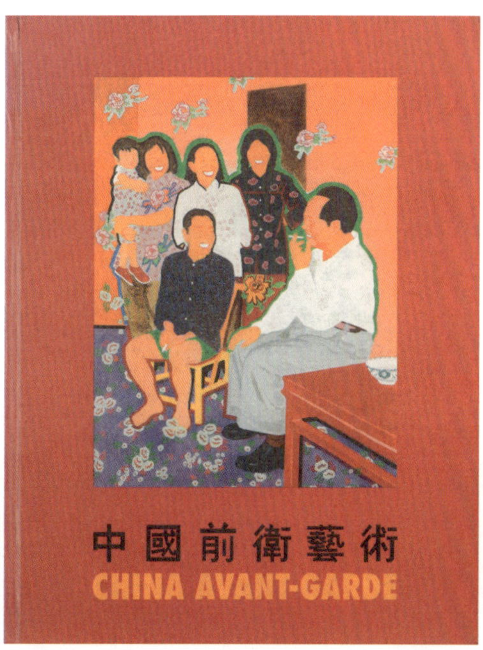

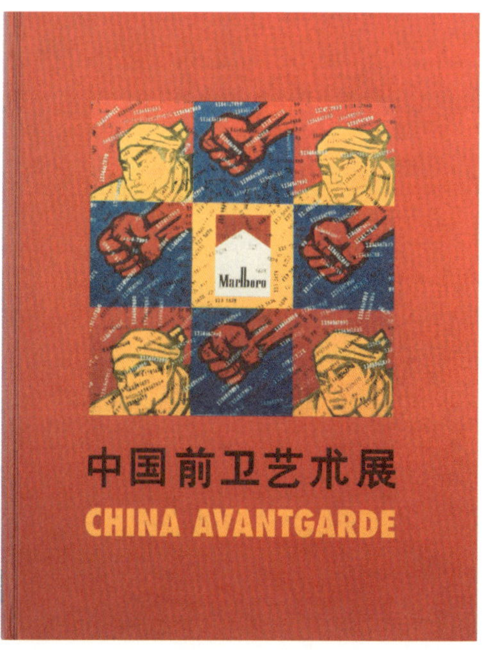

Left and center: *China Avant-garde* Chinese and English catalogues, 1993; cover image: Yu Youhan, *Chairman Mao Talking with Peasants from Shaoshan*, 1991; right: *China Avantgarde*, German catalogue, 1993; cover image: Wang Guangyi, *The Big Criticism-Marlboro*, 1990. Opposite page: Yu Youhan, *Chairman Mao in Discussion with the Peasants of Shaoshan*, acrylic on canvas, 164 × 117.3 cm, 1990, private coll.; shown for the first time after 25 years at *Hans van Dijk: 5000 Names*, UCCA, Beijing, 2014

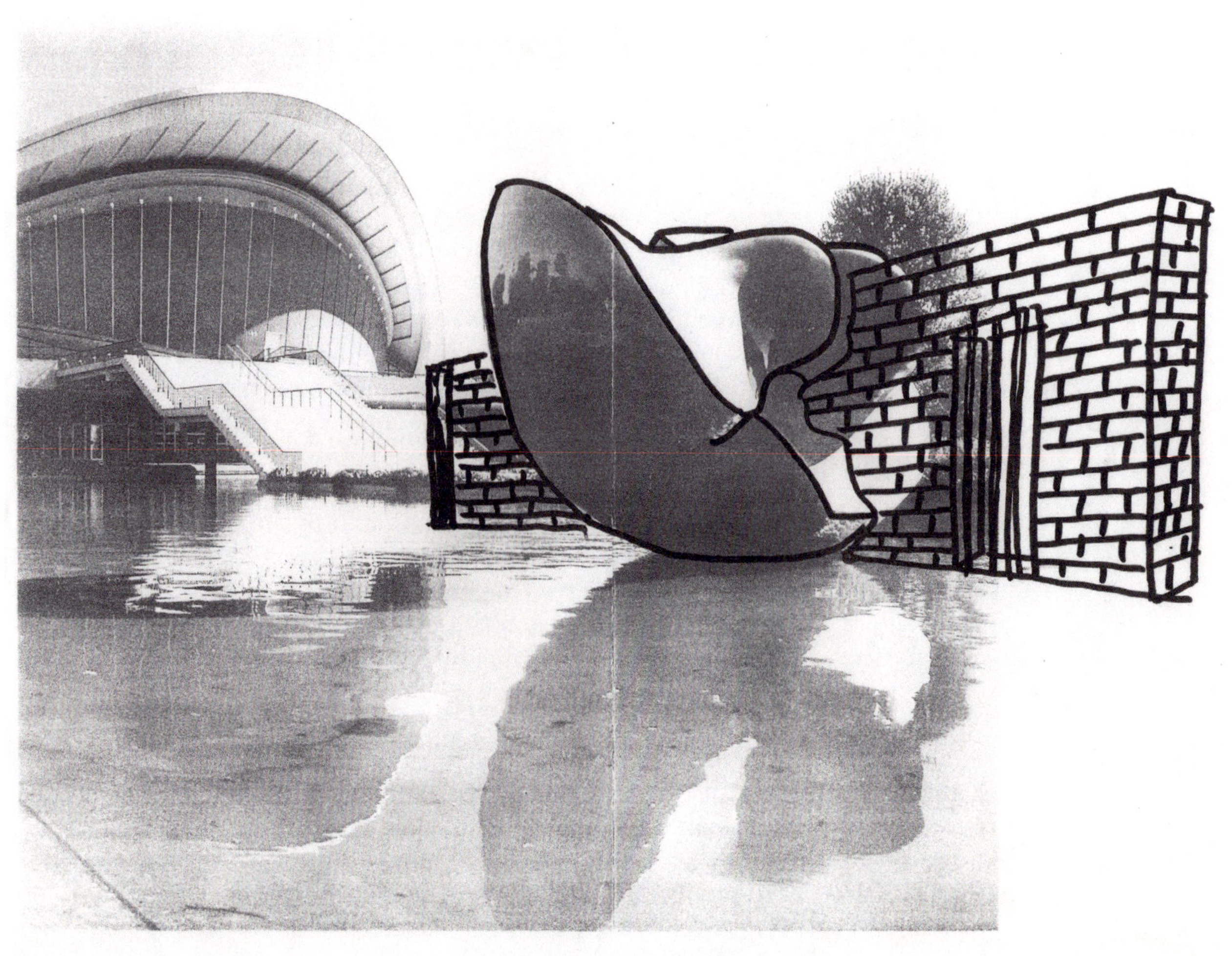

Lin Yilin, document of his proposal for *China Avant-garde*, a site-specific work encasing the large Henry Moore sculpture in the pond at the Haus der Kulturen der Welt in a brick wall, 1992; overruling van Dijk and Schmid, the proposal was rejected by HKW director Pöhlmann; reconstruction made by the artist for *Hans van Dijk: 5000 Names*, UCCA, Beijing, 2014, detail, coll. the artist

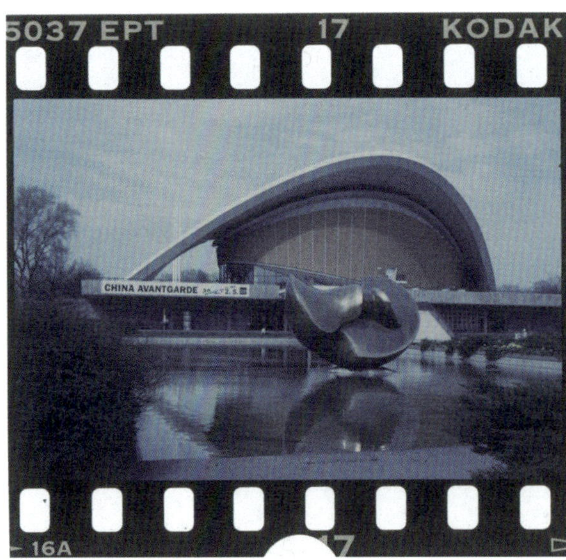

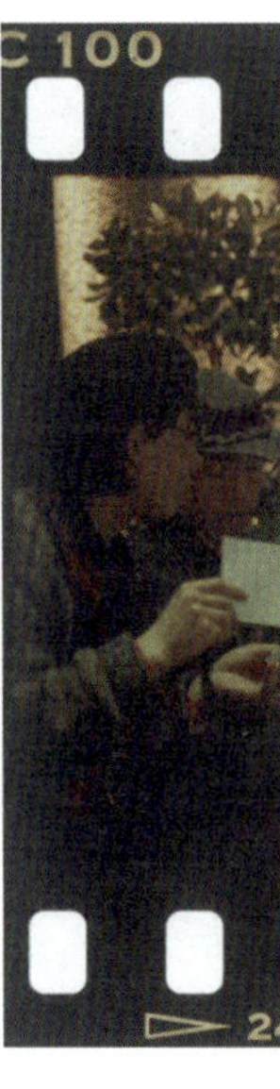

Lin Yilin, *Berlin Memory*, one of ten photographs, 15 × 20 cm, 1993; reconstruction made by the artist for *Hans van Dijk: 5000 Names*, UCCA, Beijing, 2014, detail, coll. the artist

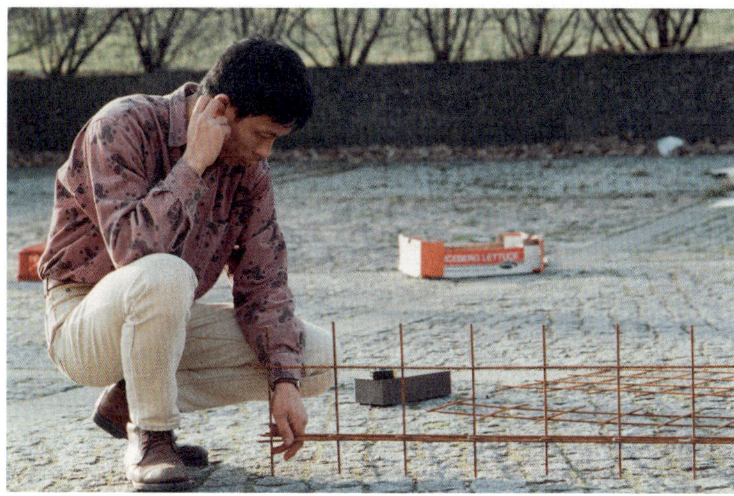

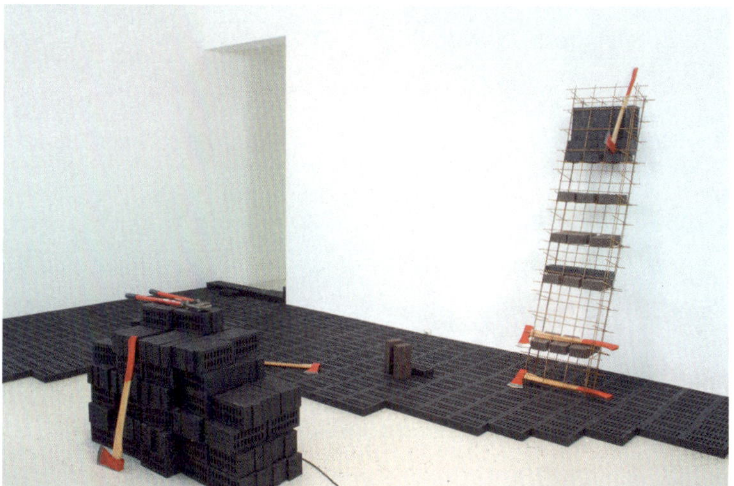

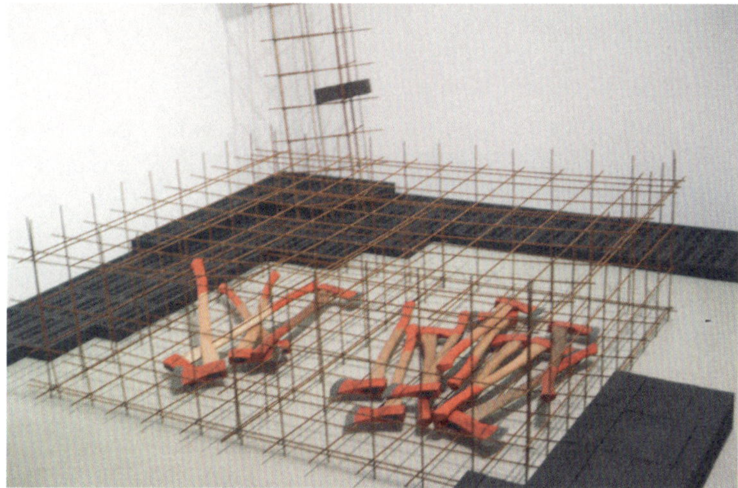

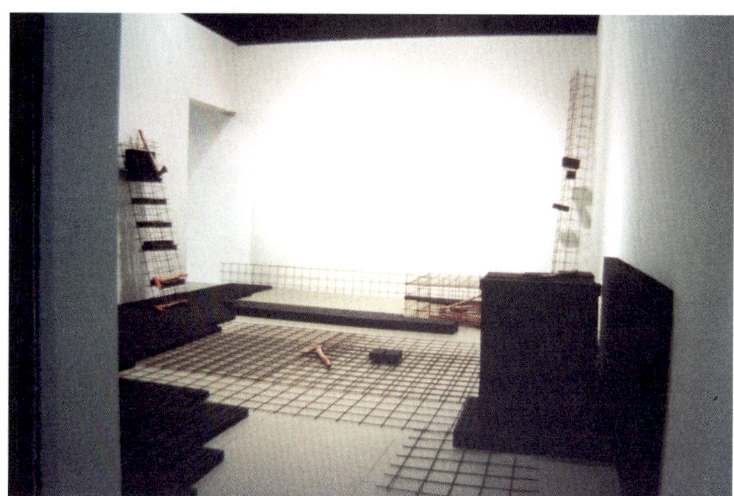

Lin Yilin working on his installation *Room No. 0* at Haus der Kulturen der Welt, Berlin, 1993, photos Andreas Schmid

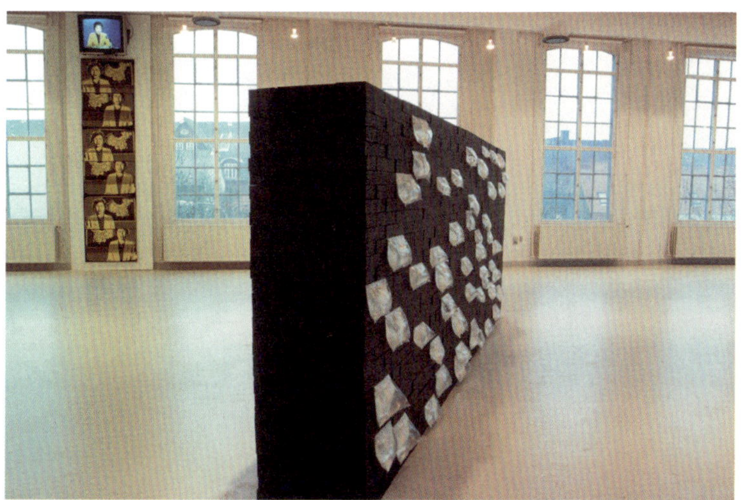

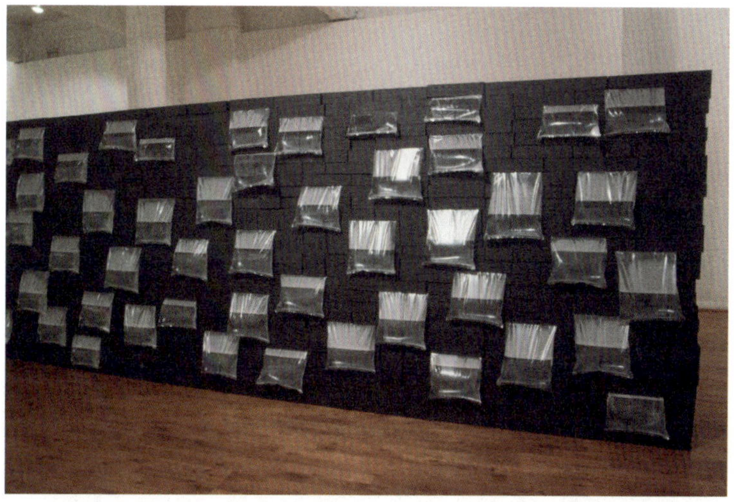

Left: exhibition view, *China Avant-garde*, Brandts Klædefabrik, Odense, 1993–94: Lin Yilin, *The Wall Itself*, bricks, plastic bags filled with water, 1993; Zhang Peili, *Water-Standard Pronunciation from the Cihai Dictionary*, single-channel video, 1991 (far left top), Zhang Peili, *The Standard Pronunciation of 1989*, oil on canvas, 1991 (far left); right: Lin Yilin, *The Wall Itself*, exhibition view *China Avant-garde*, Museum of Modern Art, Oxford, 1993, photos Andreas Schmid

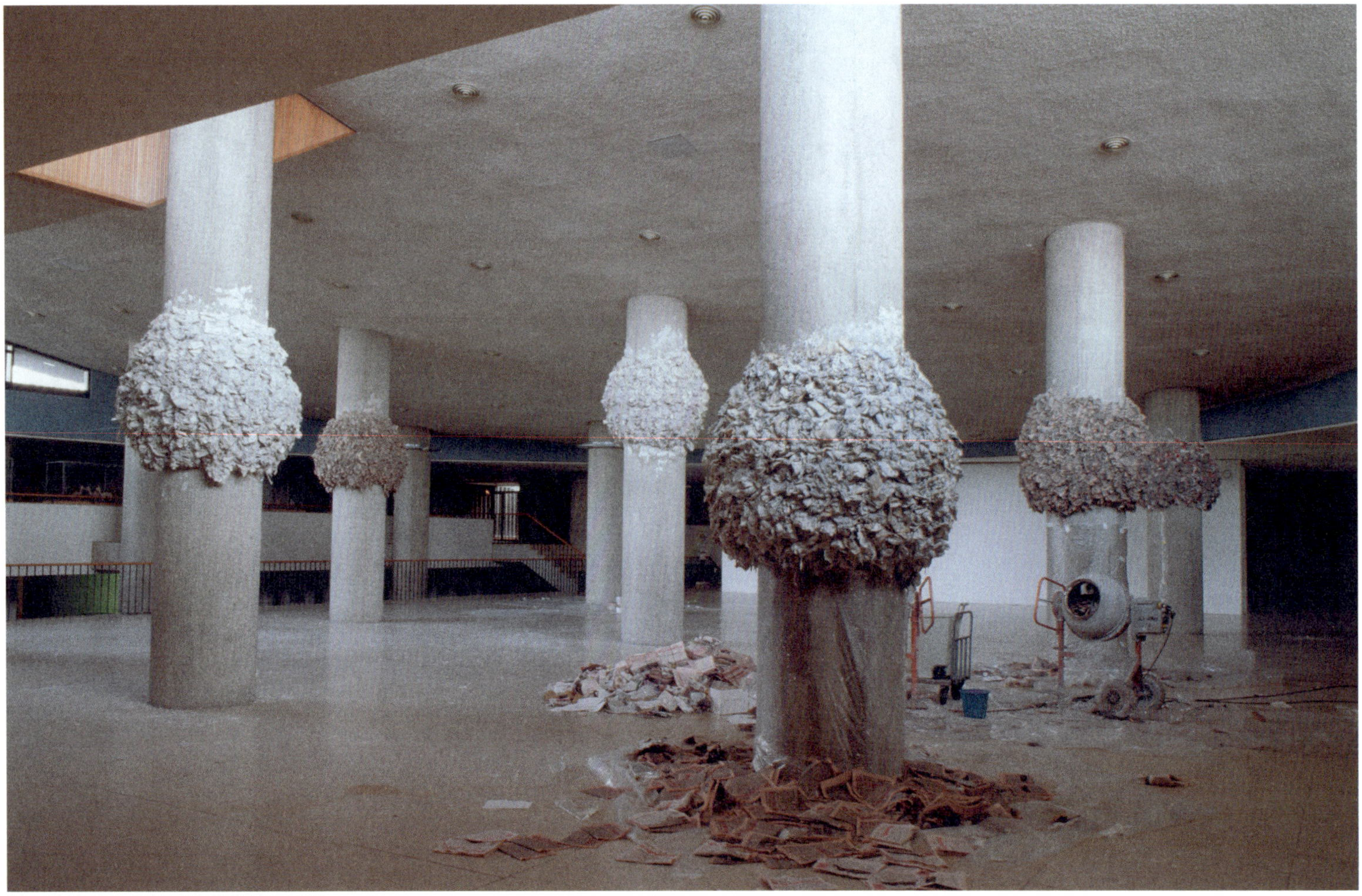

Huang Yong Ping, *Ninepins*, steel, papier mâché, 1993, *China Avant-garde*, Haus der Kulturen der Welt, Berlin, 1993, photo Andreas Schmid

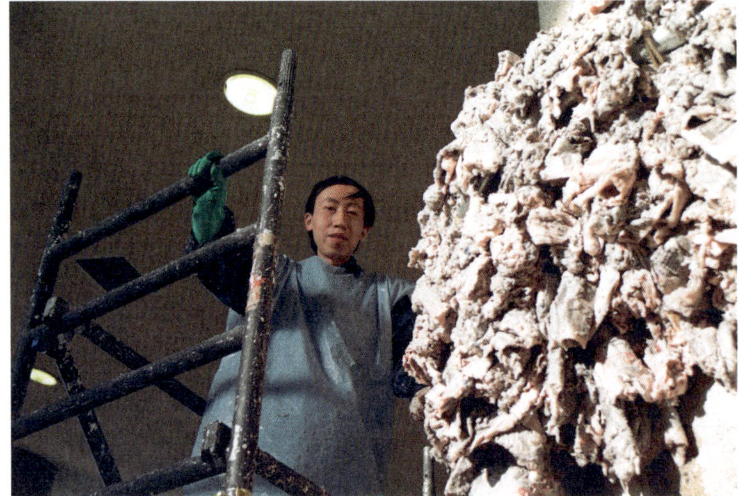

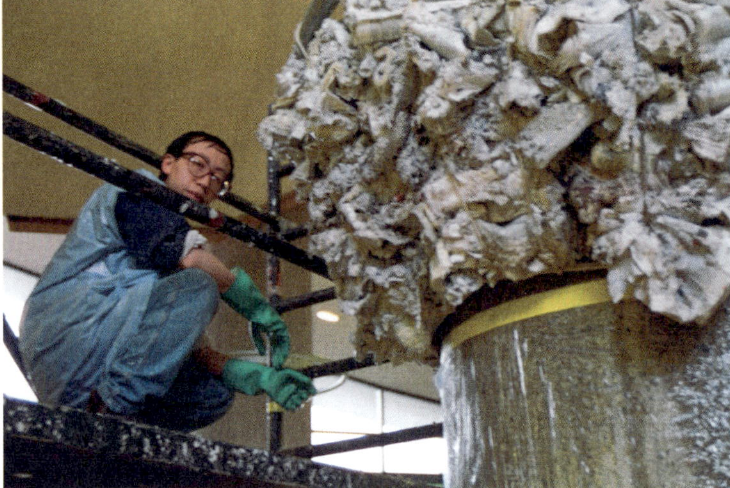

Huang Yong Ping installing *Ninepins*, Haus der Kulturen der Welt, Berlin, 1993, photo Andreas Schmid

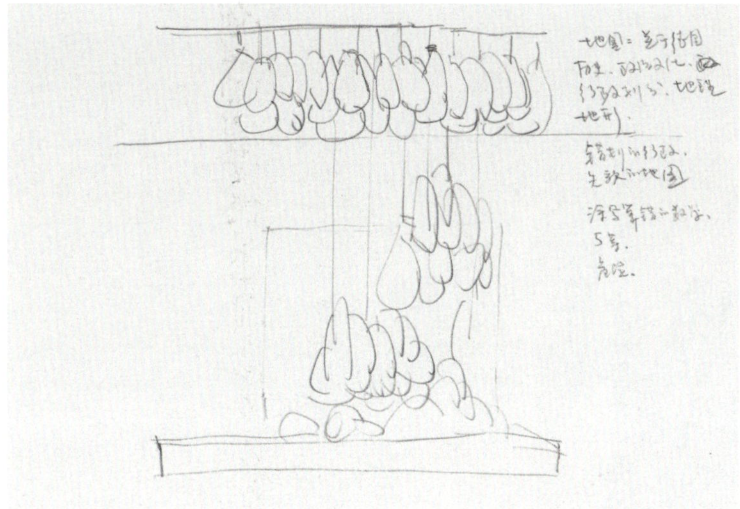

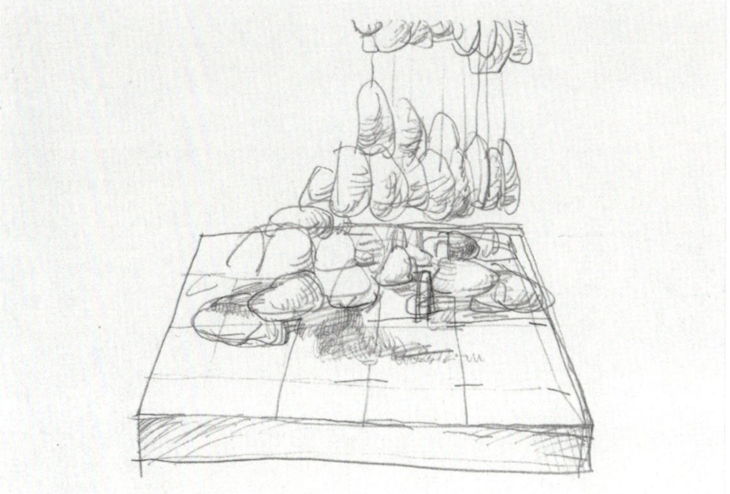

Ni Haifeng, two drawings for *Territory*, pencil on A4 paper, 1992, coll. the artist

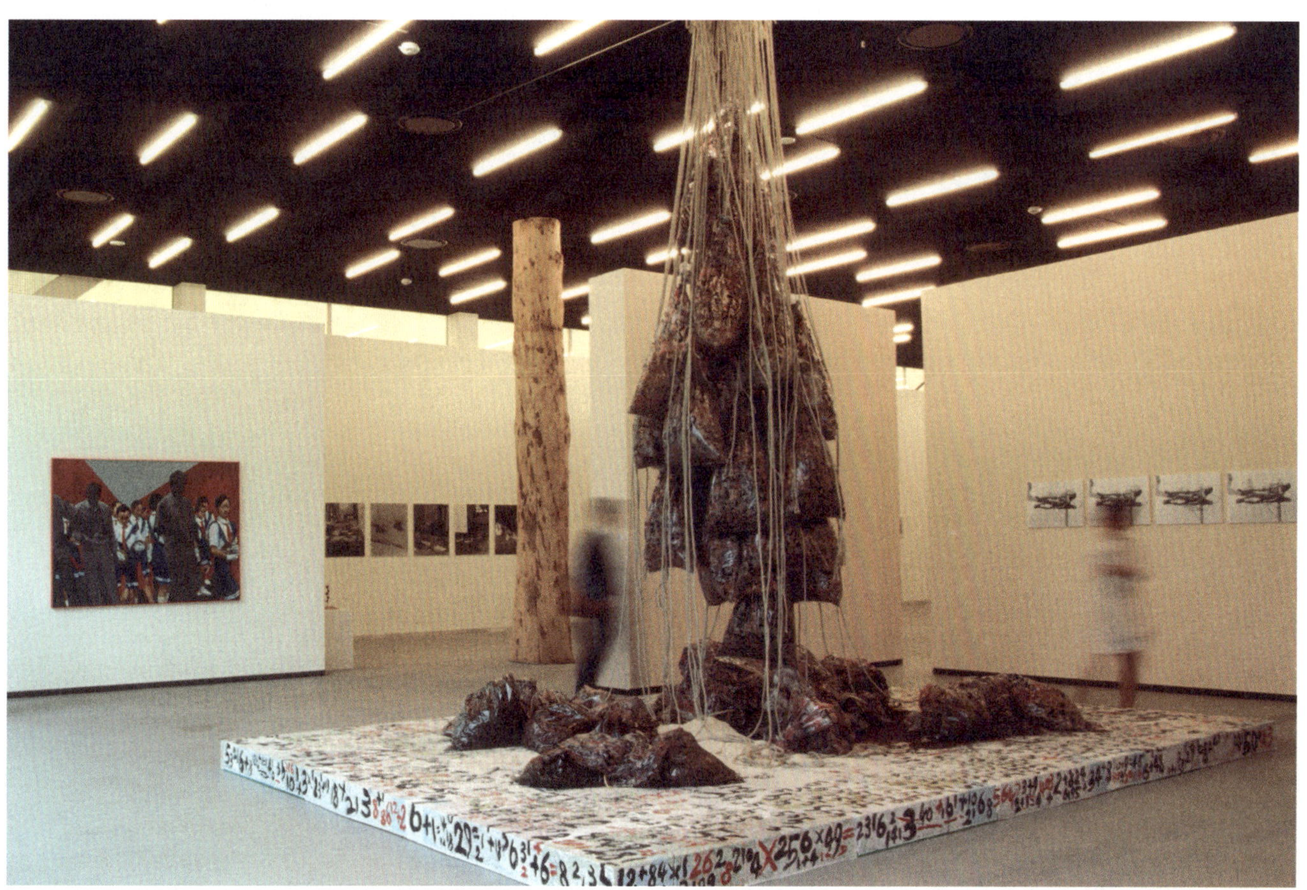

Ni Haifeng, *Territory*, wood, paint, rope, plastic bags filled with dried leaves, 1993, installation *China Avant-garde*, Kunsthal Rotterdam, 1993; Yu Hong, *Young Pioneers*, oil on canvas, 1990 (far left), photo Andreas Schmid

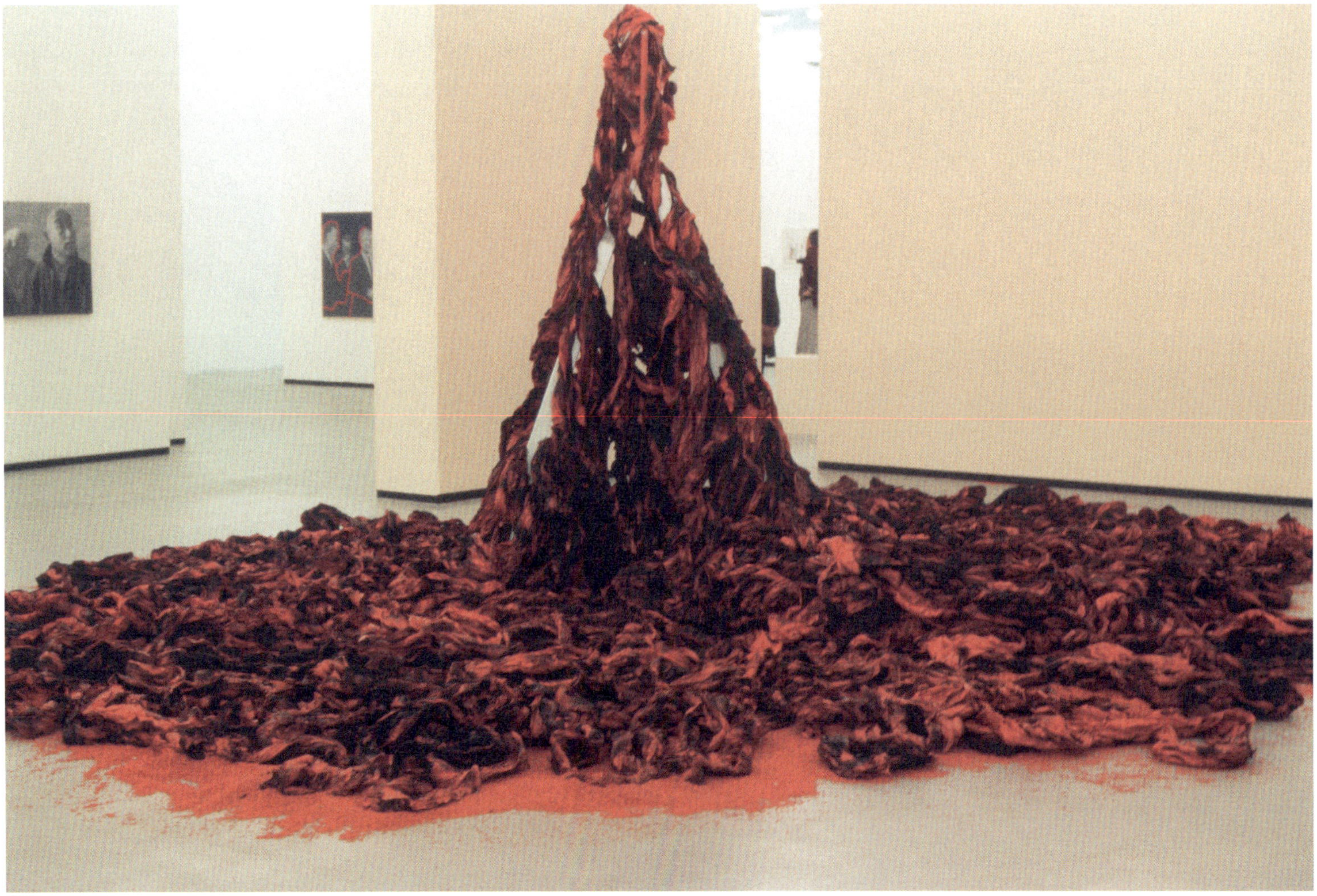

Gu Dexin, *Installation 1993-01-29*, grains, plastic, ladder, 1993, *China Avant-garde*, Kunsthal Rotterdam, 1993, photo Andreas Schmid

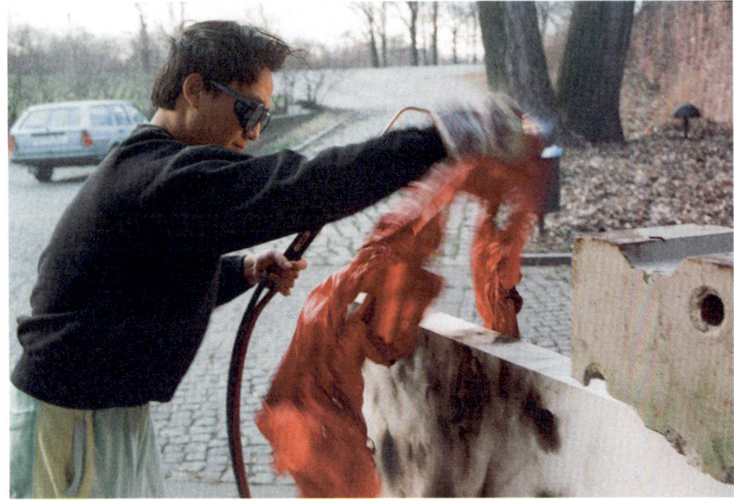

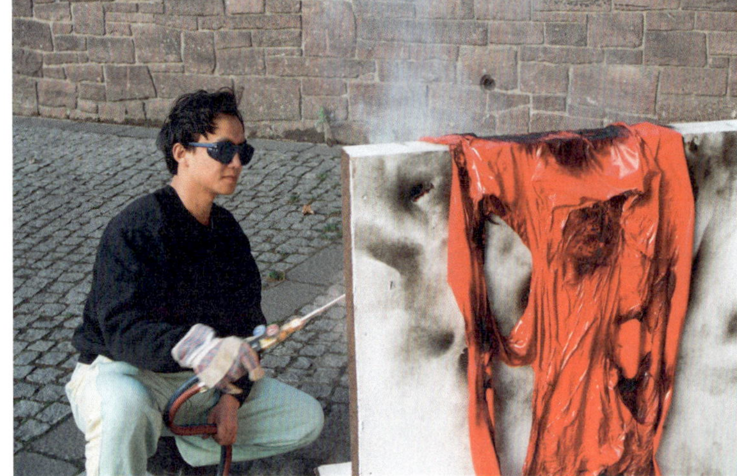

Gu Dexin melting plastic for *Installation 1993-01-29*, Berlin, 1993, photo Andreas Schmid

Ding Yi

A Dialogue of Cultural Significance
1992

Cloth Sculptures

For many years now, an estrangement has existed between art and the audience. Art has all along been closed off in the academic atmosphere between the "laboratory" and the "museum." This status quo in the development of art has caused Chinese audiences to maintain a distance towards modern art, and has continually added to the perplexity. Art seems to have distanced itself from the soil of its own survival, away from a real, practical space and environment.

The creators of the *Cloth Sculpture* series—Zhang Guoliang, Ding Yi, and Qin Yifeng—sculpted a series of static, three-dimensional works in October 1986 by wrapping up their bodies entirely, using their own bodies as the primary material, along with the most basic yellow cloth, under a natural or else urban cultural backdrop. As an artistic medium for a cultural dialogue between the individual and the group, these cloth sculptures upset customary attitudes towards life as well as the ways of viewing art for city-dwellers; this provides a beneficial reference for the audience and allows for a temporary respite in the hustle and bustle, chaos, and turbulence of the rhythm of life, allowing people to consider the links between art and life. On the actual site where the cloth sculptures are produced, and during the exhibition of the photos in the gallery, the audience can discuss this actual fact itself in succession, and provide us with quite a lot of information—that is, through the appreciation of the artworks, the excitement produced by the senses, which has been stimulated back to life by new forms.

As a means of engaging in dialogue between the individual, the group, and the universe, our cities and the empty spaces of nature are the sites—in the barren fields of the outskirts, in the architectural ruins of abandoned ports, under huge advertising signs on booming, bustling city streets, inside train stations and fast food restaurants—we can more or less sense that the universe at this point is not cheerfully illuminated by life, but rather is already an entity of existence itself. Only by letting artists occupy an equal position with the audience and nature can the audience be free of psychological barriers to their enjoyment, which causes the audience to be drawn into the work, becoming a part of the work. Such creative activities, with artists themselves as the sculptural material and with ordinary people participating as well, seemed very important and timely in 1986 in terms of the significance of the enlightenment and inspiration of modern art in China. Because creative activities are built on conditions of dialogue and exchange in close proximity with the audience, the cloth sculptures attained a greater social significance, transmitting more artistic information to the audience and pursuing greater possibilities of culturally significant dialogues.

A Silent Dialogue

We are of the generation born in the early '60s. As a political and cultural movement, the Cultural Revolution in China has stayed in our memory all these years, and often raises hazy memories of that era. Unconsciously, [we] vainly dream of a dialogue with the distinct cultural phenomena of our childhood through our lucid intellect today.

In April 1988, Ding Yi, Su Xiaosong, and others created a series of artworks mixing the environment and wrapping, *A Silent Dialogue*. We do not merely base ourselves on simple relationships between traditional painting and modern art, the past and the present reality, but are keener to expand on the mutual resonances and dialogues between artists and the audience, individuals and the social environment, to undertake an overall "wrapping up" of humans and the environment in a closed environment, using red paper as the material. Such a static atmosphere, along with the use of the artists' bodies as sculpture, consciously creates a kind of barrier and fracture from the outside world, just as the whiteness of the paper and the slogans all transmit "inert information" towards the audience. The whole environment covered by red and black, with the people wrapped up, becomes a kind of "empty" substance. All thought and words are halted, and they are presented through the environment and the texts and slogans on the walls; in other words, with external ideas invading and replacing individual thought. And this was exactly the reality of the Cultural Revolution.

In this environment, organized by art and yet suddenly unfamiliar, we wanted to point out a certain reflection at a deeper level. As a symbol, this meditative state not only hints at a deep-flowing rational spirit, but at the same time it reflects the pursuit of transcendence. A certain superficial level produced by *A Silent Dialogue* is the confirmed implication of maintaining silence, but in essence they are the spatial concepts of change, movement, respiration, meditation, and dialogue. Ordinarily, the myriad expressive conditions of language and writing are also the realization of thought and rationality; the slogan texts are annotations of the dialogue between the quiet, solemn environment and human cultural meaning. As a complete work, where all the elements are placed within a silent space and at the same time proceed to respire and spout life in common, this intimate relation of mutual resonance engenders an opposing, organic relation from the silent blockages on the surface of the work and from inner meditation. The double meaning encompassed by the work in terms of visual language, as well as the contradictory encounters, are exactly the mode of dialogue we are in search of—as a human culture and as cultured humans.

Ding Yi, *A Dialogue of Cultural Significance*, written in 1992 as Ding Yi's theoretical contribution to *China Avant-garde*

Ding Yi, *Appearance of Crosses 1991-3*, acrylic on canvas, 140×180 cm, 1991, coll. the artist; shown in *China Avant-garde*, Haus der Kulturen der Welt, Berlin, 1993

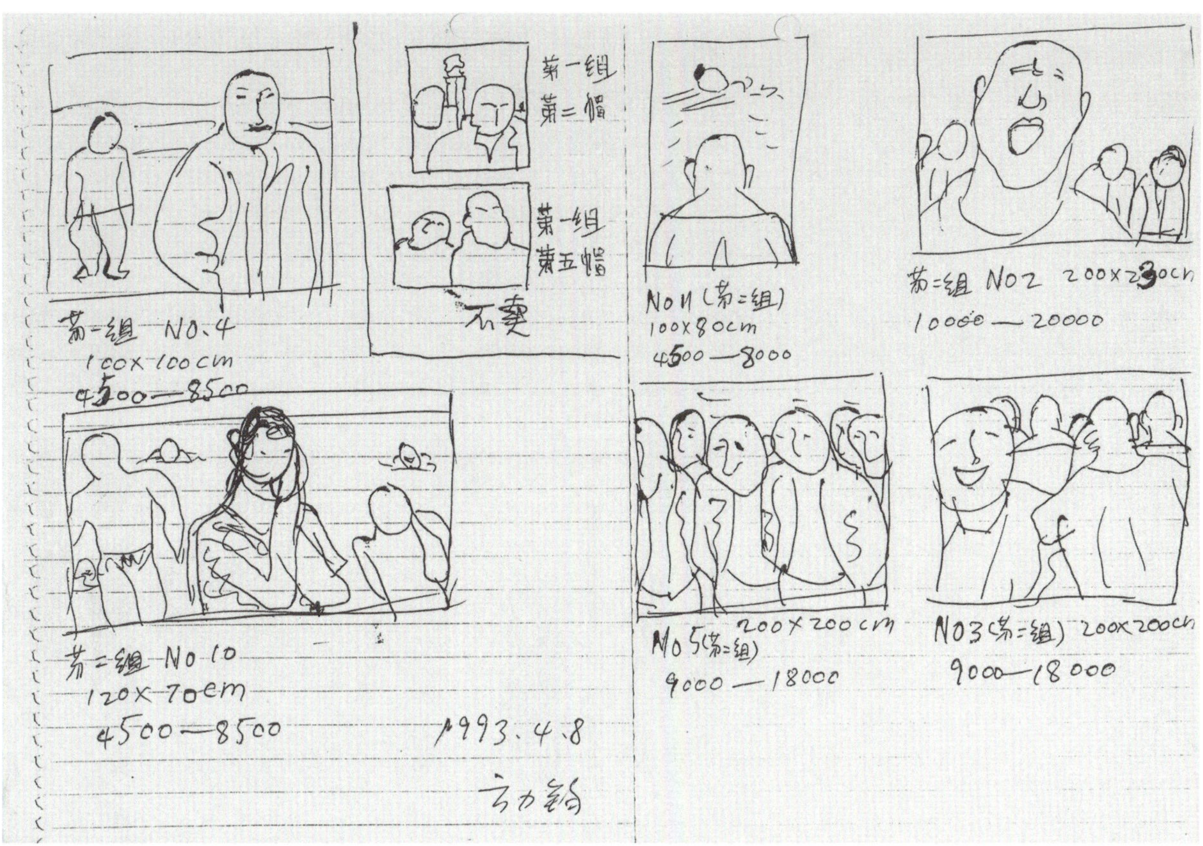

Hans van Dijk, installation sketches of Fang Lijun's works for *China Avant-garde*, 1993, coll. Asia Art Archive, Hong Kong, courtesy Andreas Schmid

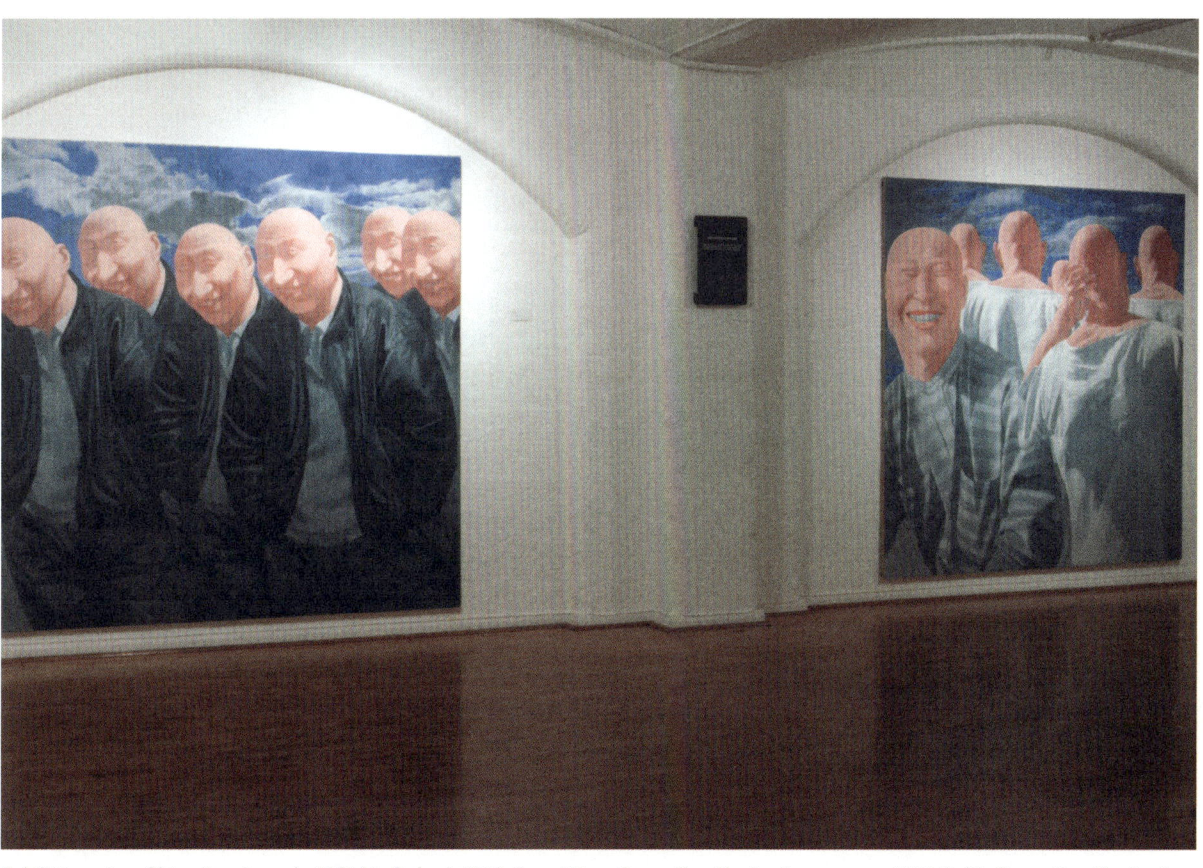

Exhibition view *China Avant-garde*, MOMA, Oxford, 1993, Fang Lijun, *Group Two No. 5*, oil on canvas, 1992 (left); *Group Two No. 3*, oil on canvas, 1992 (right); photo Andreas Schmid

Geng Jianyi

In the biographical entry for Geng Jianyi in the *China Avant-garde* catalogue, van Dijk writes:

> He mailed an official-looking form to fifty artists who had applied to take part in the *China/Avant-Garde* exhibition. The form requested detailed information on health, education, marital status, personal inclinations, cultural or political orientation, social and professional status, class, police records, et cetera. The form ended with the sentence that this data would not be stored in governmental records, but as private information. Some artists believed that this form was genuine and returned it completed with the requested photo. During the October selection meeting, Geng presented these completed forms as his exhibition contribution. He offered the artists a certificate, thanking them for their cooperation and a place in the history of art. The certificate is titled "Vegetables are not as delicious as meat."
>
> **_China Avant-garde_, exhib. cat., English edition, Edition Braus, Berlin, 1993, pp. 120–21**

Family name – Present name	Huang Yongping	Sex	Male	Family origin	Still has to be examined	PHOTO
Family name – Former name	There is none	Ethnic origin	Han	Personal social status	not clear	
Year of birth	1954	Month of birth:	2	Day of birth: 19	Sign of the zodiac: neither horse nor donkey	
Home of ancestors	Quanzhou					
Place of birth	Xiamen			Weight at birth	Forgotten	
Present profession	presently looking for one	Professional position	not yet determined	Hobby	not clear	
Salary	rising steadily month by month	Other economic income	none	Special abilities	general weakness	
Present qualification	not clear	Education	University graduate	Academic degree	B.A.	
Height	shrinking daily	Weight	Fluctuating daily	Blood group	D	
Medical History	still has to be examined			Present state of health, stamina	not clear	
State of convalescence	very good					
Membership in clubs and organizations	in no organization	What or who has a special influence on you ?	almost nothing			
Favourite plant	Plant	Favourite animal	Man	Favourite person	Animal	
Marital Status, relationships and names of members of family, attitude to work	still has to be examined					
At what time, at which place, for what reason have you recieved which kind of praise or blame ?	neither praise nor blame					
Way of life and ideological tendencies	Way of life is not yet established; there is almost no ideological tendency					

BRIEF CURRICULUM VITAE

From when (Month/Year) until when (Month/Year)	In which place, in which unit	Which specific work done	Witness
1975 - 1978	Suburb of Xiamen	Farm labour and diverse other activities	Geng Jianyi
1978 - 1982	Art College Zhejiang	Student and teacher	Geng Jianyi
1982 - 1988	Tongwen-Middleschool, Xiamen	Teacher and police-officer	Geng Jianyi

Geng Jianyi, *Investigative Form*, series of 27 forms and an audience certificate, 1988, coll. Andreas Schmid; shown here is the form filled out by Huang Yong Ping with English translation, the photo pasted on the form shows Huang Yong Ping's father

Zhao Bandi

Dear Pöhlmann, Noth, van Dijk, and Schmid:
Thanks for your hard work and outstanding achievement.
I have some ideas as follows:

1. Today's art is a hard question of study for us all. If "avant-garde" means to be enterprising and creative, I am glad to be one of them, and add my own work to it—several works of realistic style. In my opinion, there are no so-called "types of avant-garde." If there are, they must be the stale things in people's brains. Stale things are just the enemies of real creating.
2. I have been quite uneasy. My collector did not allow several of my works to take part in the show. I hope four works will be published in the catalogue. It would be more substantial.

If you choose just two, not only will I have some regrets, but also I will feel fortunate in the fact that the other four works didn't come here.
I would like to point out that the painting *Xiao Zhang* [Young Zhang] should, when printed, follow its original orientation.
I will not agree to the use of a photograph in which the painting is displayed on the wall. There are two reasons for this:

a. *Young Zhang* is not an installation work, but a pure work of painting. It should be treated just as other paintings are. As for the shape of these paintings: I don't remember anyone making any regulations about that.
b. Is the shape or angle of the work an injury to the elegance of the big book? The answer is no. In fact, it couldn't be more important and more beautiful than were it to reflect the character of artists' work honestly, especially for a book introducing modern art.

Sincerely, Zhao Bandi

Zhao Bandi, letter written in English to Wolfger Pöhlmann, Jochen Noth, Hans van Dijk, and Andreas Schmid, 17 December 1992, coll. Andreas Schmid

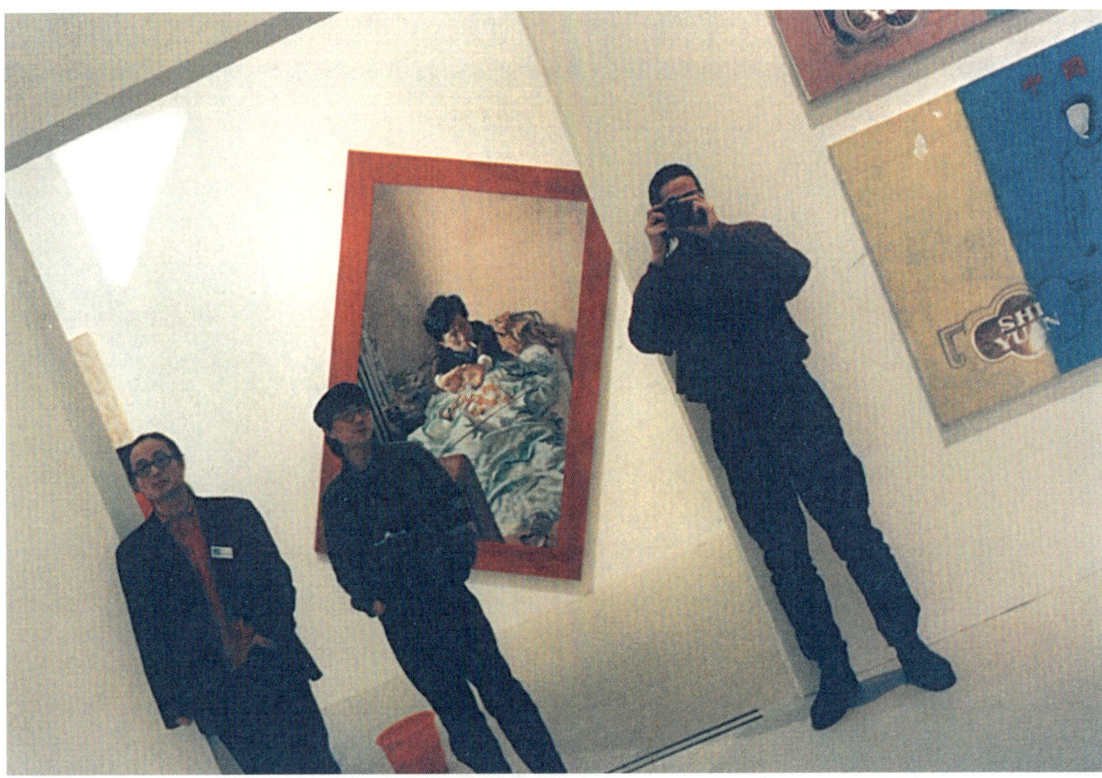

Left to right: Wu Shanzhuan, Wang Jinsong, and Ni Haifeng, in front of Zhao Bandi's painting *Young Zhang*, 1992, and Yu Youhan's *Renminbi* paintings, 1988, *China Avant-garde*, Haus der Kulturen der Welt, Berlin, 1993, photo Fang Lijun, courtesy Andreas Schmid

TOURIST INFORMATION
Concept at Large
—to whom it may concern—

As an example of the average Labourer, chinese citizen Wu Shan Zhuan is being sent by Red Humour International and in association with____________________________
to become an employee at____
from________________to_________________.
As salary he has to receive normal payment, locally being paid to an average worker.
He will work and thereby enrich____.
As a side-effect of his labouring he supplies the concept of work by the aspect of art. This can be called an example of 'over-art-work'. The labouring has to be performed without any inner movement, only its function for the customer is taking response of the action. Therefore it is concept at large, being only restricted by, from and for the customer and the custom itself.

Labour of____________
Red Humour International
Date____________

Wu Shanzhuan, *Tourist Information, Concept at Large*, 1992, private coll.

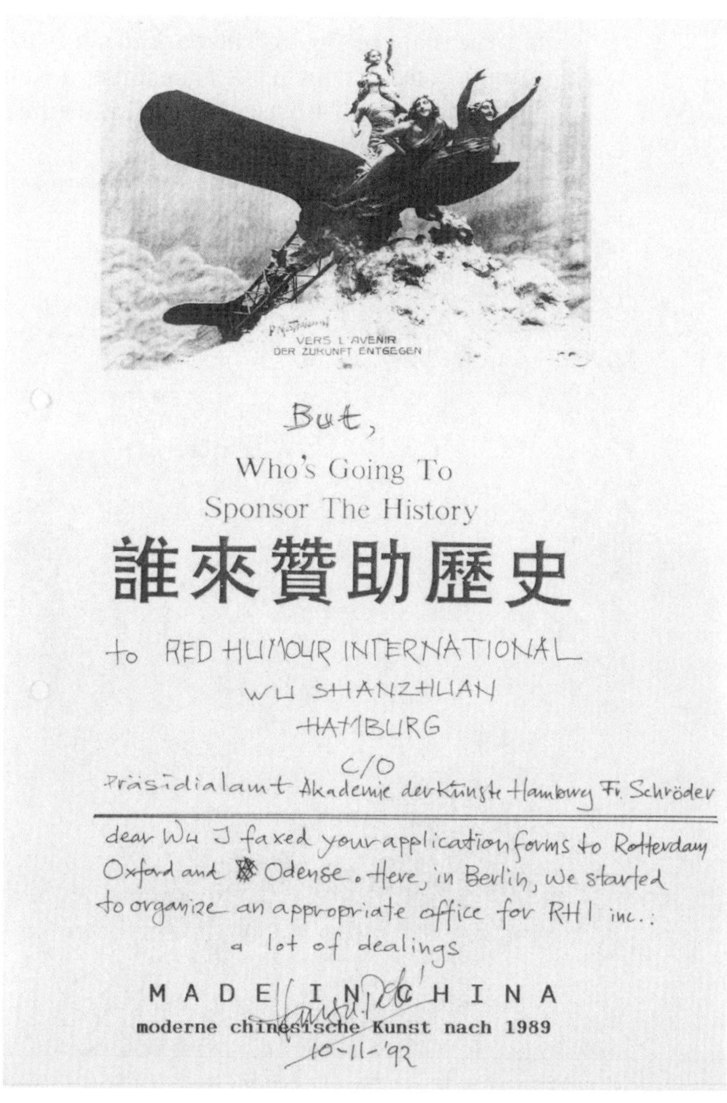

VERS L'AVENIR
DER ZUKUNFT ENTGEGEN

But,
Who's Going To
Sponsor The History
誰來贊助歷史

to RED HUMOUR INTERNATIONAL
WU SHANZHUAN
HAMBURG
c/o
Präsidialamt Akademie der Künste Hamburg Fr. Schröder

dear Wu I faxed your application forms to Rotterdam Oxford and Odense. Here, in Berlin, we started to organize an appropriate office for RHI inc.:
a lot of dealings

MADE IN CHINA
moderne chinesische Kunst nach 1989
10-11-'92

Hans van Dijk, letter to Wu Shanzhuan, sent from Berlin 10 November 1992, private coll.

TOURIST INFORMATION

Application for a labour of (Odense)

Surname: WU

Given name: SHAN ZHUAN

Nationality: CHINESE

Height: 1,74 M

Sex: MALE

Weight: 59. Kg

Date of birth: 25. OCT. 1960

Place of birth: ZHEJING CHINA

Permanent Adress: WARTENAU 16
2000 HAMBURG 76 GERMANY

Phone: 40-29843228

I hereby apply for a Labour of (Odense)
I declare that to the of my knowledge the above particulars are correct and complete

RED HUMOUR INTERNATIONAL

RED HUMOUR INTERNATIONAL

6. 11. 92
Hamburg

* PUTTING THE MONEY FOR
THE ART-MATERIAL IN BANK

Wu Shanzhuan, *Tourist Information, Application for a Labour of (Odense)*, 6 November 1992, private coll; identical applications were filed for Berlin, Rotterdam, and Oxford

17—Leo Castelli, 1907–1999, owner of the Leo Castelli Gallery in New York, world famous for its avant-garde artists.

18—Hanne Darboven, 1941–2009, conceptual artist, living in Hamburg.

THOMAS FUESSER, professional art photographer: Hans was the reason I moved to China. The *China Avant-garde* show in Berlin was the first time I ever saw Chinese contemporary art. I had been commissioned as a photographer by the Haus der Kulturen der Welt in February 1993. There I met Hans for the first time. I also met Zhang Peili and Ni Haifeng, and I remember Wu Shanzuan doing a performance where he was dressed in a Mao suit, standing on the steps of the Haus der Kulturen der Welt, greeting the visitors and bowing them in. These artists persuaded me to go to China.

I also distinctly remember a curious incident at that show: in one moment, we were all ushered out of a room in a hurry because it was announced that a VIP had arrived.

But I had forgotten my light meter in there, and when I rushed back to get it, there was gallerist Leo Castelli[17] in the room with his entourage. I knew Castelli from meeting him at Hanne Darboven's[18] studio, because I was doing all her photographs at the time. I remember thinking if Castelli is here, the show I am witnessing must be something very special indeed.

So now tell me, though I can't prove it: who pushed [famous *New York Times* journalist] Andrew Solomon to go to China in December of that year? Who else would have had that much power? Solomon was not in Berlin at the time of the show. And Solomon did his scouting for Chinese artists through Hans. With Solomon came Gueorgui Pinkhassov, the Magnum photographer from the *New York Times* who won a World Press Photo Award with his photos of Chinese artists. Hans was scouting for him, too.

I tried to get the *Frankfurter Allgemeine Zeitung* interested in my photos, but they wouldn't print them because they weren't interested in the art. Then I went to *Der Stern* magazine with them. They told me to go to China instead and report from there.

I went to China in September – October 1993. Actually *Der Stern* never did anything with my photos, though I pushed them to publish before the *New York Times*.

Hans even wrote a text in Dutch for *Der Stern*, but they never published it, and they never paid either Hans or me.

I photographed Hans several times. I once took a snapshot of him quite unaware staring out through the window, looking miles away in his thoughts. That photo is quite characteristic. I still have a slide of Hans and Li Xianting sitting together in some shoddy restaurant in Beijing near the Forbidden City, from the end of October 1993. After that I started going more often to Shanghai and Guangzhou, and then I started working in Hong Kong, because things were freer there.

MB, interview with Thomas Fuesser, Shanghai, 9 September 2012

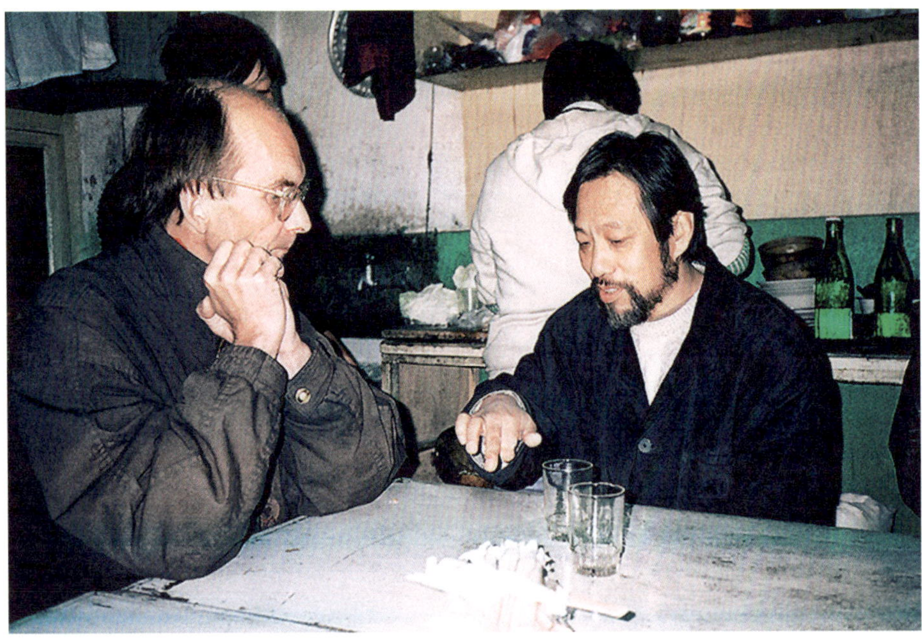

Thomas Fuesser, *Hans van Dijk and Art Critic Li Xianting*, Beijing, 1993, courtesy Thomas Fuesser

Van Dijk moves to Bejing in March. Because foreigners must live in gated communities designated by the government, van Dijk stays at the Beijing Friendship Hotel, to which he refers as a prison. One of his letters has "Friendship-hole" as his address. He wants to live in a normal neighborhood like the artists, to be part of daily life in China. His is an extremely expensive prison, moreover, since he has nothing to live off except the fee he received from the Haus der Kulturen der Welt, a rather modest 35,000.- Deutschmark (approx. EUR 27,000 today) for two years of intense work. He has to secure a job with a Chinese firm first because he needs a work permit. Until he has both, he is obliged to travel to Hong Kong every three months to renew his visa, which is not only time-consuming but also very expensive. Over time, this situation will turn into a constant source of anxiety.

Without a doubt, his experience with *Daglicht* is on his mind when he approaches the Central Academy of Craft Art (*zhongyang gongyi meishu xueyuan*) in Beijing, proposing to set up a silk-screen printing studio for artists, which do not exist in China. He also plans to establish a commercial gallery and print shop. His client base would consist of high-end diplomats and the growing expat community, and benefit from the new wealth of China's rising middle class. He wants clients with a moderate income to be able to afford art, hence the print shop. In an optimistic letter from Beijing written soon after his arrival, he tells Ernst Dinkla, who runs a profitable printing studio in Eindhoven, about his plans:

> "Are you perhaps seeking to make your fortune?" asked Mr. Wang, director of the Foundation for Silk-screen Printing of the National Printing Techniques Research Institute, after I told him about my plans. The school made a poor impression, housed in a severely derelict nineteenth-century building that looked like the revolution had just happened yesterday. Folders, machine parts, furniture, and tools were spread across every room. The central heating was running on summer mode, making it a rather chilly spring morning.
>
> I found the Institute together with an artist who had wanted to work with silk-screen for a long time. With the standard guidebook *Siwang Banhua* [Silk-screen Printing] by Dima Mala (a decent bootleg copy in Chinese), I managed to communicate well. After a few hours of chatting and a pack of Marlboros, we arrived at our shared interests, and I was to get 7,000 guilders for a silk-screen press, lighting equipment, rinsing trays with a pump, two drying racks, delivery within one month. Mr. Wang could also arrange for professional assistance and a helping hand. […]
>
> I have given myself until mid-May to find out how to set up a gallery-print shop. The conditions are good: art is definitely around, and it keeps getting better; more and more artists leave their jobs and security behind and move to Beijing to semi-legally make a living there. My reputation in the art world is pretty good (I am world famous in Beijing by now), yet relationships with artists remain complicated because of their inscrutable internal politics, but I have experience and am learning still. Luckily, there are friends who help as well.
>
> The number of prospective buyers increases, both Chinese and foreigners living here. There are a few types to distinguish: foreign professional collectors, gallery owners, art dealers, and museums. All of these will grow in number during the next year due to three big simultaneous manifestations of modern Chinese art abroad. […]
>
> Other interested parties, including a local group, consist of a few thousand of the many thousand foreigners working in Beijing. […] I have known the cultural attachés of the Dutch, Italian, and Swedish ambassadors for a few years now. They are serious collectors and are interested in my plans.
>
> The third category of clients is the least obvious and therefore the most promising: the Chinese nouveaux riches; speculators from the south; and companies that would like to do something with art (I will soon speak with someone from the Bank of China, department Shanghai, who wants to start collecting for the bank); young intellectuals, for example those who follow Chinese literature closely; and patriotic patrons who can't stand to see the most interesting art disappear abroad. […]
>
> Eventually a group of emancipated art lovers will originate in this city of twelve million. Apart from the already mentioned Australian gallery[19], there are a few others, three or four,

19—Red Gate Gallery, founded by Brian Wallace in 1991.

run by Chinese in an unprofessional way to the displeasure of the artists—often just focusing on money, not making any concrete arrangements, then suddenly closing down and disappearing.
A gallery that offers both continuity and quality therefore fills a gap in the market. […] The gallery should become a two-person business, for all sorts of contact with the government, including local authorities; it is good to collaborate with a Chinese partner. […] I am thinking about naming my gallery in Beijing "New Amsterdam Gallery," because there are too many Chinese, intellectuals and artists, not least, who have extreme nationalistic obsessions—for example, auctions like Christie's and Sotheby's in Hong Kong are called colonialist practices—but I have to discuss this with my partner.
I have shown my "market observations" and plans to the trade consul of the Dutch Embassy, Peter van Leeuwen, who immediately started giving good advice: "The best thing to do would be to rent a *hutong* (a traditional property consisting of three buildings and a gate around a square courtyard), a lot of sunlight and the gate lends itself to clear signs, then renovating, which is not expensive here. They recently renovated the embassy for eight thousand yuan. What do you think? I think it's done nicely, not cheap but done within two weeks, the entire floor. You should do something about your clothes, you are wearing two jackets right now, and more people do that here, but with clients you should appear in nicer hotels, and you should have a business card made. You know what, I'll give you the address of a friendly Belgian expert, Mr. van Hooydonk who earns $100 per hour just by advising businessmen, still as assistant general manager at the International Management Consultants, Ltd., Euro-Bitic—the biggest in China, but who wants to start his own business." […]
"Perfect," said Mr. van Hooydonk, "various constructions are possible," and then he fell into a jargon that momentarily startled me. His summary and conclusion were again spoken in a sort of Dutch: "What you need is a company with a name, an address, and a bank in Hong Kong that allows you as chief representative to open a representative office in Beijing. You still work for the firm in Hong Kong, but won't make a profit in Beijing, but in Hong Kong. That company, preferably a gallery, should exist at least for a year. It's a legal construction. If you listen to me I can manage this within two weeks," after which he gave me two addresses of companies in Hong Kong "who manage something like that by post and fax for an acceptable price."

HvD, letter to Ernst Dinkla, Beijing, 3 April 1993

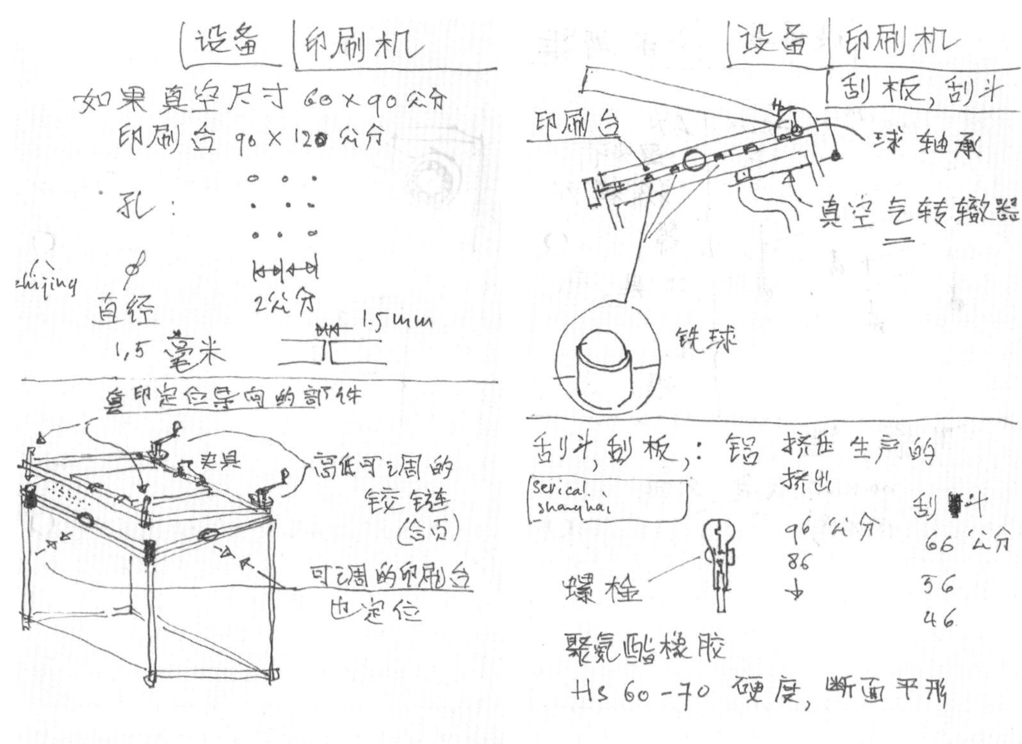

Hans van Dijk, technical drawings for a serigraphic studio, 1993, private coll.

To install the Rotterdam iteration of *China Avant-garde*, van Dijk travels to the Netherlands in May and stays for a month. When he returns to Beijing, he makes a living taking up odd jobs generously offered by Michael Kahn-Ackermann, the founding director of the Goethe Institute in Beijing. Kahn-Ackermann asks van Dijk to show German artist Jörg Immendorff around and help him install his show at the Holiday Inn. Van Dijk has little positive to say about Immendorff,[20] although his work proves to be quite important to young artists, who are excited to discover an expressionist alternative to socialist realism. During his visit in August, van Dijk is asked to introduce art critic Andrew Solomon of the *New York Times* to the art scenes of Beijing, Shanghai, and Hangzhou. Van Dijk introduces him to art critic Li Xianting and many artists, including Zhao Bandi, Ni Haifeng, Liu Wei, and Zhou Tiehai. Later that year, photographer Thomas Fuesser of the German magazine *Der Stern* arrives.

20—"Why is there so little press when I, for the first time in my life, visit Peking? I know, Baselitz is against me." HvD, letter to his friends in the Netherlands, 9 July 1995.

Hans van Dijk, English-Chinese dictionary of technical terms for silk-screen printing, 1994, coll. van Dijk family

Van Dijk continues to devote himself to the realization of his silk-screen studio. He contacts the Dutch firm of van Duppen, experts in silk-screen printing, asking for publishers' addresses and further literature. He and Dinkla start an elaborate correspondence in which Dinkla councils him on all the equipment necessary to set up a silk-screen printing press and studio. Van Dijk starts compiling a dictionary of silk-screen terms in Chinese and English. On 29 June, he writes Dinkla an update:

> Mr. Tu, the director of the Academy [of Craft Art], kept his word: he started the application to appoint a foreign specialist. It may take time of course, no one knows exactly. He did say though, that even after everything has been taken care of, he is not yet ready to integrate silk-screen into his teaching, and that I had better take care of the artists' studio for the time being. I still assume that he will pay for everything; let's see how it goes.
> The boss of the Goethe Institute, Michael Kahn-Ackermann, figured out how I can make money with a professionally managed exhibition space. Many embassies have a budget to present their national modern art here, but they can't find a reliable organization, so that is quite some money left unused. […]
> I am now looking for an English-speaking Chinese business partner, because it is still unclear how much time I will have outside of the silk-screen studio, or my tasks at the Academy. […] I started compiling an English-Chinese list of words: I now know that a squeegee is a scraping implement, Plexiglas: organic glass, cellophane: glass paper, gelatin: clear glue, and a drying rack: drying rack.
> Aside from working on that vocabulary and buying silk shirts—by the time I am an official expert, I will be the best-dressed man in the entire People's Republic—I've been spending quite some time writing short pieces like the ones you just received.[21] In the

21—Van Dijk refers to the short texts he sends his friends from time to time, full of anecdotes and *couleur locale*. One such text deals with Hong Hao's work in the China Guide office in a hotel, which "rents out part of the floor to a hospital […] doors are permanently left open […] a bookcase put in the corridor with a lounge suite behind it […] alternatively occupied by guests, editors taking a rest, or ambulant patients." Another deals with local traffic, the Huaxia Hotel where he recently moved ("one star, with almost constant electricity but no water"), and a description of the workshop of his bicycle repairman.

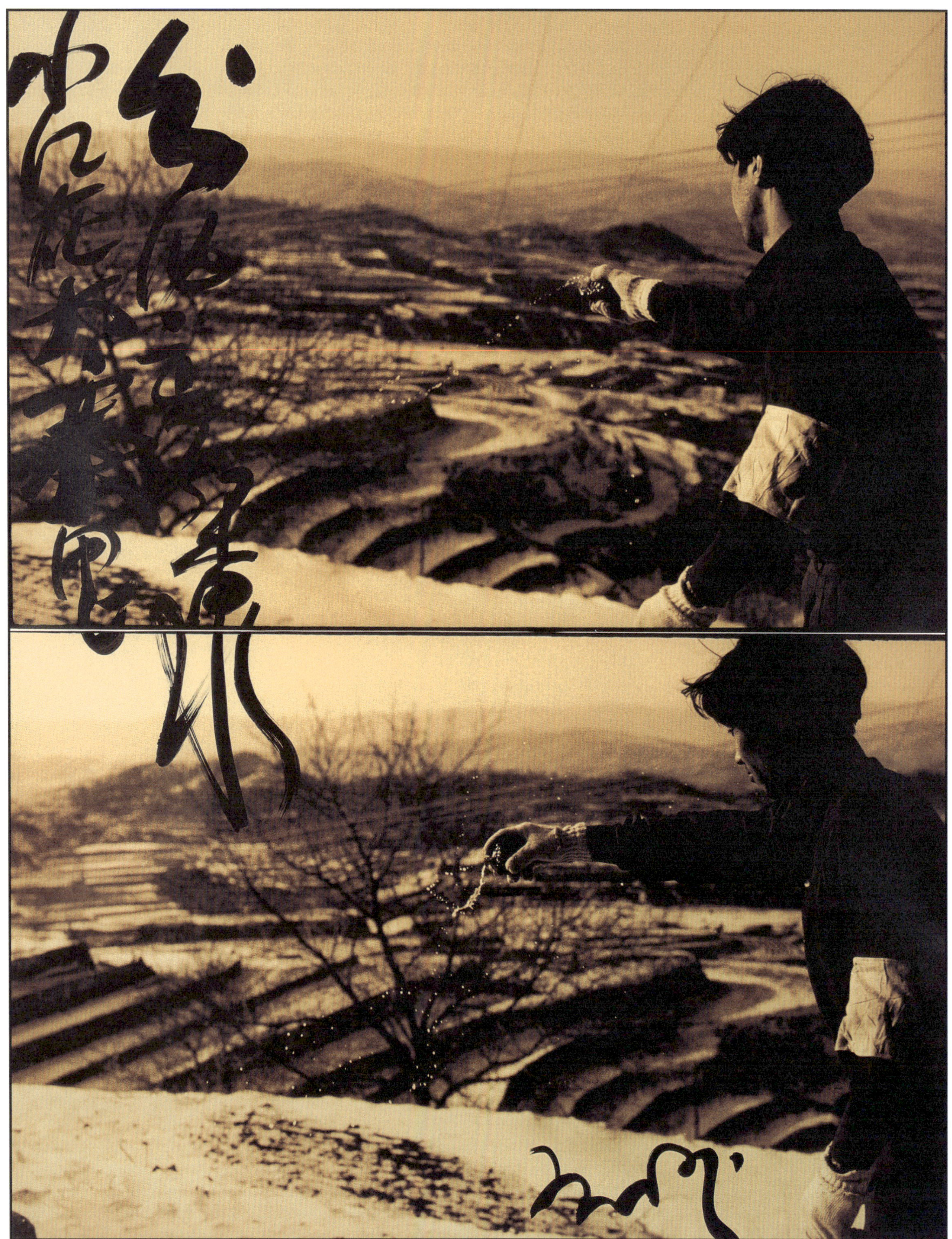

Liu Anping, *The Last Rumour of the Year 1991*, two photographs, calligraphy, 1991, private coll.

one attached, I have decided after much deliberation, to remove the worst horrors: [Liu] Anping's dreams, which he casually mentions from time to time, always ending in roaring laughter.

HvD, letter to Ernst Dinkla, Beijing, 29 June 1993

In Spring 1993, van Dijk reconnects with artist Liu Anping after running into him on the street in Beijing, and their stormy relationship. They know each other from the Zhejiang Academy, where they met in 1987. After the Tiananmen Square tragedy, Liu serves one year of jail time for counter-revolutionary activities. He subsequently moves to Beijing, where he tries to make a living without a residence permit. He adopts the nickname *Xiao Hong*, Young Red. When he meets van Dijk again in Beijing, Liu has just undertaken an action in the famous model farming commune of Dazhai, spraying perfume across the village. He shows van Dijk his photos of the action. Van Dijk proposes to pay Liu to enlarge them, which he will then sell in an edition of twenty. Van Dijk himself buys one of these works and does not take a cut of the profits. This is arguably the first time a work of action art is sold in China.

One of his rare preserved diary entries, dated 30 June 1993, shows that van Dijk has many ideas about setting up a contemporary art magazine and how to run it:

22—Leng Lin, today the president of Pace Gallery Beijing and Hong Kong, then a promising young art critic in Beijing.

I met Leng Lin[22] this morning. We'd been introduced earlier by [Zhao] Bandi at a party. According to Bandi, Leng Lin also has plans for a magazine, but in any case, he didn't mention them to me, although I did mention my own plans to him. I am looking for investors, need about 70,000.

– Under the cover of a research institute, literature and art. Nothing against the party nor against socialism. A newspaper print-style magazine, bi-weekly, print-run like that of Hanmo Yiyuan [Hanmo Art Center].
– Six editors with a rotating chief editor system and who are all payed a minimum (*gaofei*).
  Mainly young teachers, Beida [Peking University], Zhongyang [CAFA], no artists.
  Nobody makes a lot of money (everyone has another job).
  Revenue from advertisements and sales.
  Leng Lin did advertisements for *Meishu* magazine for a few years.
  He claims to be able to run the finances on his own.
  Sections: *wenxue* [literature], *meishu* [art], *huaju* [drama], *dianying* [cinema]. An ideal solution for the lack of communication between the art circles.
– Limited mission given the limited scale and production possibilities on newspaper.
  Short, clear style, correct use of language.
  Polemic themes such as:
  da Han zhuyi [Han nationalism]
  Responses to exhibitions abroad
  Critique of national art history and art criticism
  Exhibition calendar, events calendar
– In the Chinese art press, not artworks but people are judged.
  Section with debatable, grotesque statements from the art press.
  It seems humor is off limits when cultural programs and publications are concerned.
– I. Art
    Art by invitation (Wu Shanzhuan, Li Tianyuan, Geng Jianyi, Zhang Peili, Liu Anping).
    Introductions to artists and exhibitions.
– II. The Art World
    Statements, critiques, and polemics about phenomena in the art world (governmental cultural policy, arts institutions, magazines, art criticism, nationalism, supposed standards of the arts).
– Questions: How much advertisement space is needed for a commercially healthy enterprise? Division of pages between different disciplines? Color print? Management, responsibility?
– A publication which does not strive to establish or promote new trends or to explain or criticize existing ones in endless variations.
– Art, preferably original art, is more important than definitions of style.

— The exhibition calendar is more important than an article on post-modernism.
— Debate about concrete matters rather than abstractions.
— Artists and critics that speak of Chinese art cannot be considered as part of the modern art world. Modern art is an individual expression that doesn't care about which national or theoretical realm it belongs to.

In August 1993, van Dijk publishes "Double Standards," a satirical essay commissioned by his friends from *Daglicht*, on the "lugubrious world of cultural exchangers, art managers, and third-world specialists." Van Dijk categorizes the latter as "Interior Decorators, Charwomen, Conspirators, Prophets of Doom, and Sensation Mongers." It seems that he has gathered all his observations and analyses from the past years, elaborately recorded in his letters, into one sharp critique of global thinking. After praising the modest professionalism of sinologists, curators (such as David Elliott, whom he labels a Conspirator) and exhibitions (such as *Magiciens de la terre*) are examined and found wanting. The essay concludes:

> Why for God's sake is rationalism always identified with "the Western world" and everything else is labeled irrational, emotional, and mystical? China and Japan are nations where in the last fifty years the role of religion has grown increasingly smaller than in Western Europe. Identical rationalistic and philosophical trends developed simultaneously in China, India, and Greece between the fifth and third centuries. At that time, both China and India knew linguistic philosophers, sophists, and political realists, and nowadays their populations and the white race are no different from each other. Customs, language, history, and environment may differ, but they are different in Friesland and Limburg, too.
> Pictures of the most horrendous torture ever thought of by mankind, the crucifixion, are spread all over Europe, but the first documentaries on the war in the former Yugoslavia were made palatable by adding the phrase "Asian cruelty."
> **HvD, "Double Standards," in *Dossier hond & hamer. Art in Cultural Transmission*, Grafisch Atelier Daglicht, Eindhoven, 1993**

In a sign of how important of a bridge he has become between China and the West, he is tasked with guiding Andrew Solomon around the Chinese art world, which he writes about in two letters:

> Back for two days from a week-long paid trip to Shanghai and Hangzhou with writer-journalist for the *New York Times*, Andrew Solomon. [...] We have to be back in Beijing because Gilbert & George opened their big exhibition in the National Art Gallery—Andrew, 28 years, all neat and tidy from Yale, has had a thing for them since their show in Moscow, where he documented the doings of the local avant-garde for five years.
> For a payment of twenty-five thousand dollars, G & G were allowed to hang their products, some sixty works undermining family and politics in big format made after 1990—the exhibition was shown in Australia under the title "democratic images"—in this country of half a billion merciless boys. They didn't mind paying up. They were happy and content, so much so that they declared, amidst officials who were at least as content, that "China is a country full of good-looking people, China should rule the world." Better them than me.
> English humor is not instantly catching on among the intelligentsia here; "two wooden blocks" was the summation, among general approval. In reverse, the earnest question from several interested parties—which of the two played the male and which the female—didn't get across very well. G & G in unison accused the poor translator of scandalmongering, even though she had tried in vain to convince the Chinese side that if things were so clear-cut, the gentlemen probably wouldn't be homosexual.
> **HvD, letter to Ernst Dinkla, Beijing, 6 September 1993**

I just returned from Shanghai and Hangzhou, accompanying Andrew Solomon from the *New York Times* on this trip. Quite a nice young man. [...] I finally had the chance to visit Zhou Tiehai and his partner Yang Xu (the Shanghai Kreuzberger). You will see it in the *New York Times*, a delightful revolutionary couple. Andrew, though he doesn't bat for the other team, was instantly taken with their appearance: both in stylish, black Western suits, so that they can, as they explained, prepare their plans inconspicuously in the new capitalist China, namely the return of the Cultural Revolution. I suspect nostalgia for this period will be the leitmotif of Andrew's essay. Artists and intellectuals often voice such sentiments: usually it is just immature or plain stupid, but these two guys from Shanghai do something more interesting with it, and not without humor. [...] Andrew will return tomorrow. He must have interviewed at least sixty people during his three weeks here. The interviews were always one-on-one. Constant translating for five hours a day has been very tiring for me, not only because of his Yale English, but also because some artists would suddenly refuse to give certain answers. Finally, there will be an international audience for what the artists are saying.

HvD, letter to Andreas Schmid, Beijing, 9 September 1993

Little progress in all of my projects. A gallery is complicated, as they are all focused on making money fast, and because a gallery for modern art is still an unknown phenomenon here. Still, I believe it can be done. My rather detailed plan for a screen-print studio has been accepted by the school, but regarding conditions such as location, staff, visa, et cetera, I hope to have more clarity soon. It's going to be exciting.

HvD, letter to Andreas Schmid, Beijing, 14 September 1993

Fall 1993

Finding Hanmo

All the while, van Dijk has been trying to find an affordable apartment and gallery office. Rents have risen to New York levels: three hundred thousand kuai for fifty square meters a year. He manages to find several places but is repeatedly chased away by the police, often following calls made by suspicious neighbors. Finally, through Gu Dexin, van Dijk meets the artist Li Yongbin and rents a room in his apartment. His fax address remains with Michaela Raab at the Friendship Hotel.

On 8 November 1993, he sends one of his "special texts" to Jeroen Vinken and Ernst Dinkla:

About ten years ago, I bought a book by Dr. Gustav Ecke, a missionary [sic] in Hong Kong around the turn of the century who in his spare time became a connoisseur of Ming Dynasty furniture. Now I live in the capital of the current dynasty in the "Lake of Unity" [*Tuanjiehu*] area, South Neighborhood 3, Block 2, Unit No. 3, Apartment No. 601. Ecke and I never foresaw this; you can't plan such a thing.

I have rented a room from Li Yongbin, an artist who was a painter until two years ago. I had seen his work once, but that wasn't the reason I looked him up; a friend introduced me. The three of us inspected a room of a decent flat on the sixth floor. There was not much to see besides an extraordinarily clean concrete floor. We had tea after that. I liked what I saw, but Gu warned me about the weekly meetings organized by Yongbin, which ended quite loudly most of the time. Neither Yongbin nor Gu nor others of their circle had regular work, and I feared they were secretly debating art. Nevertheless, that turned out not to be as bad as expected. "You know," said Gu, "that you are dealing with the dregs of society. On Friday we discuss street robbery, and, by the way, as you already decided to take the room, the toilet is in the building across the street on the third floor...," Gu tried.

After Yongbin gave up painting, he dipped several pairs of pants in polyester. He displayed them, after hardening, in a room with crazy floral wallpaper, taking photos of them. So far that's all he has done. He sometimes reluctantly shows photos of this installation. It's about material expression, he's willing to admit.

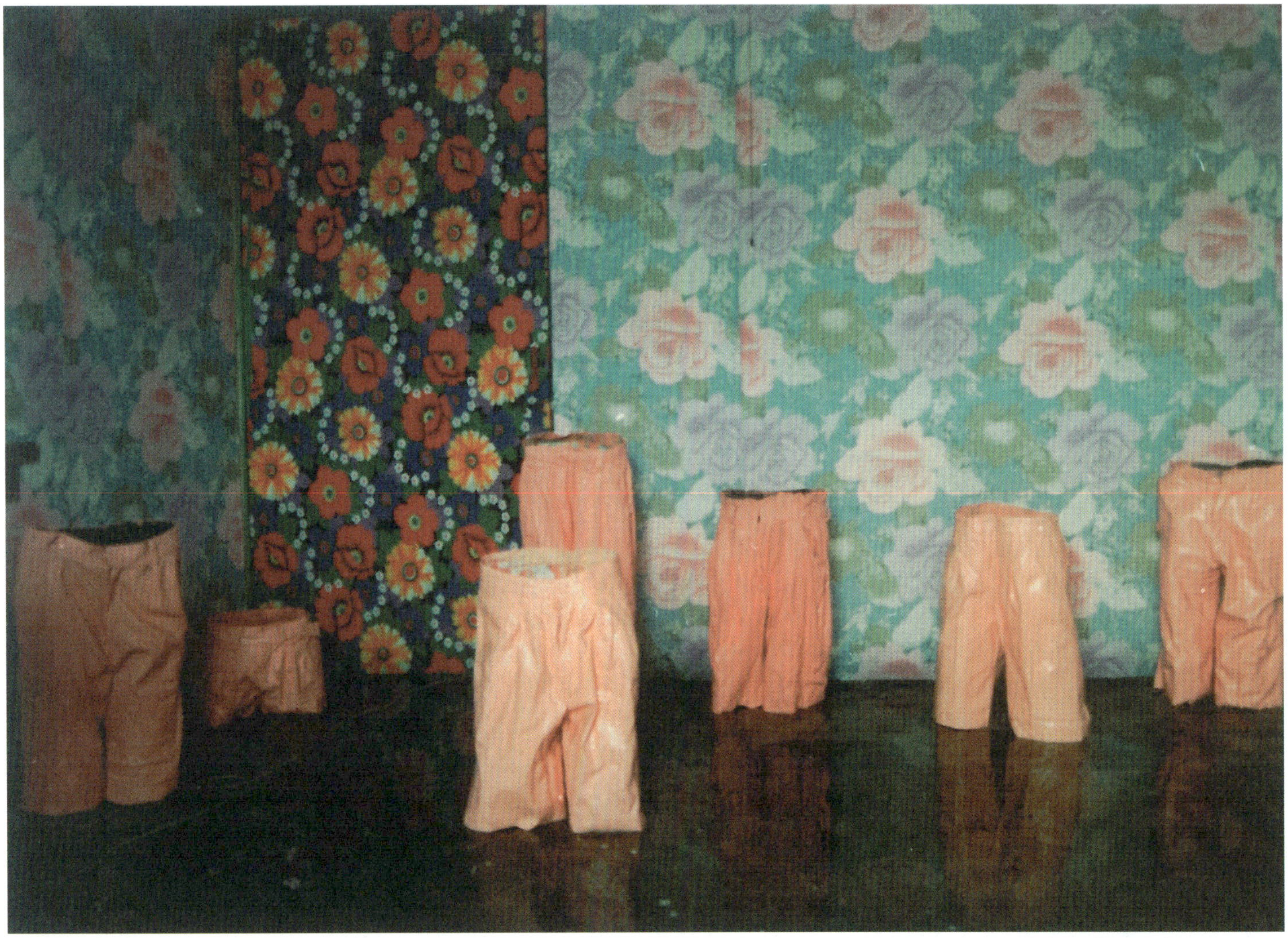

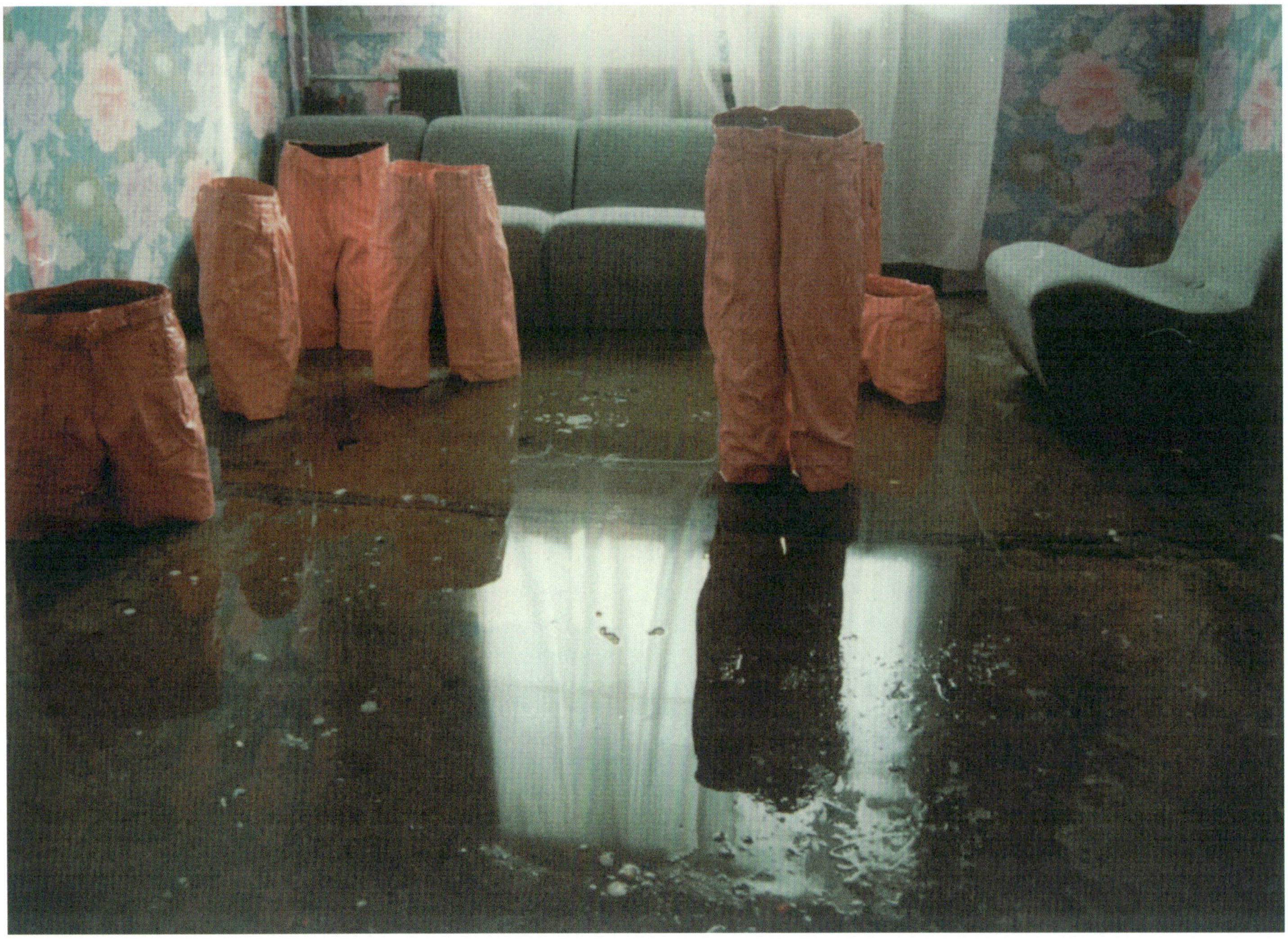

The floral wallpaper remains. He now lives and sleeps in there, after I moved into the somewhat smaller front room facing the street. We share a toilet-washroom, a hall with a fridge topped by a telephone, a TV, and a kitchen. We don't have a shower or warm water. The squat toilet is beside a rinse tank equipped with a tap, and functions as a drain. No need to be careful with water, the floor is carefully leveled concrete and well molded.
For a few days, just before I came back from a trip down south, Yongbin shared his room with a human figure spread out on the floor, made of earth and dressed in a shirt. Every day he photographs the kernels of corn he sowed into it, which are now sprouting. The stalks grow about one and a half centimeters a day, and they are already bulging through the buttonholes of the shirt.
No longer carefully separated from other citizens like a criminal, with obligatory registration formalities for anyone who takes the risk to visit, no longer having to ask for the key to your room, no longer having to be in before twelve at night.

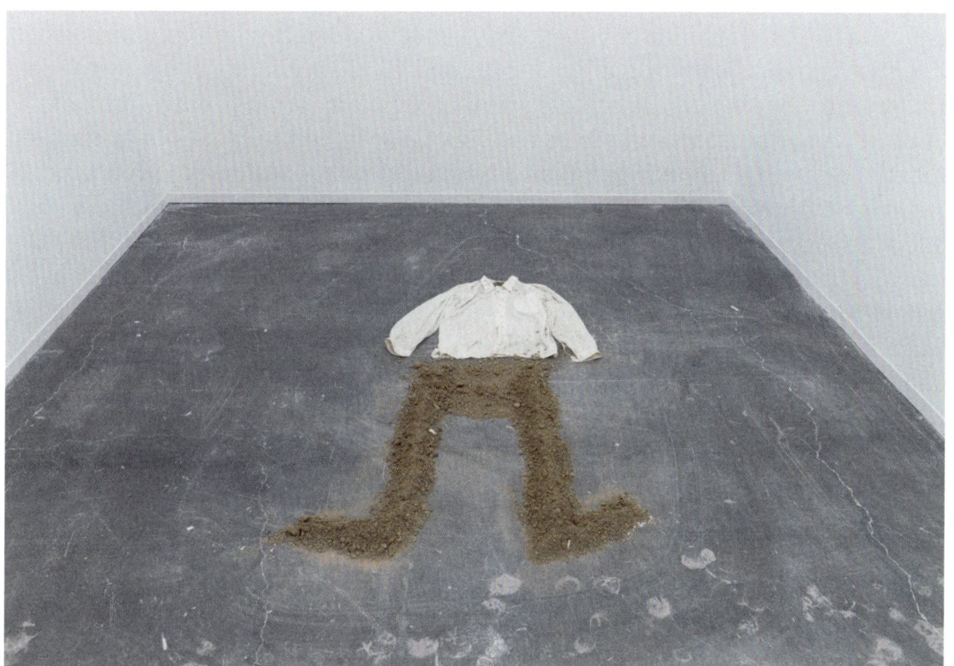

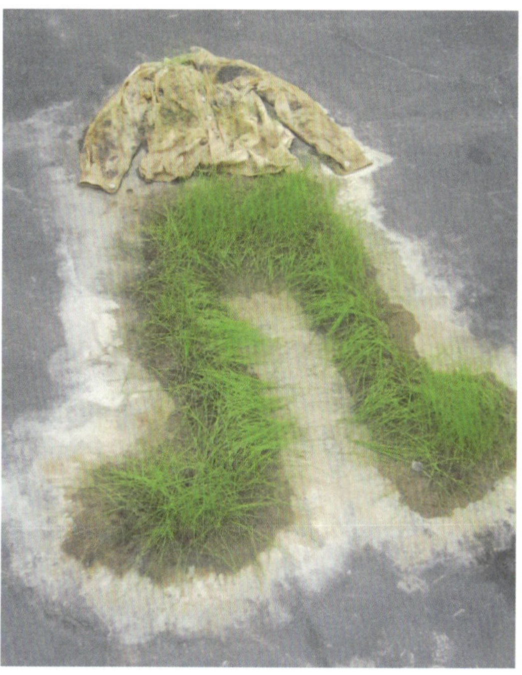

Li Yongbin, *Untitled*, dirt, seeds, water, 1993, reconstructed for *Hans van Dijk: 5000 Names*, UCCA, Beijing, 2014; left: exhibition view on the opening day, and right: four weeks later, photos courtesy UCCA, Beijing. Opposite page: Li Yongbin, *Untitled*, polyester, installation in his apartment, Beijing, 1993, photo courtesy Li Yongbin

It took half a year before anyone was found who dared undertake such an experiment with me. Several rooms were available, but every time my non-Asian appearance came up with the candidate letter, it was over. Even when it became clear that a law had been issued a year ago that made it legal for foreigners to mingle with the population after registration at the police station, distrust prevailed in this budding constitutional state. Just to sort this out, and whether it was also applicable to the area where the empty room was located, could be suspicious. After that, the fuss about getting the necessary forms, which aren't obtainable everywhere, of course, and the whining about what is this man doing here and what is that to you, how when and where did you make his acquaintance, through whom, et cetera.
The difference with Yongbin is that he and the local police chief know each other. "It was arranged in a jiffy," he said. "Why do you come to tell me this, Yongbin?" "Well, it's a foreigner." "That's not possible." "I heard there was an arrangement last year that makes it legal for foreigners after registering here." "Ok, so it's possible." "When can I come by with him for the legal formalities?" "It's fine."

HvD, letter to his friends in the Netherlands, Beijing, 8 November 1993

Several artists recall Li and van Dijk's household at the time. Li's apartment—a gift from his parents—is a very sober place; the walls and floors are bare concrete. Van Dijk and Li are extremely poor. There generally is one egg in the fridge, which belongs to Hans, and one yoghurt (a tomato in other accounts), which belongs to Li. To support the latter, some of Li's friends ask him to paint a big, colorful impressionistic landscape as an advertisement for Chen Shaoping's (a member of Xin Kedu) wife's business. Li says that of course he could do that. He made the impressionist landscape, but in black and white.

Letter to Ernst Dinkla, Beijing, 29 November 1993:

> [...] The school is a never-ending story. [...] At the request of Mr. Tu, the head of the school, I made a detailed bilingual plan for the lay-out, management, and finances of a silk-screen workshop. This led to two teachers with fifteen thousand kuai in their pockets taking off for a silk-screen fair somewhere in the north, and that was it.
> After that, I had to help a Russian photographer for the *New York Times* [Gueorgui Pinkhassov] get started, and two photographers from Hamburg [Thomas Fuesser and a colleague], who are trying right now to sell their photos and my text to *Der Stern*. I was able to publish two texts of mine about art and the art world in two local magazines. [...]
> Now I am busy with Mr. Tu getting my visa extended. [...] I am also trying through the local Holiday Inn. They have a gallery [...], and its boss is the only one of the growing number of gallery owners I visited who is not blemished by commercialism. Introduced by the Goethe Institute, I can now act as an advisor and make exhibition proposals. [...]
> When I was in Eindhoven the last time, you made me an offer that in case of a gallery, you could lend me ten thousand, and invest another ten thousand. [...] I would like to know whether your offer is still in full effect. To give you an impression of what it might be about: there are quite a lot of exhibition spaces in Beijing functioning under the name Gallery. I visited several of those to see whether they might be up for rent for a year, for instance. [...]
> After having excluded several options, [...] I am now working on two possibilities:
> The first is a space of 120 sq.m., second floor, in a former century-old consulate building, which a software firm has now rented. They are called Hanmo; the boss is a thirty-year-old art historian who currently puts eight spacious studios—the entire floor measures 3,000 square meters—at the disposition of young artists in exchange for one painting a year. It will take another two years before the building is torn down. As they move to a new housing estate, he puts the empty spaces at the service of the arts. It has to become an Art Center with its own newspaper, an artist databank, and an exhibition space. The newspaper has appeared twice; he has made quite some progress with the databank. Plans for the exhibition space excel in lack of clarity. I now try to convince him that within such a center, a professionally conducted, independent gallery for contemporary art is something different from the exhibition space he has been planning, but may very well function by attracting a new audience. It is different from what he has been imagining. Since his business success, he is accustomed to putting the name Hanmo all over his initiatives.

A fragment from an unpublished text written by van Dijk for the German magazine *Der Stern* that fall:

> The Beijing art scene is booming. It abounds with initiatives and plans for art centers, galleries, art publishers, and art fairs. New glossy art magazines appear: news, gossip, conflicts, and especially the extraordinarily high prices at which recent sales to foreigners have been made. It all feeds into a constant state of excitement. For a couple of years, artists from across the country flocked to the capital so that by now, each province and large city is represented by its most entrepreneurial outsiders. But how does an artist really survive in a society where modern art has just begun its own history, the government closes down exhibitions at random, there still is no museum of modern art, galleries barely play any role of importance, official art magazines have all the charm of a hardware catalogue, and 95 percent of the collectors and art lovers are foreigners?

On 13 December 1993, van Dijk sends a long letter to Ernst Dinkla that includes a detailed business plan in two parts: setting up a gallery in Beijing, and setting up a shareholders' company in Hong Kong. Van Dijk announces that he can now produce a realistic business proposal for his gallery in Beijing. With Hanmo Art Center, he has found a suitable gallery space situated in a small, one-story red brick building just inside the second ring road, with a metro station just half a kilometer away. The building has no running water, but there is electricity and a phone line. The façade of what van Dijk now names the New Amsterdam Gallery ("I've come up with good names before, so trust me when I say that this name will arouse interest in both Amsterdam and New York and confusion in China at the very least") is to become an artwork by artist Ni Haifeng.

> I suddenly had a terrifying vision of a perfect gallery without any art, so I started calling Guangzhou, Shanghai, and Hangzhou, and checked the willingness of artists in Beijing. The first exhibition should be a sort of introduction and give a face to the gallery. After that, I want to present one or two works by ca. ten artists. I am now sure of the participation of the most important artists. [...]
> For sales, 30 to 35% is the common brokerage for exhibited works, 20 to 25% if the work is sold straight out of storage. There are different ways of making a deal with the artist:
>
> 1. Agreeing on a selling price together and sticking to it.
> 2. Agreeing on a minimum selling price together, and whatever more the gallery manages to sell for is split following the established percentage.
> 3. Rather common here: the amount a gallerist manages to make on top of the agreed upon price with the artist, goes to the gallerist alone. I am currently most drawn to option 2.
>
> I didn't compile the enclosed business plan in a day, but I hope to hear from you very soon, as there are other competitors on the horizon. It would be good were we to open in February for Chinese New Year."
>
> **HvD, letter to Ernst Dinkla, Beijing, 13 December 1993**

In the business plan, he sums up the artists who agree to exhibit with him: Yu Youhan, Fang Lijun, Zhang Peili, Geng Jianyi, four painters from Guangzhou and Beijing, and two printmakers from Beijing. Unfortunately, due to a failing fax service, Dinkla receives the letter and business plan only in February 1994.

Catching news of van Dijk's progress with his gallery, Ding Yi writes:

> Dear Hans,
> Mr. Yu Youhan and Bo Xiaobo both have told me that you have made progress in opening a gallery in Beijing. Finally, China is about to have its first avant-garde gallery, which really excites us!
> Mr. Yu also passed onto me that I should send you some pictures of my recent works, so I selected a few photos of my paintings, including two of my most recent works.
> For almost a month, I have tried to paint on untreated canvas with charcoal and chalk, because I feel they are similar in quality and are both related to nature, which is quite interesting. Also, it is a challenge to paint with such materials, because most people may feel reluctant to collect these kinds of pieces, and I have to attract them with the content and quality of my work.
> This month, I rented a room next to my apartment, which is almost as big as my present one. Now I have a specific room for my studio. My working environment is better.
> Well, that's all I can think of for now. I will call you later.
> I wish you success in your career.
> Ding Yi
>
> **Ding Yi, letter to HvD, Shanghai, 14 December 1993**

Letter to Andreas Schmid, Beijing, 19 December 1993:

> You understand that the Arts and Crafts School has, to this day—after nine months—not finished anything, which rather decimates my hope that I will ever be able to start something here.
> However, I'm making progress with the gallery. I'm now waiting for an agreement with one of the investors after he has studied my business plan for the first year, and for a legal solution applied for by a Chinese-Japanese company at the ministry here. "New Amsterdam Gallery" (in Beijing), or something like it.

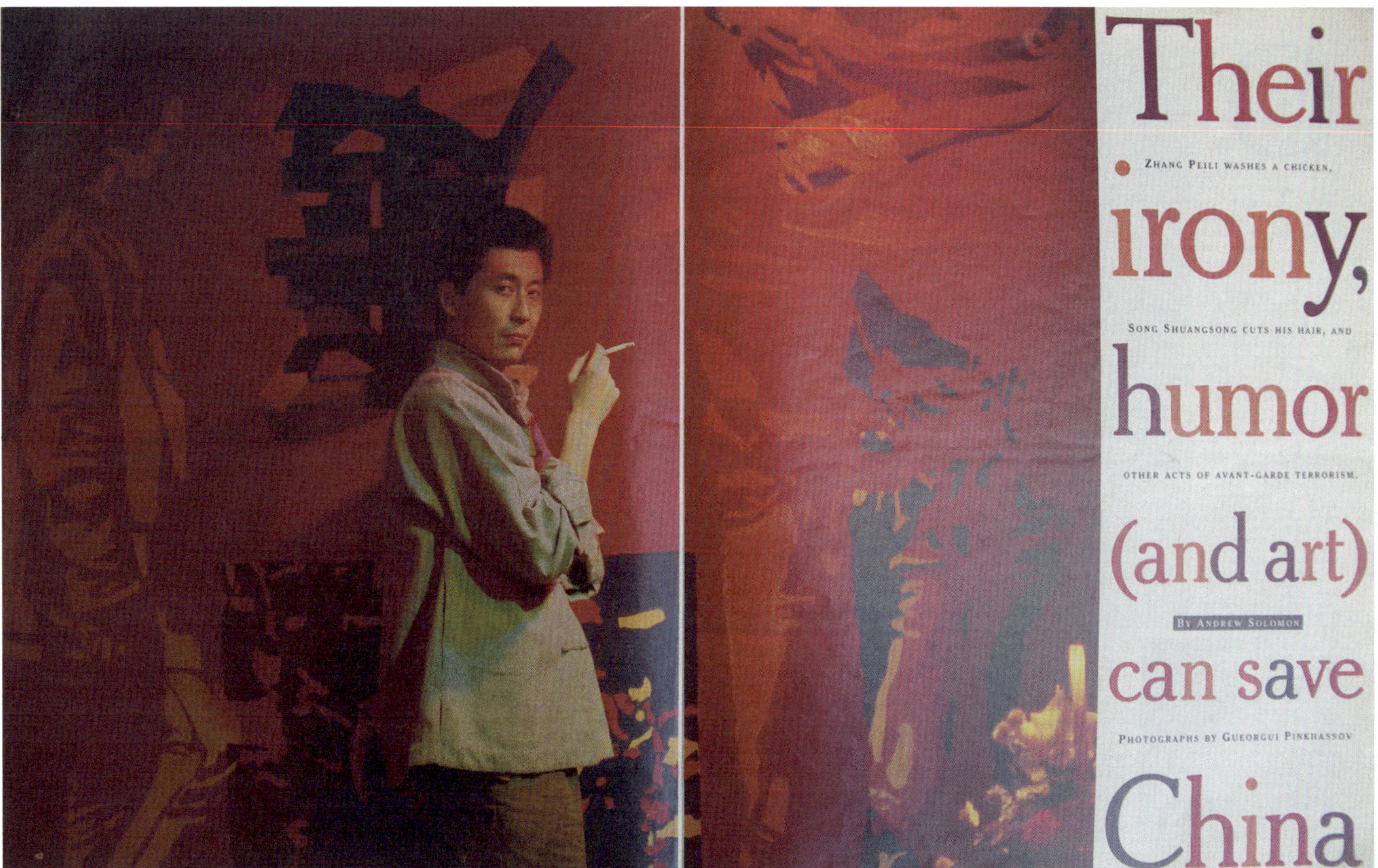

Their irony,

Zhang Peili washes a chicken, Song Shuangsong cuts his hair, and other acts of avant-garde terrorism.

humor (and art) can save China

By Andrew Solomon

Photographs by Gueorgui Pinkhassov

The New York Times Magazine, 19 December 1993, photo of Geng Jianyi on a spread for Andrew Solomon's article *Their Irony, Humor (and Art) Can Save China*

On 19 December 1993, following his visit to China, Andrew Solomon publishes "Their Irony, Humor (and Art) Can Save China," his famous article with Gueorgui Pinkhassov's award-winning photographs, in the *New York Times Magazine*. For many artists mentioned, it marks the beginning of recognition and exhibitions abroad. Solomon and van Dijk keep up a correspondence for some time.

Around this time, van Dijk receives a message that his father, who suffers from a heart condition, has fallen seriously ill. He rushes to the Netherlands and arrives in Deventer just in time to see his father before he dies.

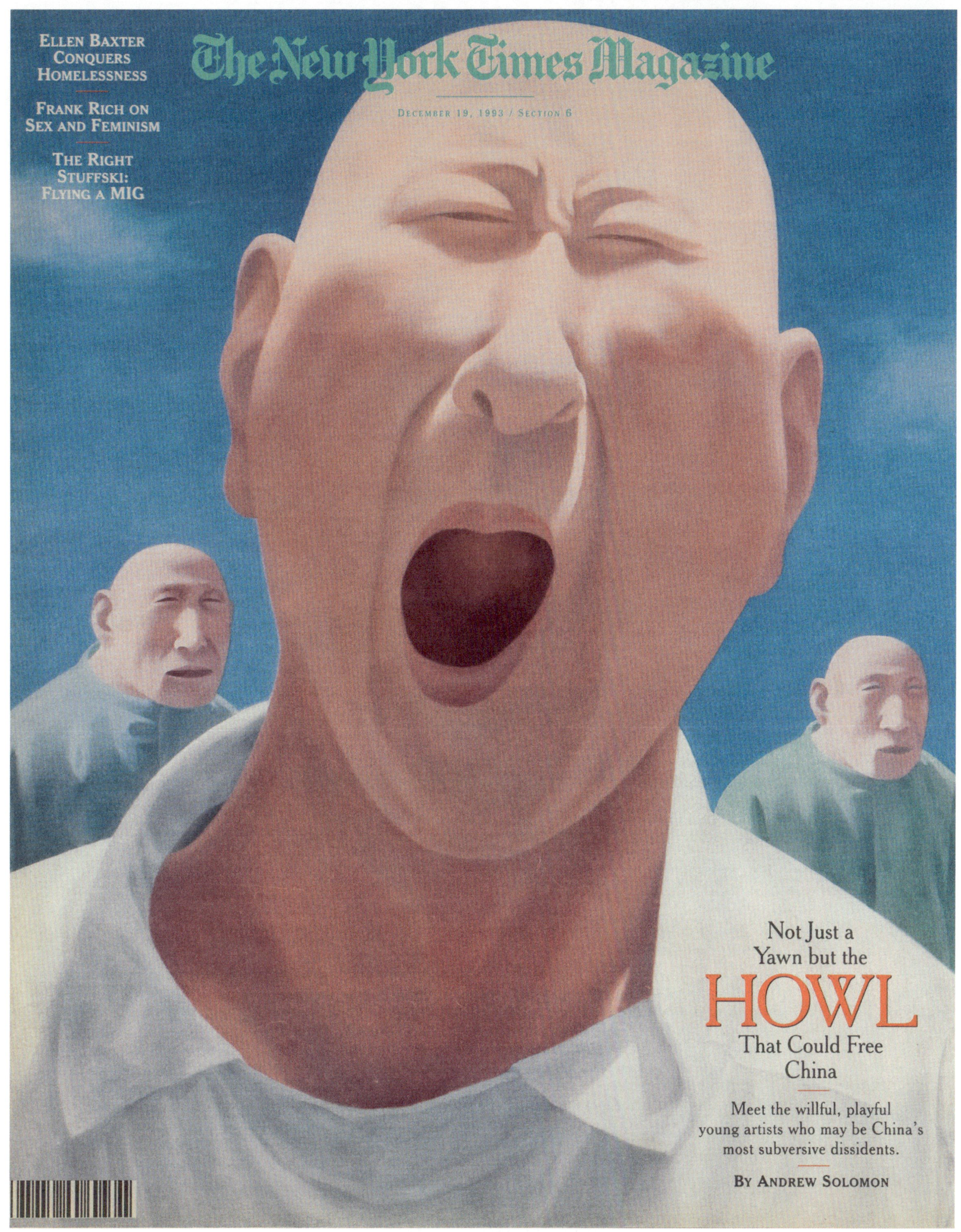

"Not Just a Yawn but the HOWL That Could Free China", cover of *The New York Times Magazine*, 19 December 1993, featuring Andrew Solomon's article *Their Irony, Humor (and Art) Can Save China*; the cover image is a detail from Fang Lijun's *Series 2, No. 2*, 1991–92

Establishing the New Amsterdam Art Consultancy (NAAC)
Beijing, 1994–1995

Hans was very independent. He was not influenced by the Chinese government nor by art critics like Li Xianting. He tried to give every independent artist a chance, not just artists who worked in one style or in a group.

Zhao Bandi

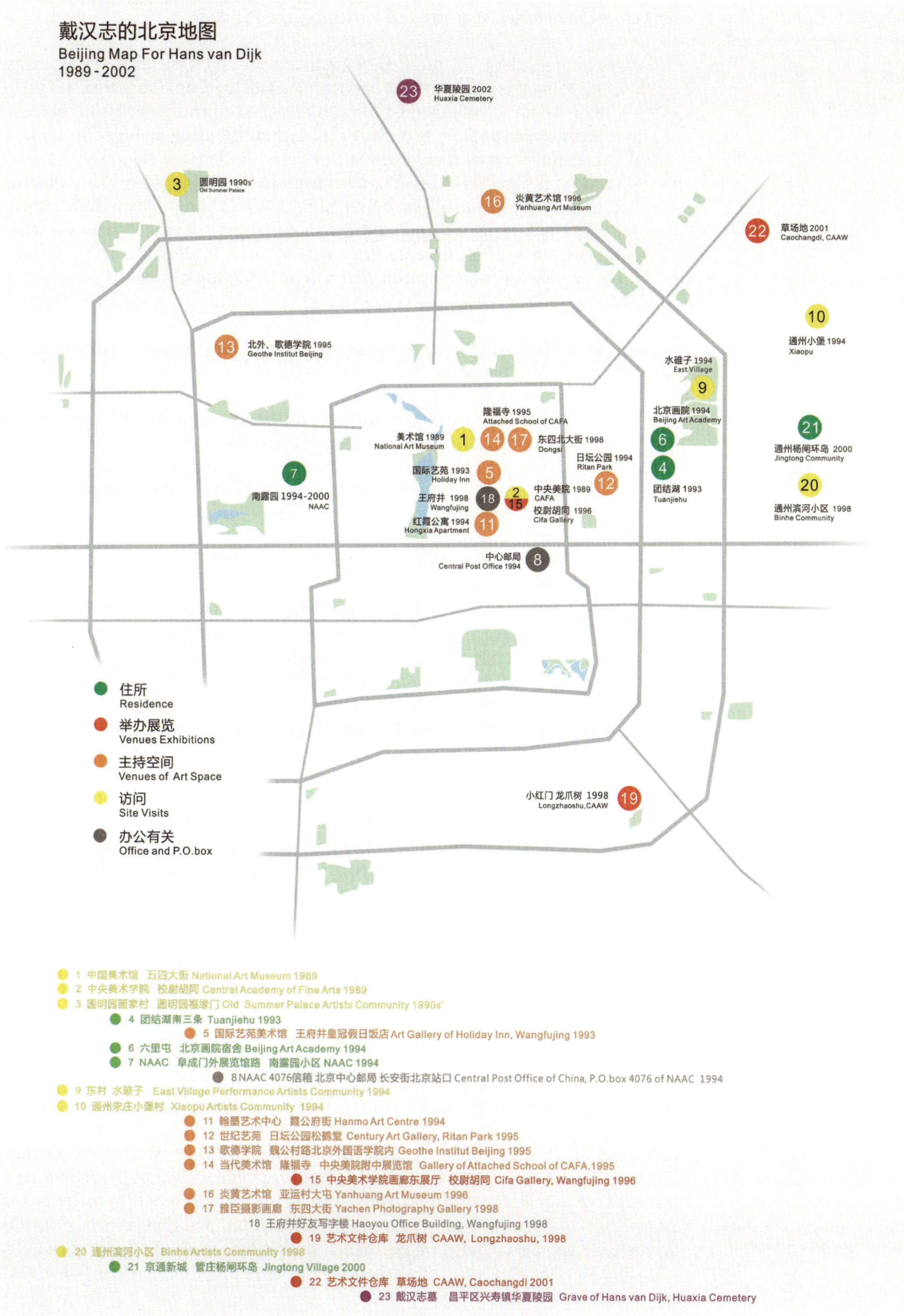

Zhang Li, *Beijing Map for Hans van Dijk. 1989–2002*, 2014

Just before Chinese New Year, van Dijk writes to Jeroen Vinken:

> My future gallery will be called New Amsterdam, and is legally the representative office of my Hong Kong firm Artfame Development Ltd. That name appeared on a list of three hundred empty Public Limited Companies offered by a firm specializing in these matters. Everything can be done by phone or fax, including buying nominee directors, and ditto shareholders, secretaries, et cetera. […]
> I no longer have any hopes for a silk-screen studio at the Academy here after the director disappeared in hospital with a liver ailment. After I have been given the run-around for a year, he plays this trick on me. I already had second thoughts about the school itself because he was the only enterprising spirit there. To work there would have made me completely dependent on him. And now he's in hospital.
>
> HvD, letter to Jeroen Vinken, Beijing, 3 February 1994

In a letter to Andreas Schmid from August, he explains how the first half of 1994 brought all sorts of big and small disasters:

> First, there were these continuous visa problems, because the Arts and Crafts School did nothing—later I understood that money was expected from me, and not just a little. Before, it was possible to get a three-month extension in Hong Kong, and then another four weeks in Beijing. Now they've changed that to two months and two weeks.
> Li Yongbin desperately needed the room where I was staying back, and in between all this Fang Lijun suddenly gets red-eyed and accuses me of having an affair with Michaela [Raab]. Michaela is panicking and wants to break off all contact for the time being—her first marriage ended similarly. For me, it means the loss of a reliable postal and fax address, and apart from that, we were cooperating on a few things [Michaela is a shareholder and board member of Artfame]. Fang Lijun knows better of course, but according to Chinese custom, we are obligated to one another [because van Dijk showed Fang Lijun's works in *China Avant-garde*]. After his international fame, and because I'm close by, he found something that will liberate him.
> Li Xianting is not so happy with what I've been doing with visitors from abroad, and he complains that he has always been exploited. My third bike was stolen, and I missed a fax at my new fax number in which my bank in Hong Kong informed me that I have a different account number than the one I was promised. One or two worried investors wonder why nothing is happening, and therefore hold onto their money a little longer. Between expensive trips to Hong Kong, I'm wasting horrible amounts of time looking at rental apartments and attempting to convince their owners that I'm not at all dangerous, but also not rich. It took three months until I found, via several attempts and with the help of various people, something for 2,000 kuai, then moved. The next day, Friday the 13th, the *gongan* [public security] woke me up and gave me three days' notice to find something else. That, too, worked out (in three months). Greetings, Hans
>
> HvD, letter to Andreas Schmid, Beijing, 4 August 1994

During these difficult times, van Dijk is nonetheless able to achieve his most important objectives: to set up a gallery and organize his first exhibitions, accompanied by professional mailings and catalogues. He writes a final business plan, which secures him Ernst Dinkla's promised loans. As he has lost his fax and postal address, Michael Kahn-Ackermann kindly puts his private fax at van Dijk's disposal. Letters are to be sent to the Goethe Institute. On 18 March 1994, van Dijk founds Artfame Development Ltd., based in Hong Kong, which provides the legal framework for the gallery in Beijing. The company has its own capital with an HKD account for expenses and a USD savings account. The shareholders are van Dijk, who holds the majority of shares, Sir Peter van Leeuwen, Michaela Raab, Frank Suffa-Friedel,[1] and Ernst Dinkla. A shareholders' agreement dated 23 March 1994 states that there can be no expectation of profit within the first two years. Van Dijk now has enough money to rent an exhibition space at Hanmo Art Center.

1—A friend of Jochen Noth working in Beijing as a freelance travel agent.

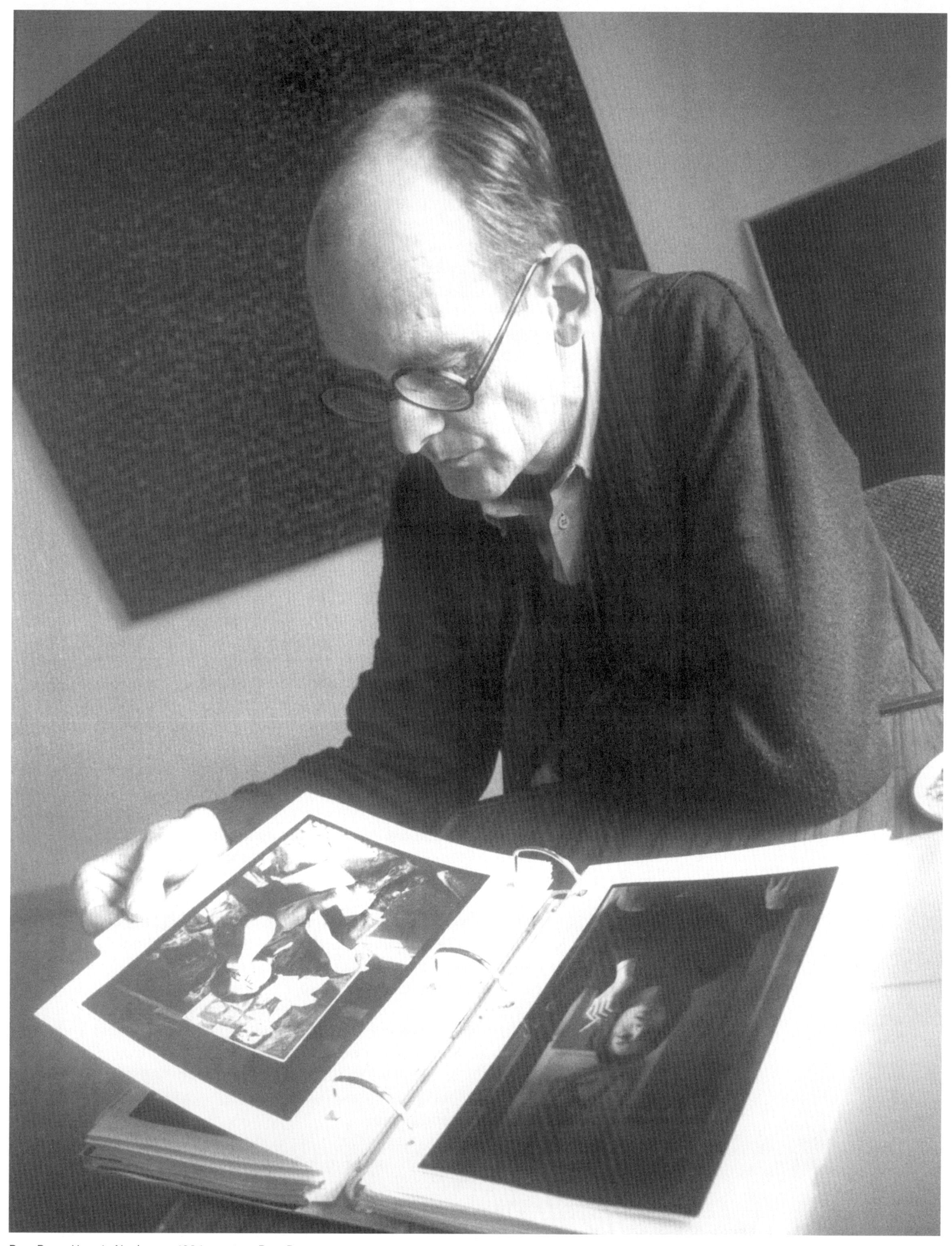

RongRong, *Hans in Nanluyuan*, 1994, courtesy RongRong

> Yesterday I agreed with the owner of the gallery space on a rental contract for three years. Next Wednesday, in my absence, Liu Anping will collect the keys, and today I did a first round of inspections with the contractor for the renovation. If all goes well, we can start mid-May.
> The first exhibition will be a representative one, with contributions by about twelve artists varying from romantically painted furniture by Zhao Bandi to a "Reassuring Action" by Zhao Shaoruo on the opening day. Shaoruo has successfully held one of these actions before, at the first national art fair last year in Guangzhou. During the opening in Beijing, many uninvited artists, overlooked critics, and worried dealers will benefit from his reassurance.
> I will invite the most expensive, and as such, the emperor of the Chinese avant-garde, [...] master Wang Guangyi, whose work is featured on the cover of the catalogue of the Berlin show, to deliver a speech about "The Problem of Arts Education in the People's Republic of China." He uses such occasions to taunt the Beijing locals by presenting his academy (the one in Hangzhou) as the most important one. Furthermore, I want to invite the folk music band that, since the ban on fireworks, enlivens weddings and parties in the neighborhood. Anping—the jailbird I've written you about before—will cheer up the event with his full-on punk hairdo, the first ever in Beijing, and as such, the true embodiment of the avant-garde. I'll be in Hong Kong and Guangzhou until the 24th: visa, banking, Artfame, and visiting artists.
> P.S. The marriage [of Fang Lijun and Michaela Raab] seems to hold.
> **HvD, letter to Ernst Dinkla, Beijing, 17 April 1994**

Van Dijk first mentions the New Amsterdam Art Consultancy (NAAC) in a letter to Dinkla in late May 1994:

> For the past eight days, I have been visiting artists' studios with two German exhibition organizers. A lucrative assignment from them will follow.[2] Two weeks ago I took Günther Uecker, now 64 years old, on studio visits. We also browsed through my archive, for which he immediately knew potentially interested parties in France and Germany. He will present an installation here in September and was looking for a venue and Chinese colleagues to collaborate with, both of which I was able to provide. It will be a rather educational project by the Goethe Institute that I can attach my name to, my name being "New Amsterdam Art Consultancy."
> The studio visits went off without a hitch. Uecker [co-founder of the *zero* movement], who is still teaching in Düsseldorf [...], proved to be an amiable character with so much educational experience that the visits to very different artists led to much enthusiasm—despite the confusing contributions by the Goethe Institute interpreter. Our visit to the artist collective *Xin Kedu* [New Measurement Group] proved to be equally successful.
> [...] A collaborative exhibition with Uecker was soon a fact, and I—naively—hoped to organize it at the Hanmo Art Center. The plan was coordinated through the Goethe Institute after receiving an affirmative message from the [Chinese] Ministry of Culture regarding the collaborative exhibition. In the end, the exhibition did not take place at all, as it was prevented by the Propaganda Department of the Party.
> A third NAAC activity is an exhibition of new work by Zhao Bandi. [...] I'm starting the program this way because of the exponential formalities of starting a gallery; an efficiently discriminatory legal system seems to prohibit foreign firms from setting up a representative office at a location of their choosing. This is what the World Trade Centers and Hiltons are for. This fact was unknown to the embassy and to my Belgian advisor.
> A foreigner setting up a gallery needs to file an official request with the Ministry of Culture, and, as such, nobody has ever done so.

2—A reference to the exhibition *Configura 2* in Erfurt, Germany, summer 1995.

To keep his clients, shareholders, and visitors informed, van Dijk regularly drafts bilingual (English-Chinese) overviews of NAAC's Chinese and international exhibitions and projects. The simple, photocopied lists are not just interesting historical records of van Dijk's achievements, they also reflect what he hoped to get done and what—for one reason or another—does not take place. According to van Dijk, he averages two successful projects out of three.

NEW AMSTERDAM ART CONSULTANCY

FINISHED AND PRESENT RELATED ACTIVITIES - 1993-1994

1. Organize visits in the Chinese artworld in Peking, Shanghai and Hangzhou for Jörg Immendorf (Hamburg), Günter Ücker (Düsseldorf), Andrew Solomon (New York Times), Thomas Füsser (Stern-Germany) (selected list).

2. Research and do curatorial work for the exhibition "Configura 2" Erfurt, Thüringen, Germany, June-September 1995.

3. Realize the exhibition "Horst Janssen" in cooperation with the Goethe Institut Peking, in the Gallery of the International Cultural Palace, Wangfujing, Beijing, April 1994.

4. Research and do curatorial work for the exhibition "Kleinplastik aus China, Süd Korea, Japan und Deutschland" (Small sculpture from China, South Korea, Japan and Germany) Stuttgart 1995, organized by the "Institut für Ausslandbeziehungen" (Institute for Foreign Relations) Stuttgart.

5. Organize the contemporary art exhibition of Zhao Bandi: "Moonflight" in cooperation with the Hanmo Art Centre, 26 June - 26 July at the Hanmo Art Centre, Peking.

6. Make preparations for the double-exhibition of Günter Ücker, German installation artist with the Chinese artgroup "New Measurement," and the related cultural program in cooperation with the Goethe Institut Beijing in the Hanmo Art Centre, September '94.

7. Research and select artists for the "Metropolis Culture Festival," organized by the Goethe Institute, Beijing autumn 1994.

SECOND HALF YEAR PROJECTED ACTIVITIES - 1994

8. Continue the above mentioned activities. (1, 2, 4, 6, 7)

9. Exhibitions in cooperation with the Hanmo Art Centre and in other locations in Peking. (i.e. the "Series Installation Exhibition" of the artists Li Yongbin, Gu Dexin and Ni Haifeng).

10. An Exhibition in cooperation with Red Gate Gallery, Peking of the artists Zhang Yajie and Wang Yigang

11. Open **NEW AMSTERDAM GALLERY**

    (NAG) September opening projected.

NEW AMSTERDAM ART CONSULTANCY P.O. BOX 4076 PEKING 100001 CHINA

a division of Artfame Development Limited, 801 Stanhope House, 738 King's Road, Honkong
Company number 417233 Bank: ABN-AMRO Bank 6099483 (HKD), 6099494 (USD)

NAAC, Finished and Present Related Activities, 1993–94, private coll.

Meanwhile, he does everything he can to make some money. Kahn-Ackermann supports him by inviting him to curate or assist with the occasional exhibition for the Goethe Institute. He also brings him in contact with Alexander Tolnay, who works for the Institute for Foreign Cultural Relations in Stuttgart, and regularly accompanies important visitors to China. For the next two years, many of NAAC's activities abroad spring from these contacts.

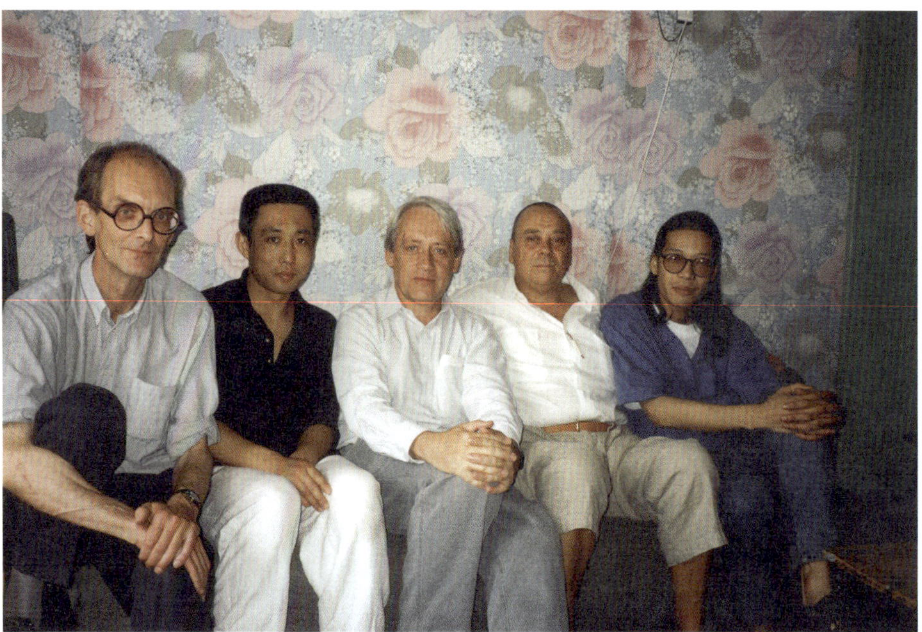

Left to right: Hans van Dijk, Li Yongbin, Alexander Tolnay, Günther Uecker, Ni Haifeng, in Li Yongbin's home, Beijing, 1994, private coll.

Van Dijk is also hiring staff: a secretary, Sui Hong, whom Andrew Solomon recommended; Jule Noth, a sinologist (and the daughter of Jochen Noth) who runs most of the contacts in Germany; and former art student Zhang Li, who will stay with him through 1996. In July 1995, he sends his Dutch friends the catalogues and invitations for all his NAAC projects to date, accompanied by a long letter of short, humorous sketches, which he calls "Fiercely Realistic Footnotes": explanations of and witty asides to his activities since his return to China. They include descriptions of his staff, foreign visitors, and NAAC projects.

> The Main Characters:
> Zhang Li is about twenty-five years old and graduated in 1992 with a degree in art history from the Central Academy of Fine Arts. Ever since, he has been performing the odd job here and there for different galleries. As he was looking for work, he admitted to a flaw that was holding him back: "Hans, I often don't know what to say, so in the end I just keep silent." I thought we could live with that. In contrast to other graduates, Zhang Li is not easily discouraged by rather unexciting jobs and chores and does not aim to make a lot of money in a small amount of time: I had to threaten to fire him before he would accept a raise. Just like me, he insists on working seven days a week and has learned so much over the past year that it felt necessary to fax him: "Zhang Li, I am so delighted that everything runs so smoothly in my absence, but at the same time I am worried because everything runs so smoothly in my absence."
> Jule Noth is the same age as Zhang Li and the daughter of Jochen, a friend and fellow "curator" of the Berlin exhibition in 1993. She was a frail girl who proved able to write such caustic business letters that I was happy never to be on the receiving end.
> The local artists (who are used to an even greater inequality between men and women than in the West) had to get used to her as well: whenever they requested to speak to me directly, Jule would firmly explain that I was caught up in other business and that she too had little time for the young man in question. She was contributing to several projects—in particular the German projects—and did so in an increasingly independent way.
> **HvD, letter to his friends in the Netherlands, Beijing, 9 July 1995**

26 June – 26 July 1994 *Zhao Bandi: Moonflight*
Hanmo Art Center, Beijing

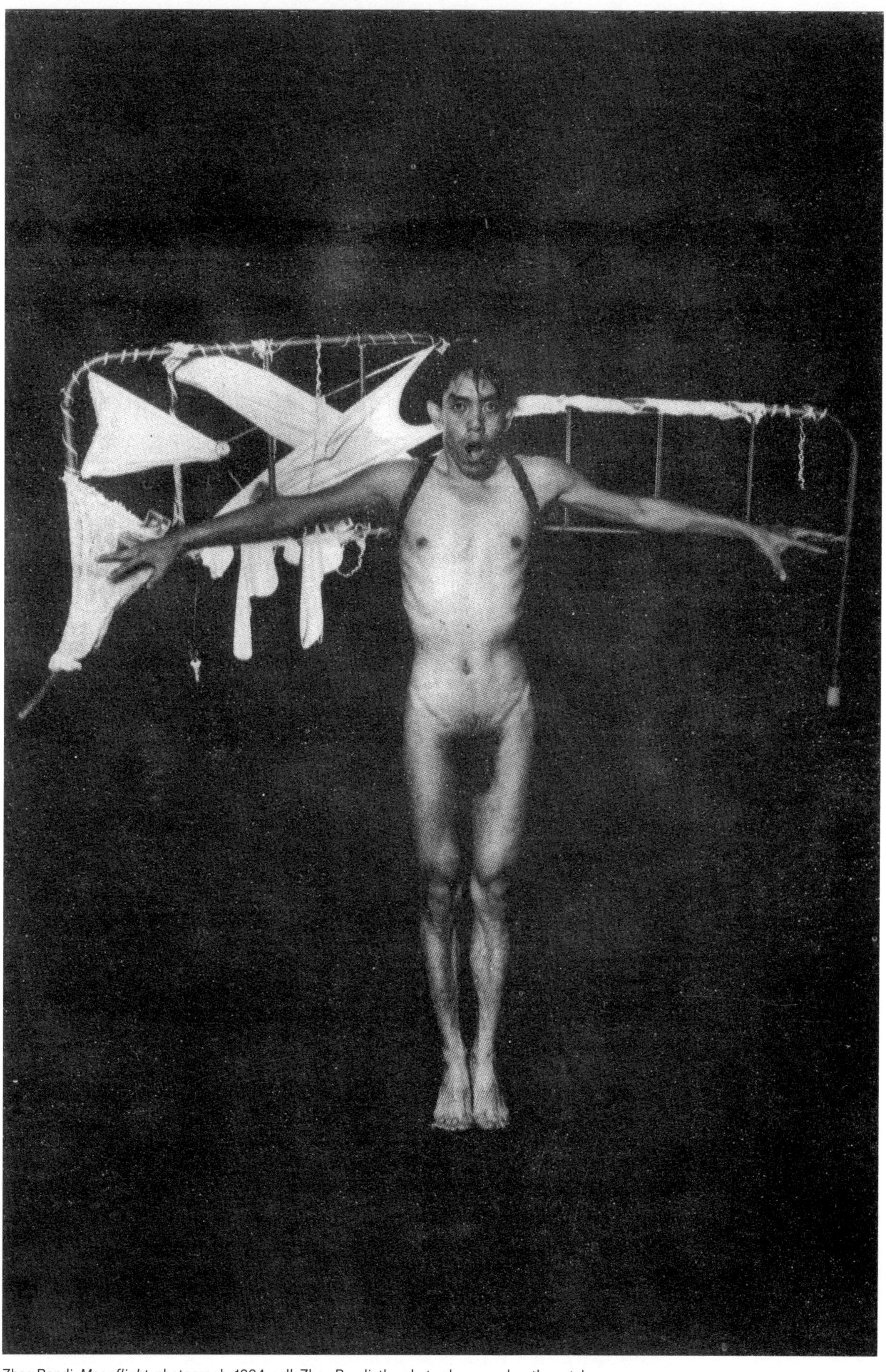

Zhao Bandi, *Moonflight*, photograph, 1994, coll. Zhao Bandi; the photo also served as the catalogue cover

赵半狄的月光号

[荷]戴汉志　张离　译

"天哪,为什么一个最有天赋的油画家放弃了他的技术,莫名其妙地做一些普通的家具、猪的肋骨和打字机一类的东西?这是对他才能的浪费,是中国现代艺术的悲剧。"这是中央美术学院赵半狄过去老师们的抱怨。

"为什么我们最有成功保障的一位艺术家离开了他的媒介?他本可以凭此财运亨通,难道他自己不知道或是他发疯了吗?"赵半狄以前作品的收藏者呻吟道。

答案很简单:赵半狄是艺术家,不是匠人,亦非商人。他不为技术、也不为金钱所左右。严格地说,他关心的不是艺术,而是生活。

不去理会90年代以来中国现代艺术圈内的潮起潮落,他仍旧坚持不解地从事他自由的现实主义风格的创作。他发展了一种对叙事性场景的描写风格。有时亲密,有时普通,但总是反映了浪漫领域中的心绪和感情,以及从激情、思念、怀旧、愤怒中变化出来的东西。很明显,赋以赵半狄以灵感的是生活本身,而不是所谓的"前卫艺术的召唤"或艺术的实验。

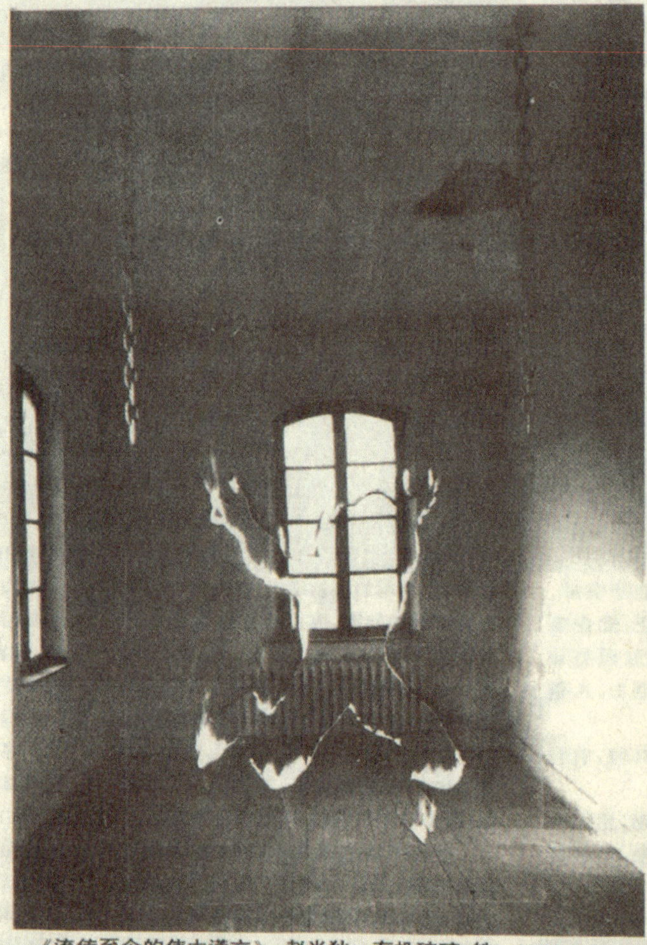

《流传至今的伟大谎言》　赵半狄　有机玻璃,铁　1994

在翰墨艺术中心其工作室举办的有12件作品的展览中,这种气质和态度并没有改变,所改变的是他所用的媒介:不再用油画,而是所有他认为适合的事物。

展览没有在展览馆、画廊等使人产生有关文化联想的地点举行。半狄偏爱他的工作室,那种半中半西、古旧不稳的、殖民地的、位于现代化的北京中心的建筑所产生的气氛,与半狄那些把普遍、匿名的现成物品和材料进行改造、有的局部绘画并赋予含意的作品十分统一。

工作室的中央悬挂着一块大尺寸的有机玻璃板,板上有一个燃烧出的跳跃人形的剪影。这是展览中最有表现力,同时也最具有非物质性的一件作品。透明的有机玻璃上只有一个剪影留下的烧灼过的边缘线,对人形的特性来作提示,也不清楚这一行动发生的时间和空间。作品题为《流传至今的伟大谎言》,是对这个独特的活跃行动的纯粹抽象的表述。它周围的作品将会一点一点地告诉我们这一绝望行动所发生的世界。

在一把旧椅子靠背的黑色人造革上,画着一个男青年轻柔地俯身在他的女友的肩膀上,她作出反应,向他的脸伸出手,触到了他的眼镜。这个色彩丰富、甜蜜、装饰在椅背中心的小画面被三个大的铁钉钉穿,使这把椅子变成了一个致命的危险的物体。作品题为《二十一世纪的流感》。与这件作品形成一个冷静对照的作品是一个对古典美貌的现代解释——《早晨好,维纳斯小姐》,一个无手臂的时装人体模型,生殖部分用色提亮,站在工作室的一角俯视着展览会场,好似一个难以企及的标准。但同时,这个腰和腿可以拆御的俗气的塑料模型与其它作品一样,远离那种优美的、平滑的、幻觉感的美术品,而带有一种笨拙的、惹人恼火的未完成感。

另几件作品,如《比我年长的侄儿》、《13月32日》、《妈妈》,同样也告诉我们一些关于外部世界而非感情方面的东西,如时间和空间。"比我年长的侄儿"中有一个上万年历史的玄武岩石块躺在一块破碎的镜子上,放在一个涂在鲜艳色彩的婴儿床里。石块好象从天外飞落,而镜子映照着,把无限的空间、时间和从一个婴儿床中开始的一个人的有限的生命过程联结起来。石块被按抽象色彩规则均匀涂刷的床栏杆所环绕。而石块底部则按印象主义的手法画成一个具体的风景,并被破碎的镜子分裂地映照出来。

赵半狄运用象征性语言的清晰性是毫不妥协的。使这十二件作品如此迷人的是他所用的使意义和事物结合在一起的质朴有力的方式。他以精湛的技艺、有时利用审美因素来构成可怕的激进因素。例如有一个天真无邪的名字的作品《一个童话》,是用10元人民币钞票做成的一只优美的花朵,在以小花瓶中的血液所浸润的肋骨顶部盛开。

注:由翰墨艺术中心和荷兰新阿姆斯特丹艺术咨询公司联合主办的《月光号——赵半狄》展于1994年5月26日至6月26日在翰墨艺术中心赵半狄工作室举行。

Hans van Dijk
Zhao Bandi's Lift-Off

"My god, why is one of the most talented oil painters abandoning his skill and doing something absurd with ordinary furniture, a pig's rib-bone, and a typewriter!? It's a waste of his capacities and a tragedy for the Chinese Modern Arts," his former teachers at the Central Academy of Fine Arts complain. "Why does one of our most promising artists leave his medium behind, he could have easily made a fortune with it, doesn't he understand or did he go insane?" his former collectors groan. The answer is simple: Zhao Bandi is an artist and not an artisan or businessman, obsessed with neither technique nor money, and strictly speaking also not concerned with art, but instead, with life.

Neglecting the latest trends or art historical categories in the Chinese modern art circles of around 1990, he continued to work in the free, realistic painting style he developed during his studies, depicting scenes sometimes intimate, sometimes common, but always reflecting moods and emotions within the realm of the romantic, varying from passion, longing, nostalgia to spleen. Obviously, life itself, instead of so-called "Avant-gardistic Summons" or artistic experiments, forms the inspiration for Zhao Bandi. And this attitude didn't change with his twelve new artworks, exhibited in his studio in the Hanmo Art Center. What changed was the medium he used, no longer oil painting but now all kinds of things he thought appropriate.

Instead of holding his exhibition in a gallery or exhibition hall, with all the connected cultural associations, Bandi preferred his studio, the environment where he made his work. The atmosphere of this half-Chinese, half-Western, century-old, ramshackle, colonial building in the center of modernizing Beijing corresponds with the common, anonymous, ready-made objects or materials that he changed, combined, and often partly painted over to load them with meaning.

In the center of the studio hangs a large Perspex plate with a burnt-out silhouette of a jumping figure. It is the most expressive artwork in the exhibition, and at the same time the most immaterial one; the Perspex is transparent, and there is only the silhouette-line of the subject; no indications are given about other characteristics of the figure, nor about the time and space he is acting in. The artwork is a pure and abstract statement about an energetic, individual action, titled *The Big Rumour Spreading Until Today*.[3] The surrounding works tell us bit by bit something more about the world in which this desperate expressive action takes place.

3—Zhao Bandi gave his work to van Dijk. For many years it hung above Hans van Dijk's bed in his apartment and NAAC office. He included it in several exhibitions, including a show at the Goethe Institute in Beijing in 1995 and several presentations at CAAW, Beijing. The work was after many years again exhibited in *Dai Hanzhi: 5000 Artists*, Witte de With, Rotterdam, 2014.

On the imitation leather of the back of a worn-out chair, a scene is painted, depicting a boy tenderly bending over his girlfriend's shoulder who, in reaction, reaches her hand to his face and touches his spectacles. The small, sweet, colorful picture, decoratively put in the center of the back, is perforated with three large nails, changing the chair into a deadly, dangerous object. The work is entitled *The 21st Century Influenza Epidemic*.

As a cool contrast to this work stands a modern version of a classic beauty titled *Good Morning Ms. Venus*: a mannequin without arms and with painstakingly painted genitals is placed in a corner of the studio, where she coldly overlooks the exhibition. The vulgar, hard, plastic model is at the same time far from a perfect, smooth, illusionistic artwork, but like the other artworks in the show, bears something of a clumsiness and, with a movable leg and waist, is provokingly unfinished.

Several artworks, like *My Older Nephew*, *A Song for Four Seasons*, *The 32nd Day of a Certain Month*, and *Mama*, also tell us something about less emotional but more external aspects,

Opposite page: Hans van Dijk, "Zhao Bandi's Lift-Off," featuring Zhao Bandi, *The Big Rumor Spreading Until Today*, burned Perspex and metal chain, 154 × 151 cm, 1994, private coll.; *Hanmo Art Journal*, translated into Chinese by Zhang Li, October 1994, private coll.

like space and time. The first mentioned above shows a millennia-old block of basalt lying on a broken mirror, placed in a colorful painted grid. The stone, apparently fallen from the universe, which the mirror is reflecting, connects infinite time and space with the contrasting limited human lifetime. The stone is surrounded by the bars of the grid, which are painted in a regular, abstract color-order. But the color used on the bottom of the stone forms an impressionistically painted, concrete landscape in fragments reflected by the incidentally broken mirror.

The symbolic language Bandi is using is uncompromised and clear, and what makes these twelve artworks fascinating is the simple and striking way he puts meanings and things together. He virtuously manages to employ aesthetic qualities in constructing his sometimes frightening, radical traps. Like the one with the innocent title *Nursery Rhyme*: an elegant flower, ingeniously made of ten-yuan bills, growing on a rib bone fed by blood in a small vase.

Hans van Dijk, "Zhao Bandi's Lift-Off," published in *Hanmo Art Journal*, Beijing, 1994.
The Chinese version of the text is by Zhang Li.

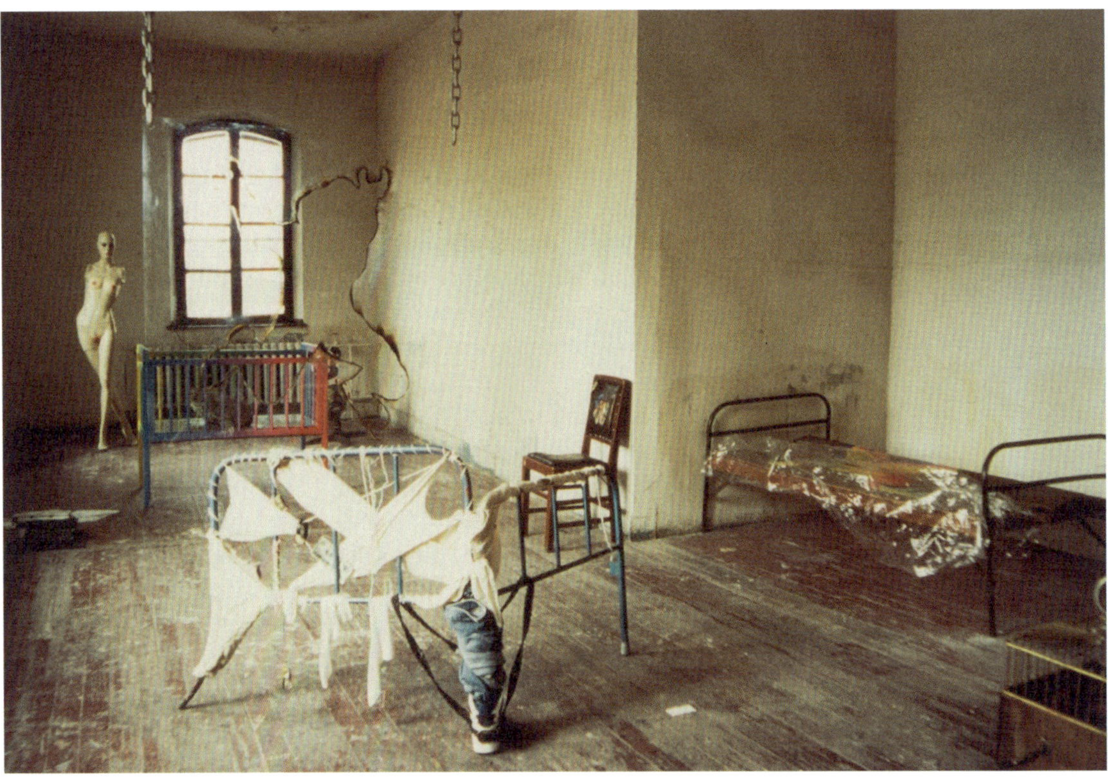

Xu Zhiwei, *Zhao Bandi, Moonflight*, exhibition view, Hanmo Art Center, Beijing, 1994, private coll.

Following the Zhao Bandi exhibition, the director of Hanmo Art Center stops collaborating with van Dijk. According to van Dijk, they start a program of their own, aiming to equal his success:

> You probably already understood that Hanmo Art Center is not my gallery. Whether I'll be welcome a second time remains to be seen. Jealousy—red eyes they call it here—is (or are) the cause. The exhibition of Zhao Bandi is generally, and rightly, seen as a cooperation between me and Bandi, and that hurts, because it is a success. There was no contribution in any form by [their] staff and personnel to the preparation of the exhibition. Only distrust for a strange intruder.
> Bandi had asked me to "curate" the exhibition in his studio. That is sort of customary here, because hierarchical thinking is so strong—so we lift each-other up, for it is a beautiful exhibition, and we already agreed before Berlin: "It's lonely at the top."
> Just before the opening, the younger brother of the boss stumbles into the space, falls down and spreads hundreds of bad photocopies (the printing of the invitations was

their responsibility too) across the floor. The A4 introduced the exhibition as an achievement by Hanmo and did not mention our "cooperation." Bandi briefly looked at the text and with a broad gesture swept the lot out of sight.
It's a national weakness, jealousy. My work with Bandi almost cost me my friendship with Liu Anping, but he recovered.

HvD, letter to Jeroen Vinken, Beijing, 7 July 1994

In the same month, van Dijk publishes the first of two short essays, "Art Theory Is Not Art," in *Jiangsu Art Monthly*. In this text, he observes, "The Chinese economy is booming because the government gave up the planned economy. Now some people have a headache because they have lost control. Chinese modern art is booming because it left behind official, traditional painting, and the art historians have a headache because they have lost control." The professional world of art critics doesn't take too kindly to what they regard as van Dijk's invasion of their territory. In a letter to Ernst Dinkla, he notes:

> I don't think very highly of the modern art world, including the Chinese version in which art critics and curators regard themselves as superior to the artists. This, however, would appear to be a miscalculation on my behalf. My attempts to reconcile the practices and thinking of my Chinese colleagues with the politicians they so often criticize, and to put the importance of theorizing (writing history) into perspective in the first place, were seen as a sophisticated attempt to seize power. And in the end, it actually did work out that way. The actors in the Chinese art world tend to think both hierarchically and strategically. Take the directors of the Hanmo Art Center, for example, who were initially very enthusiastic and happy for me to organize the exhibition with Zhao Bandi in their exhibition space (in which Bandi's studio was also located). But when they decided to organize their own exhibitions after the successful event, a few of their more remarkable shows were wrongly attributed to me by the Chinese art world; in China, most of the news is spread by word of mouth, with all its inherent inaccuracies.
>
> HvD, letter to his friends in the Netherlands, Beijing, 9 July 1995

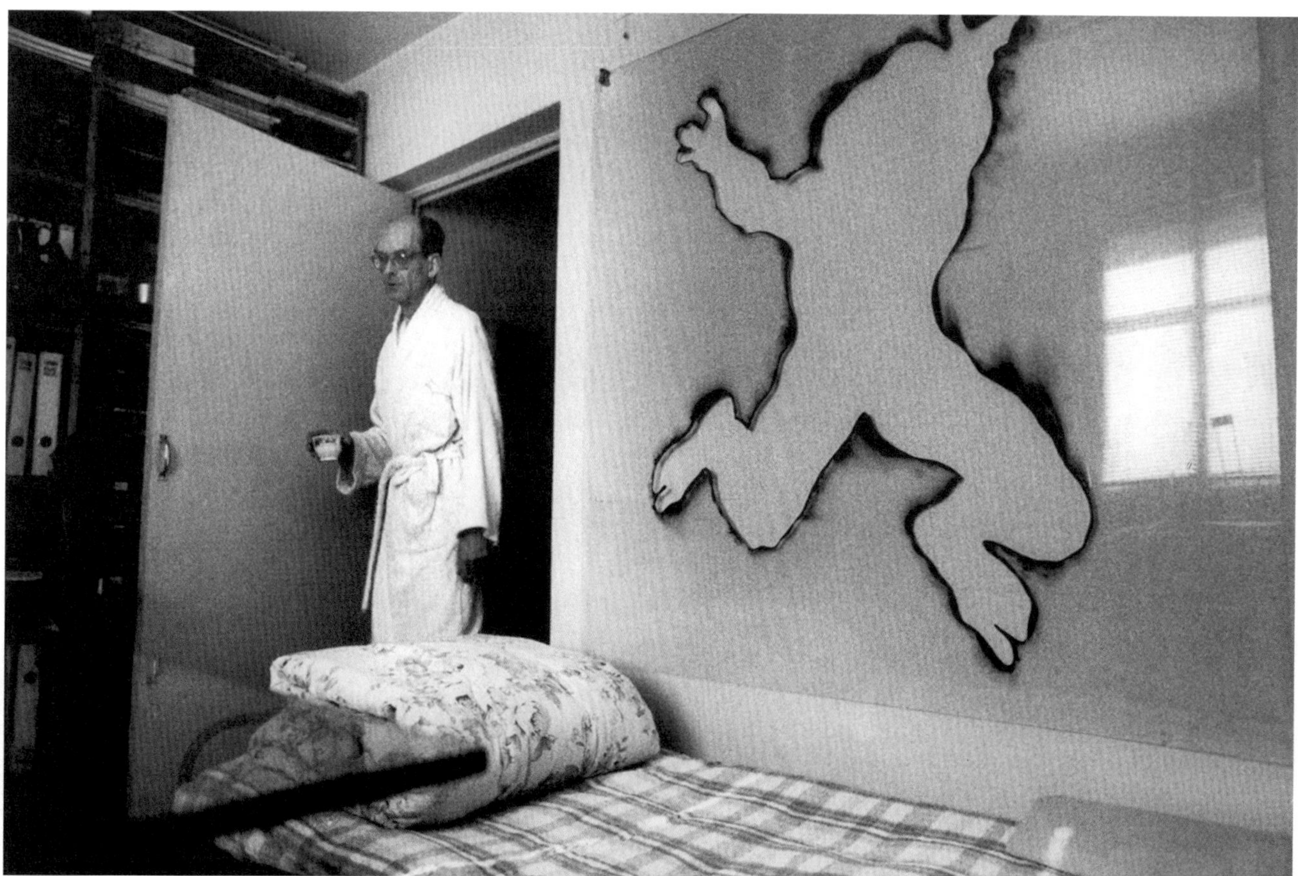

Luo Yongjin, *Hans in Pajamas*, 1996, courtesy Luo Yongjin

From time to time, van Dijk attends one of the many happenings taking place in Beijing. He is deeply impressed by Zhang Huan's performance *65kg.II.6* of 11 June 1994. The artist suspended himself on flesh hooks above a hot metal plate. The police raid the performance, and Zhang Huan is arrested along with some audience members, causing Ma Liuming, who is scheduled to perform later that same day, to flee and stay in hiding for a while.[4]

4—Note by van Dijk found in his personal archive, Beijing.

Van Dijk also attends *Trample the face*, a performance work by Cang Xin, an artist from Inner Mongolia, an ethnic minority in China often discriminated against. The performance consists of a narrow walkway in a traditional hutong neighborhood covered with plaster masks, which Cang Xin casts of his own face. Visitors to the hutong have to trample over the plaster casts, crushing them under their feet. Van Dijk collects the first cast and a photograph. They later become part of the MCAF collection.

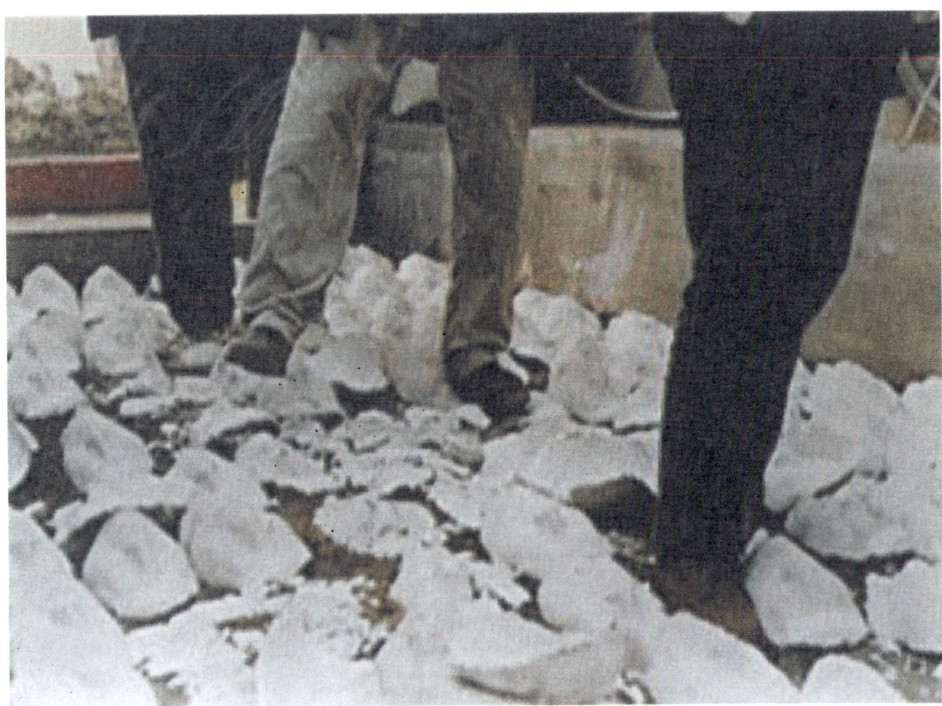

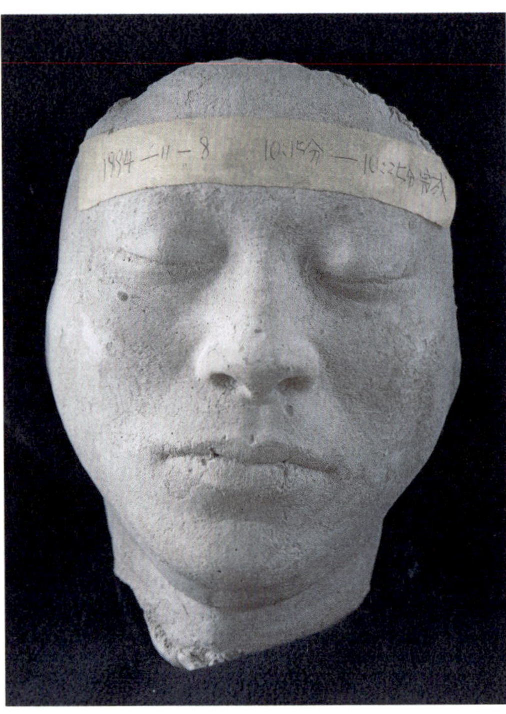

Left: Cang Xin, performance in Beijing a *hutong* with people walking on plaster masks of the artist's face, Beijing, 1994, photograph private coll.; right: Cang Xin, *Life Mask*, cast of the artist's face used during the performance *Trample the face*, plaster, 32 × 15.8 × 9.5 cm, 1994, private coll.

On 8 July 1994, the Chinese art world is invited to the Dongdan Dahua Video Theater in Beijing. The evening's program consists of a screening of *Good Morning Beijing!*, a performance video by Liu Anping and Wang Jinsong that shows them riding handcuffed on the subway as if they are under arrest. After the viewing, an unexpected happening takes place:

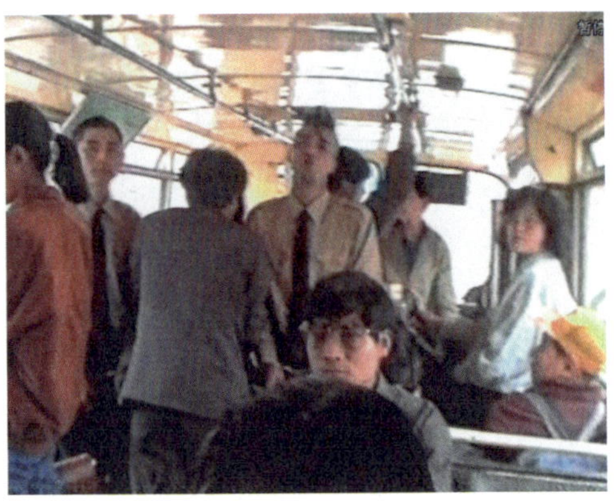

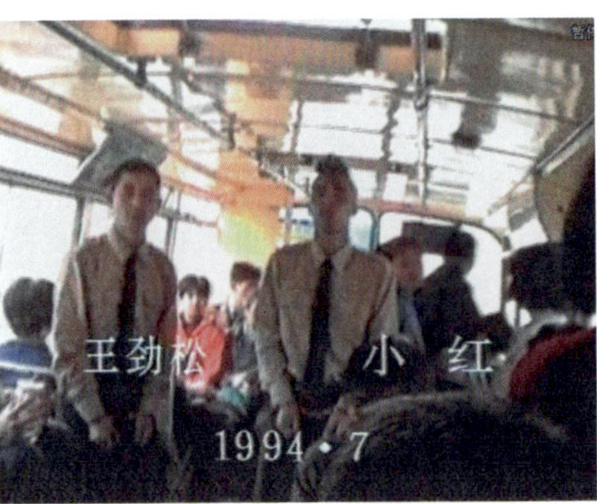

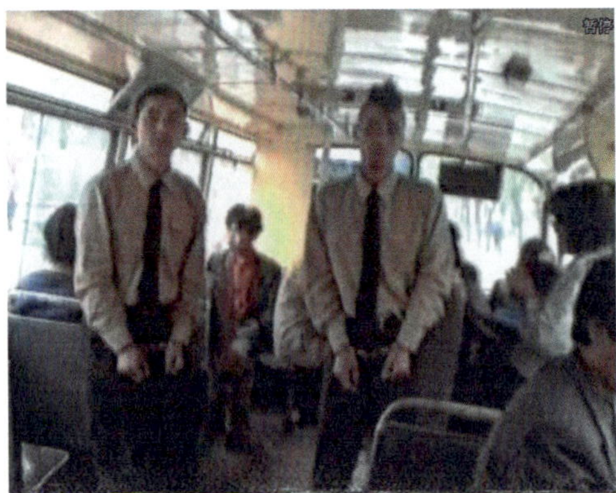

Liu Anping and Wang Jinsong, *Good Morning Beijing!*, single-channel video, 30', 1994, courtesy Liu Anping

Hans van Dijk
Ink on Top!

When Zhao Shaoruo left jail after a year, he was very fat, easygoing, and no longer interested in painting. His motto was to have fun, and not a childish sort of fun. As with Liu Anping, his fellow "artist-jailbird" from the south, it mostly leads to conflict with whomever or whatever happens to be around. It's all the same to them. First in Guangdong, where Shaoruo terrorized a national art fair with a "Reassuring Action," reassuring everyone who crossed his path with such zeal that the plainclothes security official on duty arrested him in a panic. And he then was arrested again in Beijing, this time in collaboration with Anping [...].
At the same time, a number of their colleagues who had kept painting had, on the one hand, become exorbitantly rich, yet also had serious doubts about the avant-garde content of their art. Performance art is the true avant-garde: this was the message. Anping was willing to provide the avant-garde, given adequate, which is to say one-sided, financing of the shared project. The victim was a painter who was embraced by the art world for behaving like an *enfant terrible* and had amassed a fortune with naïve realistic paintings [...].
The real success, to be recognized as a groundbreaking artist, still lay ahead. A small theater with a bar was rented, the videotape was cut—a somewhat boring work of both Liu Anping and Wang Jinsong, cuffed and guarded by police in the subway. Subtitles and nerve-racking sounds—short-wave jammer noises—were added. Forty prominent members of the Beijing art scene received invitations with tickets to the premiere. Then Shaoruo struck. On the eve of the event, he confessed to Anping that he had his doubts: it might well turn out to be your average drab screening, an evening watching video with the established jet set in Benetton and jeans. It would be best if something were to happen, some racket or whatnot. Anping was not immune to suggestions, and Shaoruo kept fanning the flames. That was the last straw. Anping exploded. "Ink on top!" he managed to say, hoarse with anger. And it was thus decided.
The theater filled up, and visitors picked seats according to their positions in the art scene (docile or self-aware, depending on the circumstances). As the first rows were almost full, the event was already a success, inscribed in the history of Chinese modern art. But the film hadn't begun yet. Shaoruo kept a low profile and gave instructions to a female photographer. Anping and Jinsong prepared for a royal celebration, and the tape began. A deafening yet rather slow show unfolded: the two artists cuffed and gawked at by fellow passengers on the subway. The tape was twenty minutes long, so it wasn't annoying when, halfway through, Anping began an elaborate photoshoot, maneuvering in front of the screen and between the front rows. At his invitation, Jinsong also came forward to bask in the success. Cameras were flashing one after another, when suddenly a rumbling, furious Shaoruo staggered forward. Angry, stout people can be very intimidating, and Shaoruo is an exceptionally gifted actor. Everyone froze. Arriving at the focal point of the glamour, with one swing of a sizable jug he lashed a liter of black ink all around the room. Ink is thin, and a liter is a lot. The posing artists, the projection screen, and the first three rows of seats with the *crème de la crème* of the art world were equally covered. The havoc was magnificent. But we only found that out later. First Shaoruo left the room after ditching the jug in the aisle. Then the celebrated artists left, followed by the front rows, one by one, looking for a place to rinse off. Everyone left ink trails and footsteps, which were more striking outside the semi-darkness of the theater than inside. With softly voiced, harsh curses, the owner of the theater entered and flicked on the lights. Unfortunately, Anping experienced another fit of paranoia, avoiding his apartment for three days. He dared return only after his informant confirmed with the police that no one had pressed charges. Now, a week later, he still jumps at every telephone call and suspects everyone and everything to be behind everything and everyone. Shaoruo had already forgotten the whole incident the next day and explained, chuckling with anticipation, how he would soon treat a celebrated art critic to a thrashing.

HvD, letter to his friends in the Netherlands, Beijing, 21 July 1994

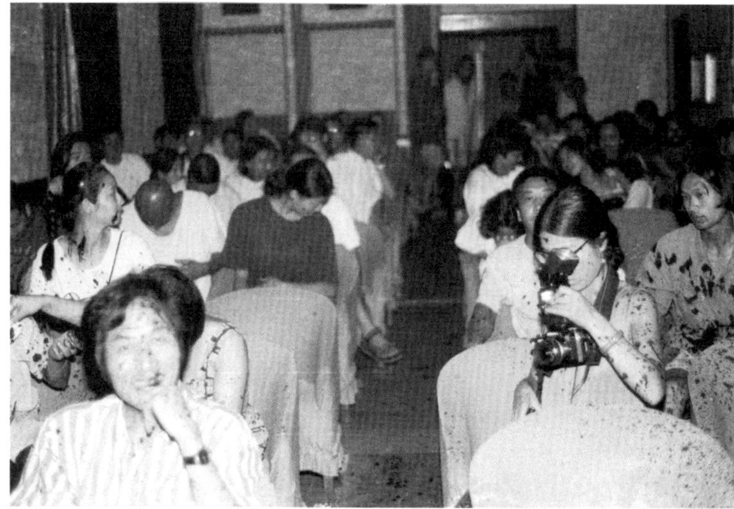
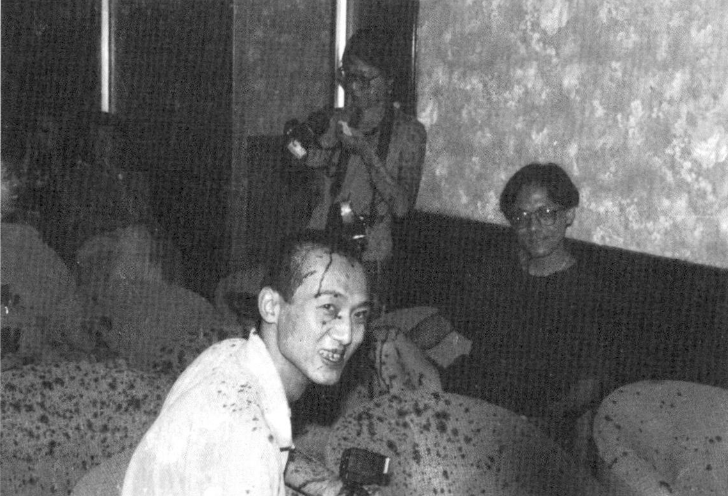
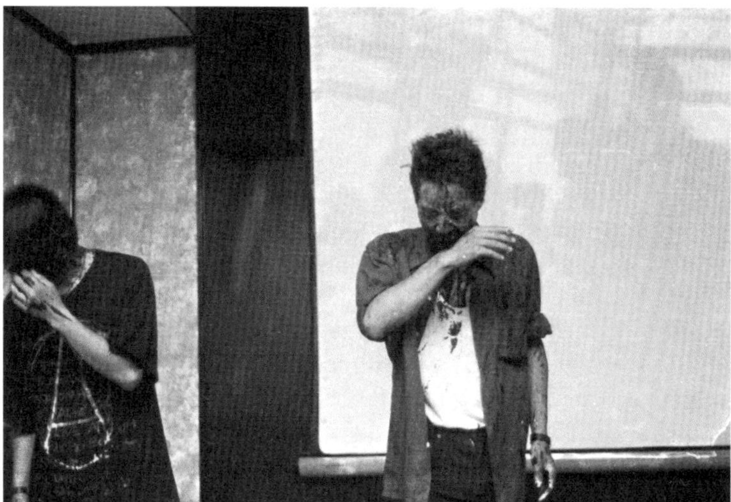
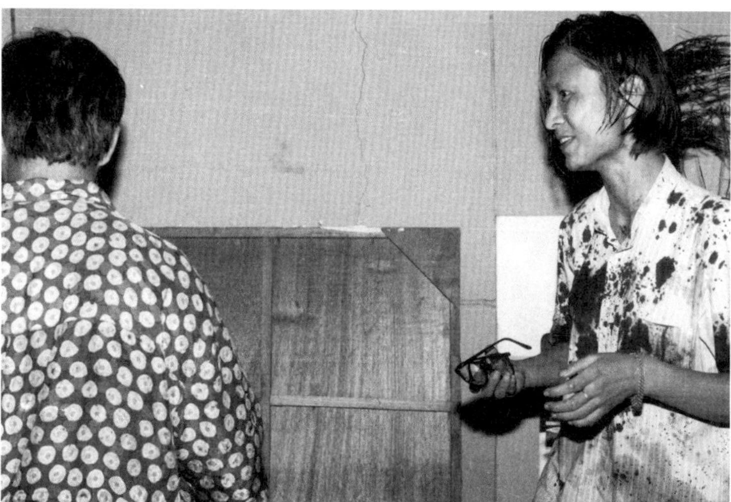
Liu Anping and Zhao Shaoruo, *Correct Action!*, Beijing, 1994, photos courtesy Liu Anping

On 17 August 1994, after a grueling six months in search of a new place to live, van Dijk finally moves into a tiny apartment, which becomes the first NAAC office apartment:

> For three months, I have been looking for an apartment in vain. [...] Time and again it turned out that any mention of the word "foreigner"—of the kind that could not be passed off as Japanese or Korean—made the rent go up dramatically, and when it became clear that registration needed to be done at the local police station, even money could not save you anymore: it was as if I suggested they commit a crime and then asked them to turn themselves in.
> [...] Zhao Yunfeng, mother and colleague of the painter Yajie, knew how to work the system. After three days, she had convinced an acquaintance to rent me a four-bedroom flat at a ridiculously cheap price. She had, however, neglected to inform the proprietor that her prospective tenant was a foreigner. The owner's first response was to shut the door on us when we visited the apartment. Luckily, her friend had quickly wedged her foot in the door. "Come on now, it's not like he's black." We had a few more of these encounters that week, but then we got lucky. Li Yongbin, my former landlord, was present at the decisive moment to advise on the tricks of officially registering: "You just tell the police he's related by marriage." That sealed the deal.
> HvD, fragment from an undated text sent to Ernst Dinkla titled "Adopted by the United Families of Asia"

August 1994

Ubu Roi Art Research Committee (URARC) Report
Beijing

Following Zhao Shaoruo's ink-throwing action, van Dijk is inspired to create the Ubu Roi Art Research Committee Report, a mock research organization including a fake advisory board, art prize, etc. Despite its satirical tone, the report contains a meaningful summary of recent art practices and an original categorization of artists. He will apply this iconographical system to his choice of artists for NAAC exhibitions in China and abroad.

> The occasion that led to the establishment of the Ubu Roi Art Research Committee (URARC) was the ink-throwing party by Zhao Shaoruo "the terrible," an artist who for political reasons was imprisoned for a year and was set free in 1990. He is now looking for danger instead of waiting to be harassed again, a respectable successor in the tradition of offending the audience. At that, Zhao Shaoruo's appearance looks a lot like Ubu Roi as portrayed by Alfred Jarry. The rest of the report is a parody of the habit in the Chinese art world of applying labels to everything. The evening before sending it out, Zhang Li and I informed Zhao Shaoruo, and it was a surprise for the other people who were mentioned in the report.
> A few artists voiced their strategic reservations, and some colleagues got really angry. "Hans is making a mess," one of them accuses me of having orchestrated the whole affair to drive him off the throne, and one author has devoted a deadly serious article to it in the Chinese edition of *Esquire Hong Kong*. Ever since, Zhao Shaoruo nags me about his award, and that is truly unsettling.
> HvD, letter to his friends in the Netherlands, Beijing, 9 July 1995

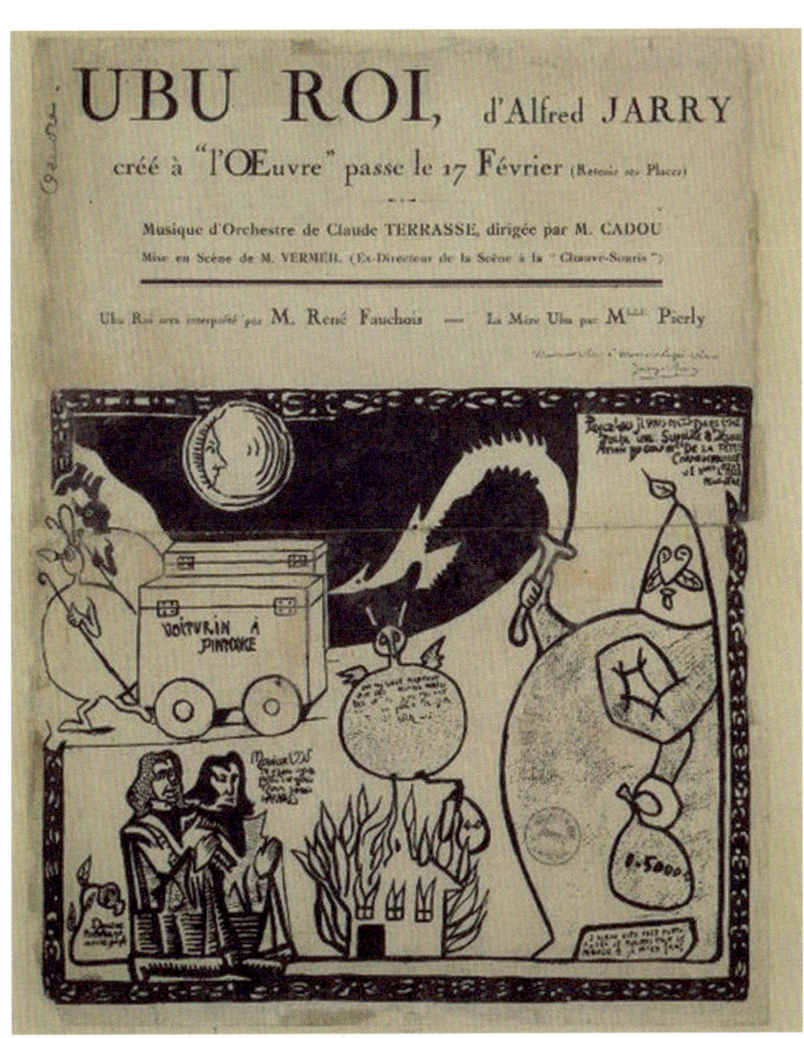

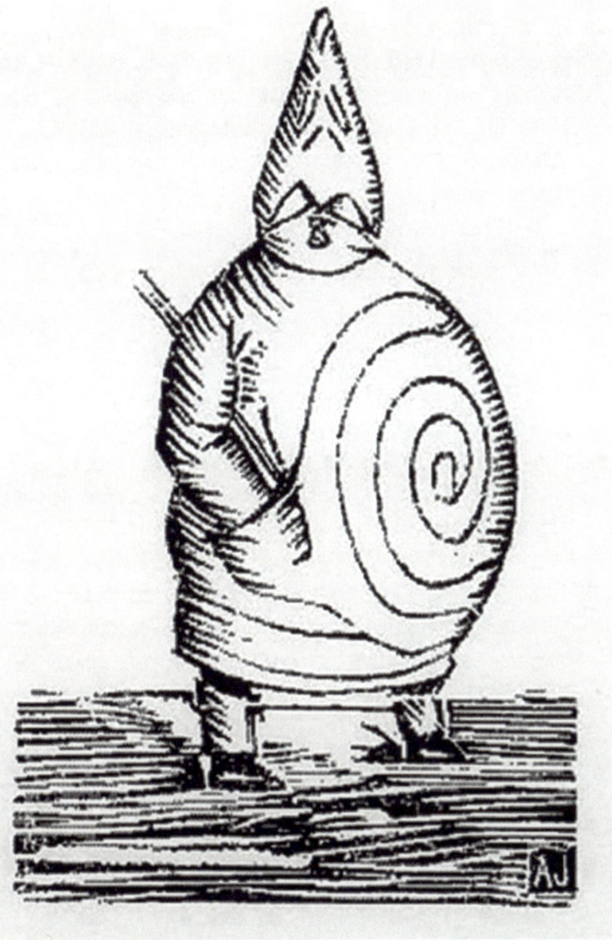

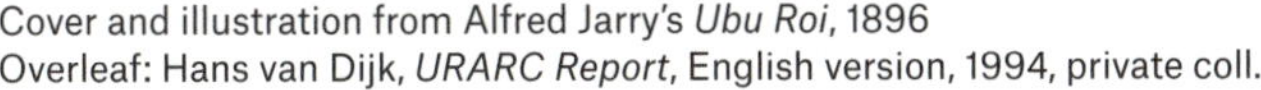
Cover and illustration from Alfred Jarry's *Ubu Roi*, 1896
Overleaf: Hans van Dijk, *URARC Report*, English version, 1994, private coll.

NEW AMSTERDAM ART CONSULTANCY

International Avantgarde Art Standards
Awards & Urgent Warnings 1994

NAAC as an international art consultancy specialized in modern Chinese art is aware of and deeply concerned with the lack of new standards in the Chinese art world. To fulfil this need the art theoretical Ubu Roi Art Research Committee (URARC) has been established wich consists of the following members

BOARD OF SPECIALISTS

Zhao Shaoruo president URARC
Hans van Dijk general director NAAC, first secretary URARC
Jule Noth assistent director NAAC, second secretary URARC

BOARD OF ADVISORS

Chen Tong art critic
Leng Lin art historian
Liu Anping board member Peking NAAC
Ni Haifeng artist
Wu Shanzhuan diplomat
Xu Tan board member Canton NAAC
Zhang Li general executive NAAC
Zhao Bandi artist

THE 1994 URARC REPORT

§I. PRINCIPLES, DEFINITIONS AND CATEGORIES

After long and intensive discussions based on profound arthistorical research, the board of specialists of the URARC is glad to present the new INTERNATIONAL AVANTGARDE ART STANDARDS by introducing contemporary CATEGORIES, SUB-CATEGORIES AND SECTIONS and their application on modern Chinese art.

THE PRINCIPLES:

1. Avantgarde art can be divided in three main catagories: NEW SOCIALISM, NEW TRADITIONALISM and the art of DING YI & MAI ZHIXIONG. (Socialism and Traditionilism both forming the main roots of the present culture of P.R. China have nothing to do with the art of Ding Yi and Mai Zhixiong, which therefore should be recognized as a main category of equal importance)

2. NEW SOCIALISM can be divided into two sub-catogies: firstly, those artworks who express or reflect a personal opinion or concept about the social surroundings or who present a certain view of the world, will be called CONCEPTUAL ART. CONCEPTUAL ART must be divided into two sections: PAINTING and SCULPTURE:
For instance the works of Cai Jin, Chen Danqing, Duan Jianyu, Fang Lijun, Feng mengbo, Hong Hao, Hu Zhiying, Li Tianyuan, Qi Zhilong, Qiu Zhijie, Wang Yin, Ye You, Yu Youhan, Zhang Gong, the Zhang Hai'er, Zhang Yajie and the older works of Zhao Bandi and Zhao Jianren can be defined as NEW SOCIALISME, sub-category CONCEPTUAL ART, section PAINTING and the works of Ai Weiwei: 'Shoe' and 'Safe Sex', both 1987, Xu Tan: 'Constant and Varying Speed' 1992 and Zhao Bandi's 'Moonflight', 1994: NEW SOCIALISM, sub-category CONCEPTUAL ART, section SCULPTURE.

3. The second sub-catagory of NEW SOCIALISM concerns works of art which only can exist or came into beeing in a certain situation. E.g. the 'Formular' of Geng Jianyi played its part in reality and came into beeing during the meeting 1988 in Huangshan preparing the Avant-Garde Exhibition 1989 in the National Gallery, Beijing, so did Sun Ping's Share Certificates (A), issued by CHINA SUN PING ART COMPANY LIMITED, October 10, 1992, in Wuhan and Yan Lei's video registration of the removal of his armpit hair, 'Claer Away' 1993, entitled and the video-artworks from 1991 and 1992 of Zhang Peili, which shows uncommented parts of the reality. and the 'Labour of Berlin' of Wu Shanzhuan which only existed during his work as a warder in the exhibitionhall and as a waiter in the restaurant of the 'Haus der Kulturen der Welt' (House of Cultures of the World) 1993. So did the artworks 'Analyses I', June 1990 and 'Analyses II', August 1992 which were the actual analysing activities of the New Measurement Group (Xinkedu Xiaozu) Beijing.
This kind of artworks can neither be seperated from the reality nor do they express a certain view on the reality, that's why URARC decided to call this kind of artworks NEW SOCIALISM, sub-category REALISM.

Other outstandings works in this sub-category are the series temporary artworks Li Yongbin realized between 1990 and 1994 in his home in Tuanjiehu, Beijing; Liu Anping spreading perfume on the acres of Dazhai and other crimes like he committed like the one in the Holiday Inn of 1992 entitled: 'The Behaviour of Young Red is Righteous' October 1992; the foam-sculptures 1993 and 1994 of Zhu Ming, realised in his studio in Dongcun Beijing before he and Ma Liuming disappeared on June the twelfth this year and the Po-Mo action of the President of URARC, Zhao Shaoruo executed in the Beijing Dongdan Dahua Video Theatre, July 8, 1994 where he spread nearly a litre black ink over half of the there invited 40 VIPs, representing the quintessence of the Peking Avantgarde Art Circle, and Zhang Huan's action the eleventh of June 1994 in Dongcun.

The last mentioned event took one hour and about 250 cc of Zhang Huan's blood, which, via medical equipment, dripped during fivty minutes out of his body (naked hanging in chains in the rafters of his studio) into a heated flat, metal plate where it boiled and curdled into a small, dark, bubbling and heavily smoking heap, gradually filling the room with an intense, a bit sweetish, smell.

4. The other main-catagory, NEW TRADITIONALISM, consists of three sub-catagories which speak for themselves:

Firstly: GARDEN-INSTALLATIONS like the works of, Gu Dexin 1989 in Paris and later in London, and paralel with Lin Yilin realized in Berlin subsequently showed in Rotterdam, Oxford, Odense (Denmark) and Hildesheim (Germany), Jiang Jie's exhibition 'Critical Point' at the Gallery of the Central academy of Fine Arts, May 1994.

Second: CALLIGAPHY-INSTALLATIONS like those of Ni Haifeng, Xu Bing and Song Haidong's recent works in Shanghai.

Third: ART THEORY-INSTALLATIONS like the artworks of Huang Yongping.

§II. AWARDS & URGENT WARNINGS

After exhausting research and deep considerations the board of specialists is proud to have the honnour to announce that the first price, the URARC GOLDEN INK BOTTLE 1994, will be presented to Zhao Shaoruo for his refreshing Po-Mo action in the Beijing Dongdan Dahua Video Theatre of July 8, 1994, and who, according to the regulations of the URARC, will be politely invited to be the President of the URARC 1995.

The URARC URGENT WARNINGS 1994 will be given to all artists who take it for granted by presenting plans instead of artworks.

International Avantgarde Art Categories Sub Categories & Sections

NEW SOCIALISM			NEW TRADITIONALISM			DING YI & MAI ZHIXIONG
CONCEPTUALISM		REALISM	GARDEN INSTALL.	CALLIGRAPHY INSTLALL.	ART THEORY INSTALL.	
PAINTING	SCULPTURE					
Cai Jin Chen Danqing Duan Jianyu Fang Lijun Feng Mengbo Hong Hao Hu Zhiying Li Tianyuan Qi Zhilong Qiu Zhijie Wang Yin Ye You Yu Youhan Zhang Gong Zhang Hai'er Zhang Yajie Zhao Jianren	Ai Weiwei Xu Tan Zhao Bandi	Geng Jianyi Li Yongbin Liu Anping Sun Ping Wu Shanzhuan Xinkedu Xiao Zu Yan Lei Zhang Peili Zhao Shaoruo Zhu Ming	Gu Dexin Jiang Jie Lin Yilin	Ni Haifeng Xu Bing	Huang Yongping	

NEW AMSTERDAM ART CONSULTANCY
P.O. BOX 4076 PEKING 100001

On 20 August 1994, van Dijk travels to the Netherlands, where he stays until 10 September. He gets rid of his room in Eindhoven and puts his belongings in storage. On 7 October 1994, he writes to Jeroen Vinken: "Things are going well, at times even great; work keeps pouring in. Besides the four projects from Germany, now also from Sweden and Belgium, the exhibition in the Shanghai Art Museum is going to be beautiful, and a next one—a dual exhibition in Beijing in December—is in the making, all showcasing art I am happy to attach my name to. Once the list is long enough, and the printing material is ready for those in Beijing, I am going to bombard that lady in Paris [Cathérine David] who is responsible for the next documenta."

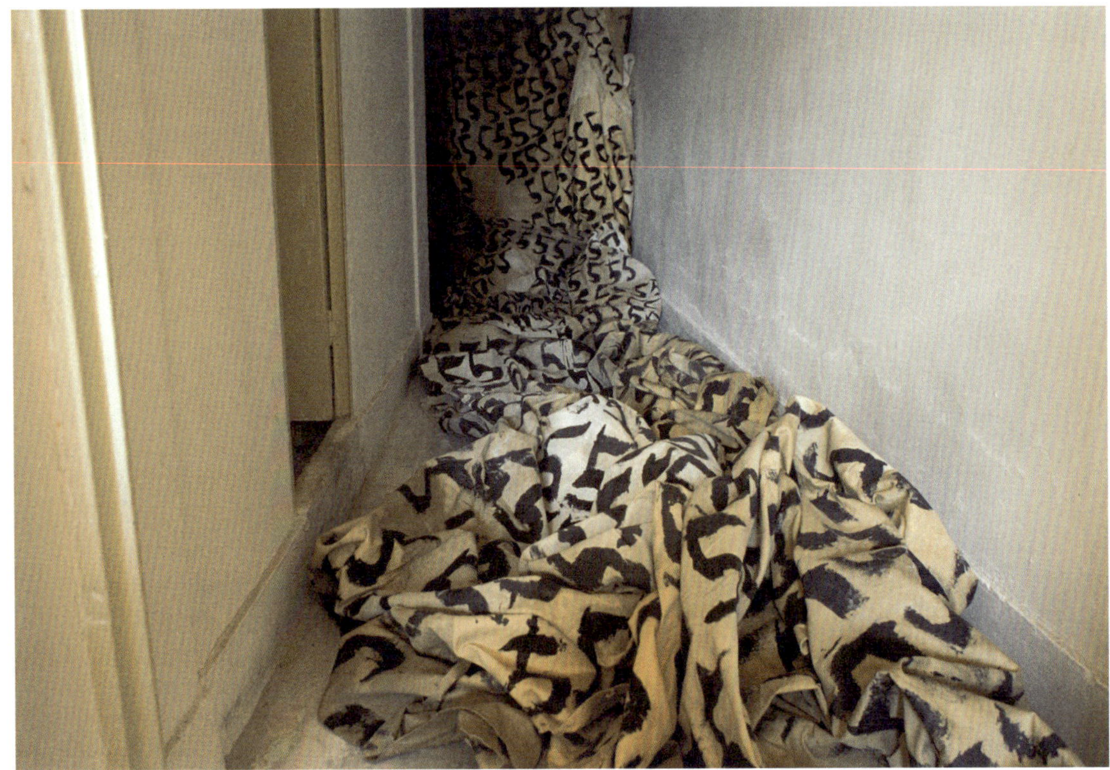

Ni Haifeng, *Heartless Passage*, painted cloth, installation in the corridor of van Dijk's apartment, Beijing, 1994, courtesy Ni Haifeng

In the fall of 1994, Ni Haifeng and his Dutch wife Roos Eijsten move in with van Dijk.

> Because of the Berlin show, I left China in 1992 to live in Germany for seven months on a grant from the Heinrich Böll Foundation. I returned to Beijing in 1993. Soon after, Hans arrived too. In Berlin, we had become good friends. Then Hans found an apartment on Fuchengmenwai. Meanwhile, I had met Roos, my wife, through Hans, and we all came to live in that apartment to save on rent. It was near the West Second Ring Road and very, very small. [...] We lived there for at least six months. As foreigners, Hans and Roos were not allowed to stay there. To go out, we had to leave after dark as much as possible. Roos had to disguise herself, wearing a scarf wrapped around her head. It was illegal to live there, because foreigners were only allowed to stay in designated compounds. But the Chinese also had a practice of renting a social housing apartment for very little money and renting it out for very high prices to other Chinese who could afford it. [...] When Roos fell pregnant, we moved out to another apartment that was very far away, outside the Fourth Ring Road. Hans stayed in the old apartment. [...] I remember he was in good spirits and optimistic about his consultancy. Soon after that, I don't remember precisely when, he was evicted from the apartment because someone reported him to the police. He said he had a lot of trouble: at least twice he invested in doing up an apartment for his office, and twice he was reported by the neighbors.
>
> **MB, interview with Ni Haifeng, Amsterdam, 4 October 2012**

13–17 October 1994

Ding Yi, Abstract Art Exhibition
Shanghai Art Museum

From van Dijk's Fiercely Realistic Footnotes:

> Shanghai is a difficult place to realize exhibition projects. Though there are many foreigners—still 99% of those who buy modern art—they are all working, in contrast to those living in Beijing. Beijing has a different tradition, in which spare time and weekends are dedicated to culture (usually by one half of the traditional diplomat couple).
> A few months earlier, the Shanghai Art Museum was approached by the Tokyo Gallery to request an exchange of exhibitions. The Japanese had shown catalogues with their impressive collection of modern art and were wondering what the Shanghai Art Museum had to offer. This turned out to be quite disappointing. Subsequently, the exhibition by Ding Yi was the first of a series in which the museum asked not for a rental fee, but for an artwork instead.
> The museum personnel were very helpful during the installation period, but appeared somewhat amazed by our demands: the captions were not to be attached to the artwork in question with the help of some sticky tape, but should be placed next to the artwork. When we showed them that the lighting on the ceiling was adjustable and could be directed at the artworks, we almost crossed the line. Moreover… it was nearly lunchtime. In the end, with the help of Ding Yi and some of his colleagues and friends, who were either foreigners or Chinese, everything came together in between lunchbreaks. The opening was a great happening.
> A Belgian business consultant, a Swiss from Hong Kong who dealt in insurance, and a German ex-Maoist bought artworks. Later in Beijing, a Brazilian diplomat and a few Swedes decided to buy as well. The reasonably well-designed catalogue was a great help in this respect.
>
> **HvD, letter to his friends in the Netherlands, Beijing, 9 July 1995**

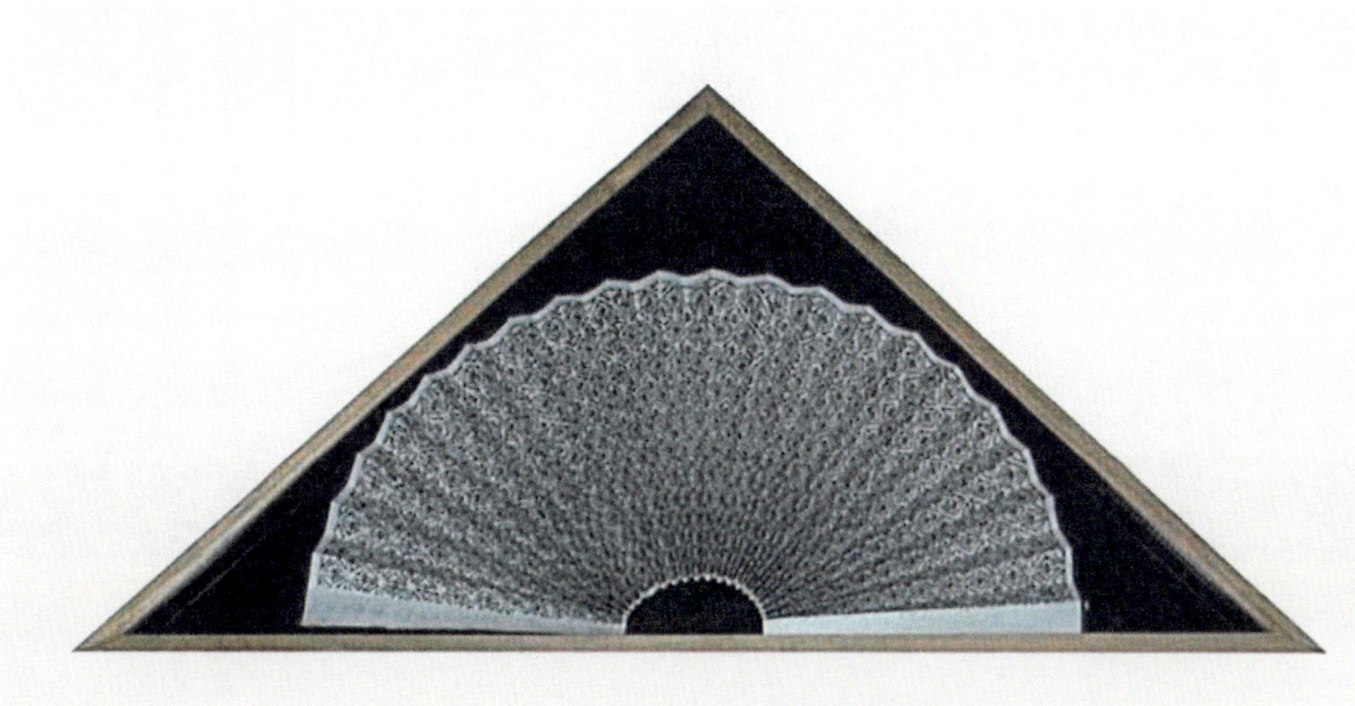

Ding Yi, *Appearance of Crosses 94-B19*, ballpoint pen and colored pencil on paper fan, 55 × 23 cm, 1994, private coll.

Ding Yi, *Appearance of Crosses 1994-10*, chalk and charcoal on linen, 160×140 cm, 1994, coll. the artist

7–18 December 1994

Zhang Hai'er
Song He Tang Pavilion, Ritan Park
in collaboration with Red Gate Gallery, Beijing

From the Fiercely Realistic Footnotes:

> Just like Ding Yi, Zhang Hai'er had an impressive list of exhibitions abroad, but had never before exhibited solo in China. Due to his fame, the opening was overcrowded. Of course, his main subject also helped: ladies of easy virtue. The elderly guard of Ritan Park was responsible for keeping order of everything that happened in his garden. He moved a photograph of a woman with a naked bosom into a quiet corner, as Zhang Hai'er had initially positioned it right across the entrance of the beautiful seventeenth-century pavilion. Everything else was allowed to stay in its original place. The day before, the artist-photographer had arrived from Guangzhou with his photographs. We worked through the night to fit all of them in passe-partouts and frames. This took especially long as Zhang Hai'er started to reminisce at every single picture.
> The exhibition, organized with Red Gate gallerist Brian Wallace, had a curious history. One of the artists represented by Red Gate Gallery had asked me to organize an exhibition of his work. Even though his oeuvre was very interesting, this could not take place without notifying Brian Wallace. Together we found a space in the Crowne Plaza on Wangfujing street, but it turned out to be too big. We had to combine the works with those of a second artist, and I suggested Zhang Hai'er. The choice of Ritan Park was determined by financial motives. At the very last moment, Brian Wallace and his artist couldn't agree on the pricing of his works, resulting in a solo show by Zhang Hai'er, of which the sales didn't disappoint: an Australian sinologist, a Canadian with a backpack, two Swiss and one Swedish diplomat, and a German "Save the Children Lady." Wallace was amazed by all the positive reviews; he didn't really value Zhang Hai'er's work.
> HvD, letter to his friends in the Netherlands, Beijing, 9 July 1995

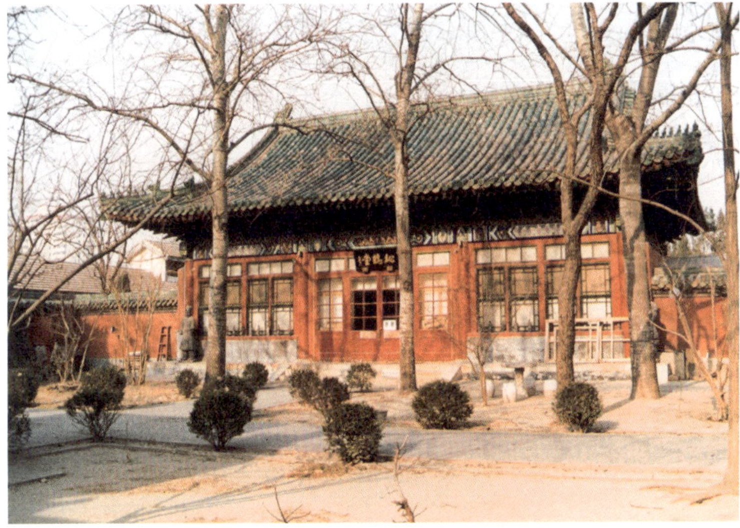

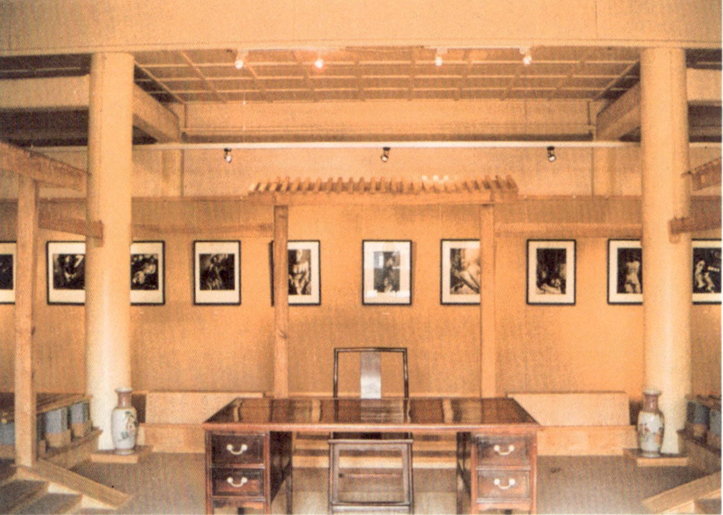

Unknown photographer, exhibition views *Zhang Hai'er*, Song He Tang Pavilion, Ritan Park, Beijing, 1994, private coll.

Jule Noth writes the introduction to the exhibition, excerpted here:

> Zhang Hai'er is illustrating his visions of sexuality, cities, time, and life, and for this purpose uses his models and sceneries. Consequently, Zhang includes photographing and its defining effect on both the artist and the model in some pictures as a second motif. Another basic theme of Zhang Hai'er's work is the description of time, the preserving of a moment, and its passing away. In his street scenes, buildings and bicycles emerge out of a deep space and gain great plasticity through extremely long exposure

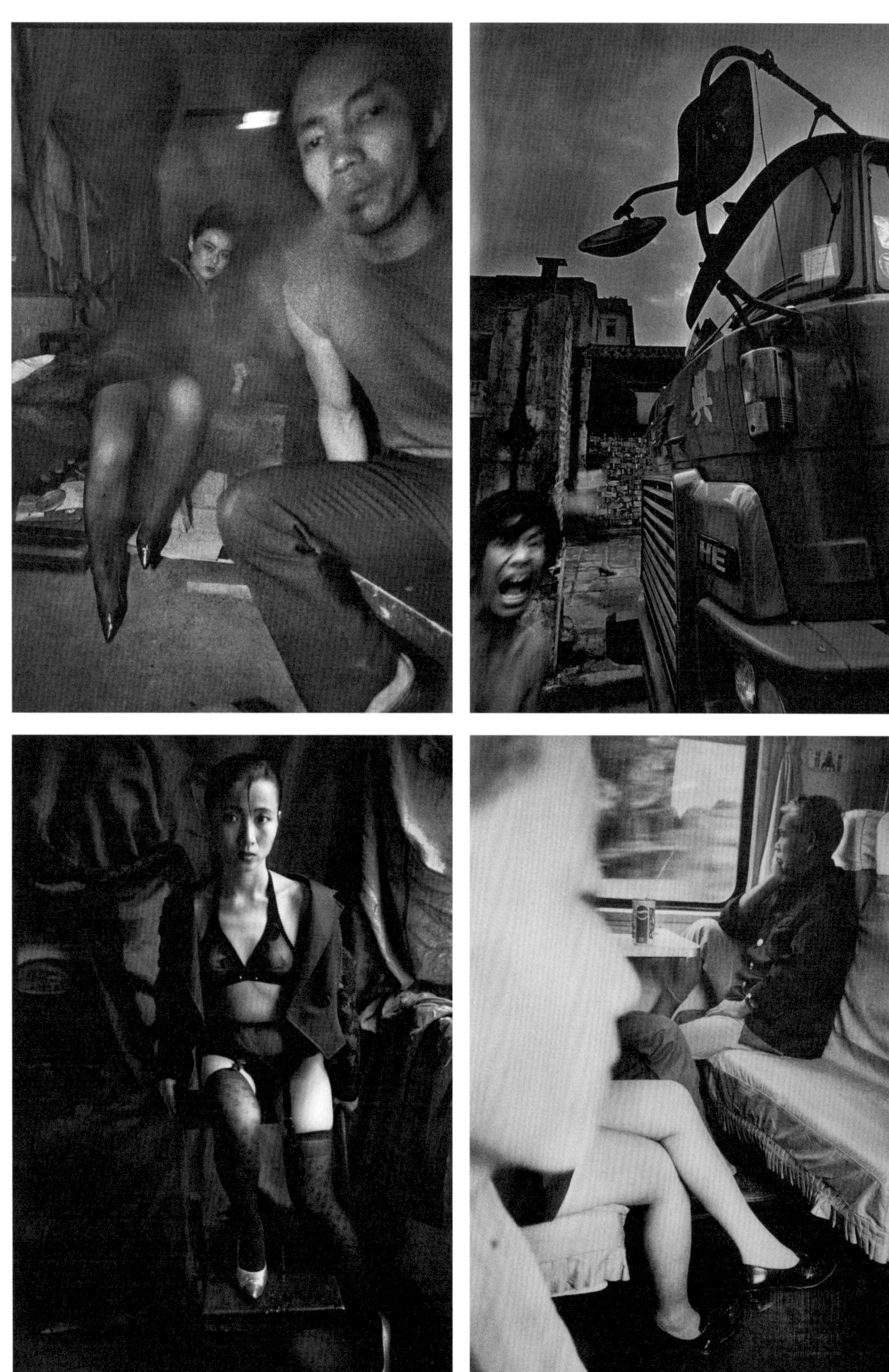

Zhang Hai'er, top left: *Untitled*, gelatin silver print, 57×32 cm, 1989, coll. Three Shadows Photography Art Centre, Beijing; top right: *Selfportrait*, gelatin silver print, 55.2×37.2 cm, 1987, coll. Three Shadows Photography Art Centre, Beijing; bottom left: *Miss H by the Window, Guangzhou*, gelatin silver print, dimensions unknown, 1987; bottom right: *Pepsi in the Train from Canton to Shenzhen*, gelatin silver print, 57.2×38 cm, 1993, private coll., also shown in *Zeitgenössische Fotokunst aus der Volksrepublik China*, Neuer Berliner Kunstverein, Berlin, 1997

times. Meanwhile the persons in these pictures, often caught in motion and placed in the immediate foreground, become temporary elements in this solid city landscape, and so their identity fades behind a feeling of passing time. Their function is that of a formal element in Zhang's composition of an atmosphere of melancholia, reminiscent of French black-and-white movies from the late fifties.
But we are confronted with a very real and existential situation in his photos taken in the train station of the small city of Shahe, where his train home stopped for 80 hours in June 1989. He reflected these days of waiting in photographs of railroads stretching out into the depths of the picture, suggesting traveling and long distances. Almost oversized, powerful engines and clear-cut wagons fill these pictures. But they cut the background off like walls, and the people clinging onto the trains or helplessly moving between them are small, weary, and forlorn.

1995

Van Dijk's new apartment houses his growing archive, library, art collection, and the NAAC office. It quickly becomes an epicenter of artistic life in Beijing. At a time when the infrastructure for contemporary Chinese art is virtually non-existent, van Dijk introduces Chinese artists to Western curatorial practices, such as crating, framing, and loan forms. It is of great importance to van Dijk to run the NAAC according to the highest professional standards. He does so despite the high production costs, limited budgets, and overall daily obstacles. It is remarkable that he publishes a catalogue for each of his shows in China. He also makes a point of supporting young art critics and writers by inviting them to contribute essays and translations.

He does a lot of curatorial work for foreigners who now come pouring in, wanting to show hot Chinese art in their home countries. Most of his work goes unnoticed and unacknowledged, while credit goes to the official organizers. The same, unfortunately, is true for his work in China itself. Even though the artists like him a great deal, and he is becoming an art world legend of sorts, official art criticism hardly acknowledges his existence. There are persistent rumors that he is making a fortune selling works, and the younger generation of critics, who are generally poor, isolated, and professionally adrift, resent him for this. The artists do not bother to discuss van Dijk's work with critics, and because art criticism itself is highly politicized, van Dijk's exhibitions represent the "foreigner's choice" to many Chinese critics. All of this contributes to a historical neglect of van Dijk's work that continues to this day.

By the beginning of 1995, van Dijk is tempted one more time into trying to set up a silk-screen printing studio for artists. This time, he collaborates with Hong Hao.

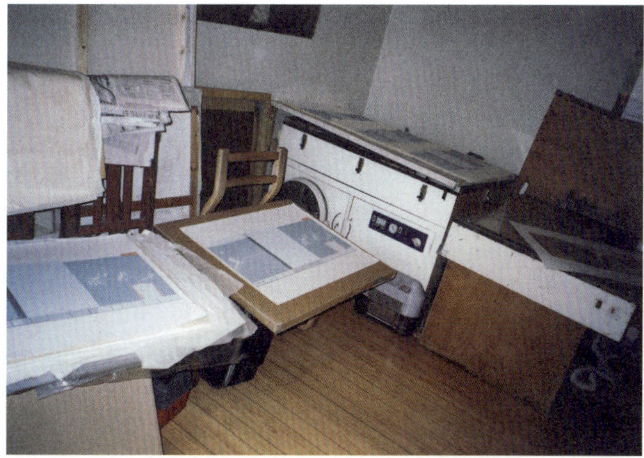

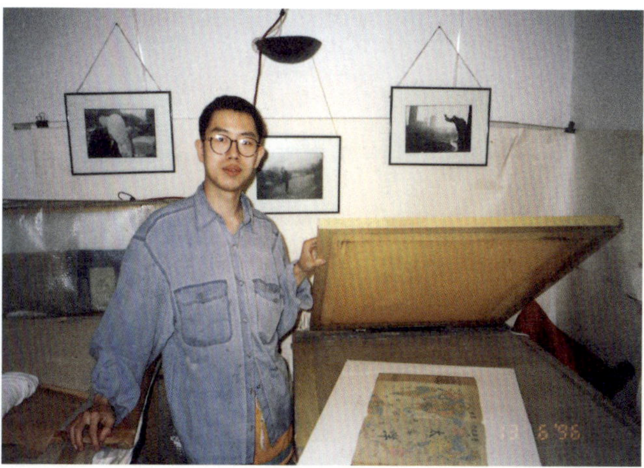

Hong Hao in his kitchen/studio, Beijing, 1995, courtesy Hong Hao
Overleaf: Hong Hao, *Selected Scriptures, page 2121, "The New Geological World"*, silk-screen print, 56 × 78 cm, 1995, private coll.

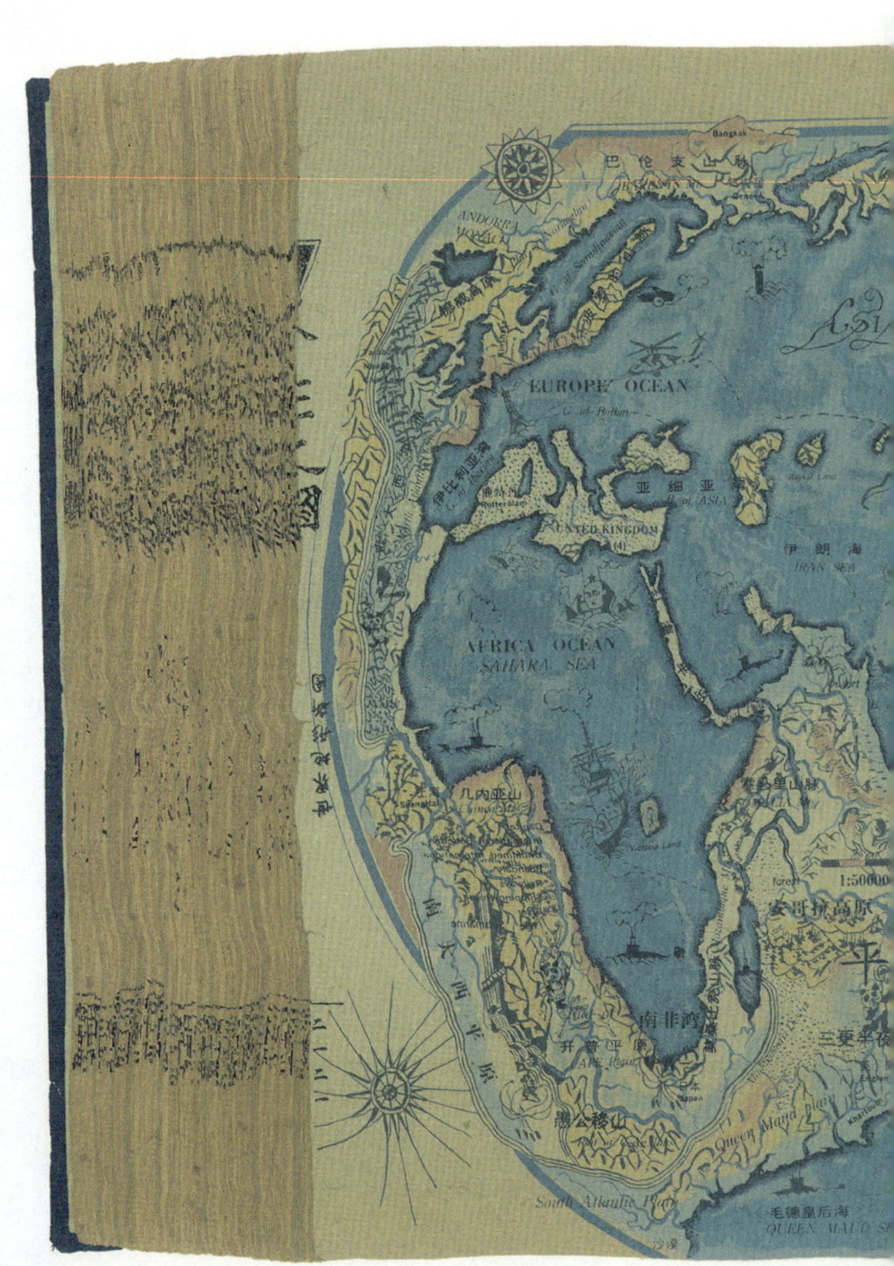

巴伦支山脉
EUROPE OCEAN
伊比利亚岛
亚细亚
UNITED KINGDOM
伊朗海
IRAN SEA
AFRICA OCEAN
SAHARA SEA
几内亚山
南大西平原
开普平原
南非湾
勰公核山
South Atlantic Plain
Queen Maud Plain
毛德皇后海
安哥拉高原
1:50000

《藏经 二二一页 世界地

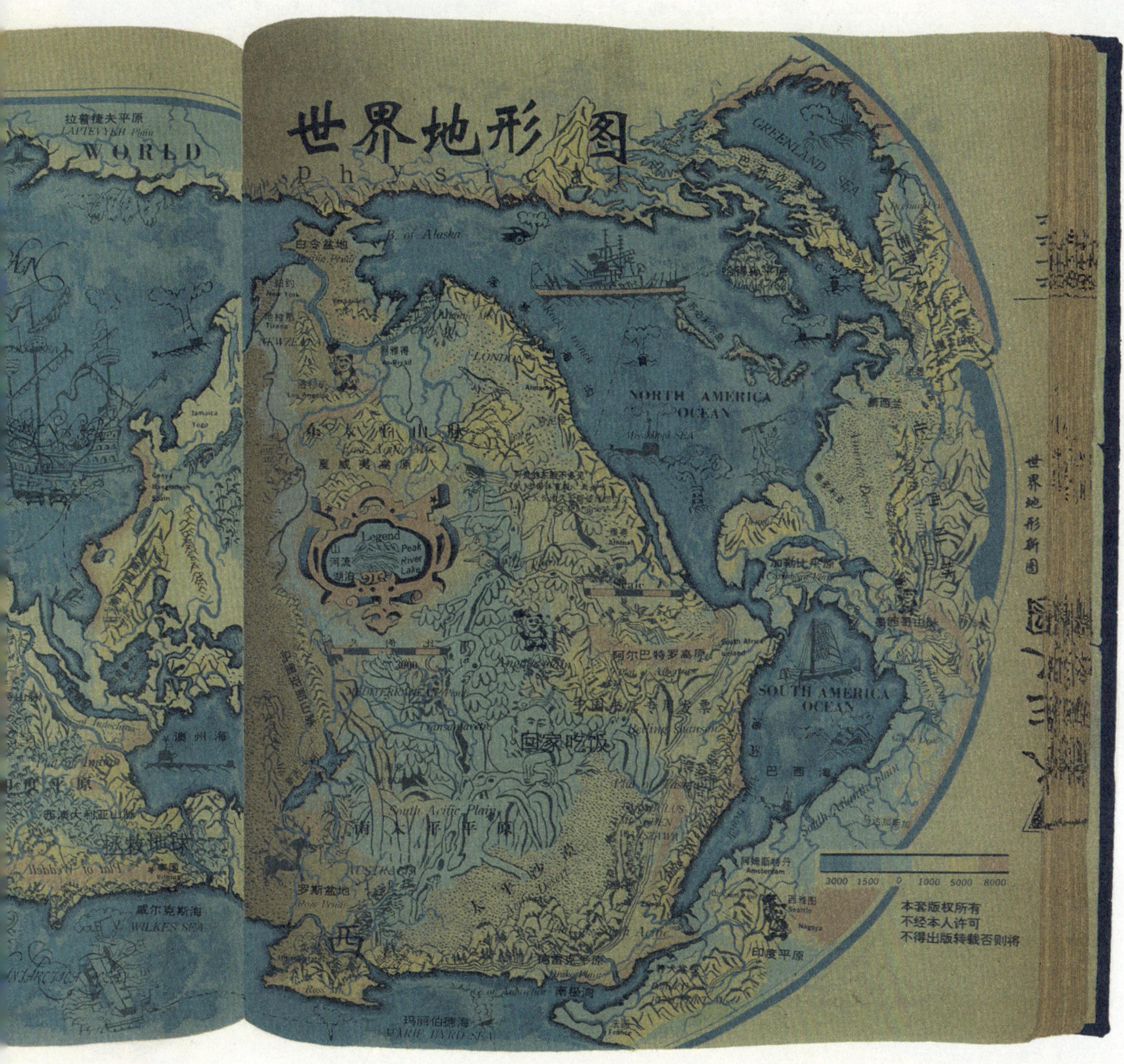

拉普捷夫平原
LAPTEVYKH Plain
WORLD
世界地形图
Physical
GREENLAND SEA
白令盆地
B. of Alaska
NORTH AMERICA
OCEAN
新西兰
Legend
Peak
River
Lake
河流
湖泊
加勒比平原
阿尔巴特罗高原
SOUTH AMERICA
OCEAN
国家吃饭
巴西海
南太平平原
South Pacific Plain
澳州海
罗斯盆地
威尔克斯海
WILKES SEA
玛丽伯德海
MARIE BYRD SEA
阿姆斯特丹
Amsterdam
西雅图
Seattle
印度平原
3000 1500 0 1000 5000 8000
本套版权所有
不经本人许可
不得出版转载否则将
世界地形新图

1/35

洪浩1995.3

From the Fiercely Realistic Footnotes:

> For the better half of 1993, I was led on by the director of the Beijing Craft Arts School, who said he wanted to realize my plan for a silk-screen printing studio but didn't do anything. Printing studios exist all over the world, except in China. Artists are invited or sign up on their own to make use of professional printing equipment for a short period under competent guidance. They donate part of the prints they produce as a payment. The studio builds a collection, and the artist can use the prints to participate in exhibitions and sell them at relatively low rates.
> Hong Hao, who prints at home on his own improvised pressing table, is very familiar with the National Silk-screen Association. He presented my plan to them, and they were interested but had no money. Chance has it that a few months ago a Swedish print studio first held an exhibition of their collection and, in addition, preached the benefits of print studios. We quickly got in touch with them, and now they are waiting for a detailed plan in Sweden to apply for start-up funding. The Swedish Embassy supports the plan—they are good collectors of Hong Hao's prints; even the ambassador is one of our customers.
> Ibid.

Van Dijk's Swedish contact is sinologist and designer Magnus Nordenhaake, his old friend from Nanjing. But even this promising initiative falls through, because the Swedish government is not willing to provide the start-up funding. With that, van Dijk abandons his ill-fated efforts to establish a silk-screen printing studio for artists in China.

Not much later, two young, enthusiastic Dutch gallerists, Martijn Kielstra and Julius Escher, who run a gallery in Amsterdam named Canvas, come to see van Dijk. Van Dijk, who hopes to establish lucrative business ties to the young gallery, takes Kielstra with him on studio visits in Shanghai and Guangzhou. Escher eventually leaves the gallery, but van Dijk continues working with Kielstra in the coming years.

In August, Jule Noth marries Liu Anping, and the couple leaves for Berlin. Van Dijk doesn't take well to this change. Work is piling up too. "I have been working non-stop since last year, seven days a week, no pause, no holidays. The same for Zhang Li, who hangs in there in spite of a relatively modest income."[5] *Jiangsu Art Monthly* publishes Van Dijk's second article, "The Myth of Art History," in its August issue.

5—HvD, letter to Jeroen Vinken, Beijing, 27 June 1995.

In September, the UN Fourth World Conference on Women takes place in Beijing. The announced attendance of First Lady Hilary Clinton makes global headlines, while the People's Republic is frantically trying to prevent more women from entering the country. Van Dijk writes to Jeroen Vinken on 22 August, "Slowly, too late, they [the Chinese Government] realized that they invited 25,000 human rights specialists. Now everyone is in a panic, visa are no longer granted, hotels suddenly have no rooms, airplanes struggle with headwinds and other forms of bad weather. To run a country like this is no sinecure."

31 January – 12 March 1995 *Förändring – Utveckling (Change – Development)*
Konsthallen Göteborg, Sweden

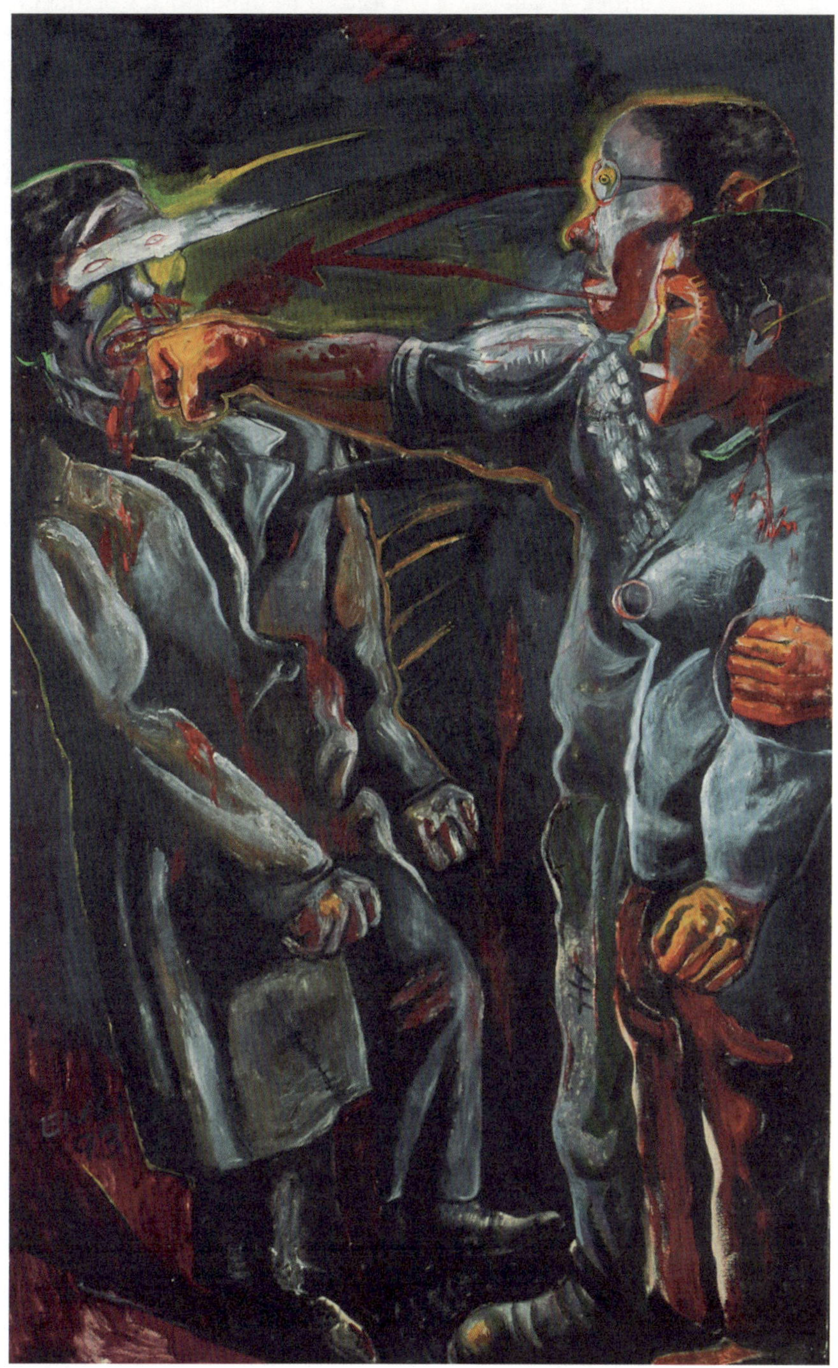

Zhang Enli, *Indignation*, oil on canvas, 160 × 100 cm, 1993, courtesy the artist and ShanghART Gallery, Shanghai

From van Dijk's Fiercely-Realistic Footnotes:

> I am thinking of starting a database exclusively dedicated to ex-Maoists: the local journalist who works for *Die Zeit*, the representative of the Ford Foundation in Beijing, my fellow director of Artfame Development Ltd. Hongkong [Frank Suffa-Friedel], a Belgian dealer in trucks [Frank Uytterhaegen], the director of the Goethe Institute [Kahn-Ackermann] and a few of their teachers, as well as the cultural attaché of the Swedish Embassy. I knew all of them already when the latter introduced me to the second Swedish specimen, the director of the Konstmuseum Göteborg: Folke Edwards. He admitted to indulgently shouting "power to the people" in the past, mainly because "people" translates to "Folke" in Swedish.

Swedes are very curt. It would be his last exhibition before retiring, and in fact, there wasn't much time or money available. Three days in Beijing and three in Shanghai. "What kind of exhibition shall I curate?" he was wondering out loud when we met each other. "It can't be as big as the one in Berlin. It's October now, we open in January, and we'll have a catalogue." This was as far as his deliberations would go, after which we each went on studio visits. After he returned to Sweden, he faxed me a selection of artists that was twice as big as the budget I had drafted in Shanghai. I told him I was honored by his increased trust in my capacities (the Dutch are like the French compared to the Swedes) and drafted a new budget. Meanwhile, I kept up the work, as there was not much time left. "A lot of money, but OK, fine." Following his faxed instructions, the exhibition kept on growing, a fact of which I deliberately kept reminding him. Nils Ericsson, cultural attaché, came to the opening. The ex-Maoist returned and was particularly impressed by the ceremony performed by the Swedish queen. "Maybe, Nils, but I think my queen is better dressed than yours." That left him speechless. Jule and I published a piece of writing in the catalogue together."

HvD, letter to his friends in the Netherlands, Beijing, 9 July 1995

Following van Dijk's recommendation, one of the works shown at the *Förändring – Utveckling* exhibition is *Indignation* by Zhang Enli. Another early discovery by van Dijk is the work of Ai Weiwei. Van Dijk met Ai Weiwei in Beijing in 1993, after the artists returned from New York. Exhibited in Göteborg was *Violin with Egg*, Ai Weiwei's first work ever shown in Europe.

16 – 25 April 1995

Xu Zhiwei, The Arts' Environment
Eighty photographs of artists in Beijing 1992–1994
Ammonal Gallery, Beijing, shut down by police on 15 April

Xu Zhiwei documents the art world in Beijing, the East Village in particular, where many artists, such as Fang Lijun and Ai Weiwei, live and work. He captures artist studios, exhibition openings, happenings, along with street life in the East Village. When van Dijk proposes to exhibit his photographs, Xu himself finds the venue for the show, the Ammonal Gallery, located beneath a small theater. Together they make a catalogue with an essay by Karen Smith.

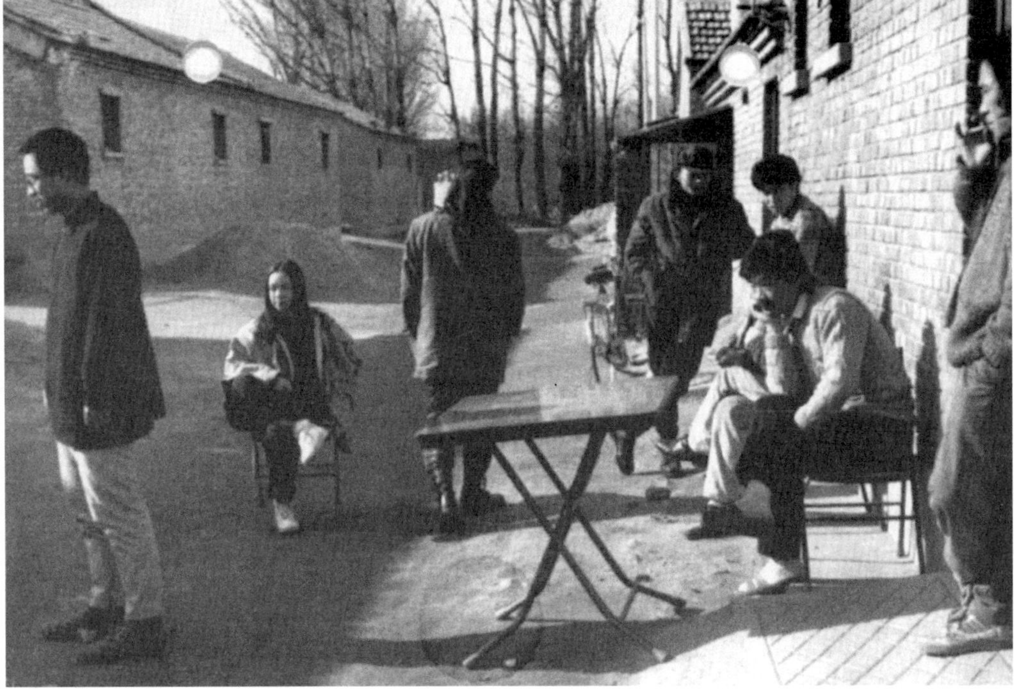

Xu Zhiwei, East Village, Beijing, postcard, private coll.
Opposite page: Karen Smith, catalogue essay for Xu Zhiwei's *The Arts' Environment*, 1995

The theme of Xu Zhiwei's photographs is an examination of the daily lives, the living and working environments of contemporary artists in Beijing. It looks at the flip side of a world often overshadowed by the glamour of grand exhibitions, glossy magazine coverage and notoriety. The world of studios, of cramped spaces, bare necessities and earning the daily bread is very real to the artists themselves who live and make their art within contemporary Chinese society. Its constraints and the possibilities it offers, like those of each and every culture in countries spanning the globe, are fundamental to the art that results. The importance of this context is often glossed over by those unfamiliar with either the circumstances of a contemporary artist in modern China, or the art historical background against which new art is made in its radically changing society. The romanticism often attributed to the artist's garret has never been associated with artists in China. However the traditional metaphor of the creative genius rising like the lotus from the mud remains apt, and in evidence in modern times.

Just as by looking at scribbles made in preparation for finished art work often reveals much about the way in which an artist works and the way a concept or image develops, images of artists' working environments equally reveal much about individual outlook; social, aesthetic and economical. Clutter, artistic paraphernalia, works in progress, those completed or those abandoned, provide an insight into the individual creative processes often invisible in the finished work offered for public view. Within each process, struggle and failure is as important as success achieved; indeed without working the wrong path once or twice, no concern for finding the right one - a more succinct one - is possible. Documentation plays an important role for understanding both progress and change.

Photography is particularly significant here with its emphasis on the moment, effecting images of instances that are not necessarily retained in the memory. Photographs become the memory, reminders of environments that especially in modern China, are subject to constant flux.

The majority of Xu Zhiwei's photographs were taken between 1992-1993 in numerous locations around Beijing. This includes a two-month period in the summer of 1992 when Xu lived in the midst of one artistic community, observing daily life at first hand. This afforded him the opportunity to capture moments that span domesticity to the creative sublime. During the years that have passed since that time, the circumstances of several of the artists photographed by Xu Zhiwei have changed dramatically. Thus his images also highlight the dramatic and meteoric swings in fortune and maturity attained in a brief span of two years. Beyond the insight they give to the general public, such images are a yardstick against which the artists themselves can look back and measure their own personal development. Reflecting working relationships, friendships, communal social and artistic activities of the period, these photographs indicate how each of these elements has shaped the trends and diversity in Beijing's current contemporary art scene.

As documentary evidence that captures the mood of the time and places which he visited, Xu Zhiwei's photographs offer a photo-journalistic impression of an art scene that, having established a broad base since the early eighties, more than ever demands recognition of the potential it has already begun to realize.

Karen Smith
March, 1995

Xu Zhiwei
Born 1961, Beijing. Selftaught photographer.
Since 1987 art editor of the "China Photo Press".
Since 1988 photojournalist of the "Consumer Times".
Winner of the second prize in the photography competition of the 5th UN International Week of Science and Peace.

organized by NEW AMSTERDAM ART CONSULTANCY tel/fax : 832 7949 p.o.box 4076 Beijing 100001

The exhibition is shut down before it even opens. According to Xu, the Chinese title (*chujing*) alone is too sensitive for the authorities. "To them it had a negative connotation, because in Chinese it can be understood as hinting at a method of torture. Van Dijk and Zhang Li took a mini-cab together to the opening; however, they never got out of the car, because the police had already arrived, claiming a violation of fire safety regulations. If the police had seen a foreigner there, things would have gotten even more complicated.[6]

6—MB, interview with Xu Zhiwei, Beijing, March 2014.

From the Fiercely Realistic Footnotes:

> A few days before the opening, the gallerist was visited by the local police with a report from the local fire department saying the lighting of the exhibition did not comply with safety regulations. They told him to show this report when people ask why the exhibition was canceled. The government fears social gatherings now that the month of June is drawing closer. Every year it worsens during the months before that feared date. This shows that ideas about human rights don't differ that much internationally, despite what's said by the government and some sinologists. A shame about those 1,000 invitations that have all been sent off, 350 within China and Hong Kong, 650 abroad. A shame about the already paid gallery fee, frames, et cetera. Starting a gallery in Beijing is an increasingly less attractive idea. Shanghai is more liberal, but building a clientele would take half a year to a year. At least the Goethe Institute in Hong Kong said they are interested in the exhibition: it's in the works for January 1996.
>
> **HvD, letter to his friends in the Netherlands, Beijing, 9 July 1995**

Van Dijk is able to stage the exhibition at the CIFA Gallery of the Central Academy of Fine Arts (CAFA) in Beijing instead, from 9 to 13 December 1995. It is a small space, but beautifully located next to the Academy itself. From 5 to 20 January 1996, it is shown at the Agfa Gallery of the Goethe Institute in Hong Kong.

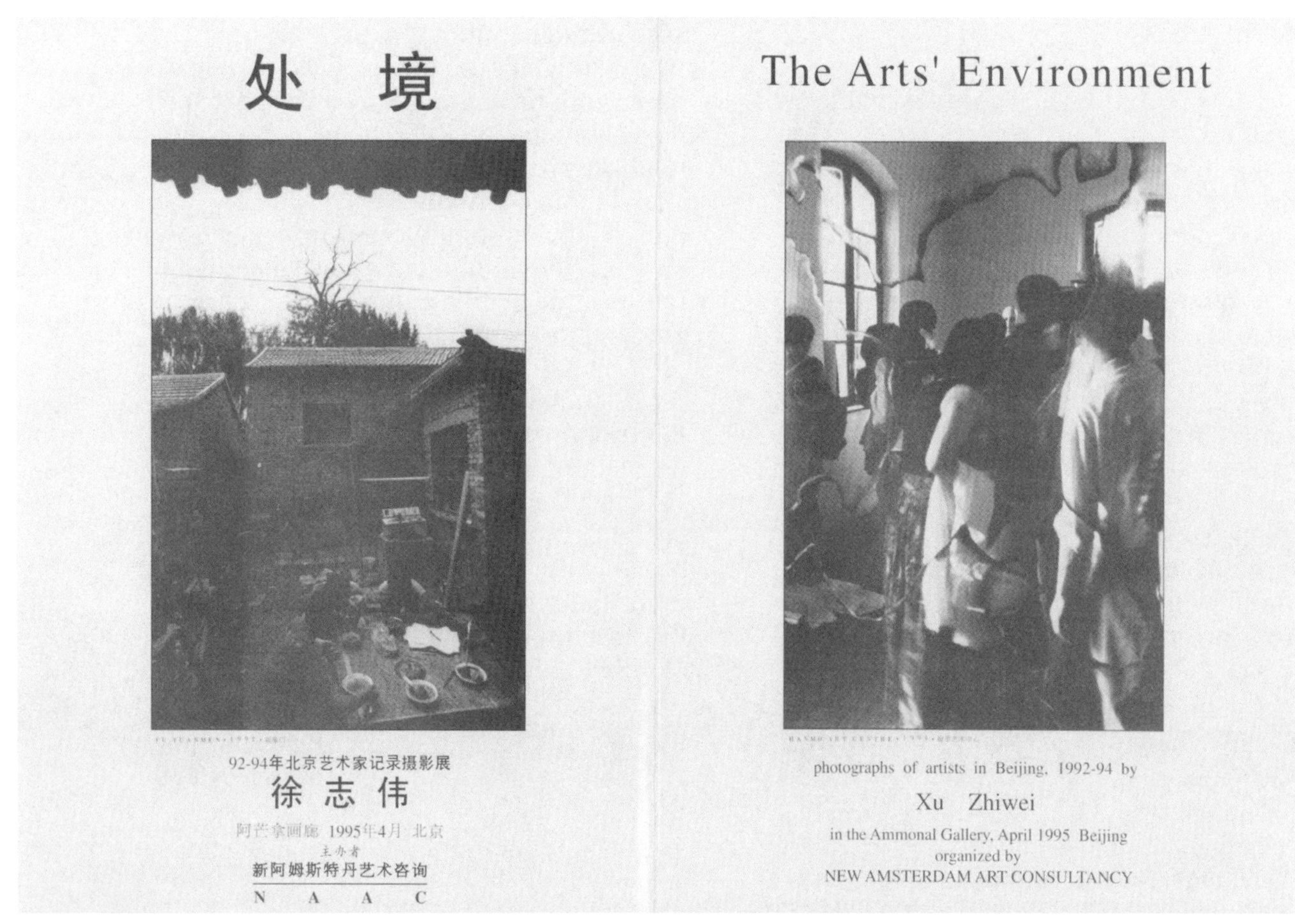

Xu Zhiwei, The Arts' Environment, Eighty Photographs of Artists in Beijing 1992–1994, exhib. cat., publ. NAAC, Beijing, 1995, private coll.; left: East Village, Beijing; right: opening of Zhao Bandi's *Moonflight*, Beijing, 1994

21 May – 21 July 1995

Modern Chinese Art in the Goethe Institute
Goethe Institute, Beijing

From the Fiercely Realistic Footnotes:

> German Angst, part III. I was invited by the new director of the Goethe Institute, Herr Kempf, to brighten up the Institute's building with modern Chinese art. Later I found out that this plan was a suggestion from his staff. I made a proposal and demanded to be exclusively in charge. The Goethe Institute had become one of the few lively cultural centers of Beijing under the guidance of Michael Kahn-Ackermann and his staff: lectures, film screenings, modern art adorning the walls, and a well-equipped, and public, library. Kempf's invitation soon provoked jealousy from my surroundings. He was warned to expect trouble with the Ministry of Culture should he continue working with me. I am almost sure that this story was an attempt by someone to take over the commission. Should the Ministry truly hold anything against me, it would be extremely easy for them to take matters into their own hands. But Kempf was not easily reassured. He went to the Ministry to ask for permission, but they had no clue what he was talking about, so they redirected him to the Ministry of Education. There, he was told he could do as he pleased, as long as there wouldn't be too much publicity.
> Meanwhile, half a year had passed since our first meeting. I already understood that he really just wished for a prohibition on exhibitions. There was little chance that would happen though, as the Goethe Institute had finally, after years of negotiating, acquired the right to organize cultural events besides merely education- and language-related projects. When the visitor numbers of their events exceeded his expectations (not because of their efforts, but because news spreads easily in Beijing), he phoned me up at night, telling me in a panicked voice that the exhibition had to close. The next morning, he withdrew his demand, but it turned out that visitors were denied access to the exhibition because of vague reasons. Other events initiated by staff of the Goethe Institute were, one after another, shut down by a frustrated Kempf: the end of the Goethe Institute.
>
> **HvD, letter to his friends in the Netherlands, Beijing, 9 July 1995**

Summer 1995

Geng Jianyi, Liu Anping, *Action/Solution*
Installation project, Huashan Art School, Shanghai, unrealized

For this installation project, Liu Anping and Geng Jianyi plan to enter the real estate market and establish an interior decorating company. Liu Anping is to be the manager. Geng Jianyi is interested in the tastes of the nouveau riche Chinese middle class, such as neo-classical hotel lobbies and gilded baroque interiors. The exhibition consists of creating a modern, posh apartment within the school. The exhibition period is the time it takes to renovate. *Action/Solution* is inspired by a line from *Records of the Grand Historian* by Sima Qian: "All actions and solutions are perfectly appropriate, similar to painting and drawing."

> Mr. Jiang Qun, Hello! The joint exhibition of Liu Anping and Geng Jianyi is now titled *Action/Solution*. Geng Jianyi's work is titled *The Standards of Interior Decoration of the Modern Family Home*, using cardboard printing to decorate a bedroom, living room, kitchen, and toilet as an example of popular standards of fashion. Liu Anping's work, entitled *King of Drawing*, exhibits the paintings, drawings, and photographic works that he purchased from more than twenty artists, using eggs as a theme to hold a mock sale event at the exhibition venue. This also relates to consumer attitudes towards the modern family.
> The issues we need to discuss regarding the exhibition space of the Huashan Art School:
> 1. This exhibition, including the printed invitations and flyers, is an art action in the form of a mock commercial sale by the artists. It is not a real business.
> 2. The exhibition is expected to be held in mid- or late November and last for ten days, preferably including two weekends.
>
> **HvD, letter to the director of the Huashan Art School, summer 1995**

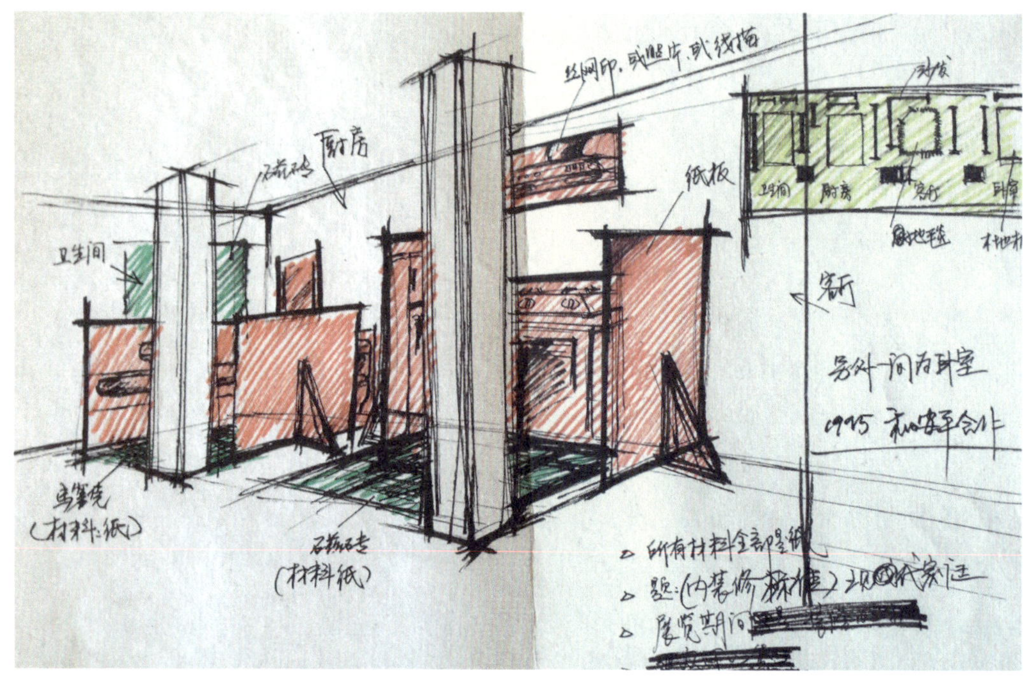

Geng Jianyi, *Modern Family Home,* exhibition proposal for *Action/Solution*, pen and felt pen on paper, folded A4 paper, 1995, private coll.

2 June–16 July 1995

Xin Kedu and Günther Uecker, *Brief an Peking/Arbeit III*
Neuer Berliner Kunstverein, Berlin

Xin Kedu, or the New Measurement Group, is active between 1989 and 1996. It consists of Gu Dexin, Chen Shaoping, and Wang Luyan, who all belong to the first radical post-Mao generation in Chinese art. Founded in 1988, Xin Kedu makes its first public appearance in *China/Avant-Garde*. Denying the validity of artistic self-expression, the group aims to erase all traces of subjectivity from their art. Meeting on a regular basis, the three adopt rules with the goal of regulating every aspect of artistic creation, from drawing tools to working procedures.

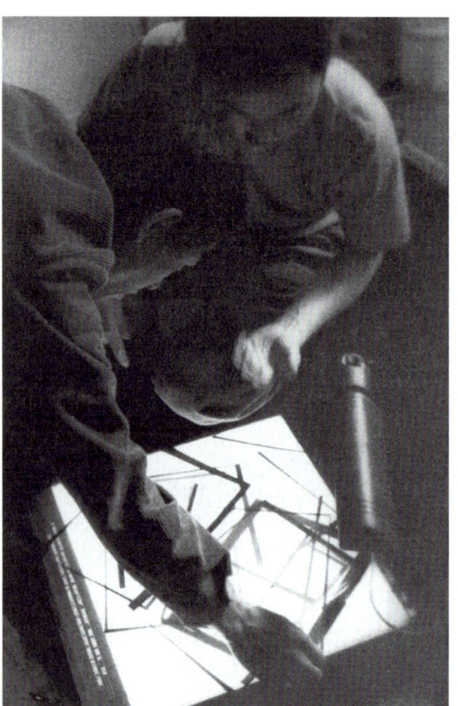
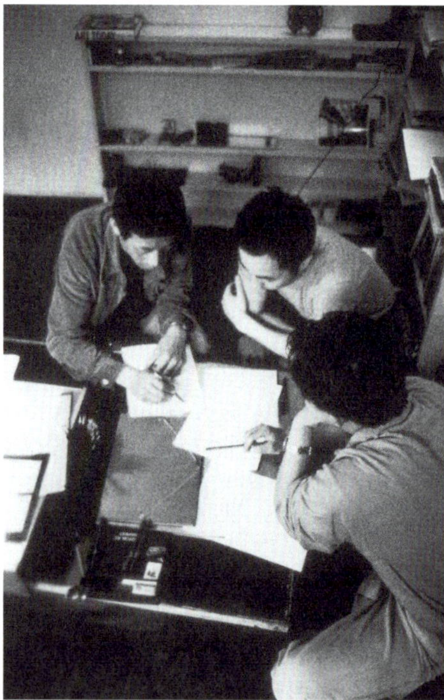
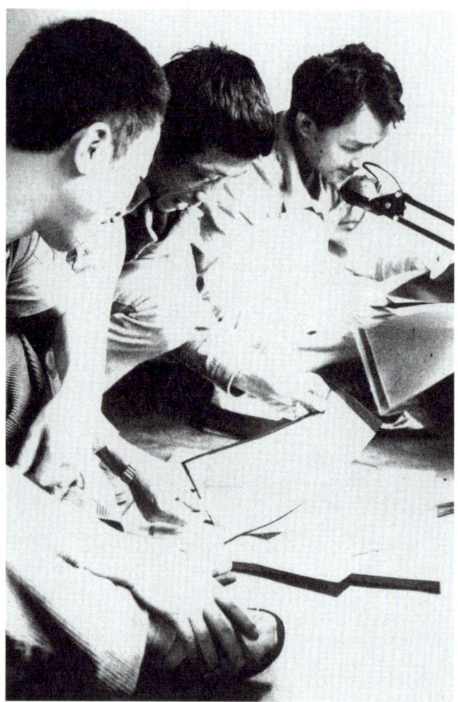

Xin Kedu during working sessions, *China/Avant-Garde*, Beijing, 1989, courtesy Xin Kedu

Between 1990 and 1996, the group produces five books that record the deconstruction process through which objects, human behaviors, and situations are transformed into graphs. In late 1995, in view of the conflict between its radical founding principles and the inevitable absorption of their work by the art system, the group calls a final meeting and decides to destroy all its documents and drawings as a final "measurement" required to terminate its mission.

From the Fiercely Realistic Footnotes:

> When visiting Beijing last year, Günther Uecker was sixty-four years old and just as active as he was thirty years ago, when he was taking lessons given by his Dutch friend and colleague Henk Peeters[7] at the Academy of Fine Arts in Arnhem. Günther Uecker, Heinz Mack, and Otto Piene (German); Henk Peeters, Jan Hendrikse, and Armando (Dutch); and Piero Manzoni (Italian) were breaking new ground at the time under the name "zero-group." They mainly reacted to the idea, dominant in Western Europe, of the proliferating romanticism surrounding the artist, which since World War II had taken the form of "Abstract Expressionism" (Karel Appel and associates). The statement "Why would I hang the painterly immortalized misery of someone else on my wall?" was, I suspect, uttered by Armando. The zero-group represented simplicity, often realized through provocative vulgarities: Uecker made reliefs using nails; Peeters mounted cotton balls behind netting, and filled refrigerated bags with colored water, calling them "watercolors"; Armando covered a wall in the Stedelijk Museum Amsterdam with coasters of Amstel Beer (after negotiating with Heineken, well-paid of course); and Manzoni managed to have his canned feces become part of multiple museum collections.
>
> **HvD, letter to his friends in the Netherlands, Beijing, 9 July 1995**

7—Van Dijk's former art teacher.

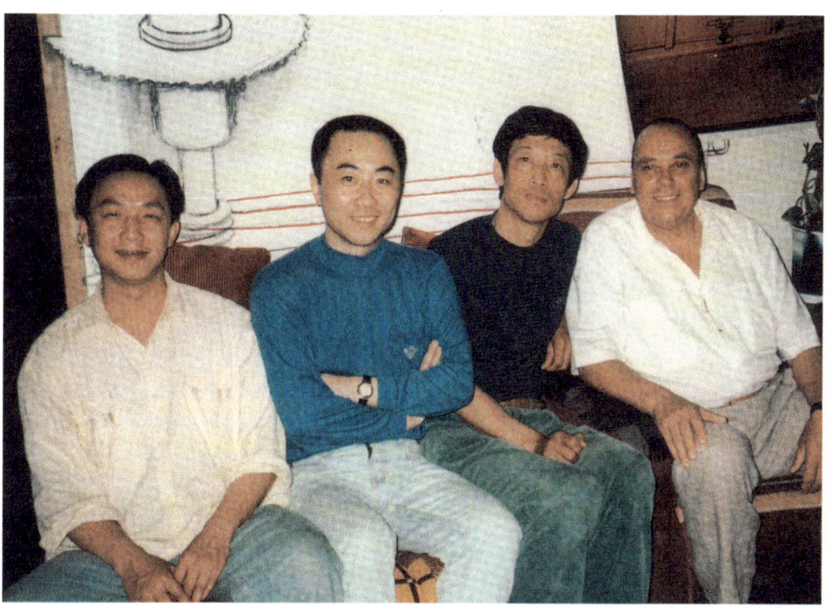

Left to right: Xin Kedu (Gu Dexin, Wang Luyan, Chen Xiaoping) with Günther Uecker in Wang Luyan's home, Beijing, May 1994, courtesy Xin Kedu

Before visiting Beijing in 1994, Uecker wrote *Letter to Beijing* (*Brief an Peking*), which is to be part of the dual show with Xin Kedu. The Xin Kedu artists design their *Work III*[8] for the exhibition, taking Uecker's *Letter to Beijing* and gradually transforming it into a graph. Van Dijk originally hopes to publish it for an exhibition at Hanmo Art Center in 1994. The design of *Arbeit III* is finished but the book unprinted when Xin Kedu is forbidden by the authorities to take part in the show because Uecker's letter mentions human rights. Uecker returns to Germany. When Alexander Tolnay becomes the director of the Neuer Berliner Kunstverein soon afterwards, he immediately invites Xin Kedu to exhibit in Berlin with Uecker. *Arbeit III* is Xin Kedu's artwork in the show.

8—*Die Arbeit III der Gruppe "Xin Kedu", Ein Dialog mit Günther Uecker*, 23 June to 22 August 1994.

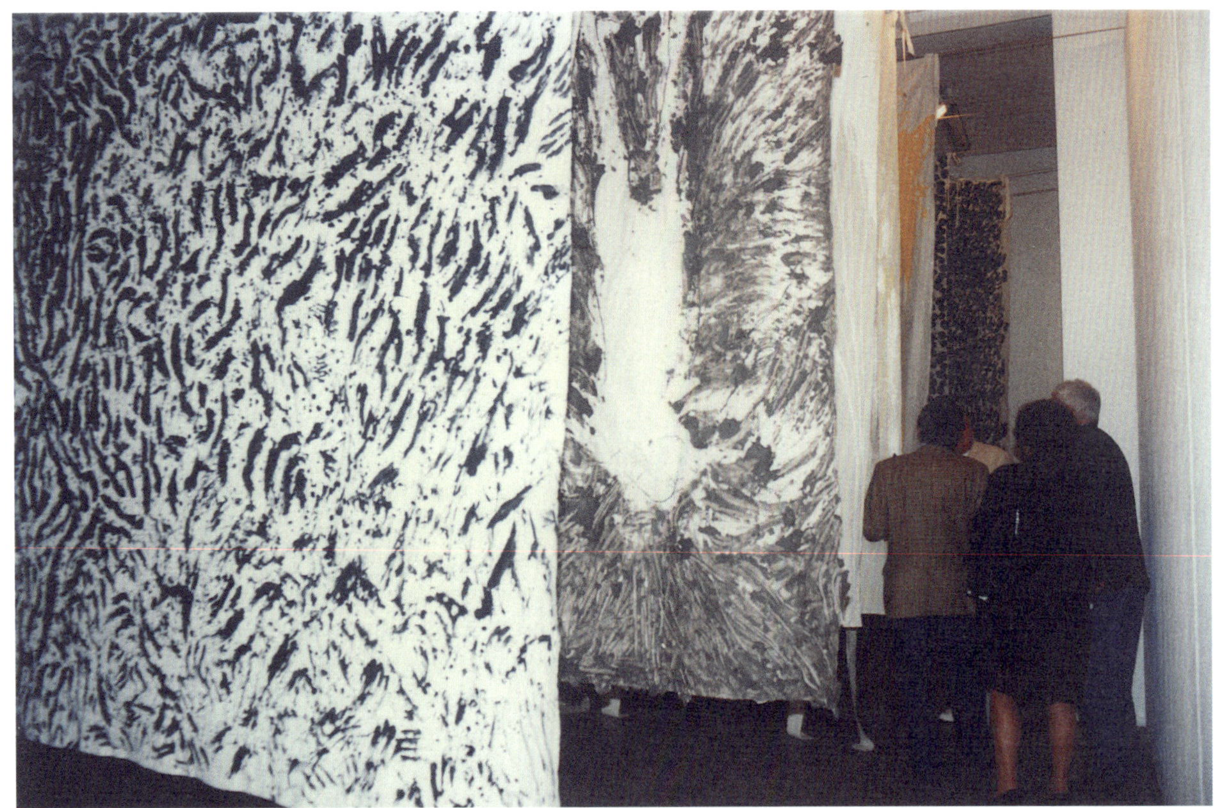

Günther Uecker, *Brief an Peking*, Neuer Berliner Kunstverein, Berlin, 1995, exhibition view, courtesy Xin Kedu

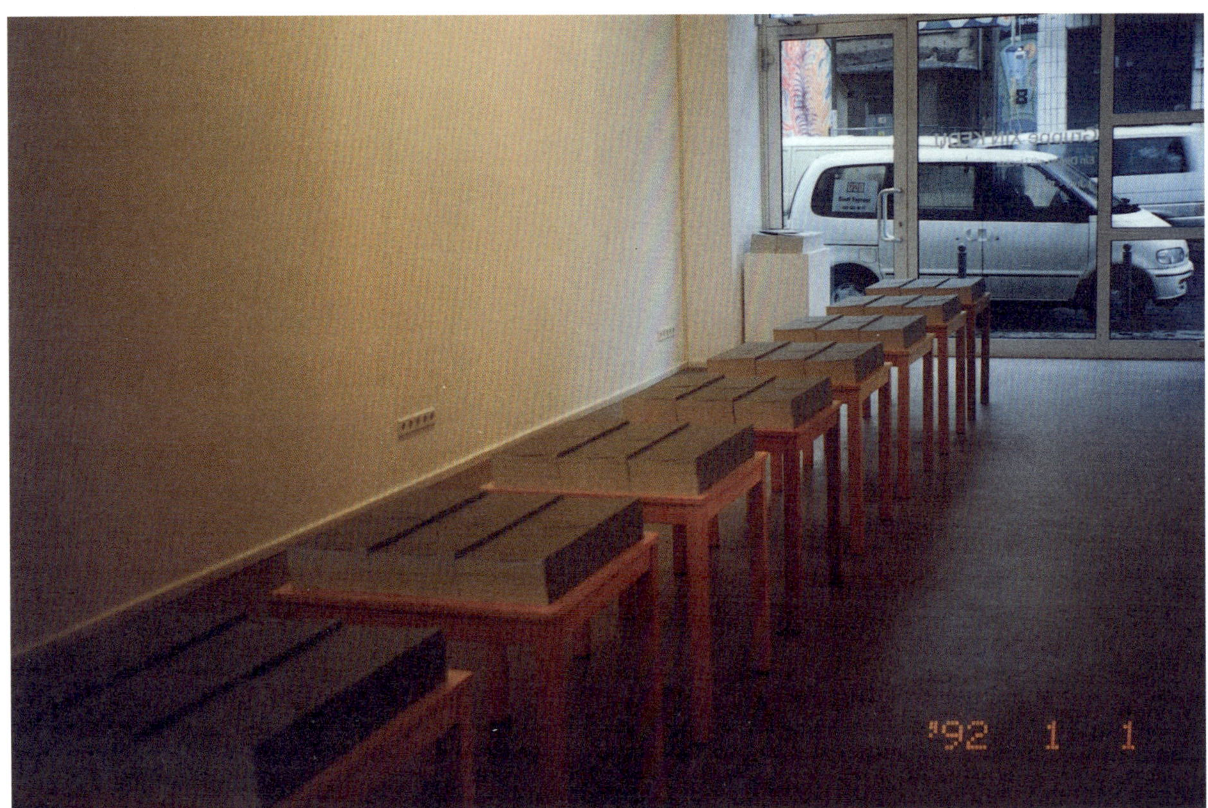

Xin Kedu, *Arbeit III*, Neuer Berliner Kunstverein, Berlin, 1995, exhibition view, courtesy Xin Kedu

1994–1996

Las Meninas/Beijing 1995
European Multimedial Project, unrealized

Since mid-1994, Hans van Dijk has thrown himself heart and soul into a fantastic scheme called *Las Meninas*, conceived by Belgian artist Bart Vanwalle.

From the Fiercely Realistic Footnotes:

> A project at risk of exploding like a balloon. As funds applied for from the Belgian Government were held off, the posh, mustachioed initiator Vanwalle responded by taking the project to an even grander level. His fellow countryman, ex-Maoist truck trader Frank [Frank Uytterhaegen], calls this "launching turbo's." Vanwalle, a fifty-year-old artist, thinks big. "Romanticism, yes, we will deal with that in the 21st and 22nd century."
> The plan is to build a multimedia center in Beijing with an internet relationship with Barcelona, Brussels, Eindhoven, and Berlin. He's already granted me the directorship of the center, but besides a lot of paper, there is little money or anything else. Every now and then he visits for a few days, recently informing me he made it clear to the embassy that he couldn't work this way any longer: the three million francs should make their appearance soon. Also in Brussels, they would have to come forth with their money.
> HvD, letter to his friends in the Netherlands, Beijing, 9 July 1995

The only tangible outcome is the foundational meeting between van Dijk and "ex-Maoist truck trader" Frank Uytterhaegen[9], a Belgian businessman and fledgling art collector. A friendship springs up between the two men; by the end of 1995, Uytterhaegen becomes the business director of NAAC. Uytterhaegen, who has his own art contacts in Belgium, proposes that van Dijk organize an exhibition of Belgian art at the privately owned Yan Huang Art Museum in Beijing. The exhibition is titled *3×3 On Paper – Three Generations of Flemish Artists* and takes place in July 1996. The participating artists are selected by a Belgian gallery.

9—Frank Uytterhaegen, owner of the trading company Chinalink, studied history and philosophy in Ghent, Belgium. He is married to Pascale Geulleaume.

17 June – 10 September 1995

Configura 2 – Dialog Der Kulturen
Erfurt, Germany

Van Dijk is the curator/consultant and organizer of the Chinese part of this large-scale project that aims to exhibit art from across the globe. Participating Chinese artists include Ai Weiwei, Feng Mengbo, Ni Haifeng, Xin Kedu, Zhang Huan, and Zhang Peili. Jule Noth continues to assist van Dijk with his many Europe-based projects from Berlin, including *Configura 2*. She contributes to the catalogue with a text entitled "Outsiders," while van Dijk writes the essay "Politik, Dollars, Wiedergutmachung und Ruhm" ("Politics, Dollars, Retribution, and Fame").

From the Fiercely Realistic Footnotes:

> "East Germans Discover the World" would have been a better title. Two serious-looking Germans travel the world with a well-prepared *Ausstellungskonzept* [exhibition concept] and a budget of three million marks (which I didn't know of at the time). This meant traveling from Hilton to Hilton, nine in total. They turned into nervous wrecks each time, hoping the Hilton bus would deliver them at the airport in time to travel on. The first morning in Beijing, they manned up—beards up high, teeth clenched—and stepped into a touristy decorated rickshaw, which drove them around the city like kings. When they got out, the driver asked them for 100 USD each, which they paid of course. Afterwards, they stepped into a fancy restaurant, where they ordered the cheapest dish on the menu. Of course, the waiter came to announce that the dish wasn't available at the moment, suggesting another, similar dish, which unfortunately turned out to be much higher priced, et cetera, et cetera.
> During each (very tense) studio visit, they needed to have their ecumenical concept affirmed, after which they would congratulate each other, relieved and smitten with

their visionary gifts. Whenever the visits weren't so successful, the world concept would be explained again to the artist, very slowly and explicitly this time, making it clear that his participation in this international exhibition was at risk.
Their visit coincided with Günther Uecker's, and I followed his advice to continue working with them: you just choose great artists and ignore the stories that are told about them. Jule Noth took care of the organization of the Chinese part of the exhibition, and we both wrote a nice piece for the catalogue.

HvD, letter to his friends in the Netherlands, Beijing, 9 July 1995

Xin Kedu

Arbeitsbuch IV is Xin Kedu's work for *Configura 2* in Erfurt, Germany. The work is based on nine recipes for original dishes from the participating countries, which they obtain mostly by writing to the relevant embassies. At the opening, the members of Xin Kedu prepare dishes from the recipes.

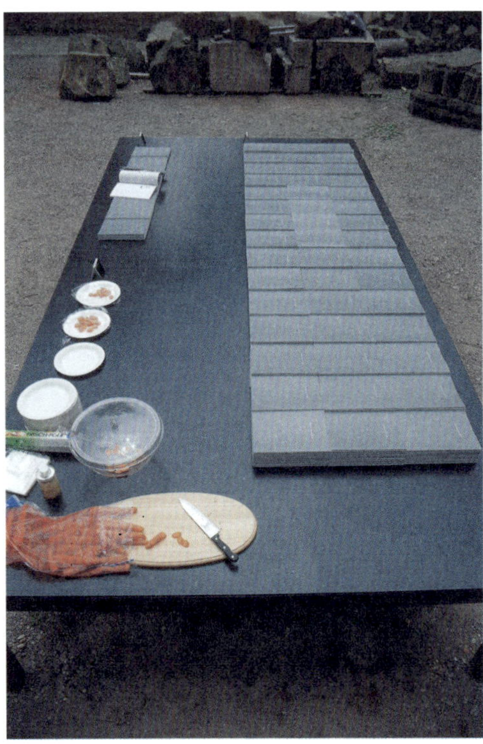

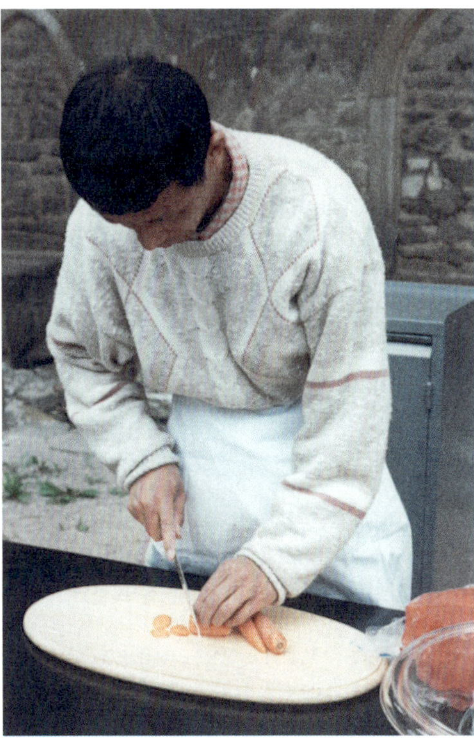

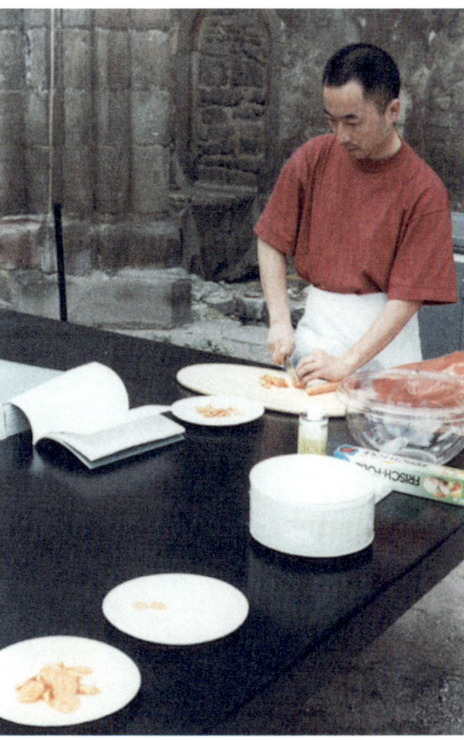

Xin Kedu, *Artbeitsbuch IV*, action on the opening day of *Configura 2 – Dialog Der Kulturen*, Erfurt, Germany, 1995, courtesy Xin Kedu
Opposite page: Xin Kedu, Original recipe for kebabs, Chinese translation, and two printing proofs (left to right) for *Arbeitsbuch IV*, 1995, private coll.

Kebab

Zutaten:

1 kg	Hackfleisch vom Rind oder Lamm
1	mittelgroße gehackte Zwiebel
2	gehackte Knoblauchzehen
1/2 TL	schwarzer Pfeffer
1/4 TL	Zimt
1 TL	Salz
1 EL	Petersilie
2 TL	Öl

Zubereitung:

Alle Zutaten mit Ausnahme des Öls in einer Schüssel vermengen und 45 Min. ziehen lassen.
Das Fleisch zu länglichen Würsten formen und der Länge nach auf Grillspieße stecken. Während dem Grillen regelmäßig wenden und mit Öl bestreichen, bis es gar ist.
Die Kebabs vor dem Servieren vorsichtig von den Spießen streifen und mit Pommes Frites und etwas Petersilie servieren.

A页-1

a,-1 埃及

烤肉串(KEBABS) ·埃及·

〈配料〉

肉馅(牛肉、羊肉)	1公斤
洋葱(中等)(切碎)	1个 ~~(剁碎或搾碎)~~
蒜 (切碎)	2瓣 ~~(剁碎)~~
黑胡椒	½匙
肉桂	¼匙
盐	1匙
欧芹	1大汤匙
橄榄油	2匙

〈作法〉:

1. 将所有配料(除油外)在碗里搀合在一起 然后放置边上腌制45分钟。
2. 将制成的肉馅搓成肠形串在铁扦上,在烤架下烧烤时,不断转动铁扦,并往肉上抹油。
3. 上桌前将肉串从铁扦上轻轻取下,配以法国炸土豆和一些欧芹。

A-1 a,-1

①-1

O A B C D E F G H I J K L M

Kebab	Koupe-pia	Edikan-g	Zutate-n:	(Dolm-dhakia)	Ikong	1	Zutatn:	(Efik/	kg	500	Ibibio)	Hackfl-eisch
1	¼	g	mittelg-roße	Tasse	Spinatb-lätter	gehack-te	Zitro-nensaft	1	Zwiebel	2	kg	2
er	1	Rinder-haxe	Pfeffer	EL	(nach	½	Zimt	Be-lieben)	TL	1	300	Zimt
EL	1	(nach	Peter-silie	große,	Be-lieben)	2	Kleing-ewürfe-lte	300	TL	Tomate	g	Öl
	50	Palmöl		60	1	Öls	Weinbl-ätter		in	1	1	einer
Min.	Wasche-n	Seesch-necken	Ziehen	und	oder	lassen.	in	Musche-ln	Das	sieden-dem	(nach	Fleisch
und	weichk-ochen.	3	der	Mit	gr.	Länge	kaltem	EL	nach	Wasser	ner	auf
Grillen	Reis,	und	regelm-äßig	eine	40	Wenden	gehack-te	Min.	und	Zwiebel.	kochen.	mit
gar	Einen	aus	ist.	TL	dem	Die	der	Topf	Kebabs	Füllung	nehmen.	vor
den	die	Schnec-ken	Spieße-n	Seiten	hinein-geben	streif-en	der	und	und	Länge	weiter-e	mit
Peters-ilie	gefüll-ten	und	servie-ren.	Seite	Spinat-blätter	Fisch	her	putzen.	in	lose	in	
1	dünste-n,	Topf	Glas	die	geben.	Zitron-ensaft	Tomate	Auch	Salz	und	das	schwar-zer
Glas	in	15	warmes	die	Min.	Wasser	Pfanne	kochen	1	legen	lassen.	Zwiebe-l
EL	zudeck-en.	Maggi	Pflanz-enöl	damit	unterr-ühren.	3	sie	Zudeck-en	Tomate-n.	nicht	und	geschä-lt
Lauchs-pitzen	Koupe-p-ia	Gehack-te	Zubere-itung:	bedeck-t	Zwiebe-ln	Fisch	sind.	hinein-gebenm	mit	den	um-rühr-en	Zitron-ensaft.
und	Flamme	Min.	30	garen	kochen	min.	lassen.	lassen.	ziehen	Tan-doo-ri	Umrühr-en	lassen.
warmem	8	Cassav-a	Wasser	Knobla-uchzeh-en	Fufu	in	1	Von	der	TL	weicher	Rührma-schine
einem	30		sauber-en	g	Sauerk-ohlsup-pe	Tuch	Zwiebe-ln	Zutate-n:	auspre-ssen.	15	500	Das
ergebe-n:	15	1	bei	g	Zwiebel	Bedarf	Papaya	1	kann	(falls	Karotte	die
wer-den.	Braten,	Stärke	Die	1	1	Zwiebel	EL	EL	in	Zitron-ensaft	Tomate-npürre-e	den
dünste-n.	oder	Zubere-itung:	dann		Das	die	Lebens-mittel-farbe	Rindfl-eisch	Tomat-en,	60	in	die
	Prise	Sauerk-ohl	beigeb-en.	Safran	mit	Nach	(nach	etwas	Belieb-en	Belieb-en)	Wasser	mit
Fisch	Garam	kochen.	in	Masala	Das	den	Zum	Fleisc-h	Topf	Servie-ren:	und	geben.
garen	gemahl-en	geben.	lassen.	½	Die	Jiaozi	TL	Karott-ensche-iben.	(Chine-sische	Kaleba-ssenbl-ätter	die	Ravioli-i)
Weizen-mehl	Man-gop-ulver	kurz	200	2	anbrat-en	ml	TL	und	warmes	Zitron-ensaft	auch	Wasser
Schüssel	wasche-n.	und	geben.	Zwiebe-ln.	Stärke	das	Knobla-uch.	verrüh-ren.	Wasser	Ingwer	anbrat-en	unter
anschl-ießend	einer	bis	den	feinen	20	Teig	Paste	Min.	kneten.	verrüh-ren.	köchel-n	Zudeck-en

Z 栈

①⅓-1

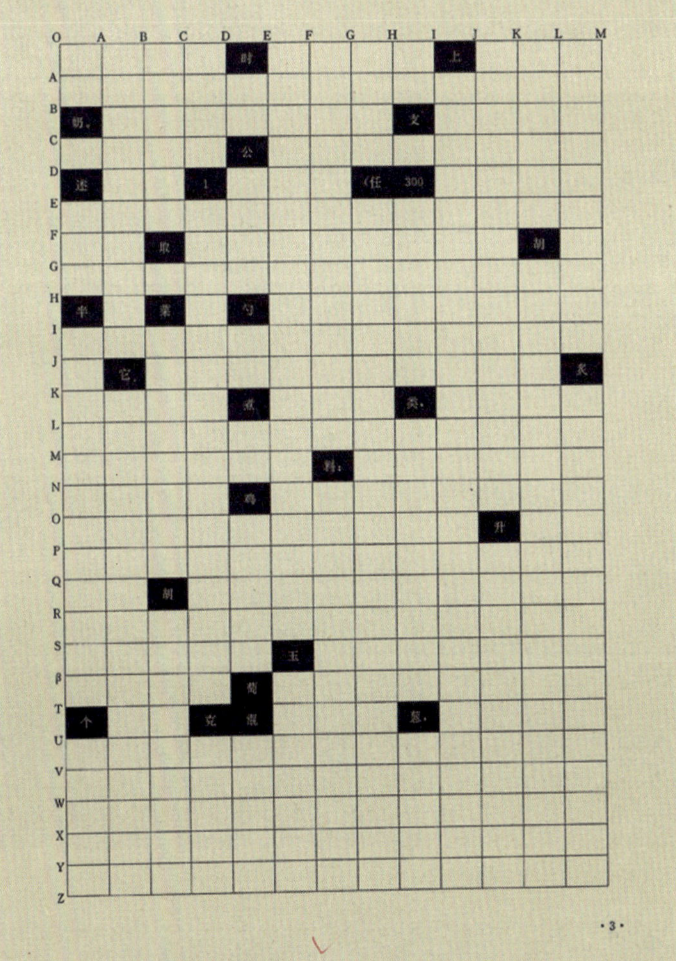

Feng Mengbo

Feng Mengbo, under thirty years old and one of the youngest amongst the group of interesting artists, hopes to escape from the traditional arts circuit with his self-designed video games. Since graduating two years ago, a number of serious sales of (sadly never exhibited) older works to a Hong Kong based art dealer-gallerist and a Japanese writer has allowed him to devote all his time to his own work. Until recently, futuristic plastic toys and popular video games were his main source of images. [...]
On the recently purchased computer, he works on a series of images about an opera he grew up with: *How Yang Zirong Conquered Tiger Mountain*, the only opera that was performed during his years in primary school. The series starts with a no-smoking sign, followed by a quote from the great chairman taken from his 1942 lecture on arts and culture. To many artists, the recent past and the current stormy process of modernization are heavy and dramatic subjects, yet for Feng Mengbo they prove to be material that generates an unstoppable flow of images of a cool, disturbing beauty.
HvD, fragment of an unpublished text written in fall 1993 for *Der Stern*

Taking Tiger Mountain by Strategy is first exhibited in *Configura 2*, Erfurt, Germany, where it takes the form of a game consisting of nine episodes. It is considered the first computer-generated video work made in China, yet is shown for the first time in China only in 2014 as part of the exhibition *Hans van Dijk: 5000 Names* at UCCA, Beijing.

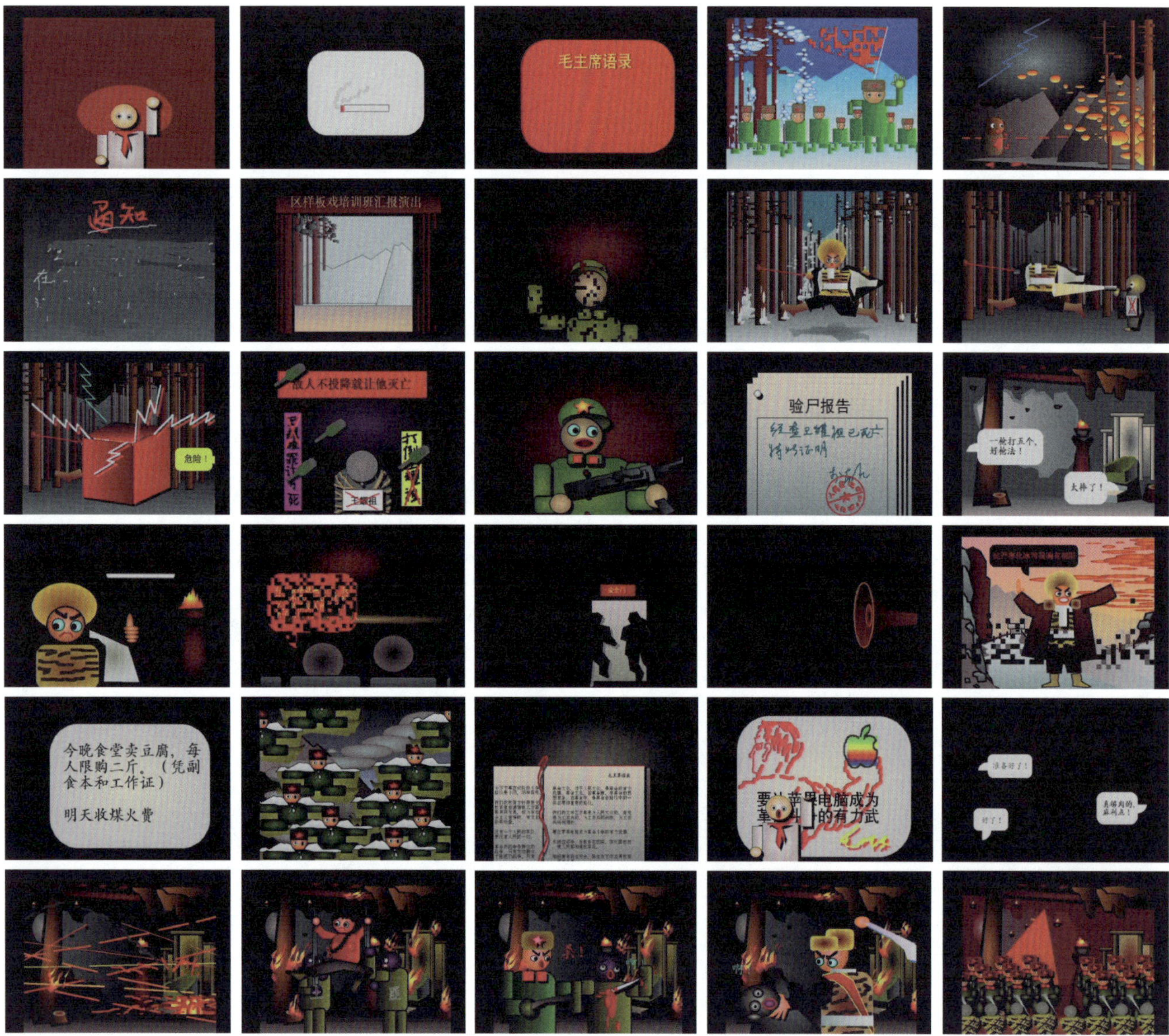

Feng Mengbo, *Taking Tiger Mountain by Strategy*, Macintosh LCII, System 7, Aldus Persuasion V2., 1994, courtesy Feng Mengbo and Chambers Fine Art

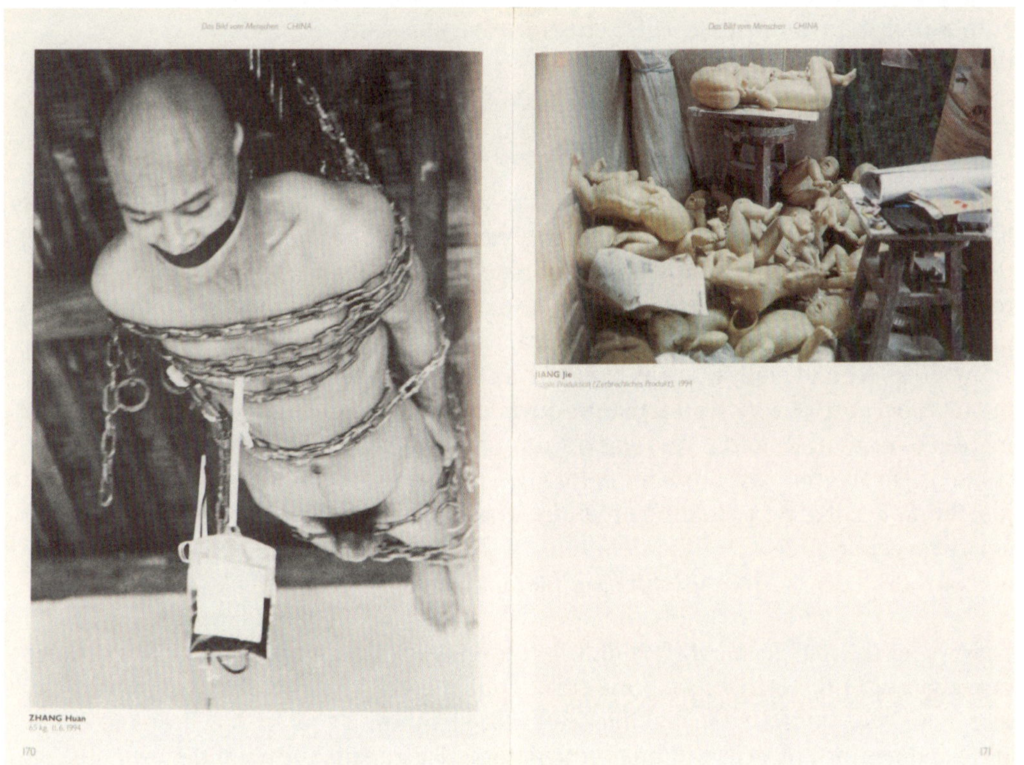

Configura 2 – Dialog Der Kulturen, Erfurt, Germany, 1995, exhib. cat., chapter "The Image of Man-China"; left: photo of Zhang Huan's performance *65 kg.II.6*, Beijing, 1994; right: Jiang Jie, *Fragile Production*, 1994, private coll.

2–10 September 1995

Kvindelig Kinesisk Avantgarde
Kvindemuseet, Aarhus, Denmark

For the exhibition *Kvindelig Kinesisk Avantgarde* (*Women of the Chinese Avant-garde*), part of the Aarhus Festival Week, van Dijk suggests an interesting combination of works by Chen Haiyan, Chen Yanyin, Duan Jianyu, and Jiang Jie. For financial reasons, only Chen Yanyin and Jiang Jie exhibit at the Kvindemuseet (Women's Museum). Chen Yanyin shows a two-part video installation entitled *Original Point* and *Abortion*; Jiang Jie exhibits *Fragile Production*, an installation of wax baby dolls. Also as part of the Festival Week, Zhang Hai'er has a solo exhibition at the Image Gallery.

From van Dijk's Fiercely Realistic Footnotes:

> The Swedes disappeared, and the Danes made their entrance. Simultaneously with the Aarhus Festival on 21 September, an exhibition opened with two female artists, Jiang Jie from Beijing and Chen Yanyin from Shanghai. They were given a warm welcome by Jette Sandahl, Merete Ipsen, and Wiesia Struzik-Westergard in the Aarhuser Kvindemuseet. Jule, who immediately started learning Danish, and Zhang Li, who looked after the Chinese ladies, took on this project as I was busy with Yasuhiro Ihara of the Ihara Ludens Gallery in New York—just call me Hiro. The very distinguished Japanese gentleman told me he was looking for his roots in China after spending twenty years in New York. Initially rather taken aback, I suggested he do some studio visits together with Togolese Amouzou-Glikpa-Akouette (whose business card says Artist, Sculptor, Painter, Percussionist). Both were very pleased in the end. Two years earlier, Amouzou had successfully acted as the Chinese-French interpreter for Russian photographer Gregory Pinkhassov of the *New York Times Magazine*, who needed to be shown around. (They called him Pinky.)
>
> **HvD, letter to his friends in the Netherlands, Beijing, 9 July 1995**

14 October 1995 –
14 January 1996

6th Triennial of Small Sculpture 1995, Europe – East Asia
LB Forum Südwest, Stuttgart, Germany

From the Fiercely Realistic Footnotes:

> This project was taken over by Jule via Alexander Tolnay. A money matter, due to various issues. Jule and I presented our budget to a visiting Oberbürgermeister [super-mayor]—the chair of the exhibition association—and decided to set an ambitious goal. Herr Oberbürgermeister was still slightly dizzy, as he had just arrived that morning, but livened up quickly upon Jule's appearance. The deal was almost instantaneously finalized. […] Thereafter—we had eight months to export five artworks—Jule made a small spelling mistake, because of which an artist produced a work measuring one cubic centimeter instead of one cubic meter. This was obviously very beneficial to the transportation costs. […] At the very last moment before the art transport, a third artist told us that he just didn't feel like participating anymore. Thankfully, this only happened once in my entire career.
>
> HvD, letter to his friends in the Netherlands, Beijing, 9 July 1995

Gu Dexin's work for the 1995 *Triennial of Small Sculpture* is the result of a translation error: instead of "one cubic meter," Jule Noth writes "one cubic centimeter." The artist notes, "I would probably not have been interested in making a work for this show if the size had been one cubic meter. But I liked the idea of a cube of one centimeter."[10] He kneads the meat between his thumb and forefinger for days until it shrinks and desiccates. Gu makes a similar work in 1997 for the exhibition *Another Long March* in Breda, the Netherlands, for which he kneads a slightly larger piece of meat. The meat is put on display in a mirrored vitrine, while a framed photograph of Gu's hand kneading it is hung in a secluded spot. Van Dijk buys the photograph and later adds it, with other works from his collection, to the Modern Chinese Art Foundation.

10—MB, interview with Gu Dexin, Beijing, December 2013.

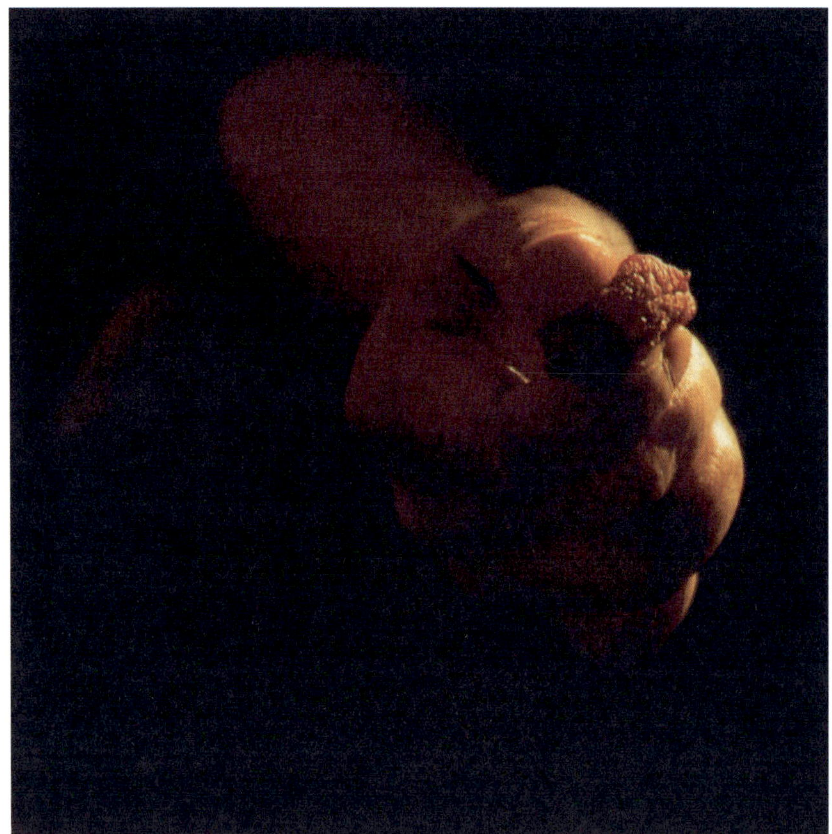

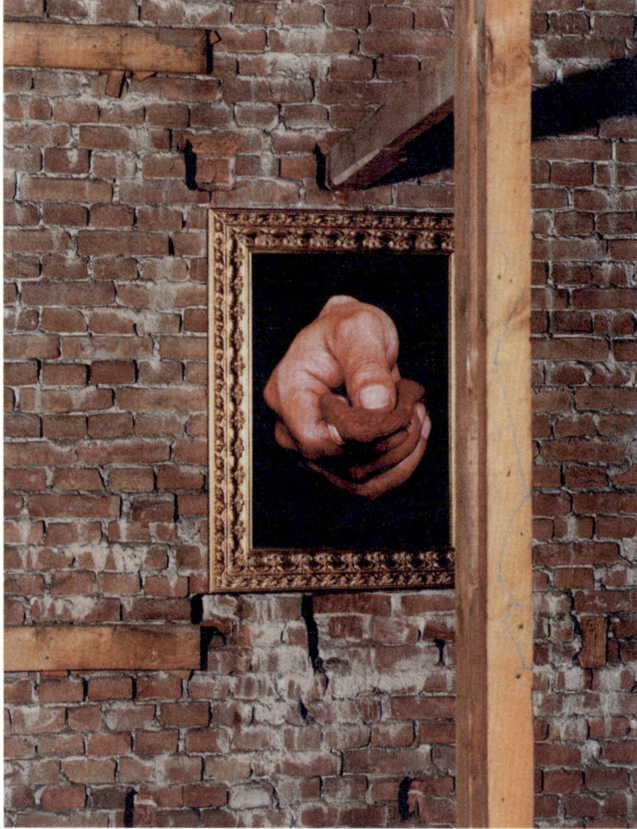

Left: Gu Dexin, *Meat*, 1995, private coll.; right: Gu Dexin, *Meat*, framed photograph, 1997, exhibition view *Another Long March*, Chassé Kazerne, Breda, 1997, private coll.

Han Lei, *Alienation*
Contemporary Art Gallery, Beijing

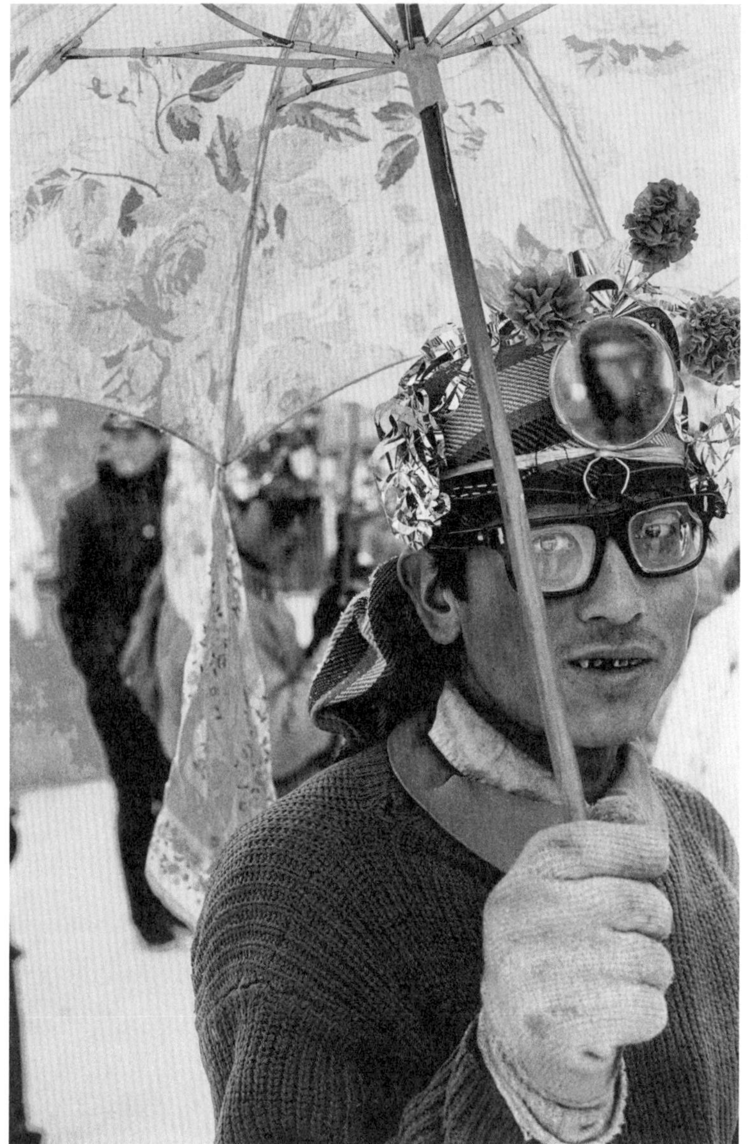

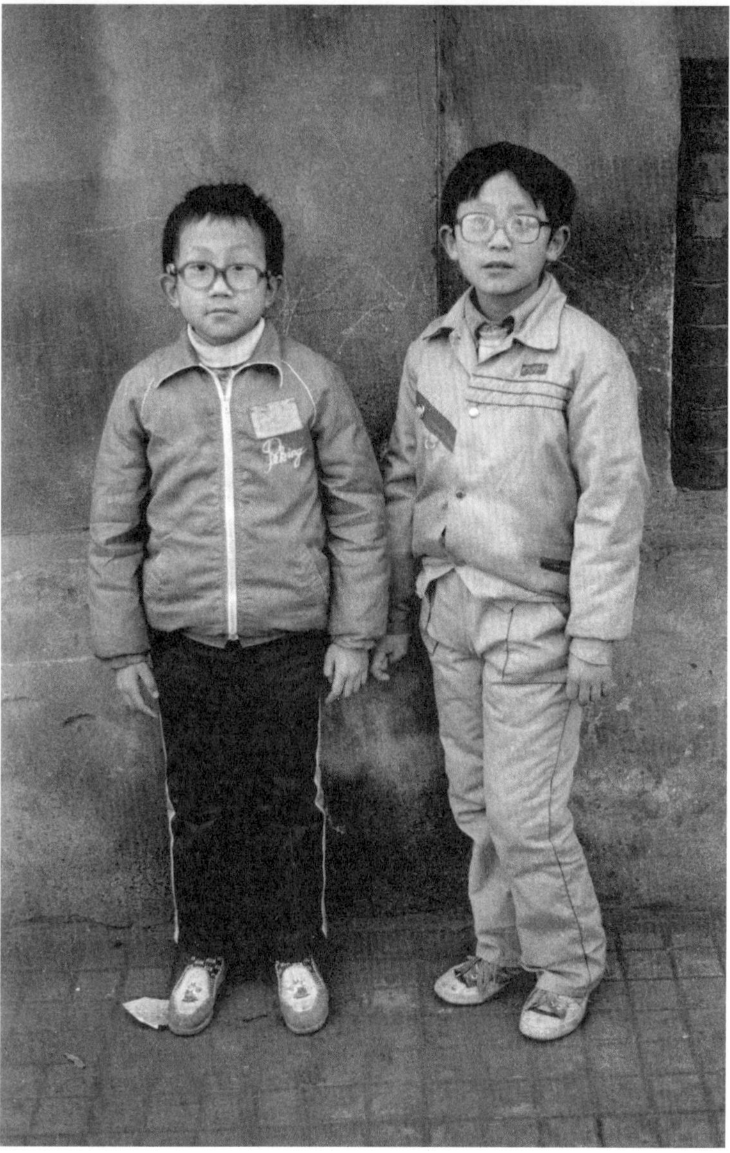

Han Lei, left: *Luochuan*, 1989; right: *Beijing*, 1988, gelatin silver prints, 120 × 80 cm, courtesy Han Lei

On the occasion of *Alienation* by Han Lei, the NAAC publishes the following exhibition announcement:

> To whom it may concern:
>
> May I present to you the works of Han Lei. Enclosed is a catalogue of an upcoming exhibition to take place in Beijing's Contemporary Art Gallery during the month of October.
>
> The exhibition is a survey of the last ten years of Han Lei's photographic endeavors. The works are shot in various locations around China. They reflect Han Lei's constant occupation with wandering, observing the solitary and violent nature of humans within society, within themselves. Han Lei attempts to present an untold reality—dense with its multilayered forms of fare and hypocrisy in a simple photograph.

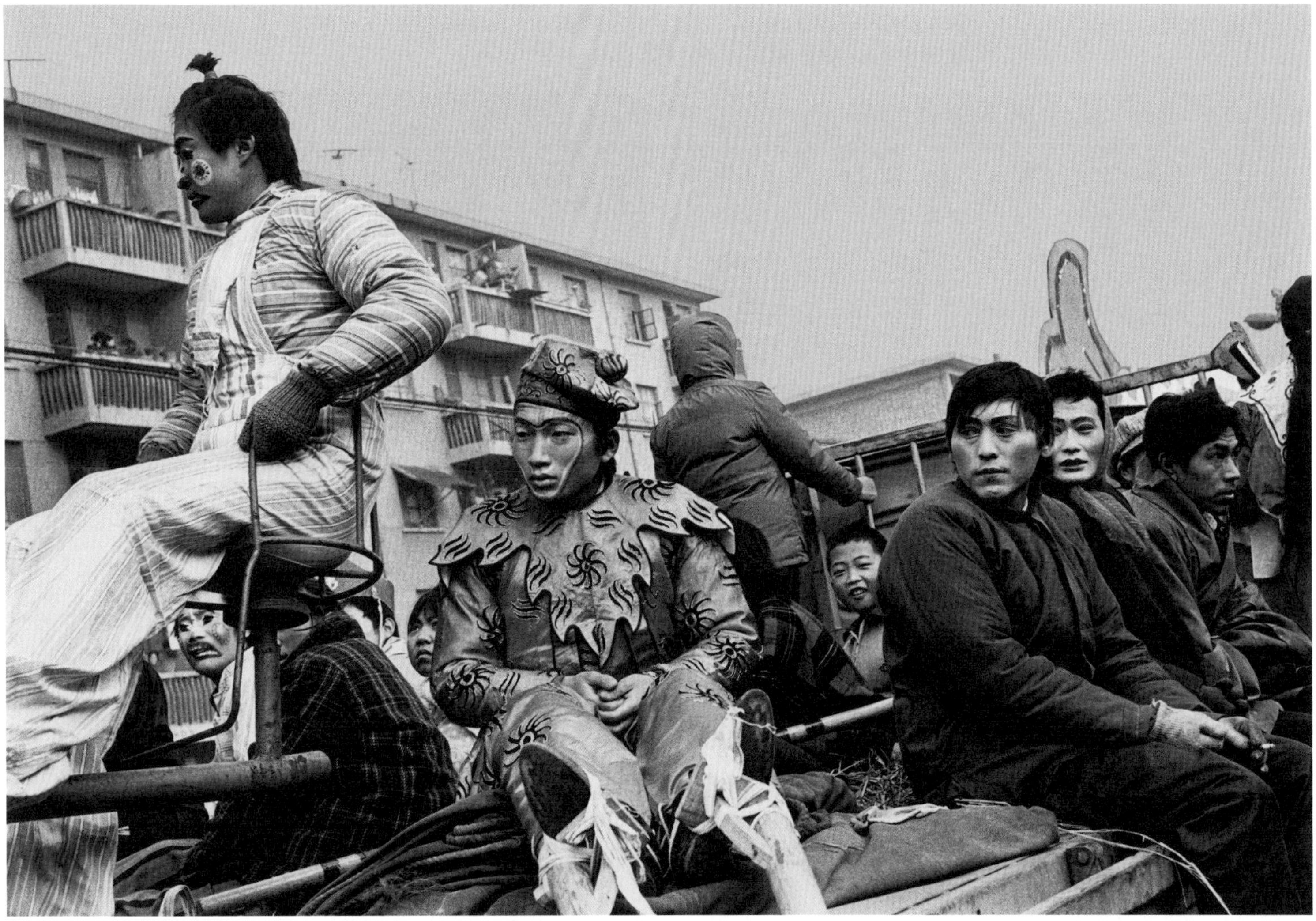

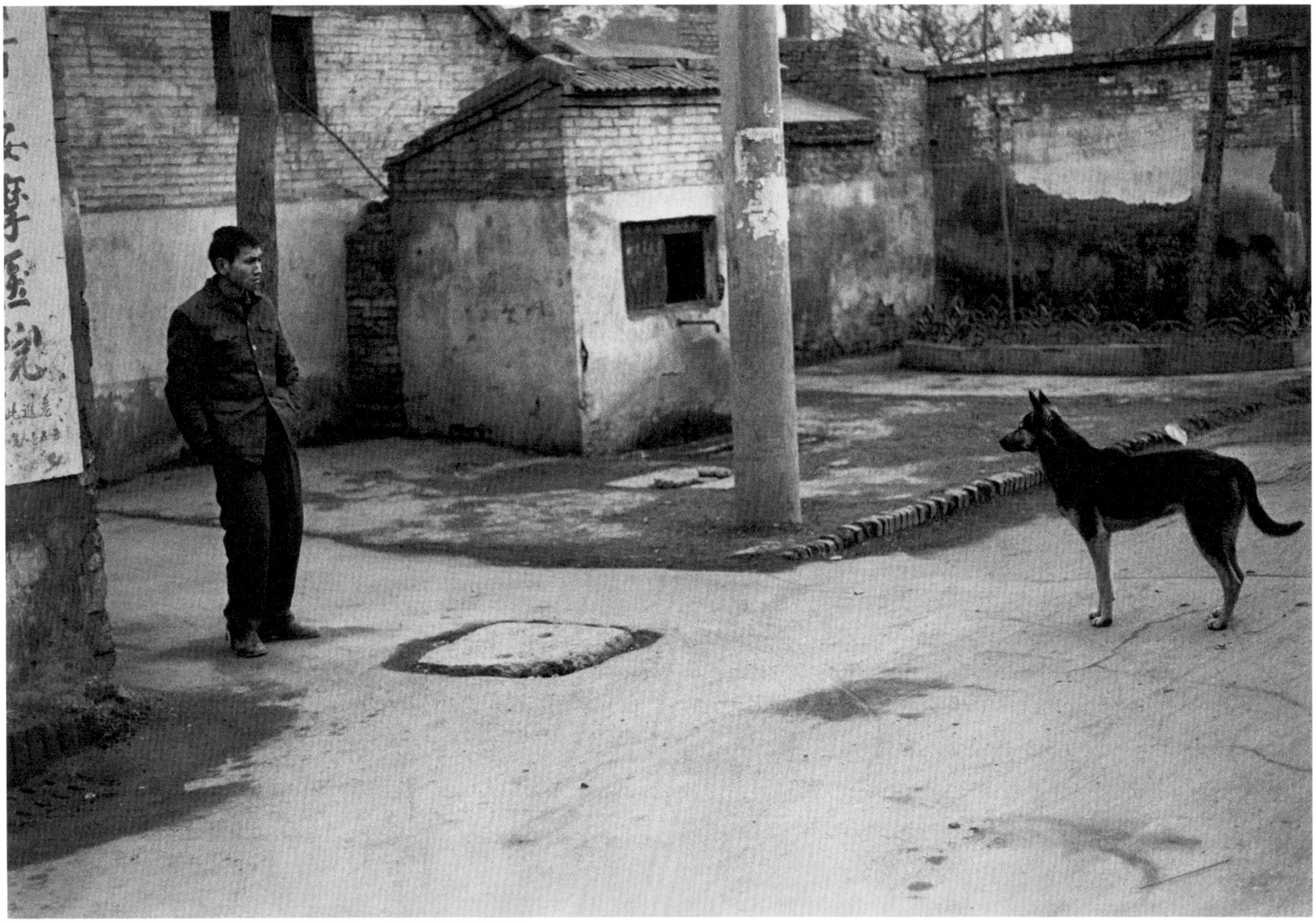

ALIENATION

and the Significative World of Photos

foreword to an exhibition by Han Lei

Alienation starts off in the darkness and returns to the light and its enemy.
Alienation is not what is in the mind of the common. If the idea is of definite content and is in possession of the mind, it might already become alienation.
It is no less ordinary than being described, dependent upon the extension of linguistic rules.
Nothing exists beyond the photograph.
A formal fabrication, which flies off to make love and cry, hires in advance the symbolic rights of alienation.
The alienator, therefore is the existent.
The essence of photography is the light of witness.
A photograph is not likely the extension but rather the re-movement or remarriage of a familiar idea. What the film obtains, usually, is incantations, traces, and pre-narrative systems. There exist no photographs of facts, but only meta-photography.
Perception may repeat the same thing in different situations. Yet is it possible to be distinguished from the other elements of a shared situation?
Two key elements: time presumed as A while space as B. The paternal time and maternal space do not produce photographs, but they become the possible A and B because of the photographs.
In between death and birth, the alienator and the alienated interact as the object and the image.
Reality becomes possible because of the traces, but the allusion cannot elicit absolute reality. The present tense is composed of the staying power of the past tense.
All reasons, are results, just as all photographs are the past of the present and the present of the future.
The storage of time is the opponent of any history.
The absolute value of aesthetic alienation is like the flow of water. It is complicated in all but pure in one.
The referent is negative reflection of imitation.
The alienator turns to the finite for help and allocates the camera as the god of reproduction. Simple and fictitious.
Or take alienation as the extension of the rules of the present world, if you like.
Interpretation is not assertion, but a meta-depiction instead. Statement is a kind of picture.
Photography is not the media between language and the world, but rather the visual hygiene that allows for distinction of this kind.
Alienation is the only necessary craft.
As autocracy over digits, the weapon of alienation is the camera of the photographer, and the camera of alienation transcends and replaces nihilism.
The photography of the alienator consumates the final moral clinic.
Whiter than dark, but darker than white. The universe is named and stated from the lips of light. Photography entrusts the sender, the addressee, and the referent to the open lens.
The human landscape belongs to the other fields of post-alienation.

by
Daozi

Translated by
Qian Zhi Jian

Foreword to Alienation, signed Daozi, translated by Qian Zhijian, exhib. cat., ed. Hans van Dijk, publ. NAAC, Beijing, 1995
Opposite page: Han Lei, top to bottom: *Kaifeng*, 1986; *Kaifeng*, 1986, gelatin silver prints, 80 × 120 cm each, courtesy Han Lei

New Amsterdam Art Consultancy (NAAC)
Beijing, 1996–1998

Hans' role in the Chinese art world was pivotal in a way. He was the only serious curator in China. There was no one else who understood the art really, from looking at the art. Hans never looked at what was trendy or hyped, never followed groups or fashions.

Karen Smith

1996

Within three months of the Xu Zhiwei exhibition at CIFA Gallery, van Dijk succeeds in renting the space, small but very centrally located next to the Central Academy of Fine Arts, for half a year. Zhang Li is appointed director after CAFA relieved the previous director of his post for alleged fraudulent behavior. Between March and August, van Dijk curates some of the most iconic exhibitions of his career at a breakneck pace, including the first solo presentations of painter Wang Xingwei and photographer Luo Yongjin, and four group shows of drawings, photos, and paintings from China's main art centers—Canton, Shanghai, Beijing, Hangzhou, and Luoyang—showing the scope of his ambitions as a gallerist. As always, he designs all invitations and cards himself. He simultaneously undertakes the scouting and organization for the 1996 Chinese Cultural Weeks in Munich, a massive project that includes theater, music, and the exhibition *China: Aktuelles aus 15 Ateliers* (China: News from 15 Studios). The events, however, are canceled by the Chinese partners at the last minute, causing enormous political upheaval. Of the numerous planned events, only *Aktuelles* takes place.

By May 1996, van Dijk appoints a new assistant director for the gallery, Yang Qing. Zhang Li is the manager, Zhang Wei the assistant manager, and Jule Noth acts as "Berlin representative." Artfame, the NAAC shareholders' company, has expanded its shareholders, adding Ding Yi, Francesca Dal Lago, Xu Tan, Liu Anping, and a few more. On 1 September 1996, he writes to Jeroen Vinken that Zhang Li wants to leave. "I hope he carries on a little longer working with someone twice his age who grumbles all the time about Chinese peasant habits, and complains about lack of experience, knowledge, and dedication in the local art world [...]. You forty, me fifty (well, this year). When I risked turning forty I went to China, and I don't regret it. Let's see how it works out for you Jeroen?—ship's doctor on the Holland-America Line? Fang Lijun is just 30 years old and is about to move to Holland[1] with his wife Michaela Raab. He does serious business there." In this period, around two thirds of van Dijk's projects fail to materialize. Sales commissions are slow to come in, and he sells next to nothing from new shows. He spends all the money he earns buying art and helping artists, while he also pays back Ernst Dinkla's loan with due interest and gives the Artfame shareholders their cuts.

1—Fang Lijun stays at the artist residence of the Stedelijk Museum in Amsterdam during the second half of 1997 and has a solo exhibition there in the spring of 1998.

By the end of 1996, Zhang Li leaves the NAAC to finish his studies–interrupted in 1989—at the Central Academy of Fine Arts, and proposes that his relative Zhang Wei replace him as the new assistant to the director. Van Dijk acts as a mentor to both Zhang Li and Zhang Wei, teaching them about curating and contemporary art practice.

> ZHANG LI: I worked for Hans as an assistant full-time from 1994–96 and part-time in 1997. I first started when Hans moved to the apartment in west Beijing around 1994. There was a spare bed for guests in the office. There were a lot of catalogues and books in the archive, old magazines and catalogues from the fifties and sixties. People were always calling there. Once Ni Haifeng and his Dutch wife Roos came to live in the apartment. Hans designed his own furniture: he designed his office desk to make it fit the space, and he designed the living room table by taking the wooden legs off an old table and putting a glass top on it instead. In my memory, Hans was always working on his very old computer with a black-and-white program called Works. He said its database was like heaven. Later on, he worked with a database called Access. You put in a query, and it found the connection. We had the CIFA Gallery for half a year only. Before we had that space, we would work in sporadic locations. Then I found this small space [CIFA] for a low rent, and we bought a bit of equipment and renovated for little money. We made six or seven exhibitions there, but we spent so much money on them that it couldn't last. Also the big project for Munich was getting started by that time, and we couldn't do both, moneywise. I felt so disappointed and guilty toward Hans that I couldn't make the gallery work that I quit and returned to my hometown for three months. In 1997, Hans contacted me again for the show *Zeitgenössische Photokunst in China* at the Neuer Berliner Kunstverein in Berlin. That was my last project with him. It was a very important show. Hans did the project with Andreas [Schmid]. I established the contacts, and traveled with Andreas. [...] Working with Hans, I learned the curatorial approach from him: to really pay attention to what the artist is doing and respect that.
>
> **MB, interview with Zhang Li, Beijing, 11 September 2012**

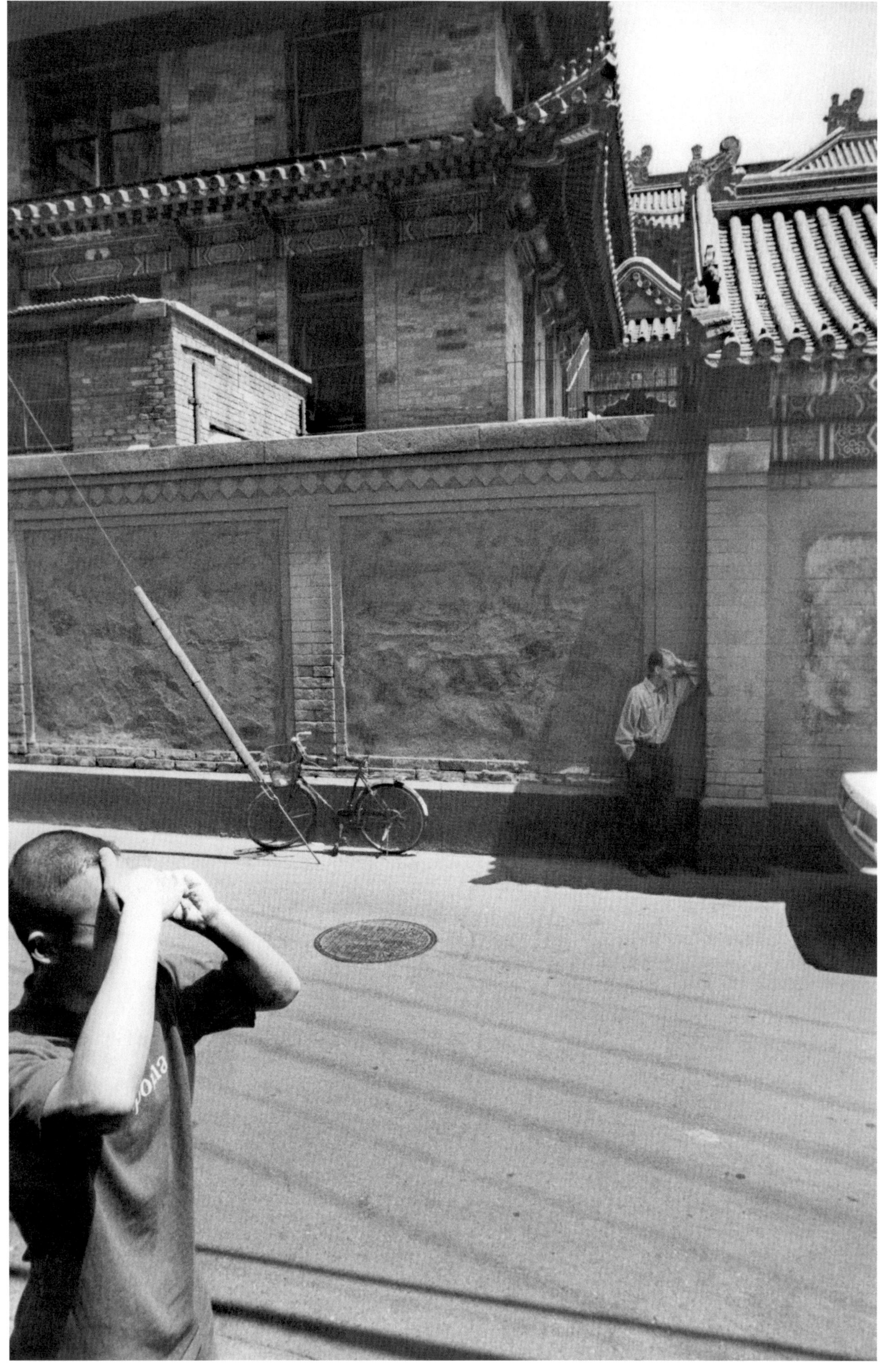

Luo Yongjin, *Zhang Li Waiting*, 1996; Zhang Li and Hans van Dijk (far end) waiting for a delivery of artworks in the courtyard of CIFA Gallery adjacent to the Central Academy of Fine Arts, Beijing, 1996, courtesy Luo Yongjin

ZHANG WEI: I had just graduated from university when I moved to Beijing for my internship. It was when the CIFA Gallery had opened, and they needed somebody to take care of the space, clean the floor, and go to the post office. That is when I started working with Hans. I learned from him how to write letters, how to put addresses in the computer, or works on the wall; how to frame them, and how to clean the glass of the photo frames. Back then I really thought that it was a hard job. It was very difficult working in the gallery, as we had to avoid the policemen every day. As we were really scared that somebody would come in and check on us, we used to speak carefully about everything, in another language.

The way of working was underground. I thought that it was a bit too much for me, and I was thinking that after my internship I would have to find another job, and maybe work for a foreign company, which was really a way to make a living.

But then we did shows with Zhou Tiehai and Wang Xingwei. Talking to them, I found that it was very interesting for me to find new perspectives with these kinds of people, by observing their way of thinking. So then, before finishing my internship, Hans asked me whether I would like to work in his office, as Zhang Li wanted to leave at the time. At this point I would like to explain the story of CIFA Gallery.

Hans used all the money he received from selling works, which by that time was about 40,000–45,000 RMB, to run CIFA Gallery for six months. Still, as he didn't sell anything during these six months, he was forced to close the gallery and move back to his office again, with the room and his bed. He then proposed that I work with him there, and I accepted. From then on I somehow got more intrigued. I became the only person helping him with projects, but it was, indeed, really tough, as we had nothing to eat. In a day, we might eat a piece of fruit and dumplings, and only occasionally rice boxes. By the end of each month, we had to look everywhere in our pockets to find money to pay the rent. Sometimes I had to talk with the landlord to postpone the payment. But the amazing thing was that Hans was always very relaxed. Since I was also doing bookkeeping, project management, and basically everything, I once told him that we didn't have any money left. He just replied, "Ok, it will come." I don't know how, but eventually the problem would be solved somehow. For the three years I worked with him, we struggled to maintain the space. Still, what was magical for me was that, because of his passion, he himself became the institution. At every point I thought it would end, after a few days something would change and the problem would be solved.

Zhang Wei, fragment of *Hans van Dijk: Dialogues in the Development of Contemporary Art in China*, Salon Talk for Art Basel Hong Kong, 16 May 2014

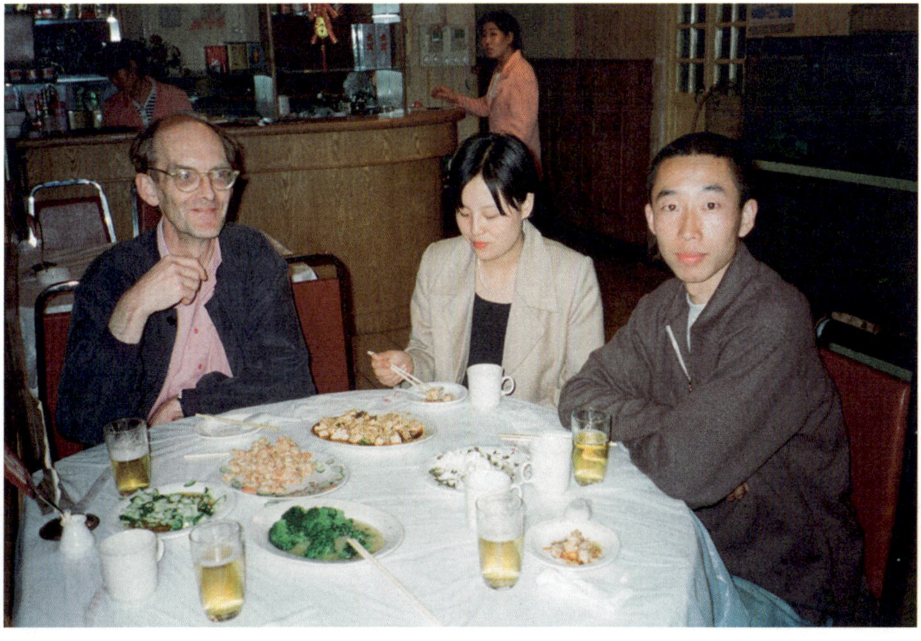

Left to right: Hans van Dijk, Zhang Wei, and Zhang Li, Beijing, 1996, photo Andreas Schmid

23–30 March 1996

Wang Xingwei, *The Dust of the Romantic History of Male Heroism* CIFA Gallery, Beijing

The first show van Dijk organises at CIFA is of works by the painter Wang Xingwei, who was introduced to van Dijk by Zhang Li. It is Wang's first solo show, named after one of his paintings, *The Dust of the Romantic History of Male Heroism*.

> Between 1991 and 1993, Wang Xingwei painted a large triptych showing a group of fighting young people. The northeastern part of China, where he grew up and lives, is known for those frequent outbursts. The formation of the figures in the painting is classical, static in symmetry with an inside action. It is painted in a realistic fashion, slightly tending to cartoon-like character style. Like other paintings from that period, Wang used realism to reflect and document his social surroundings. Violence remained the theme in the paintings *To Hurt* (1994) and *All Happy Families are Similar No. 1 and 2* (1994), but in *To Hurt* he used a more monumental style, less realistic, as an effort to define the essence of violence. [...] After his works first received recognition, he preferred to live in a rather small city, enjoying family life and better working conditions, unlike many artists who moved to Beijing. Since then he finished around twenty works, showing situations by using artworks and images from the history of Western art, Chinese social realism, propaganda art, and recent history to confront and test their meanings and values by applying them to his own surroundings and daily life. In several of them he plays the principal character, like in *Mein Kampf – Wang Xingwei in 1936* where he stands as a complacent adolescent beside Hitler, who just has been convinced by Wang Xingwei of the theories of Gandhi. *Mein Kampf* is burning at their feet. In *The Testimony of the Hare*, painted in the style of Caravaggio, he interrogates the animal to find out what really happened when Beuys did his performance with the dead hare in his arms. In *Still No A-mark* (1998) he rebukes his son for his shortcomings. The title, like the posture of the boy, is derived from a work around 1940 of the Russian painter Reshetnikov, a painting used for copying at many art academies in China. Wang Xingwei is sitting on pop-art furniture from the English artist Allen Jones in a posture derived from a sculpture by Michelangelo against a canvas painted in American hard-edge style as a background "to make it more stage-like," he explained.
>
> Hans van Dijk, introduction to the inaugural exhibition of the Modern Chinese Art Foundation, exhib. cat., Ghent, 1999

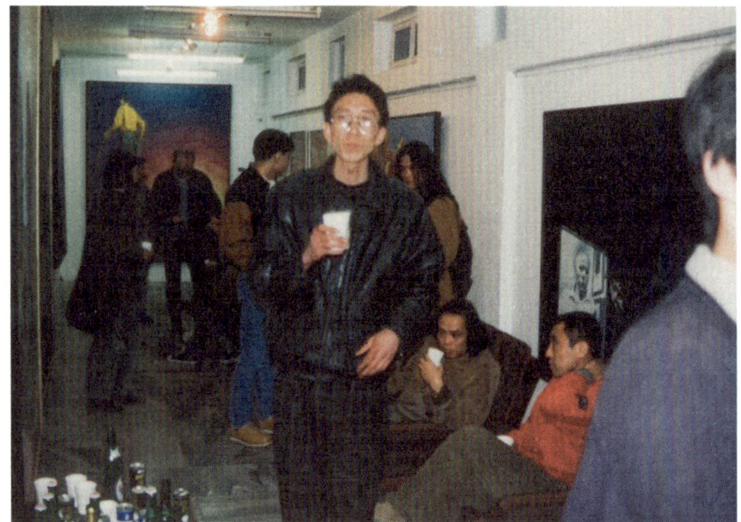

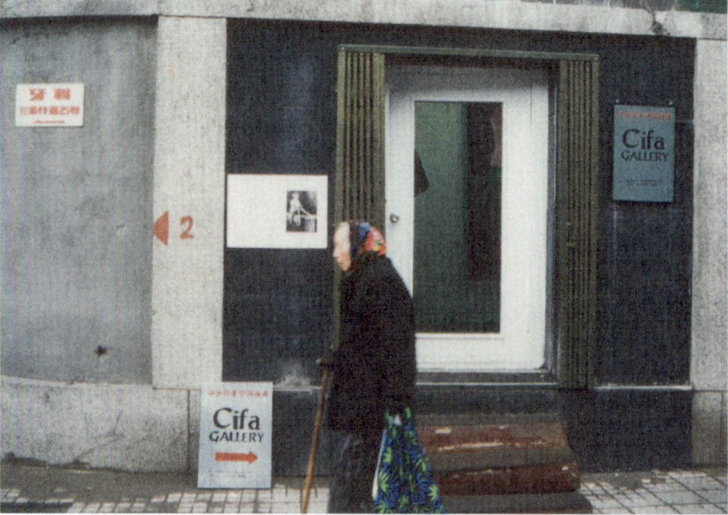

Left: Wang Xingwei at the opening of *The Dust of the Romantic History of Male Heroism*, CIFA Gallery, Beijing, 1996, private coll.; right: entrance to CIFA Gallery during Wang Xingwei's exhibition *The Dust of the Romantic History of Male Heroism*, 1996, private coll.

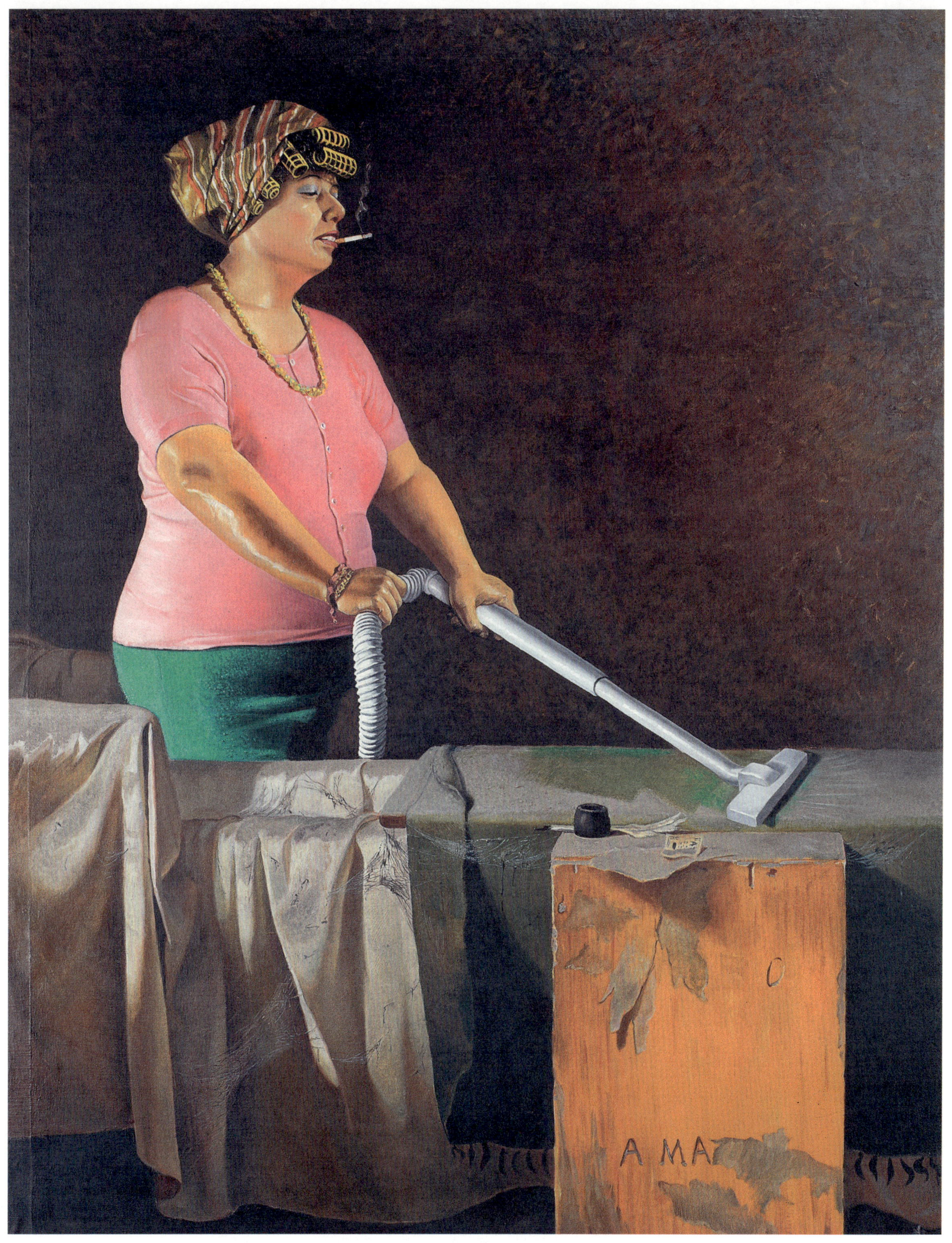

Wang Xingwei, *The Dust of the Romantic History of Male Heroism*, oil on canvas, 155×200 cm, 1996, private coll.

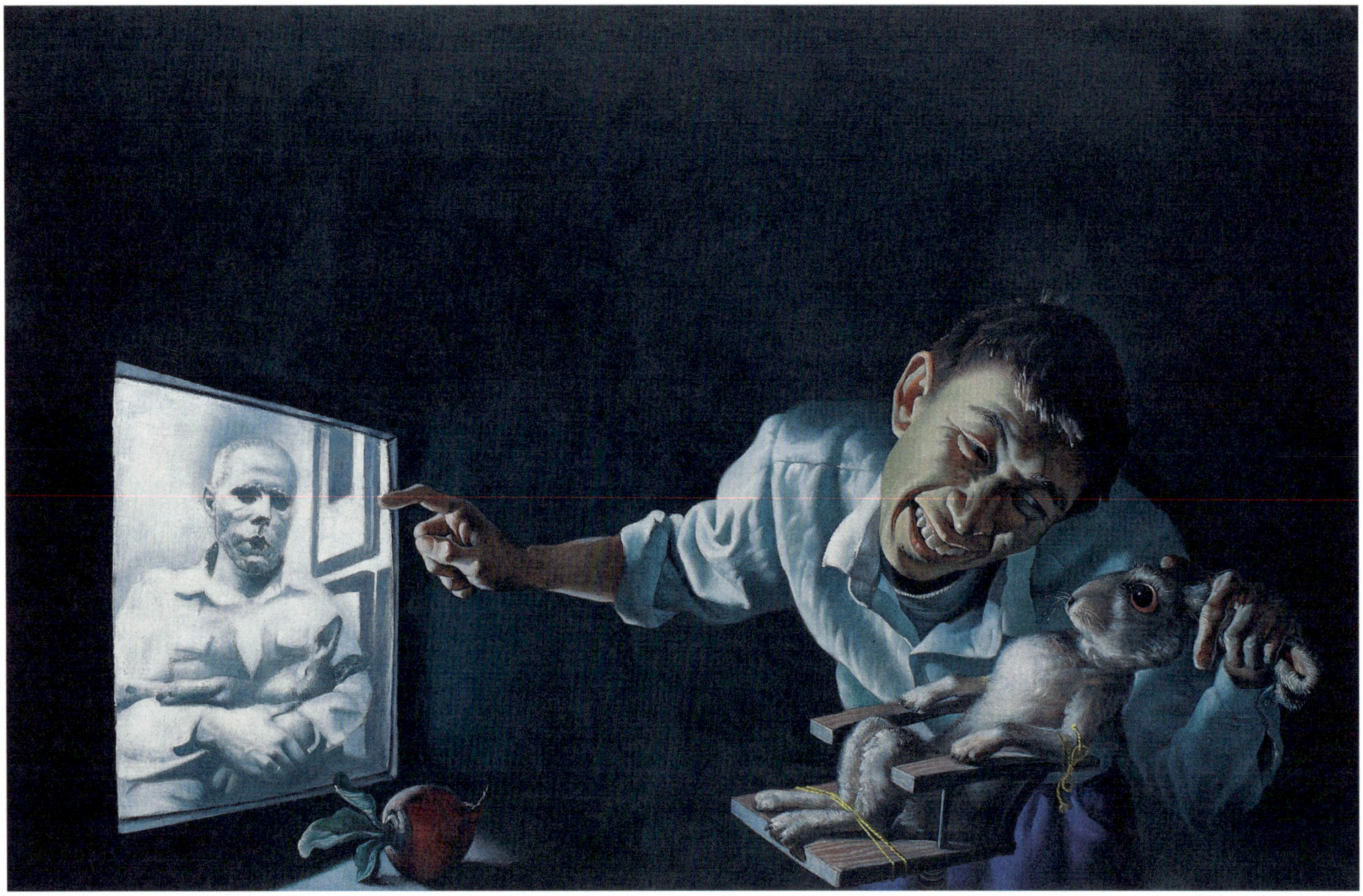

Wang Xingwei, *The Testimony of the Hare*, oil on canvas, 124.5 × 200 cm, 1995, private coll.

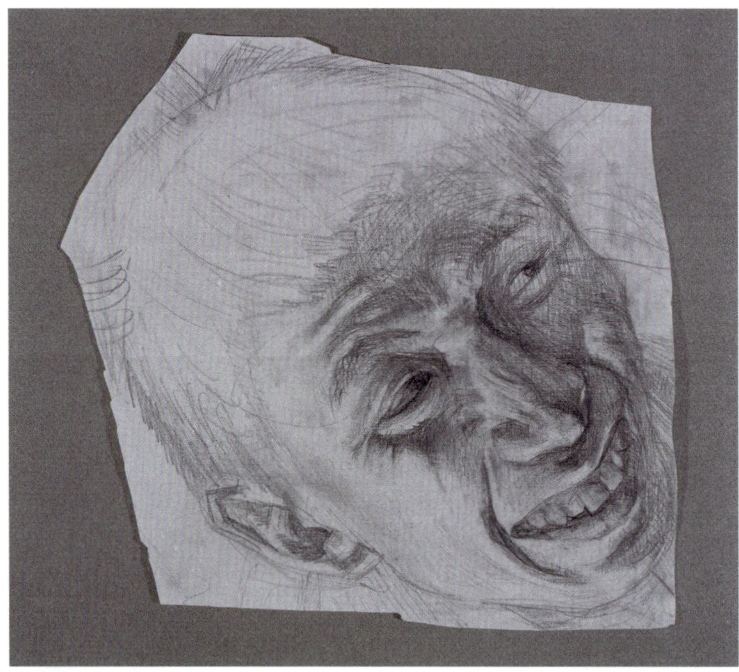

Wang Xingwei, *Study for the Testimony of the Hare (self-portrait)*, pencil on paper, 1995, private coll.; Wang Xingwei gave the drawing to Hans van Dijk as a thank you gift

26 April – 8 May 1996

Zhou Tiehai, *Too Materialistic Too Spiritualized* CIFA Gallery, Beijing

With this show, van Dijk introduces Shanghai-born Zhou Tiehai to Beijing. Zhou is a painter and conceptual artist with highly complicated, multi-layered works. The show is characteristic of Zhou's recent work at the time, which consists of intentional mystifications of and critical puns on the art worlds of both East and West. It includes one of Zhou's very large, collaged drawings, entitled *I want to carry her in my Louis Vuitton bag*, and the first six of his now famous "Magazine Covers," which include a fake *Time* magazine cover of himself as Person of the Year.

> Museums were clumsy, Soviet-style architectural dinosaurs that hardly collected new art. Official art magazines were fighting new developments, and although valiant attempts were made to create a market, to publish alternative art magazines, and to promote new art to center-stage, it was a very slow development that is only now [2001] paying off. It is partly for this reason that some attitudes of resentment and mockery of the West appeared. It is easy to perceive Western initiatives as patronizing. Zhou Tiehai's magazine covers are a joke in this direction. They play on the desire to appear or comedy of appearing on the most famous Western magazine covers.
>
> Eduardo Welsh, "Unanticipated Sights and People" in *Portraits, Figures, Couples and Groups*, exhib. cat., MCAF (Beijing) and BizArt (Shanghai), 2001

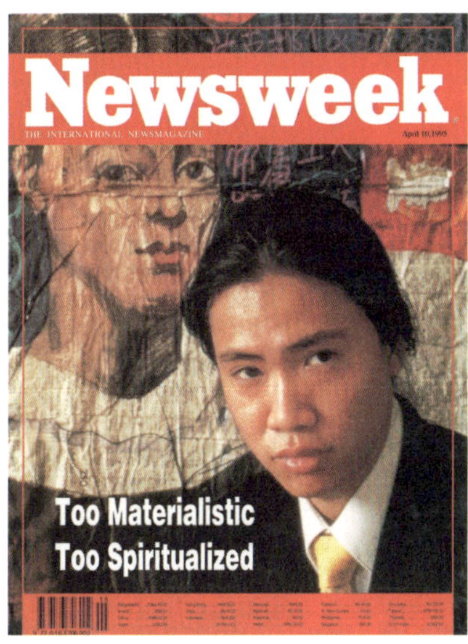

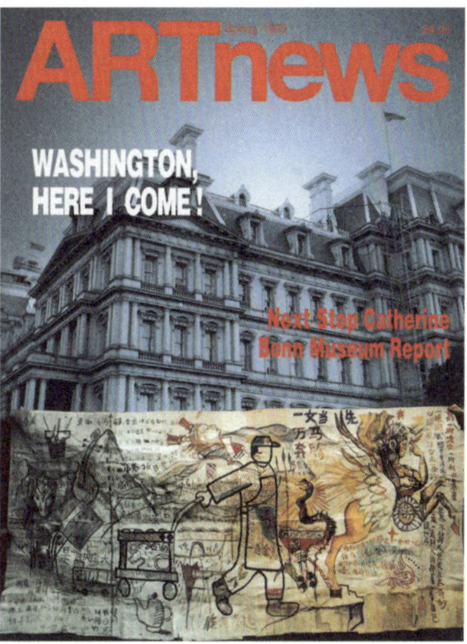

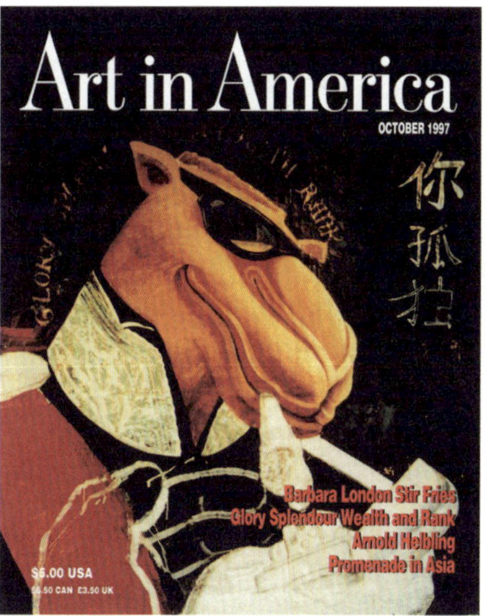

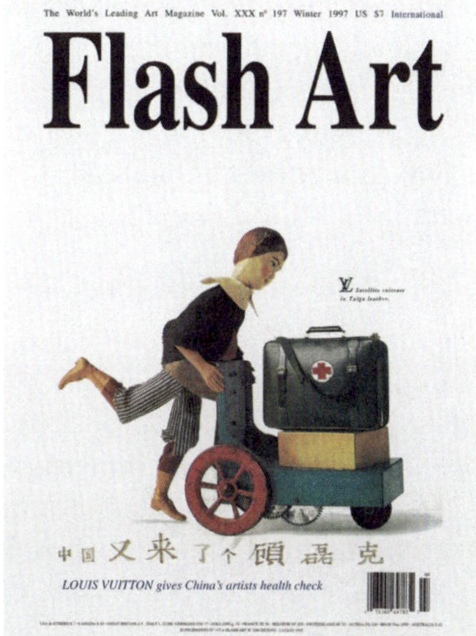

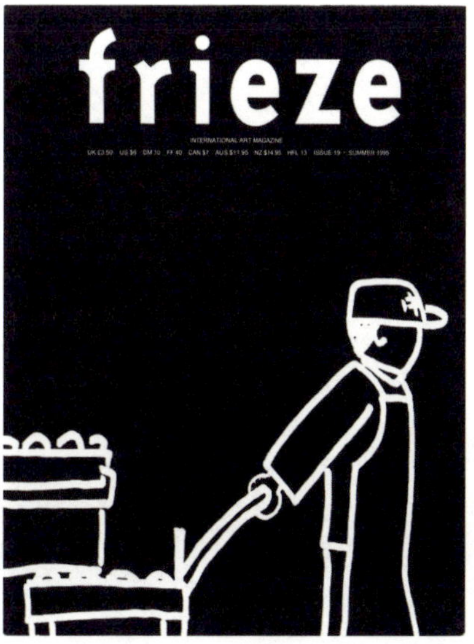

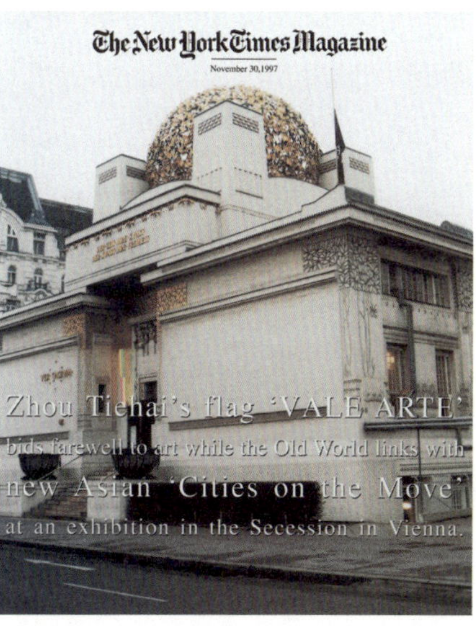

Zhou Tiehai, *Newsweek*, print, 27.6 × 21 cm, 1995; *ARTnews*, print, 27.6 × 21 cm, 1995; *Art in America*, print, 27 × 23 cm, 1997; *Flash Art*, print, 27 × 20.5 cm, 1997; *Frieze*, print, 30 × 23 cm, 1995; *The New York Times*, print, 29 × 24.5 cm, 1997; all images courtesy Zhou Tiehai and ShanghART Gallery, Shanghai

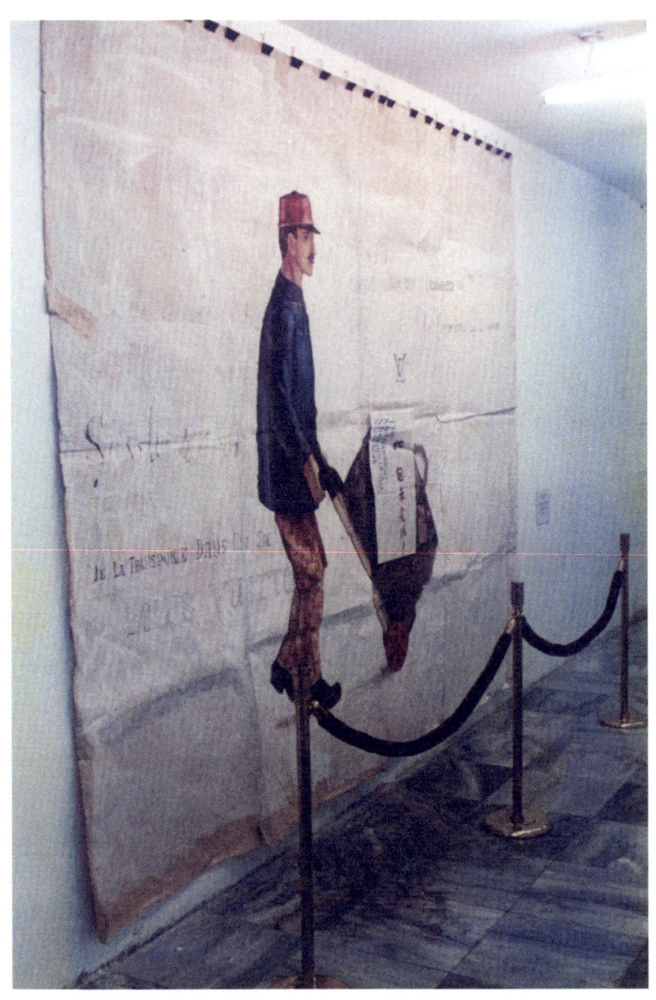

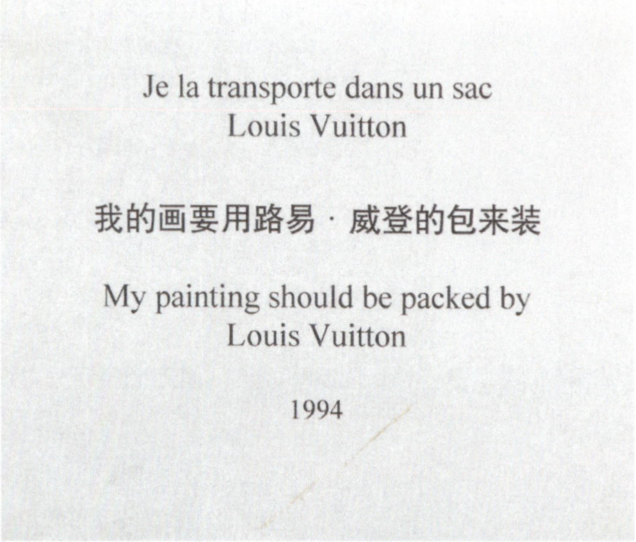

Exhibition view Zhou Tiehai, *Je la transporte dans un sac Louis Vuitton / My painting should be packed by Louis Vuitton*, gouache, pencil, and paper collage on packing paper, 250 × 400 cm, 1994 (work now lost), CIFA Gallery, Beijing, 1996

10 – 22 May 1996

Luo Yongjin, *Celebrations & Celebrities*
CIFA Gallery, Beijing

Much of Luo Yongjin's oeuvre consists of portraits, with photographs of his artist friends holding a strong presence throughout. Aware of the rapidly changing times, he ironically titles the series portraying artists such as Zhang Peili, Zhang Hai'er, and Ding Yi "Celebrities," and pairs the series with "Celebrations," in which he documents everyday life in modern China, where old customs and new developments are increasingly entangled. Van Dijk's role in the promotion of Chinese photography cannot be overestimated. The role of photography in China was exclusively documentary; it was never thought of as art. As is typical of his approach, van Dijk does not theorize about photography; he shows his engagement with the medium by exhibiting it equally alongside other art forms from the outset.

> LUO YONGJIN: I had my first exhibition with him [Hans] at CIFA in 1996. The year after that I was in Hans' Siemens show [*Face to Face*] with Thomas Struth in one of the first new art spaces in Beijing next to the lobby of the Holiday Inn on Wangfujing Road near the National Art Museum of China. [...]
> Making an exhibition with Hans was the simplest thing, no problems selecting works, or deciding on materials or framing. [...] All the frames for my photos in the Wangfujing show were done by Ai Weiwei. I was surprised because they were so well crafted: solid, with thick wood and real joints, not at all like the no-good frames one got in the market. Hans told me that the frames were more expensive than the works themselves.
> I remember that the crates for Thomas Struth's works were better and more expensive than the furniture in my own home.

His importance for photography was almost like a landmark—for Chinese artists to know that there are other ways of photography, not just documentary photography like in magazines or books. And also that photography can be a form of a free expression like painting or drawing or sculpture. Hans made me feel that I could carry on: he encouraged me a lot. That's why I decided to leave the army, because I was convinced I could make better pieces outside of the army. I was in the army language school [as a photographer] for twenty years, documenting meetings, et cetera. During that time, I studied for one year in the art school in Zhejiang in 1985, and three and a half years at the Guangzhou Academy of Fine Arts, where I took photos with Zhang Hai'er, played video games with Xu Tan, and played football with Zheng Guogu. I don't remember Hans ever asking questions about my photos, the subject or content, or quality or technique, nothing. Just simple. He never said "great" or anything like that, but he called or maybe wrote me a few months later and said how about an exhibition here, and which series would you like to show?
Without Hans, Chinese contemporary art would be less known or would have developed later. From him, the artists learned there were other attitudes toward art. The Chinese art critics were still too young or not paying attention to contemporary art. We mentioned Hans to them, but we never seriously talked with them about him. Hans was the only one doing this and gaining nothing from it, not like the art market. Once, in 1998 when I was living in Beijing, he asked me to take documentary color photos when the Prime Minister of Belgium came to a reception [of the Permeke exhibition]. That was my first paid job as a photographer.

MB, interview with Luo Yongjin, Shanghai, 21 January 2013

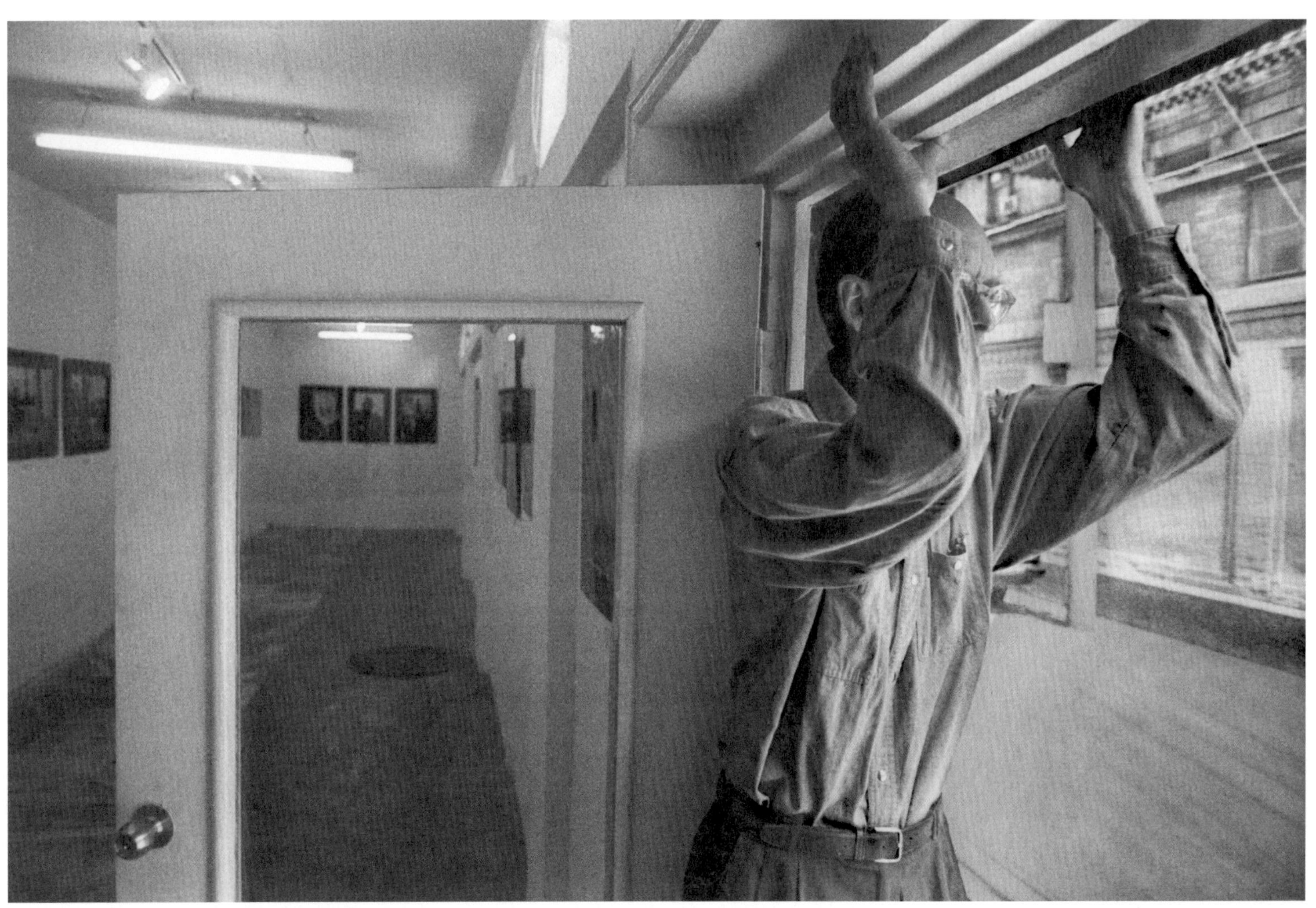

Luo Yongjin, *Gallery Door*, 1996; Hans van Dijk at CIFA Gallery during Luo Yongjin's exhibition *Celebrations & Celebrities*, Beijing, 1996, courtesy Luo Yongjin

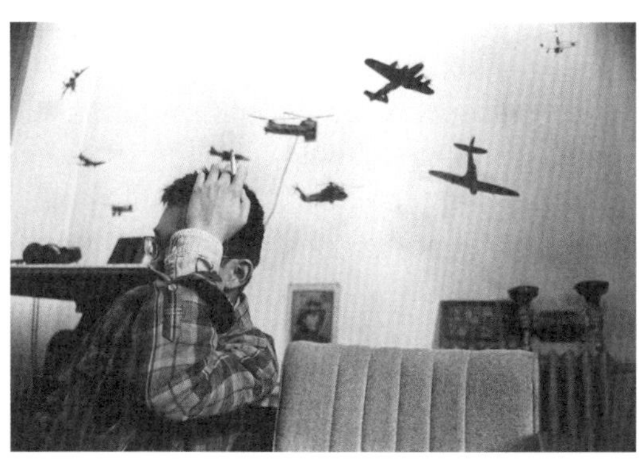

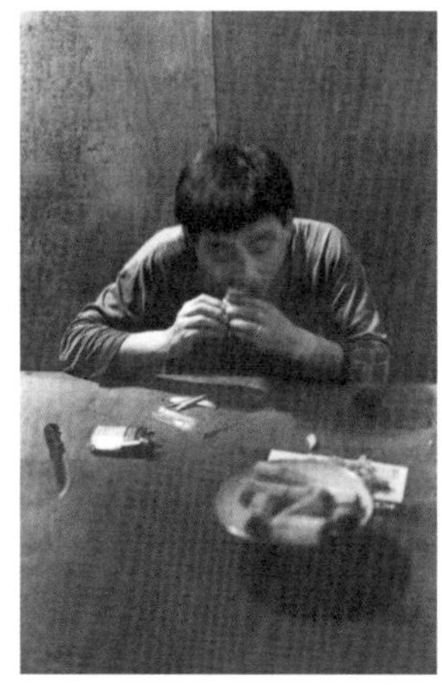

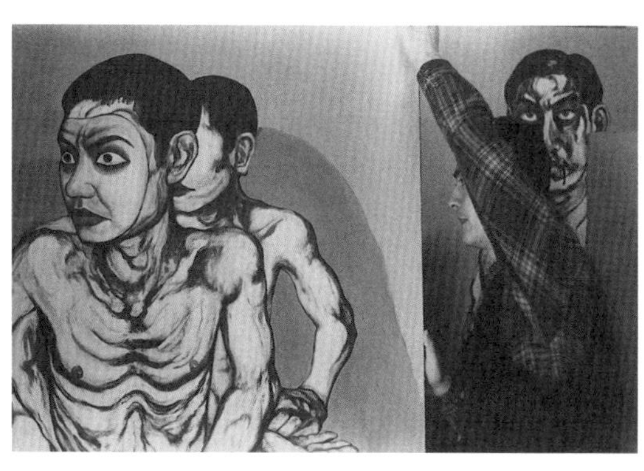

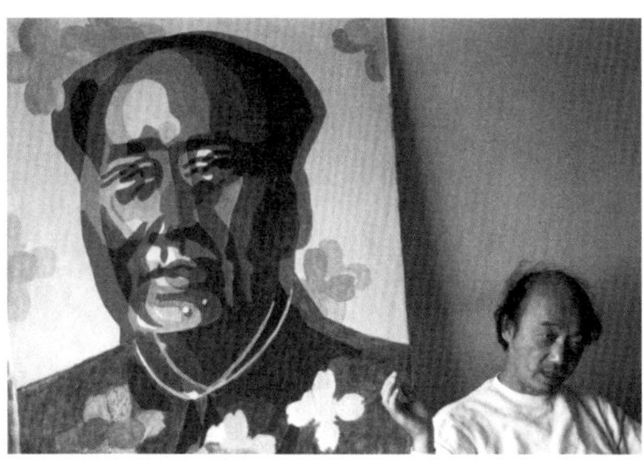

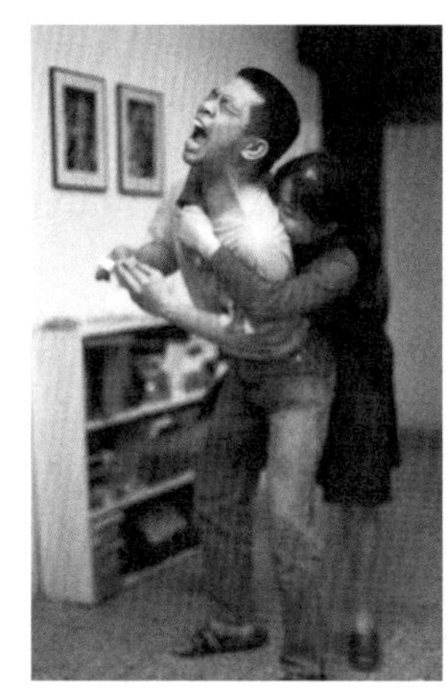

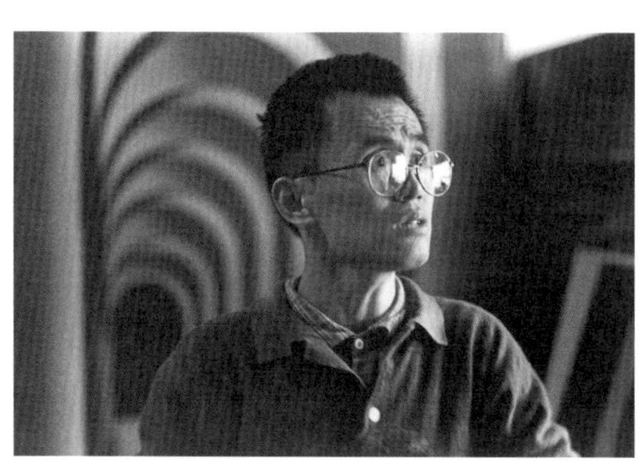

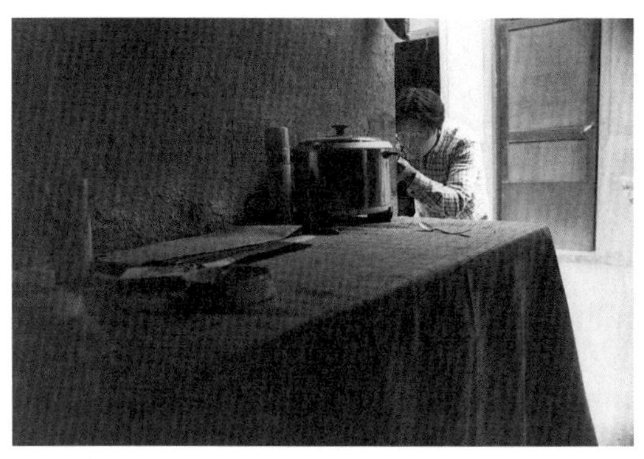

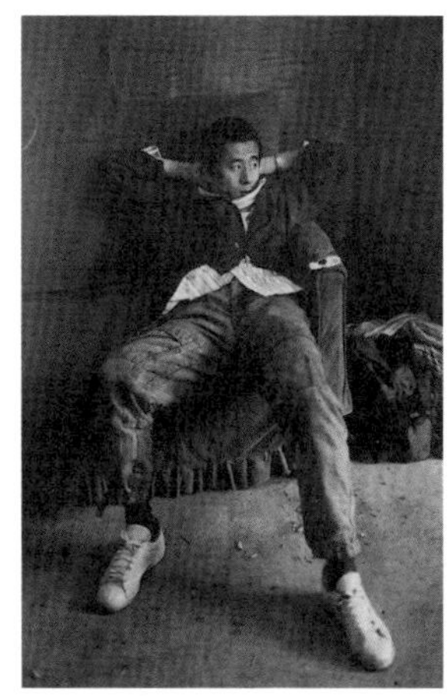

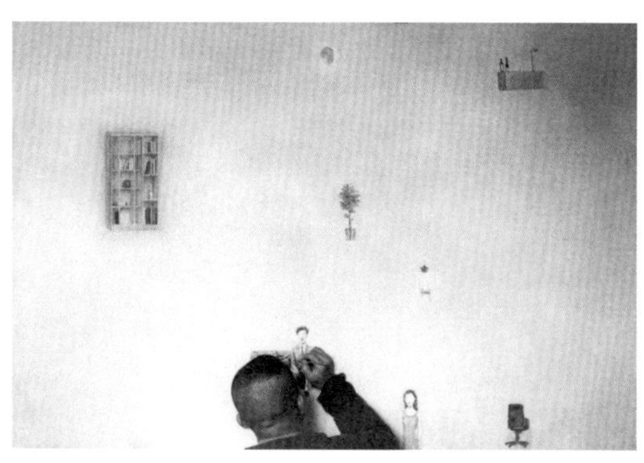

Luo Yongjin, *Celebrities and Celebrations*, series of black and white photographs, 87.5 × 66 cm and 66 × 87.5 cm each, 1992–97; installation scheme of *Celebrities*; left to right: *Feng Mengbo, Wang Jinsong, Zeng Fanzhi, Yu Youhan, Zhang Hai'er, Shu Qun, Ding Yi, Zhang Peili, Zeng Hao*, courtesy Luo Yongjin

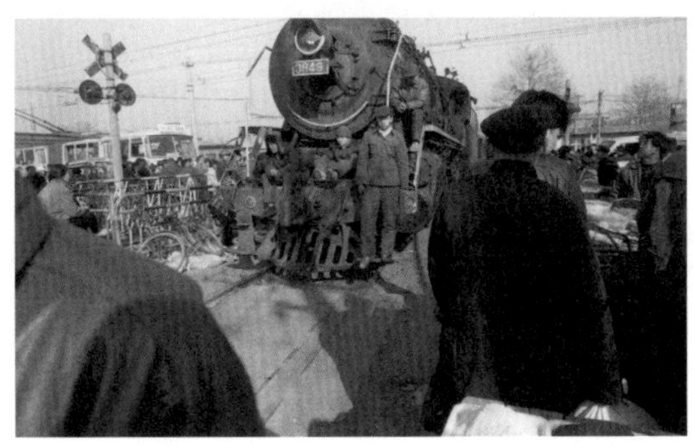

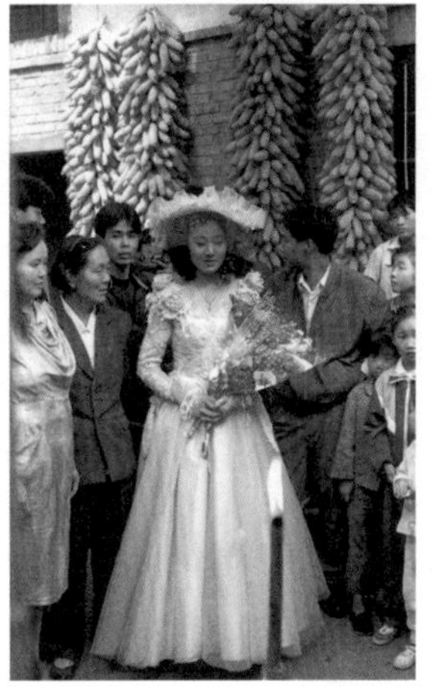

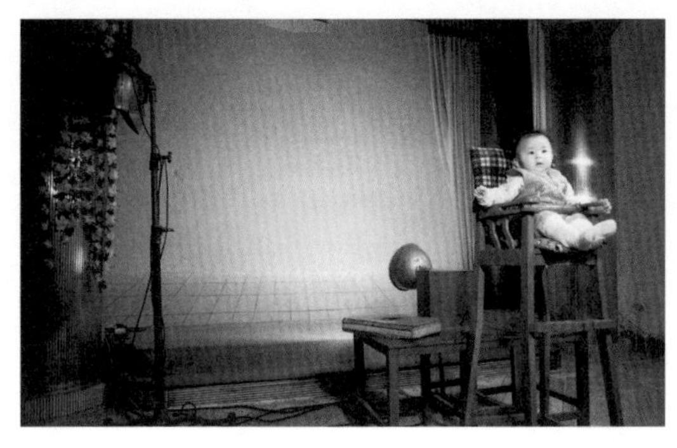

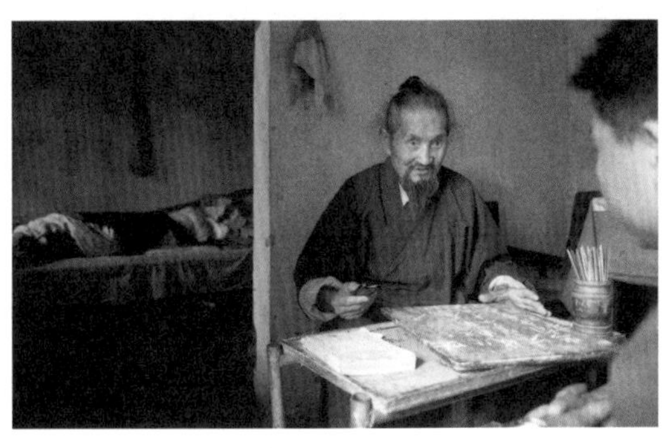

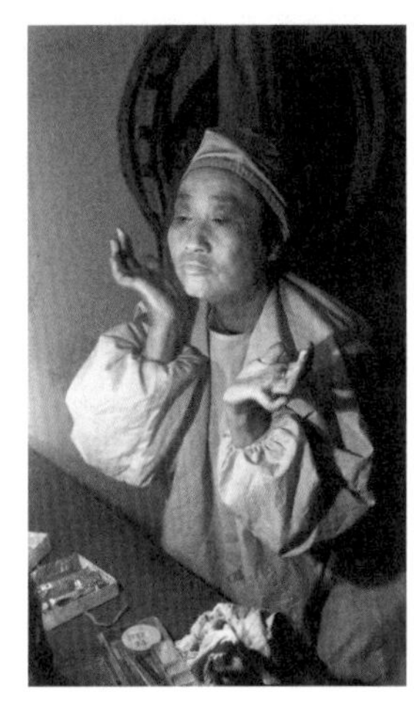

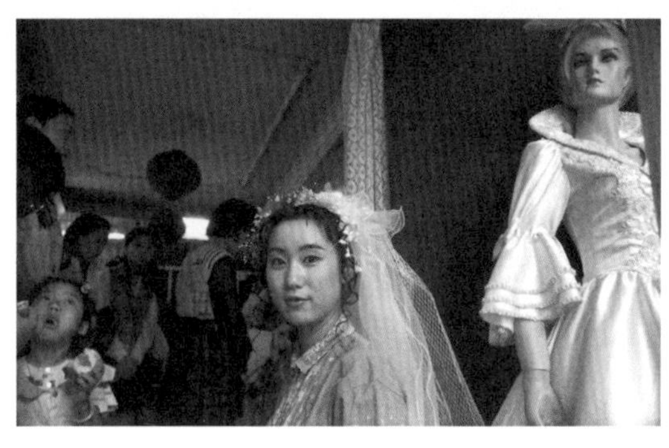

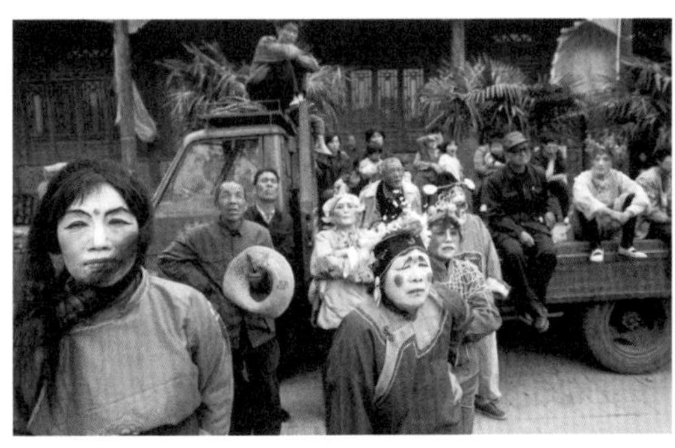

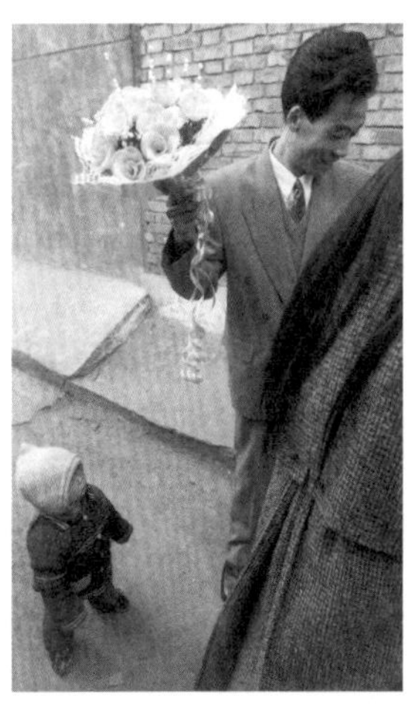

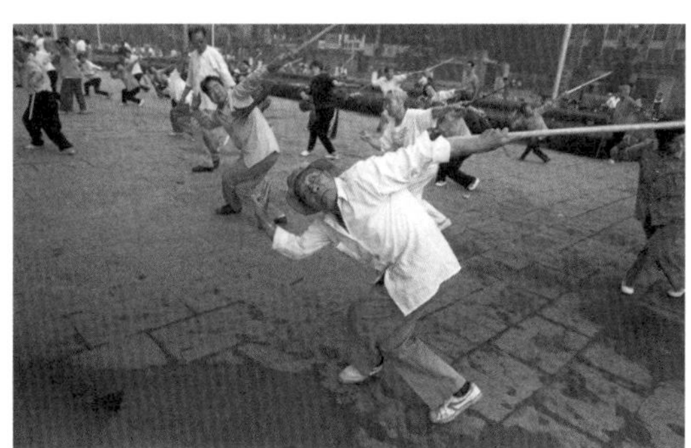

Luo Yongjin, *Celebrities and Celebrations*, series of black and white photographs, 87.5 × 66 cm and 66 × 87.5 cm each, 1992–97; installation scheme of *Celebrations*; left to right: *Locomotive, Wedding, The One-Hundredth Day, Fortune Telling, Pantaloon, Tu Lei, The Fire Agent, Luo Baoheng, Swordsmen*, courtesy Luo Yongjin

30–31 August 1996

Li Yongbin, *Video Art*
CIFA Gallery, Beijing

First a self-taught painter, Li Yongbin becomes interested in more conceptually driven work in the early 1990s, increasingly dealing with time and the temporality of worldly phenomena. He makes his works in the very personal setting of his small Beijing apartment. Li's first video is a portrait of his mother, which he makes after her death in 1995. His second video, *Face I*, is filmed between 1995 and 1996. He borrows a photograph from his neighbor, an old woman, and projects her image onto his own face as he sits on a stool in front of the video camera. The piece is shot at night. The old woman's face overlaps with Li's almost imperceptibly. Since then, he has made many *Face* films, which he always shoots in his apartment at night. They are filmed in real time and undergo minimal post-production editing. The CIFA show comes at the suggestion of Zhang Li.

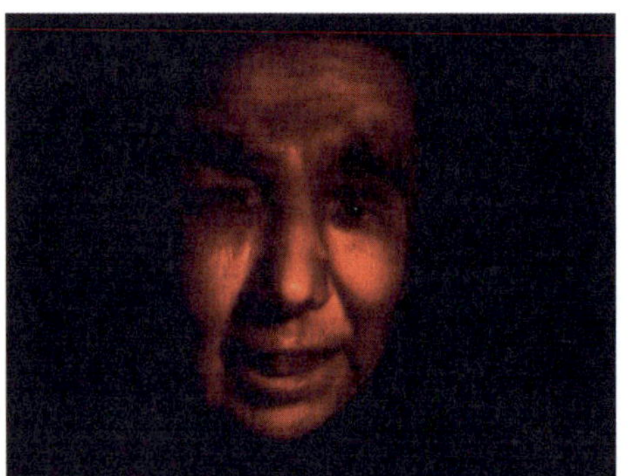
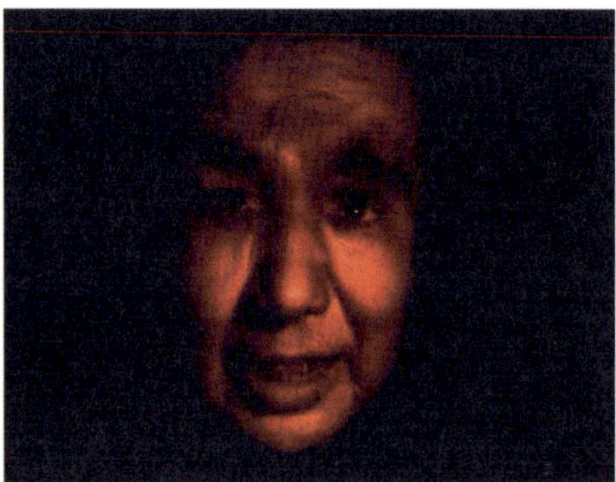
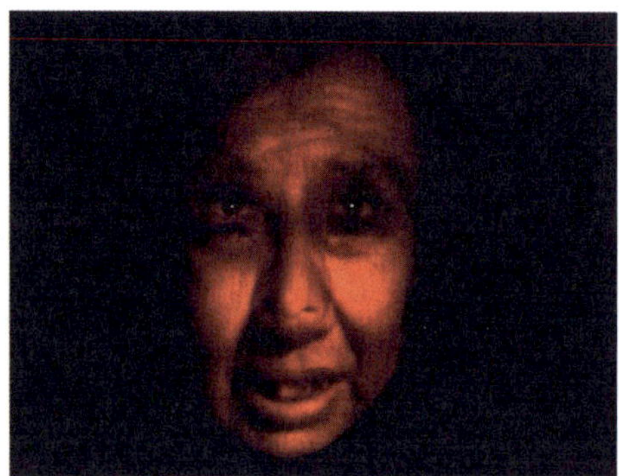

Li Yongbin, *Face (No. 1)*, video, 35′, 1995–96, courtesy Li Yongbin

14 June–21 July 1996

China: Aktuelles aus 15 Ateliers
Reithalle / Alte Kaserne, Munich

In the summer of 1995, van Dijk guides German curator Dr. Inge Lindemann through China in preparation for the exhibition *China: Aktuelles aus 15 Ateliers*, which takes place in Munich in 1996. Erika Kiffl, a German photographer, accompanies them.
Van Dijk acts as the China consultant and organizer for this exhibition and all related programs during *China Today*, the China Cultural Weeks in Munich. These span theater, exhibitions, music, and films. Organizers are Jochen Hahn, head of Hahn Productions, and the German gallerist Alexander Ochs. A festival week on German arts and culture in China has also been planned. The festival is part of a German-Chinese open door policy for culture and trade. The political situation between China and Germany becomes tense in spring, however, following human rights protests at an exhibition of Chinese painting in Bonn and an official condemnation of China's treatment of Tibet by the German Parliament. On 1 April, van Dijk writes the organizers in Munich, warning them against escalation:

> The works for the exhibition were shipped yesterday. We are now busy preparing the travel schedules for the artists and the theater people. Many of them need to apply for a passport, so I want to ask you to please be careful. If the press starts to directly link the exhibition to politically sensitive themes like human rights, war games, or other things, the project is doomed.
> The Chinese artists who were represented in the exhibition in Bonn are still encountering problems: they have to answer for themselves with local governments, with their school administrations, and with other officials, just because the organizers in Bonn believed that a scandal in the press was the only way to rescue their exhibition.
> I believe that much art can speak for itself, and that artists don't need to deliver political statements. All they must do is show their individual worlds.
> **HvD, letter to Lucas Lessing, Beijing, 1 April 1996**

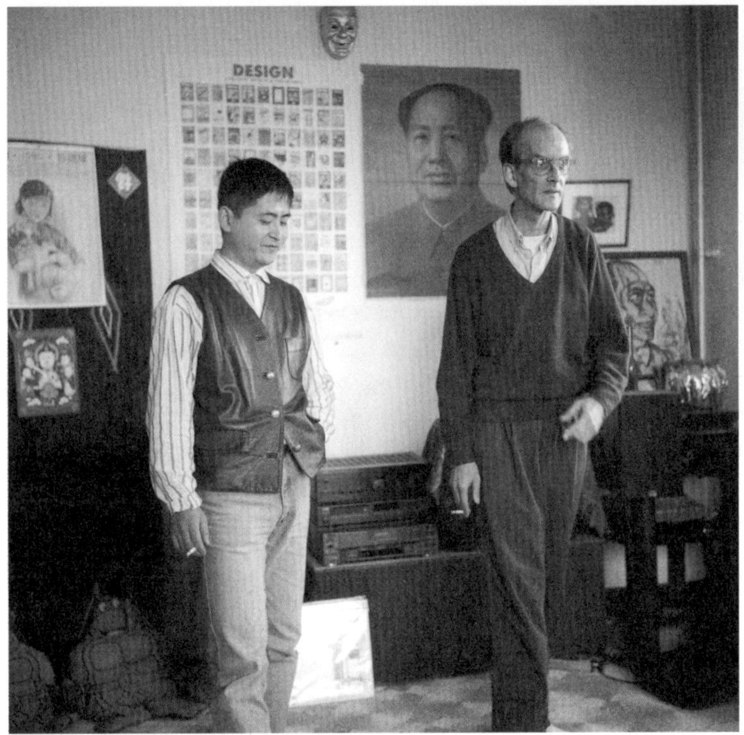

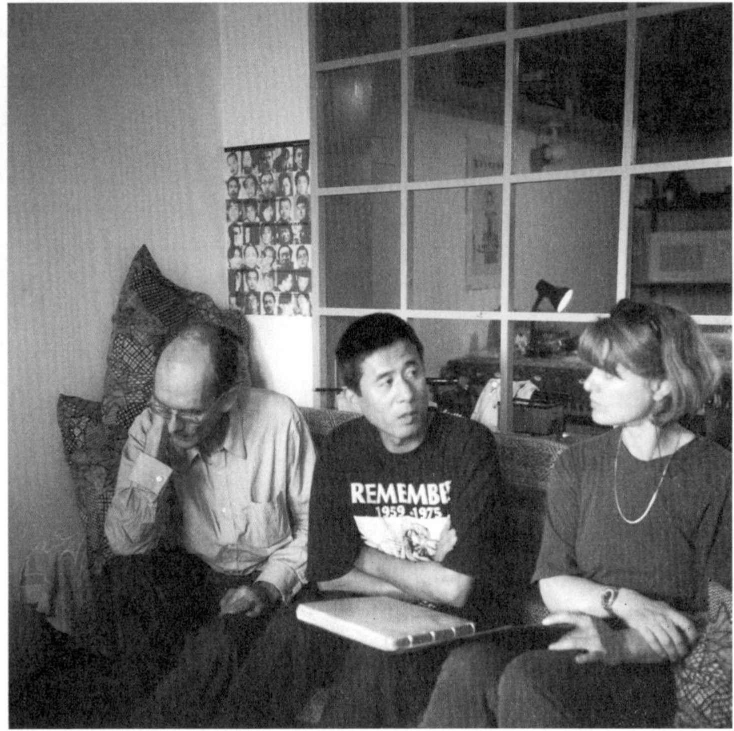

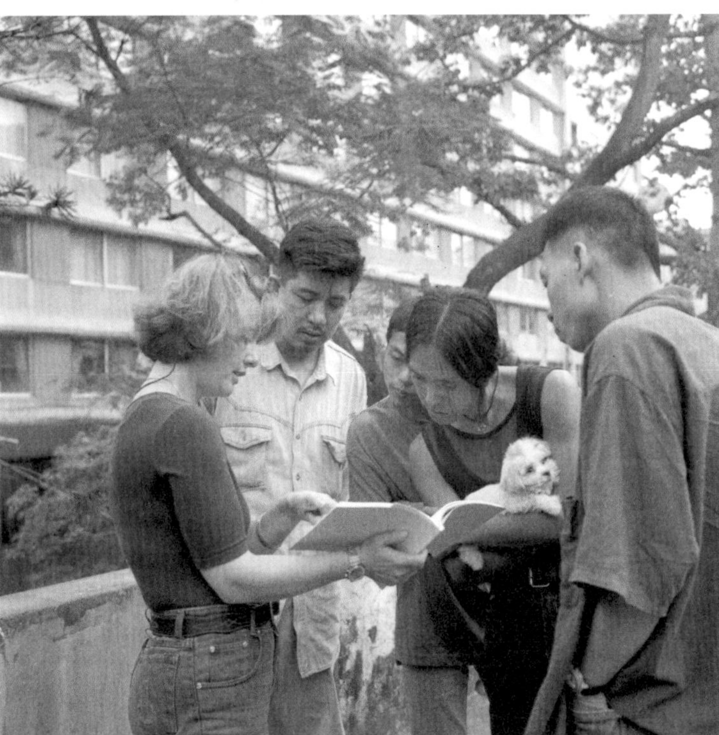

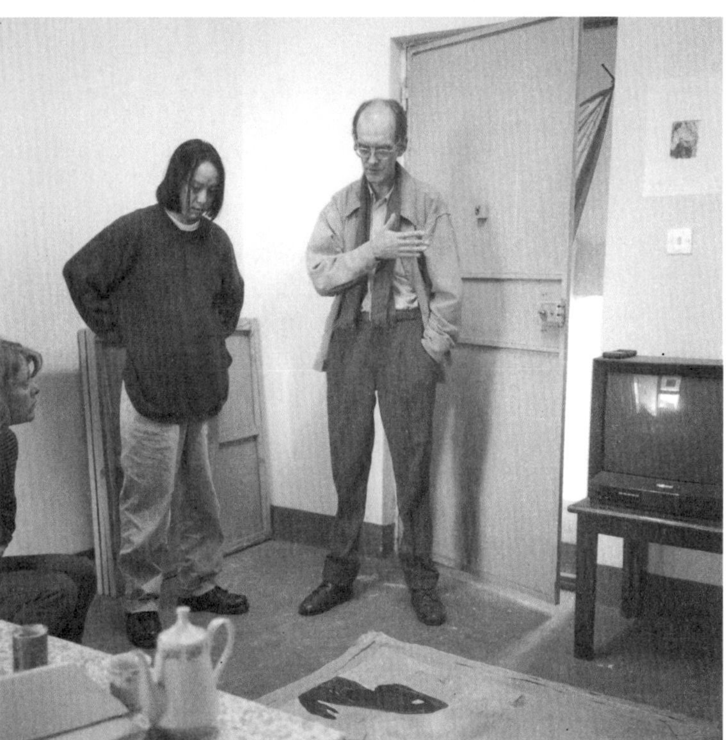

Erika Kiffl, photos of Chinese artists in their studios, 1995; above, left to right: Hans van Dijk and Zeng Fanzhi, Beijing; Hans van Dijk, Zhang Peili, and Dr. Inge Lindemann, Hangzhou; bottom, left to right: Dr. Inge Lindemann, Xu Tan, Zhao Bandi, Lin Yilin, Guangzhou; Shen Xiaotong with Hans van Dijk, Chengdu, courtesy Erika Kiffl and Archive of Artistic Photography of the Rhineland's Art Scene (AFORK), Kunstpalast, Düsseldorf

To make matters worse, the Dalai Lama is to visit Germany from 13 – 15 June 1996. Officials threaten to close down the Goethe Institute in Beijing. At the very last moment, the Cultural Weeks are canceled by the Chinese partners controlled by the Chinese government, causing an enormous upheaval in the German press. Of the numerous events scheduled in Munich, only *Aktuelles* takes place. Van Dijk manages to find other venues for the scheduled ballet and theater performances in France, and the shipment of props and decors is redirected. He also tries to arrange for Zhang Li to visit Europe, but Zhang cannot obtain a passport in time.

Munich Hahn Production
Beijing, 24 May 1996

Dear Jochen Hahn,
It is with mixed feelings that I send you this fax to formally inform you that China will not attend the Munich Cultural Weeks. As you may know, just before the opening ceremony we were notified that someone added several discussions on Chinese politics to the schedule without our knowledge. This action has broken our agreement in the most barbaric way. Although the Chinese side paid several visits to the relevant German departments and clearly stated our viewpoint, it is said that one of the German patrons nonetheless insists on the inclusion of these discussions in the schedule. Due to this situation, China will not go to Munich.
We fully understand your enthusiasm for the Cultural Weeks. We also have undertaken a lot of preparatory work based on our agreement. The materials have already arrived in Germany. Neither of us expected or wished for the current situation. Those who proposed these discussions and targeted China for political reasons should be held responsible.
We would like to take this opportunity to express our deep regret at the loss of this chance to introduce modern Chinese culture to the German public. We feel even worse that we had to end our cooperation such a short time before the start of the Cultural Weeks. Our company had such a good collaboration with your Hahn Production in the early phases.
However, we still hope both sides can continue to work together with mutual understanding to settle the problems caused by our non-participation.

Best Wishes,
China Foreign Cultural Exchange Company

Aktuelles includes the paintings *The Testimony of the Hare,* and *To Hurt* by Wang Xingwei, prints by Hong Hao, photographs by Zhao Shaoruo, and an installation consisting of a large earth pyramid by Xu Tan. Zhao Bandi's *30×30×30cm Exchange of Earth Between China and Germany* is a stunningly original earth work. Zhang Peili's split-screen video installation *Related Rhythm* is commissioned as a site-specific work, the first multi-channel video installation by a Chinese artist.

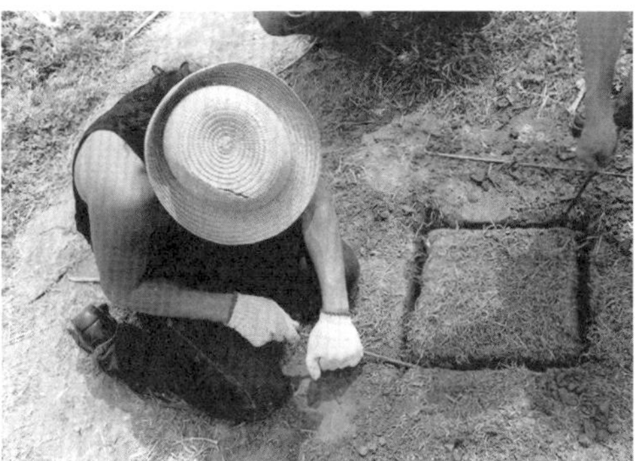

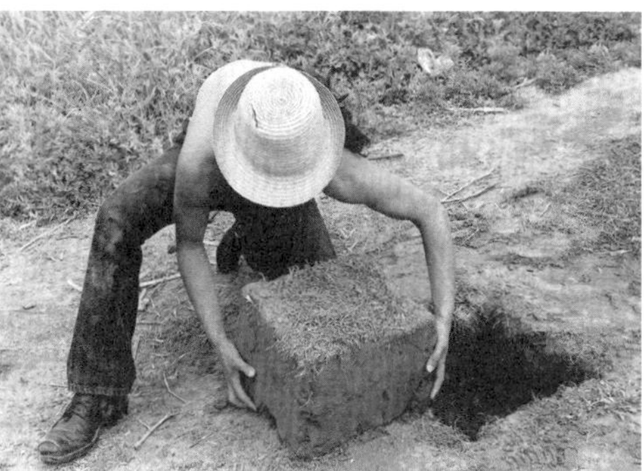

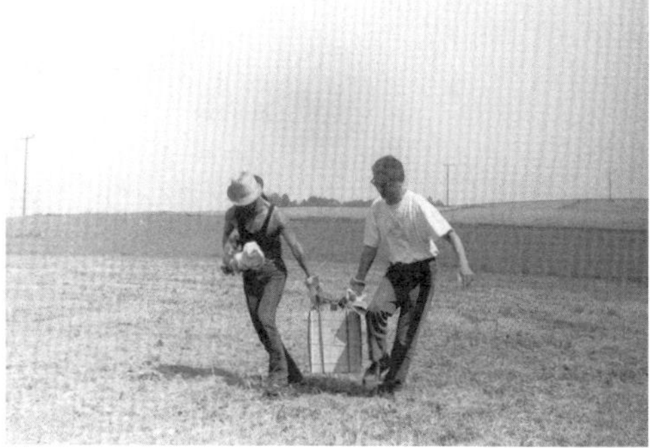

Zhao Bandi, *30×30×30 cm Exchange of Earth Between China and Germany*, 1996; left: Zhao Bandi delineating a plot of earth in Beijing; center: Zhao Bandi digging out 30×30×30 cm of soil in Beijing; bottom: Zhao Bandi and Zhang Peili carrying the soil to be buried in a field in Munich, courtesy Zhao Bandi

Paintings by Mai Zhixiong and drawings by Sun Kai proposed by van Dijk are not approved by the organizers, while Chinese authorities do not allow some of the artists to travel to Munich. Xu Tan is requested to appear before the Board of Directors of the art academy in Guangzhou to explain his involvement with the show, which he is ultimately forbidden to attend. Van Dijk unsuccessfully tries to arrange the necessary papers for Zhao Shaoruo to travel to Munich to save him from the Chinese police. The artist is already in danger, and soon after this is forced to leave for Hong Kong.

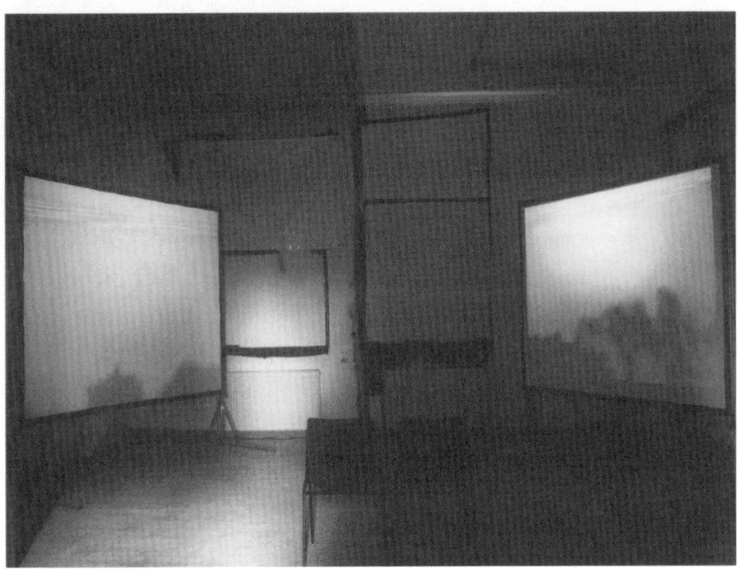

Zhang Peili, *Related Rhythm*, two-channel video installation, 27', 1996, *Aktuelles aus 15 Ateliers*, Reithalle, Munich, 1996; reconstructed by the artist and first shown in China during *Hans van Dijk: 5000 Names*, UCCA, Beijing, 2014

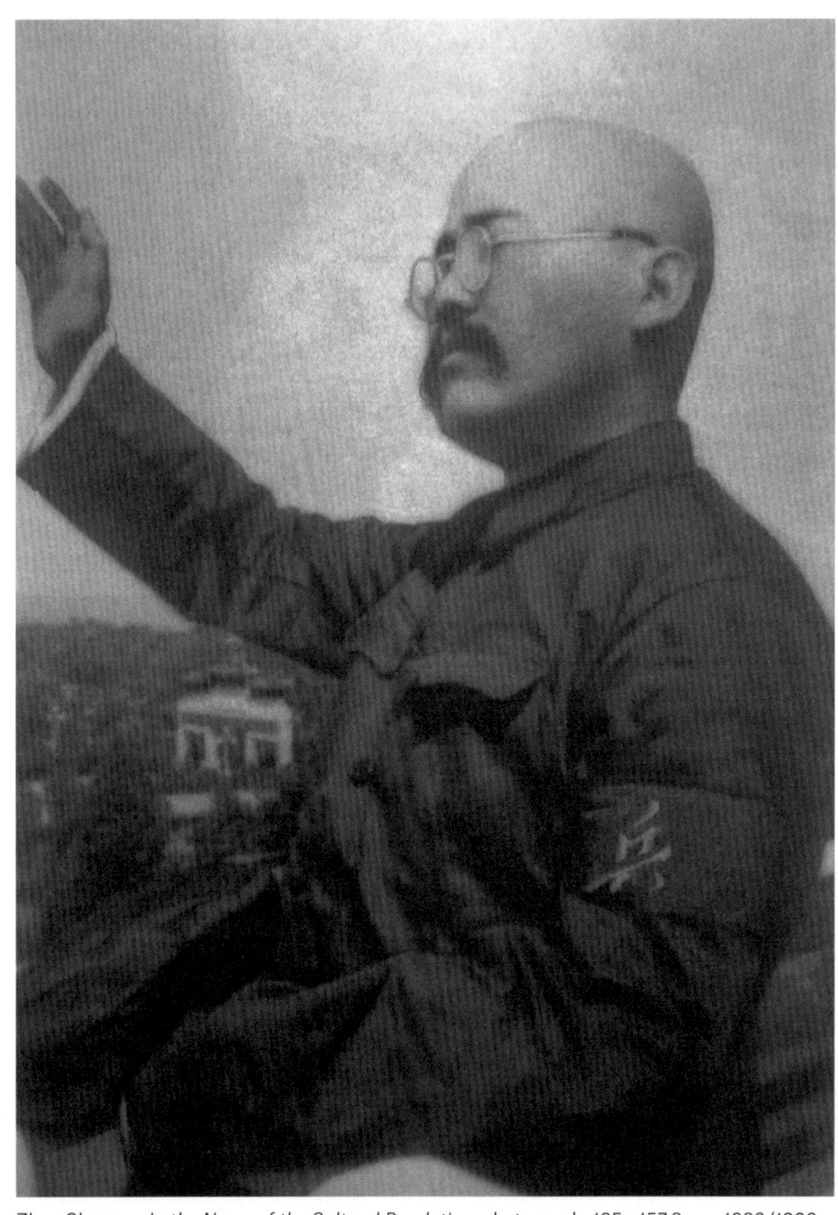

Zhao Shaoruo, *In the Name of the Cultural Revolution*, photograph, 125 × 157.8 cm, 1989/1993, courtesy Zhao Shaoruo

Zhao Shaoruo
My Approach To Imitating God Brings Me Huge Success
1995

> Judging by Western standards, I am already successful. I feel honored: even though I am still young, my accomplishments and reputation are those of a great personage after middle age, after death, even. I am very excited. Every time I see myself, I am carried away by happiness. The greatness of my achievement rivals that of the most magnificent leaders (only in the visual field, of course). I can objectively see that the elder generation's great accomplishments are the results of following Marxist thought; that Marxism was born in Germany is, I believe, truly one of Western culture's most outstanding achievements. I followed them closely, unwilling to fall behind and unceasingly imitating them, such that today I am successful and famous. I have a sense of "enjoying success while young." I'm "riding on the crest of success." I hope to strike the iron while it is hot. In the near future, whether in Frankfurt, Paris, London, Amsterdam, or even in the whole of Europe, my name will resound across the land.

Because *In the Name of the Cultural Revolution* is prominently featured on the cover of the Guangzhou International Art Fair booklet in 1996, the police intend to put Zhao in prison for a third time. However, with the help of van Dijk, Zhao successfully makes his escape to Hong Kong, where he lives on Lamma Island. Van Dijk seeks help from Sir Christopher Patten, Britain's last Governor of Hong Kong, as well as from a representative of the United Nations Human Rights Council. As a political refugee, Zhao is given HKD 7,000 dollars a month for two years by the Hong Kong government. Afterward, Zhao moves to Finland where he will live for several years. Between 1996 and 2002, van Dijk sells works by Zhao with a total value of EUR 20,000. This money allows the artist to survive in exile.[2]

2—MB, interview with Zhao Shaoruo, Beijing, March 2014.

In a fax to Lindemann, van Dijk writes, "Please don't use Zhao Shaoruo's photos with the Mao propaganda versions. He is again on the run at the moment, and the catalogue could sooner or later cause new trouble for him and for us. His work is about THE FAME OF ZHAO SHAORUO, and that is not a concession."

After the exhibition, a selection of works travels on to Littmann Kulturprojekte, Basel. From there, they are scheduled to travel to Tokyo. Among them are five paintings by an artist from Guangzhou. His works were insured for an unusually high amount, with a fine if they are not sent back in due time. Unfortunately, Littmann fails to return the works. Nobody seems to actually know where they are. Instead of being sent to Tokyo, it turns out that at least one of them is in Ghent. Frank Uytterhaegen travels to Ghent in a frenzy to bring the paintings back, but because they are not on time, van Dijk is sued for USD 150,000. Van Dijk is obliged to seek legal assistance, while the artist in question is shunned by the art community and ultimately gives up being an artist.

1997

The year takes off promisingly. Van Dijk has been invited by the prominent German firm Siemens to organize a German-Chinese art exhibition program to support its cultural activities in China. The program is called *Face to Face*. It starts in spring, and is scheduled to continue well into summer.

In summer, van Dijk travels to the Netherlands because his mother falls gravely ill. His father has already passed away in 1993. Since van Dijk is very close to his mother, her death a few weeks after his arrival has a big impact on him.

From 1997 to the end of 1998, van Dijk rents a small office in an office building in Wangfujing, but still has no permanent exhibition space at his disposal. In August 1997, van Dijk signs a contract with the Kempinski Hotel to install contemporary art shows in its lobby and first floor. The connection proves extremely useful, because van Dijk will be able to hold his seminal *Mondrian in China* exhibition there in 1998. But for now, the NAAC announcement, betraying a blatant commercialism, states:

> The project integrates contemporary Chinese art in the architecture, interior design, and overall ambience of the Kempinski Hotel. Color and forms of the interior design as well as the exceptional lighting conditions of the Kempinski Hotel offer an extraordinary setting for the arts. On the one hand, the works are distributed between the ground and first floors; on the other hand, the second floor allows one to take in almost all the works at a glance. Thus, gallery visitors and incidental guests encounter the artworks. [...] Visit the abstract *Crosses* by Ding Yi, the cartoon-like book pages of Hong Hao, the tricolored machine visions of the young artist Mai Zhixiong, Zhao Jianfei's Cubist series, which in fact consists of triangles, Fang Lijun's famous bald heads, and Zhang Hai'er's black-and-white photographs of fashion and folk.

In the fall, van Dijk realizes a seminal exhibition of Chinese photography at the Neuer Berliner Kunstverein in collaboration with Alexander Tolnay and Andreas Schmid, which establishes Chinese photography abroad.

New galleries begin sprouting up across China, while van Dijk still has no residence permit and therefore cannot set up a space. In 1997, the Chinese government again changes its visa policy, shortening the maximum duration of stay from two months to one. The easiest visa run is to Hong Kong. The round trip from Beijing takes about a week by train. In the past, van Dijk has always stayed over in Guangzhou to see his friends. Traveling to Hong Kong every month is now impossible unless by plane, which is very expensive.

Until this point, NAAC is just about the only organization in China acting as an intermediary between Chinese artists and the outside world that also operates without any direct commercial interest. Van Dijk has succeeded in building his idealistic business model at a great cost to himself. But while he is known among art scholars in the US and Australia, he lacks a high-end business network with international art institutions, as well as a solid base in China, depending on NAAC commissions ad hoc.

Others are able to jump into that gap. The Courtyard Gallery opens in Beijing in 1996 with Karen Smith as its main curator; in Shanghai, ShanghART Gallery, founded by the Swiss Lorenz Helbling in 1996, becomes increasingly influential. Because there is little concept of gallery loyalty, artists frequently sell to the highest bidder. Several of van Dijk's close artist friends leave him for other galleries. One of them argues the case: "I really like Hans, but he cannot make me famous." Van Dijk is forced to renegotiate his position in the Chinese contemporary art world. With Helbling, he bitterly agrees to split up the country: all Hangzhou- and Shanghai-based artists, such as Zhang Peili, Geng Jianyi, Zhou Tiehai, and Zhang Enli, are to work with Helbling. The artists based in Beijing are to stay with van Dijk. Of those, Hong Hao soon changes to the Courtyard Gallery, and Zhao Bandi switches to ShanghART. Ding Yi, his closest artist friend, continues working with both. Unfortunately, Beijing artists are famously divided into factions, which is the main reason van Dijk was always reluctant to work with them. Guangzhou, where he has many loyal artist friends, remains neutral territory.

Van Dijk still acts as a consultant to many foreign collectors. He advises Uytterhaegen on buying contemporary Chinese art. His old acquaintance from Nanjing Robert Bernell[3], who arrives in Beijing from Hong Kong in 1995, starts investing in Chinese video art and photography, with van Dijk as his advisor. Van Dijk also plays an important role in building up the collection of Uli Sigg[4], whom he takes to the studios of various artists in the mid-1990s, when Sigg is the Swiss ambassador to China.

3—Robert Bernell, sinologist, driving force behind the 798 Art District in Beijing. Founder of Timezone 8, a bookshop, art space, and bilingual art publishing house.

4—Today, Ulli Sigg is a world famous collector of Chinese contemporary art. The M+ museum in Hong Kong houses a major part of his collection.

5—Silvie Seidlitz, Swiss-born art dealer, lives in China for fifteen years.

> More and more art is being bought. Sigg, the Swiss ambassador, has built an interesting collection over the past three years. Seidlitz[5], who has been collecting for a longer time, here, in Moscow, and in Hong Kong, doesn't want to be left behind and asked me to mediate for her. There is talk of Chinese collectors, but nobody knows who they are. One dealer who works for them flaunts a lot of money and a lot of artists, including Li Yousong. Later this year, two contemporary art auctions are to take place, and both of them have approached me about Ding Yi.

Starting last year, Chinese Contemporary [a gallery] is active in London. They have a Wang Xingwei on consignment from me after I sold three other works by him to Sigg. In Berlin, Alexander Ochs runs Asia Art Now. He has also been pulling my sleeve a lot. Also in Berlin is the opening on 26 September of *Zeitgenössische Fotokunst aus der Volksrepublik China* [*Contemporary Art Photography from the People's Republic of China*] at the Neuer Berliner Kunstverein, directed by Alexander Tolnay. The exhibition includes fourteen mainland artists. A lot of work, little money, but they sell through us, and some sales have already been made. [...]
Now and then I hear of debates in the Western art press about "new realism versus conceptual art," et cetera. Also the upcoming exhibition in Berlin is positioned explicitly as "Photographic Art," while TZ Art in New York and Frederieke Sanders Taylor[6] speak of "Conceptual Photography." Photography or painting are no longer sufficient; people want something new. If ever you encounter anything of this new genre, do let me know.
HvD, letter to Dutch art advisor Marina Betist, 17 June 1997

6—Frederieke Sanders Taylor, owner of TZ Art Gallery, New York.

With the foreign galleries, foreign art dealers arrive, not all of them honest. Art business in China, painting especially, has become very lucrative. Deals are being closed with collectors in which the artist doesn't even know the price; sometimes a zero or two are added under the table, away from his prying eyes. As a possible competitor, van Dijk, too, is being crossed by dealers touring the country with foreign investors and collectors; often now, he isn't even visited.

Young Chinese art critics have now come of age and are demanding to be heard. Foreign curators, too, are flocking to China, kicking off a wave of exhibitions and diminishing van Dijk's importance as a mediator to the art scene in China. Although van Dijk has been extremely knowledgeable when providing advice on Chinese contributions to nearly all important early exhibitions of Chinese contemporary art abroad, the Western art world has hardly acknowledged or appreciated him as an independent curator. The internet is becoming important in China as well. People are getting email and portable phones. By the end of 1997, Robert Bernell starts a hugely successful website, ChineseArt.com.

ROBERT BERNELL: At the time, the local critics and curators were not empowered. They didn't have money, nor did the artists. For them Chinese art was overtly influenced by foreigners in power. When I started my website, I was careful to minimize my role to a degree. In most cases it was just putting the exhibitions online, with the curators sending us the images. To further minimize my role, I would ask a Chinese art critic to write for us, and then also name the next critic to write.
Hans wasn't driven by the commercial viability of a work, only by his interest in it. You saw those wildly popular Cynical Realism and Political Pop shows, and then you went to Hans and you would see something completely different, photographs, let's say, and wonder how he paid the rent.
Hans was the first to direct interest into photography and conceptual photography in China. He was interested in gender and politics. He was interested in performance art from the East Village artists, but he didn't like violent work. He preferred ironic comments related to fame and money like Wang Jin's *To Marry a Mule*, or Zheng Guogu's *Sky Stories*. Gu Zhenqing was doing a lot of this slicing up of animals and sleeping inside the carcasses, and Hans didn't like that at all.
When I started collecting art myself, about half the artists in my collection came through Hans. I got Zheng Guogu through him, and a lot of photography in particular. I was the largest collector of Chinese art after Uli Sigg at that time; I owned about 150 pieces. In 2002, I sold my collection to Frank [Uytterhaegen].
I think Hans realized that what motivated his contemporaries was a quest for power that legitimated them to shape discourse. Who owns Contemporary Chinese Art was always the issue, and it is still there. Hans was political in the sense that he didn't like politics. He didn't like the political nature of artists and critics and the games they played. He stayed out of it as much as possible. Hans' way of thinking, to not have a political agenda, must have been quizzical, a bit of an anomaly.
MB, interview with Robert Bernell, Beijing, 11 and 13 September 2012

Face to Face, an exhibition series showing Chinese and German artists in Beijing
Organized by the Siemens Cultural Programme in cooperation with NAAC
Part one: Photography, part two: Painting, part three: Video

Siemens
Kultur
Programm

Press Release **Munich, February 1997**

Face to Face

Luo Yongjin & Thomas Struth

Photography

An exhibition series of Siemens Cultural Programme in Beijing

The aim of the exhibition project of Siemens Cultural Programme in Beijing is to give Chinese and German artists the opportunity to work closely together. This personal contact will encourage them to exchange opinions and experiences and to jointly discover new forms of intercultural activity. It will enable the national characteristics found in the production and design of visual art to be viewed in a cross-cultural context. The first exhibition will feature the work of the photographers Thomas Struth and Luo Yongjin.

In the mid-seventies Bernd Becher was appointed Professor of Photography at the Dusseldorf Art Academy. His clear and unspectacular perspective has had a formative influence on numerous young artists - among them Thomas Struth. Struth views his objects from a distance, and allows the camera to adopt a human perspective. At the same time the photographs reflect an objective view of the situation, they do not intervene in the scene. From his own individual artistic perspective, Thomas Struth addresses the human image, even in photographs where people are absent. His photographs with architectural themes focus on public areas which symbolically reflect mankind's principles of organization, while his family portraits focus on privacy and intimacy. Reality is not artificially created, interpreted or dramatized; instead it is exposed by the camera. This is also a characteristic of Luo Yongjin's work. But he abandons distance, and becomes actively involved in the scenes. In effect, he becomes part of the action. The main themes of his photographs are the traditional Chinese celebrations and rituals marking the rights of passage such as birth, marriage and death. His other motives are daily life in the streets and on market-places.

Three joint exhibitions, each featuring a Chinese and a German artist, are planned as part of the ›Face to Face‹ series of events. The different artistic media that will be featured include photography, painting and video and will offer an overview of contemporary artistic trends in both cultures as well as contribute to direct and constructive contacts between Chinese and German artists. In June Katharina Grosse, Dusseldorf, and Ding Yi, Shanghai, will arrange a joint exhibition.

Duration: **22 February to 2 March 1997**

Place: **Art Gallery of the Beijing International Art Palace**
Holiday Inn Crowne Plaza
48 Wangfujing Dajie
Beijing 100006

The exhibitions will be realized in cooperation with NAAC Beijing and in the curatorial care of Claudia Albrecht and Hans van Dijk. A catalogue will be published in each case.

Information: Siemens Cultural Programme • Leonore Leonardy • 80 312 Munich
T: +49 89 234-3594 • F: +49 89 234-3615

Face to Face, Luo Yongjin & Thomas Struth – Photography, press release, Munich, 1997, private coll.

22 February – 3 March 1997

Face to Face, Luo Yongjin & Thomas Struth – Photography
Art Gallery of the Beijing International Art Palace

This is the first time a Chinese artist is allowed to exhibit in China together with a foreign artist. The exhibition is a success, the formula much appreciated, but Luo Yongjin's work receives loud criticism from the Chinese press, possibly instigated by the China Photographers Association (Luo is not a member).

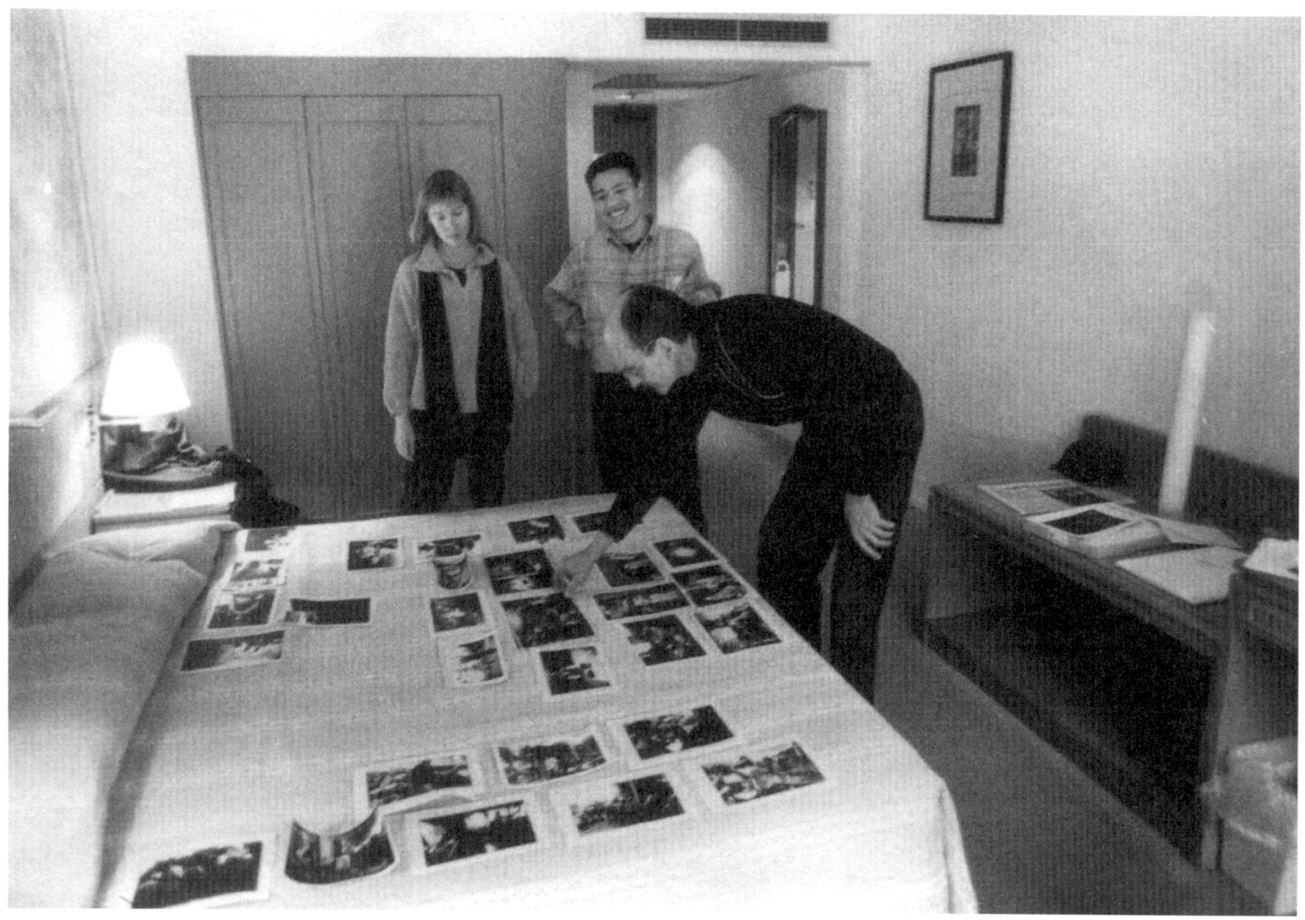

Unknown photographer, Hans van Dijk and Luo Yongjin selecting works for *Face to Face*, Beijing, 1997

In the meantime Ding Yi travels to Germany to visit Katharina Grosse to prepare for the second show. He brings small-scale models of the exhibition spaces, and Grosse and him choose the works together. Van Dijk asks his friend Monica Dematté, who has been living and working in China since the late eighties, to write an essay about Ding Yi for the catalogue.

> Dear Monica, Thank you for your fax. In Beijing it is very exciting, too much work, too much bureaucracy, and neither freedom nor money. But there is a lot happening; we get a lot of reactions from different parts of the world. I have one growing problem: I have to get legal status, the sooner the better. I need to get registered some way. Do you have any ideas? The dates for the Ding Yi – Katharina Grosse exhibition are now fixed: 13 – 22 June. The Germans need your text urgently. What can I tell them? All the best, Hans
>
> HvD, note to Monica Dematté, Beijing, 7 April 1997

The catalogue is never published, however. Perhaps afraid of another Munich debacle, Siemens stalls on the remaining exhibitions, and abandons the project without informing van Dijk or the artists, even though the date for Ding Yi and Katharina Grosse has been set, and van Dijk is preparing for the exhibition with Zhang Peili and a German video artist. It leaves everyone with a large gap in their agenda and a lot of work done in vain.

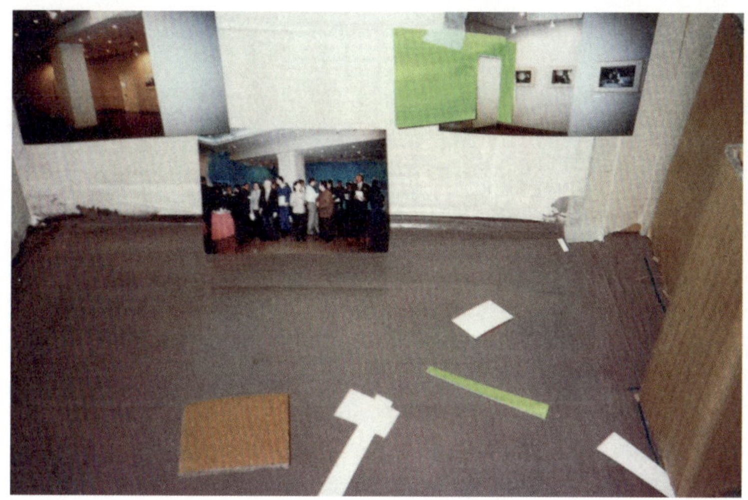
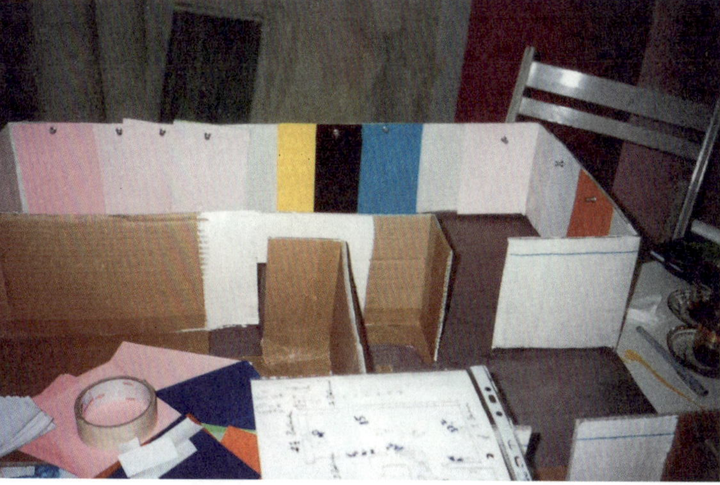
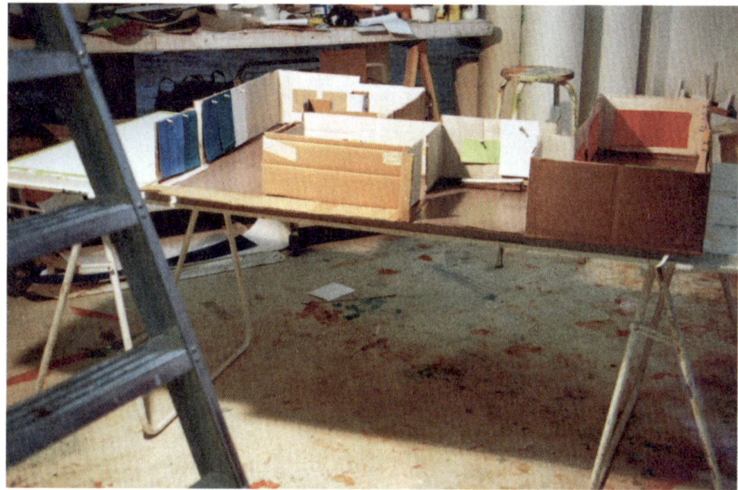
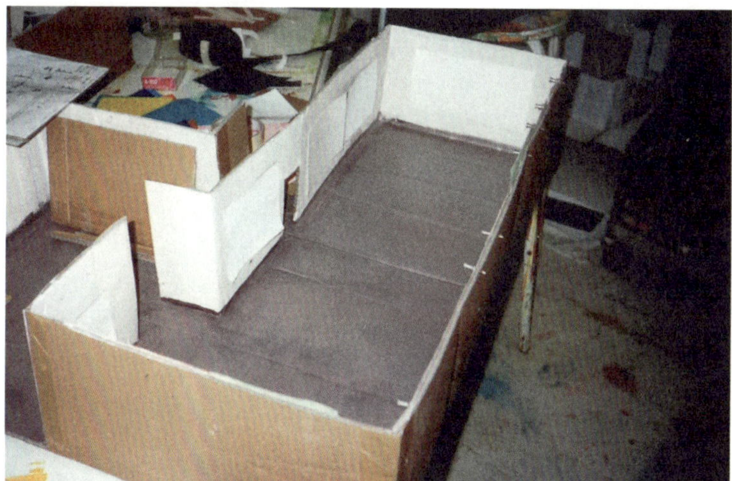

Ding Yi, scale models for the second *Face to Face* exhibition, 1997, private coll.

Summer 1997

The joke of documenta X

Van Dijk, Yan Lei, and Hong Hao, having a beer together one evening in van Dijk's apartment, devise a practical joke together. They write a letter addressed to a substantial number of Chinese artists, letting them know that a certain Mr. Ielnay Oahgnoh (Yan Lei Hong Hao backwards) has been commissioned to curate a Chinese show for *documenta X*, and that he is now starting the process of selecting the Chinese artists. He will travel to China shortly to visit the artists. However, because timeline is too short for the show to open with *documenta X* in June, it will start in September under the title *From the Other World—China Avant-garde* at 16 Gnakupul, Kassel. A floorplan of the exhibition space is included with the letter. The joke causes enormous furore, and Hong Hao and Yan Lei later apologize in *Jiangsu Art Monthly*, without revealing, however, that the floorplan is actually that of van Dijk's apartment. Gnakupul is a reversal of "Lupukang," the area in Beijing where the apartment is situated.

> BRITTA ERICKSON: I have a vivid memory of talking with Hans at a China Art Archive and Warehouse (CAAW) exhibition of Yan Lei's work. Hans was delighted to tell me the real story behind Yan Lei and Hong Hao's "invitations," a devilish prank that played on artists' desire to be included in major European exhibitions. Many were incredibly excited when they received the fake invitation to appear in a special section of documenta. Hans helped with the plot, arranging for the invitations to be mailed from Europe. The floorplan of the supposed exhibition space was that of Hans' apartment. He had the driest wit I have ever encountered, understated yet impish! I wish there had been time to get to know him better. There is no one at all like him today.
>
> **Scholar, artist, and curator Britta Erickson, email correspondence with MB, 2012**

Dear Sir/Madam

documenta in Kassel has existed since 1955. This year the tenth documenta will take place from 21 June onwards, that is for the duration of exactly 100 days.
This exhibition is a sign of acknowledgement of the extraordinary position of Chinese contemporary art in the art world. We feel obliged to offer the Chinese artists this unique opportunity. The title of the exhibition is *From the Other World—China Avant-garde—* it reflects the galloping development of Chinese art.
Unfortunately, due to limited time, we can only announce this exhibition at very short notice. It is no longer possible even now for this special exhibition to fully coincide with documenta. *From the Other World—China Avant-garde* will therefore be opened in September 1997. We hope that you appreciate this situation. The exhibition venue will be No. 16 Second Quarter Gnakupul, Kassel. The author of this letter was appointed curator of this exhibition and will travel to China from 30 June to 30 July in order to meet the artists and make all necessary preparations.

Hoping to see you in China,
Sincerely yours, Ielnay Oahgnoh—curator of the exhibition

Invitiation letter to *documenta X*, signed Ielnay Oahgnoh, Beijing, 20 May 1997

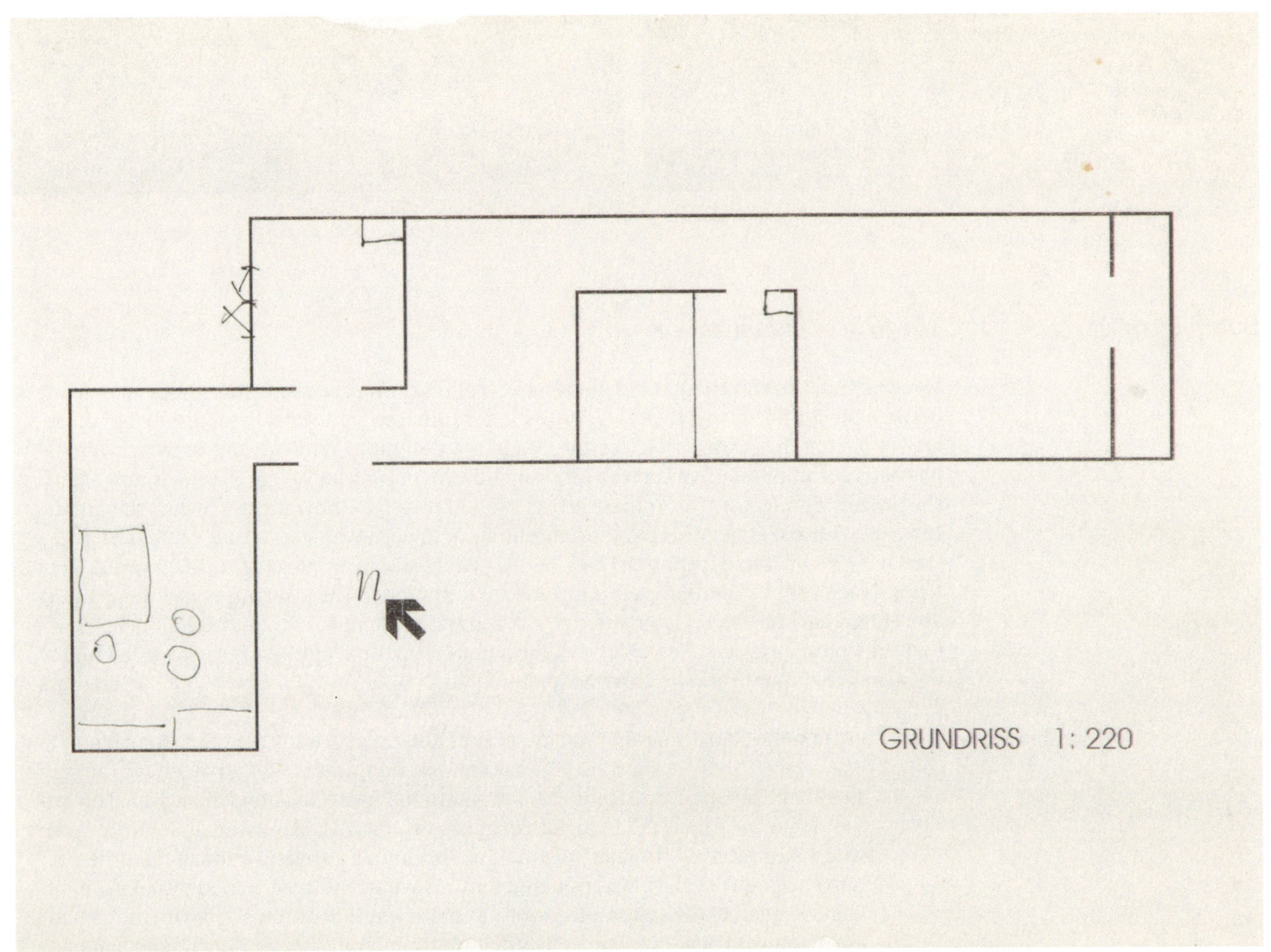

Hans van Dijk, floorplan of his apartment drawn at a fictitious scale, 1997, private coll.
Opposite page: fake invitation letter to *documenta X*, Kassel, Germany, signed Ielnay Oahgnoh (Hong Hao, Yan Lei), Beijing, 1997, private coll.

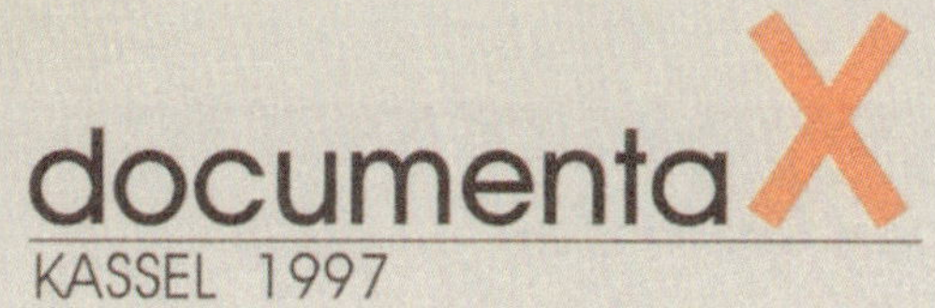

5 - 20 - 1997

Liebe(r) Frau/Herr Hans van Dijk

Seit 1955 gibt es die documenta in Kassel. Dieses Jahr wird die zehnte documenta statt finden und zwar vom 21. Juni an genau 100 Tage.

Der Träger der Ausstellung freut sich, Ihnen mitteilen zu können, daß dieses Jahr besondere fianzielle Mittel zur Verfügung sstehen, die für eine Sonderausstellung mit zeitgenössischer chinesischer Kunst verwendet werden sollen.

Diese Ausstellung ist ein Zeichen der Anerkennung für die besondere Stellung der zeitgenössischen chinesische Kunst in der Kunstwelt. Wir fühlen uns verpflichtet, den chinesischen Künstlern diese einzigartige Gelegenheit zu bieten. Der Titel der Ausstellung heißt "Aus der anderen Welt - chinesiche Avantgarde" - er spiegelt die galoppierende Entwicklung der chinesischen Kunst wieder.

Aus Zeitgründen können wir diese Ausstellung leider nur kurzfristig ankündigen. Schon jetzt ist es nicht mehr möglich, diese Sonderausstellung gleichzeitig mit der documenta stattfinden zu lassen. "Aus der andere Welt - chinesiche Avantgarde" wird deshalb im September 1997 eröffnet werden. Wir hoffen, daß Sie für diese Situation Verständnis haben. Der Ausstellungsort wird No.16 Second quator Gnakupul, Kassel sein.

Der Autor diese Briefes wurde zum Kurator der Ausstellung ernannt, und wird vom 30. Juni bis zum 15. Juli nach China reisen, um die Künstler zu treffen und alle nötigen Vorbereitungen vorzunehmen.
(Tel 010 6507 3384, Fax 010 6507 3363)

In der Hoffnung, Sie in China zu sehen

Hochachtungsvoll

Jelnay Oahgnoh

Kurator der Ausstellung

Jehang Oahgnoh

No.16 Second quarter Gnakupull ,Kassel , Germany TEL: 49561 - 65918 FAX: 49561 - 65103

27 September –
9 November 1997

Zeitgenössische Fotokunst aus der Volksrepublik China
Neuer Berliner Kunstverein, Berlin

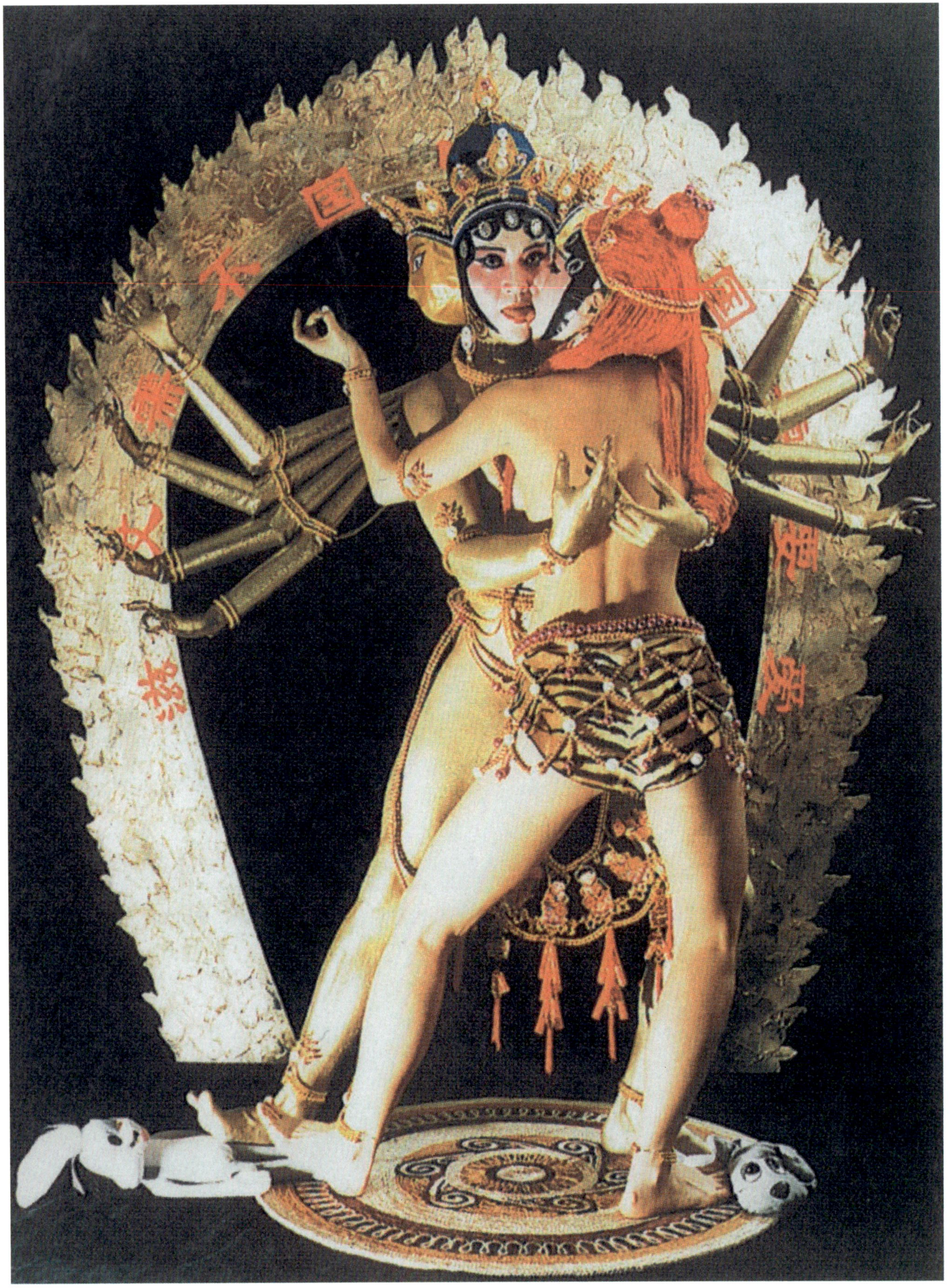

An Hong, *China Doesn't Need Aids, China Needs Love*, photograph, 61 × 47.8 cm, 1997, private coll.; shown at *Contemporary Art Photography from the People's Republic of China*, Neuer Berliner Kunstverein, Berlin, 1997

Drawing attention to Chinese photography with a historic overview, and featuring sixteen eminent artists (Ai Weiwei and Gu Dexin among them), this is the first exhibition of its kind in Europe. The exhibition is initiated by Alexander Tolnay and Andreas Schmid, who is the curator of the show. They travel to China together to choose the artists. As their advisor, van Dijk travels with them part of the way, asking Zhang Li to act as their guide in Hong Kong. One of the artists van Dijk recommends is Zheng Guogu, then a young and very promising artist.

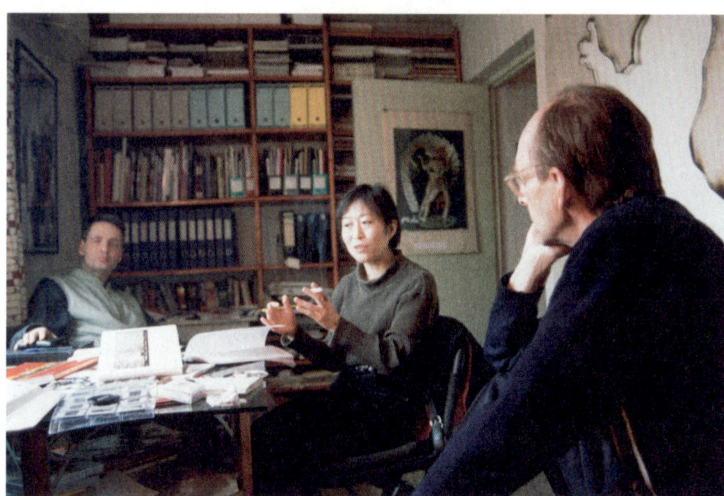

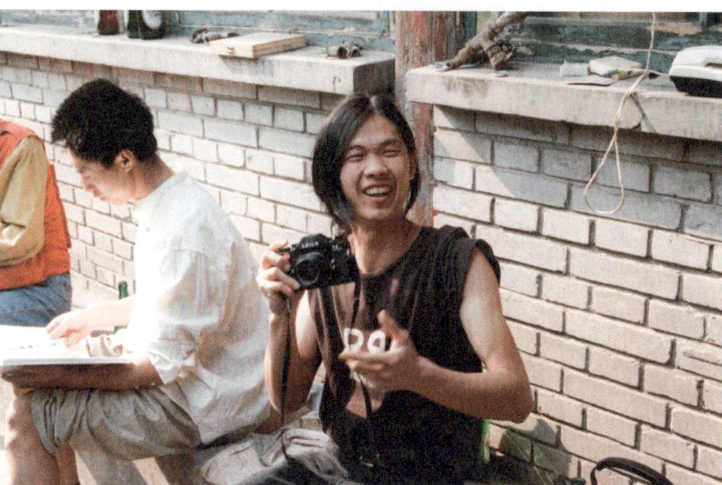

Preparing for the photography exhibition in Berlin: Andreas Schmid, Shu Kewen (Editor of *Sanlian Life Weekly*), and Hans van Dijk (left to right) in van Dijk's apartment, Beijing, 1996; a print of An Hong's work *China Doesn't Need Aids, China Needs Love* hangs on the door; on the wall to the right hangs Zhao Bandi's *The Big Rumour Spreading Until Today*; right: photographer RongRong in Beijing's East Village, 1996, photos courtesy Andreas Schmid

ZHENG GUOGU: I first met Hans around 1996, or perhaps before that. At that particular time, Hans was working on an exhibition with Andreas Schmid called *New Conceptual Photography in China*, and he wanted to meet me because Xu Tan and Chen Tong had introduced my work to him. I had just finished the Academy and started making art on my own. Because of that exhibition, we got to know each other better. Hans took some of my works to his gallery in Beijiing, both for showing and for selling. I was very happy, because I didn't know then that photos could also be collected.
There was a big difference then between "real" artists and photographers. Back then, people didn't think photos could be artworks. This situation lasted for years before that exhibition in 1996. For example: already in 1993, I made art in the form of photos, but people didn't accept them as art, and I got kind of stuck in that situation. I was lucky at this stage that I met Hans, because many people older than me who struggled with that same concept didn't get that chance, and very often they quit making art altogether. Hans enabled me to get to that conceptual break in thinking about photography.
MB, interview with Zheng Guogu, Guangzhou, 17 January 2013

ZHUANG HUI: If I remember correctly, I visited Hans' office for the first time in 1996. I may have met him at exhibitions here or there before that, though. He asked me to bring a print of my new work to NAAC entitled *One and Thirty – Workers*. My work was shown for the first time at the Neuer Berliner Kunstverein show in Berlin. That show was very important. [...] Ai Weiwei wrote an article on my work in 1997. I knew Ai Weiwei because we worked together on the black and white books, and I was the editor.
I would talk with Hans when I made a new work, but not otherwise. I would just explain to him how I had made that work. I would talk most of the time, and Hans would say very little; mostly he nodded, saying, "Very good" or "Hmmm." In my memory, Hans was not a talker, but to my surprise I found a photo in my archive of Hans at a party around 1998 in a bar drinking beer with many artists. I put that photo in my work from 2003 called *Ten Years*. It consists of a hundred photos of ten years of my life, and this picture is one of them because I wanted to commemorate Hans with it.
MB, interview with Zhuang Hui, Beijing, 11 September 2012

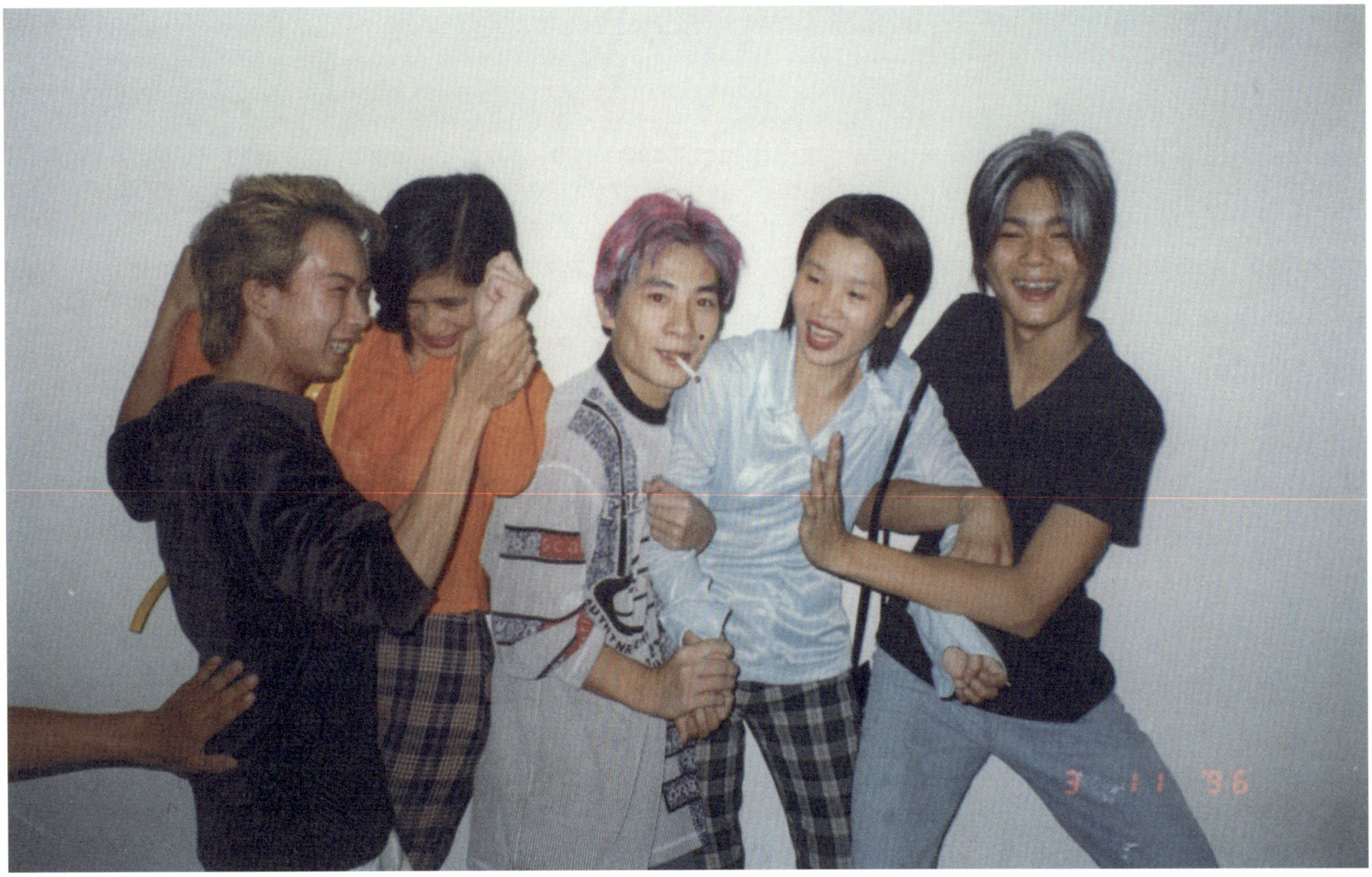

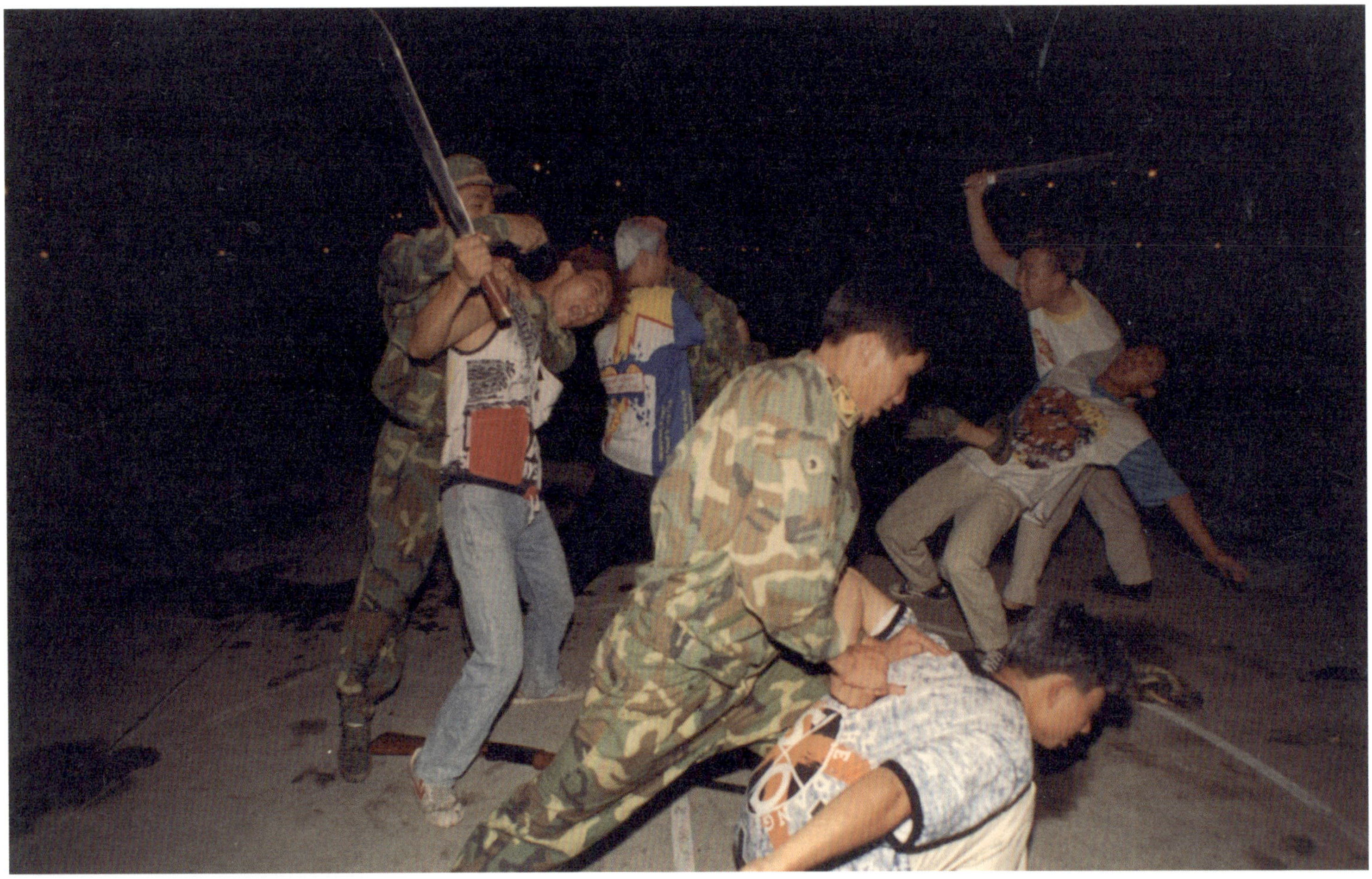

Zheng Guogu, *The Vagarious Life of Yangjiang Youth*, 4 from 15 chromogenic prints, 61×100 cm each, 1996, courtesy Zheng Guogu and Vitamin Creative Space, Beijing, Guangzhou

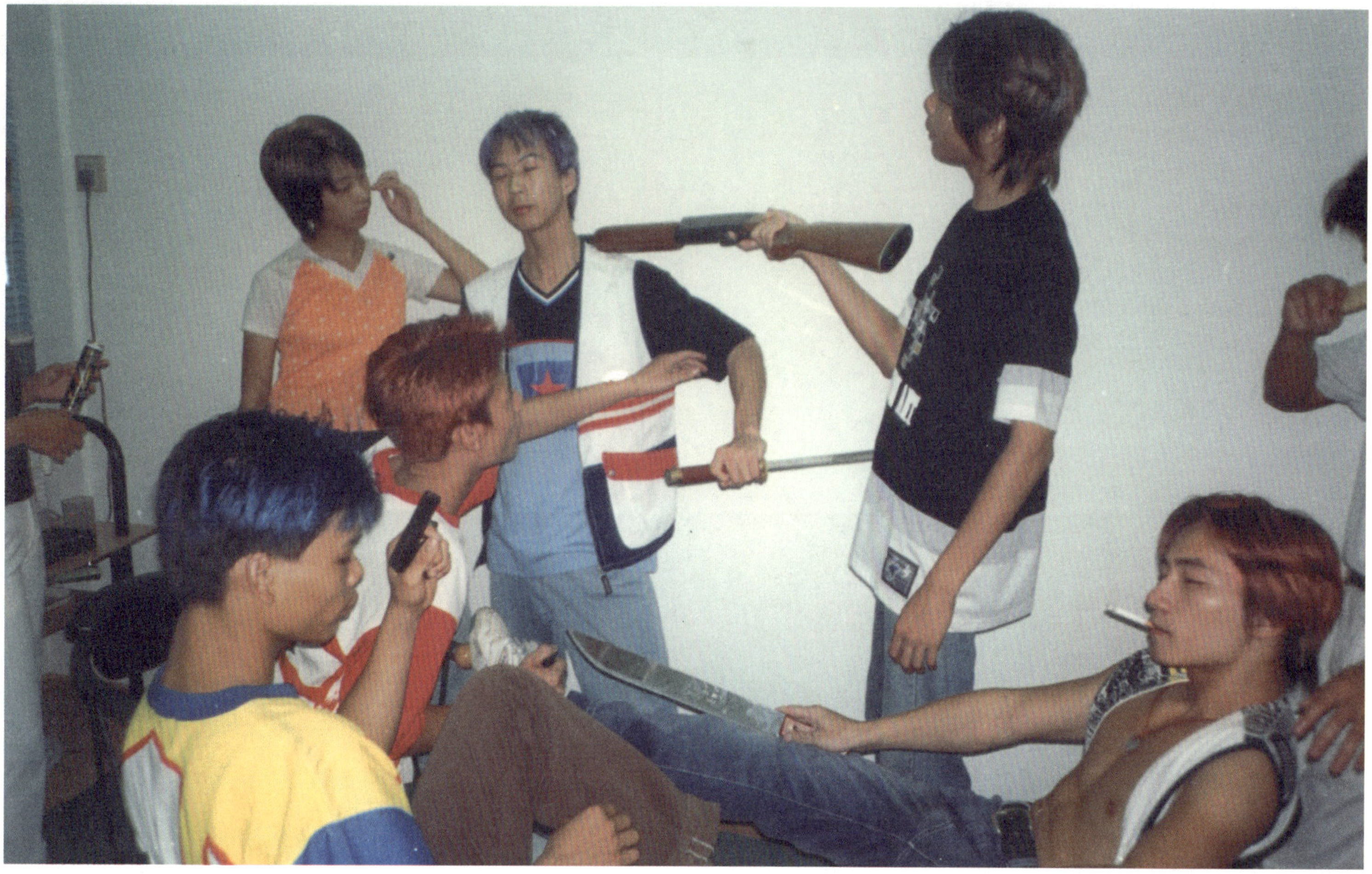

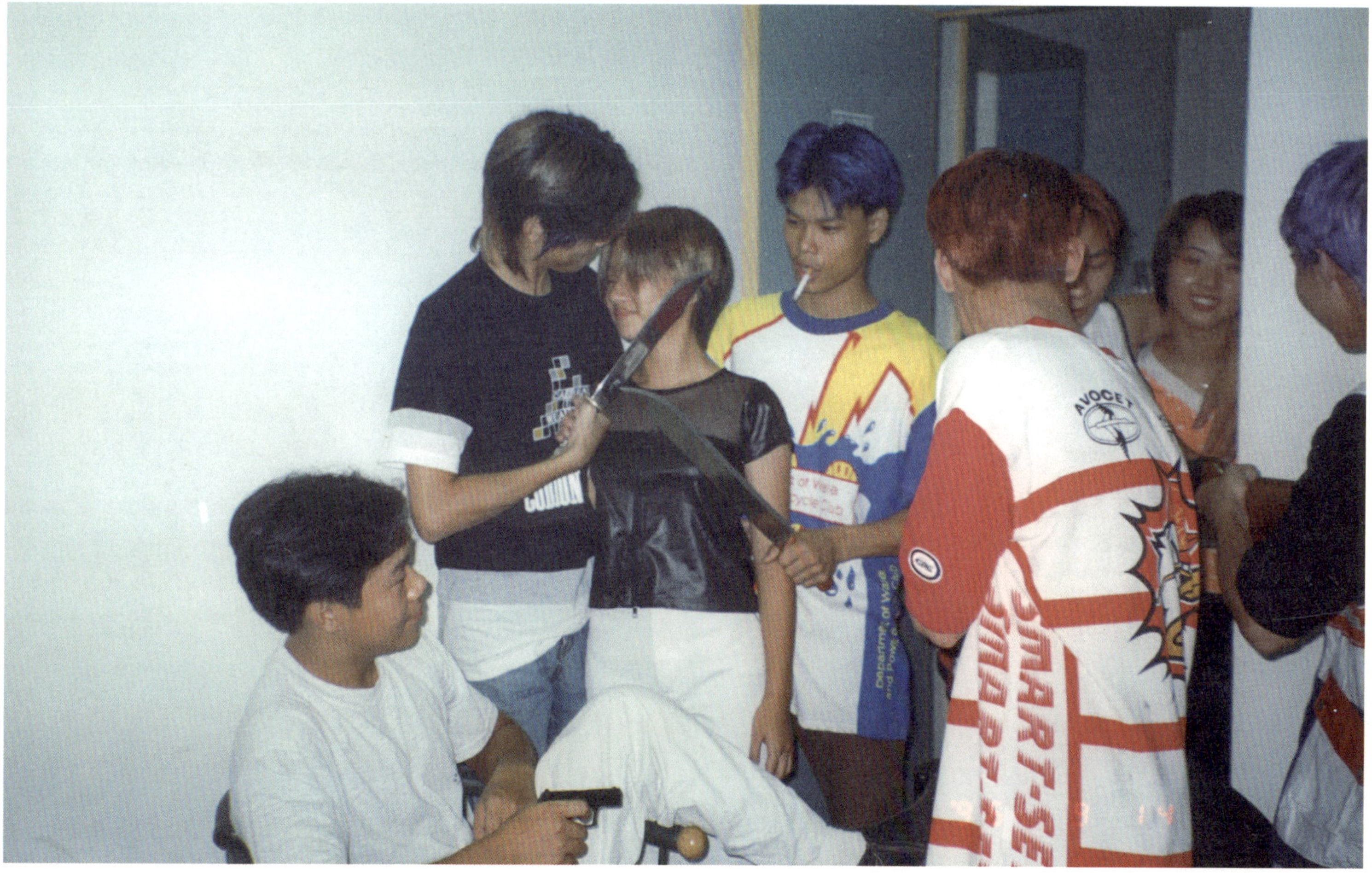

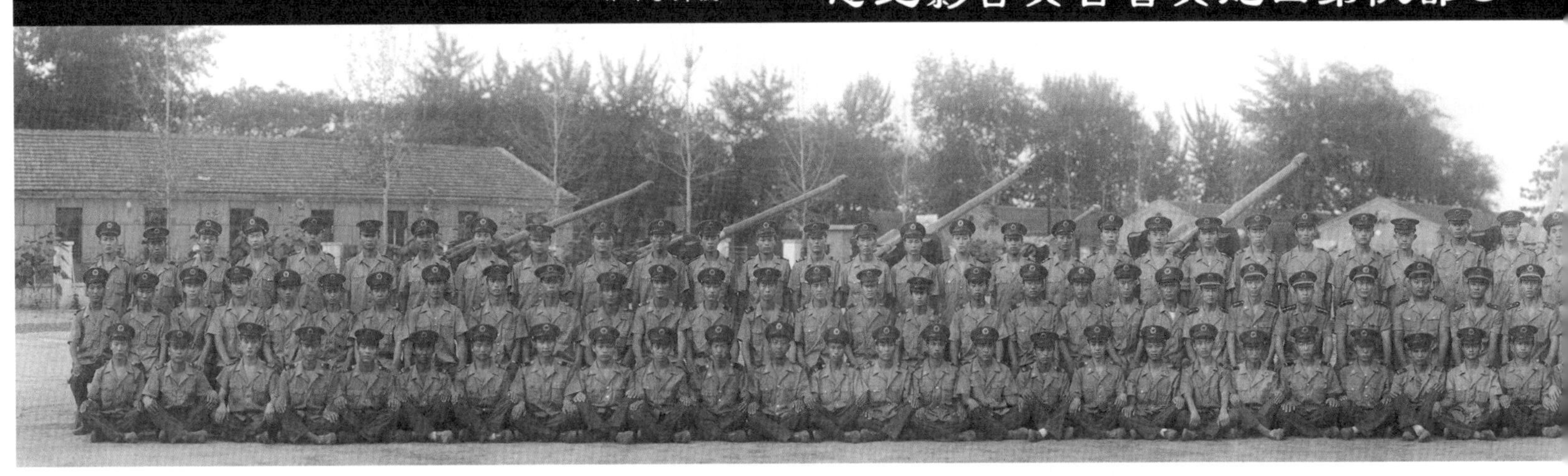

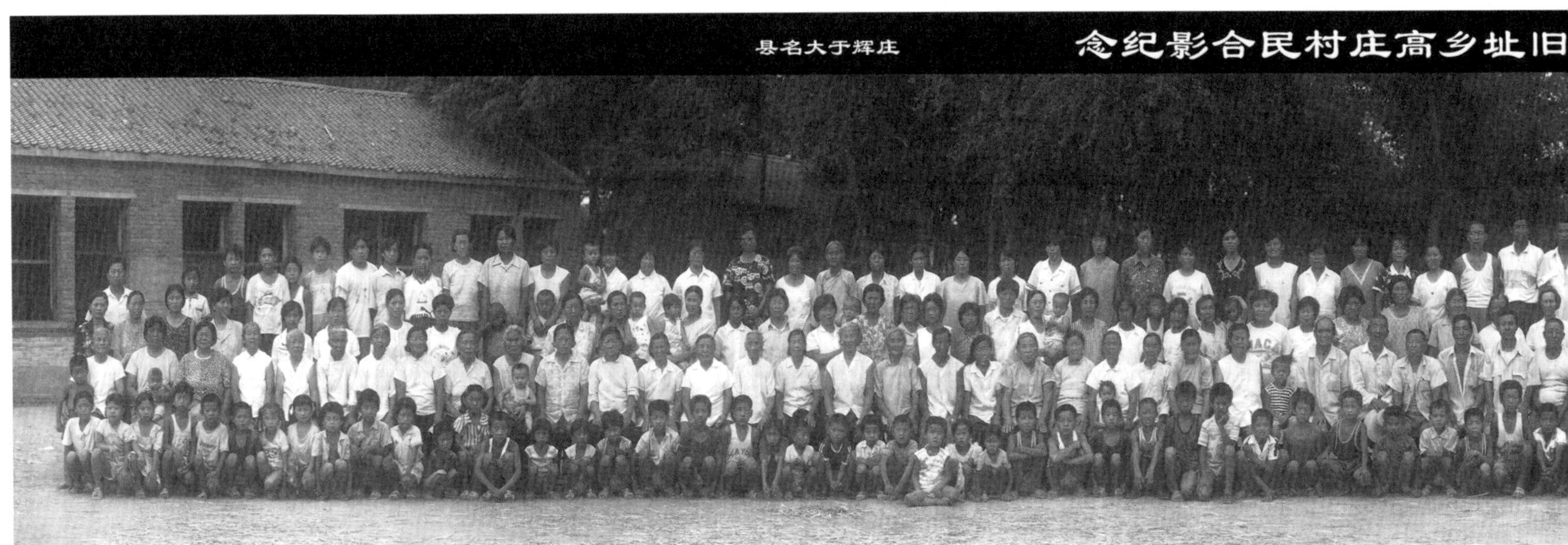

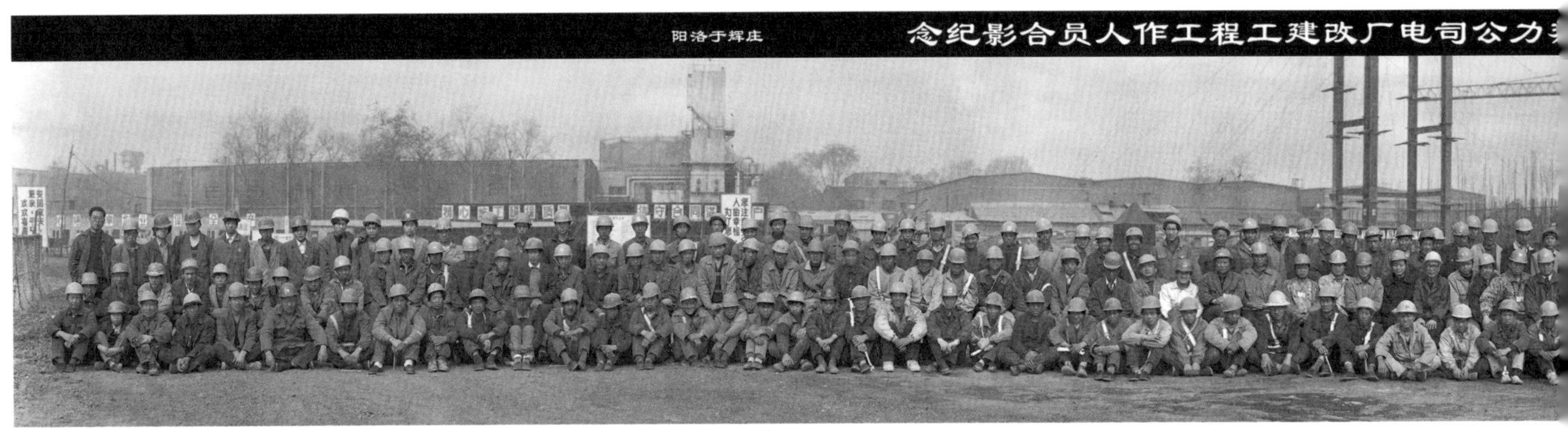

Zhuang Hui, top: *The Officers of No.4 Battalion and Artillery of Unit 51410 in Handan City, Hebei Province, July 23, 1997*, photograph, 16.4 × 74.2 cm, 1997, private coll.; center: *The People of Gaozhuang Village, Jiuzhi District, Daming County, Hebei Province, August 13, 1997*, photograph, 16.4 × 98.7 cm, 1997, private coll.; bottom: *The Entire Staff of Shuangyuan Energy Source Company, Henan Province, March 26, 1997*, photograph, 16.3 × 125 cm, 1997, private coll. All photos courtesy Zhuang Hui

五市郸邯省北河日三十二月七年七九九一元公

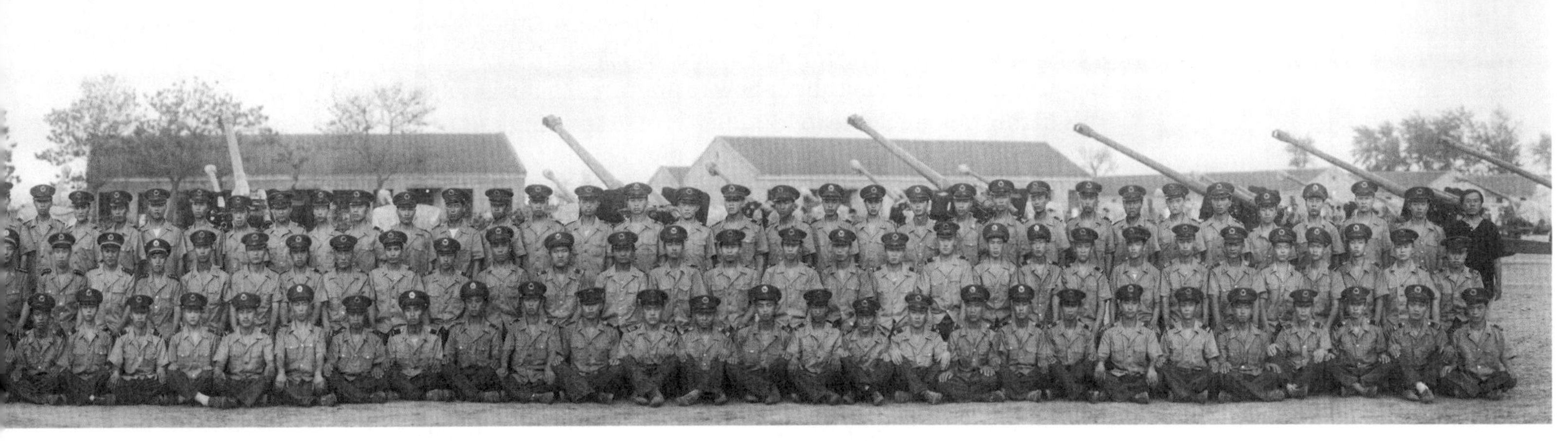

大省北河日 三十月八年七九九一元公

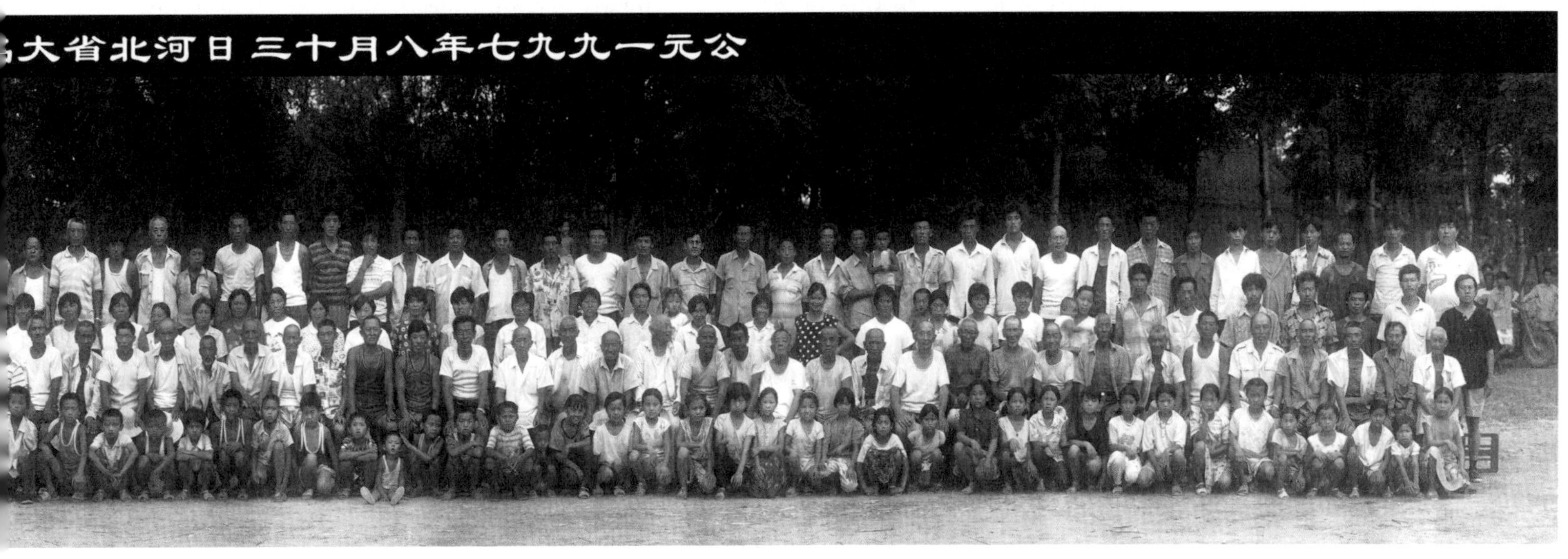

阳洛司公六建省南河日六十二月三年七九九一元公

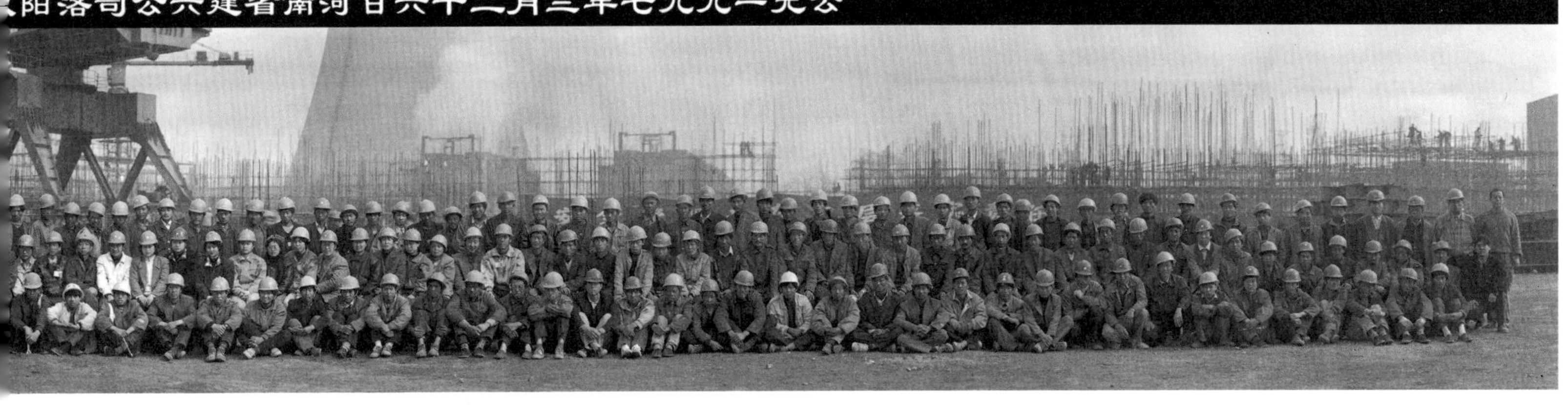

Around Chinese New Year, van Dijk writes to Ernst Dinkla:

> NAAC flourishes; we now have a "management director," Frank Uytterhaegen, and a "project manager," Li Zheng, who spits and hawks up all day. I am "art director" now, and at loggerheads with Frank about how to interpret Zhang Wei's function of assistant director. It's hardly possible to reappoint her as assistant director to both of us. She makes her own program anyhow; a month ago she decided to go to Guangzhou to continue our salutary work at the home of her new fiancé, Hu Fang. [She] decided *en passant* to tackle the editing, publication, and production of a catalogue in which she also appears as an author. She had never done anything like it before, but that is how she plans. Upcoming author Hu Fang and painter Mai Zhixiong and his wife, all the same age as Zhang Wei, occupy two floors of an apartment building in Guangzhou and have offered me hospitality for many years during my regular visa travels to Hong Kong. Then there is the "public relations" lady, Bettina Eichmanns. Office assistant Zhang Che is now three days on her way to buying a NAAC washing machine. They all have portable phones; I don't. The website for the time being is http://ourworld.compuserve.com/homepages/China/.
> HvD, letter to Ernst Dinkla, Beijing, early 1998

Also this year, the artist Sun Hongbin joins NAAC as an assistant. Along with all his other projects—a big Ding Yi exhibition, both in Shanghai and in Beijing; his fantastically original traveling exhibition *Mondrian in China*; a big solo exhibition by Zheng Guogu at the Wangfujing Photo Gallery, and one or two minor commercial projects—van Dijk is persuaded by Uytterhaegen to act as Chinese liaison for a monumental retrospective of the famous Flemish Expressionist Constant Permeke (1886–1952) at the National Art Museum of China. But without a regular gallery space, and without a working permit and visa, it becomes harder and harder for van Dijk to keep NAAC afloat, even when working with a very generous business director. Dutch tourists even confuse NAAC for a travel agency every now and then. Normalizing the situation becomes more and more urgent. By the end of 1998, he asks Uytterhaegen and his old friend Ai Weiwei for help.

11–14 January 1998

Ding Yi: Crosses '89–'97
Beijing International Art Palace, Beijing
In cooperation with ShanghART Gallery

For the first time since their rift, van Dijk and ShanghART director Lorenz Helbling are working together on a shared Ding Yi show. In December 1997, *Ding Yi: Crosses '97* opens at the Shanghai Art Museum, immediately followed by *Ding Yi: Crosses '89–'97* in Beijing. The text by Monica Dematté, originally commissioned for the second *Face to Face* show, is now printed in the catalogue accompanying the two exhibitions.

> Monica Dematté
> *Theorization of Casualness*
>
> Ding Yi started to paint the *Cross* series in 1988. Using a very simple and neutral pattern, "+", which was prompted by his knowledge of printing techniques (the cross marked and divided the surface of the sheets), he challenged himself to transform its simplicity and functionality into a pictorially rich and variegated subject. The ten years since Ding Yi's original conception have served to prove the richness of that transformation.
>
> The evolution of Ding's paintings reveals a progressive maturing of a process that began in cold, mental determination and developed towards a more open and relaxed relationship with himself and with the world. The young Ding neither wanted nor needed to be identified as a "Chinese" artist; rather, he contrived to overstep the boundaries of nationality. Indeed, his geometric structures are so far from the Chinese tradition that we would never be inclined to search for any relationship with that tradition. Only in looking deeper can we find surprising analogies.

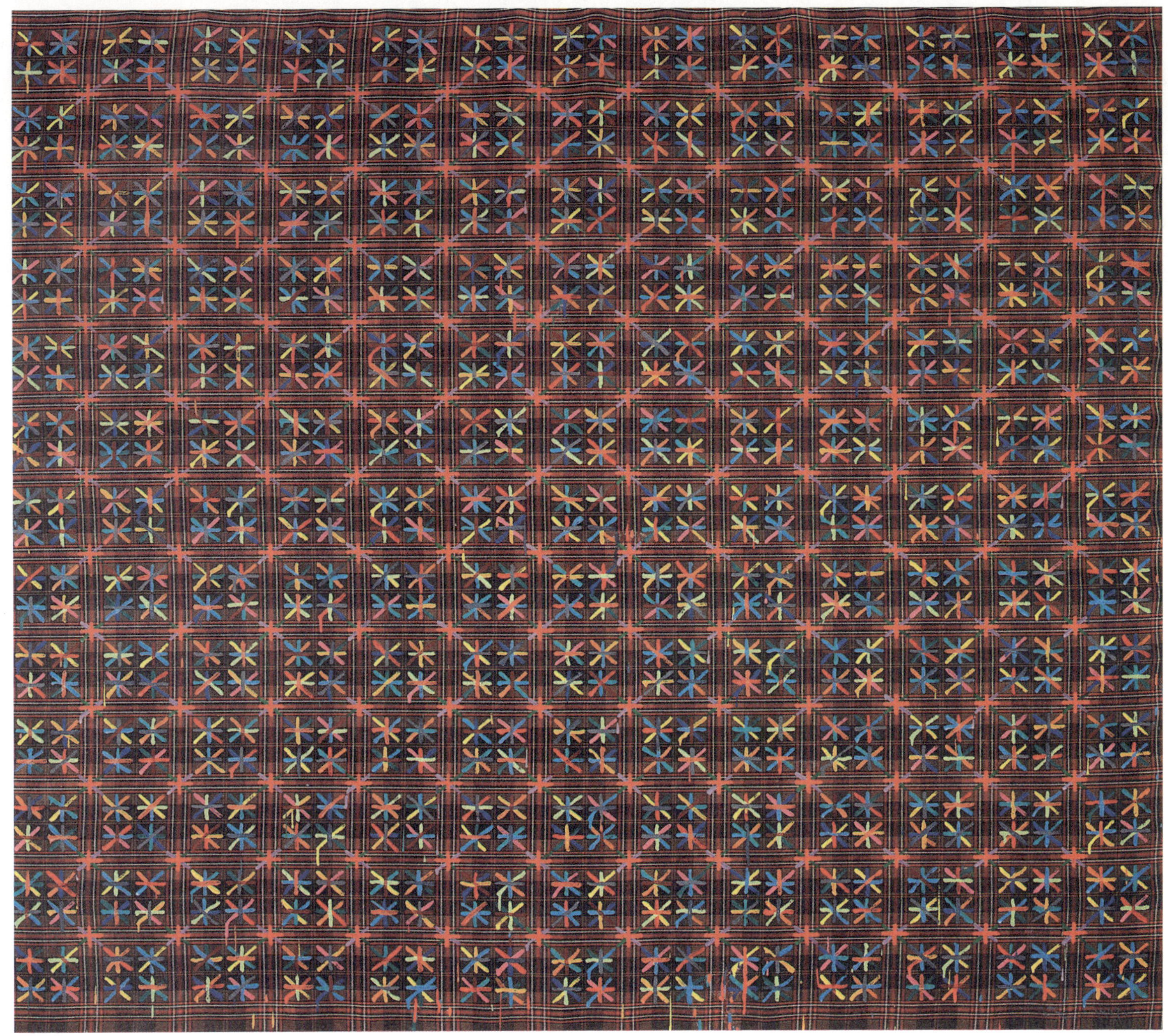

Ding Yi, *Appearance of Crosses 97-18*, acrylic, tartan, 140×160 cm, 1997, private coll.

In his mid-twenties, Ding decided to spend his days bent over large canvases for hours and hours, covering each of them methodically and precisely with colorful pigments he randomly juxtaposed. Imposing this hard, physical discipline upon himself, he cultivated a close relationship with the canvas that might justly be considered a kind of meditation. Renouncing any display of his technical skill and virtuosity—to draw lines seems to require patience rather than mastery—he chose to undergo a humble apprenticeship, pushing for a higher achievement in the future. In using such an approach, Ding recovered its original meaning and value: his intuition was that any knowledge, any mastery, and any evolution required a period of interiorization, of mental "digestion." So if the start of his *Cross* phase was purely theoretical, the way it developed showed a close link to a more fully appreciable ground of both manual dexterity and understanding of the materials. The interplay of such dexterity and technicality with a somewhat spiritual impetus (if we can keep such aspects separate) recalls the long learning process involved in Chinese traditional painting (*zhongguo hua*). I think it far from inconsequential that Ding Yi actually studied *zhongguo hua* even though he had then written a thesis criticizing its conservative stillness.

From the early works to today's paintings, the *Cross* series shows a surprisingly wide variety of appearance, color, and materials. After the precise line of the original, Ding went on to conceive more relaxed structures that did not need measurements, and so the play of positive-negative is evident in his black-and-white works. He then experimented with different materials: chalk and charcoal took the place of the more even acrylic on untreated canvas, producing a texturally rich result.

Ding Yi likes to mention the casualness of nature. He did so when we first met in 1992, talking about the way he puts together different colors, and he still does now, when he refers to the "tartan" fabrics he has recently chosen as a basis for evolving his art further. Apparently nothing less resembles nature than this kind of support, yet Ding compares the feeling he has when he is in front of a new tartan, deciding how to "intervene" on it, to the one of a landscape painter who has to translate a natural scene onto the canvas. The artist becomes a medium between what he sees and what he wants to convey—and in this case, both the landscape and the tartan motifs are a predetermined and complex basis for compositions emerging upon a blank canvas.

At the same time, Ding is aware of the strong "industrial" implication of machine-produced fabrics, and, taking up another challenge, he wants to be able to raise such to the status of art. The challenge is even more daring if we consider that the brush-stokes he applies are not a display of pictorial skill but are rather simple, [marks] any person familiar with the brush could produce. In this sense, Ding Yi openly disagrees with the traditionally held belief that technical skill should always be visible and apparent.

To look at details of the paintings and to look at the whole picture evoke different responses. While the details, even considering the unevenness of the freehand strokes, give an impression of regularity and monotony, the larger view adds spontaneity, richness, depth, and casualness to the supporting medium. A support chosen for its flatness, regularity, and predictability becomes something else. Again, it is a challenge, which Ding has proved himself to be a master of.

Monica Dematté, catalogue text in *Ding Yi: Crosses '89–'97*, published by ShanghART Gallery and NAAC, 1998.

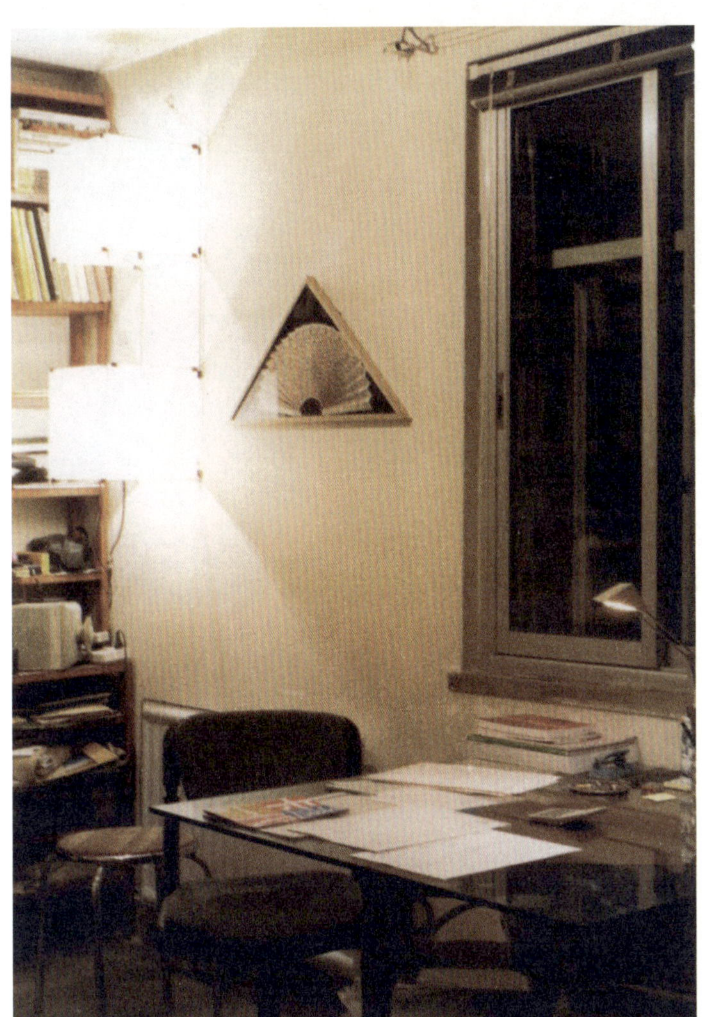
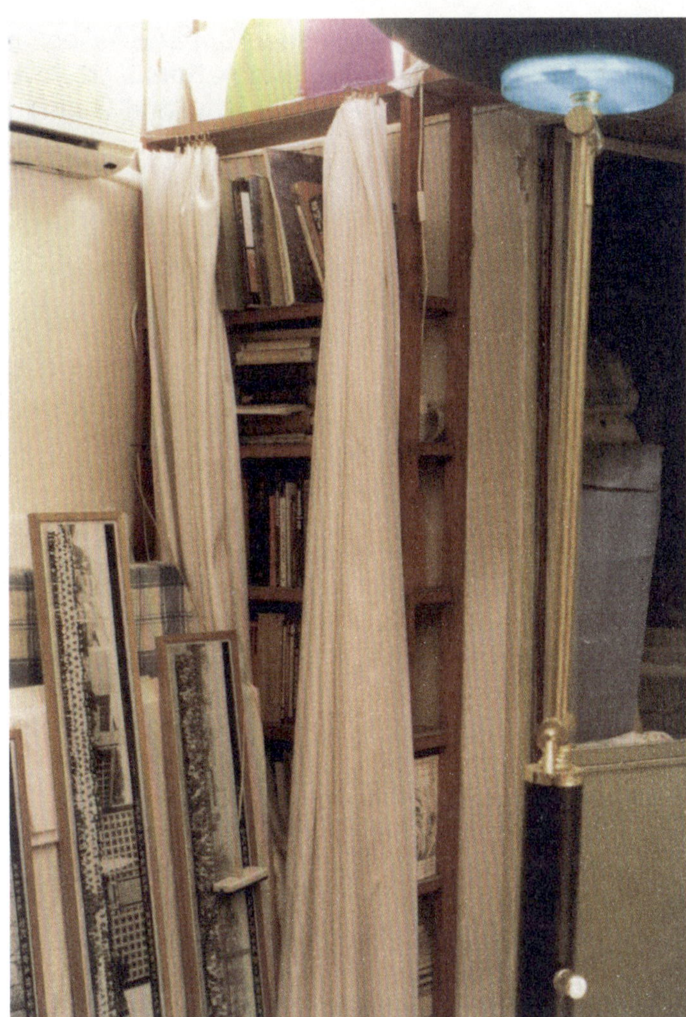
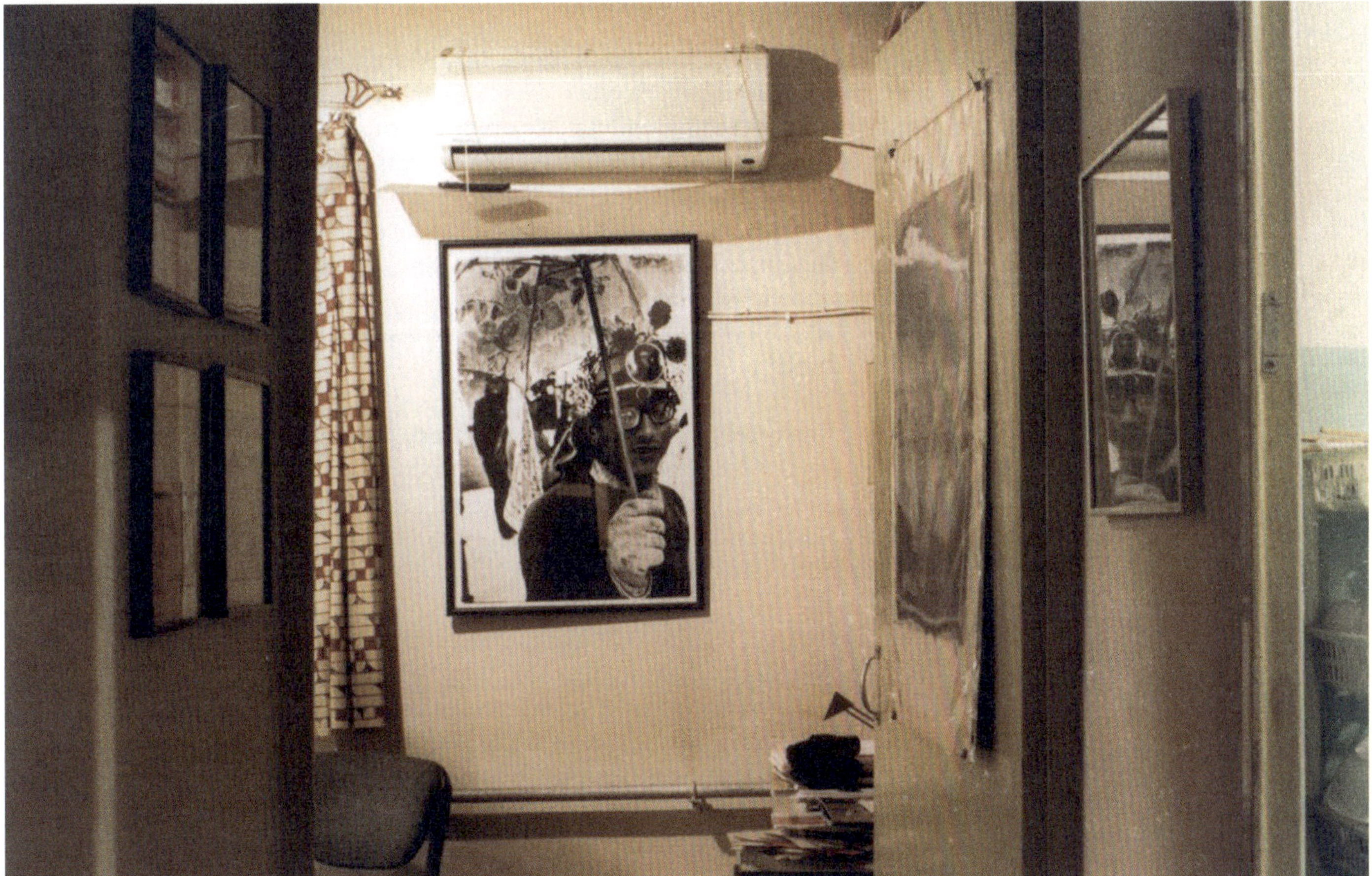

Mai Zhixiong, Hans van Dijk's apartment and NAAC office, 1997–98, courtesy Zhao Lelin

14 March – 24 May 1998 *Mondrian in China – A Documentary Exhibition with Chinese Originals*
Beijing International Art Palace, 14–29 March; New Library, Shanghai, 23 April–2 May; and Guangdong Art Museum, Guangzhou, 16–24 May

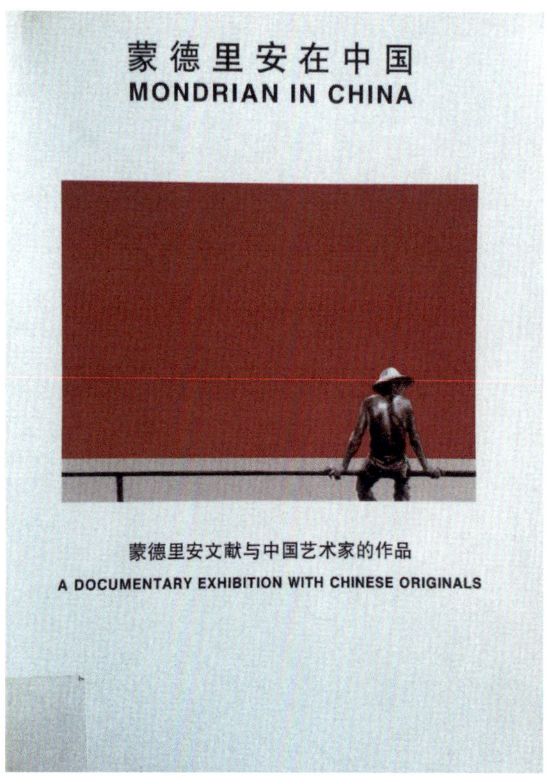

Mondrian in China, exhib. cat., 1998, design by Chen Tong and Hans van Dijk, editing by Hu Fang and Zhang Wei

The Dutch Ministry of Foreign Affairs wants to promote Mondrian worldwide. Exhibitions have already been held in Brazil and elsewhere. The formula is always the same: Mondrian is paired with paintings by artists from the host country. No original Mondrian paintings are ever shown in any of these exhibitions. The Dutch part of the shows consists of reproductions of original works, posters, and other educational material. The same is true for *Mondrian in China*, for which van Dijk is the curator. Since the project is entirely sponsored, van Dijk seizes the occasion to show often overlooked Chinese abstract painters like Ding Yi, Luo Qi, and Yi Ling, pairing them with figurative artist Liu Ye, who has been fascinated by Mondrian all his life, and Mai Zhixiong, whose preoccupation with modernity and religion results in uniquely abstract paintings of landscapes and machines.

The publicity image for the project is Li Huimin's 1986 painting *Red*, which van Dijk, while studying in Nanjing, saw in *Jiangsu Art Monthly*. Van Dijk asks Chen Tong, artist, teacher, publisher, and owner of the Libreria Borges Institute for Contemporary Art, to edit the book. Libreria Borges is a famous bookshop and library in Guangzhou, where Chen Tong organizes experimental performances from 1993 to 1996. It is the first time van Dijk and Chen Tong work together.

> CHEN TONG: Between 1993 and 1996, I organized events, and Hans wanted to do something together. We met in the winter in Beijing, where I had organized something in a gallery called Hanmo on Wangfujing Road. Hans had asked if we could meet there. One thing I do remember clearly: the first time I met Hans he was holding two ledgers, two thick documents—they were the portfolios of various artists. My first image of him was him holding these two thick files. That's why this winter impressed me so much: there was Hans holding two documents and talking to someone about cooperation, and that is also what I do. I hold books and files, and I talk to people about doing things together. But this was the first time I saw a Westerner doing this.

And he was full of passion. He didn't care whether I had the means or not, but he saw me as the best potential partner in southern China. Perhaps he had tried elsewhere many times before. Later, we met very often. I would see him every three months.
He mostly stayed with Hu Fang and the painter Mai Zhixiong, and we would all have dinner together in the restaurant close to their building. Zhang Wei and Hu Fang met in Guangzhou through Hans, well before they started Vitamin. I knew Hu Fang in 1993 when he was still a journalist, and he came to the opening of my bookstore. That Hu Fang became part of the art circle in Guangzhou was due to the bookstore.
Mondrian in China was the first exhibition Hans and I worked on together. Hans asked me to do the catalogue. It wasn't at all difficult to edit the catalogue: all the photos were there, and we didn't need a designer because he had all the pages ready. During this collaboration, I came to understand that there were three types of artworks in the exhibition: abstract art, artists that were influenced by Mondrian, and those who respected Mondrian. I also came to understand that this exhibition had sponsors, so I realized that there was a business aspect to it, because I was paid for my work. By doing this catalogue, I also got to know the painter Liu Ye; there was a picture of his of a girl standing in front of a Mondrian-like background. And Mai Zhixiong was also in that show.
I never visited Hans in Beijing. We always met in Guangzhou, so I never saw his archive. But I remember that he once was looking for documentation about a Guangzhou artist from the thirties named Zhao Shou. He found it, and also some of Zhao Shou's works later on. He even went to visit the building where Zhao had lived. Zhao belonged to the first group of artists in southern China who were influenced by Western art.
Hans was different from ordinary gallerists, art dealers, and researchers in that he didn't want to just document current art, but go to the roots of it, to its origins. In China, we have a saying that when people meet coincidentally they are destined to meet: "Yuanfen." Maybe it's an intuitive feeling, but I think that Hans had a kind of missionary spirit, that maybe he could sacrifice himself for art in China, and that that was his fate.

MB, interview with Chen Tong, Guangzhou, 19 January 2013

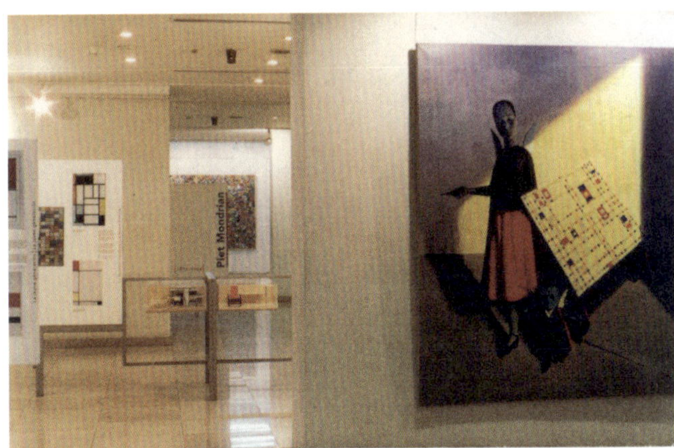
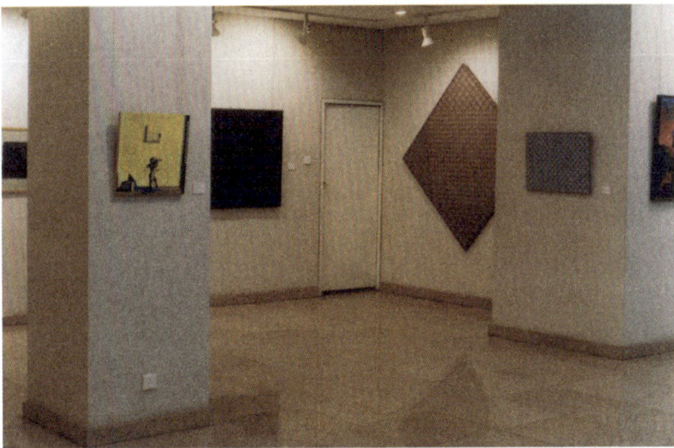
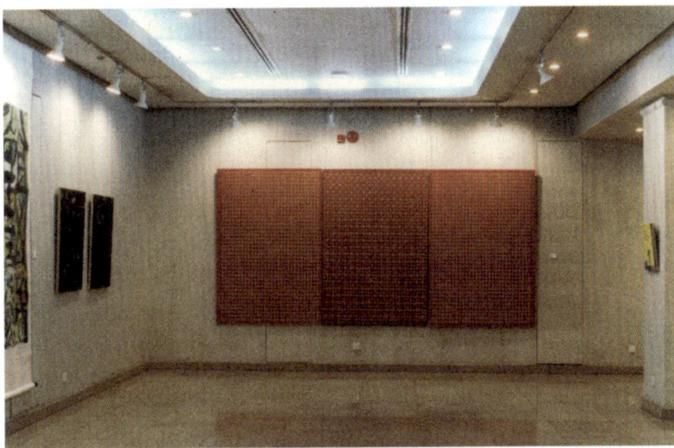
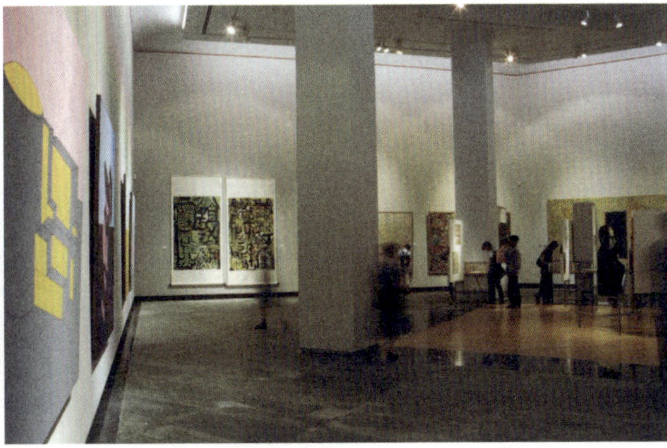

Mondrian in China, Beijing International Art Palace, 1998, exhibition views, photographer unknown, private coll.

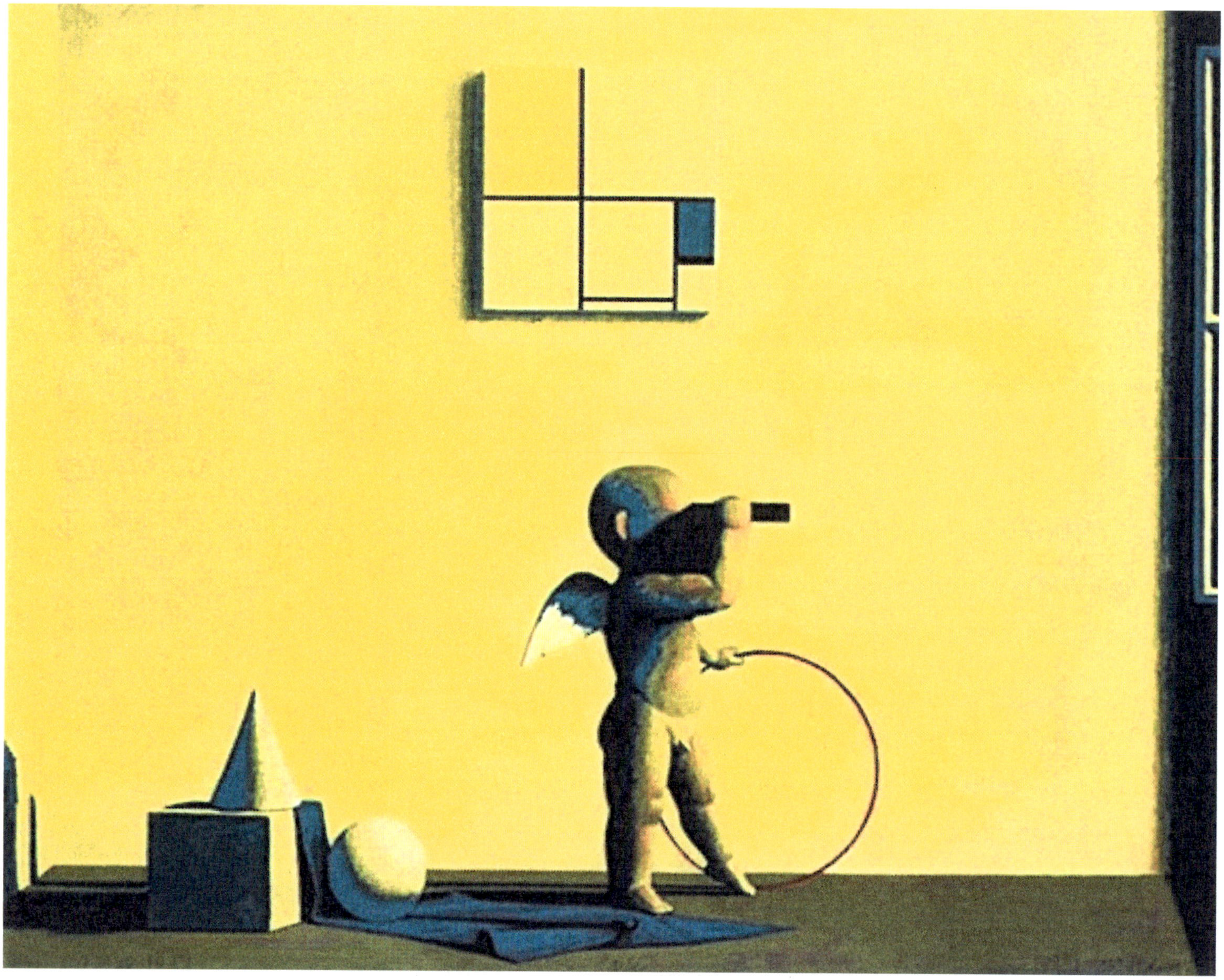

Liu Ye, *For M's Yellow And Blue*, oil on canvas, 45 × 45 cm, 1995, private coll.

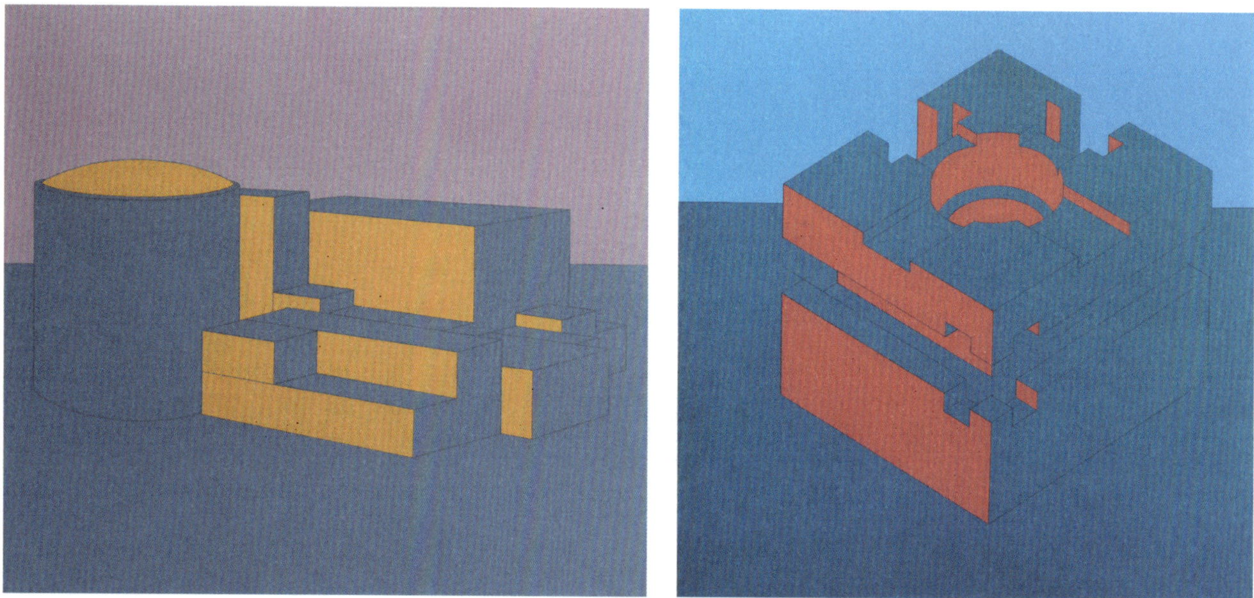

Left: Mai Zhixiong, *Landscape Series No. 5*, acrylic and pencil on canvas, 182 × 200 cm, 1995; right: Mai Zhixiong, *Machinery Series No. 2*, acrylic and pencil on canvas, 200 × 200 cm, 1994, coll. Redtory Culture & Art Organization, Guangzhou

4–12 July 1998

Zheng Guogu, *Sixteen of the Ten Thousand Customers and Other Works*
Beijing Photo Gallery

ZHENG GUOGU: In 1998, I had a solo show organized by Hans in Beijing in a space on the second floor of a commercial photography studio. It was my first time in Beijing, so I don't remember where it was exactly. The show was called *Sixteen of the Ten Tousand Customers and Other Works*. The background was that Hans told me that in the West, artists would make maybe a hundred copies from their original work and sell them for 50 to 100 dollars, and I thought: what if I made 10,000 copies of each work and sold each copy for 500 dollars? So the idea came from there. Hans told me the rules of the market, and I thought I should set the rules within my own heart. I would search for those 10,000 customers throughout my life, because to me 10,000 customers were a conceptual entity, and as soon as there appeared a real customer who wanted to buy my real work, this would be part of the realization of my work. Because of this idea, Hans decided to hold this 1998 exhibition.

To me it's like this: in 1993, I broke the rules of the art world through photography, and in 1998, I again broke the logic of the art market. Since then, nothing is unbreakable for me. What exists in reality is easier to break than what exists in the mind.

In 2000, Hans held another exhibition in the old CAAW space in the south of Beijing, *Zheng Guogu: More Dimensional*. Hans called me "Mr. Multidimension," because he thought I was capable of getting from the first dimension to the fourth and then back again. The exhibition was specially curated, because there was little space for photography and a lot of space for three-dimensional works. I felt stressed because it was huge for a single artist to handle. So I filled that space with paintings and installations, including the prototypes for the *10,000 Customers*.

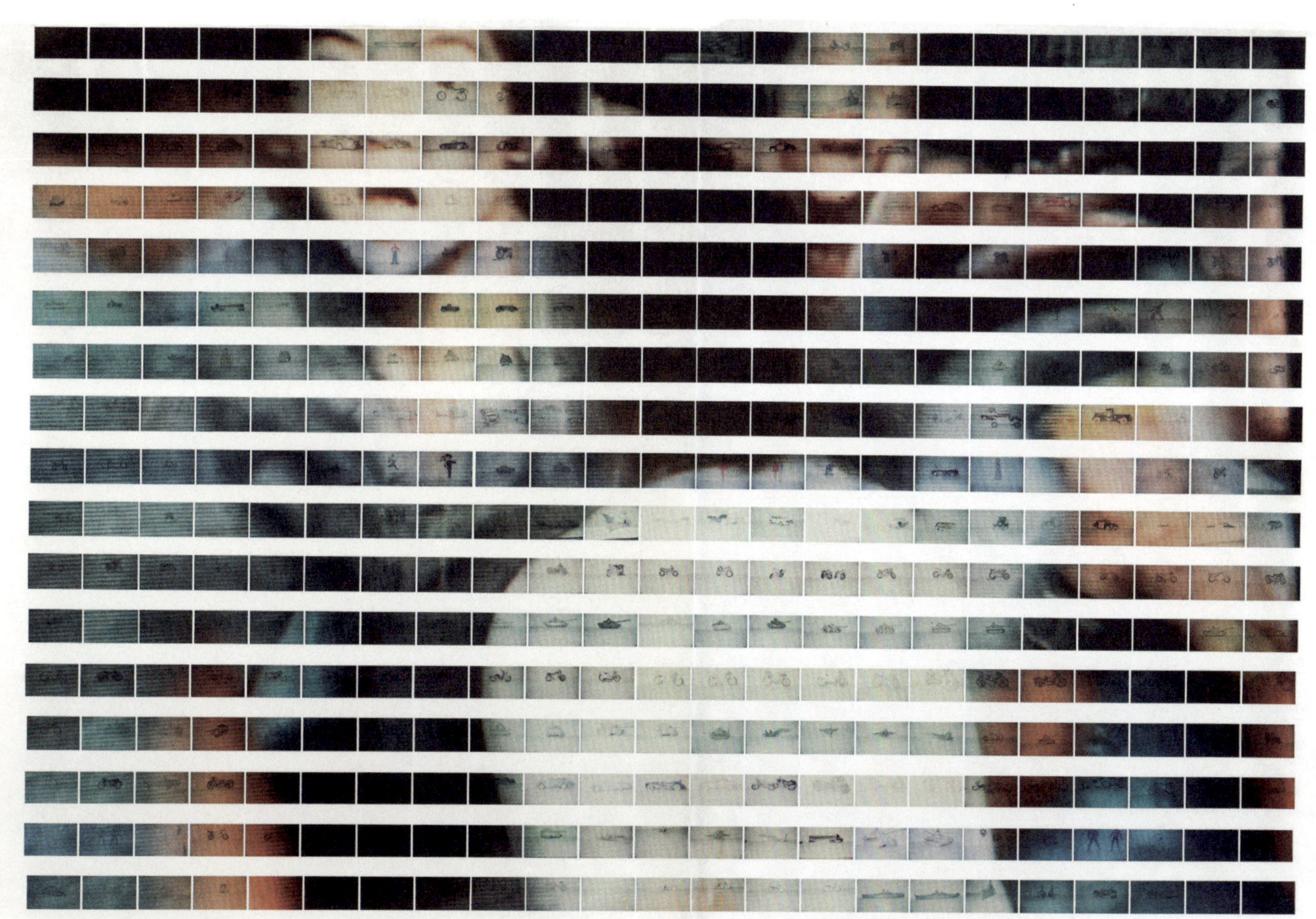

Zheng Guogu, *Sixteen of the Ten Thousand Customers* (detail), 1998, private coll.

In 2001, there was an art space in Shanghai called BizArt. *More Dimensional* traveled to that space, and the title changed to *Multidimensional Travel*. During 2001 and 2002, Hans and Lorenz Helbling, that is to say CAAW and ShanghART Gallery, had an artist exchange program. Zhou Tiehai was with Lorenz and was going to show at CAAW, while I was with Hans, which resulted in my presentation in Shanghai. But the show with Tiehai in Beijing never happened, because Hans died. We then established the Yangjiang group in Shanghai and showed with Lorenz. The show was called *2002 in Shanghai, Yangjiang Some Event Occuring*, which referred to Hans' death. There is a saying "When big events occur in Yangjiang, bigger things happen in Beijing, and even bigger ones in the world." The state of contemporary art in China was partially built by Hans. When Hans first came to China, the situation of art in China was really conservative. Young artists, for example, would not have the chance to hold exhibitions in art museums. What Hans did was to create a safe space, a shelter where young artists, curators, and art agents were protected and could grow.

MB, interview with Zheng Guogu, Guangzhou, 17 January 2013

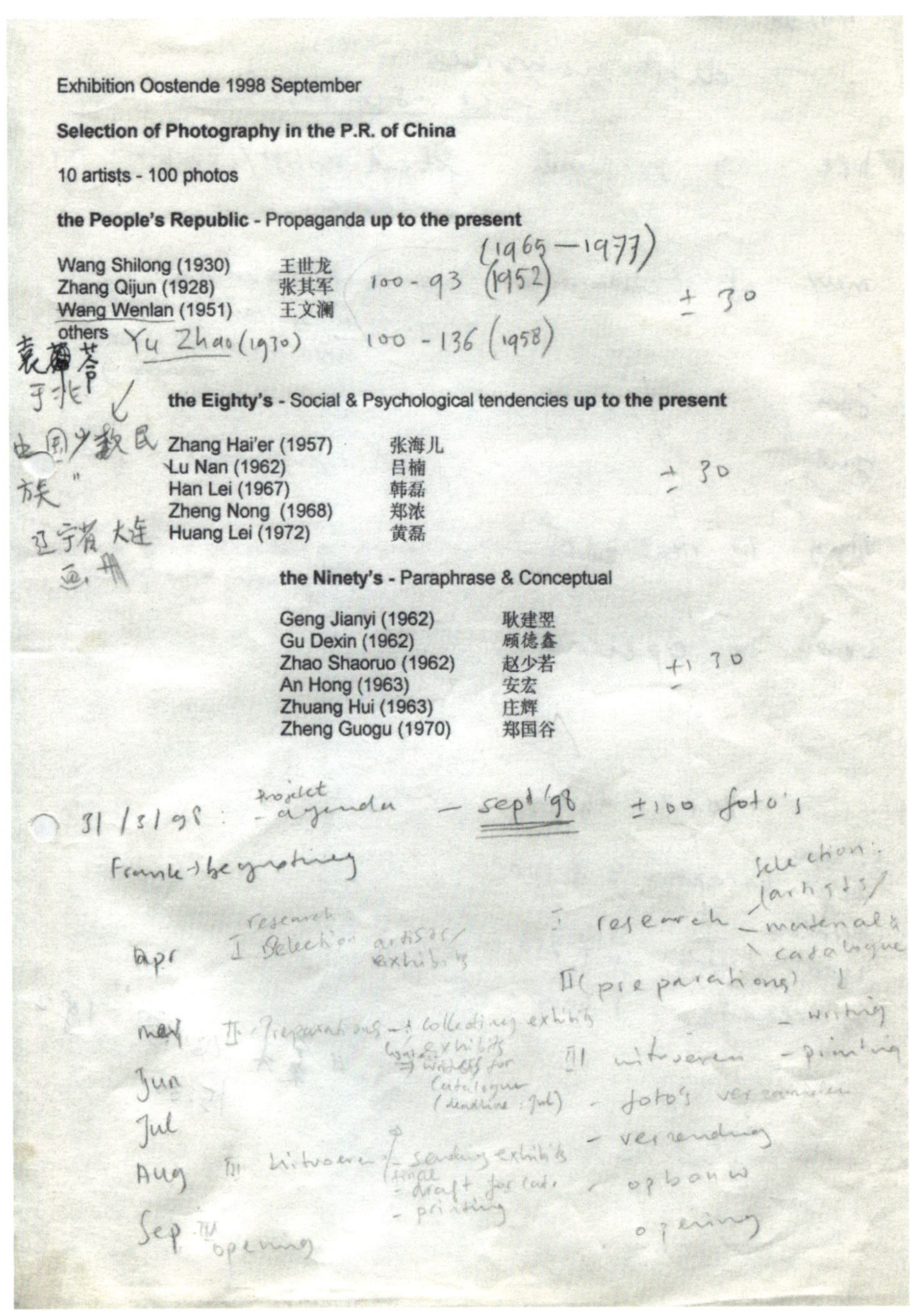

Exhibition Oostende 1998 September

Selection of Photography in the P.R. of China

10 artists - 100 photos

the People's Republic - Propaganda **up to the present**

Wang Shilong (1930) 王世龙 (1965—1977)
Zhang Qijun (1928) 张其军 100 - 93 (1952)
~~Wang Wenlan~~ (1951) 王文澜 ± 30
others Yu Zhao (1930) 100 - 136 (1958)

the Eighty's - Social & Psychological tendencies **up to the present**

Zhang Hai'er (1957) 张海儿
Lu Nan (1962) 吕楠 ± 30
Han Lei (1967) 韩磊
Zheng Nong (1968) 郑浓
Huang Lei (1972) 黄磊

the Ninety's - Paraphrase & Conceptual

Geng Jianyi (1962) 耿建翌
Gu Dexin (1962) 顾德鑫
Zhao Shaoruo (1962) 赵少若 ± 30
An Hong (1963) 安宏
Zhuang Hui (1963) 庄辉
Zheng Guogu (1970) 郑国谷

31/3/98: project agenda — sept '98 ±100 foto's

Hans van Dijk, exhibition concept for *Different Worlds*, Provinciaal Museum voor Moderne Kunst, Oostende, 1998, print and pencil on A4 paper, private coll.

21 November 1998 – 10 January 1999

Different Worlds – Photography from the People's Republic of China
Provincial Museum for Modern Art, Ostend, Belgium
Unrealized Exhibition

The project is commissioned by Willy van den Bussche, director of the Provincial Museum for Modern Art in Ostend, Belgium, whom van Dijk met through Frank Uytterhaegen while preparing the Permeke restrospective *Constant Permeke, the Belgian Master* at the China National Gallery in Beijing.

For unknown reasons, the exhibition never takes place, although van Dijk almost finishes all the curatorial work for the project, and the date of the exhibition was set. The exhibition would have presented a unique combination of historical photographs from the early days of the People's Republic of China paired with photographs by contemporary Chinese artists and photographers. The Ostend show is practically the only exhibition from which van Dijk's preliminary drawings, notes, and listings are conserved. They give a rare insight into his curatorial considerations.

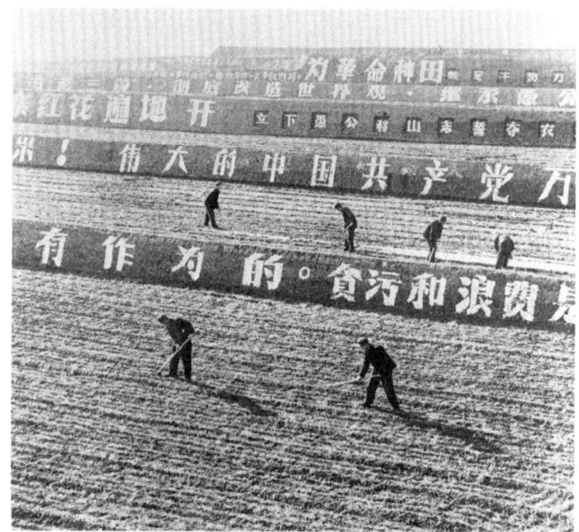

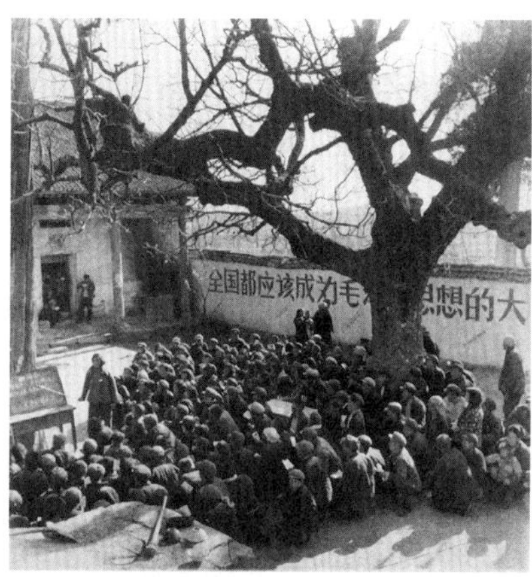

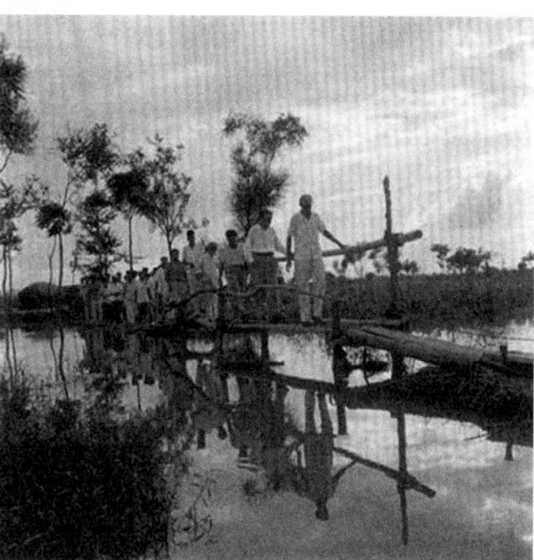

Wang Shilong, left: *Terraces at Wang Wu Mountain*, 1966; center: *Studying Mao Zedong's Thought*, 1975; right: *Mao Zedong Visiting the Countryside*, 1958; photographs, private coll.

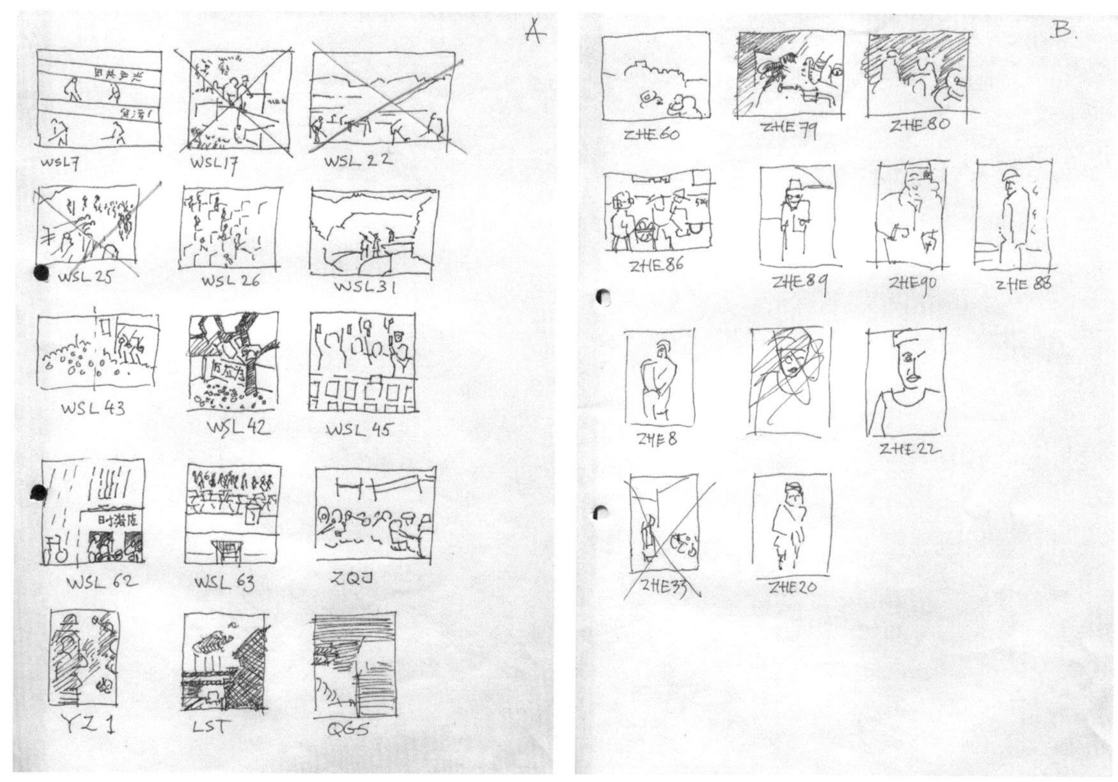

Left: Hans van Dijk, sketches of works by Wang Shilong and others in preparation for *Different Worlds*, pencil on A4, private coll.; right: Hans van Dijk, sketches of works by Zheng Guogu in preparation for *Different Worlds*, pencil on A4, private coll.

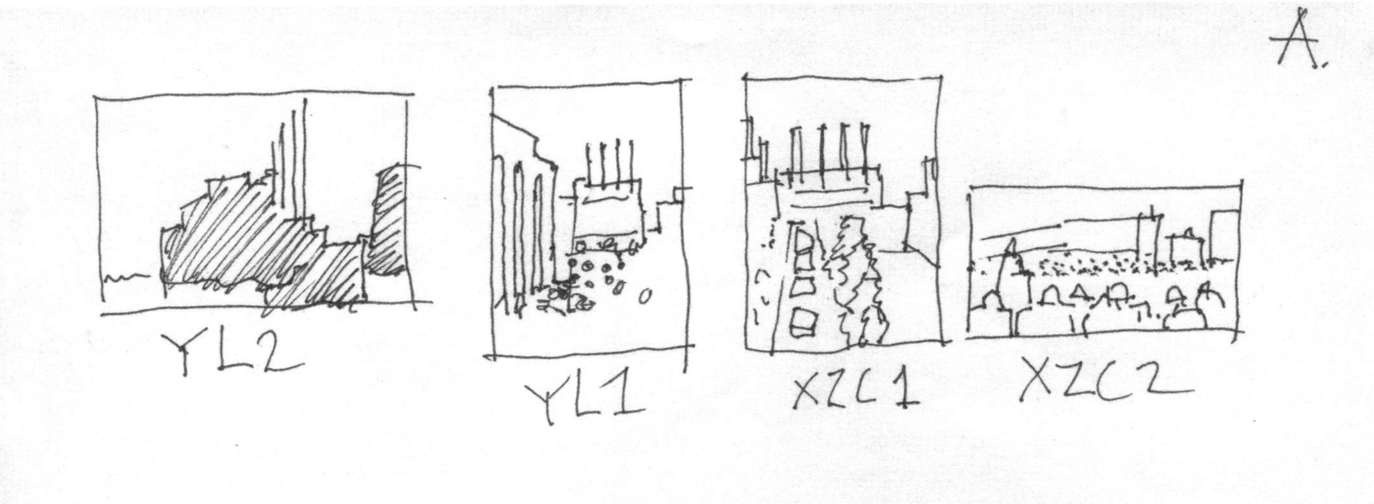

Hans van Dijk, sketches of works by Yuan Ling (left) and Xu Zhicheng (right) in preparation for *Different Worlds*, pencil on paper, 1998, private coll.

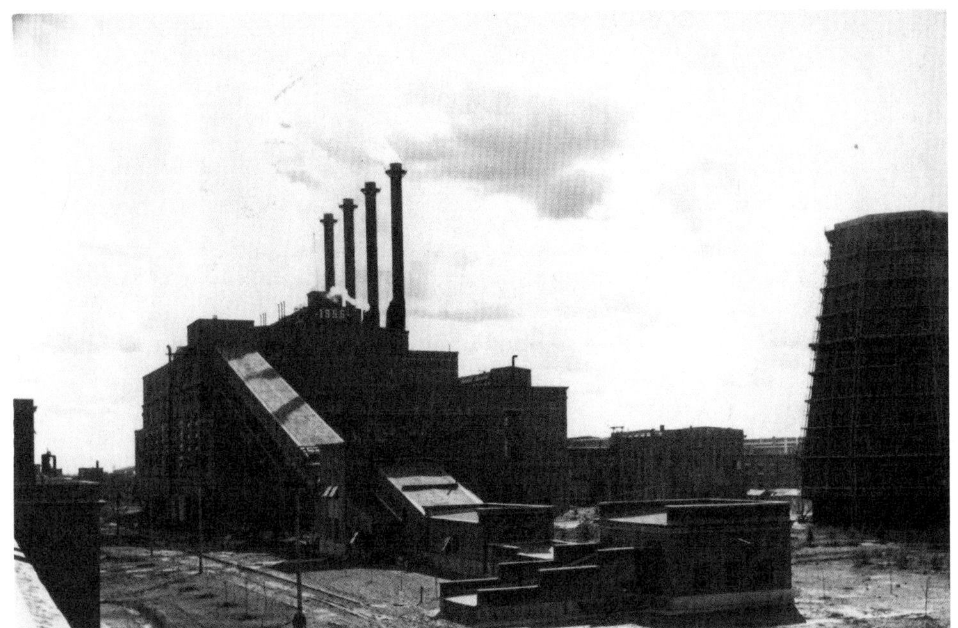

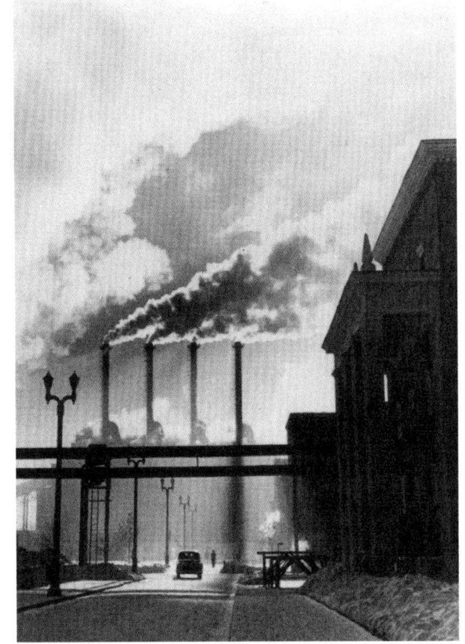

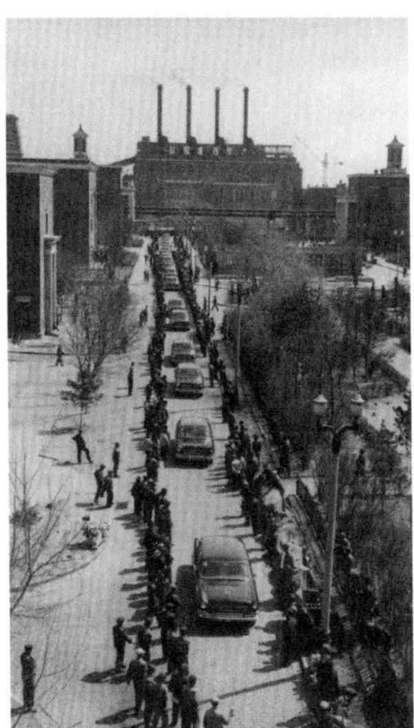

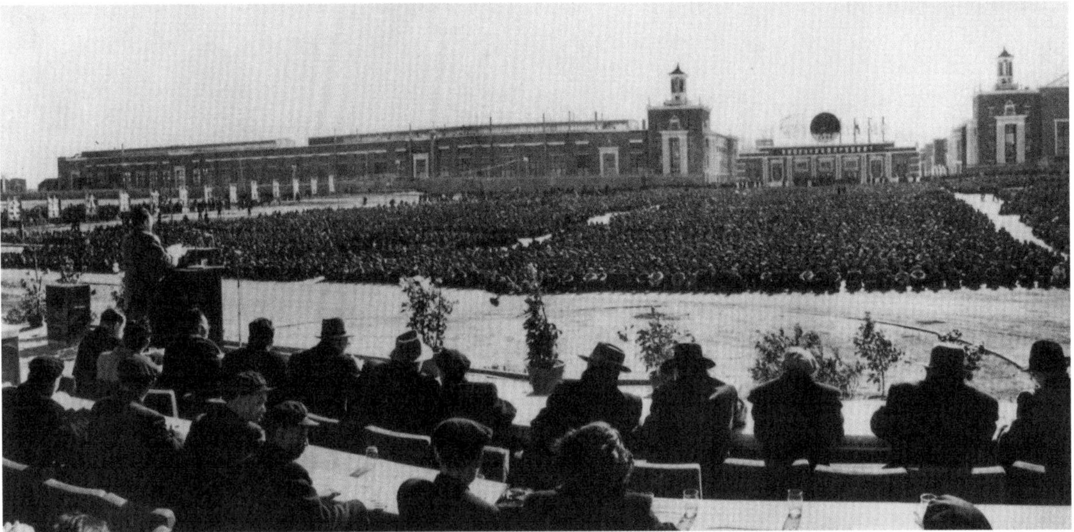

Photos for *Different Worlds*, 1998, all photos black and white; prints private coll. Top left: Yuan Ling, factory, title unknown, date unknown; right: Liu Sitai, *FAW (First Automobile Works) Car Factory, Changchun*, 1958; bottom left: Xu Zhicheng, *The First Domestically Produced Chinese Passenger Car, the Hongqi Luxury Sedan, Leaving the Factory, Changchun*, 1958; right: Xu Zhicheng, title unknown, 1956

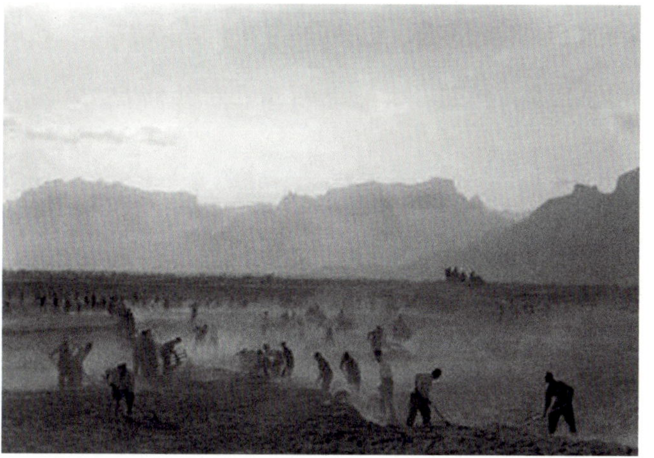

Wang Shilong : 1930 Runan (汝南)
– A photographer of "Potato School" ; China Photograph, vol. 3, '93
" I prefer natural beauty ... My idea is that auspicious and beautiful ~~people~~ things fall within the scope of art.
→ I want my audience to see beauty directly from the pictures and also get benefits through the themes reflected in my pictures ". p. 5/6 "中原文苑".

Left: Wang Shilong, *Reclaiming Land*, photograph, 1974, private coll.; right: Hans van Dijk, notes on Wang Shilong in preparation for *Different Worlds*, pencil on paper, private coll.: "Wang Shilong: 1930 Runan—A photographer of 'Potato School.' 'I prefer natural beauty...My idea is that auspicious and beautiful things fall within the scope of art [...] I want my audience to see beauty directly from the pictures and also get benefits through the themes reflected in my pictures.' *China Photograph*, vol. 3, 1993, pp. 5–6"

This (unrealised) exhibition, marks the end of an era. Van Dijk is now given a job: director of the China Art Archives and Warehouse. He enters the art market and acquires his desperately needed visa. Here, the history of the NAAC ends, and with it the archive all but ends too. Apart from a few exhibition photographs, it contains almost nothing on the coming years: the transition to the CAAW, or the CAAW's and Modern Chinese Art Foundation's activities. Van Dijk's personal correspondence—one priceless source of information—has by now almost petered out. The reason could well be the internet. Starting 1997, van Dijk—with all the rest of the world—gets e-mail, and not even van Dijk thinks of keeping print-outs in all cases. As for CAAW, it has its own website from the start, incorporating NAAC's exhibition history, Ai Weiwei's black, white, and grey books, and CAAW's exhibition data, images, and texts on artists. Perhaps they felt that a paper archive was redundant at best. The data on the CAAW exhibitions featuring in the following chapters were copied from its website just before it was shut down in 2012, and from a CD-Rom of information taken from van Dijk's computer by his assistants after his death.

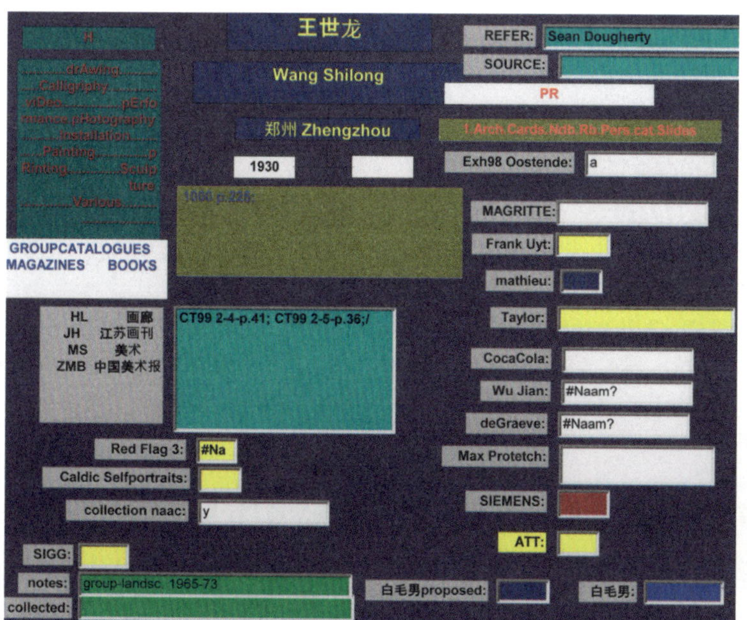

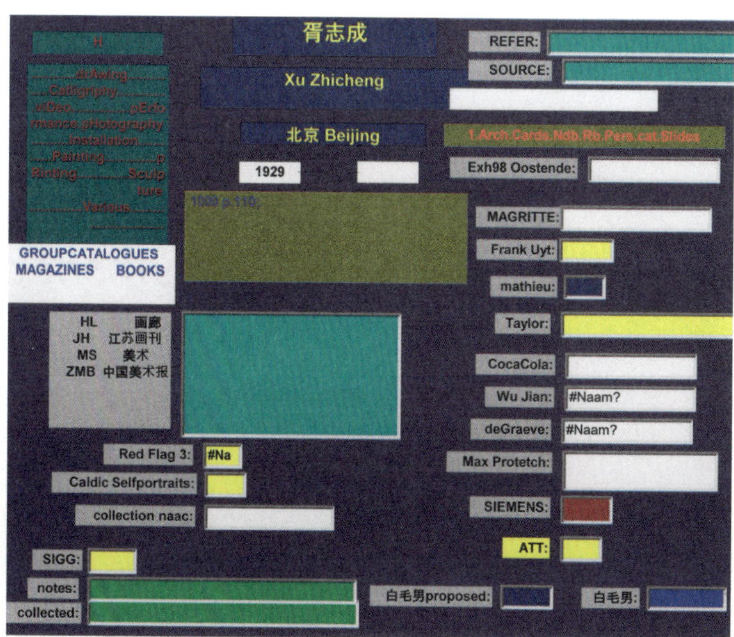

Hans van Dijk, entries from his digital archive of Chinese photographers, 504 entries in total, CD-ROM, 1999, coll. van Dijk family; this list is made and designed especially for the *Different Worlds* exhibition and it is likely the first time van Dijk uses his database this way

Founding the China Art Archives and Warehouse (CAAW) and the Modern Chinese Art Foundation (MCAF) Beijing, 1999–2002

Hans was different from ordinary gallerists, art dealers, and researchers in that he didn't want to only document current art, but wanted to go to the roots of it, to its origins.

Chen Tong

When later the art market grew more and more, he was always a reminder to every artist that you should understand art from a different perspective.

Duan Jianyu

Entering the art market

> XU TAN: In the old days, Hans used to come to the south because he had to renew his tourist visa in Hong Kong every three months. He used to stay at Hu Fang and Mai Zhixiong's house, or sometimes with Lin Yilin. We saw each other very often until 1997. Whenever I had to be in Beijing, I used to stay at Hans' home, which was also his office. If Hans was not there, Zhang Wei would arrange for me to stay there. We were both very poor. Sometimes we only had money for food, sometimes for just one meal between us. When Hans got his work visa in 1998, he stopped coming to Guangzhou so often. The last time he went to Guangzhou, he had become very interested in the art market, and he wanted to do that in a big way and go into business with Ai Weiwei. He said it was really important to do that. He said, "The art business is interesting, not because of the money or doing gallery business, but I find entering the art market interesting." At the time, no one in China thought about the art market, because art was still very underground. I was so strongly against the art market that we really clashed in our opinions. Now I have changed my mind: Hans had the right idea then. I think he felt it coming, this movement in China toward the art market.
> From 1997 on, my generation started to travel and exhibit abroad, and I got less and less information from him. The image of Hans for me is not so much the art market or politics; it is first and foremost the image of a friend.
> MB, interview with Xu Tan, Guangzhou, 5 June 2013

Over the last years, van Dijk has become very good friends with Frank Uytterhaegen, his wife Pascale Geulleaume, and their family, their daughter Aiko in particular. They even have a Dutch nickname for him: "Het benig geheel," best translated as "Bones." The Uytterhaegen family now wants to settle down in China for good. Uytterhaegen acts like a true maecenas, both in China and in Ghent, where they mainly have lived until now.
To realize a fully functional gallery, Uytterhaegen, van Dijk, and Ai Weiwei, set up a new foundation together, the China Art Archives and Warehouse (CAAW). It is the end of the NAAC, and the beginning of the new CAAW gallery, which Uytterhaegen supports financially until it can support itself. Uytterhaegen rents a large space, an abandoned factory that he completely refurbishes as a gallery, in Longzhaoshu, a village in south Beijing. It is mainly a carpenters' village. Ai negotiates with the villagers to accept a gallery and foreigners in their midst. Access is difficult because the place is hard to find, and because of the muddy country roads.

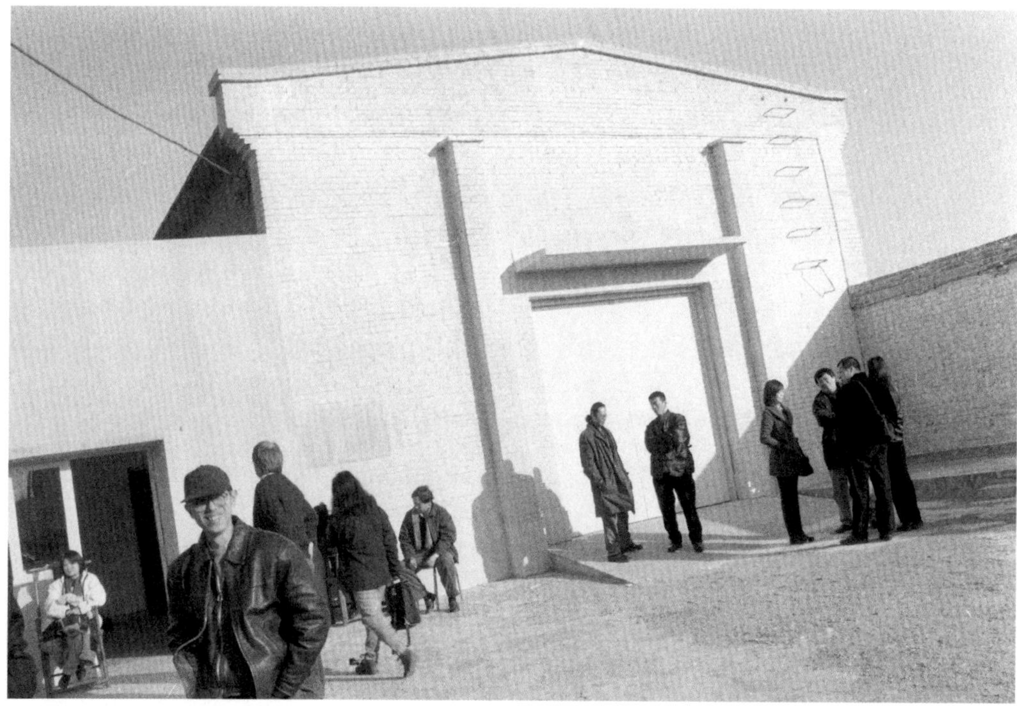

Feng Mengbo (front) and others at an opening at CAAW, Longzhaoshu, south Beijing, circa 1999–2000, photo Sun Hongbin

Van Dijk and Ai are the artistic directors, with a mutual agreement that they would not interfere with one another's work. Only van Dijk gets a salary. Uytterhaegen is the business director, and Sun Hongbin and the newly hired Xie Wenyue the assistants. Sun Hongbin, an artist photographer, joined the NAAC in 1998. He stays at CAAW until 2003, a year after van Dijk's death.

Xie Wenyue, a graphic designer, joins the team in 1999. He mainly works as a technician, taking care of the artists' installations in particular, but he also helps design the gallery's catalogues. He stays until Uytterhaegen's death in 2012.

> SUN HONGBIN: I met Hans in 1998. Hans was aware that I could speak English. We talked for about half an hour. Two months later Hans asked me whether I was interested in the job of assistant. I took the job and moved to Beijing.
> Hans had a large collection of Chinese novels and cassette tapes of a popular singer from the early nineties. In the end, he only listened to Bach. We often discussed together why Hans chose certain artists. He chose them not so much for their individual works of the moment, but for the way they reflected the whole of society and culture. Often Hans wouldn't have the money to buy work, but Frank would lend him the money. These were hard times for CAAW; it wasn't easy to sell. Frank had his own taste, like the works of the older Liu Wei. In the early years of CAAW, Frank and Pascale stayed relatively little in Beijing, more in Europe. When Hans came back from Burgundy [where the Uytterhaegens had a house] in 2001, he had not yet fully recovered. He felt weak and took a lot of different pills. He didn't drink beer that much, but drank a lot of black coffee and had no physical exercise.
> Hans had no grand scheme, no grand idealistic ambitions, but he was a great scholar with a sharp mind and eye. He was no thinker, always preferring action. He loved to make things.
> **MB, interview with Sun Hongbin, Beijing, 11 September 2012**

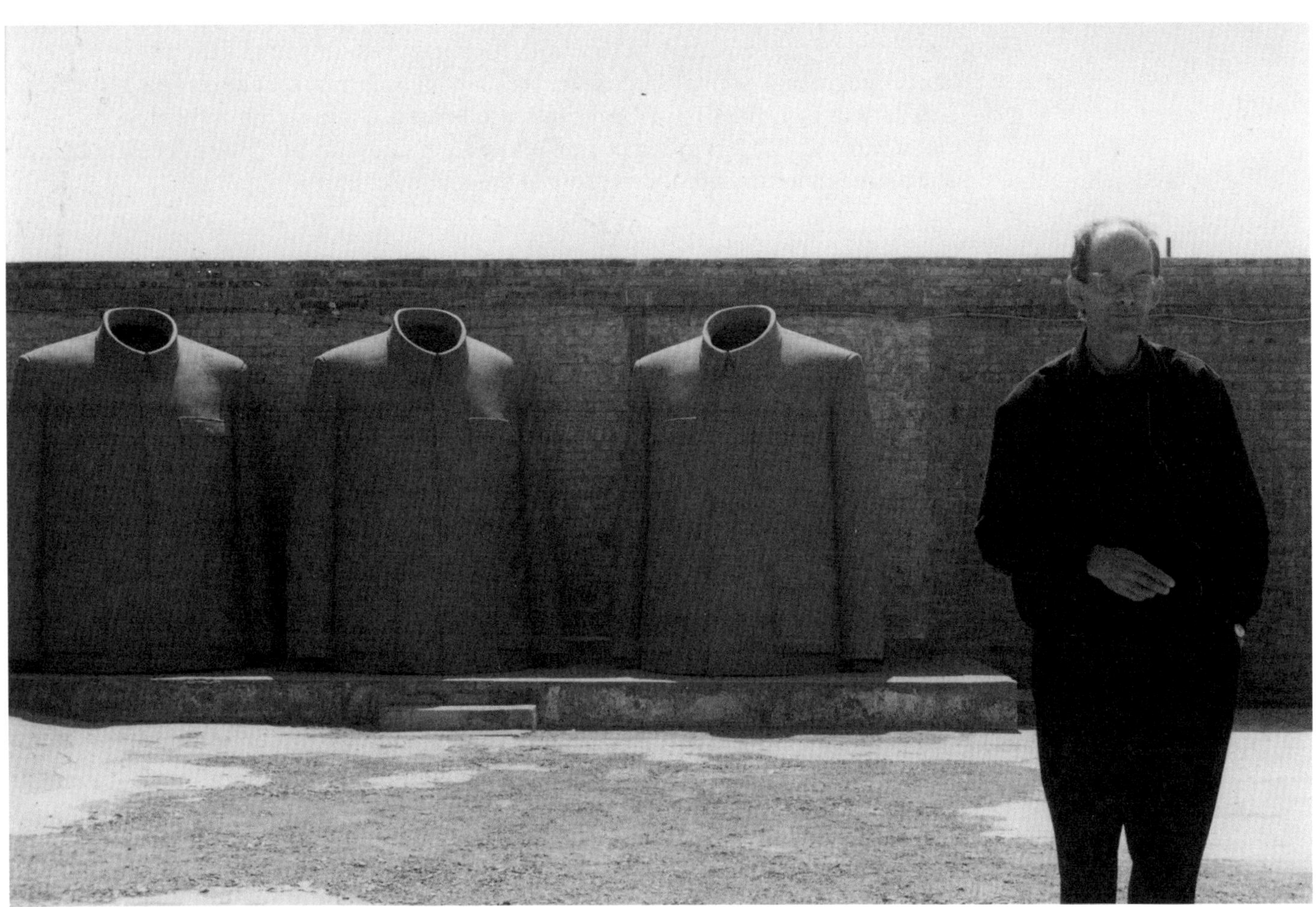

Hans van Dijk in the CAAW courtyard, Longzhaoshu, south Beijing, 1999; Sui Jianguo, *Legacy Mantle*, 1997 (far end), photo Sun Hongbin

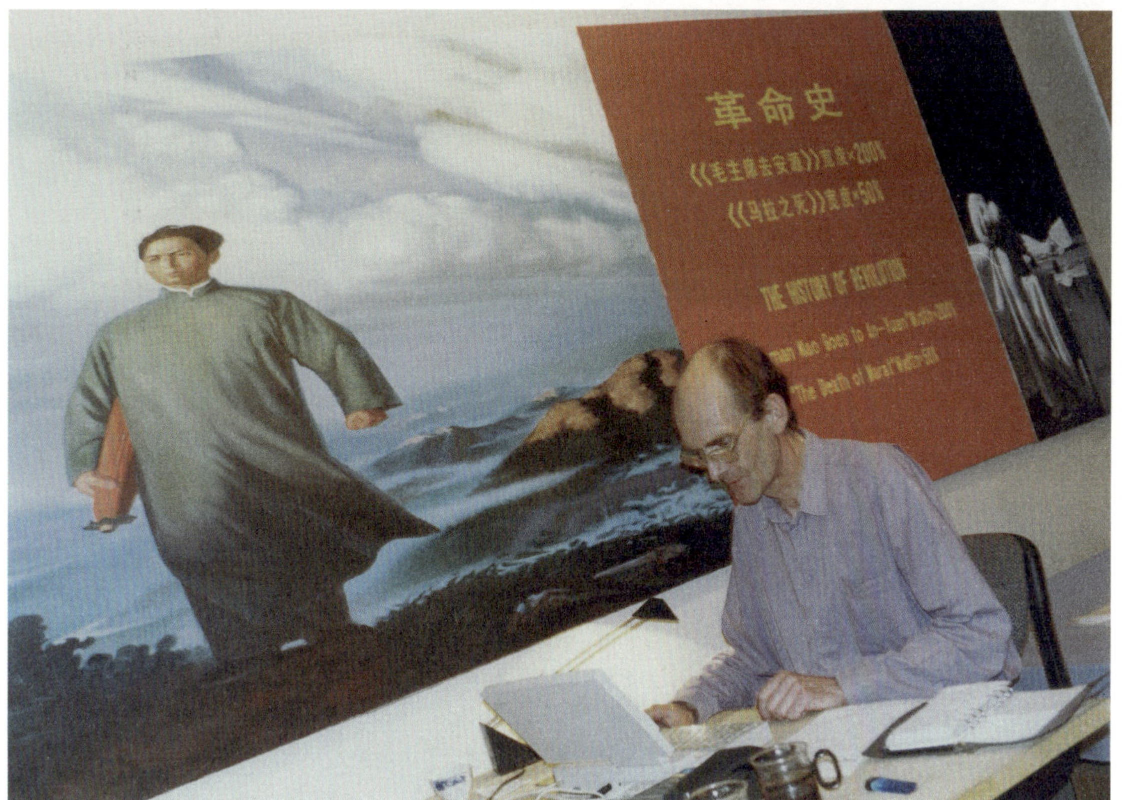

Hans van Dijk in the CAAW office, Longzhaoshu, south Beijing, 1999, photo Sun Hongbin

XIE WENYUE: Hans wanted to do a book about the entire history of Chinese contemporary and modern art. That was his life's work. That was the archive. The book was to be an encyclopedia containing the names, biographies, and bibliographies of the artists. There were to be no pictures in the system for the book. The system was alphabetical by artist name, not chronological. The system also included the library: he put notes in the catalogues, written on little stickers that he would paste on particular pages. He would collect all the information on one particular artist, cross referencing the artist's name with data on which pages and in which catalogues they appeared. For example, he collected all the material he could find about the Stars, and [artists] well before that. He had already put that system on his computer by 1998. Before that, he had a filing system on cards. He did it all by himself and kept updating the files.

The files were copied onto the new office computer in 2001. Hans kept the old computer himself, but kept updating both computers. But Hans died far too soon and too suddenly, and we didn't understand the program on his computer. That is to say, we understood what was in the system, but not the system itself of Hans' references and cross references.

Hans came to the office every day at nine a.m. He stayed on until six p.m. Whenever there was no exhibition [to install], he worked on his files. He always used a bike, but after we moved to south Beijing, he started taking taxis. He seldom mentioned his personal life. By 2000, it became much easier in China to openly say that one was gay. But during the photofestival in Aachen in 2000, some Chinese artists jeered about homosexuals with him. Perhaps they didn't realize how serious an issue it was with Hans.

Hans was the one who mainly decided on the exhibition program. He didn't do the PR for CAAW though; that was mainly Ai Weiwei. Hans stayed in the background.

Ibid.

1999 The CAAW gallery in south Beijing opens on 27 February 1999, just after Chinese New Year, with *Innovations Part I*, a group show with many of his old friends. Even within a commercial gallery structure, van Dijk maintains his standard of meticulously researched and curated exhibitions. CAAW has a unique formula: it is both a gallery and a research center. It includes van Dijk's art archive and library, which is installed in the office and is open to visitors for consultation.

The space in Longzhaoshu is only temporary, though. Uytterhaegen and Ai Weiwei plan to move to Caochangdi, a village northeast of Beijing, which is rapidly becoming a new artistic center, and for which Ai designs one new building after another. Van Dijk is offered the opportunity to have his own quarters built there too, but he declines. As always, he prefers to remain independent. In 1999, with the inheritance from his parents and a small loan from Uytterhaegen, he buys a small, newly built apartment in Chaoyang District in east Beijing.

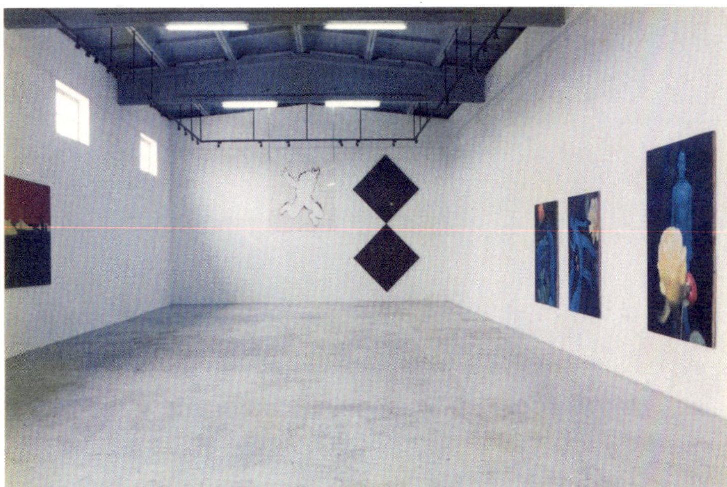

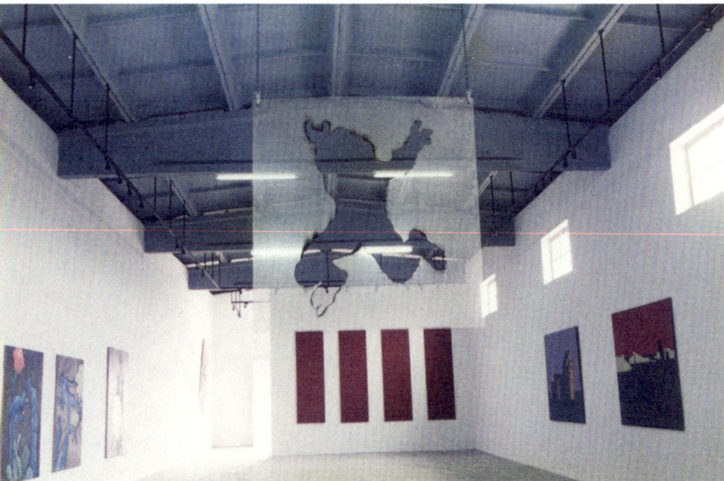

Left: CAAW, Longzhaoshu, south Beijing, exhibition view, works by (left to right) Mai Zhixiong, Zhao Bandi, Ding Yi, and Xie Nanxing, 1999–2000; right: CAAW, Longzhaoshu, south Beijing, exhibition view, works by (left to right) Xie Nanxing, Liu Ding, Mai Zhixiong, and Zhao Bandi, 1999–2000, private coll., photos Sun Hongbin

30 October –
26 December 1999

Duan Jianyu & Li Tianyuan – Recent Works
CAAW, South Beijing

DUAN JIANYU: Xu Tan introduced Hans to me while I was still studying at the Art Academy in Guangzhou. That was in 1994. Xu Tan told me that Hans wanted to see my work. In those days, the situation was so different because there were no art galleries, I was obliged to do a lot of my artwork in my spare time after classes, outside the regular curriculum. As a student, in general there is always some kind of push to not create like the mainstream. In my mind Xu Tan was not like an official artist—he created strange things, kind of avant-garde, so when Hans said that Xu Tan was great, as a student of his I was quite happy. Hans encouraged me a lot; he had a large impact on my work.

Hans came to Guangzhou about every three months, so he visited me regularly. After I finished university in 1995, I started to work as a teacher. By that time I had a lot of works, no good place to put them, and very bad living conditions. Once when Hans came to visit me, he scolded me, saying that I didn't treat my works well. This was the first time I seriously considered the question of how an artist should conserve and handle her own work. After he saw my work in 1998, he took some of my paintings to CAAW in Beijing.

Hans also inspired me: in 2000, he showed me some photos of paintings by Wang Xingwei, and I also went to Beijing to see the real works. My understanding then was quite different from now. I didn't understand how good they were, only much later. I now think Wang Xingwei is one of the best Chinese painters, so Hans was like a guide to me. Even today, a lot of artists that Hans introduced are all good artists where I'm concerned.

I think he had a really great understanding of art, and he gave me a special understanding of it as well.

We never discussed the subjects of my works. Instead, Hans would sometimes show me pictures of rebellious works by foreign artists, and because I was very young and obstinate, I would say I didn't like them at all. I didn't know then that Hans had given up everything, sold all his belongings to come to China. Now of course I feel very stupid.

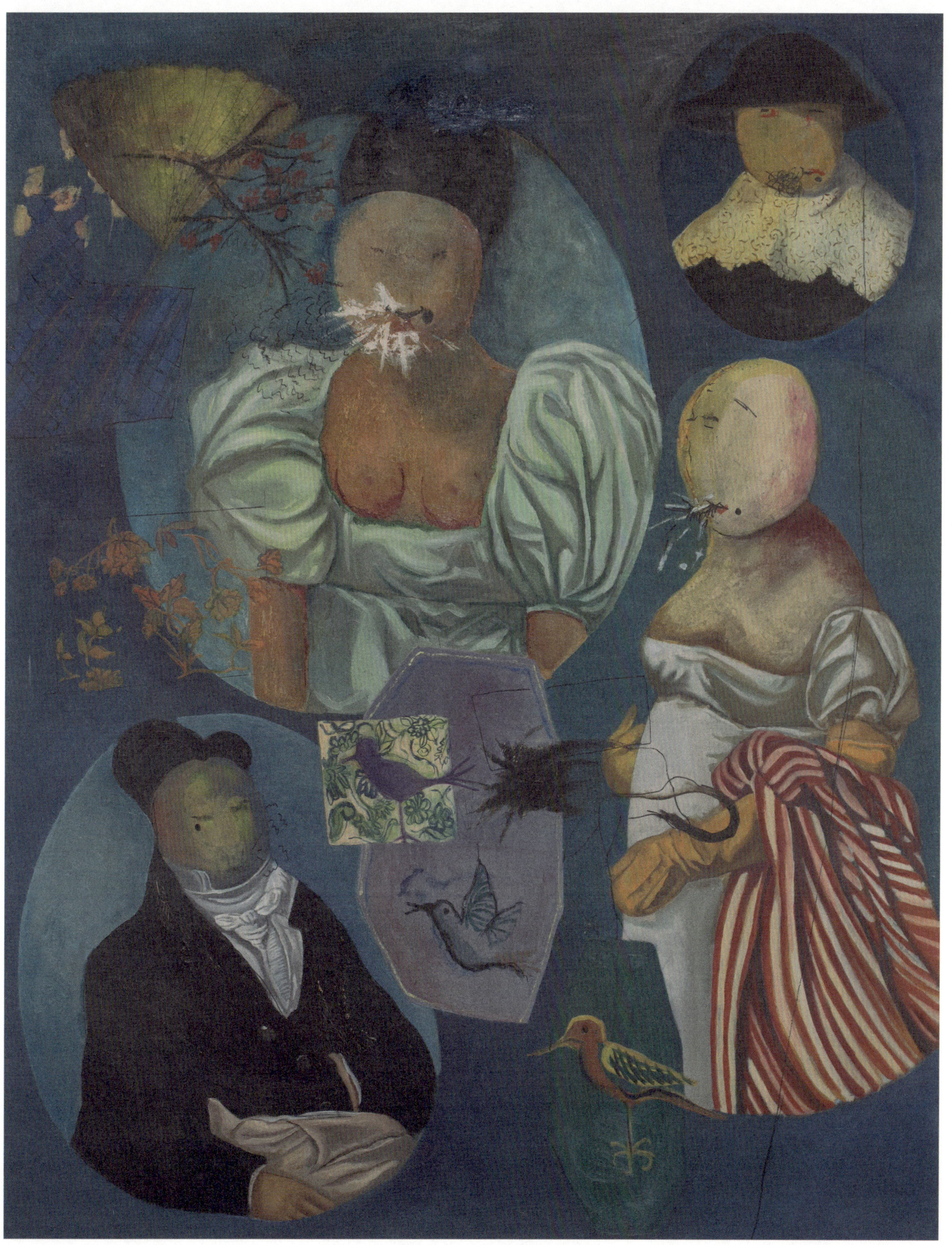

Duan Jianyu, *8 5-4*, oil on canvas, 180 × 140 cm, 1998, courtesy Duan Jianyu and Vitamin Creative Space, Beijing, Guanggzhou; shown at *Duan Jianyu & Li Tianyuan – Recent Works*, CAAW, South Beijing, 1999

I wanted to be a special person but didn't know how, and he showed me how. I still regret not having been good enough to him, not to buy him more cigarettes, for he was always smoking. I wish I could go back to that time.
When Hans was in hospital, we had to go see him one by one, for half an hour maximum each day. Everyone only had a few minutes, but I spoke to him for fifteen minutes: I held his hand, and when I came out everyone blamed me for taking too long. I think Hans was a treasure for Chinese contemporary art, and in the beginning his contribution to the Chinese art scene was very important. When later on the art market grew, he was always a reminder to every artist that you should understand art from a different perspective. I was lucky to meet him, because not everyone had the chance to be with him, since he was not so many years with us in China.

MB, interview with Duan Jianyu, Shanghai, 20 January 2013

8 January – 8 March 2000 *Lost Paradise – Recent Works by Meng Huang* CAAW, South Beijing

Meng Huang began his *Lost Paradise* series in 1996. These are night view paintings, both idyllic and intimidating, of factories and farmhouses, water and mud: impoverished industrial landscapes at the edge of the urban wasteland.

Meng Huang is introduced to van Dijk by Sun Hongbin. The exhibition at CAAW, where he shows a selection of his works, is the artist's first solo show. Van Dijk buys *Paradise 28*, the largest in the series, for his own collection in 2000. He hangs it in the bedroom of his apartment, where it stays until his death. Uytterhaegen and Geulleaume buy a selection of the smaller paintings. In 2002, Meng Huang moves to Berlin, where he lives today.

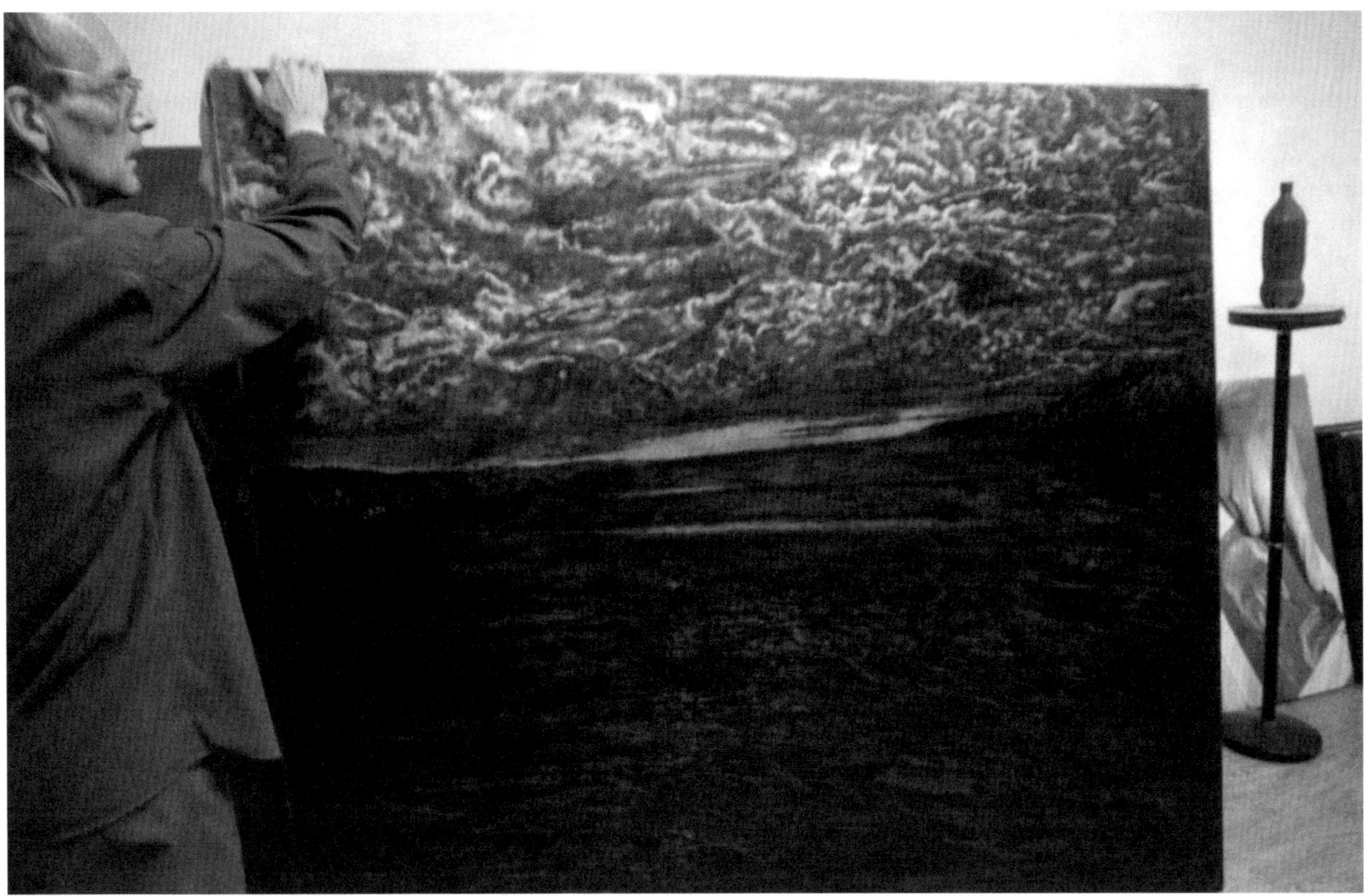

Luo Yongijn, *Photograph of Hans with Painting Paradise 28 by Meng Huang*, photograph, 2000, courtesy Luo Yongjin; on the right stands a sculpture by Zheng Guogu

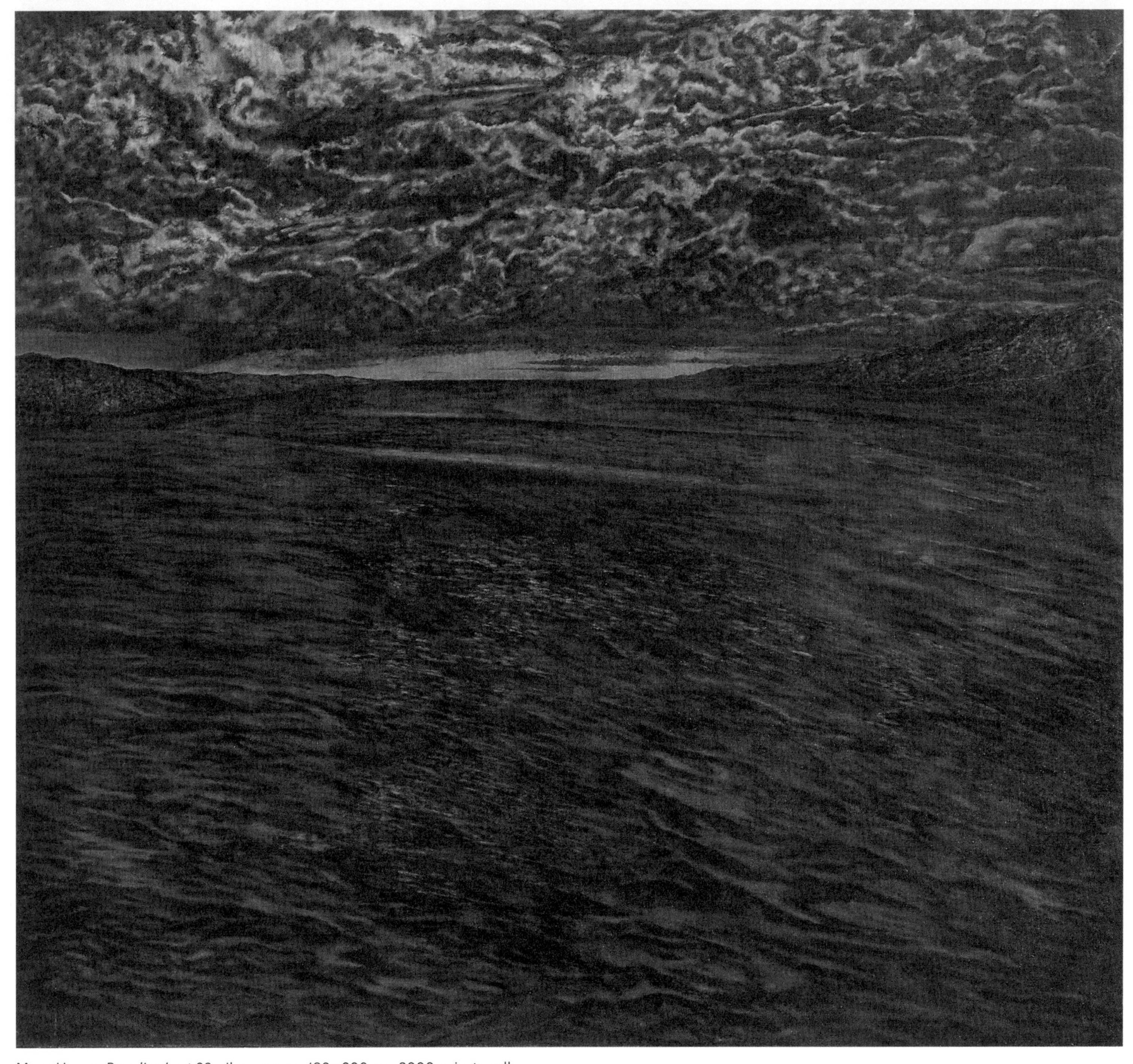

Meng Huang, *Paradise Lost 28*, oil on canvas, 180 × 200 cm, 2000, private coll.

25 March – 23 April 2000 *Caught & Arranged – Photography*
CAAW, South Beijing

29 April – 5 June 2000 *Arranged & Caught – Photography*
CAAW, South Beijing

The titles of these two exhibitions, with recent works by ten young photographers from Beijing, Shenzhen, Yangjiang, Shanghai, and elsewhere, refer to a discussion about opposing working methods as delineated by Wang Shilong[1], a photographer from Zhengzhou. When he worked for the People's Liberation Army, and later for other government institutions, debates arose about whether an artist should catch their subjects and then arrange or manipulate the results, or first arrange or construct a scene until the desired effect is reached and then caught.

1—Wang Shilong (1930–2013), a member of the "Potato School" of photography from the 1930s.

In the meantime van Dijk continues to broaden his contacts with the West. He curates an exhibition with western artists at CAAW, and works as a consultant for sometimes prestigeous exhibitions in Europe and the US. In 2000 he assists with the realization of the exhibition *Beijing, Shanghai, Shenzhen: Cities of the 21st Century*, at the Bauhaus in Dessau, Germany. For the "Thematic Area" of EXPO 2000 HANNOVER, he acts as a consultant, advising on the works of Lin Yilin, Wang Jin, and others. He tirelessly advocates Chinese photography abroad. He shows works at photography festivals in Aachen, Germany; Naarden, the Netherlands; and at the *Rencontres Internationales de la Photographie* in Arles, France.

In 1999, van Dijk meets the young Italian artist and Tibetologist Davide Quadrio (whose Chinese name is Dadou). Quadrio wants to establish an alternative art space in Shanghai and to develop a new business model for it. He has long conversations with van Dijk about his plans. They become good friends and work together on big projects, of which Zheng Guogu's *More Dimensional* is the first.

> DAVIDE QUADRIO: I came to China in 1997 after having spent a couple of years in Tibet. Hans and I were introduced by common friends, perhaps by Monica Dematté, in Beijing in early 1999. I went to see him at the old CAAW in southeast Beijing, where we had a very long talk. He told me about his archive, and I told him that I wanted to start something in Shanghai. When he came to Shanghai that year, we went to see the *Art for Sale* show[2], in which I participated as an artist. All the artists seemed to know that Hans was in town, and I was amazed to see this long line of them all queueing up for Hans with their portfolios. Then I looked into the possibilities of opening a space in Shanghai. Together with Katelijne Verstraete, who also was a friend of Hans', we put some money in. I was talking a lot with Hans about what to do and how to do it. We carried the name of BizArt from 1998 on, but we moved around a lot until I found this place in Huaihai West Road where Red Town [today a sculpture ground also housing the Minsheng Museum] is now and decided to open a new space there, and I wanted to invite Hans to do something there. I went to Beijing for a few weeks and went to see Hans again, who had an exhibition by Zheng Guogu, and we said let's bring the exhibition down to Shanghai. So that was the first exhibition in our space, called *Multidimensional Travel*. Hans came down and stayed here for ten days with Xie Wenyue, and we had a lot of time together talking about what to do with the archive and the gallery, because they were about to move to Caochangdi. After that, we decided to do another show during the Shanghai Biennale. The exhibition was called *Portraits, Figures, Couples and Groups*, consisting of the collection of the Modern Chinese Art Foundation.
> I had wanted BizArt to be something like a creative laboratory from the start. I didn't want to make money from selling works, but from other activities, by doing design or services in the business sector. This would keep the artistic content of our activities completely free. Times were changing very fast: more private money was coming in, and I was also more comfortable with doing PR than Hans. Hans and I differed in this.

2—*Art for Sale* took place in a supermarket situated on the unoccupied fourth floor of a popular Shanghai mall. The works were integrated into the supermarket.

3—Hsieh Tehching, b. 1950, Nanzhou, Taiwan, internationally acclaimed master of extreme performance art.

To him, CAAW, even though it was selling artworks, was always a not-for-profit thing. It never was purely a gallery: it was also a research center emanating out of Hans' activities. Financial support of course came from Frank. Frank bought a lot from Hans' exhibitions, and so the intellectual and creative framework of CAAW was Hans'.

In November 2000, he called me because Hsieh Tehching[3] had come to China. He was an artist from Taiwan who had been doing seminal performances from 1978 – 99 and now lived in New York. So we had this presentation [lecture] of his work at both CAAW and BizArt.

We shared a lot of info this way. Hans was really like a mentor to me. I was so young, and I really had the energy and the enthusiasm: I think that must have also been a beautiful thing to him. We didn't talk about the art as much: mostly philosophy or exchanging ideas for projects.

At one point, we really thought of becoming a joint venture, because he also talked about leaving CAAW. In the middle of 2001, he came down to us. He said he was so exhausted in Beijing. We proposed that he stay and work with us, but he felt he needed to go back. He was already pretty sick, easily tired. In the summer I was in Italy, and Hans called me from Europe saying that he was in hospital, and Frank was taking care of him. Then he went back to Beijing, and I came back from holidays. We were supposed to meet around Christmas, but when I was finally able to go up to Beijing, Meng Huang called me to say that Hans had died.

MB, interview with Davide Quadrio, Shanghai, 23 January 2013

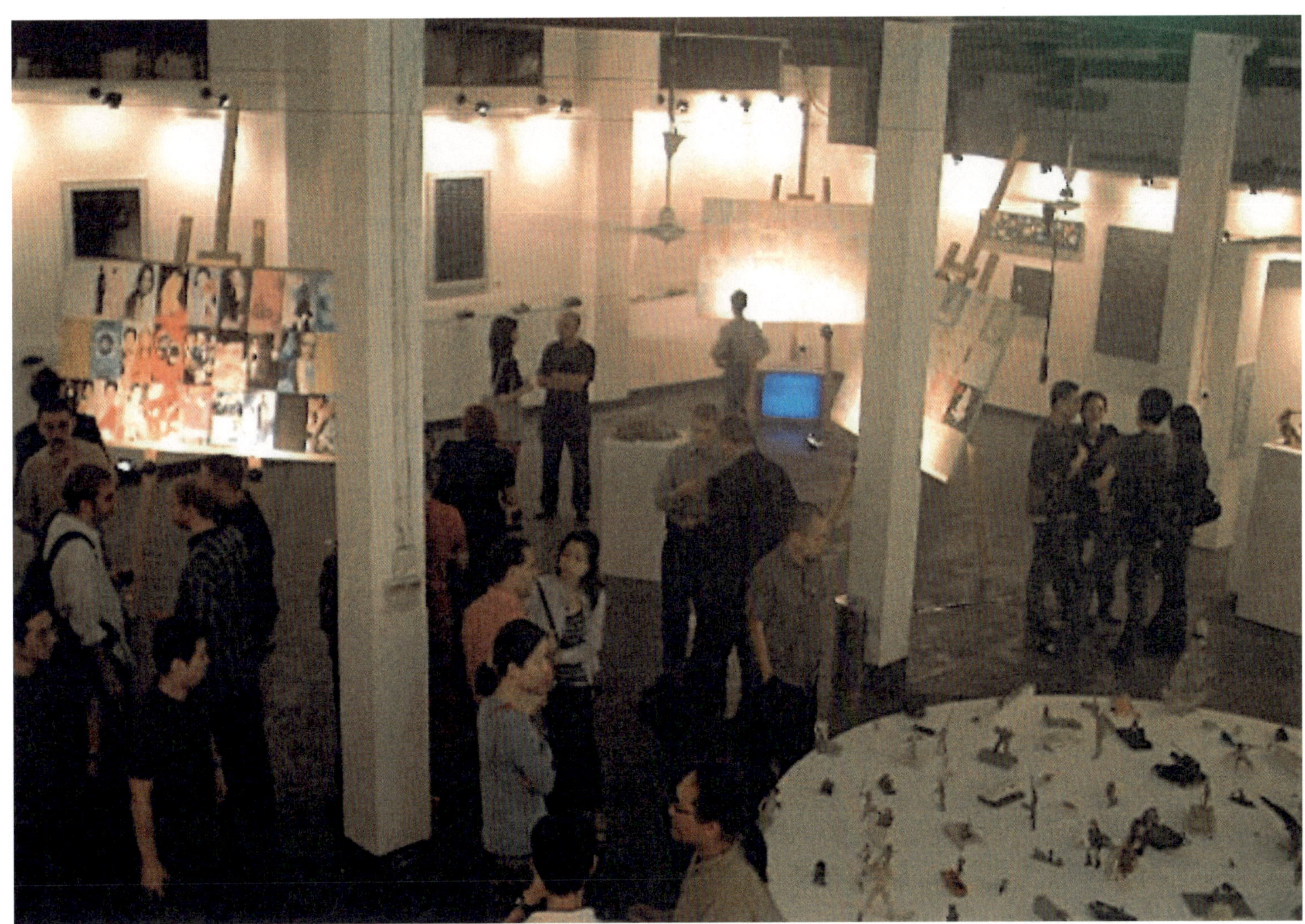

Zheng Guogu: Multidimensional Travel, exhibition view, BizArt, Shanghai, 2000, private coll.

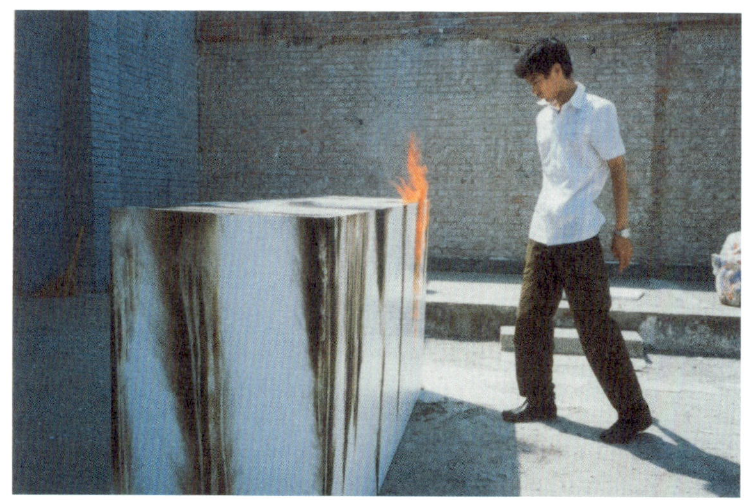
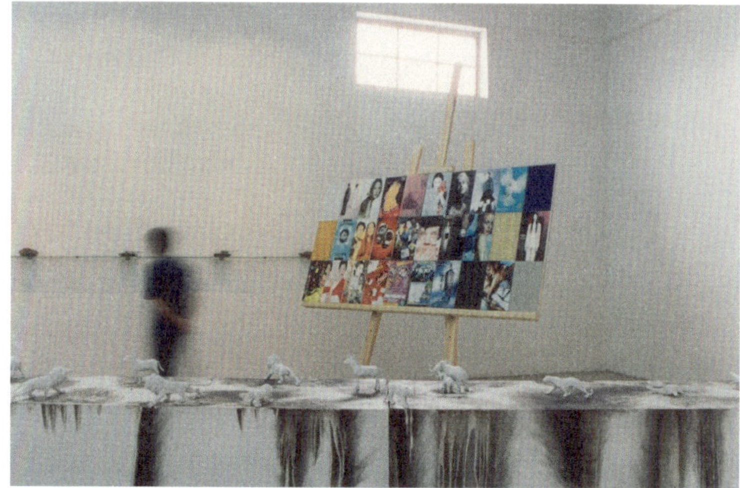

Left: Zheng Guogu preparing his works for *Zheng Guogu: More Dimensional* in the courtyard of CAAW, south Beijing, 2000, photographer unknown, private coll.; right: *Zheng Guogu: More Dimensional*, exhibition view, CAAW, south Beijing, 2000, private coll.

10 June – 30 July 2000	*Zheng Guogu: More Dimensional* CAAW, South Beijing
13 September – 10 October 2000	*Zheng Guogu: Multidimensional Travel* BizArt, Shanghai

In a forthcoming exhibition, CAAW hosts a collection of artworks by Zheng Guogu, including photography, oil painting, and sculpture. Born in the China of the 1970s, Zheng has acted both as a witness to and as an active part in the growth of a new, flourishing consumer market.

Zheng's artwork represents not only the feelings of his generation but also his tight bond to his colorful but also bleakly contradictory home province, Guangdong, where the glittering proximity of Hong Kong constantly beckons.

His subject matter pivots around consumption and human behavior in a quickly developing, affluent young society; around relations between men and consumer products; and between real and/or animated commercials and lives.

His latest art inventions include bottle sculpture and oil paintings. His bottles, which began life as a mere commercial arrangement on a supermarket shelf, are then brought to a new existence through other materials, such as steel and brass. Similar in thought are his oil paintings, with pasty colors set on thick cotton canvas, more durable than standard photo paper.

HvD, invitiation card for *Zheng Guogu: More Dimensional*, 2000

1998–2000

Creating the Modern Chinese Art Foundation

Although preparations were well underway from 1998 on, the Modern Chinese Art Foundation (MCAF) is officially established as a nonprofit association by Uytterhaegen and his wife Pascale Geulleaume in their home in Ghent on 9 June 2000. The MCAF is a private initiative "aiming at collecting, documenting, and promoting modern Chinese art and at being instrumental in promoting the ongoing art movement in China," as the mission statement reads. The foundation brings private collections of Chinese contemporary art together and sets up touring shows. MCAF comprises van Dijk's collection as well as Uytterhaegen and Geulleaume's extensive collection of Chinese contemporary art. It later includes Robert Bernell's collection of video and photography. Van Dijk is the curator of the foundation, comparable to a museum curator's role, where he can fully deploy his knowledge of Chinese art history and iconography. He only gets to curate two exhibitions, the *Modern Chinese Art Foundation Collection* in Ghent in 1999, and *Portraits, Figures, Couples and Groups* in Shanghai in 2000.

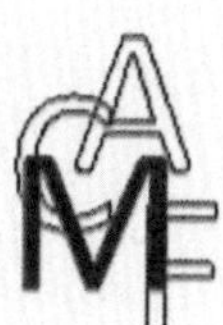

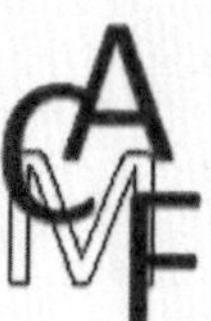

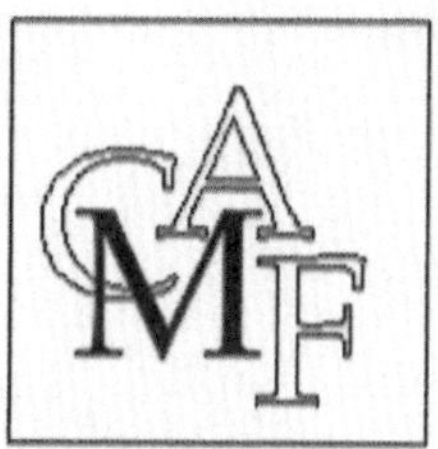

MCAF logo designed by Hans van Dijk, Book Antiqua 72 pt. font, 1999

12 November–
5 December 1999

Modern Chinese Art Foundation Collection
Caermersklooster, Ghent, Belgium

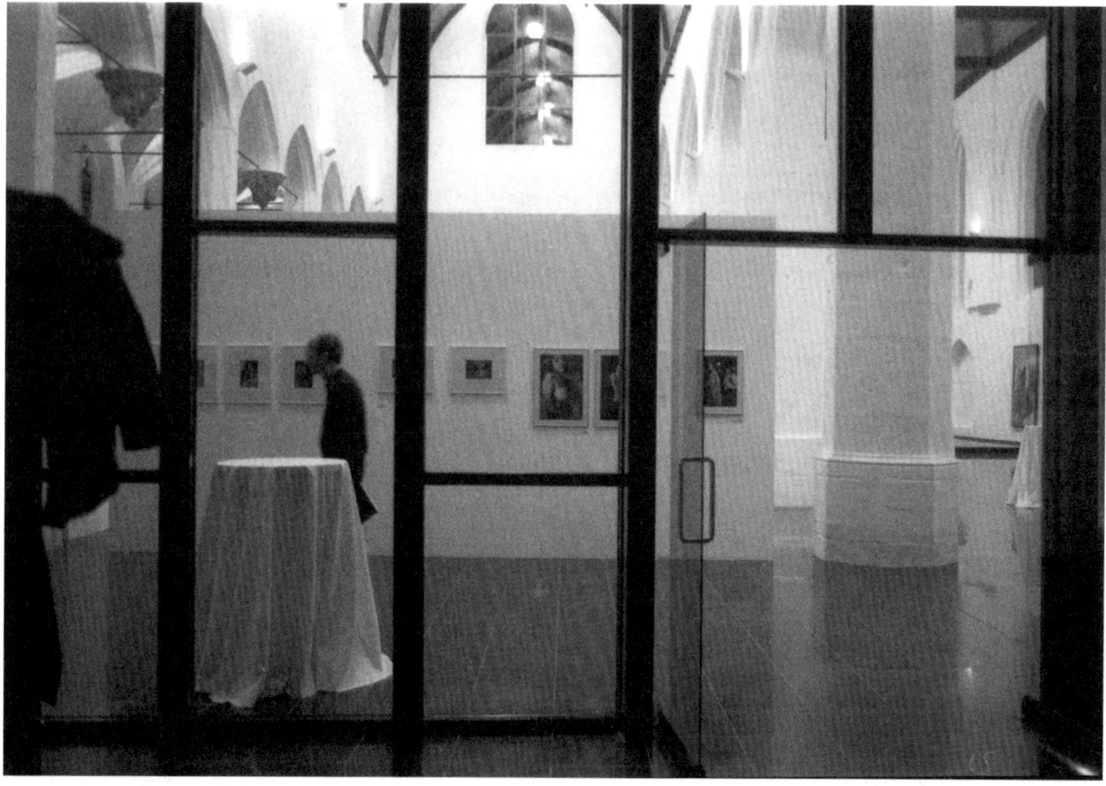

Hans van Dijk installing the collection of the Modern Chinese Art Foundation, Caermersklooster, Ghent, 1999, photo Xie Wenyue

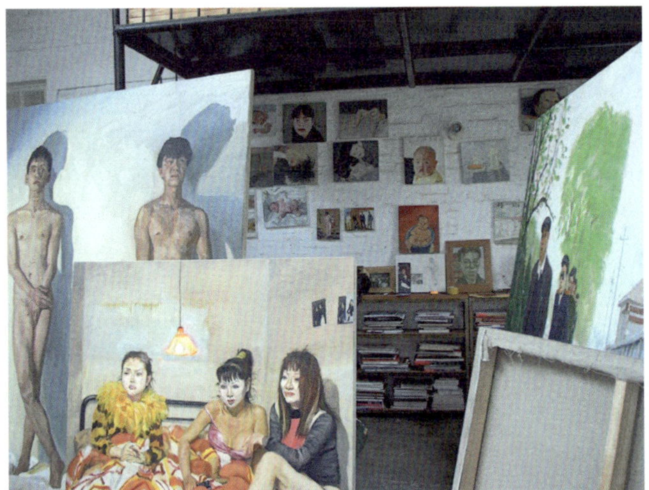
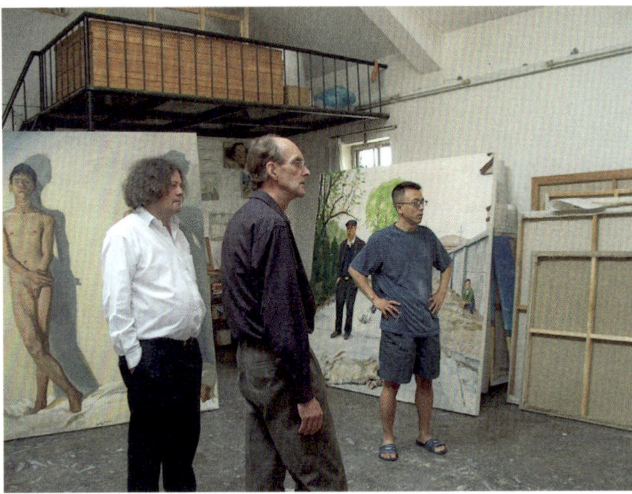
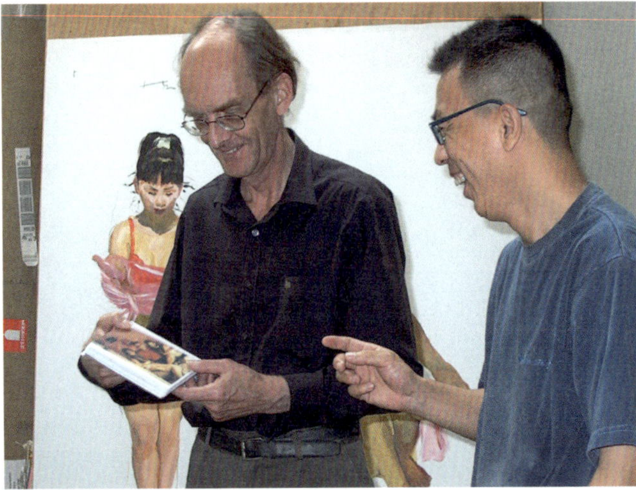
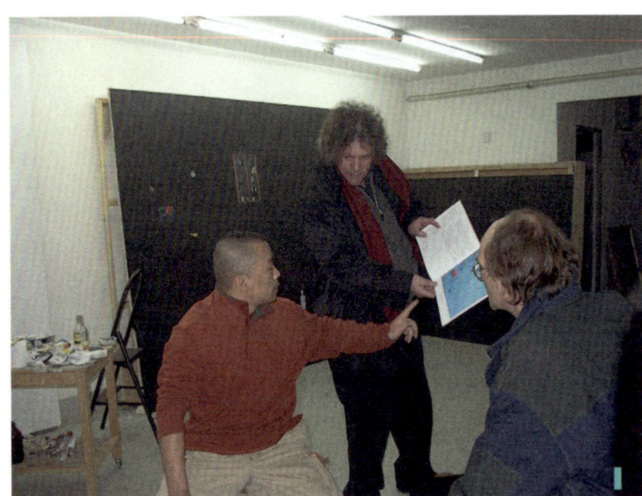

Top left to bottom left: Hans van Dijk and Frank Uytterhaegen visiting Liu Xiaodong in his studio, Beijing, circa 2000, photos Pascale Geulleaume; bottom right: Hans van Dijk and Frank Uytterhaegen visiting Zeng Hao in his studio, Beijing, circa 2000, photo Pascale Geulleaume

8 November – 4 December 2000

Portraits, Figures, Couples and Groups MCAF at BizArt, Shanghai

DAVIDE QUADRIO: The exhibition was curated by Hans, and it was beautiful to work with him on this. The exhibition at BizArt was really a chance for Hans to present a kind of overview of the last fifty years of Chinese contemporary art, starting with a lot of old photographs from the sixties. And we had beautiful images of the Cultural Revolution. We discussed mediums in art in China a lot, and for Hans the functions of all the various mediums were very similar—there was no hierarchical difference. We discussed each individual piece in the show, and what I remember is the pure love with which Hans spoke of them. It was not just about curating that exhibition per se, but his long-standing connection to all those works. It's my understanding that he was not only showing the collection as such, but actually presenting a sort of reader of what for him was the history of contemporary art in China. It was a very full exhibition. Talking about how to display the works, going through the spaces, he would put some artists together, not chronologically but all based on the intimate correlations between pieces. This exhibition was incredibly important in its curatorship.

MB, interview with Davide Quadrio, Shanghai, 23 January 2013

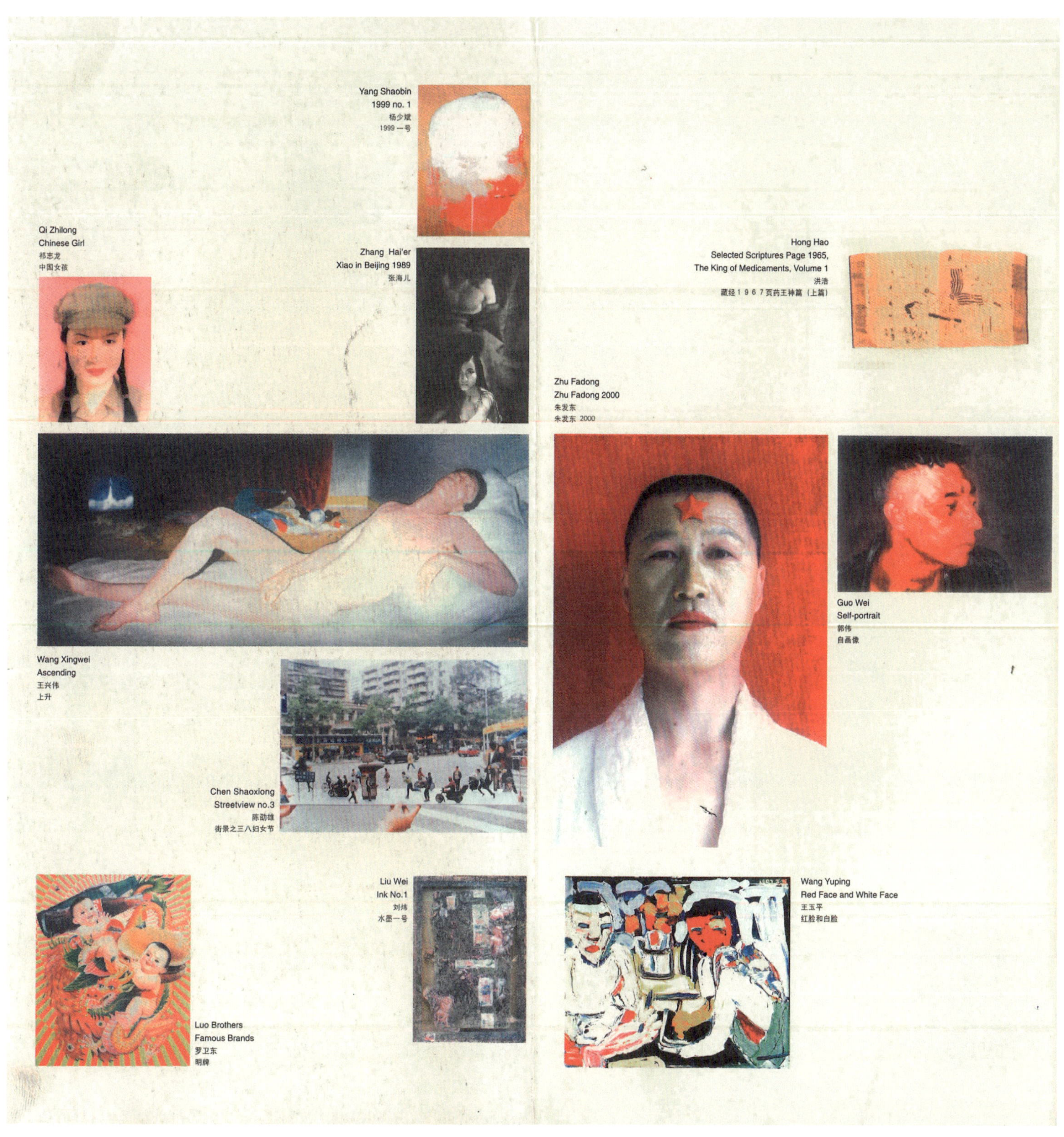

Portraits, Figures, Couples and Groups invitation card, page 1, works by Qi Zhilong, Yang Shaobin, Zhang Hai'er, Wang Xingwei, Chen Shaoxiong, Luo Brothers, Liu Wei, Hong Hao, Zhu Fadong, Guo Wei, and Wang Yuping, 2001, private coll.

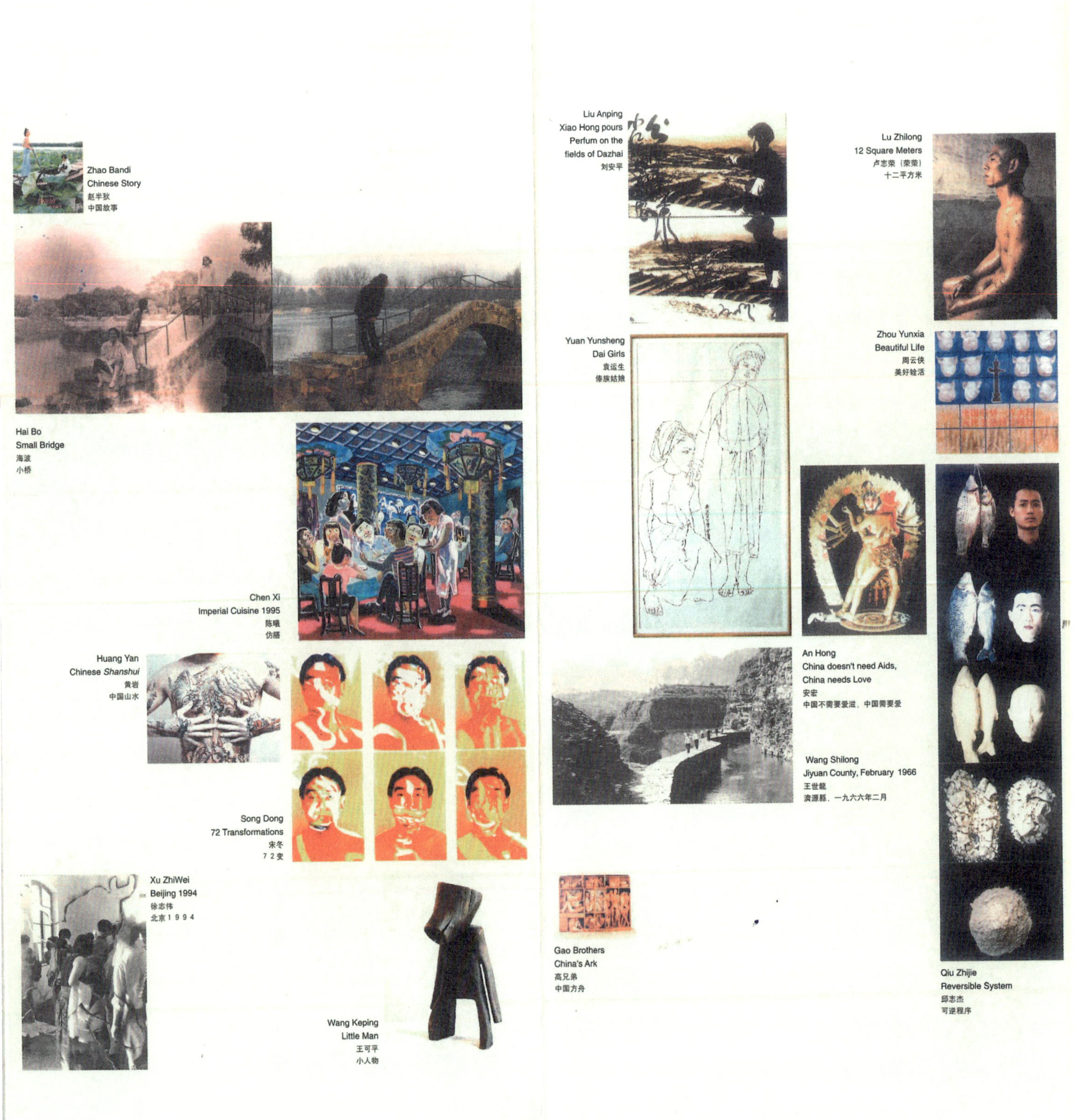

Portraits, Figures, Couples and Groups invitation card, page 2, works by Zhao Bandi, Hai Bo, Chen Xi, Huang Yan, Song Dong, Xu Zhiwei, Wang Keping, Liu Anping, RongRong, Yuan Yunsheng, Zhou Yunxia, An Hong, Wang Shilong, Qiu Zhijie, and Gao Brothers, 2001, private coll.

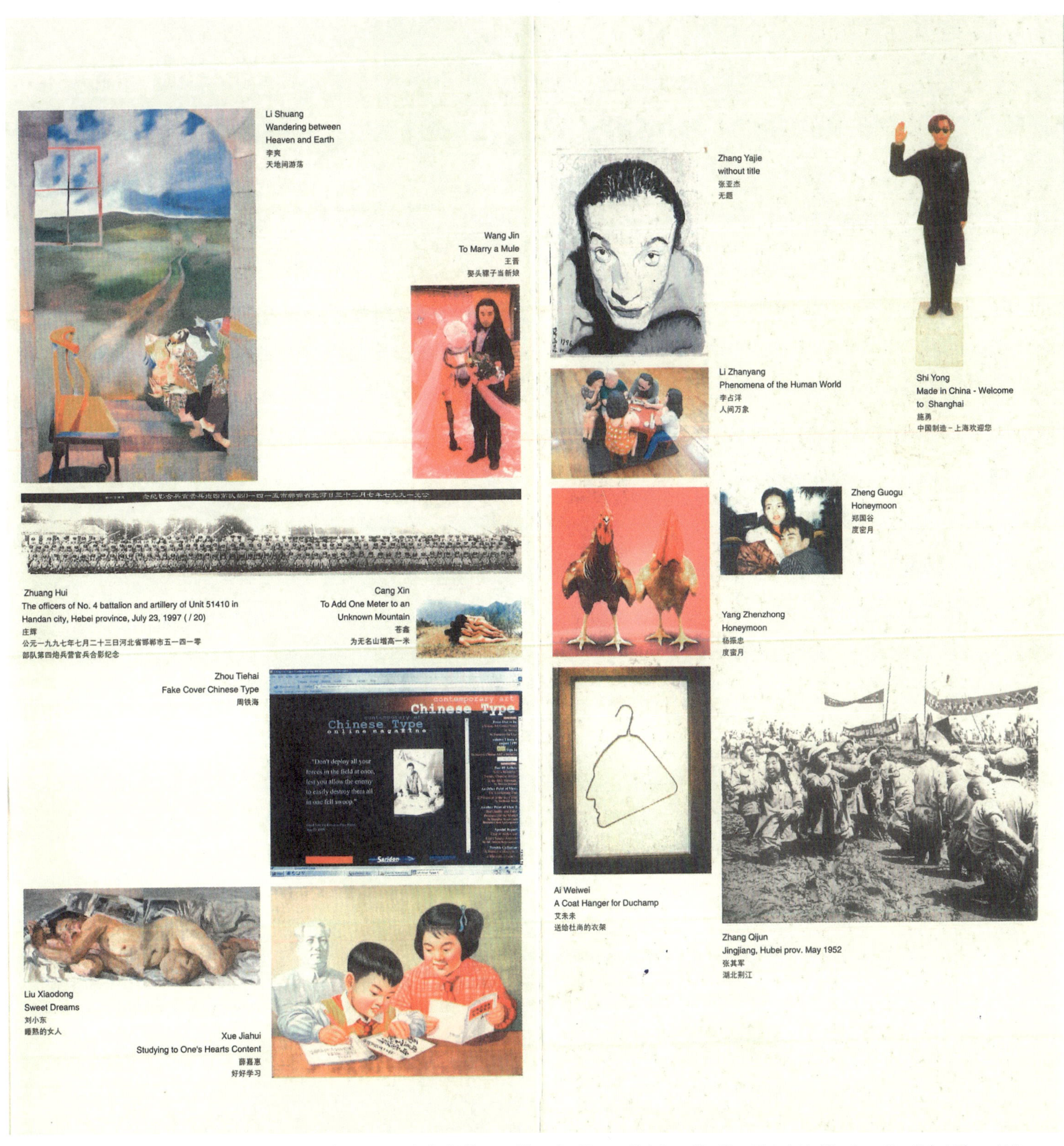

Portraits, Figures, Couples and Groups invitation card, page 3, works by Li Shuang, Wang Jin, Zhuang Hui, Cang Xin, Zhou Tiehai, Liu Xiaodong, Xue Jiahui, Zhang Yajie, Shi Yong, Li Zhanyang, Yang Zhenzhong, Zheng Guogu, Ai Weiwei, and Zhang Qijun, 2001, private coll.

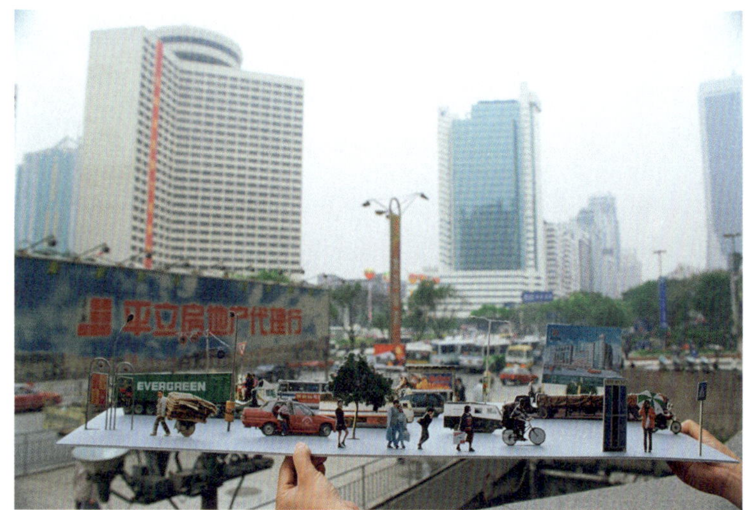

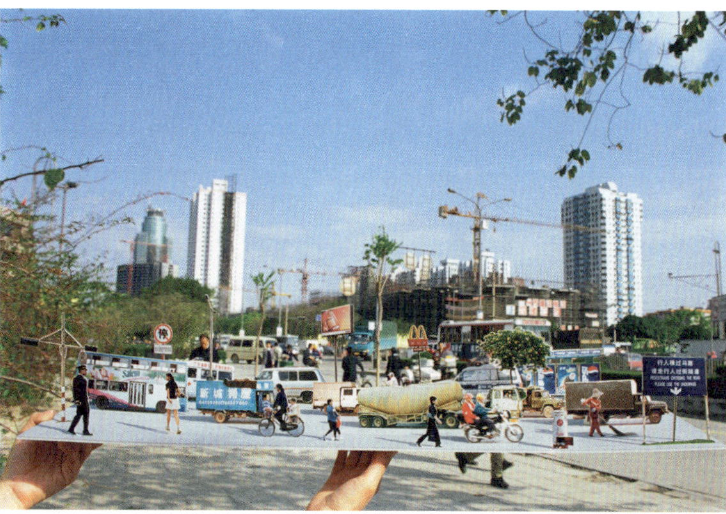

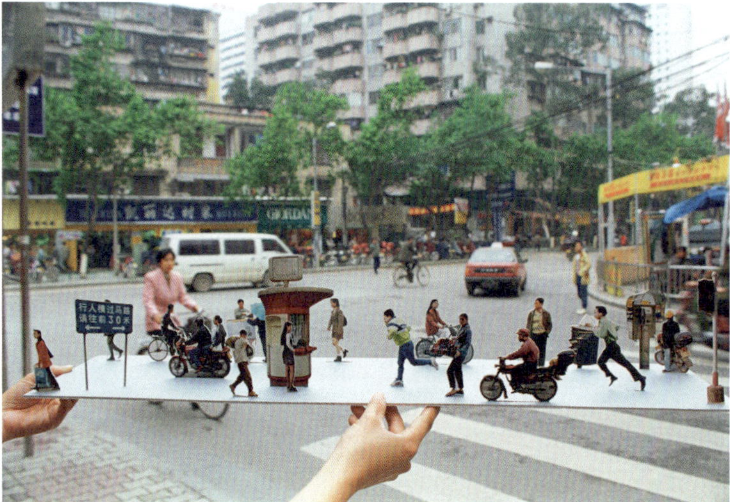

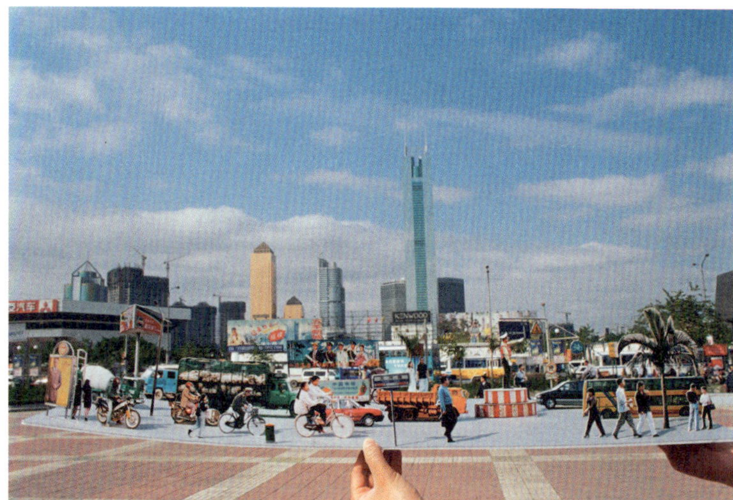

Chen Shaoxiong, *Street 1; Street 2; Street 3; Street 4*, photographs, 85×127 cm each, 1998, courtesy Chen Shaoxiong and Boers-Li Gallery, Beijing

Hans van Dijk
Introduction to the catalogue

Portraits, Figures, Couples and Groups is a selection of the artworks in the MCAF collection, which could be categorized as such. Maybe seventy percent or more of the present total collection exists of work with human figures. Without claiming that the present MCAF collection is representative of contemporary art of the Chinese mainland, it shows at least that the depiction of characters and defining identities plays a crucial role in the art world.

“Portraiture” as a classical art discipline has been applied as a critirion for selecting and arranging the works: face-detail, face-on, face-half, profile, face-profile, torso, full-length figure, et cetera. The result is eigthy-odd art works in various media of forty-one artists from all over China. The oldest work dates from the fifites, while the majority of the works are from the nineties.

On the one hand, showing eighty artworks by forty artists doesn’t do justice to the artist; their works being rigorously, without any reference to their oeuvres, put into a formal system. On the other hand, the formal character of this presentation denies propagation of a chosen stylistic unity and excludes a preconceived message, meaning, or intention dominating the artworks.

By applying the discipline of portraiture, an artist unavoidably shows an approach to the model, and with that, shows fundamental aspects of his or her attitude towards society and often to the supposed role art should play in it. Although few artists, also among those who worked in the past under more or less strict political guidelines, will really hold up that they represent or represented the people of the People's Republic of China, the resulting summary here of those attitudes and approaches certainly reveals essential social aspects from the worlds the artists lived and worked in.

Through all the categories, techniques, and periods, a line can be drawn between works made to depict and catch characters and scenes after life, unidealized, and as sincere and direct as one is able to, and works defining identities, which are made after considerations or plans, often to fulfill certain ideological purposes varying from political, social, or artistic ones, and sometimes in close cooperation with the model.

The division at work is similar to that of Realism-Classicism in the nineteenth-century French art world, where Realists intended to reveal and un-idealize what Classicists ignored and exalted. The emergence of these two types in mainland China should not be seen as following a simplified linear art historical process where one replaces the other. Although propaganda art of the sixties and seventies vanished after that period, similar approaches used posed, staged, and arranged models and situations, but now based on other conventions. These are common in the art world and are now known as "conceptual art." And although reality-revealing photography and painting started in the eighties as a reaction to the idealizing art before that, it continues to deliver many astonishing works made in contemporary Chinese art.

Portraits, Figures, Couples and Groups, ed. Hans van Dijk, published by the Modern Chinese Art Foundation, Ghent, 2001

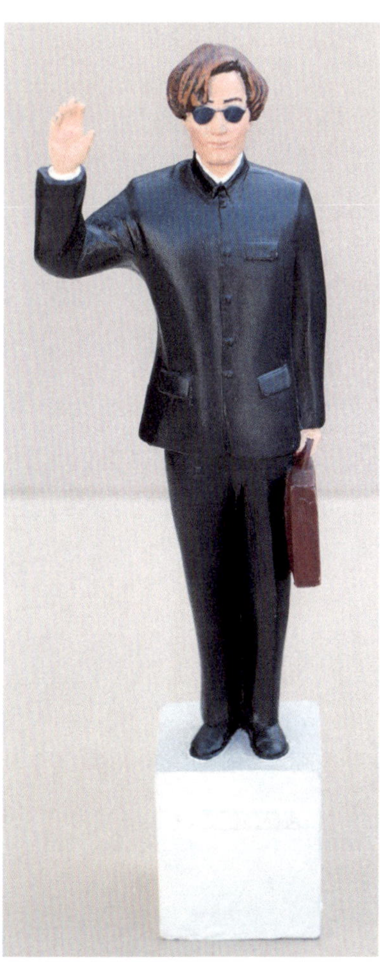

Shi Yong, *Made in China – Welcome to Shanghai*, hand-painted plaster, 8 × 10 × 30 cm, 1999, courtesy Shi Yong and ShanghART Gallery, Shanghai

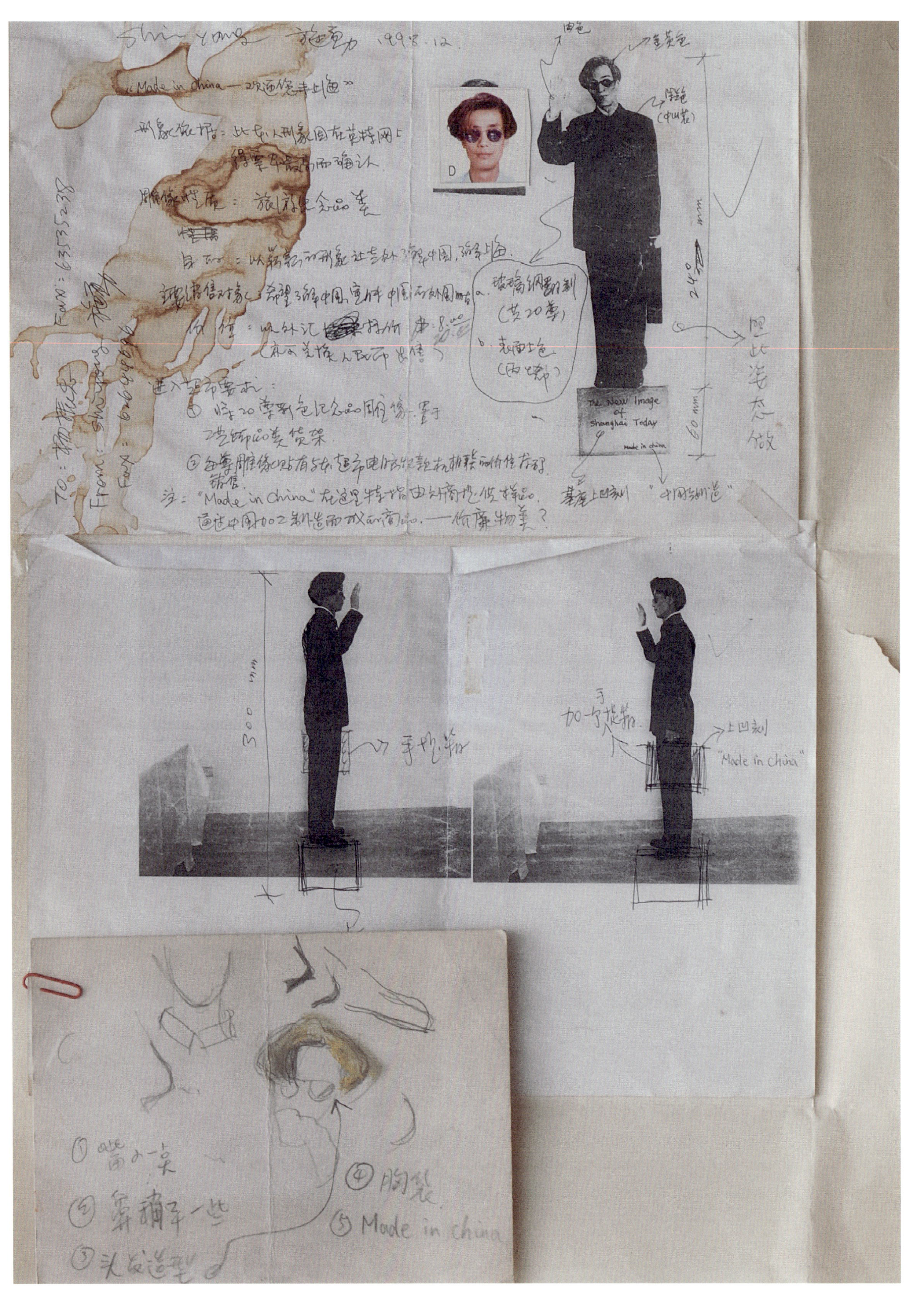
1998.12
The New Image of Shanghai Today
Made in china
"Made in China"
Made in china

One of the works in the exhibition is a small plaster statue by Shi Yong entitled *Made in China – Welcome to Shanghai*. Shi Yong lives in Shanghai and never worked with van Dijk, but he has vivid memories of van Dijk being his first collector.

> SHI YONG: I met Hans in 1994. It was very hard at that time to be a contemporary artist. Through Hans, many Chinese contemporary artists got to know Western art history, and he was the source of news from abroad as well. He was extremely important to the beginnings of Chinese art. Without Hans, I wouldn't have known what to do as an artist at an early age, and I don't see how Chinese art could have grown and flourished. It was a very harsh environment, both spiritually and materially.
> Hans was the first person ever to buy a work of mine. That was in 1999, when I participated in *Art for Sale*, a group show organized by BizArt. I had made a group of 100 small statues based on research I had done on the internet. The title of the work was *The New Image of Shanghai Today – Welcome to Shanghai*. Hans bought one statue for 180 yuan for his Modern Chinese Art Foundation. He later included that work in a show by CAAW at BizArt on Huaihai Road, which was the most interesting non-profit space in Shanghai at the time.
> Later in Hans' life, he opened the CAAW, an archive in south Beijing accessible to everyone. It was very hard to get to the old CAAW: you had to go through back alleys, and when it rained the roads were terribly muddy. And then suddenly you found yourself inside this pristine big white cube! The archive itself consisted of photos, slides, index cards, and catalogues. There used to be an album he had that looked a bit like Ai Weiwei's black and white books, with similar compilations of the most avant-garde artists. Hans would always generously provide info to anyone, also to foreigners who came to visit. The info he would give out typically consisted of clippings, printouts, photocopies, reviews, and handouts stapled together. We had very little in the way of information in those days. Even before meeting him, I was already influenced by him because of the international exhibitions he organized.
> **MB, interview with Shi Yong, Shanghai, 9 September 2012**

Another work in the exhibition is a photo series of a performance by Zhu Fadong, entitled *Person for Sale*. Zhu Fadong is a performance artist of the same generation as Cang Xin and Ma Liuming. One of his first performances is *Person for Sale*, in which the artist walks around Beijing in a blue worker's suit with a patch on his back declaring, "This person is for sale, price negotiable." Anyone could avail themselves of his services. Zhu Fadong's work is likely inspired by a real life situation. One day, Wang Xingwei announces that he will be coming to Beijing to bring some of his new paintings for van Dijk to see. Because van Dijk cannot personally pick up Wang that day, he hires Zhu Fadong to receive him at the train station and accompany him to CAAW. As Zhu and Wang don't know each other, van Dijk provides Zhu with a copy of his own ID card. Zhu is to show this card and his employee ID to identify himself. Both identity cards are now part of the CAAW archive.[4]

4—MB, interview with Zhang Li, April 2014.

Opposite page: Shi Yong, *The New Image of Shanghai Today*, collaged script, 53 × 37 cm, 1998, private coll.

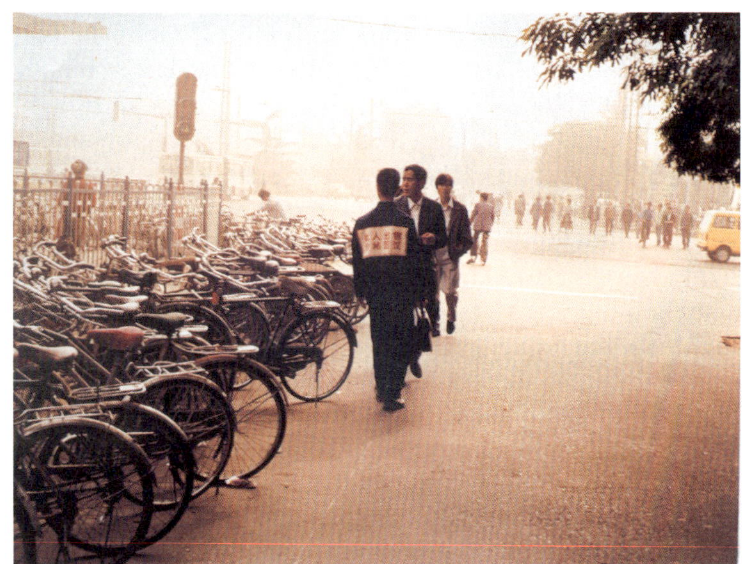

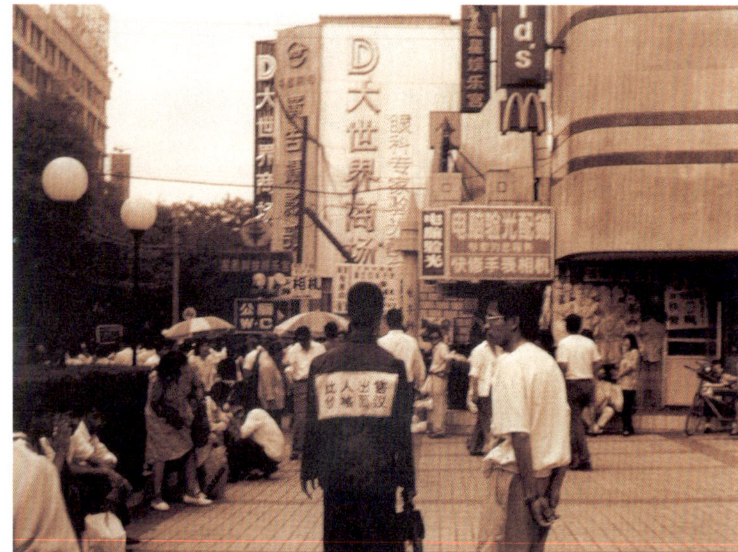

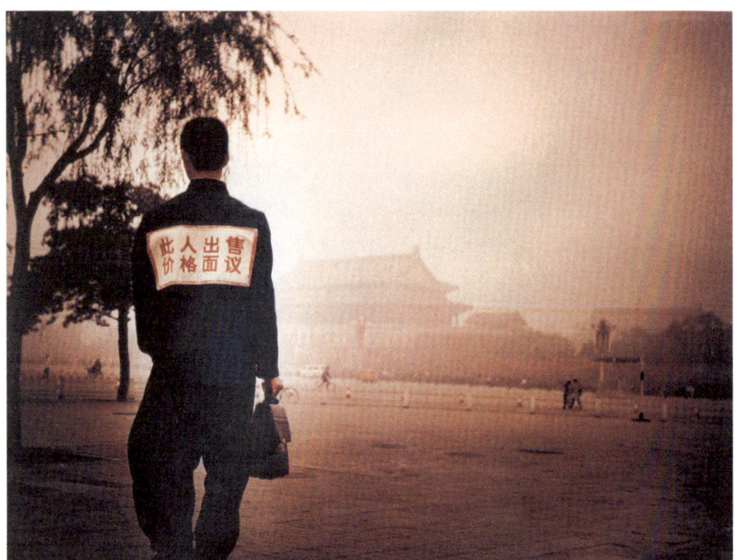

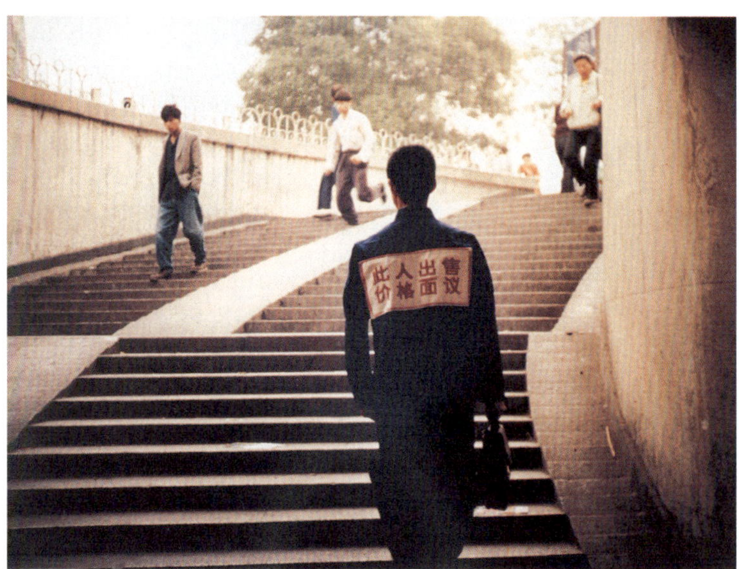

Zhu Fadong, *Person for Sale: Price Negotiable*, photographs, 42 × 55.5 cm each, 1999, private coll.

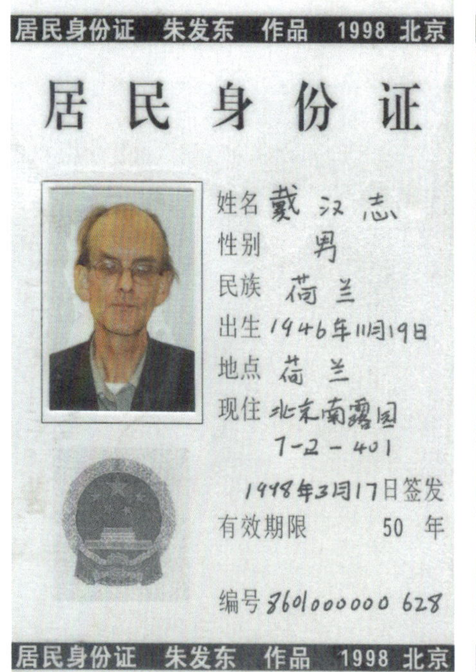

居民身份证 朱发东 作品 1998 北京

居 民 身 份 证

姓名 戴汉志
性别 男
民族 荷兰
出生 1946年11月19日
地点 荷兰
现住 北京南露园 7-2-401

1998年3月17日签发
有效期限 50 年

编号 3601000000 628

居民身份证 朱发东 作品 1998 北京

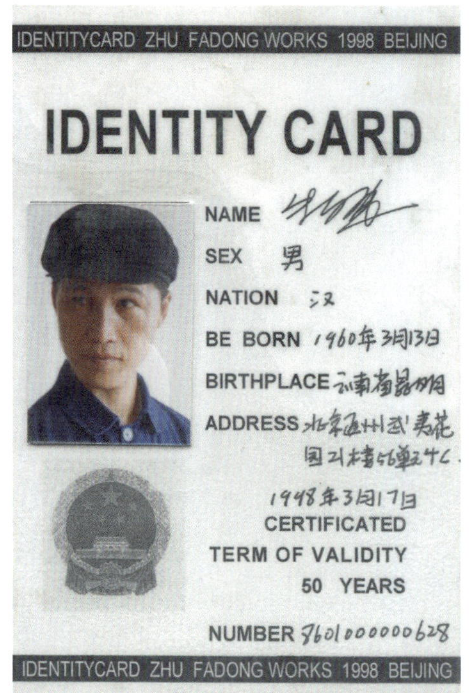

IDENTITYCARD ZHU FADONG WORKS 1998 BEIJING

IDENTITY CARD

NAME
SEX 男
NATION 汉
BE BORN 1960年3月13日
BIRTHPLACE 云南省昆明
ADDRESS 北京通州武夷花园 [illegible]

1998年3月17日
CERTIFICATED
TERM OF VALIDITY
50 YEARS

NUMBER 3601000000628

IDENTITYCARD ZHU FADONG WORKS 1998 BEIJING

Left: Hans van Dijk, identity card, 1998, private coll.; right: Zhu Fadong, identity card, 1998, private coll.

2001

CAAW, Caochangdi, Beijing

Released in English and Chinese at the opening of the new building in Caochangdi, 1 January 2001:

> Mission Statement,
> China Art Archives & Warehouse
>
> First known under the name NAAC, the China Art Archives & Warehouse—CAAW—is one of the most prominent Beijing galleries showing contemporary Chinese art. Since 1993, CAAW has closely monitored the development of Chinese contemporary art, and this research resulted in the largest currently available database in this field. This database is available in Beijing and will be made available through the CAAW website in the near future. CAAW was the first gallery to set up a Beijing exhibition space that could meet the standards of the international art scene: being totally independent and capable of housing large works.
>
> Recently, CAAW moved into its new premises in the north of Beijing, where it now disposes of an impressive exhibition space and all modern facilities. Its prime location and exceptionally spacious display capacity makes it a much sought-after exhibition location. Its main exhibition hall covers an area of 27 × 12 m with 6 m high walls and enables CAAW to display even the largest works. Adjacent to this large hall are more intimate exposition areas and the CAAW offices.
>
> CAAW's objective is to establish durable links with contemporary artists and to host high quality exhibitions. CAAW features monthly exhibitions. Its opening receptions are very well-liked events, attended by artists, curators, art collectors, and visitors from both within and outside of China.
>
> CAAW's activities extend well beyond Chinese borders; apart from exhibitions in China, CAAW organizes and participates in international exhibitions such as, recently: the Venice Biennale; the exhibition *Beijing Shanghai Shenzhen – Cities of the 21st Century* in Dessau, Germany; Fotofestival Naarden; Hot Pot Norway; Lyon Biennale; et cetera. During the Shanghai Biennale in 2000, Ai Weiwei, one of the two CAAW curators and contemporary artist himself, organized the controversial but much-noticed exhibition *Fuck Off* in Shanghai. Also during the Shanghai Biennale, Hans van Dijk, curator of CAAW, organized the successful exhibition *Portraits, Figures, Couples and Groups*, exhibiting about eighty artworks by thirty-six artists, including sculpture, oil paintings, drawings, prints, photography, and video from the Modern Chinese Art Foundation. CAAW people were at the forefront of the establishment, in 1999, of the Modern Chinese Art Foundation, established in Ghent, Belgium. The Modern Chinese Art Foundation holds an extensive collection, illustrating Chinese art and its development during the last decades. It has permanent exhibition spaces in both Beijing and Ghent. Through its close collaboration with the Modern Chinese Art Foundation, CAAW ensures its presence in Europe.
>
> Art Directors Ai Weiwei, Hans van Dijk
> Business Director Frank Uytterhaegen
> Partners Sun Hongbin, Xie Wenyue

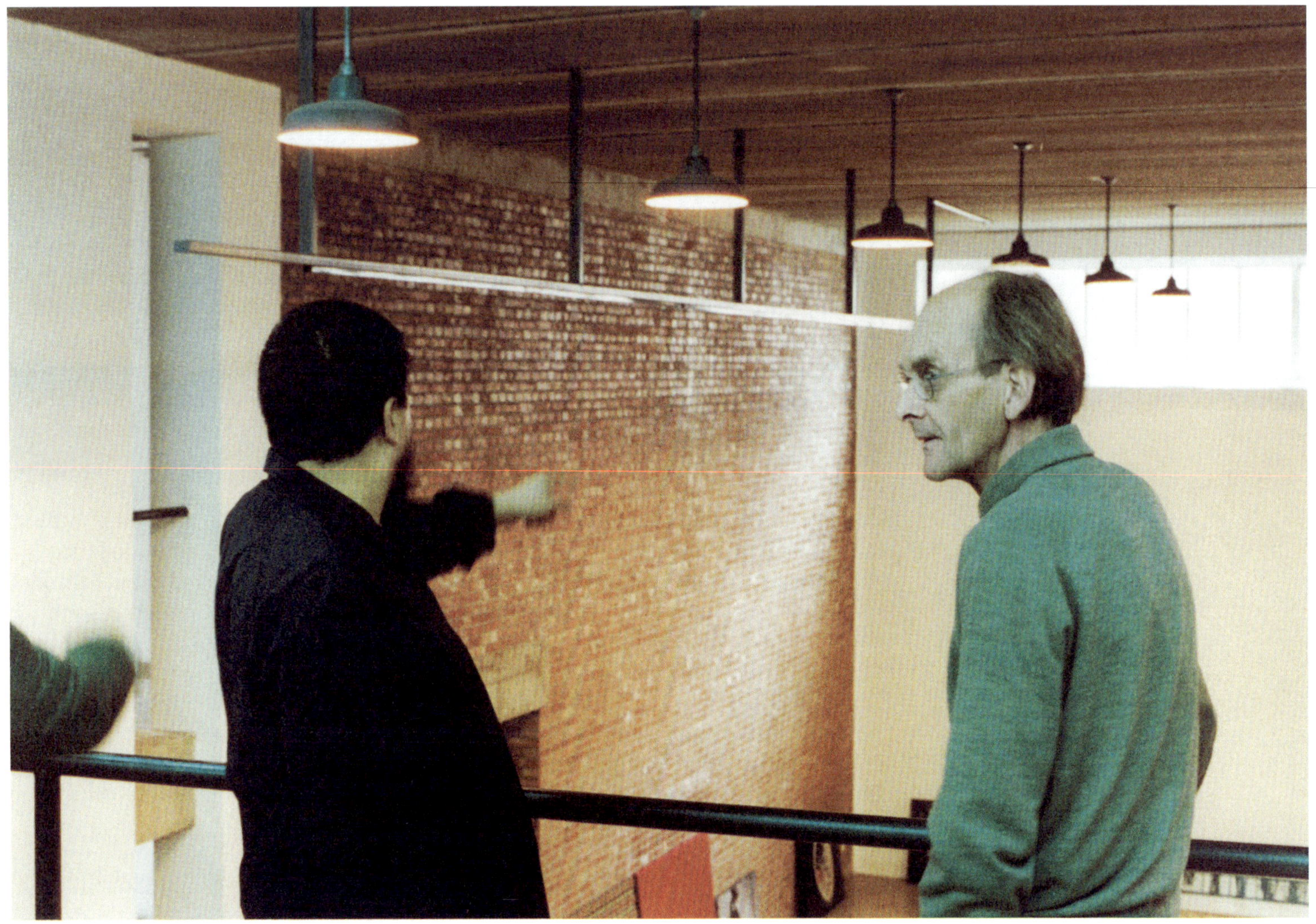

Ai Weiwei and Hans van Dijk at CAAW, Caochangdi, Beijing, 2001, photo Xie Wenyue

1 January –
17 February 2001

Inaugural Exhibition of the New Gallery
Group exhibition, CAAW, Caochangdi, Beijing

The show includes an older generation of artists like Wang Xingwei, Sun Kai, Xu Hongming, Zhang Enli, and Meng Huang, but also introduces artists of a younger generation. The young artist Liu Ding is part of this group exhibition, where he exhibits his nail polish paintings for the first time.

> LIU DING: Hans had no boundaries about what was or was not art. That has interested me to this day. Hans spoke a lot about modernizing the categories of Chinese art. He was very aware of history and modernity. When he revisited the past, he did not base his thoughts on existing assumptions or categories. I remember Hans would show me works of the Cultural Revolution and discuss them with me.
> Now that I think about it, I was very young and constantly talking about my ideas of how to be more radical. Hans would always respond to my anxiety in a very light manner, never answering me directly. After I made the nail polish paintings, I was so scared of what I had done that I stopped making art for two years.
> I did my very first show at CAAW with Hans in 2001. At CAAW, Hans was doing better. Ding Yi fetched high prices by then, Yan Lei was getting known, and Zheng Guogu was beginning to get known as well. There was very little support for abstract painting to begin with. After Hans died, so many artists stopped working, because there was no more interest in abstraction with rational thinking behind it.
> MB, interview with Liu Ding, Beijing, 17 September 2012

17 March – 28 April 2001

Yan Lei, *International Scenery*
CAAW, Caochangdi, Beijing

Yan Lei first meets van Dijk in 1987 when he is studying at the Zhejiang Academy. From 1993 to 1997, he lives in Beijing, working as a graphic designer for a journal about theater and film, visiting van Dijk from time to time for drinks and conversation. In 1995, Yan Lei photographs himself as a wounded man with blood streaming down his face and his back flogged, making up a story of having gotten into a fight "trying to make performance art." According to the artist, it is part of trying to find ways to "get into important exhibitions."[5] In 1996, he makes printed works: *Are you included in the show in Germany?*, *May I see your work?*. In 1997, with Hong Hao and van Dijk, he creates the *documenta X* hoax, consisting of fake invitations for artists to documenta.

5—MB, interview with Yan Lei, Hong Kong, 5 September 2012.

In 1998, having moved to Hong Kong, Yan Lei starts a project with the Dafen village, which is famous for producing copies of works by famous artists. He has them copy black and white photographs of (urban) landscapes he took throughout the years. In 2000, while in Hong Kong, van Dijk stays in his apartment and sees the large, black-and-white landscape paintings. One of them is of Hangzhou Park's West Lake, where Yan Lei and van Dijk first met. Van Dijk invites Yan Lei for a solo exhibition at CAAW. The exhibition included six large, conceptual paintings and two enlarged photographs from 1996 of Yan Lei's made-up wounded face and made-up flogged back. After the exhibition, postcards are made of the paintings.

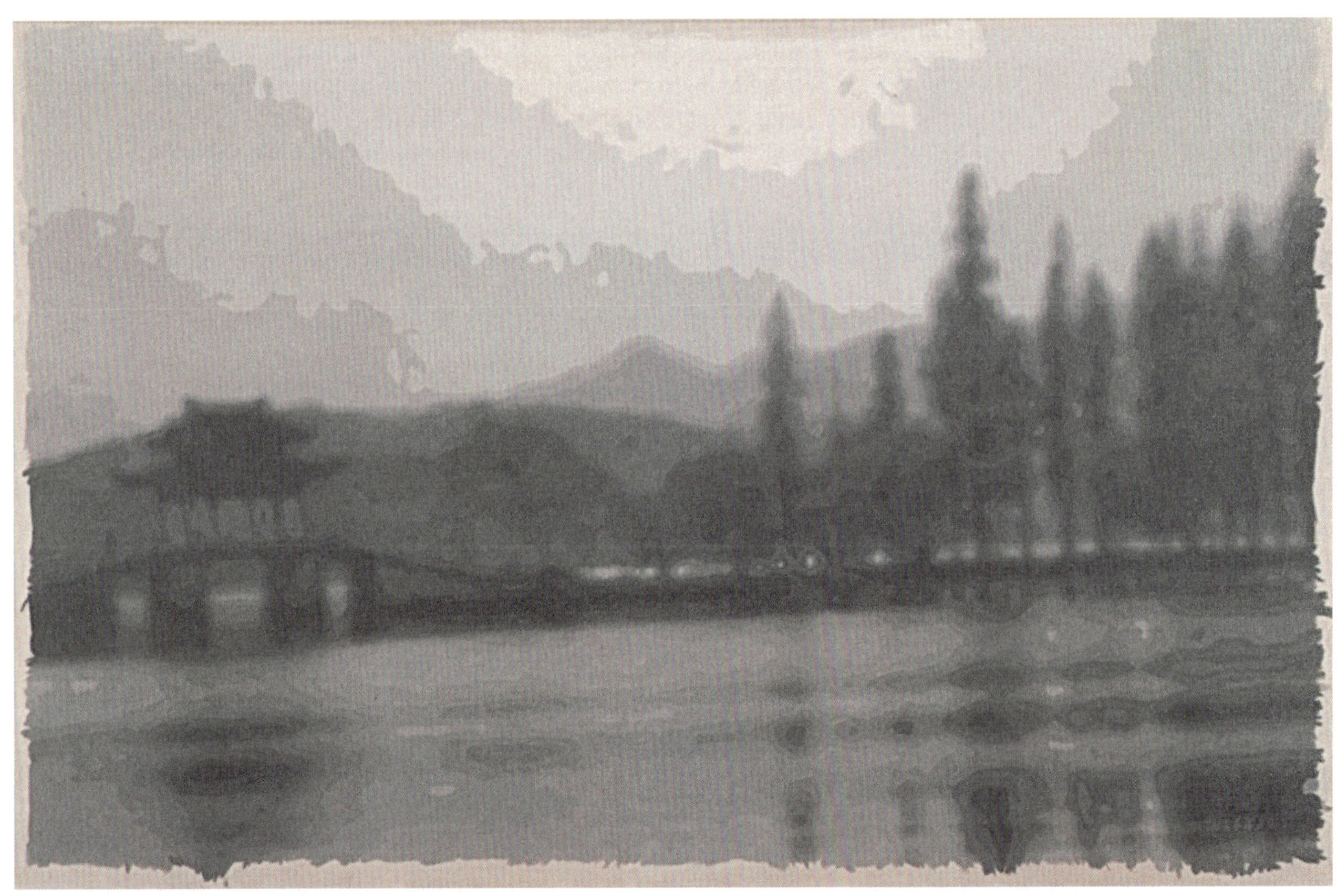

Yan Lei, *West Lake*, acrylic on canvas, 150 × 200 cm, 2001, private coll.; West Lake in Hangzhou was where Yan Lei and Hans van Dijk first met

28 September – 18 October 2001

Still Paint – Chen Danqing & Wang Xingwei
CAAW, Caochangdi, Beijing

Hans van Dijk

Related by Marriage

About a year ago, I courted one of our artists rather zealously, but in vain. As the story of my efforts started to circulate, the Chinese art world proved to be too small. Although many knew of or suspected my preferences, I never paid it much attention. [...] But the affair was so hilarious that I not only received reactions from all over the country, but even from New York. Altogether the tendency was more or less, "Hanzhi, now you are definitely one of us." Reactions varied from, "When are you coming to spank me?" to, "Go on a date with you? That will have to be in a park," and, "When are we going to get drunk together?" to an artist from Nanjing who came to show his new work on a CD entitled "Gay." It was so cheerful and silly that it was quite touching, though far from homosexual.

The most intriguing reaction came from Wang Xingwei, an artist from the far north with whom I have worked for almost eight years, and who has turned out to be the most bizarre and virtuoso artist I know. I think—and I am not the only one—he is simply a genius. He chooses a style, a method of painting that fits his current subject. Each time it is different, and each time it hits the mark. When he sent me his last work by email, I knew that [this time] I was the victim. He told me that he wanted to put this work in a nation-wide exhibition in central-southern China and asked whether that was OK by me. What else could I do? I went there eventually. This time, he used a photo of an over-the-hill popular singer. The photo was a still from one of the star's promotional films. Wang Xingwei enlarged it to 2×3 m. and painted it in a somewhat impressionistic style, titling it *No Matter How Busy He Is, Brother-in-Law Won't Forget You*.

HvD, letter to his family and friends in the Netherlands, Beijing, undated, 2001

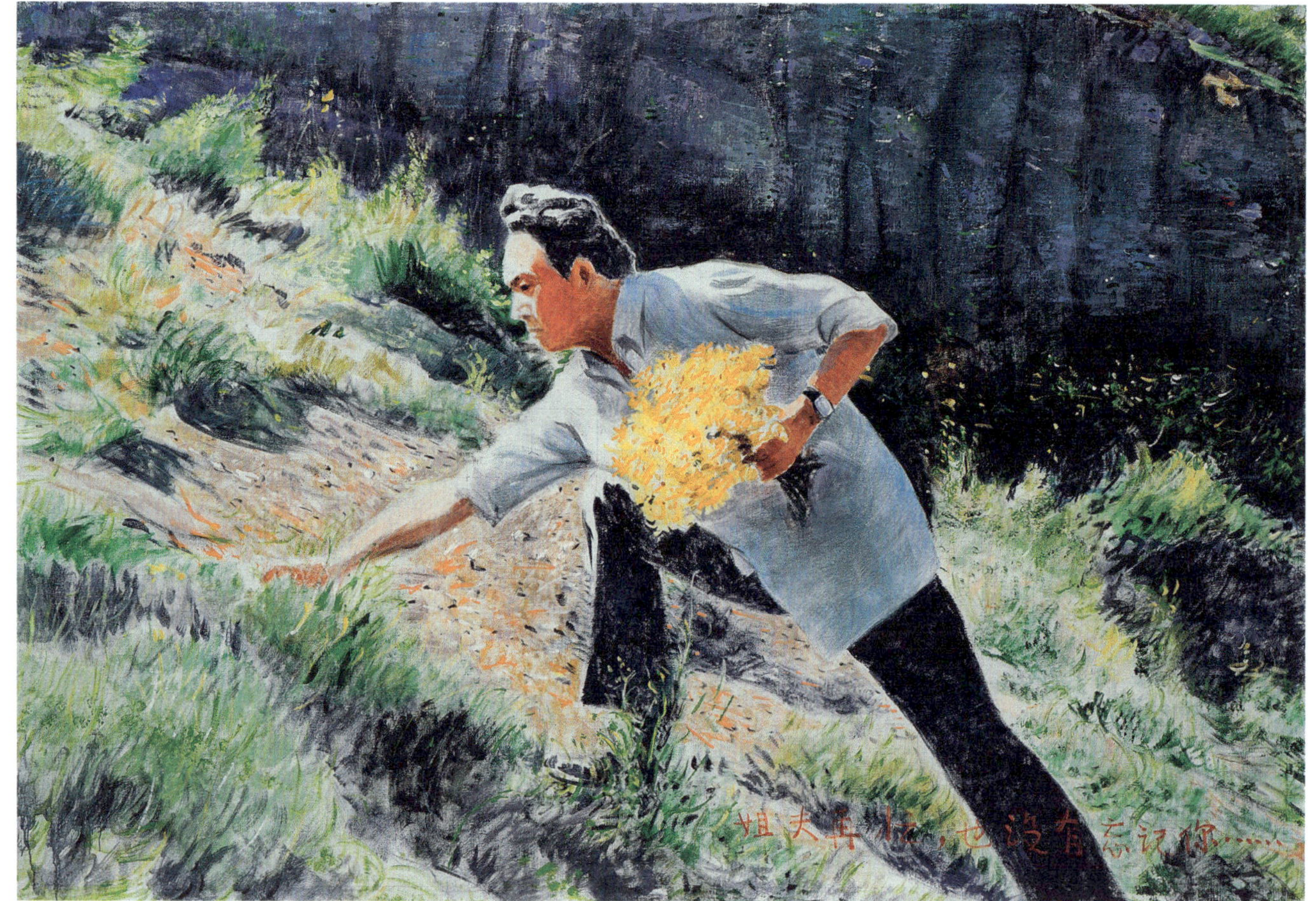

Wang Xingwei, *No Matter How Busy He Is, Brother-In-Law Won't Forget You*, acrylic on canvas, 200×300 cm, 2001, coll. Tian Jun

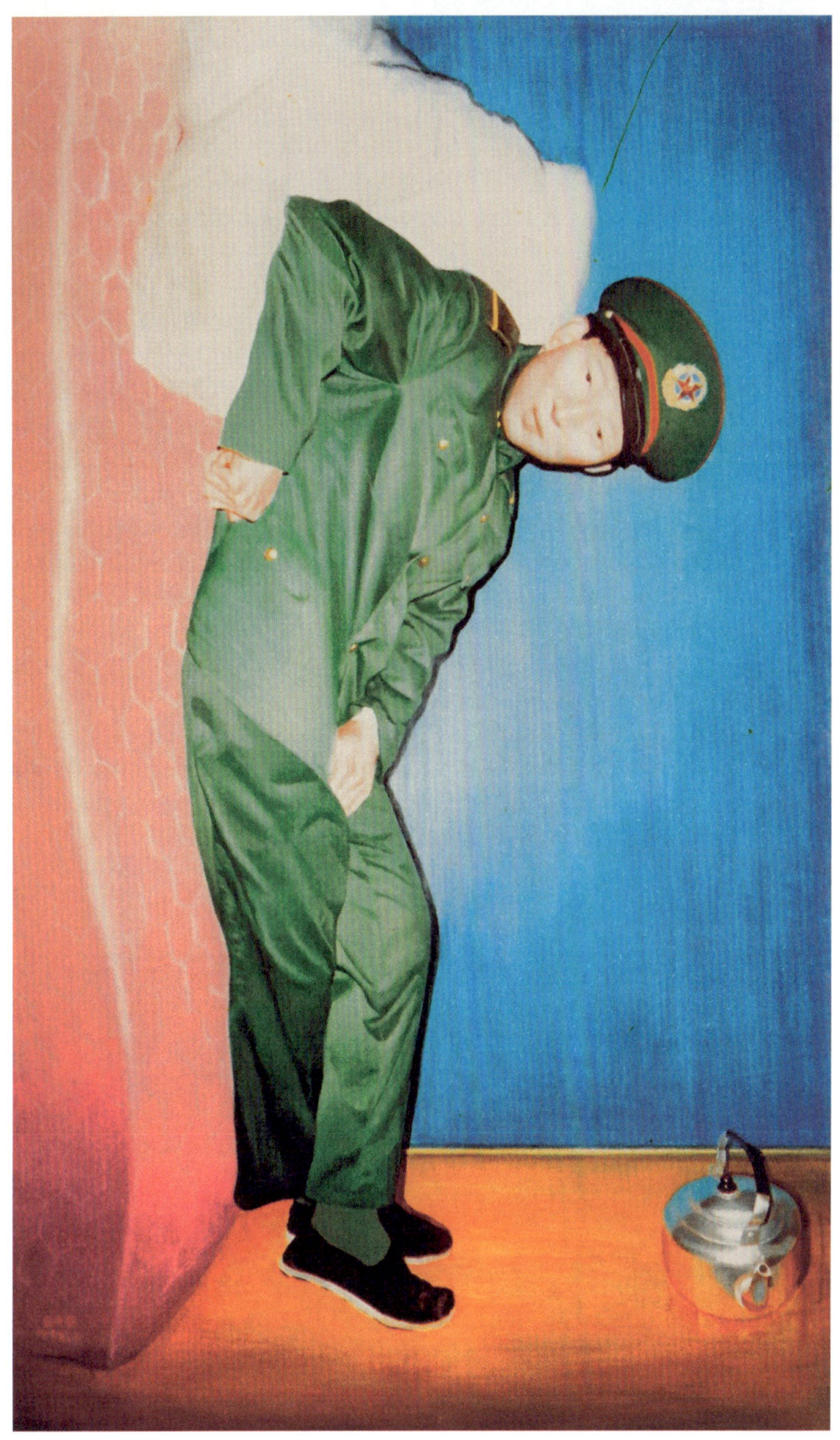

Wang Xingwei, *Recruit*, acrylic on canvas, 196 × 120 cm, 1998, coll. Sinopia East Asia Fine Arts Collection

Dear Ernst, Here's a request for help. Around 1930, an artist published a woodprint about Japanese soldiers stationed in northeast China at the time. The print bears the title *Newcomers*. The same title appeared under a photo with soldiers who are commanded from the provinces to Beijing. It was published in the state newspaper *China Daily* in May 1989, just before those boys were brought in to start their gruesome job. That photo should be somewhere in my papers about that period I left with you long ago [...]. Wang Xingwei, one of our artists, produced a painting a few years ago entitled *New Soldier* in Chinese, which I translated as "Recruit," but it could very well be that he—always digging into art history, both Chinese and Western—has known about that woodprint for a long time. One never knows with him; he is rather cryptic about his work, to which he has every right, of course.

HvD, email to Ernst Dinkla, Beijing, 26 February 2002

Illness and death

Both CAAW and the Modern Chinese Art Foundation are running successfully. CAAW turns a profit for the first time in 2001, making 11,000 USD a month on average. Van Dijk, Xie Wenyue, and Sun Hongbin consider buying a car to save on the huge taxi expenses. They are undecided as to who will take up the responsibility of getting a driver's license.

Years of poverty and sacrifice are taking their toll, however. Van Dijk travels to the Netherlands in spring to attend the 2001 edition of *Fotofestival Naarden*. It has a China focus this year, and Hong Lei is exhibiting. He goes to see Jeroen Vinken, who is surprised and worried seeing van Dijk walking out of the station painfully slowly, shuffling like an old man.[6] His condition worsens over the summer. From October, van Dijk spends a long period recovering in France at the Uytterhaegen home in Le Creusot. He takes a trip to the Netherlands to attend the funeral of his beloved nephew Julian. Soon, he seems to be better; he takes long walks again. By December, he is back in Beijing, where photographer Hai Bo, who has an exhibition at CAAW, comes by and takes his portrait. It is the last of many portraits of Hans taken by artists and friends. To his old friend Deborah Nash, he sends a rather melancholic letter, the first ever to reveal his plans with his lexicon.

6—MB, interview with Jeroen Vinken, 2013.

Refusing to take pills from his French doctor any longer ("that alcoholic from Burgundy prescribed me anti-depressants, I soon stopped that, they made me crazy, let him take them himself "[7]), he stuffs himself with aspirin. He continues working as always, though. He is on the brink of finishing his lexicon—the pages are designed, the frontispiece is done, and all that remains is the introduction text and corrections.

7—Hans van Dijk, email to Ernst Dinkla, Beijing, 22 February 2002.

Xu Hongming, *Extending Diamond in Black 2*, 1998, mixed media, 160 × 200 cm, private coll.

10 March–14 April 2002

Xu Hongming Works (1998–2001)
CAAW, Caochangdi, Beijing

Xu Hongming is one of the abstract artists van Dijk champions. Xu is an ardent admirer of Mondrian, and he and van Dijk share long discussions about Mondrian's paintings. *Xu Hongming Works (1998–2001)* is the last exhibition entirely curated by van Dijk. Two works in the show are subsequently bought by Uytterhaegen and Geulleaume for their collection.

27 April–14 May 2002

WXY
Curated by Ai Weiwei
CAAW, Caochangdi, Beijing

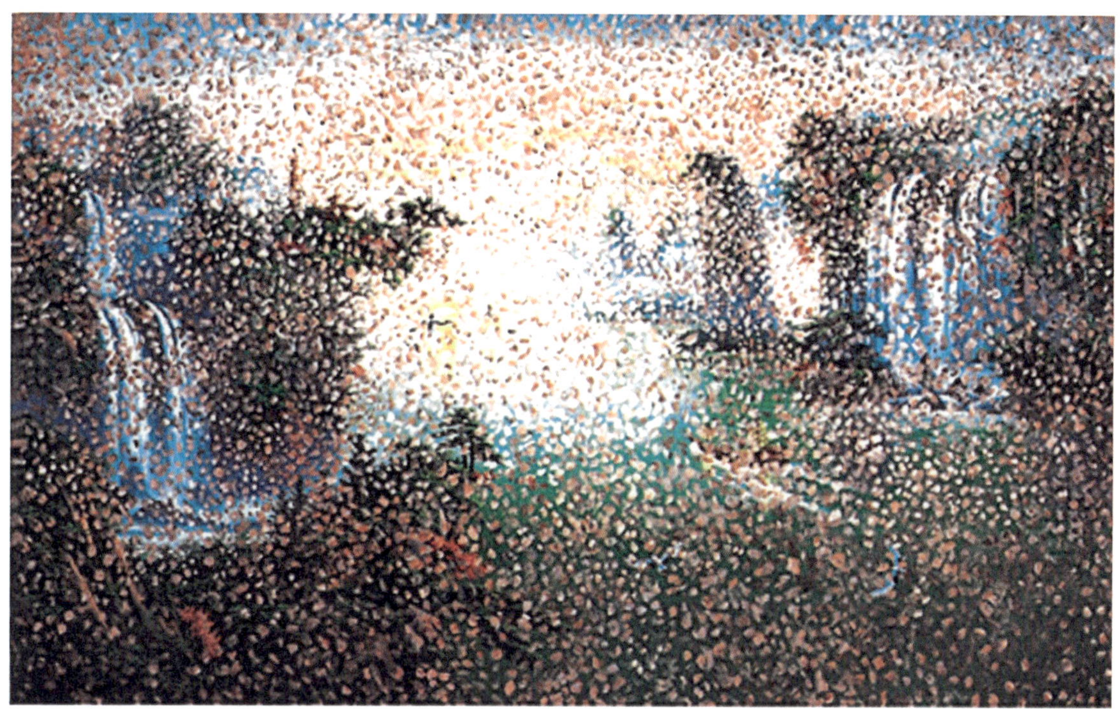

Wang Yin, *Sandstorm*, oil on canvas, 180 × 300 cm, 2002, coll. Huang Yu

The exhibited paintings of Beijing-based artist Wang Yin (1964) are visually captivating because of their fascinating colors, brushstrokes, and compositions, while at the same time they consciously form a unique art historical and topographical hybrid.
Wang Yin painted them in cooperation with an artisan-folk painter working in Henan, who paints mainly landscapes in a popular, realistic painting style.
Similar kitschy styles developed over several hundred years in various Asian countries after realistic pictures, paintings, and decorations incidentally arrived from Western European countries, resulting in colorful mixtures of adaptations and interpretations of local official art with imported Western examples, different and attractive for perspective and color applications, for popular use.
Continuing until today, people in China frequently applied oils onto wood for furniture and architectural use, embroidery screens, pottery, and ceramic tiles used on walls inside and outside countryside dwellings. It represents the vulgar esthetic world of the main part of Chinese society of the last centuries until the beginning of the twentieth century. Wang Yin chose this style to combine and confront it with the newly introduced Western painting art of the twenties and thirties, brought in by Chinese intellectuals and painters like Xu Beihong and others who introduced modern Western realistic and expressionistic painting styles.

Unfinished text by Hans van Dijk on the work of Wang Yin for the exhibition *WXY*, 2002, private coll.

Weeks after his last e-mail to Dinkla, while preparing a new exhibition and working on his lexicon, van Dijk suddenly falls very ill. Because it is the middle of the night and Frank is away in Belgium, he doesn't want to disturb anyone by calling them. He finally phones Sun Hongbin in the morning, who alerts Ai Weiwei and cancels van Dijk's immediate appointments. He is rushed to the hospital, where he is given life-saving treatment for what turns out to be a stomach perforation. Frank Uytterhaegen and Pascale Geulleaume, Ai Weiwei and his wife, and Brian Wallace of the Red Gate Gallery—everyone is mobilized into frantic action, taking charge of hospital matters, medicine, doctors, and insurance.

He is hospitalized for weeks, receiving expert medical care. While his brothers prepare to travel to Beijing, the artists flock to the hospital to say goodbye to Dai Hanzhi. The doctors allow only one person to stay with him at a time for a maximum of fifteen minutes. Outside the hospital, there are long queues every day.

Hans van Dijk dies of complications from gastrointestinal bleeding in Beijing on Monday, 29 April 2002. On 7 May, van Dijk is cremated in the Babao Mountain Crematorium, attended by his brothers and more than a hundred artists from China's avant-garde; in the afternoon, a social gathering is held at CAAW, where the exhibition *WXY* is on view.

Uytterhaegen and Ai vow to continue CAAW in van Dijk's spirit. Three months later, Italian art writer and curator Beatrice Leanza is appointed the new managing director of CAAW. Many artists retrieve their works. Quite a few of them, including Ai, change over to the Swiss gallerist Urs Meile.

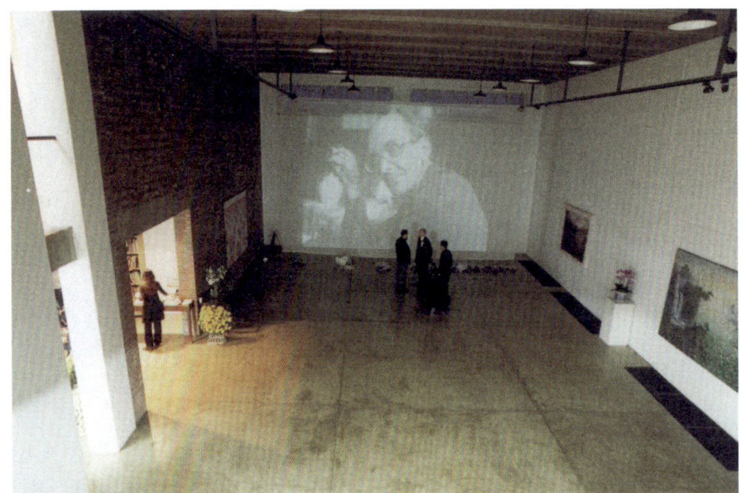

Memorial service for Hans van Dijk at CAAW, Caochangdi, Beijing, 2002; Wang Yin's painting *Sandstorm* hangs on the right, photo courtesy Xie Wenyue

6–30 September 2003

Hans van Dijk Polaroid Photos
Curated by Ai Weiwei
CAAW, Caochangdi, Beijing

When going through van Dijk's belongings in the archive, Ai Weiwei discovers three iron boxes full of hundreds of early Polaroids by van Dijk. Most of the photos were taken by van Dijk during his early years in Nuenen. Ai chooses a selection and exhibits them framed and enlarged at CAAW, and publishes a catalogue in his memory.

> The content of the photographs is light, casual, and ordinary, the immediacy and ephemerality of the Polaroids strike me as being a reflection of Hans' life: a reverie of light and shade, the form inseparable from its shadow, and gone in the blink of an eye.
> Ai Weiwei, "Hans's Photos," introduction to *Hans van Dijk: Polaroid Photos*, exhib. cat., CAAW, Beijing, 2003

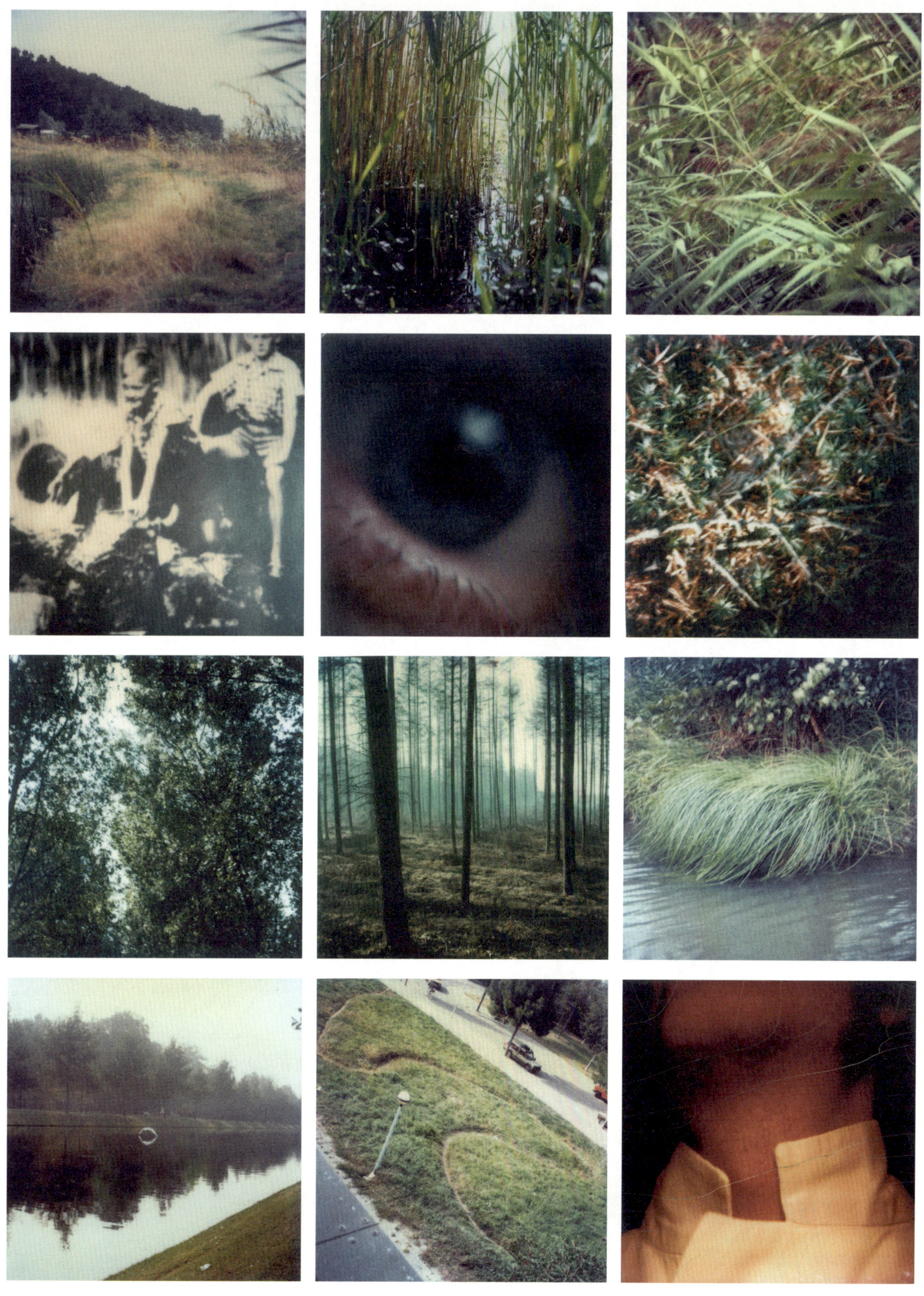

Hans van Dijk, Polaroids, undated, probably made between 1972 and 1989, private coll.

2004

In January 2004, on a date considered auspicious, van Dijk's ashes are buried at the Huaxia Cemetery, thirty kilometers northeast of Beijing, after a careful Feng Shui analysis commissioned by the artists. Ai Weiwei designs the tombstone; the artists pay for it together. Van Dijk's brothers commission three memorial stones to take to the Netherlands. Pieter van Dijk writes in a letter:

> In China, very few people are buried or have a grave. [...] The Huaxia Cemetery is the prestigious cemetery for artists and scientists of repute. That is the community of great spirits where Hans belongs. Two roads lead to the cemetery that go separately at first, then join together crossing two rivers. Rivers stand for riches and wellbeing; the deceased has left streams of wellbeing along his way in the past. The cemetery is at the foot of a hill. Wooded hills symbolize a wealth of offspring: many will owe him a great deal in the future. Finally, Huaxia lies exactly on the axis that traverses the middle of the Imperial Palace of Heavenly Peace 30 km further south.

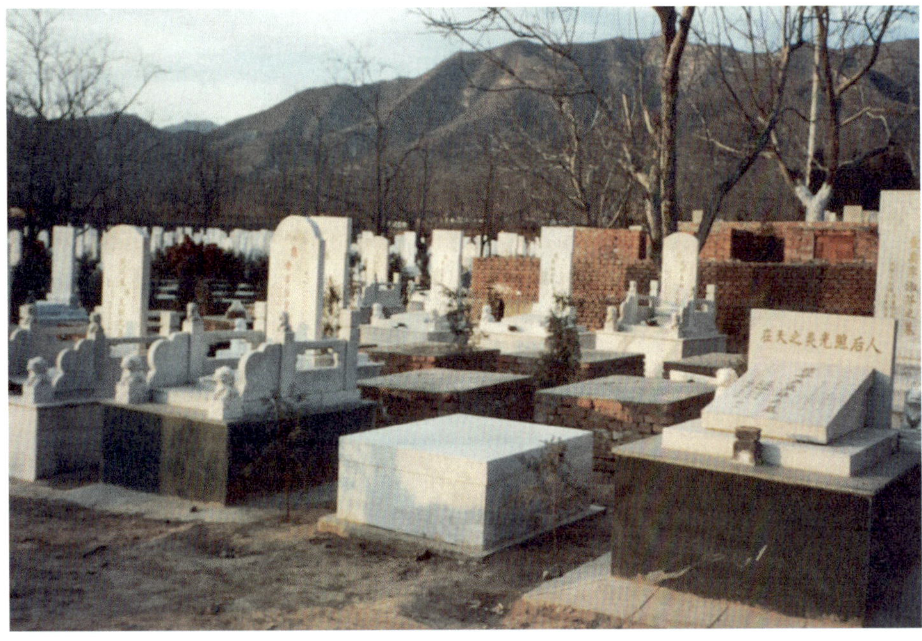

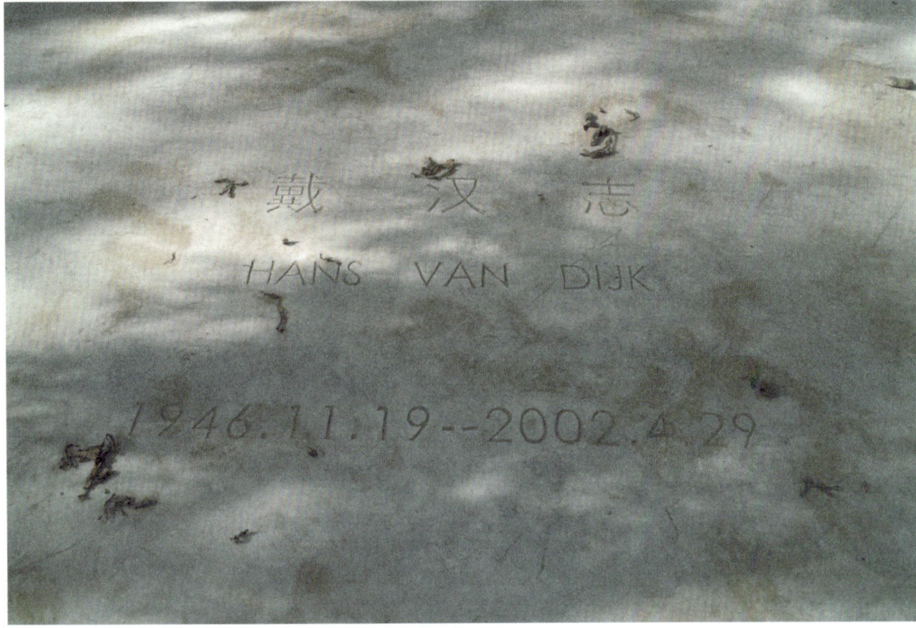

Top: Hans van Dijk's tomb at Huaxia Cemetery, Beijing, designed by Ai Weiwei, photo Zhang Li; bottom: Hans van Dijk's tomb, photo Zhang Li

16 May – 20 June 2004

Persona 3
Ai Weiwei, Ding Yi, Wang Xingwei
CAAW, Caochangdi, Beijing

It is customary in China to commemorate the dead at several intervals after their parting. The first one is after two years. Van Dijk's best friends, Ding Yi, Ai Weiwei, and Wang Xingwei organize a show in van Dijk's memory. Each artist makes a work in the style of one of the others. It is not revealed who makes each work. The artist is free to do whatever he wants with the work made in his style, which then becomes his own work and is credited as such.

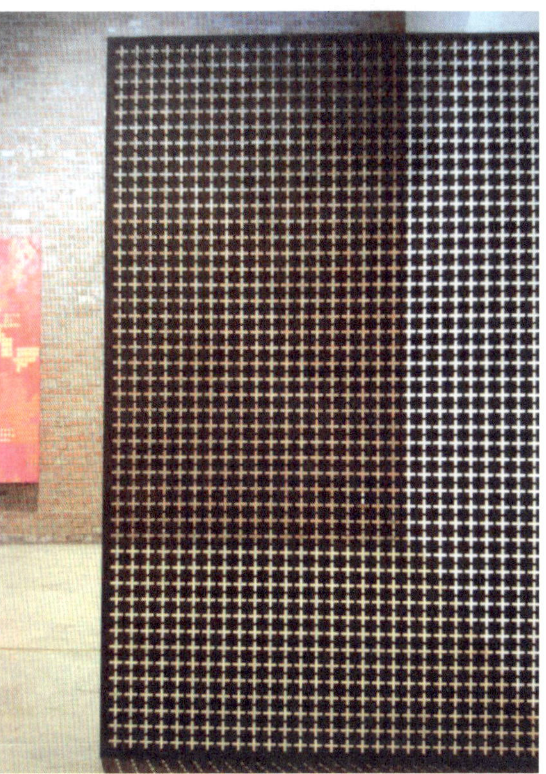
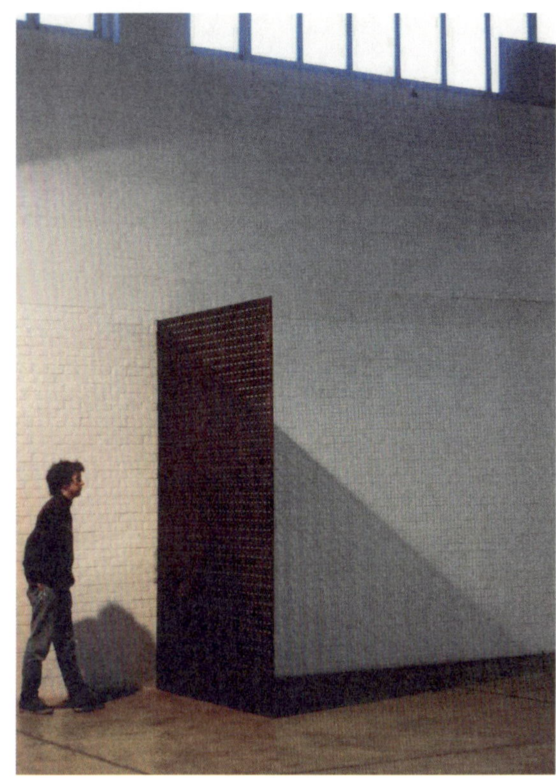

Ding Yi, *Appearance of Crosses*, made for the exhibition *Persona 3*, in memory of Hans van Dijk, CAAW, Caocangdi, 2004, courtesy Ding Yi

2004 – 2012

Over the years, Uytterhaegen and Ai try to preserve van Dijk's legacy. After Beatrice Leanza leaves, however, CAAW and the archive slowly fall into disrepair. Uytterhaegen asks the Asia Art Archive (AAA) in Hong Kong to digitize the archive. In December 2011, Uytterhaegen passes away. Ai Weiwei closes down CAAW for good. Shortly afterwards, AAA begins digitizing the files and restores the CAAW office, which remains closed to visitors. The NAAC/CAAW website is taken offline.

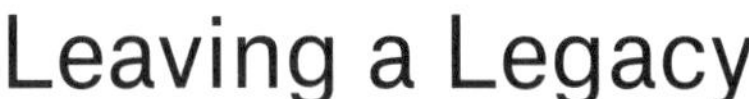

Leaving a Legacy

If Hans were alive today, and his space still running, I think he would be the most important figure in contemporary Chinese art. Not as a dealer, but as a scholar, able to influence the entire discourse on art.

Wang Guangyi

Chapter VII

Dear Deborah,

It was a long time ago that I received your letter. That's why I took a Sunday afternoon off to answer it: switched off mobile, pulled out telephone connections, didn't read e-mail, and didn't care for the mess at home. I apologize for this computer-typewritten letter, but in my handwriting I am very slow. Besides, pens don't offer Microsoft spelling and grammar checks, so every mistake, clumsy expression, awkward remark, or unintended insult is not my responsibility, but Bill Gates'.
Many of the people I know here, from more than ten years ago, are now living in quite luxurious conditions. You remember the dirty, small, packed rooms they lived in, alone or together. Now several of them possess apartments of eighty or more square meters, with all the facilities you can think of. Some have built houses plus studios, and live in the south or abroad in the winter. The sympathetic thing is most of them didn't change a bit. Still the warm hospitality and the same friendly, open approach as ten years ago. They didn't complain about the limited conditions then and are just using the better ones now. Down to Earth, if tomorrow it all collapses, so what? And also, the same energy, like we experienced back then, now brings all this exposure to Chinese contemporary arts in the West.

I'm doing rather well too, bought an apartment using the inheritance of my parents who passed away in the last few years. Five years ago, I met a Belgian businessman and art collector who has been visiting China for twenty years. [...] He recently built the best-equipped art gallery in China, which I run together with him and a Chinese artist: Ai Weiwei, of the same generation as Qu Leilei. Ai Weiwei spent thirteen years in New York and came back to Beijing, like me, in 1993. Since then, we have followed each other's activities and three years ago started to do things together. [...] I shouldn't say that the cooperation with the two is without complications, but that's normal: to some famous artist-friends, I confess "it's lonely at the top." They confirm and understand and hand over a cigarette.

Like many people, I'm a bit fed up with the modern art world: too much what's new, what's hot. Writing this, in front of me are those rectangular aluminum food tins from the Nanjing Arts Institute, in which I used to put cards with dates about artists. Now I'm adding the dates on those cards into a database about artists I started in Berlin in 1991, when I bought my first computer. I know I'm good at archiving. It's not new and hot but will be useful. There is a Chinese expression [about] denying short-term success, "*xiao congming*"—small smart. I believe in that.

HvD, letter to Deborah Nash, Beijing, undated, probably fall 2001

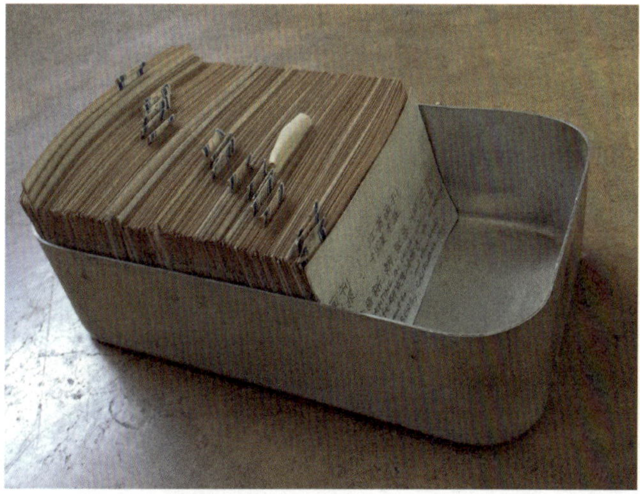

Hans van Dijk, index cards in metal lunch box, 1986–89, private coll., photo Marianne Brouwer

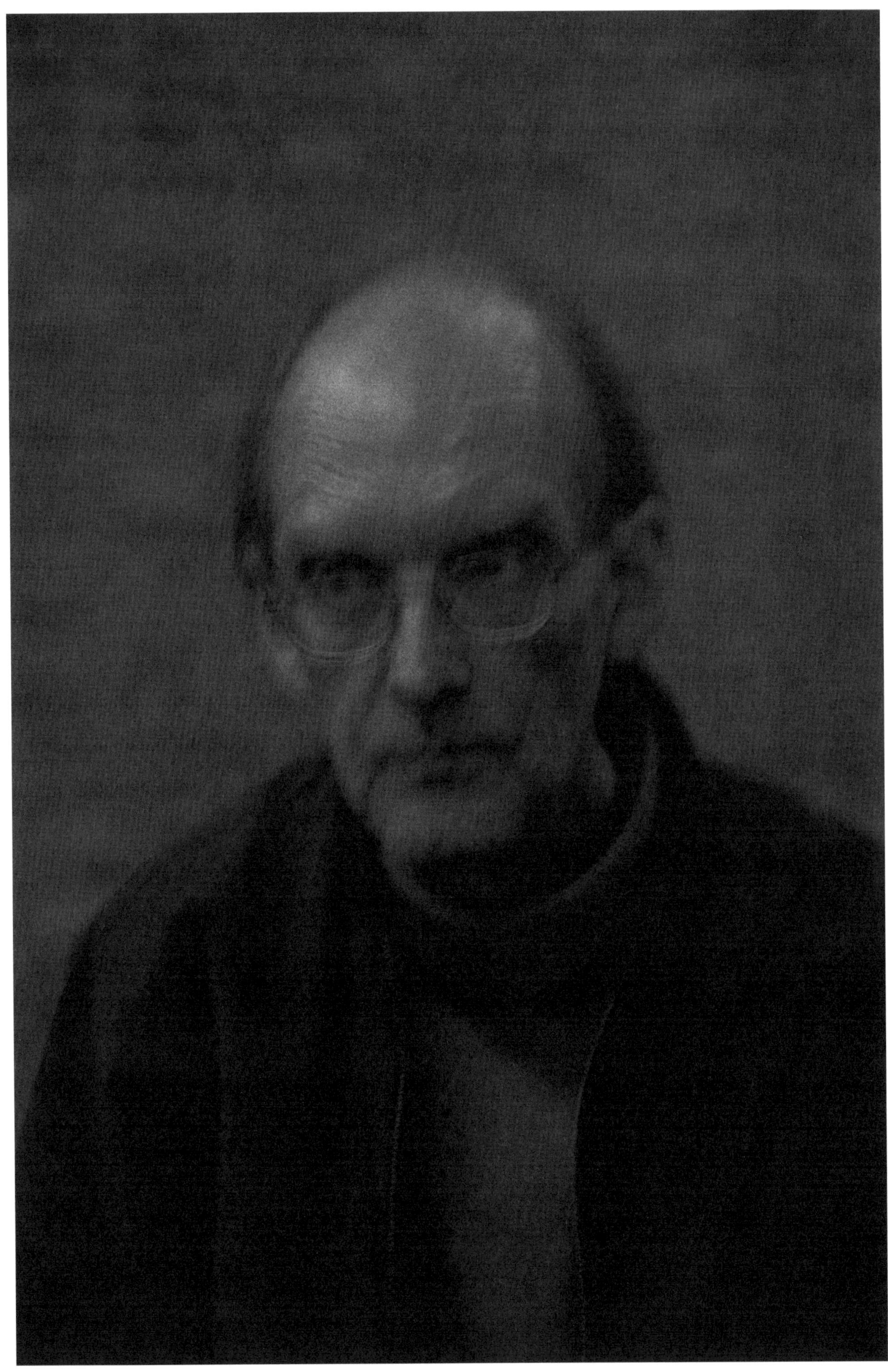

Hai Bo, *Portrait of Hans van Dijk*, photograph, 90×60 cm, 2001, courtesy Hai Bo

Artists Lexicon and Database

In 1986, while still a student in Nanjing, van Dijk begins compiling his archive. A natural-born scholar and researcher, everything he sees and reads pushes him toward important questions: Where does this new art come from? What is its history? How do we value it? This leads him to collect every piece of data he can find on modern art in China. He researches the Stars and other art collectives, conducts field research, and spends a lot of time "pester[ing] the artists for every little bit of information," as he puts it.

With the advance payment he receives for the *China Avant-garde* exhibition, van Dijk purchases a computer in 1991 and begins digitizing his files. As his archive grows, he realizes that a comprehensive compendium of artists would be an invaluable asset to a gallery of Chinese contemporary art. As part of his consultancy, he creates a system of artists' files that allows him to offer information to every type of visitor, and answers to every conceivable question on Chinese modern art. The database is sortable according to many categories, with the ability to cross-reference artists' names, dates, bibliographical references, locations, and media. Art historian Thomas Berghuis, while writing his dissertation *Performance Art in China*, comes to van Dijk for information and advice, and receives a stack of printouts. So does John Clark, a China expert from the University of Sydney. From 1999 on, van Dijk designs specific databases as a curatorial tool for his exhibition projects, well ahead of even Western museum practices at that time. Several digital versions of the database exist, and each has more than 5,000 artists, an arbitrary target van Dijk set for himself. Although van Dijk talks about the ever-increasing number of artists in his database, he doesn't disclose much else, not even to close friends.

The uniqueness of van Dijk's archive is not just the sheer number of artists, quite unthinkable in the early nineties; rather, it lies in its initiation of a historical lexicon for modern China, including over a century of artistic practices beginning with artists born as early as 1880, from the generation of leading literary critic Lu Xun. It is hard to overstate the exceptionality of this project. Periods and people are regularly edited out of Chinese history for political reasons, with modern and contemporary art history being particularly sensitive topics in this respect.

The format of the lexicon and its unbiased indexing circumvent these types of censorship and competitive claims within the Chinese art-critical field. At the same time, his research and choice of artists implicitly allows him to make a claim for his own inclusive vision of Chinese modern art history. It will take experts from many fields and with great knowledge of China during the twentieth century to interpret van Dijk's vision because, in contrast to the usual Chinese art-historical lexica, van Dijk includes artists from all disciplines, including photography, printmaking, and folk art, on an equal plane with what is traditionally deemed high art.
The lexicon is originally meant to be available as a trilingual (Chinese-English-German) book and database. Toward the end of his life, van Dijk narrows it down to Chinese-English. He dedicates a great amount of time to it, continuing to edit. Every day after work, he goes home and enters information from his index cards into his PC, copying the data onto the office computer the next day. At the time of his death, van Dijk has finished the book's layout, designed the title page and key, and started an introduction.

Following van Dijk's death, his oldest brother Pieter, who takes care of his legacy, writes in a thank you letter to friends and family, "The great English-Chinese lexicon, in which more than 5,000 artists have been carefully documented for the first time, is shortly to appear. Hans was able to finish the manuscript just before his passing." The CAAW staff sets out to posthumously publish his lexicon. This turns out to be impossible. Nobody besides van Dijk can make the database work the way it was intended. Moreover, the digital key to access it is stored on his private computer, for which no one has the password. When the office computers are discarded, the lexicon too is forgotten. It is rediscovered in 2013 on a CD-ROM containing the files that Sun Hongbin and Xie Wenyue copied from the office computer just after van Dijk's death and gave to his brother Ronald. Van Dijk's own PC, which could probably have been accessed with today's technology, has sadly been lost.

(Chinese)

FIVE THOUSAND ARTISTS ACTIVE IN CHINA
BORN BETWEEN 1880 AND 1980

Five thousands artists active in China, covering one hundred years is a kind of guarantee / confirmation / pledge of the incompleteness of this lexicon, besides it presents a far from objective selection.

The work started around 1986 and then was only intended to organize the load of information, which like an explosion appeared inside China. Ten years after that - the world suddenly had awoken - the number of publications abroad also grew yearly. I tried to update and also started at the same time to add information about earlier periods from the history of the Chinese modern art.

Result: description periods and where they underrepresented

One person's work, there will be mistakes which I'm therefore responsibly for

Hans van Dijk, *Five Thousand Artists active in China born between 1880 and 1980. Artists Lexicon & Library*, title page, design Hans van Dijk, digital file, 2002, courtesy van Dijk family

目录 CONTENTS

用法说明 GUIDE TO THE USE OF THE LEXICON

例子:Example

Wang Qianwei (f) 王前卫 Beijing, 1975, 绘画, 装置, 摄影 painting, installation, photography *[Priv. Publ. Beijing 2001]*, JH90-9-pp.7,14,19; CT99 2-5-p.6;158 171 254 pp.20-23; 296 p.14; 314 pp.20,21,38, pic.pp.36,37;

(f) = 女, female
residence is last known residence (Chinese)
p. = 页, pp. = 及格页, pic. = 图
文字两个 *[...]* 之间查看个人画册
Text between *[...]* refers to one-man publications
号码两个空 之间查看杆物号码
Numbers between spaces or at the end of a paragraph refer to publication (group-catalogues, books etc.) code.

JH87-5-6 = 江苏画刊 5 月 6 页. Jiangsu Huakan May 1987, page 6.
(Chinese) Idem for the magazines:

HL =画廊 Hualang
MS =美术 Meishu
MSSC = 美术思潮 Meishu Sichao
YSJ = 艺术界 Yishu Jie
XMS = 新美术 Xin Meishu
ZMB =, 中国美术报 Zhongguo Meishu Bao
CT 98 1-5-p. 45 = Chinese Type 1998 Volume 1, Issue 5, page 45.
(website www.chinese-art.com hard copy)

Hans van Dijk, *Five Thousand Artists active in China born between 1880 and 1980. Artists Lexicon & Library*, user guide, design Hans van Dijk, digital file, 2002, courtesy van Dijk family

1

A Budu, 阿不都, active ca.: 1985, 102 p.113;

A Ge (f), 阿鸽, Shanxi prov., 1948, 17 p.284; 289 pic.p.388; 290 pic.p.553;

A Lao (Lao Xianhong), 阿老（老宪洪）, Beijing, 1920, 43 no.405; 264 pic.16, 188; 289 pic.p.197;

A Liang, 阿亮, active ca.: 1997, JH98-2-pp.7-9;

A Lo, 阿龙, active ca.: 1950, CT98 1-5-p.16;

A Man, 阿曼, 1937, 102 p.108;

A Xian (Ah Xian), 阿仙, Australia, 1960, CT99 2-6-pp.95, 96; 21 40 pp.67, 68; 49 no, 159; 212 232 pic.p.279;

A Xing, 阿兴, Shanghai, 1944, 103;

A Ya, 阿雅, Jilin prov., 1957, 31;

Ai An, 艾安, Beijing, 1963, *[Yimen Art Productions, Beijing 1997],* HL97-1, 2-pp.9-13; JH97-4-pp.22-26; CT97 1-1-pp.2, 14; 24 p.27; 98 160 162;

Ai Maiti, 艾买提, Xinjiang, 1935, 65 102 p.99, 117;

Ai Minyou, 艾民有, active ca.: 1991, 102 p.135;

Ai Shizhi, 艾石之, 1930, 102 p.36;

Ai Weiwei, 艾未未, Beijing, 1957, HL95-5, 6-pp.5; CT97 1-1-pp.12; CT99 1-6-pp.7, 8, 9, 10; CT99 2-4-pp.3, 13, 18; CT99 2-6-pp.50, 96; JH99-9-p.9; Sabine "Aufbruch in China", Art Nr. 5, 2000 (p.30); 10 15 16 29 40 pp.42-51; 41 pp.8-21, 37; 79 91 97 104 119 pp.9, 10, 37, pic.pp.8, 11, 36; 189 pp.40-43; 219 220 p.36; 221 p43; 232 pic.p.83; 254 pp.12-15;

Ai Xin Jue Luo (Jin) Lian Xiu (f), 爱新觉罗（金）廉锈, Beijing, 1936, 17 pp.142, 310;

Ai Xiuqi (Mu Shi), 艾秀琪 (牧石), Hebei prov., 1947, 71;

Ai Xuan, 艾轩, Beijing, 1947, MS83-1-p.39; parcticipated in 参加了: "国际艺苑第一回油画展" Beijing 1986: MS86-9-pp.0, 58; JH91-4-pp.18, 19, 24, 25; 36 pic.130; 42 p.16; 52 80 97 102 p.112; 155 160 162 232 pic.pp.43, 47, 48;

Ai Yan, 艾炎, 1914, 289 p.167; 290 pic.pp.339, 464;

Ai Zhongxin, 艾中信, Beijing, 1915, 22 36 pic.46. 57; 58 pic.44; 89 no.941; 97 102 pp.17, 115; 127 195 229 p.7; 234 pp.55, 70, 94; 264 pic.306, 326;

An Bin, 安滨, Beijing, 1962, 24 p.27;

An Hong, 安宏, Beijing, 1963, Lu Zhirong et al., "New Photo 3" Beijing, 1997; CT99 2-2-p.10; CT99 2-6-p.97; 64 94 96 98 119 pic.p.61; 222 223 291 p.182;

An Kang, 安康, 1925, 1000 p.49;

An Lin, 安林, active ca.: 1946, 116 pic.p.167;

An Xiaotong, 安晓彤, 1971, CT99 2-4-p.37; CT99 2-5-p.34;

An Zhengzhong, 安正中, Xi'an, 1934, 71;

Aniwar, 艾尼瓦, Beijing, 1962,

Ba Menghua, 岜梦花, active ca.: 1998, JH98-8-p.11;

Ba Te, 巴特, active ca.: 1991, 102 p.136;

Ba Ya'er, 巴雅儿, Inner Mongolia, 1959, 24 p.192;

Bai Chonglu, 白崇禄, Shenyang, 1940, 57 p.117;

Bai Chongmin (f), active ca.: 1999, 175;

Bai Di, 白砥, Hangzhou, 1965, 205 p.181;

1

Hans van Dijk, *Five Thousand Artists active in China born between 1880 and 1980. Artists Lexicon & Library*, first page of the lexicon, design Hans van Dijk, digital file, 2002, courtesy van Dijk family

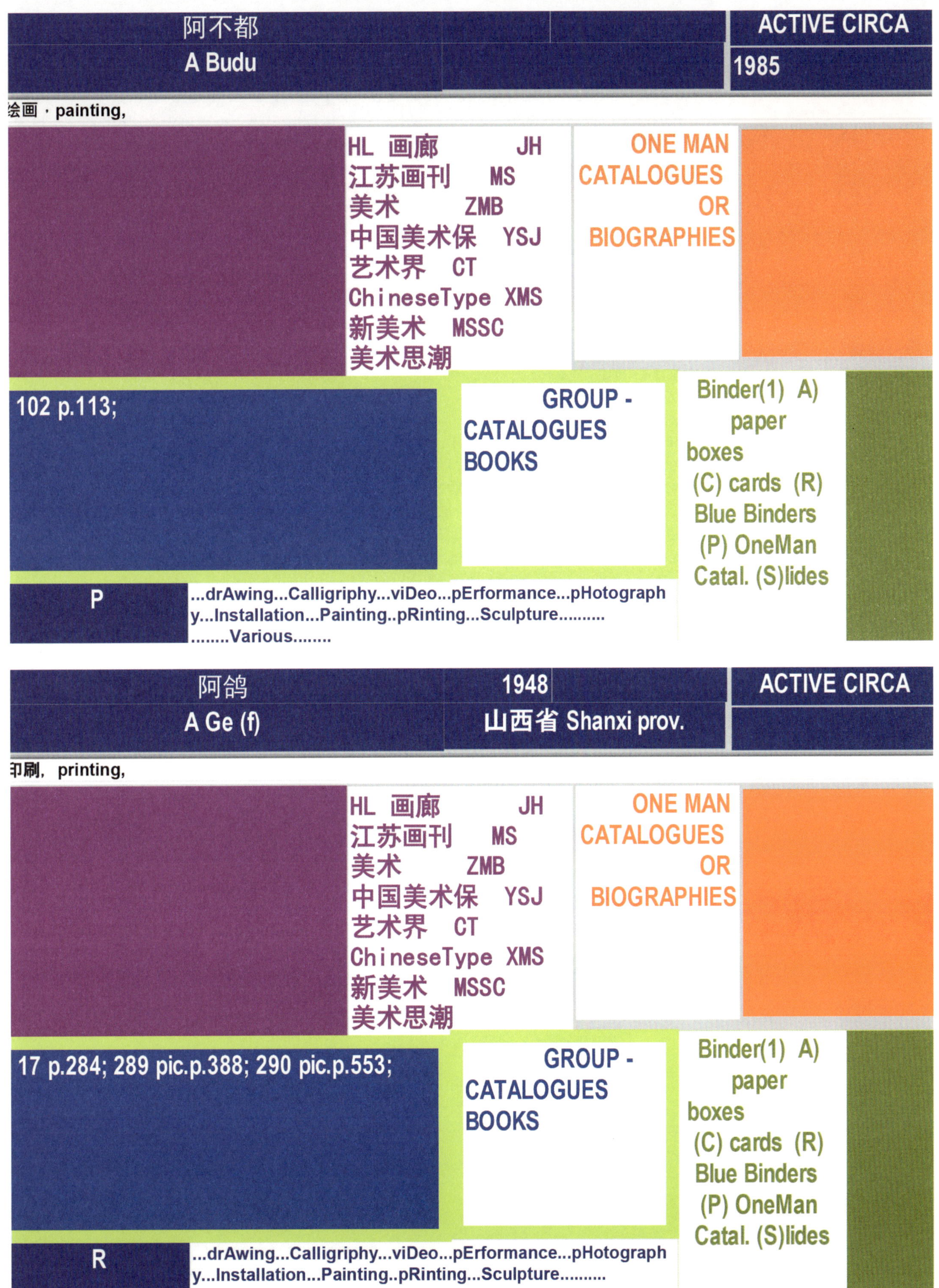

Hans van Dijk, artist entries from his digital database, 2002, courtesy van Dijk family

A New Model for Art Spaces in China

With the New Amsterdam Art Consultancy and China Art Archive and Warehouse, van Dijk creates a new, unique model in China for art gallery spaces. It is a rare model even for Western alternative art spaces. The combination of warehouse, library, and art consultancy pairs an art space that produces and exhibits art with a research center and commercial business.
The NAAC/CAAW-model is a laboratory for thoughts and projects. The tiny NAAC office/apartment becomes the Warehouse office, both hubs for intellectual encounters between visiting artists and art professionals, with a library of over a thousand books and catalogues as well as sixteen years' worth of Chinese art magazines. Van Dijk's physical archive includes 480 artists' files and photographs; his database contains 5,000+ artist entries. All material can be accessed in order to respond to visitors' questions. Two very influential art spaces in China are directly based on van Dijk's model: Vitamin Creative Space in Beijing and Guangzho, and the BizArt Art Center in Shanghai.

BizArt, Shanghai

BizArt Art Center is Shanghai's first autonomous, not-for-profit art space run as an artists' collective in the true sense of the term. It is founded by Davide Quadrio, an Italian artist and curator, in 1998, and in 2002 artist Xu Zhen formally joins the organization as artistic director. The aim of BizArt is to support the practices of local, emerging artists outside of governmental and commercial spheres and encourage discussion. Due to the bureaucratic impossibility of registering as a non-commercial entity in China, the name of the organization (formally considered a company by the government) was ironically chosen to underline its not-for-profit aims.

At the time of BizArt's founding, independent exhibitions were held in improvised spaces such as basements and parking lots. BizArt provides a professional place for emerging artists to create and curate their own shows, thereby fostering local visibility and validation. BizArt has organized around 280 shows and activities in more than a decade of operation, presenting the work of over 400 artists.

Vitamin Creative Space, Beijing and Guangzhou

Vitamin Creative Space is founded in 2002 in Guangzhou by van Dijk's former assistant Zhang Wei and her husband, the writer, art critic, and curator Hu Fang. It follows van Dijk's unique gallery model: an art archive and commercial warehouse gallery, as well as a laboratory and meeting ground for artists. Vitamin Creative Space proves to be highly successful in China and abroad. The couple opens a second office in Beijing in 2008. From the day the spaces are founded, van Dijk's portrait adorns a wall in each Vitamin office. Today Vitamin is one of the most recognized and internationally prominent Chinese galleries, maintaining a uniquely experimental character and environmental philosophy.

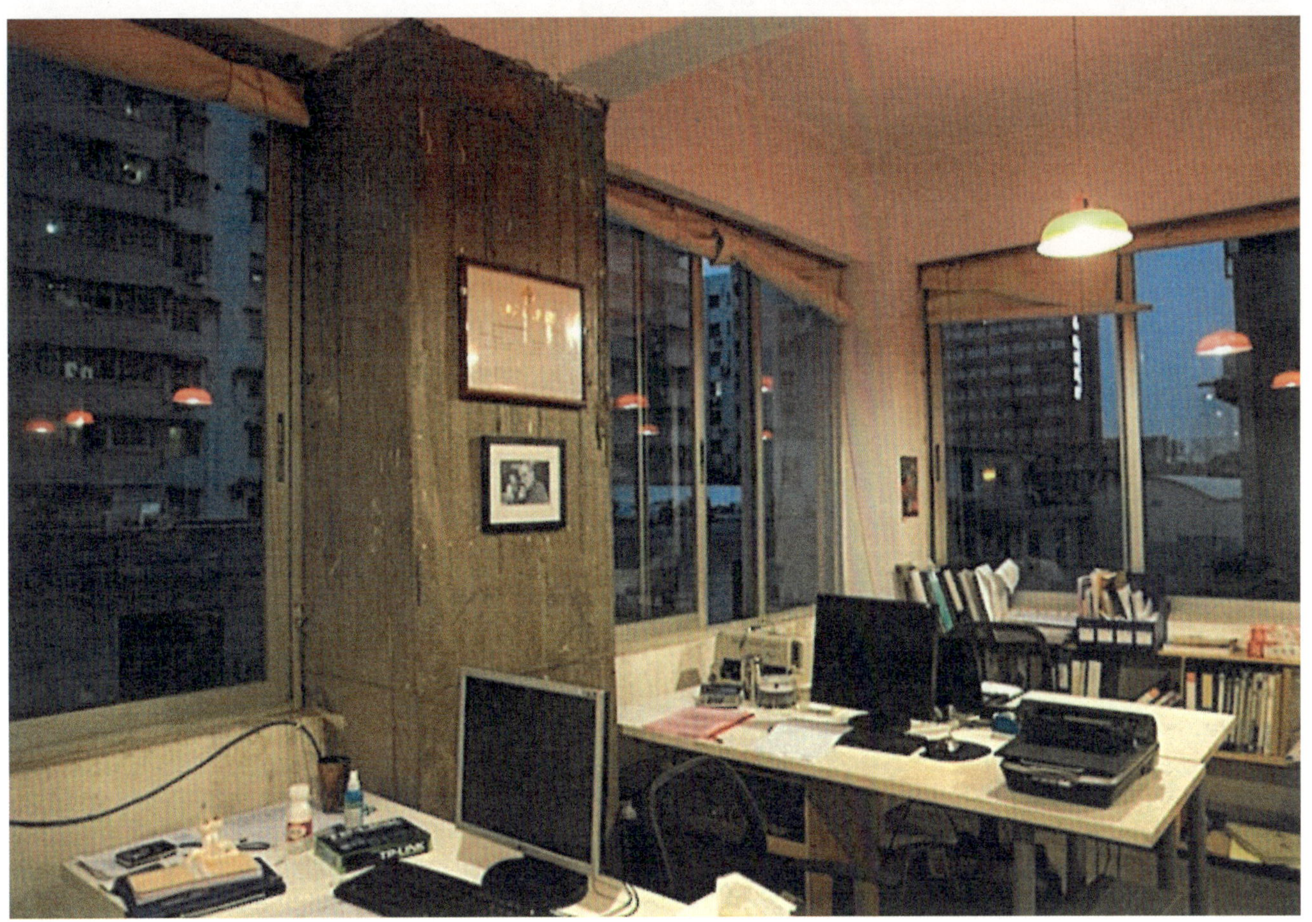

Vitamin Creative Space Guangzhou office with portrait of Hans van Dijk, 2014, courtesy Vitamin Creative Space, Beijing and Guangzhou

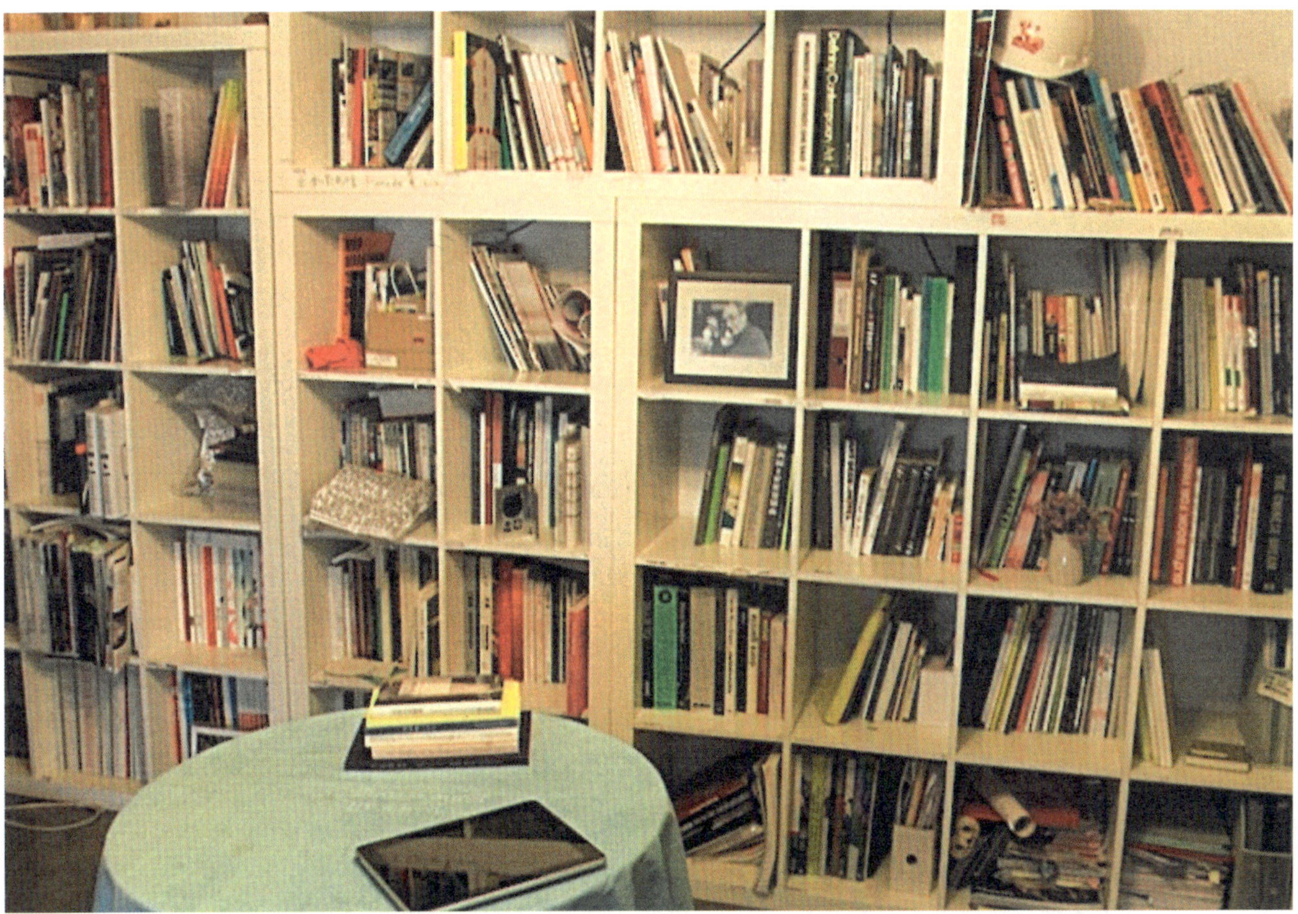

Vitamin Creative Space Beijing office with portrait of Hans van Dijk, 2014, courtesy Vitamin Creative Space, Beijing and Guangzhou

Hu Fang and Zhang Wei,
Guangzhou, Easter 2014

Facing the light you could not see directly
— To Hans van Dijk

Then, you
smiled
slyly, bashfully,
dropped the hand with the cigarette
and turned

In the gaze of your youth
a windblown vessel
calmly plying the ocean's plane
elegant as a piece of Ming furniture
almost casually
bore you to China

in that dream the small, black cat, wide-eyed,
always accompanied you

if winter in Beijing is too harsh
(the suburbs, dead branches stretching like ink washes,
remind you of a long-past trip to Germany)
then you are welcome in the warm South
where at the food stalls friends excitedly discuss
Sartre and Teresa Teng,
post-colonialism, sex and the war in Bosnia
the humid climate may relieve
your longing for Amsterdam's waterways

you stare at the tabletop
the beer glass spilling foam
and a pack of the "Dubaos" (都宝) the artists always smoke

is it
the delicacies of the South that are so intoxicating
while the frozen dumplings, sole contents of your northern icebox, alert you
to focus
on not letting your space get consumed by things
there, faint shadows
thrown upon the white wall
at daybreak
disappear
with the sun's rising

so, in the first light
from a cup of coffee
and a copy of the *China Daily*, you start
to enter
the dialogue with
those times and momentous times and trivial
times and times of serenity and of turbulence
—no matter what
following some Mondrian-like order, the world
gives everything its corresponding destiny
and no one has the luxury of exception
just like night
allows countless naked gasps to simultaneously resist
the pull of history
and eastern rays flatten the rushing pedestrians
into silhouettes
turn concrete architectural pastiches
into historical documents
facing the light
you could not see directly
are the details of life
we cannot overlook
you brought us together
made us become us

with the infinite firecrackers
about to set off the New Year
friends invite you back South
you gracefully decline, as though to say,
"I have yet to become
the person I envisioned"
the photographs you took in your youth
now sealed forever in a metal box
you watch the dead, fallen leaves
and one by one the names cross your mind

there, the sea is still calm,
the coffee in the pot, too, stays calm

P. S. Oh, yes
the Zhao Shou (赵兽) you were seeking,
we found it
it was many years later, at an exhibition
called "Mystical Wildness"
catching our breath, we saw 1930's *Violent Waves* (骇浪)

Translated from the Chinese by Andrew Maerkle

Pascale Geulleaume
29 March, 2014

Hans had taken a special liking to the library in our house. It was a slightly elongated room with a dark wooden floor, cream-colored walls, and thick red curtains. A few bookcases, a couch, and comfortable armchairs lined the room. Above them, some old, withered frames with drawings and pictures of long-deceased ancestors. At the far end were a Chinese desk and a chair with a piece of calligraphy hanging behind. Books and scrolls were stacked here and there on the floor, on a small table, and on the desk. The desk was further adorned with an Art Deco plaster bust. It was autumn 2001. Hans would spend hours in that room, concentrated and undisturbed. Sipping coffee, smoking cigarette upon cigarette, working, and pondering things.

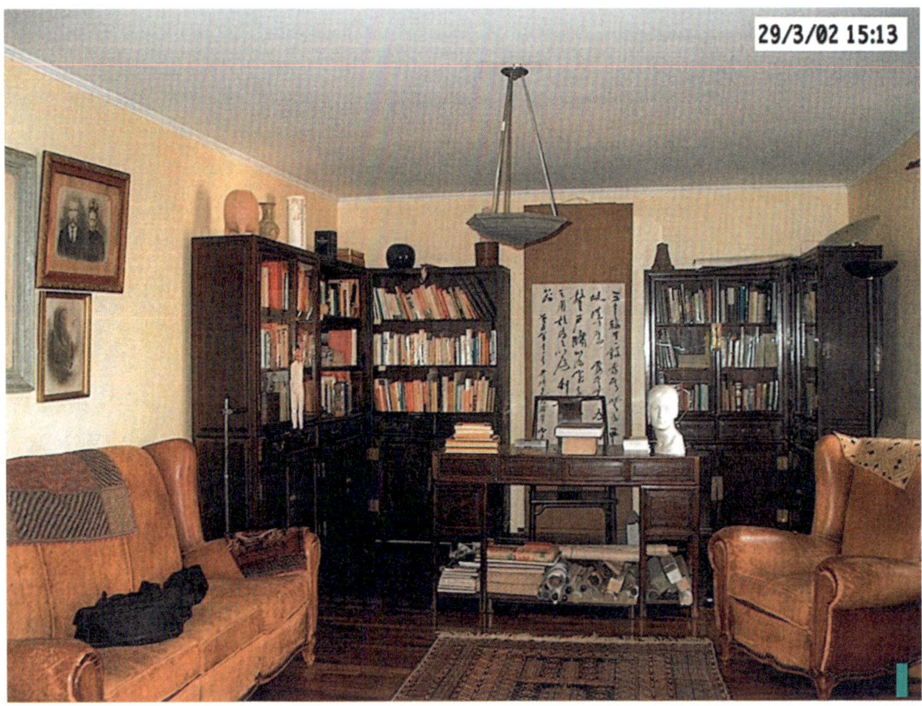

Library at the Uytterhaegen-Geulleaume residence, Burgundy, France, 2002, photo Pascale Geulleaume

On that particular day, our nine-year-old daughter had invited some friends over, and they were rushing all over the house playing hide-and-seek. From an adjoining room, I saw a small boy rush through the living room and dash into the library in a flurried urge to find the perfect hiding spot. I wanted to ask him not to disturb Hans and followed him to the door of the room.

There he stood, halfway in the room, stopped cold in his tracks. Very still, very small. His shoulders slightly raised and his arms dangling alongside. He just stood there staring at Hans, who was sitting behind the desk at the far end opposite from him.

Hans, startled by the sudden commotion, didn't move. He looked very thin, very tall, his complexion white and pale. He was dressed in black and grey as usual, and his hair was probably undone. He looked rather stern behind his glasses, and most certainly quite gaunt. He simply sat there, gazing back at the little boy.

The scene must have lasted only a few seconds, but it had this most particular quality of timelessness to it.

The first one to move was the little boy. He raised his shoulders even further and with a scared tremble in his voice asked, "Are you the master of the house?" In truth, it sounded more like he meant to ask whether Hans was the master of the dungeon or some other ominous abode.

Hans, whom the whole thing had really taken by surprise, still didn't move. He looked like he was trying to catch the full extent of both the moment and the question.

I must have made a sound. The boy turned around and saw me. My presence gave him wings and he fled the room with the look of someone who has just been given a second chance at life.
That left Hans and me staring at each other. We both started giggling and broke into a fit of laugher, and I could see Hans' face mellow out. He had sparkles in his eyes and, as always when he was laughing, he pouted his lips as if to contain the excesses of pleasure. It was not a big event and certainly not one that typified Hans and his intellectual endeavors. Nor me, for all it's worth. It was just a moment of shared lighthearted fun and enjoyment. The kind of moment in which you lower your guard and let yourself go. This is a memory I cherish, and one—amongst many—I like to remember Hans by.

Hong Lei
Excerpt from *Hans and I*
Shanghai, 12 May 2002

[…] We met and bade farewell on the same street, which to my mind seems like some mysterious sense of fate. It was a spring day when Brian [Wallace] brought me, Liu Ding, and others across the bustling Mishi Avenue to the rear entrance of the Beijing Union Medical College Hospital and into the Intensive Care Unit. Hans lay on the hospital bed with his mouth stuffed full of tubes of all shapes and sizes, breathing heavily. His eyes were open wide, but I knew he was completely unresponsive. His labored breathing was aided by a medical device next to his bed. I couldn't bear the sight of it. At that instant, I thought of Don Quixote on his deathbed. Yet Hans wasn't as fortunate as Don Quixote, who before his end could lie in his own garden, viewing the wild landscape in his place of birth, shaded by an awning, recollecting the fictitious exploits of his life. Hans struggled to keep his eyes open, only to see chaos. He was about to die in a foreign land, far away from home.
Don Quixote was defeated by reality. Hans was not—he was ravished by the demons of illness, because an even crueler reality was futile against Hans' steely determination. I always thought Hans was a Don Quixote-esque character: his slender, towering figure and his unyielding confidence in his work were proof enough that he was a warrior of futility. Yet he lacked a Sancho to accompany him in pursuit of his ideals. Some say Hans was a contemporary Norman Bethune; I think he was more than that. Borges, in a book critiquing Don Quixote, said, "The tissue of that whole plot consisted in the contraposition of two worlds: the unreal world of the books of chivalry and the common, everyday world of the seventeenth century." Hans, a Dutchman who thought nothing of traveling ten thousand miles to come to China, had a heart full of ideals, but every day he had to face the complications, competition, chaos, and senselessness of contemporary China. Because of his aloofness, he was very lonely. He was gay, I surmise, because his idealism had always occupied the greater portion of his mind. Adding to that his aloof personality, and for years we never saw him with a lover. Every day, aside from work, he would sit quietly by himself in the gallery courtyard, drinking strong coffee and reading in a sunny corner.
Last year in Amsterdam, I suddenly felt Hans had gotten old. At the end of last spring, after the *Fotofestival Naarden*, a friend of Hans', Martijn, the owner of a gallery in Amsterdam, invited me, Wang Jinsong, Zheng Guogu, Zhang Hai'er, and his wife on a boat tour of Amsterdam, this city of water, dropping Hans off at the train station along the way. We all had a great time that day, with Martijn steering the small motorboat and cutting through the crisscrossing waterways. Hans sat next to me, and I held Martijn's bronze horn, constantly calling out at oncoming boats large and small. I blew especially hard through the red-light district. We noisily laughed and joked the whole way, and Hans never stopped smiling. Later, we arrived at the pier near the train station, and we sat down for a beer at the outdoor bar next to the pier. After one drink, Hans got up and said goodbye. Alone, staggering, he dragged a suitcase towards the railway platform. I asked him, Hans, are you okay?

Why don't I send you off? He said, no, it's okay, no need for that. He obstinately tugged his suitcase along and left without even turning back. I saw Hans' faltering silhouette fade away into the teeming crowds at the Amsterdam train station. My eyes were moist. Hans had gotten old.

Since the early 1990s, Hans was constantly moving his New Amsterdam Art Consultancy (NAAC) in Beijing, all while quietly undertaking his meticulous archival work. Artists and art events, large and small, he recorded them all. Yet at the time, some Chinese critics completely dismissed him. I went to his home, all four walls were crammed full of artists' works. This made me so jealous, and I thought to myself how great it would be if my works could hang there.

Hans slipped away in a way that was hard to predict. His career had really just begun, from the New Amsterdam Art Consultancy to the China Art Archive and Warehouse, first in Longzhaoshu and now in Caochangdi. The hardships Hans endured I'm afraid no one really understood. At the gallery, he often couldn't eat regularly. After work alone at home, he still didn't have any good food to eat. Han Lei had seen how Hans often bought frozen dumplings at the supermarket for dinner; that, along with smoking those shoddy Dubao cigarettes and drinking strong coffee, wreaked havoc on his stomach. [...]

Last night, my mother prepared some paper money, and I brought two of my catalogues. We burned them together [as an offering] for Hans. Hans was never able to see my catalogues. I could only express my grief in this Chinese manner. Because when Hans fell seriously ill, I called Sun Hongbin, who was busy day and night rushing between the hospital room, the doctors, and Hans' relatives, and asked what I could do for Hans. Each time Sun would wearily and helplessly tell me there was nothing I could do to help. And just like this, Hans left us and slipped away?

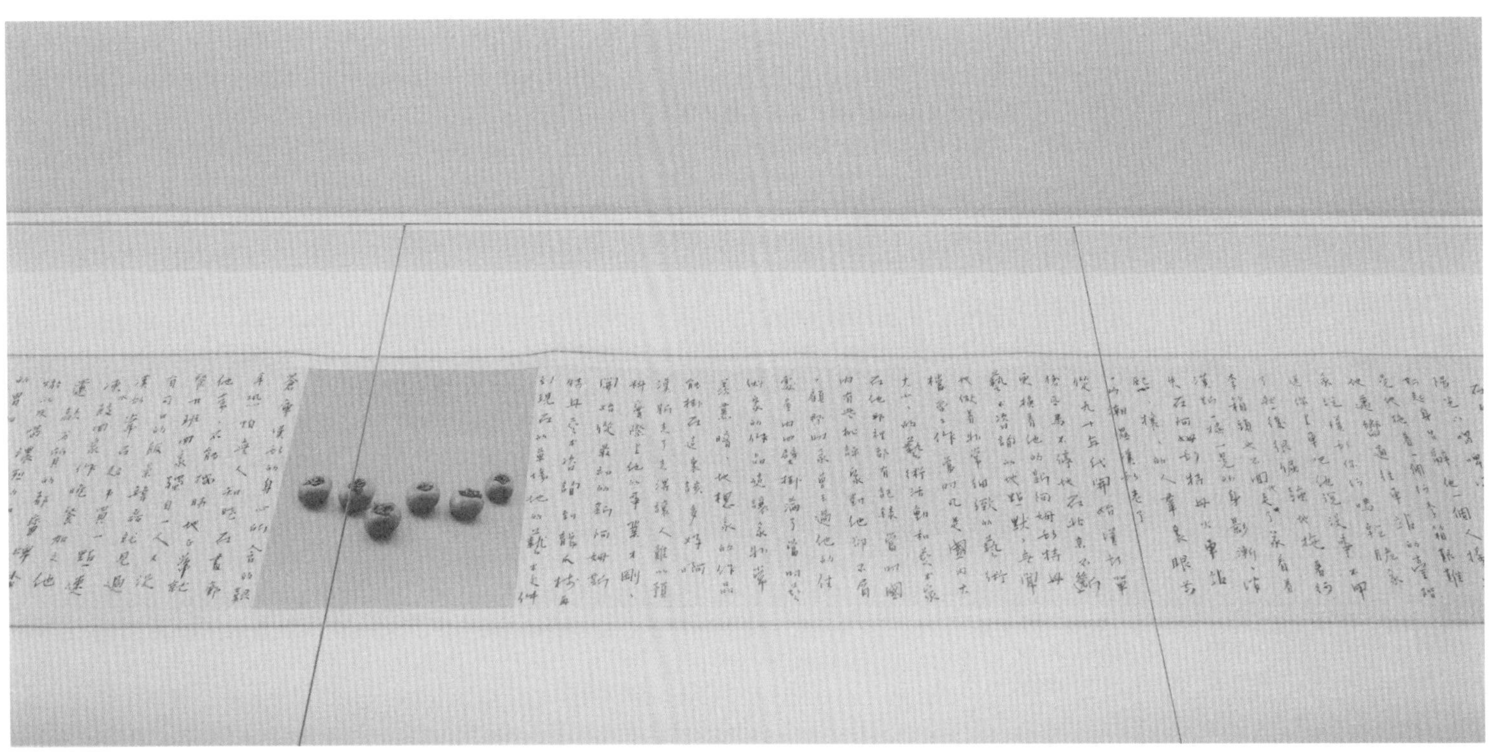

Hong Lei, *Hans and I*, ink on rice paper, shufa calligraphy, 1022 × 40 cm, 2014, coll. the artist; made for the exhibitions *Hans van Dijk: 5000 Names*, UCCA, Beijing, and *Dai Hanzhi: 5000 Artists*, Witte de With, Rotterdam, 2014

Zhao Shaoruo
Letter addressed to the Kingdom of Heaven: Remembering Hans van Dijk
5 May 2002

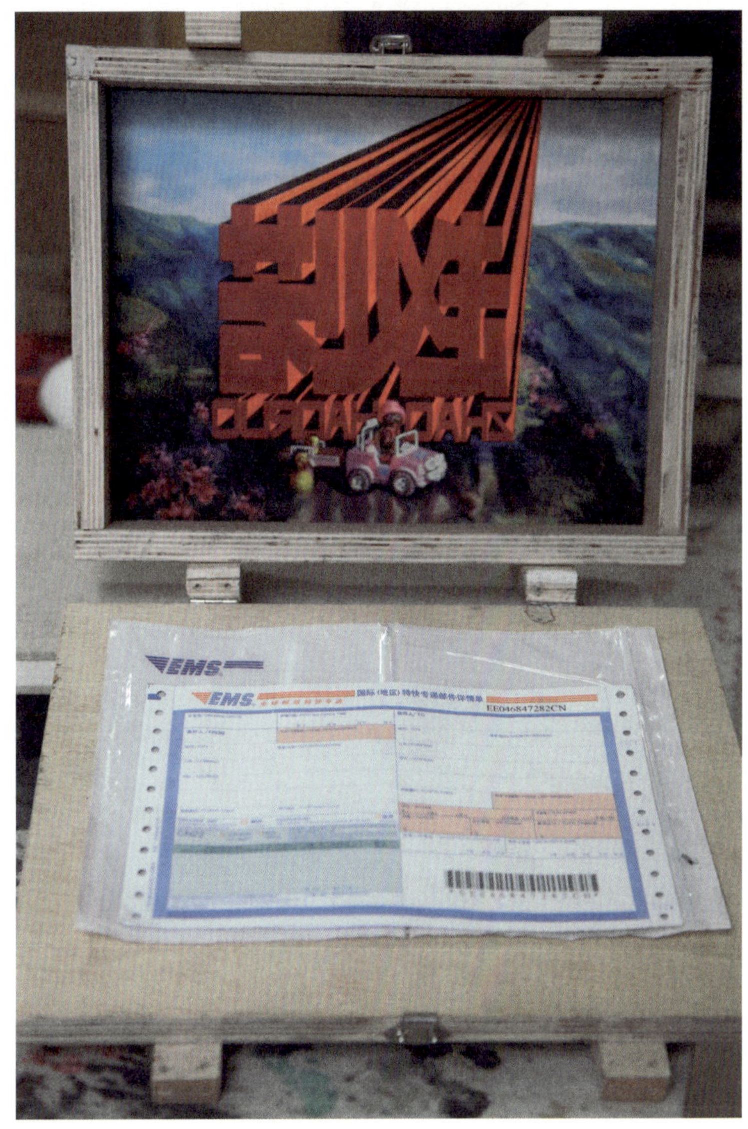

Zhao Shaoruo, *In the Name of Heaven – Gift Sent to Hans*, painting and letter in wooden box with China Post and EMS stamps, 33×26×8.5 cm, 2014, coll. the artist

Hans, Hello! Some days ago, a friend sent you some works of mine that were at her place. You responded to say how happy you were to see them and how much you liked them. I thought to myself: it has been quite a while since I've contacted you. I ought to organize my recent things and send them over, along with my regards. I felt I didn't have to rush, and that I'd see to it after this busy period ended. A few days ago, I opened up my computer to see your email. I was excited, but I also felt a bit guilty and apologetic.
So I rushed to open it, but it was pitch black, and reading further down… I felt as though the long, gloomy northern European night had descended again.
Perhaps you had already heard about what happened to me last year that almost caused me to pass away before you. If that had been the case, I certainly would have waited for you myself, just like how I waited to meet you at Hong Kong's Star Ferry pier in 1997. But now the tables have turned so quickly. It looks like I won't ever have the chance to greet you again.
It was about 1993 when you rushed back to Holland for your father's funeral. You returned only after quite some time. One time after you came back, we were out for a meal together. We were joking with you and asked if your father left an inheritance, a will,

some final words, or whatnot. You said there were a few final words, just one sentence. You told us how your father beckoned you to his deathbed and said, "Hans, you must also go to see God." We said, "Really?" You said, "Perhaps. Who knows!"

From the second half of 1996 through the first half of 1997, you often had to go to Hong Kong because of visa problems. For a while, you came almost every two weeks. Each time you would stay at my place, and each time we'd chat quietly. I remember that each time you came, I would routinely prepare your mattress, towel, slippers, and whatnot. As soon as you arrived, you always would take a cold shower, eat, and then go for a stroll at Hung Shing Yeh Beach. The last time you came, I had a little puppy who loved to harass people. You didn't like it, but you just said to it dead seriously, "Go away, will you? We are not friends." I remember the last time I sent you off back to mainland China. You said you were feeling a bit cold, so I got a jacket and insisted that you wear it. You couldn't deter me, so you put it on. [...] In Sheung Shui on your way to the Lo Wu border crossing, you were set on taking the jacket off and returning it before we parted. Your reason was it would be hot in Guangzhou, so I ended up wearing it and sweating the whole way home. I remembered thinking I would definitely mention this the next time you came. Who knew this would be the final farewell...

I can't remember how many times we talked about that passport of yours, your visa in constant need of renewal. Yet you would never tire of it, waiting for when you could return to Beijing. We joked that if one day [the world] were no longer divided by states and nations, we would be completely free of visas.

Of course, accompanying us on each stroll was the beach in the afternoon sun, the meandering path between the ridges, the sea breeze whirling among the coconut trees, and an endless expanse of wilderness blanketed in golden blooms. I always said it was just like the May Seventh Cadre School, where my father spent time when I was little. You said it was even more like your native Holland. I once asked you why you liked it here so much. You just murmured, "It's quiet here." We firmly believed that when we were truly old and couldn't do anything, we would come and live here. Our custom was to quietly walk and talk facing the setting sun at dusk. All this is in the past now, yet it seems just like yesterday, right in front of our eyes. Our shared ideal has become an unreachable dream.

Perhaps, Hans, you are already there. We all firmly believe that where you're going is a land with no need for a visa. We have faith that because of your personality, you'll still be sitting in front of a window with soft sunlight pouring in, your desk strewn with proposals and sample works. Next to a dangerously hot cup of coffee, you will meticulously categorize them and think of ways to exhibit them in some site in the universe outside of the world of man or hell. It's true, you certainly will continue doing this; otherwise you wouldn't be you. You will soon meet new friends from all around, as well as a few old friends from the past. Come to think of it, it seems we don't need to feel so insecure or afraid; even if things end in failure or lack of accomplishment, as long as there is the will to live for the sake of art, for an honest view of life, for our once-held dreams, for freedom and everything, then we will follow to where you are, we will continue collaborating with you. We all believe that where you are, there certainly won't be too many troubles or manmade pain, which shouldn't exist in the first place. Even if you smoke more cigarettes, drink more liquor, and never sleep or eat, you will still be healthy. At least the demons of illness will never have any luck with you, and pain and sadness will never reappear. Not only this, you will also never again walk alone, as your companions will be greater and greater in number. Go in peace, Hans!

Duan Jianyu
A Treasure Left in the Mundane
2014

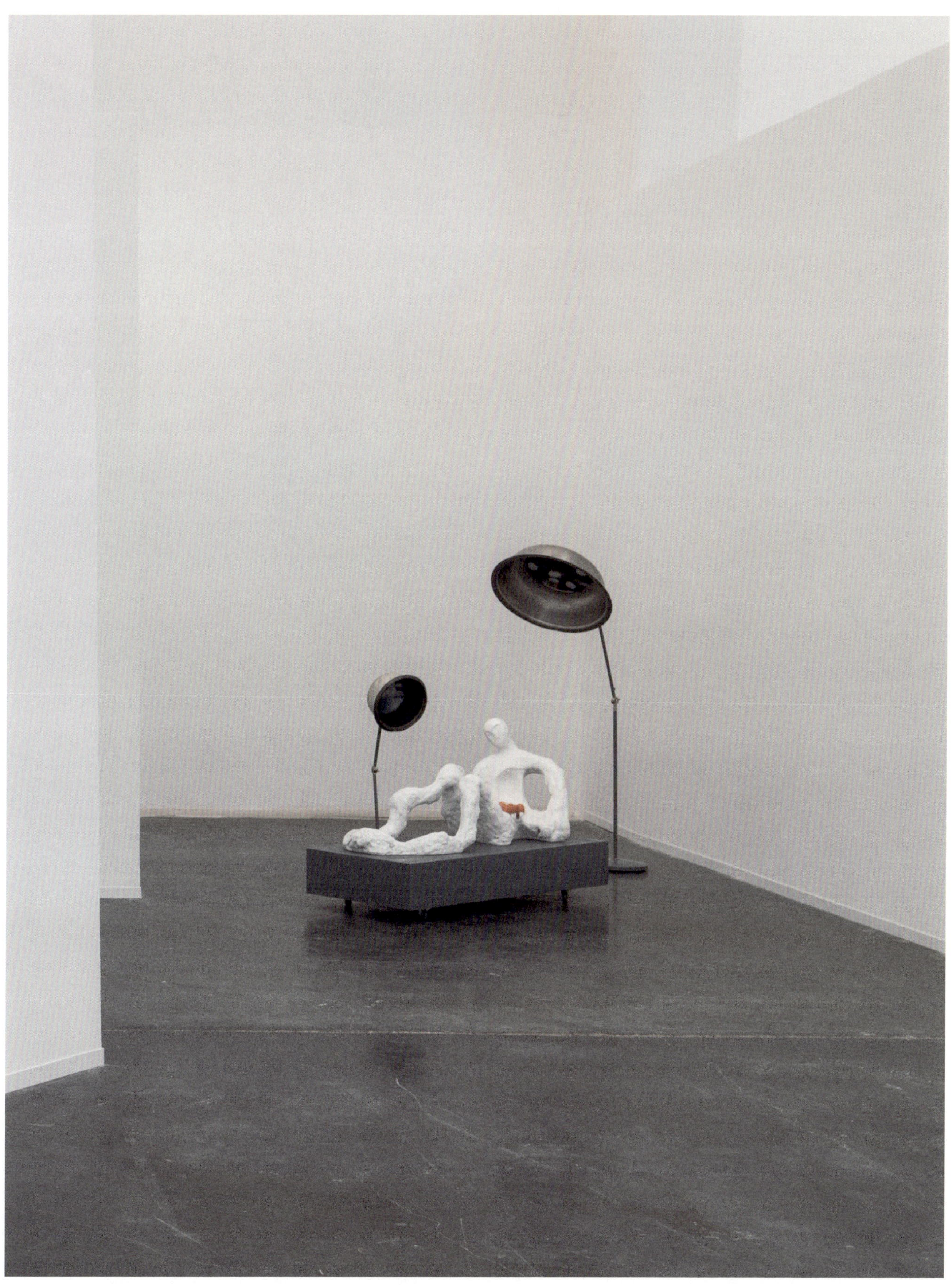

Duan Jianyu, *A Treasure Left in the Mundane*, fiberglass, egg carton with eggs, lamps painted on the inside, 130 × 60 × 54 cm, 2014, courtesy Duan Jianyu and Vitamin Creative Space, Beijing and Guangzhou; the artist made this work especially for *Hans van Dijk: 5000 Names*, UCCA, 2014

Sun Kai
Remembrance of Hans
3 April 2014

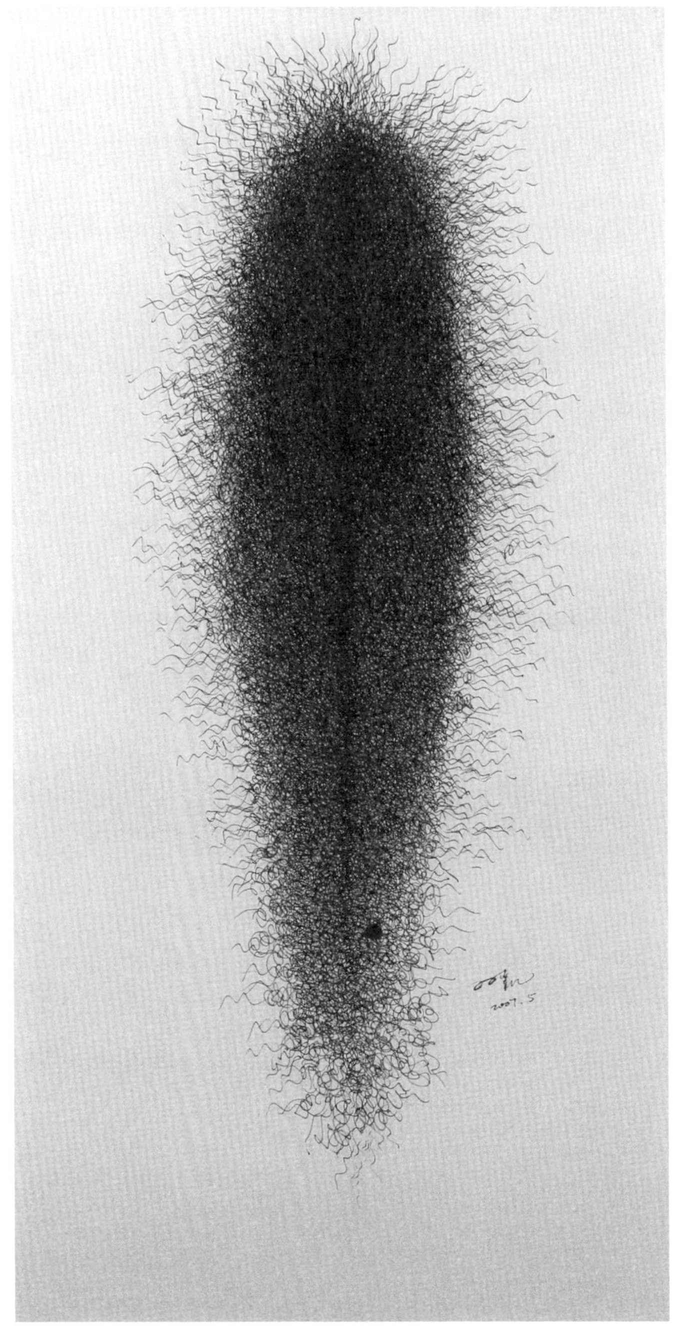

Sun Kai, *Untitled*, carbon ink on paper, 137×69 cm, 2007, coll. the artist

On the afternoon of 17 May 1995, I printed some photos of a set of paintings. On 2 June, Hans and Zhang Li came to my place to see the originals and were quite interested. At the time, he intended to recommend me for the Chinese art exhibition to be held in Munich in 1996, but I didn't manage to participate in the end. Hans explained to me that it was not up to him alone to decide. My understanding was my works were not good enough to meet the requirements. I also knew very few people liked my experimental works on paper. Hans was the only one who approved of my works. Never did he show any doubt or hesitation about the value of my work. Hans always expressed interest in my work from the very beginning, even though no other people accepted me. That was when everything started, from scratch. Hans would travel a long way on a crowded bus to visit the artists he wanted to meet. He never asked me to come to his place with my works. Later, I moved to a place owned by Old Shan in Shijingshan, which was actually very far from the city. Hans still came to see me and my work. The first time he came to my home, sitting on my Simmons mattress on the floor, he said he also found a place to live, eyes shining with excitement. He was trying to rent a house at that time. I didn't say anything, just gave him a suspicious glance. I didn't think he was serious, because he would occasionally joke with people. His humor was quite pleasant. [...] I often miss Hans. Thin and a little hunchbacked, he was always staring ahead of himself. It seemed he had something to bear. Was it hardship? This is supposed to be carried by us. Was it doubt? Or sympathy? I could feel the shining love in his eyes, which convinced me that life is beautiful. Such beauty can only be brought by a saint, a good heart. His goodness was expressed through his eyes, as well his hands, those soft hands. He only enlightened and guided people, without any interference. This is also soft, and full of love. Like his heart, his hands are nimble, good at working. I miss him a lot sometimes, and also worry about him. He could never live without cigarettes, black coffee, or beer. Sitting in a chair under the sun and staring out, he grew depressed, slow, and weak. In 2002, I was on a performing tour with my colleagues in the theater for two months. In Shanghai, I was told the news that Hans was severely ill and was in hospital. I was very anxious. Later, I heard he had passed away. I even missed his memorial service. What I could do was donate some money to help build his headstone. I feel very sorry every time I think about it. In my diary, I wrote down my deep sorrow, which I can hardly contain.

Zheng Guogu
Hans' brain
2014

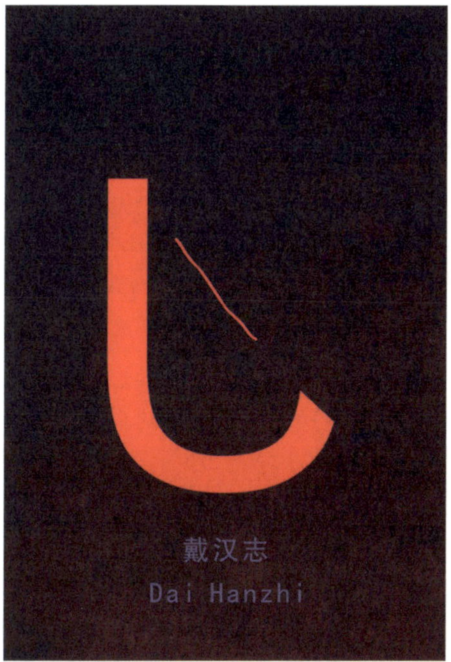

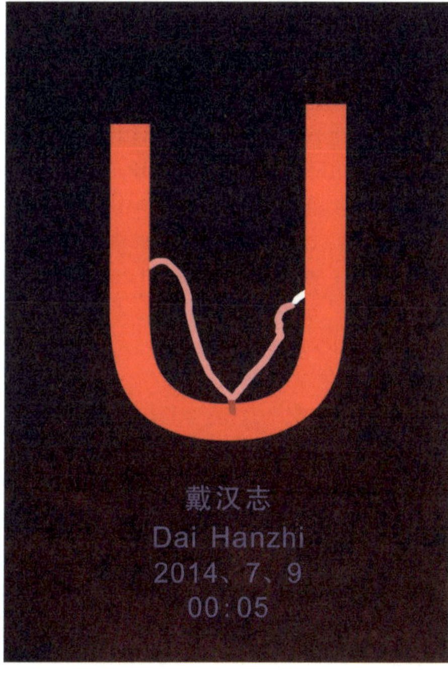

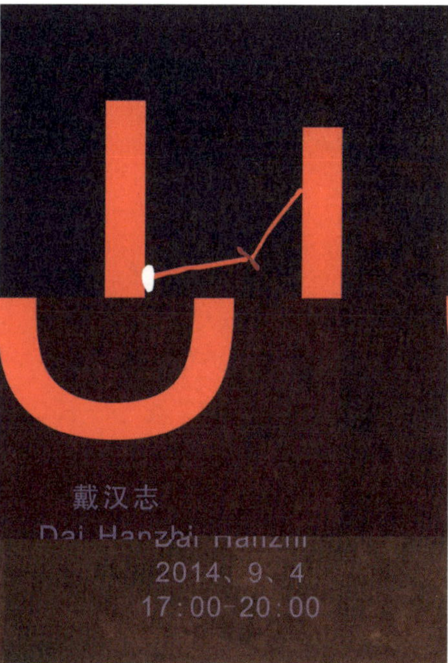

Zheng Guogu, *Hans' brain*, three digital prints, 2014, courtesy Zheng Guogu

In 2006, Zheng Guogu started a series of works entitled *Computer Controlled by Pig's Brain*. In contrast, he also began a series of paintings portraying the insides of wholly original minds or brains, including those of Leonardo da Vinci, Joseph Beuys, and Marcel Duchamp. The portraits of van Dijk's brain are the latest addition to the series and Zheng's personal contribution to the exhibitions dedicated to van Dijk's legacy at the Ullens Center for Contemporary Art in Beijing and Witte de With Center for Contemporary Art in Rotterdam.

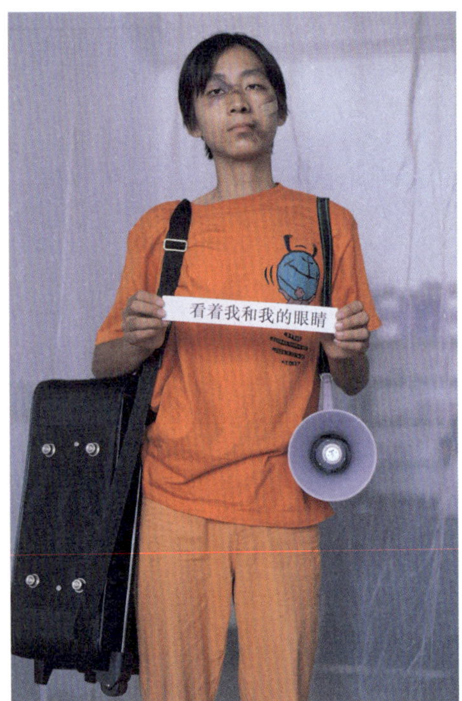

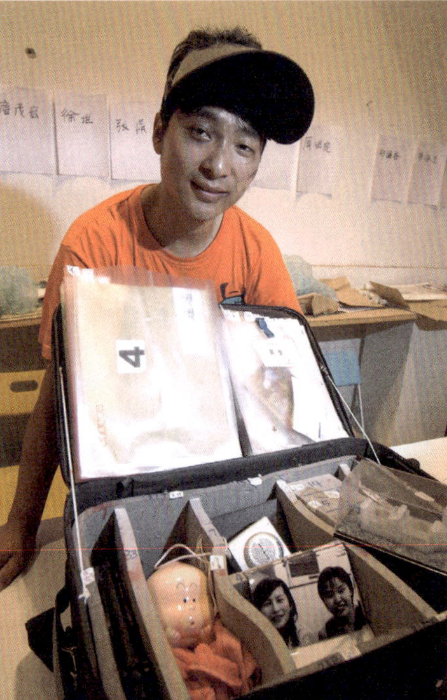
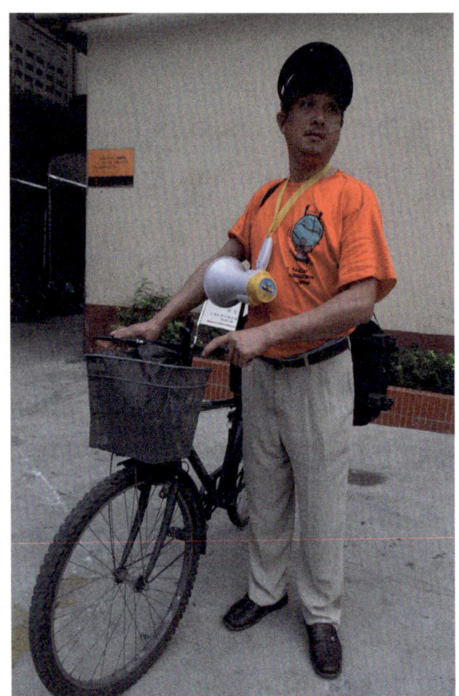

Couriers and participants during *62761232*, Shanghai, 2004, photos courtesy Quadrio and Shi Yong

Davide Quadrio and Shi Yong
62761232
2004

For *Dai Hanzhi: 5000 Artists*, at Witte de With in 2014, Davide Quadrio and artist Shi Yong contributed extensive original materials from *62761232*, a BizArt project from 2004. *62761232* was a "portable" exhibition involving artists and couriers from a local messenger service. The couriers were taught to do a performance, explain a conceptual work, and exhibit contemporary artworks. When someone called the titular phone number, a courier brought them a suitcase filled with pocket-sized artworks made especially for this project. As a tribute to van Dijk, Davide Quadrio and Shi Yong reconstructed the suitcase and its contents in a dedicated exhibition space at Witte de With, alongside videos and photographs of the performances.

Exhibition Statement:
62761232 is the telephone number for a courier in Shanghai. From September 10th to September 20th, from 10am to 10pm, no matter where you are in the city, you will be able to have an exhibition brought to you.
What is the position of contemporary art in Shanghai? In this landscape of economic and social changes, contemporary art is under a continuous change. With this unusual art event, we break the common exhibition mode. This exhibition is curated by a team of artists from Shanghai and will collect artworks from 40 artists from all around China.
Participating artists: Ba Zhenlong, Fei Dawei, Chen Shaoxiong, He An, Xu Tan, Xiang Liqing, Fan Mingzhu, Jiang Zhi, Chen Xiaoyun, Geng Jianyi, Shao Yi, Ni Jun, Hu Jieming, Alexander Brandt, Jia Bu, Jin Feng the elder, Shi Qing, Huang Kui, Kan Xuan, Davide Quadrio, Jin Feng the younger, Yu Ju, Jin Jiangbo, Liu Wei, Mao Dou, Zhou Zixi, Yang Fudong, Zhou Xiaohu, Liu Jianhua, Shi Yong, Song Tao, Zhang Qing, Zhang Ding, Xu Zhen, Tang Maohong, Yang Qingping, Wu Jianxin, Zheng Guogu, Ding Yi, Wang Xingwei, Yang Zhenzhong, Zhu Yu, Ni Jun.
Couriers: Gu Yunzhong, Pang Wenhui, Li Chunzi, Cui Kemin, Li Wenzan, Gao Liming, Xi Zhihua, Hu Shijun, Qin Desheng, Li Xianlun, Shi Xiujiao, Chen Delin, Xu Xinjiang, Shi Xiuhao, Wang Zhengxuan.

Liu Ding
1999
2014

1999 is a semi-autobiographical, multi-media work describing the cultural atmosphere of the late nineties in China, when Liu Ding first met Hans van Dijk. It consists of a set of twenty-one texts written and designed by Liu Ding in the form of a calendar. Each calendar is accompanied by a speaker softly playing a selection of Chinese pop music from the nineties—at the time mostly produced in Hong Kong. The work was made for *Dai Hanzhi: 5000 Artists* at Witte de With, Rotterdam, where the calendars and speakers were hung throughout the exhibition.

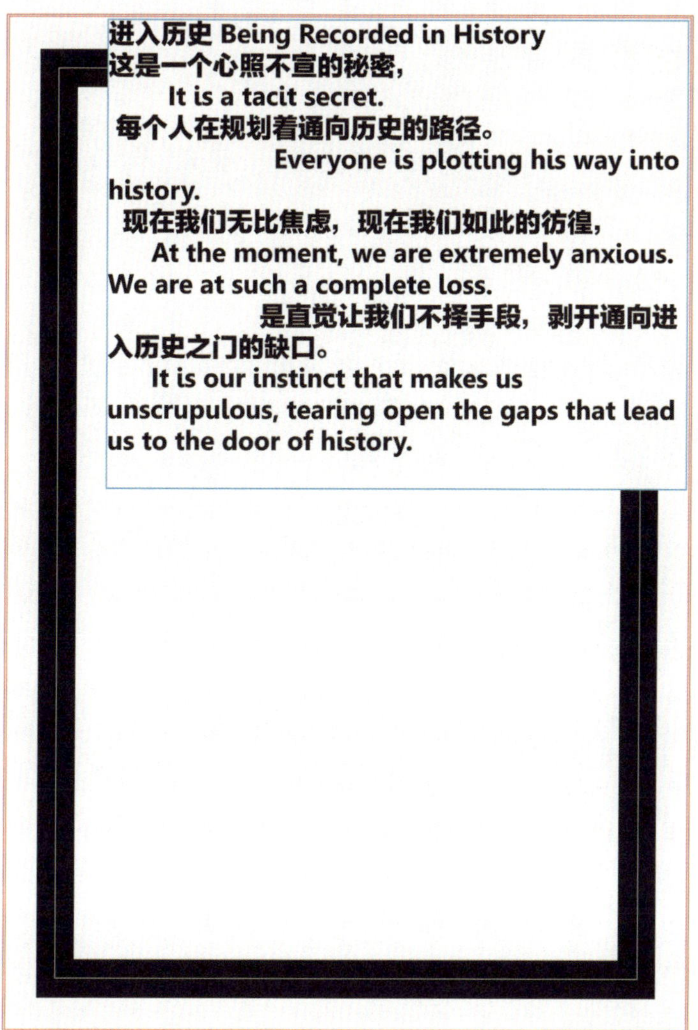

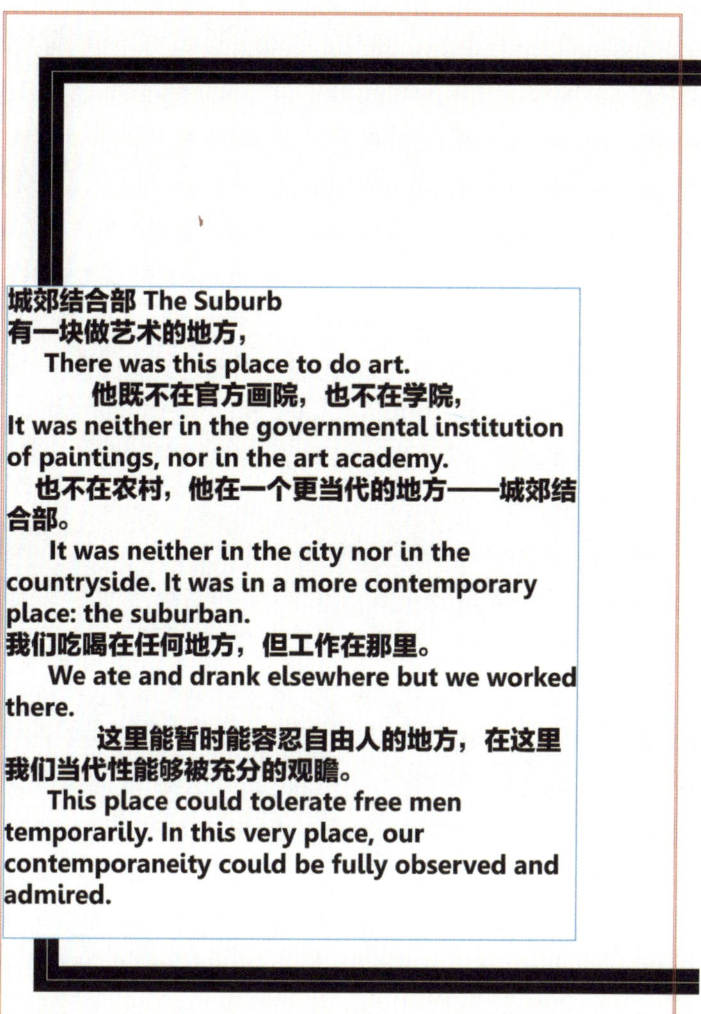

Liu Ding, *1999*, 21 texts in Chinese and English on A3 paper, spiral binding, speakers with Chinese pop songs, edition of 10, 2014

The Exhibitions

Hans van Dijk: 5000 Names
Ullens Center for Contemporary Art,
Beijing, 24 May–10 August 2014

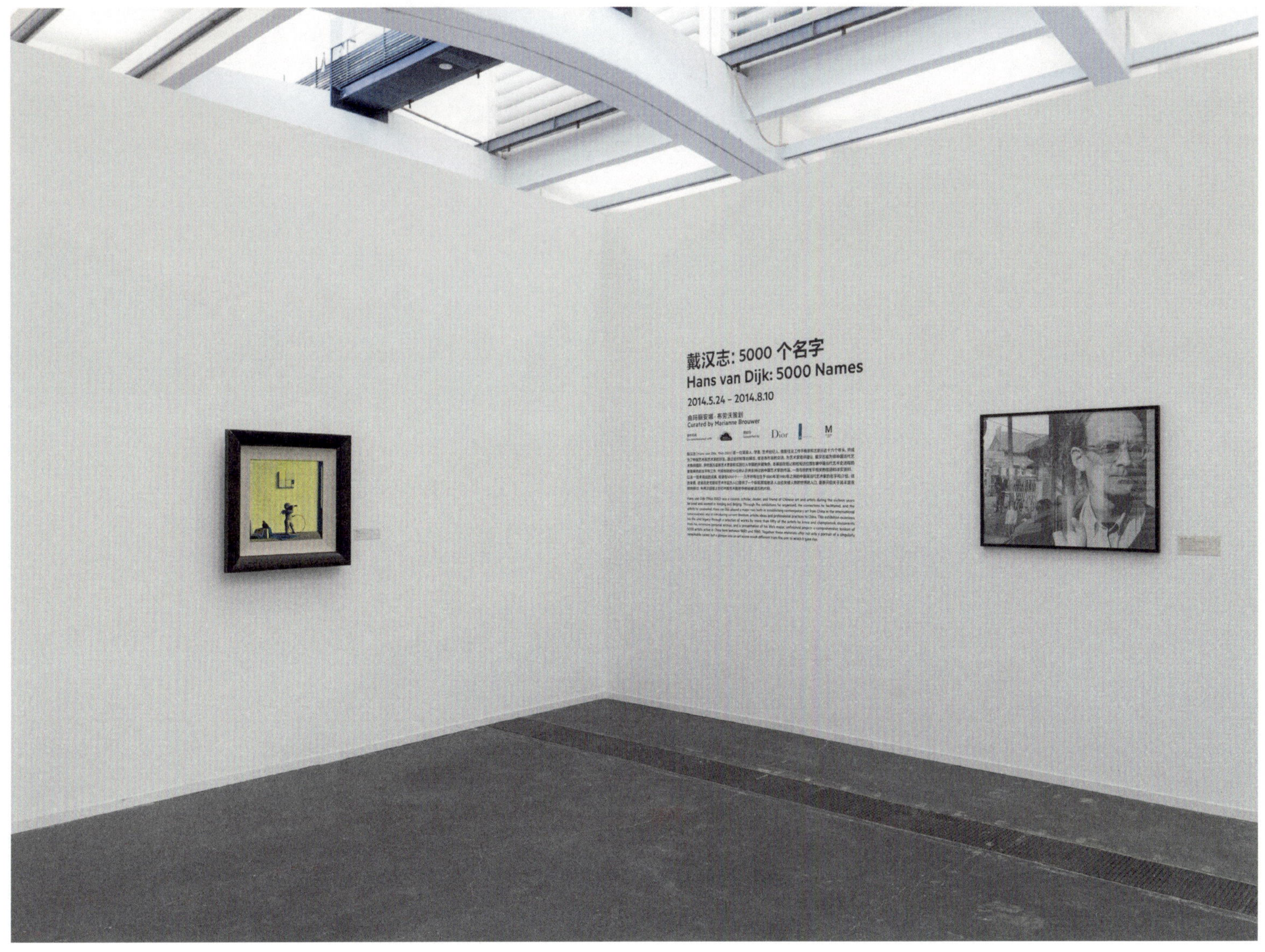

All images courtesy Ullens Center for Contemporary Art, photography Eric Powell
Left: Liu Ye, *For M's Yellow And Blue*, 1995 (→ p. 200); right: Thomas Fuesser, *Hans van Dijk (Beijing 1993)*, 1993

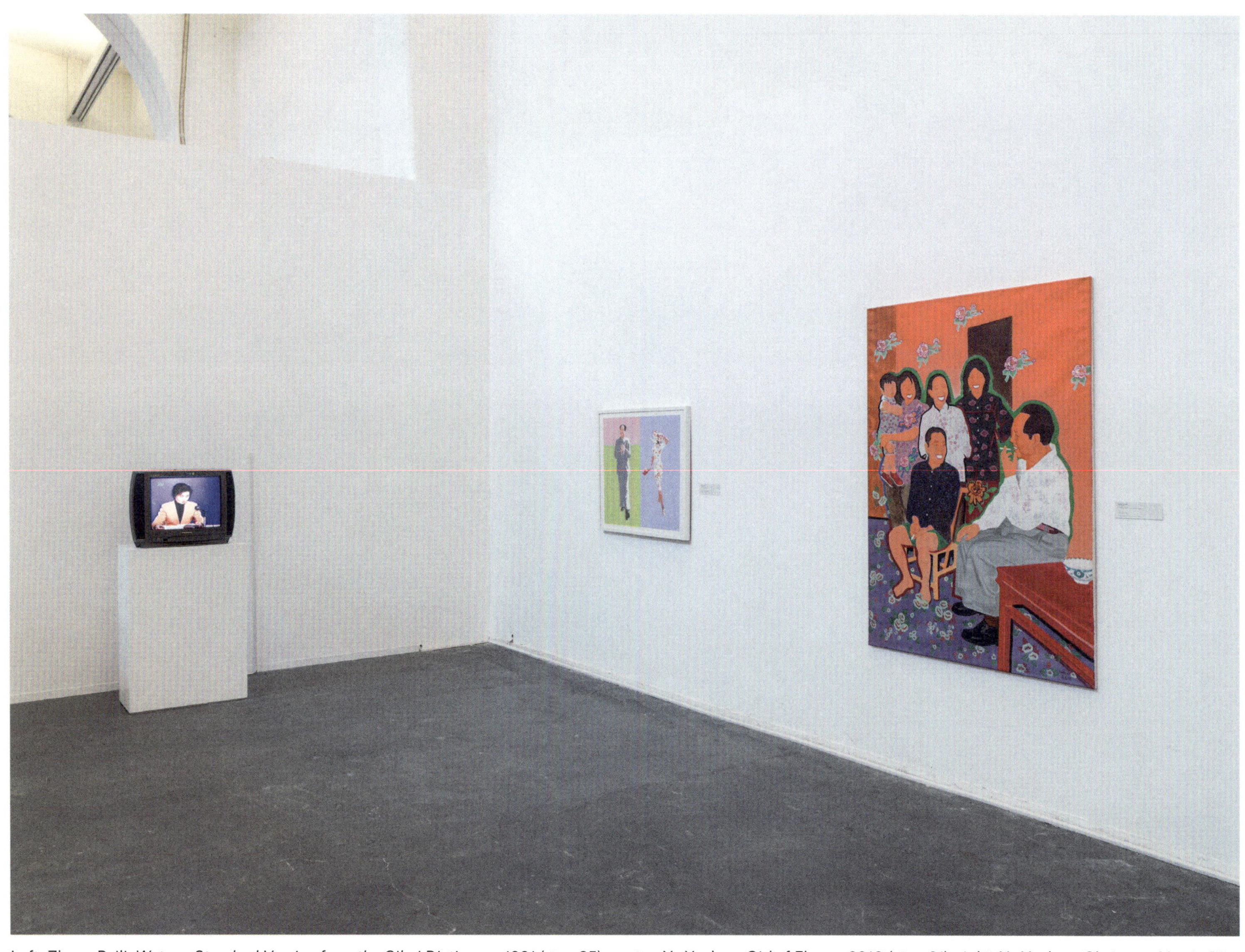

Left: Zhang Peili, *Water – Standard Version from the Cihai Dictionary*, 1991 (→ p. 85); center: Yu Youhan, *Girl of Flower*, 2010 (→ p. 91); right: Yu Youhan, *Chairman Mao in Discussion with the Peasants of Shaoshan*, 1990 (→ p. 92)

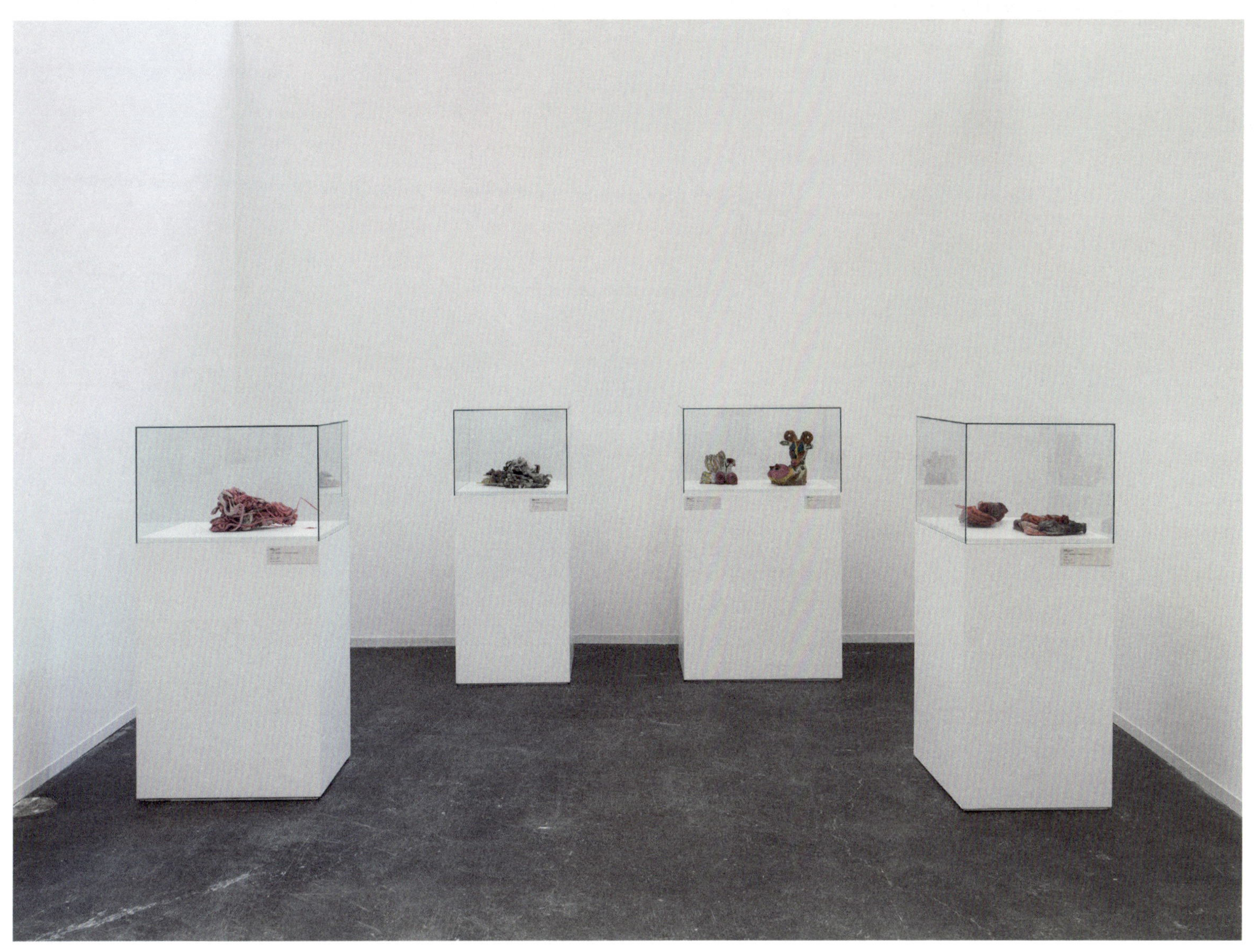

Left to right: Gu Dexin, *Untitled (Plastic Sculpture 1)*, 1983–84; *Untitled (Plastic Sculpture 2)*, 1983–84; *Untitled (Clay Figure 1)*, 1982–83; *Untitled (Clay Figure 2)*, 1982–83; *Untitled (Plastic Sculpture 3)*, 1983–84; *Untitled (Plastic Sculpture 4)*, 1983–84

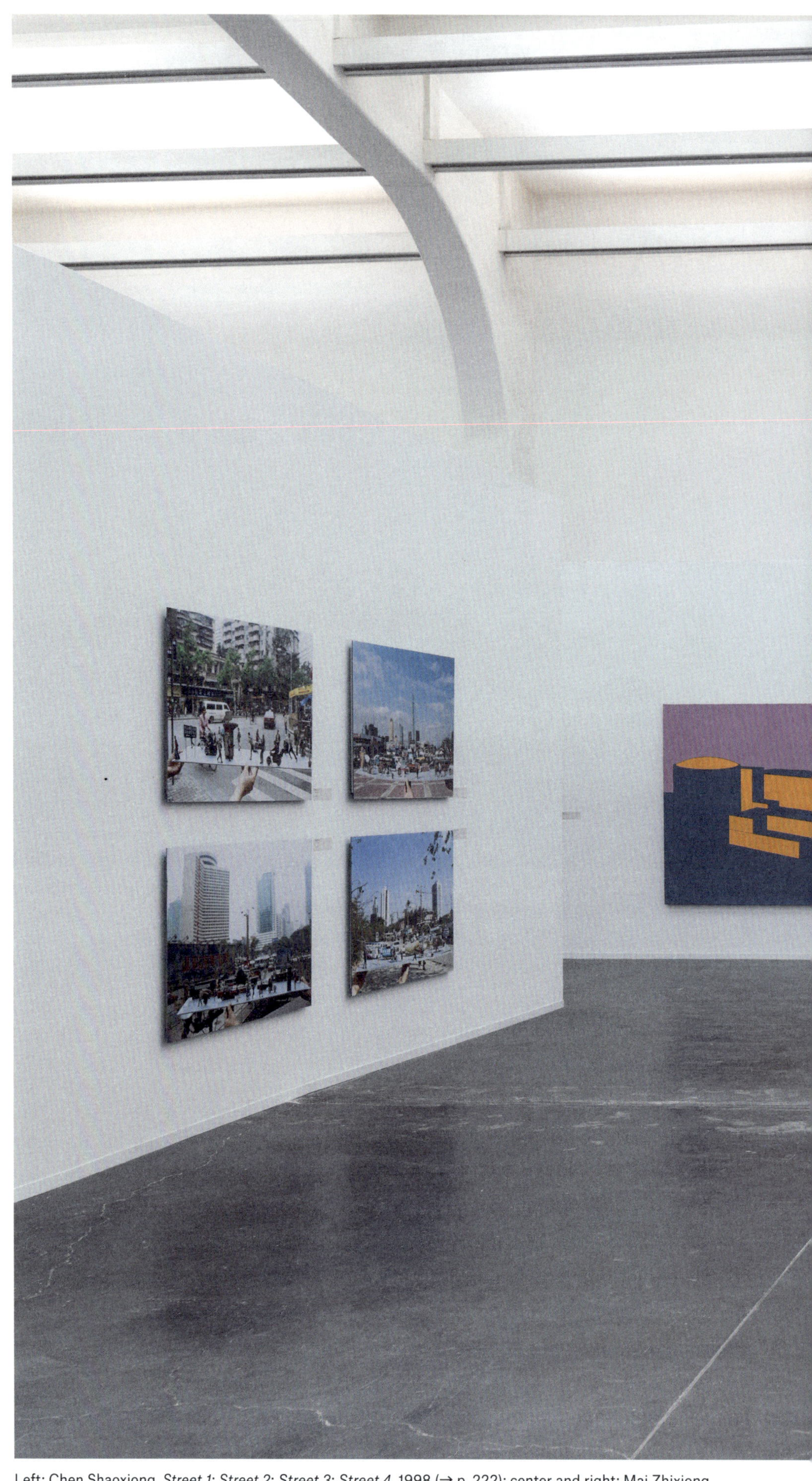

Left: Chen Shaoxiong, *Street 1*; *Street 2*; *Street 3*; *Street 4*, 1998 (→ p. 222); center and right: Mai Zhixiong, *Landscape Series No. 5*, 1995 (→ p. 200); *Machinery Series No. 4*, 1996; *Landscape Series Sanctuary No. 3*, 2010; *Landscape Series Sanctuary No. 4*, 2010

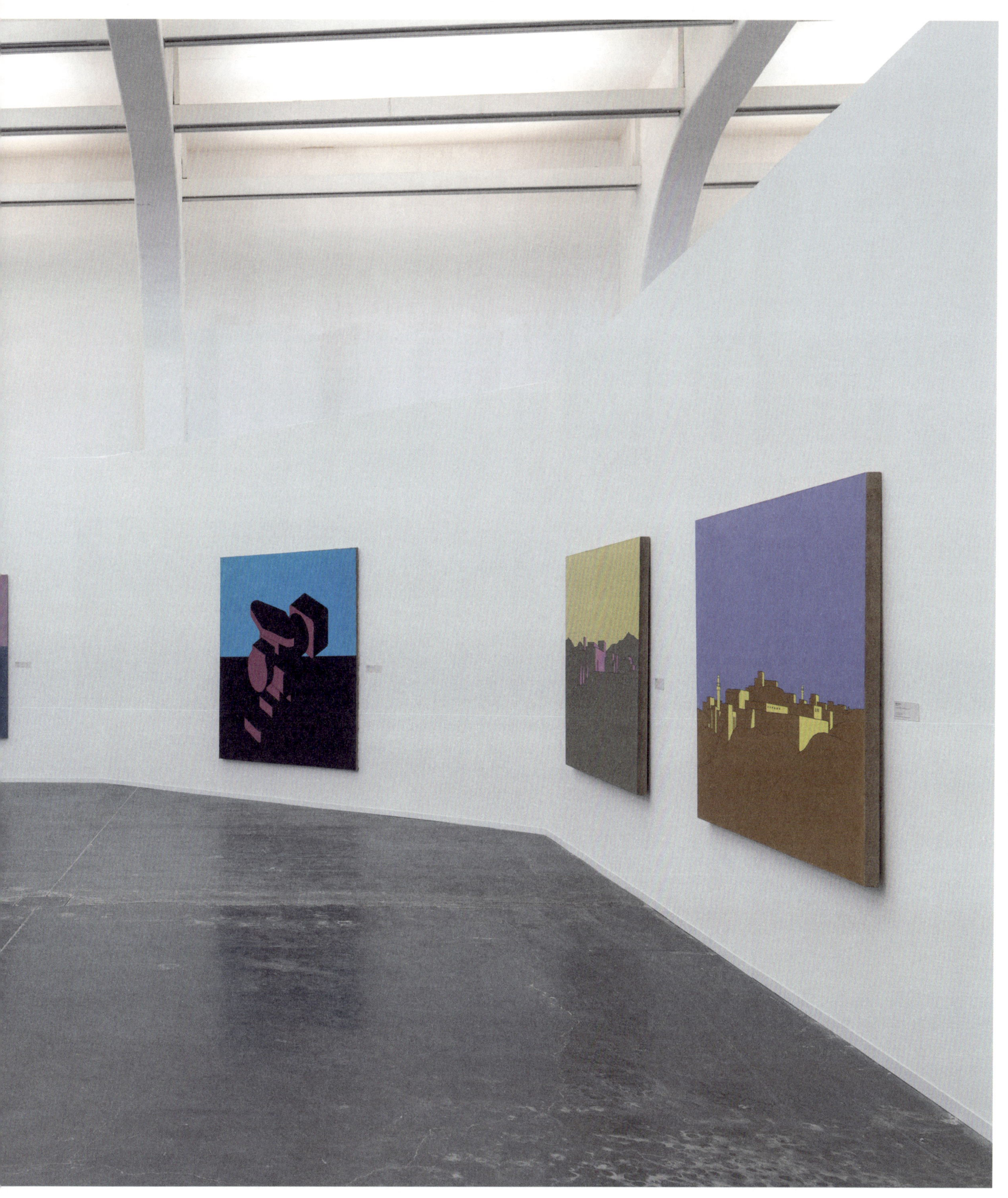

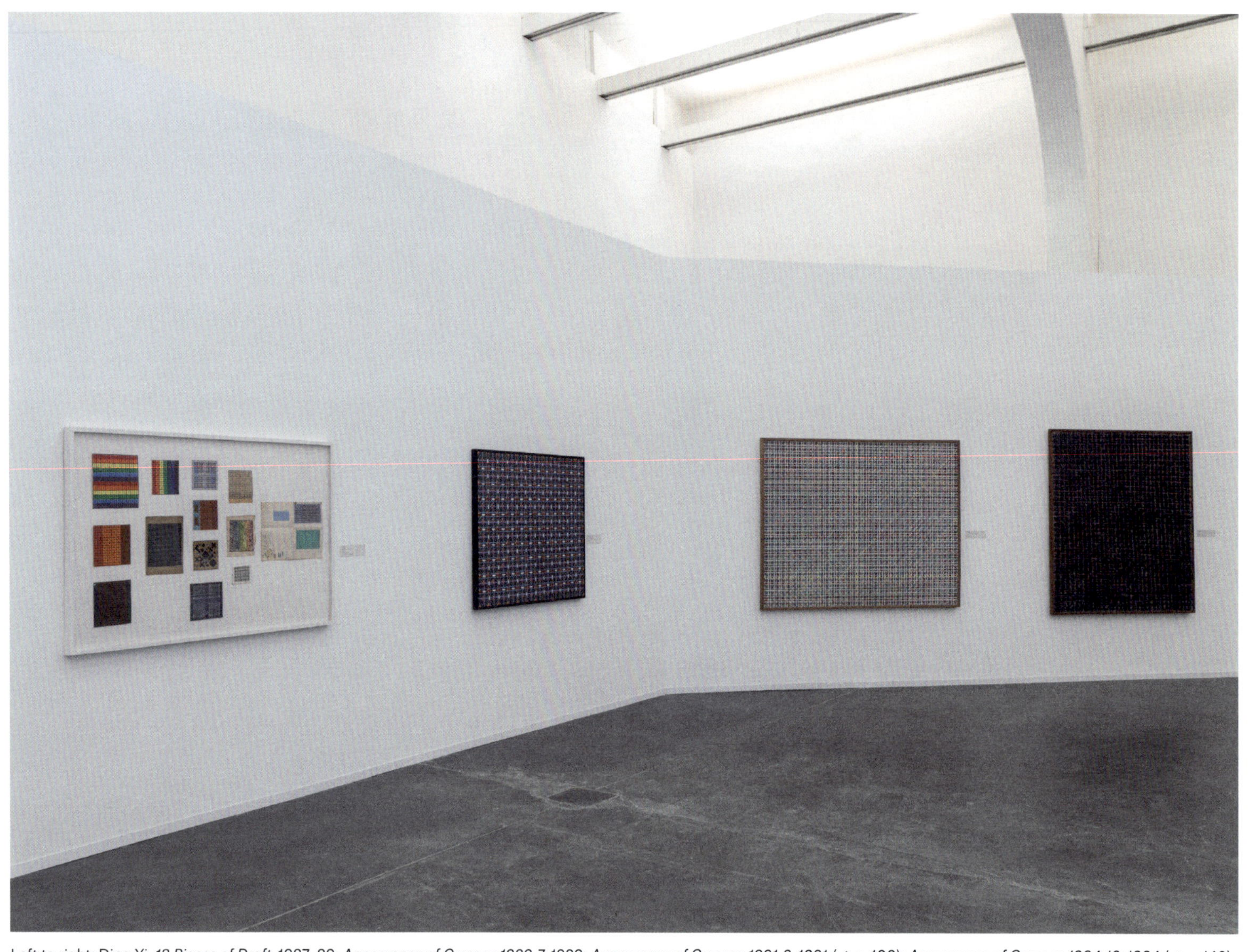

Left to right: Ding Yi, *13 Pieces of Draft*, 1987–89; *Appearance of Crosses 1989-7*, 1989; *Appearance of Crosses 1991-3*, 1991 (→ p. 100); *Appearance of Crosses 1994-10*, 1994 (→ p. 140)

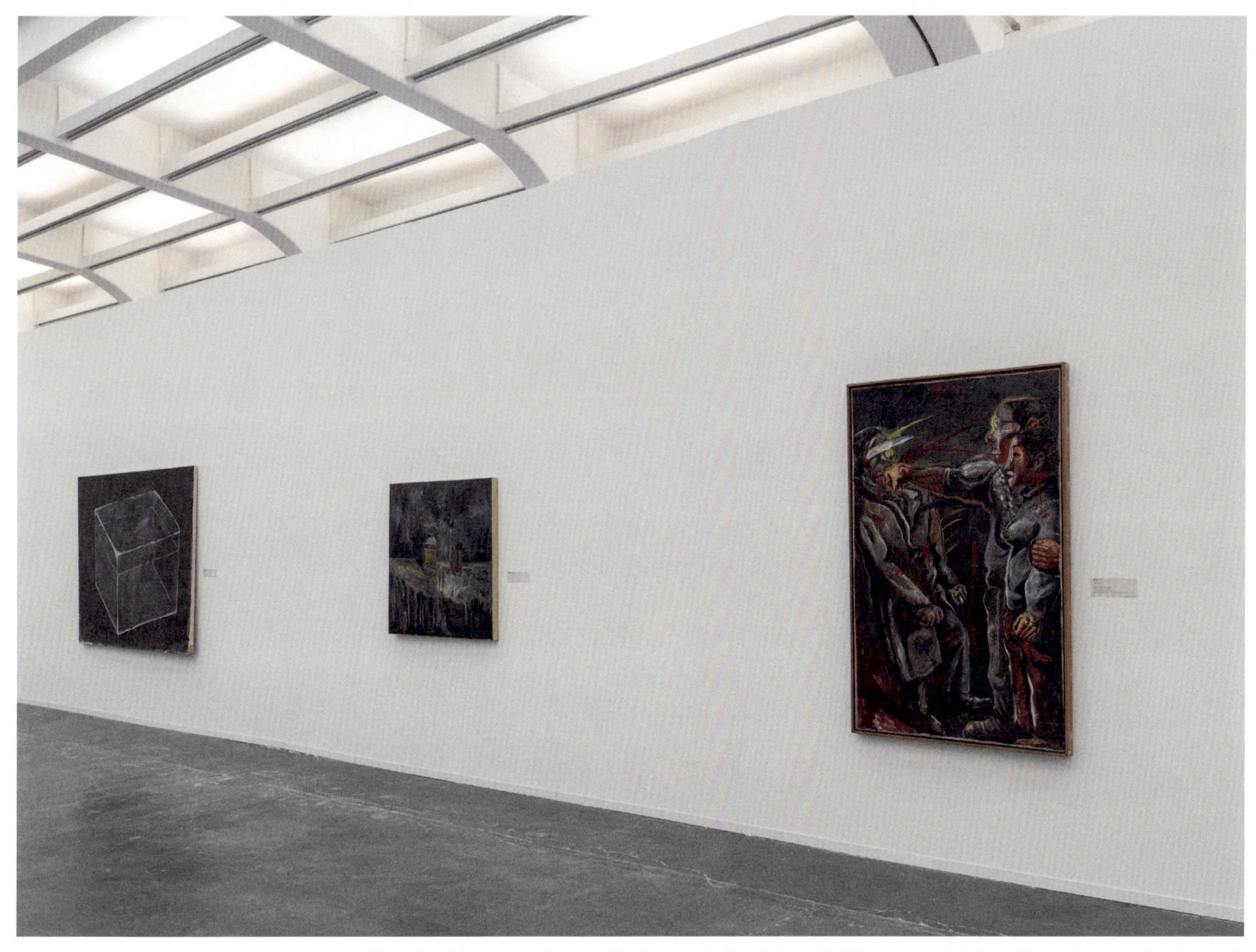

Left to right: Zhang Enli, *Container 5, 2003; Vessel (2)*, 1998, exhibited in the *Inaugural Exhibition of the New Gallery*, CAAW, Caochangdi, Beijing, 2001; *Indignation*, 1993 (→ p. 147)

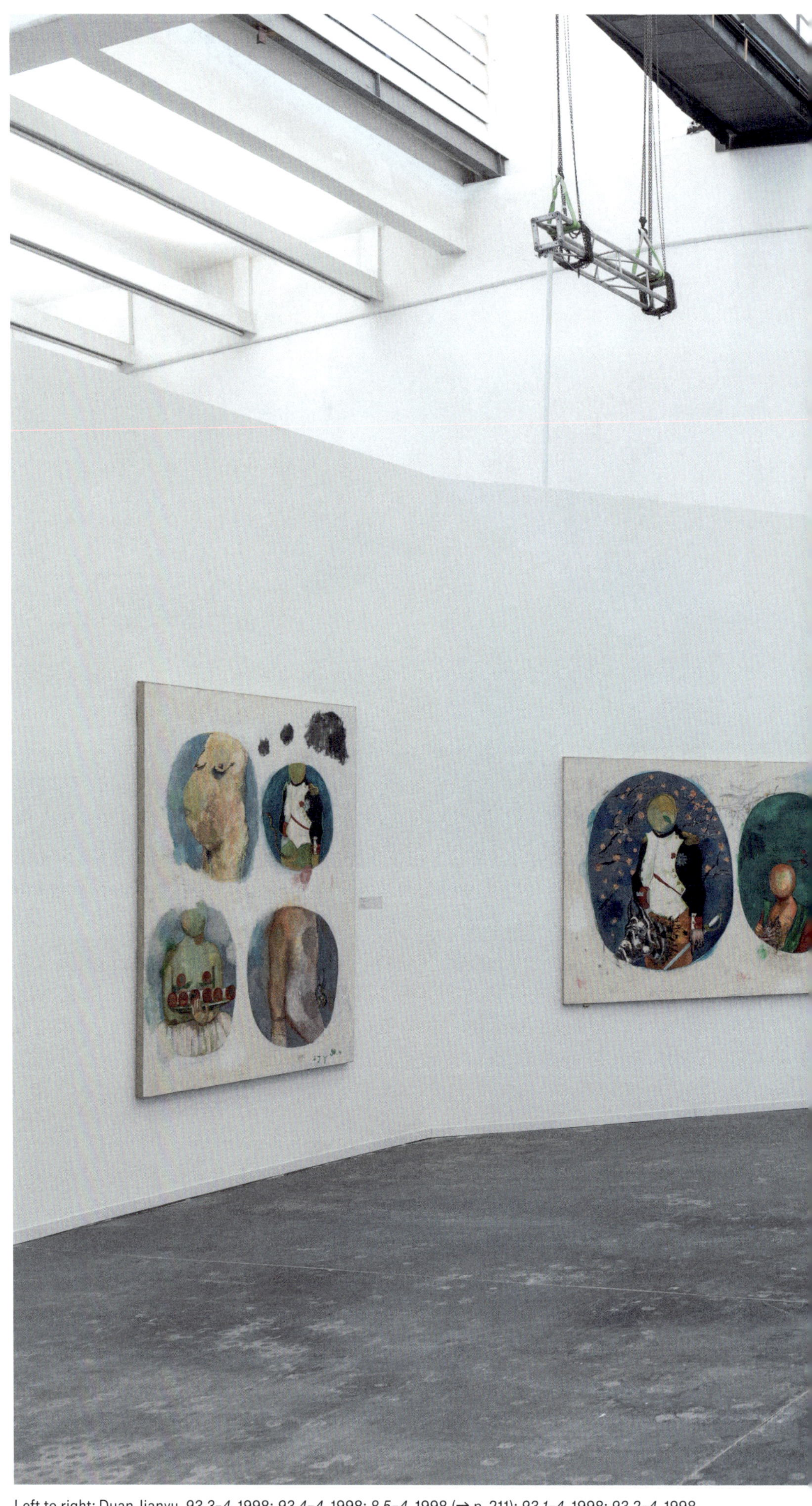

Left to right: Duan Jianyu, *93 3-4*, 1998; *93 4-4*, 1998; *8 5-4*, 1998 (→ p. 211); *93 1-4*, 1998; *93 2-4*, 1998, all exhibited during *Duan Jianyu & Li Tianyuan – Recent Works*, CAAW, south Beijing, 1999

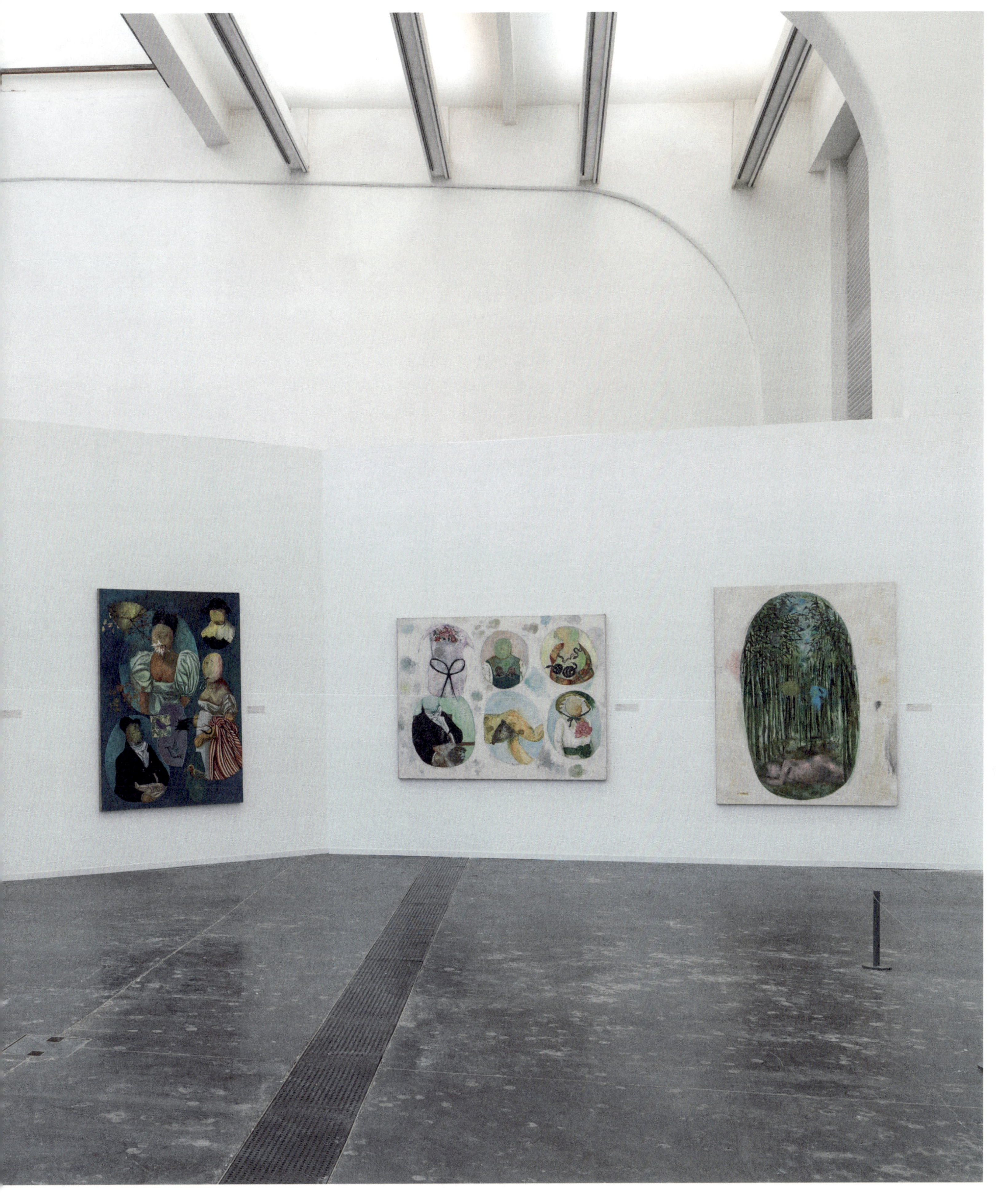

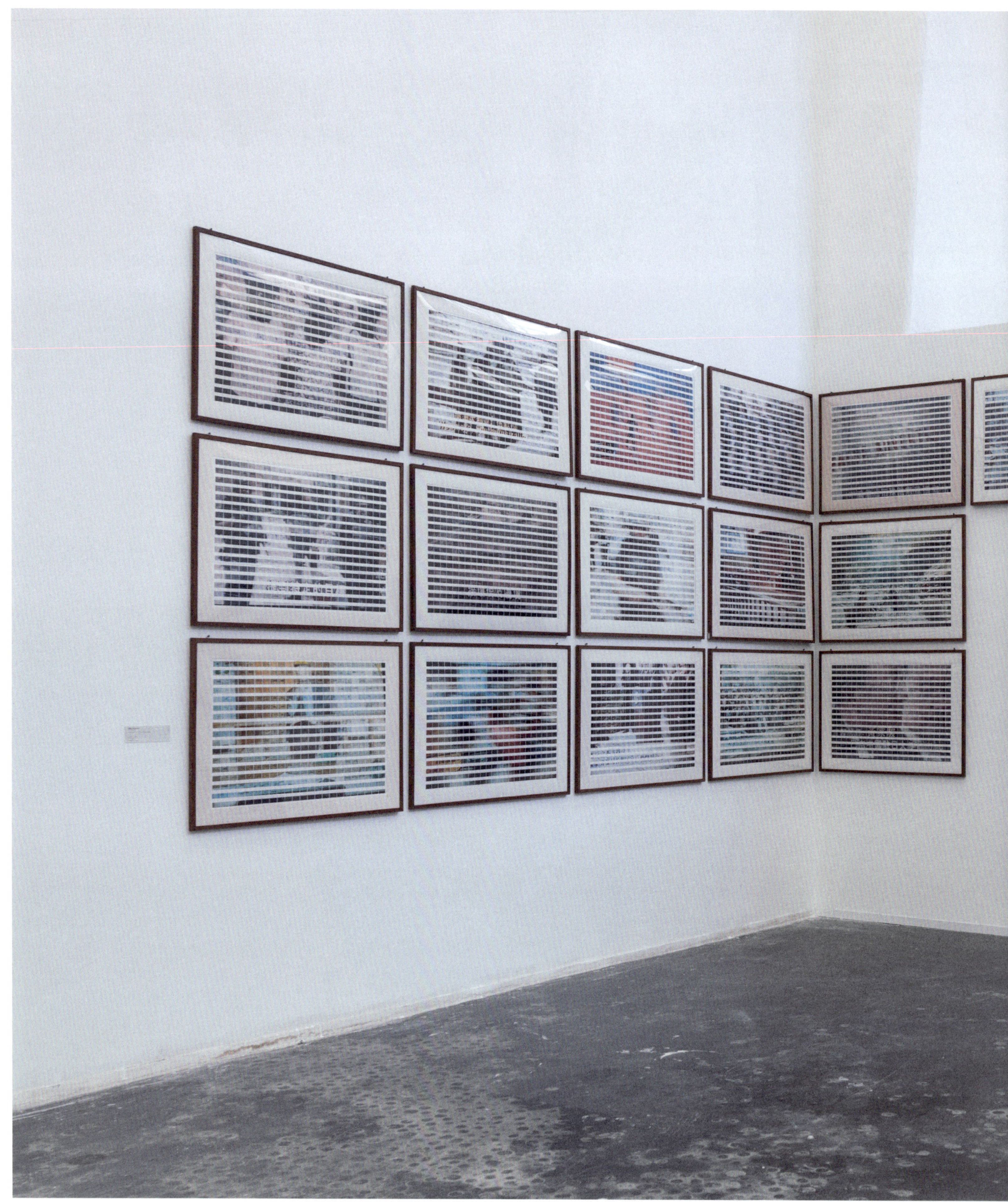

Left to right: Zheng Guogu, *Sixteen of the Ten Thousand Customers*, 1998 (→ p. 201); *The Inside of the Brain of Dai Hanzhi*, 2014, oil painting made for *Hans van Dijk: 5000 Names*, UCCA, 2014 (→ p. 257)

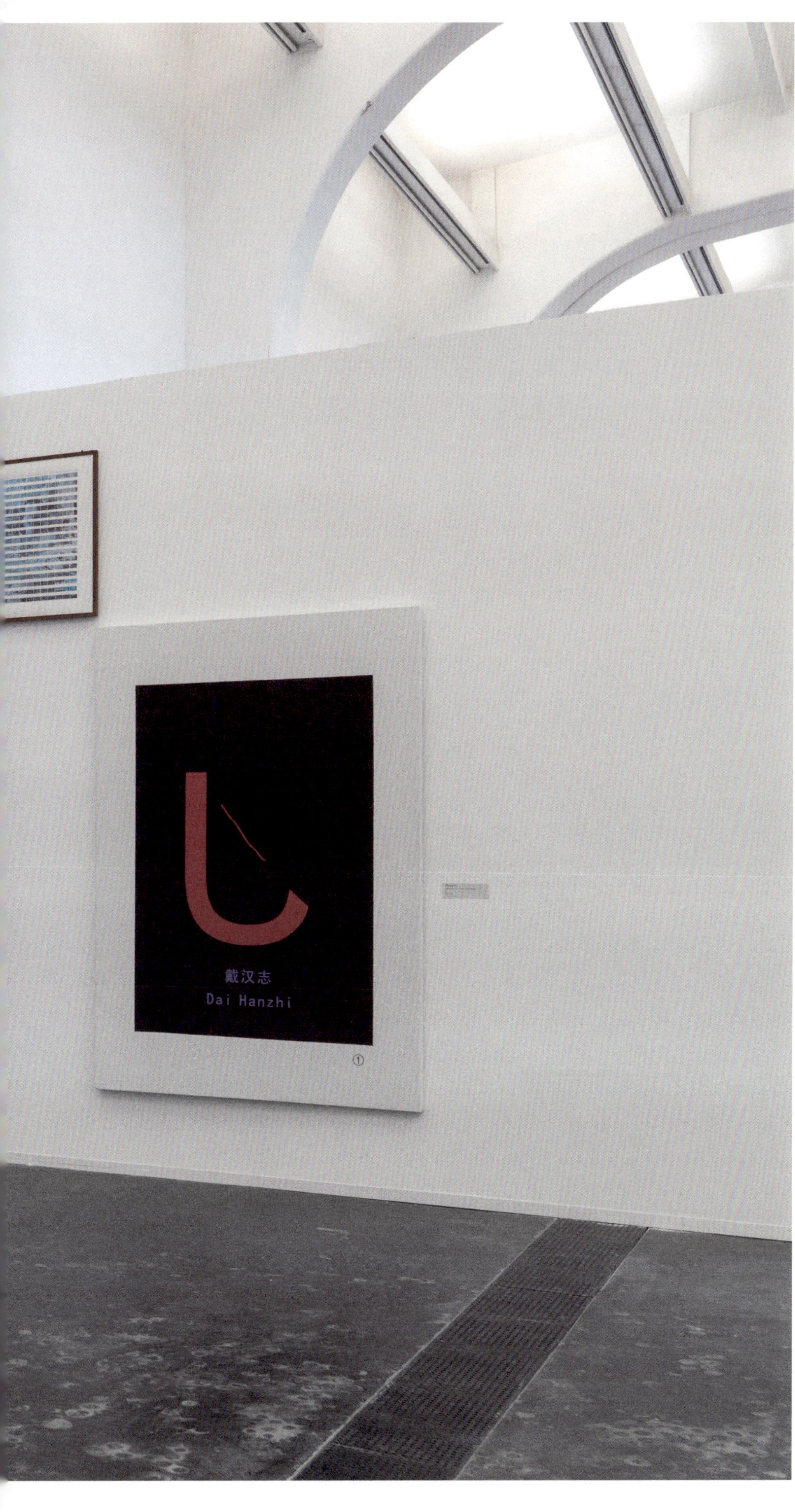
戴汉志
Dai Hanzhi

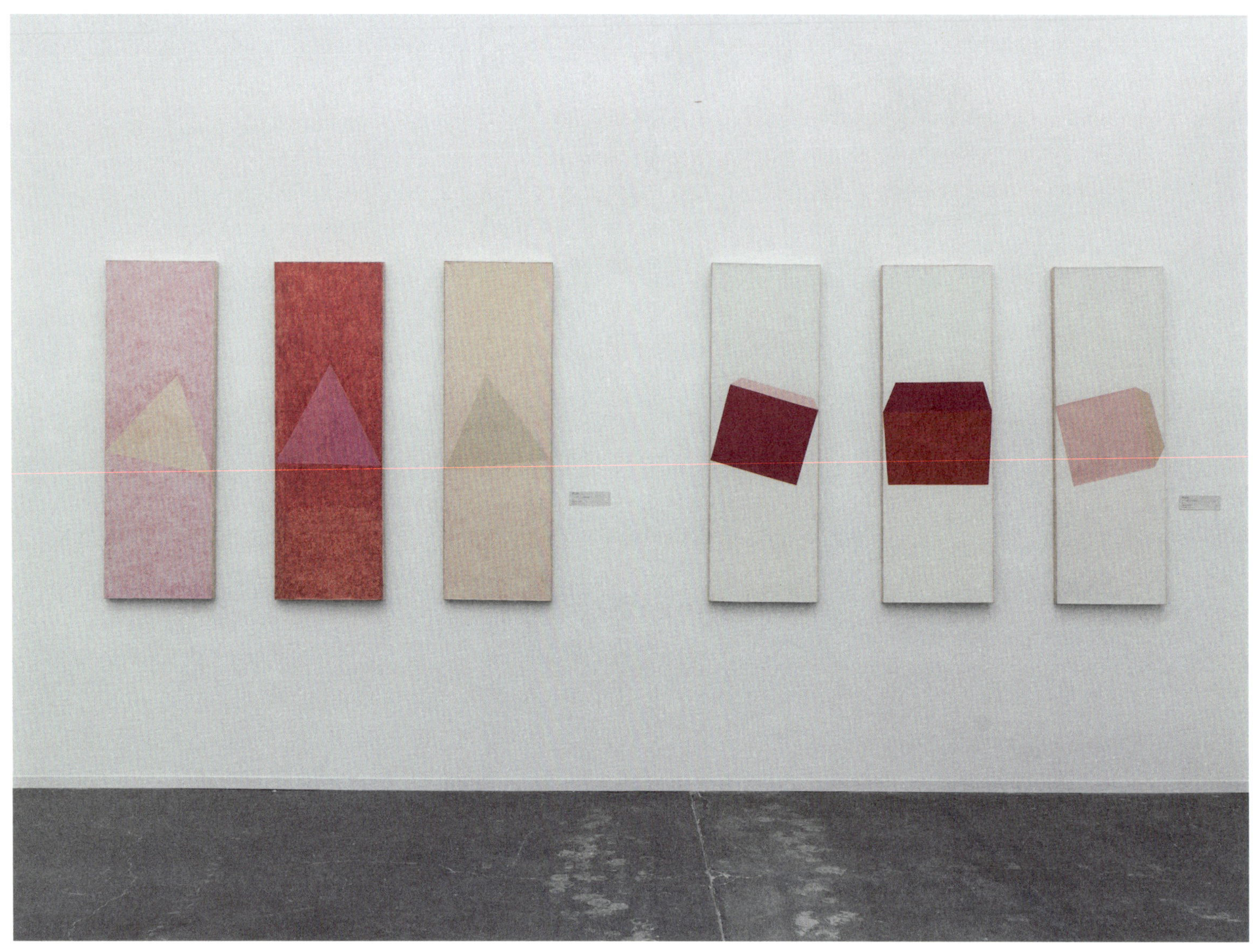

Left to right: Liu Ding, *Fuck 1*; *Fuck 2*; *Fuck 3*; *Sugar 1*; *Sugar 2*; *Sugar 3*, all 2001 (→ p. 228)

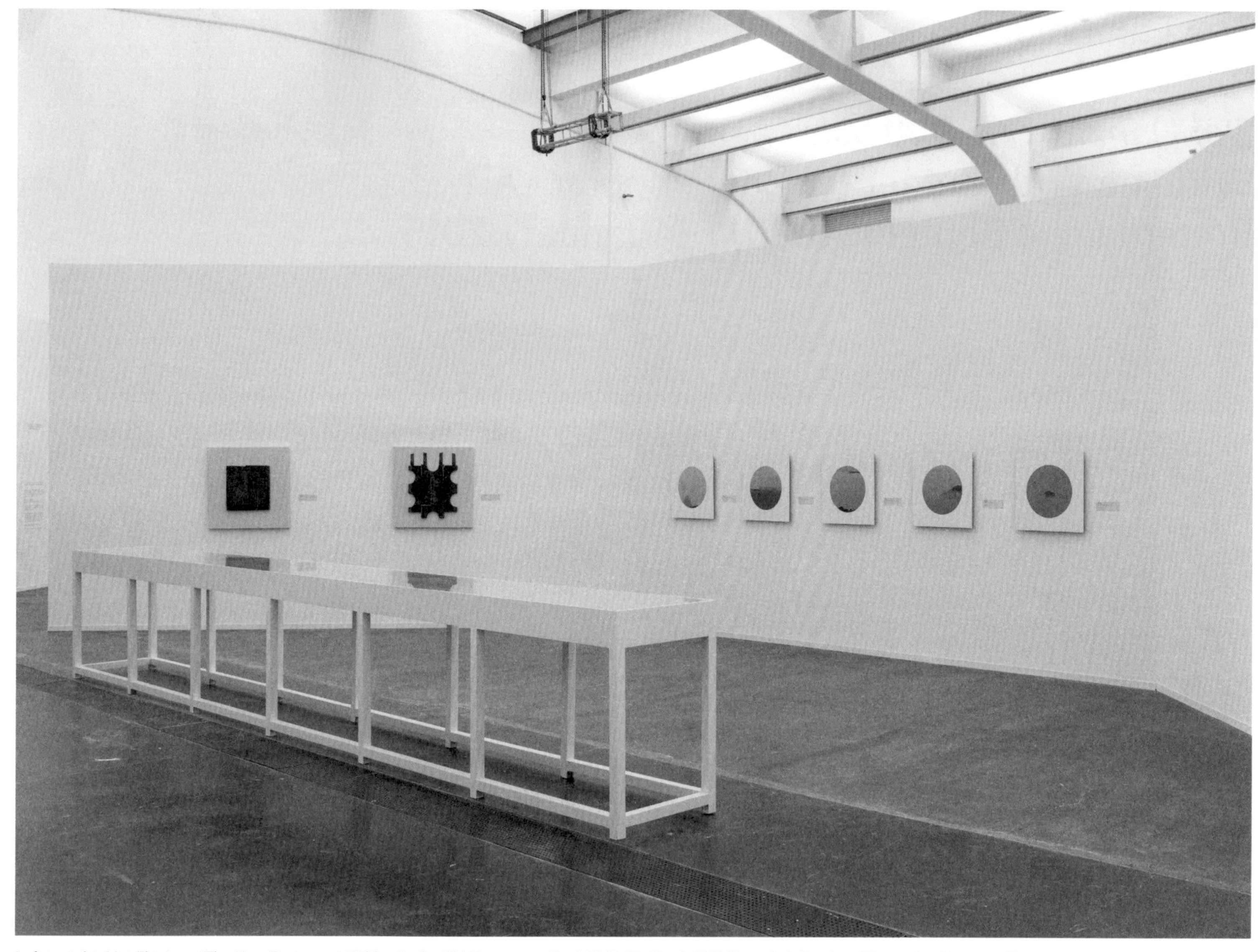

Left to right: Mai Zhixiong, *The New Testament Hidden in the Old Testament No. 1*, 2011; *Sin No. 1*, 2011; Hong Lei, *Yandang Mountains, Yueqing, Zhejiang*; *Taihu, Dongshan, Suzhou, Jiangsu*; *Qiandao Lake, Chun'an, Zhejiang*; *Mount Lu 2, Jiujiang, Jiangxi*; *Mount Lu 1, Jiujiang, Jiangxi*, all 2000; foreground: vitrine with Hong Lei, *Hans and I*, 2014 (→ p. 251)

The Exhibitions

Dai Hanzhi: 5000 Artists
Witte de With Center for Contemporary Art, Rotterdam, 4 September 2014–4 January 2015

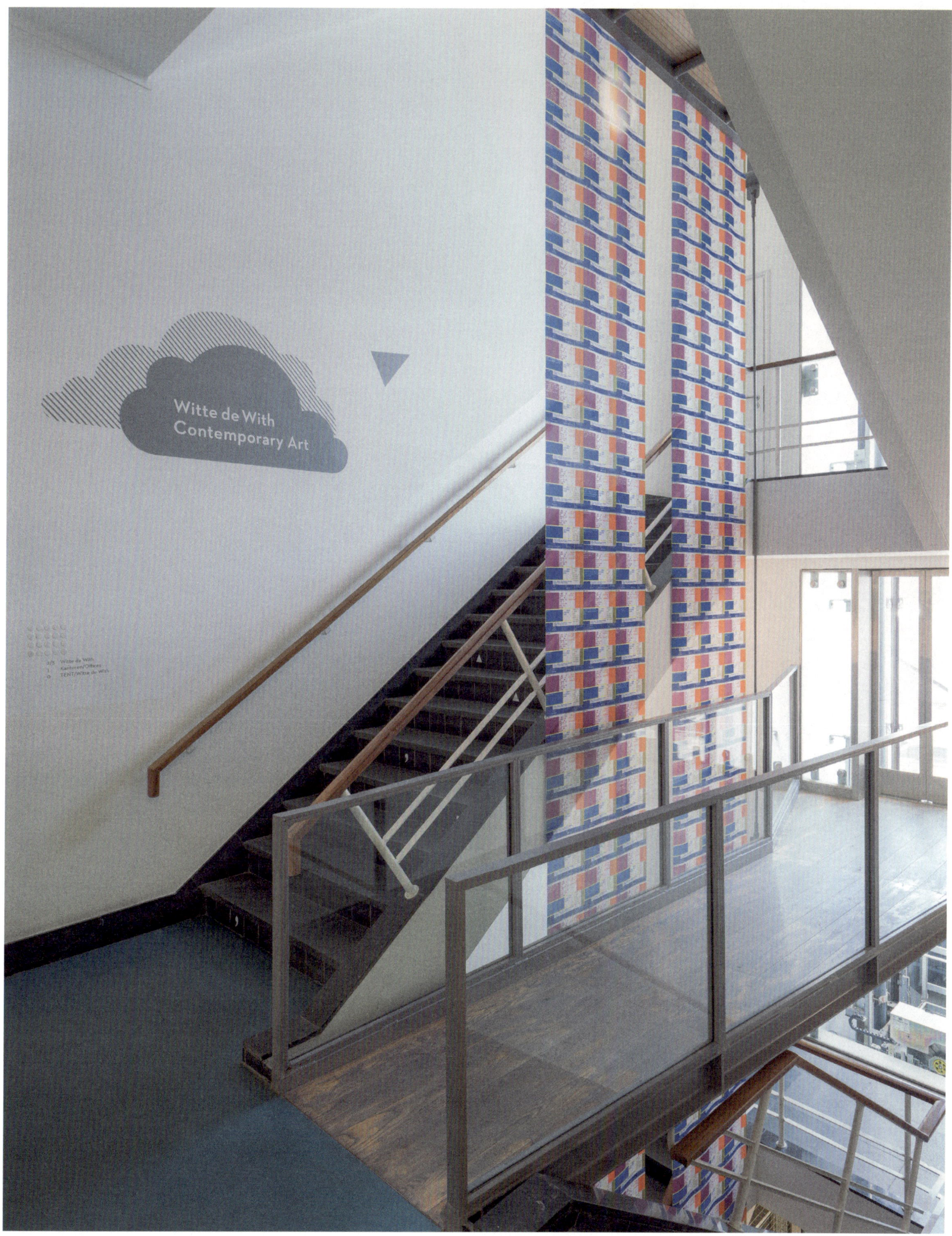

All images courtesy Witte de With Center for Contemporary Art, photography Cassander Eeftinck Schattenkerk
Banners running across three floors showing artist entries from Hans van Dijk's digital Lexicon (→ p. 245)

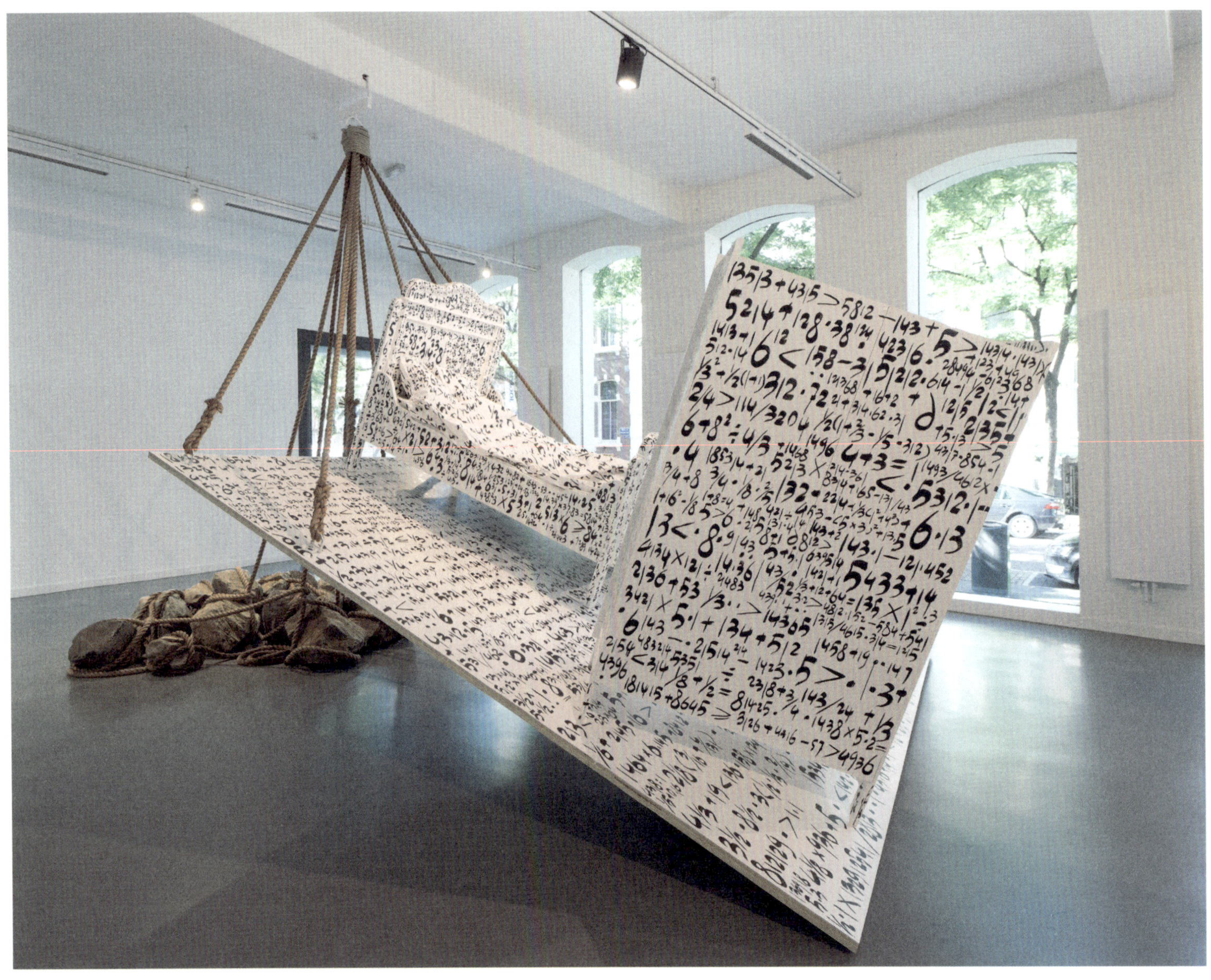

Ni Haifeng, *The Angle*, 1995/2014, originally made for *Configura 2 – Dialog Der Kulturen*, Erfurt, Germany, 1995 (→ see p. 155) and painted in red, white, and black; Ni Haifeng omitted red in the remake he produced for the exhibition at Witte de With in 2014

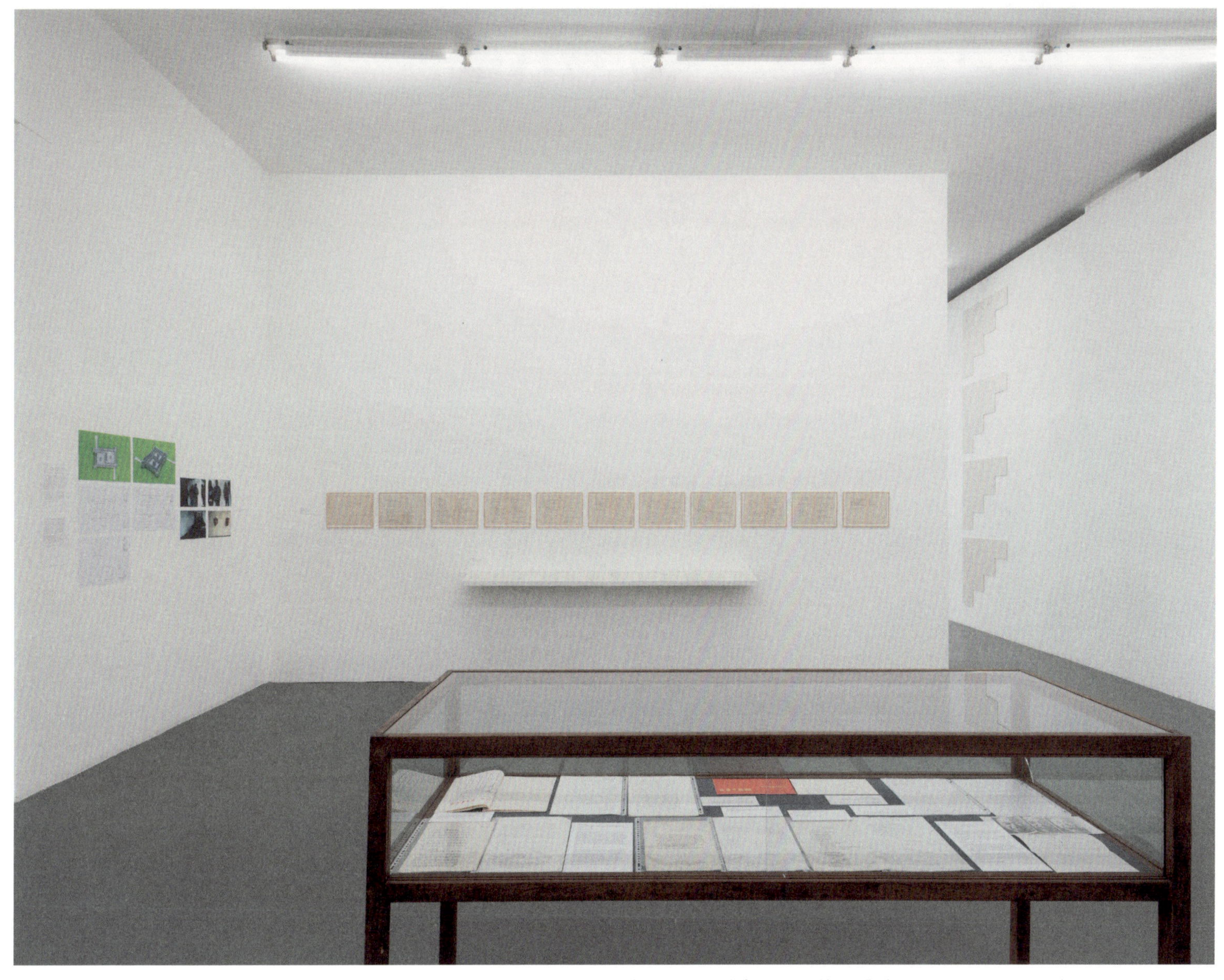

Left: Geng Jianyi, *Water Factory, (The owner has the right to (re)construct the work)*, 1987/2013 (→ p. 49); far center: Zhang Peili, *Art Project No. 2*, 1987 (→ p. 46)

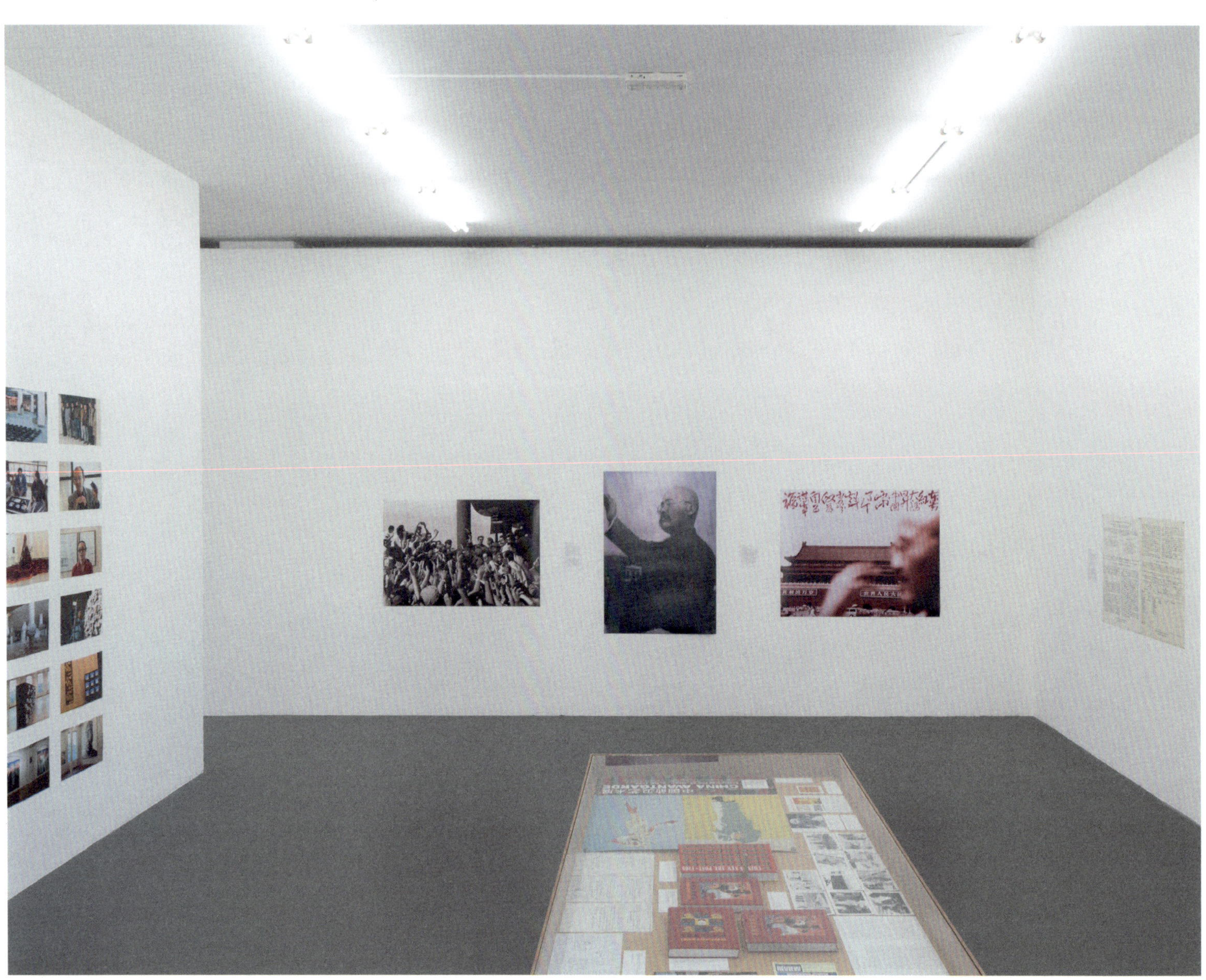

Left to right: archival images of the *China Avant-garde* exhibition, 1993; Zhao Shaoruo, *In the name of the Red Guard Youth*, 1989/2005; *In the name of the Cultural Revolution*, 1989/1993 (→ p. 179); *In the name of the Red Sun*, 1988/1991; Hans van Dijk, URARC report, 1994 (→ p. 135)

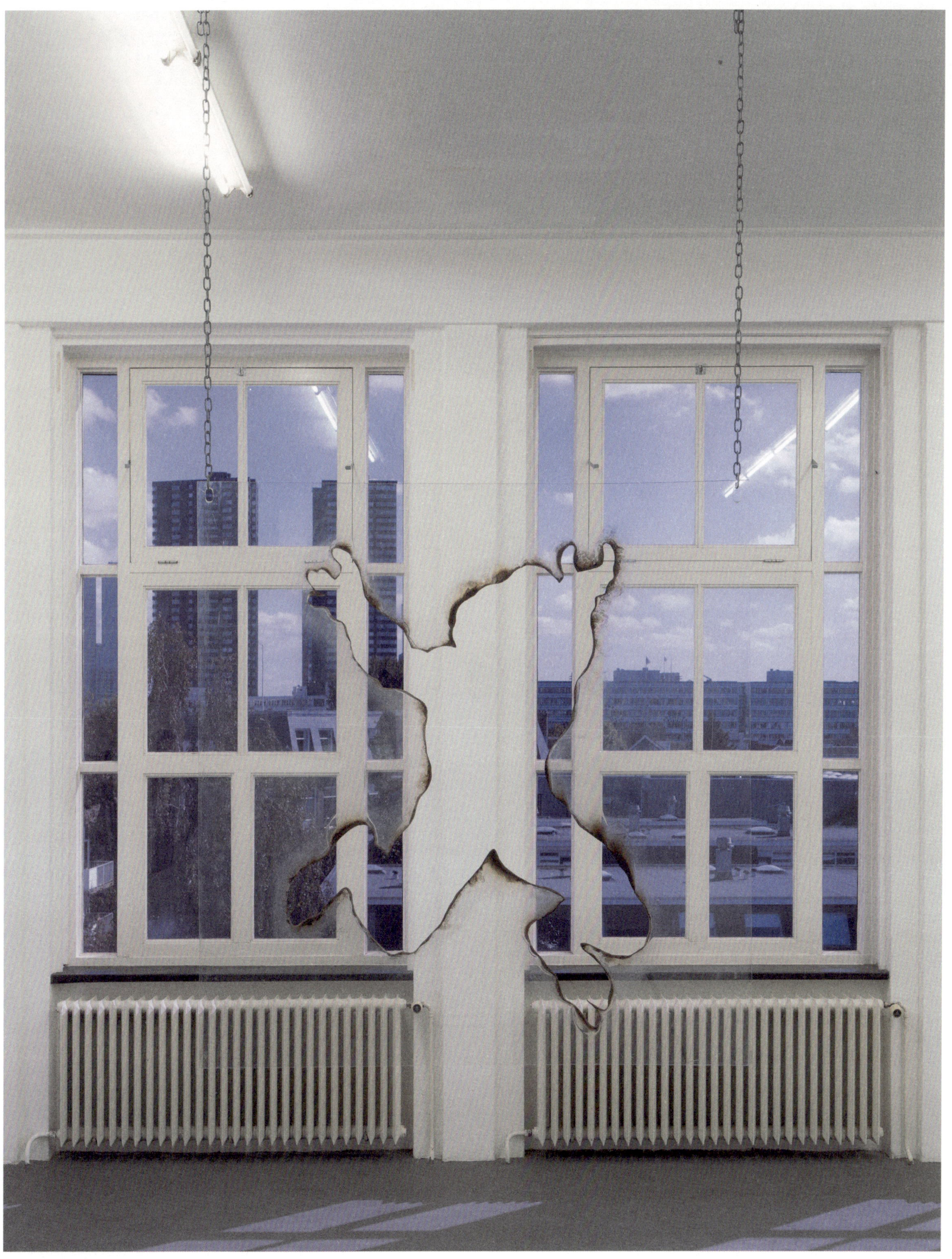

Zhao Bandi, *The Big Rumour Spreading Until Today*, 1994 (→ p. 128)

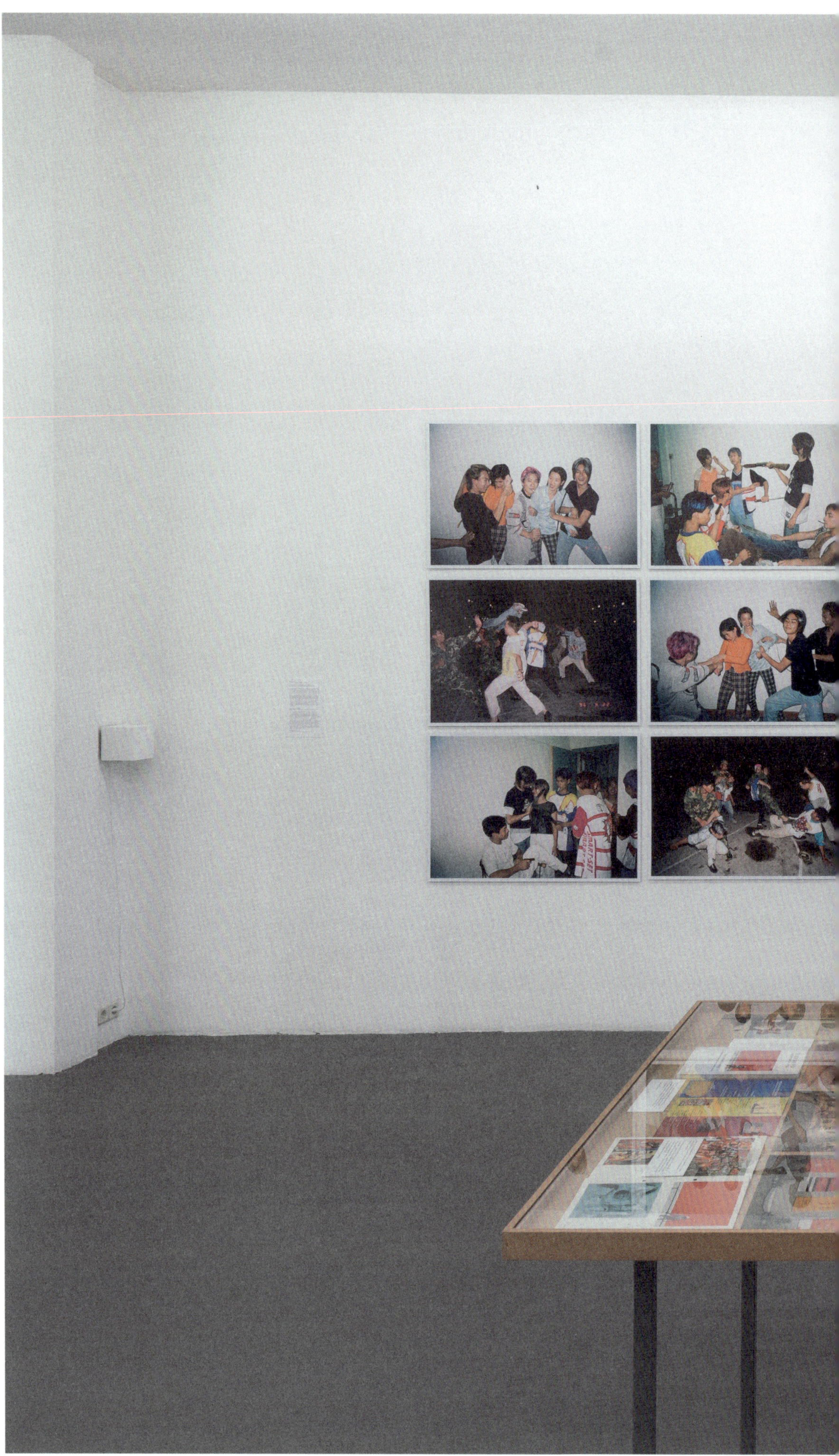

Zheng Guogu, *The Vagarious Life of Yangjiang Youth*, 1996 (→ p. 190)

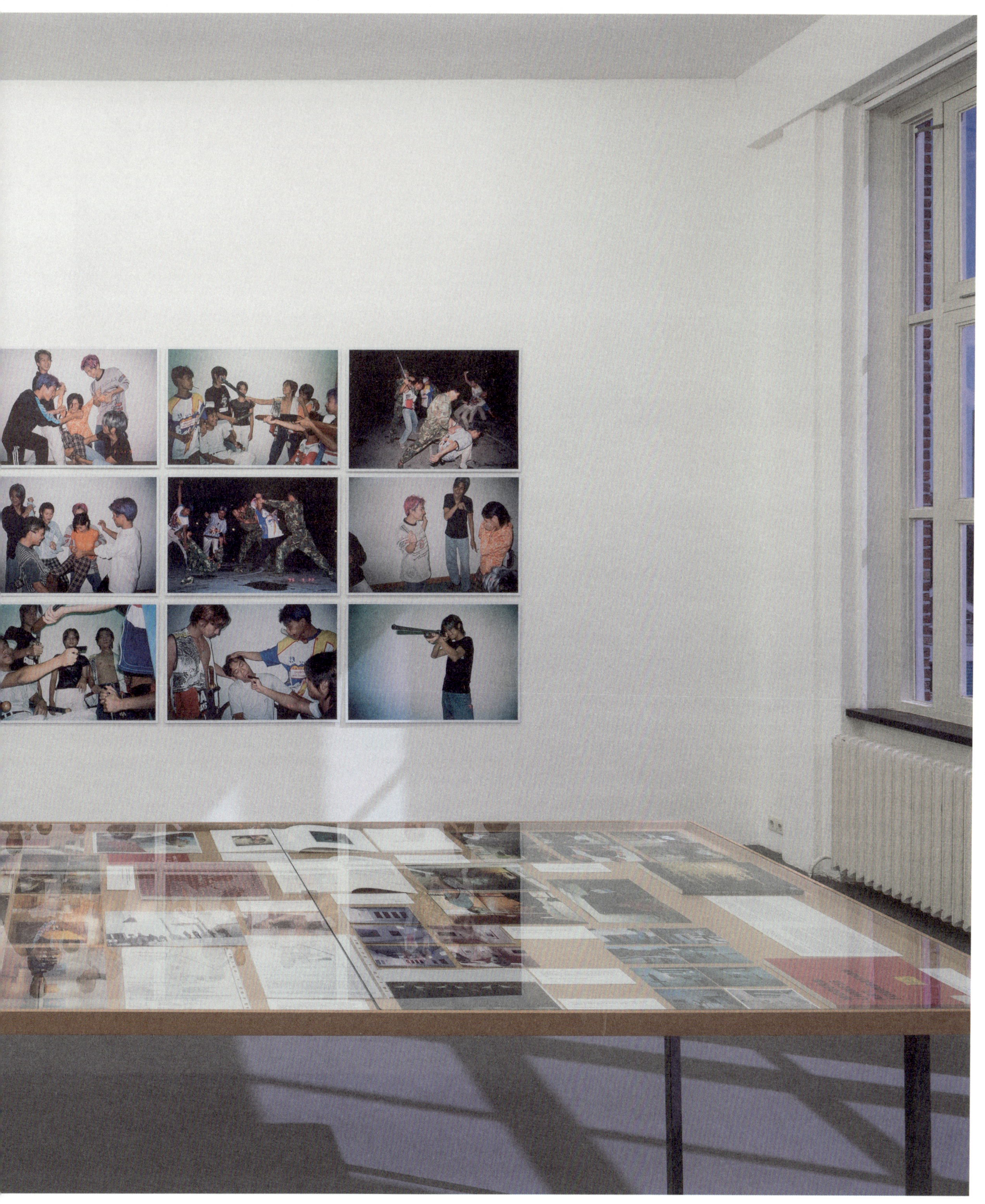

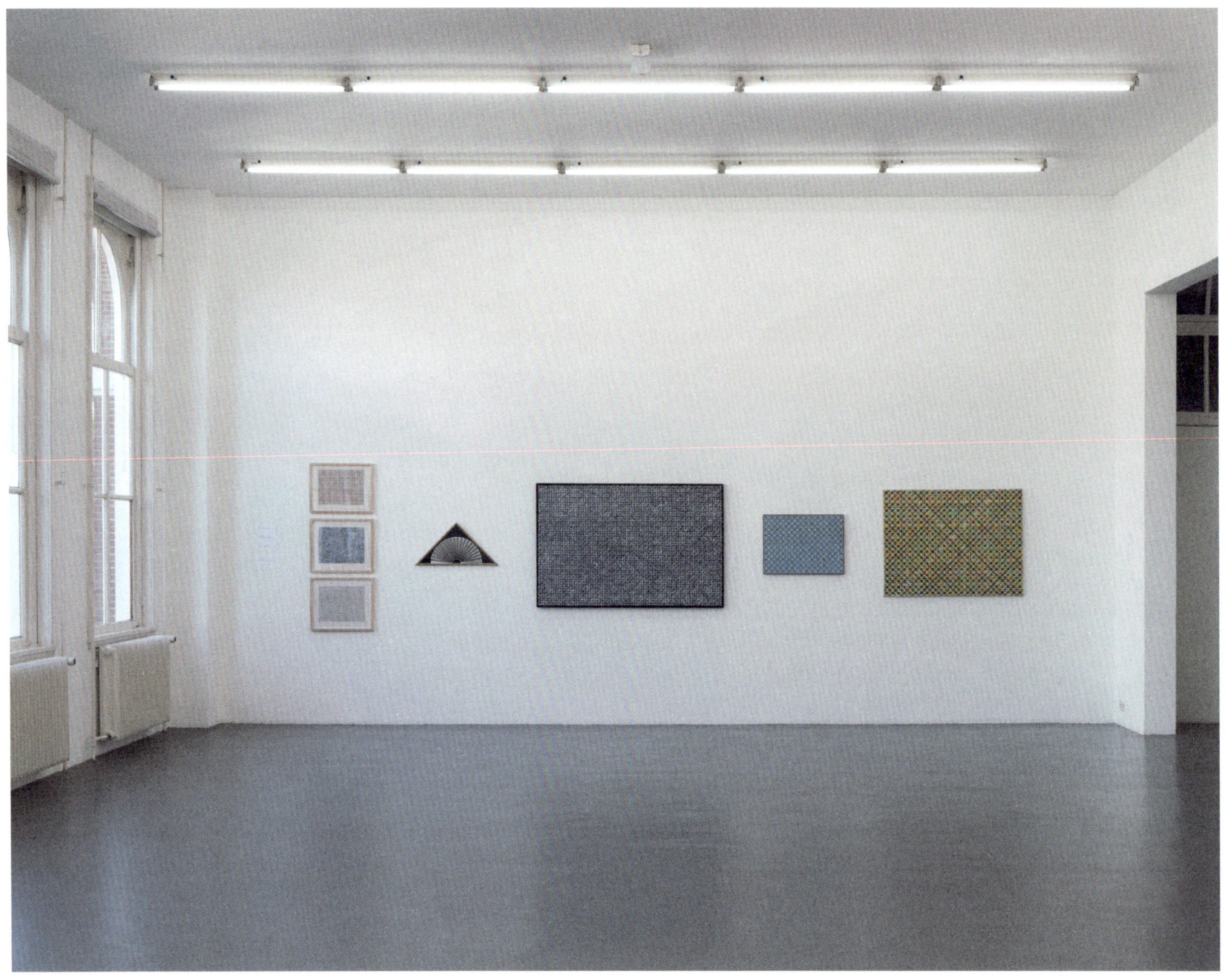

Left to right: Ding Yi, *Appearance of Crosses 91-B6*, 1991; *Appearance of Crosses 92-B20*, 1992; *Appearance of Crosses 93-B3*, 1993; *Appearance of Crosses 94-B19*, 1994 (→ p. 139); *Appearance of Crosses 93-2*, 1993; *Appearance of Crosses 89-6*, 1989 (→ p. 54); *Appearance of Crosses 90-7*, 1990

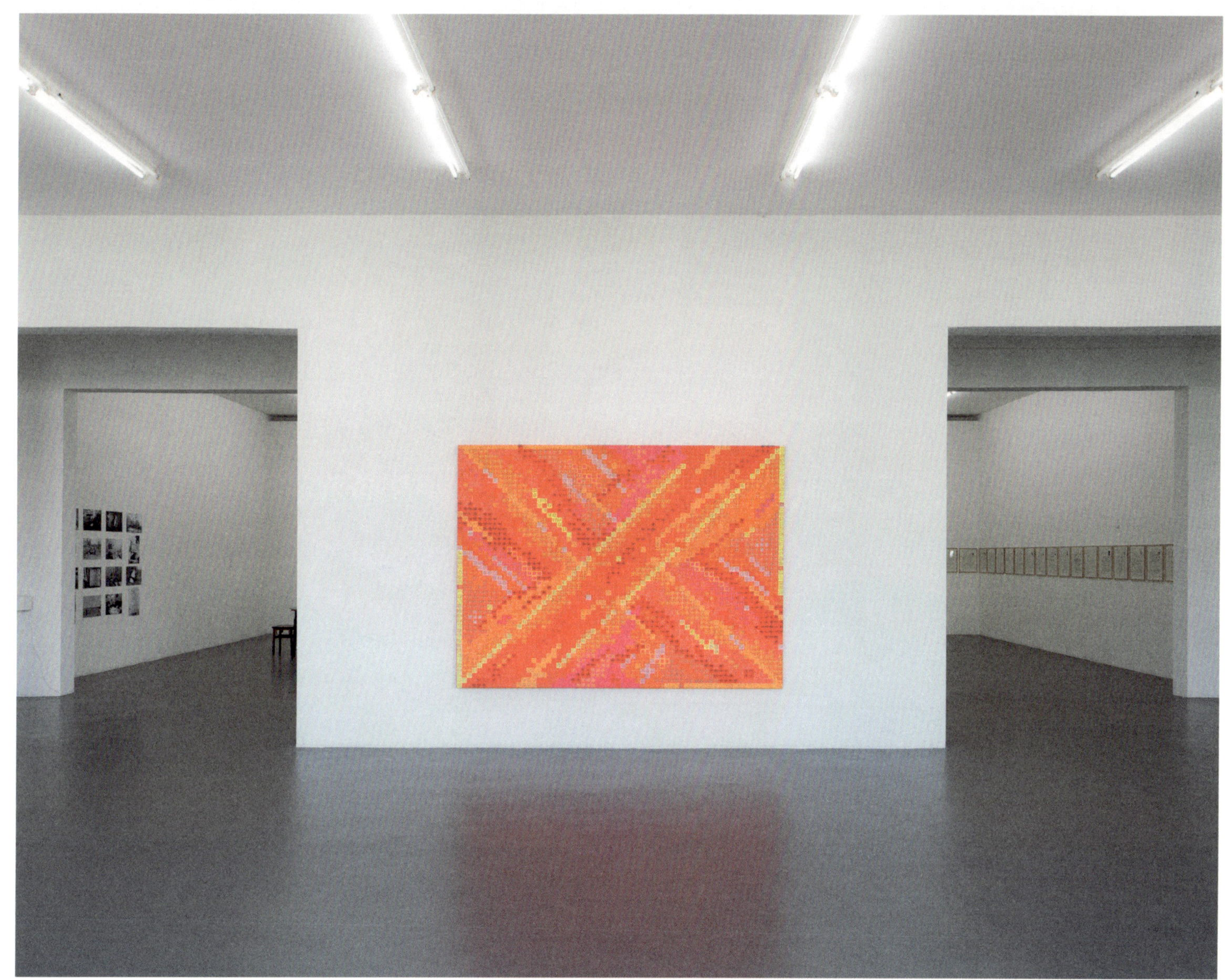

Ding Yi, *Appearance of Crosses 2007-11*, 2007

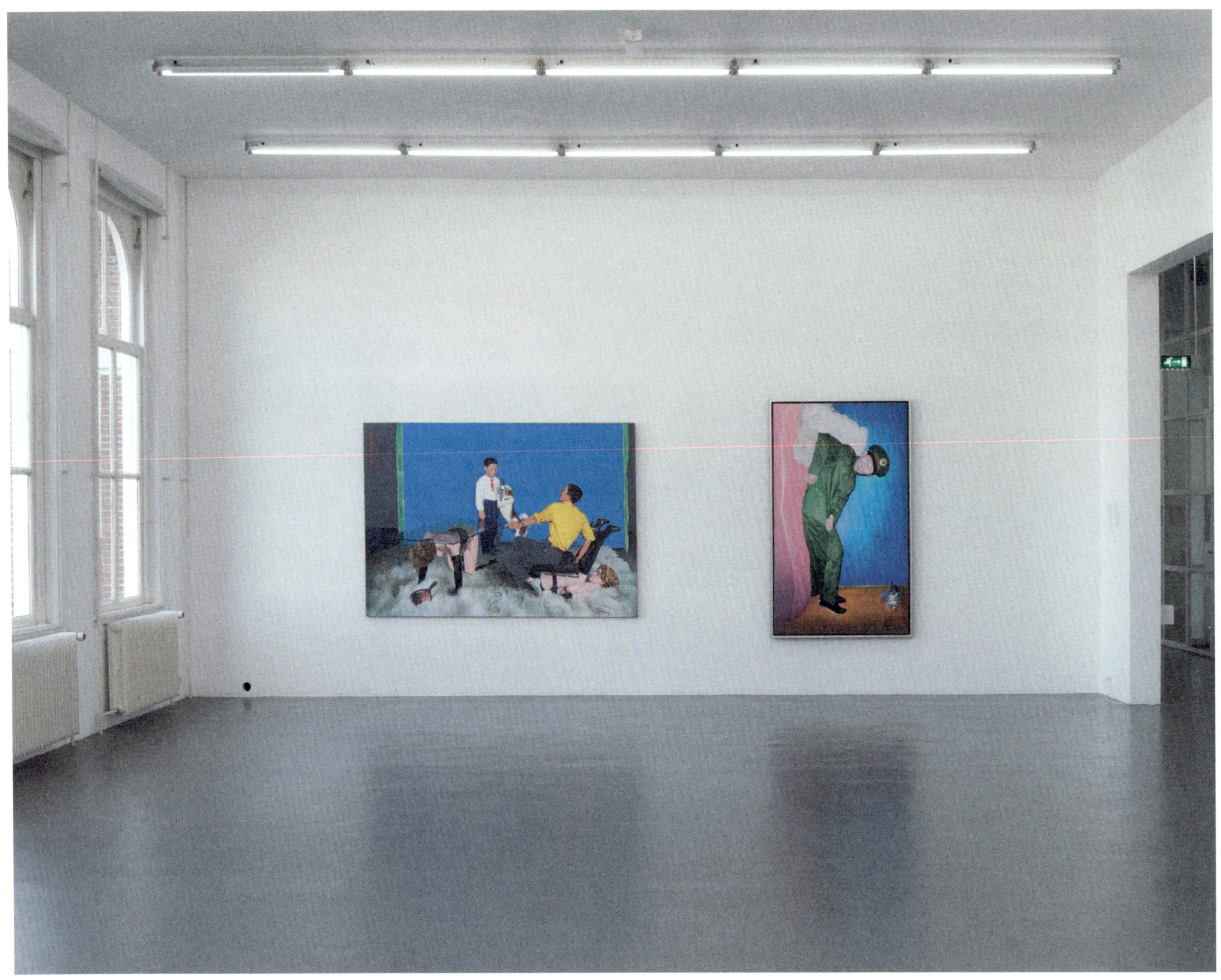

Left to right: Wang Xingwei, *Still No A-mark*, 1998; *Recruit*, 1998 (→ p. 231)

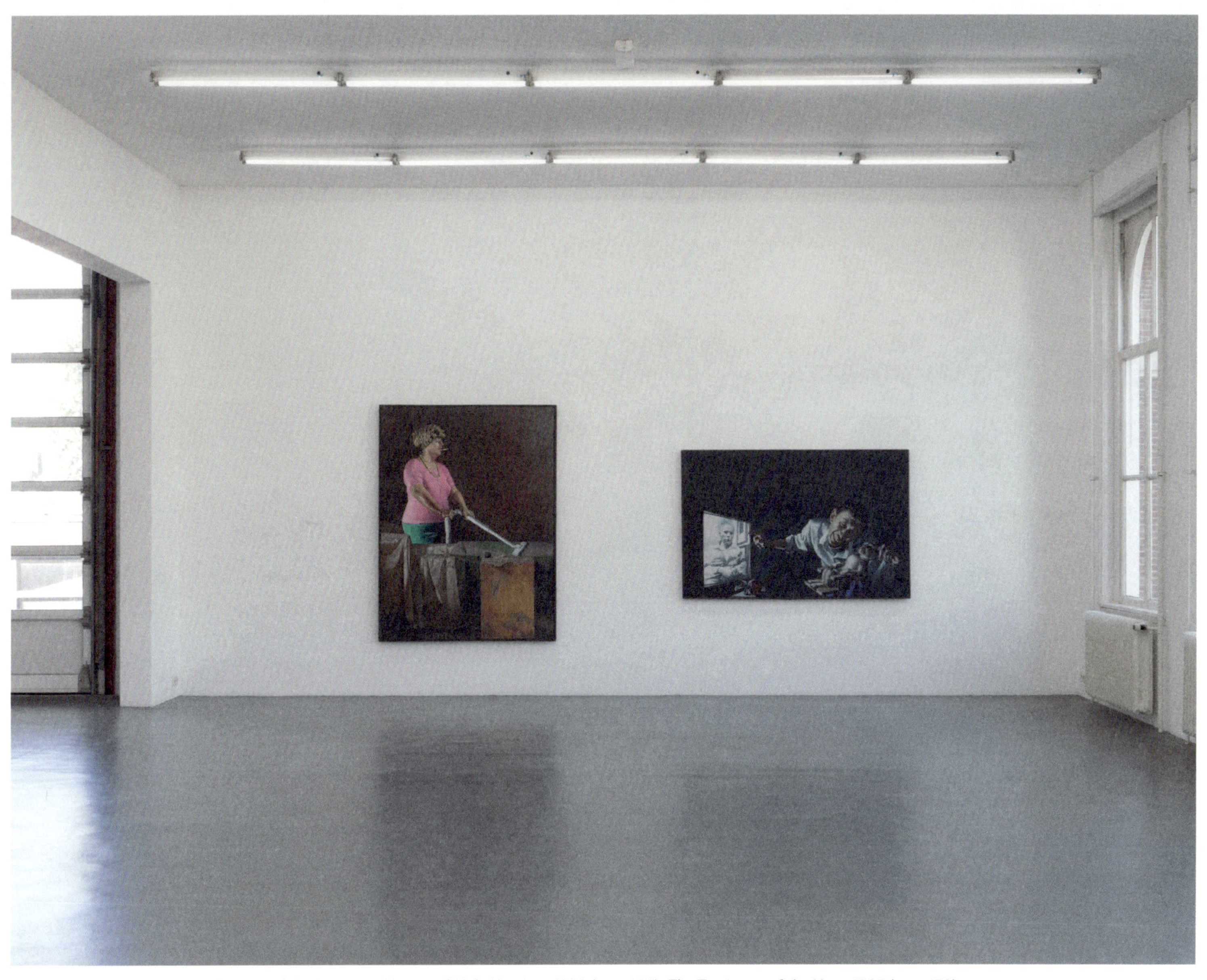

Left to right: Wang Xingwei, *The Dust of the Romantic History of Male Heroism*, 1996 (→ p. 169); *The Testimony of the Hare*, 1995 (→ p. 170)

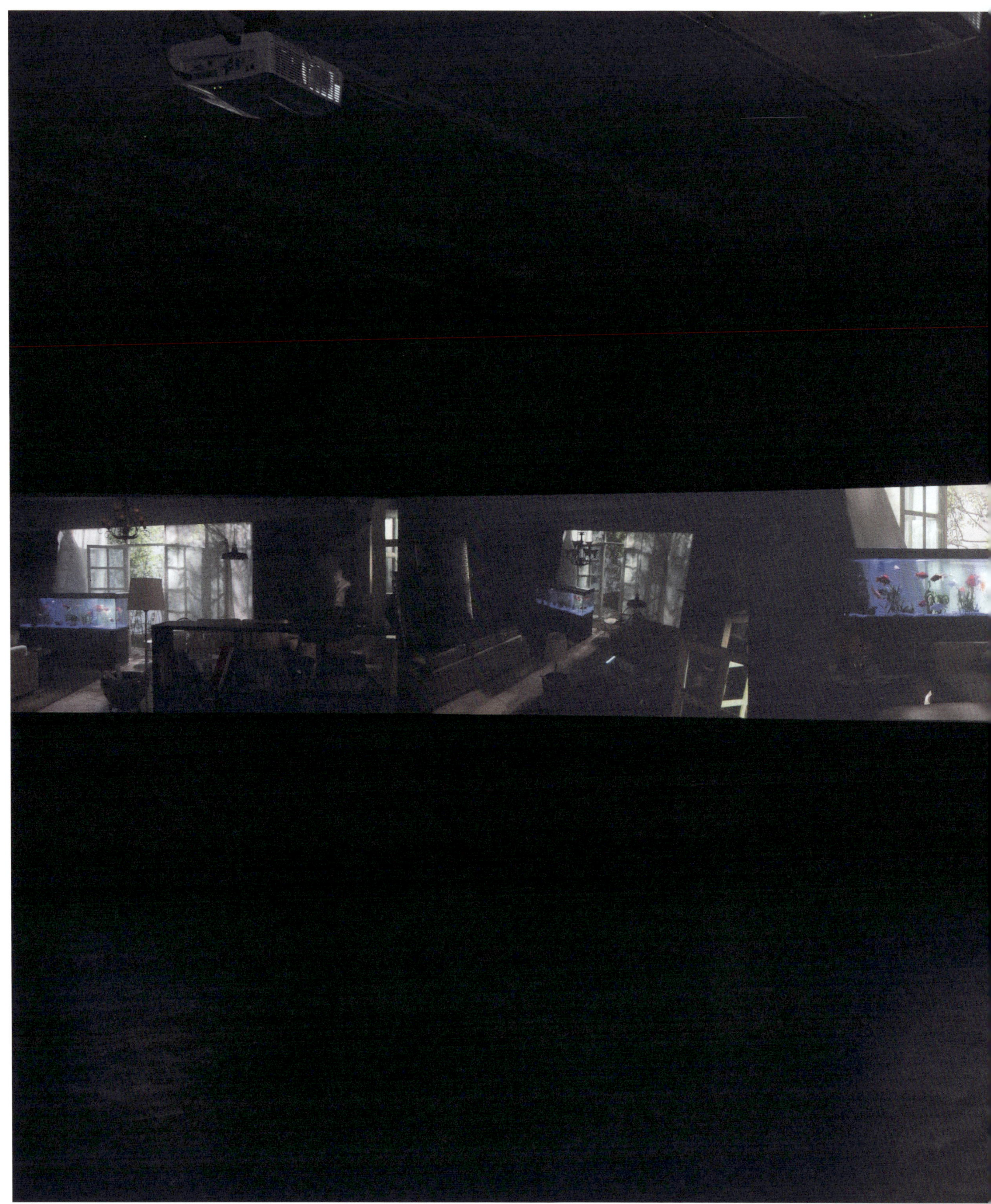

Zhang Peili, *A Gust of Wind*, 2008

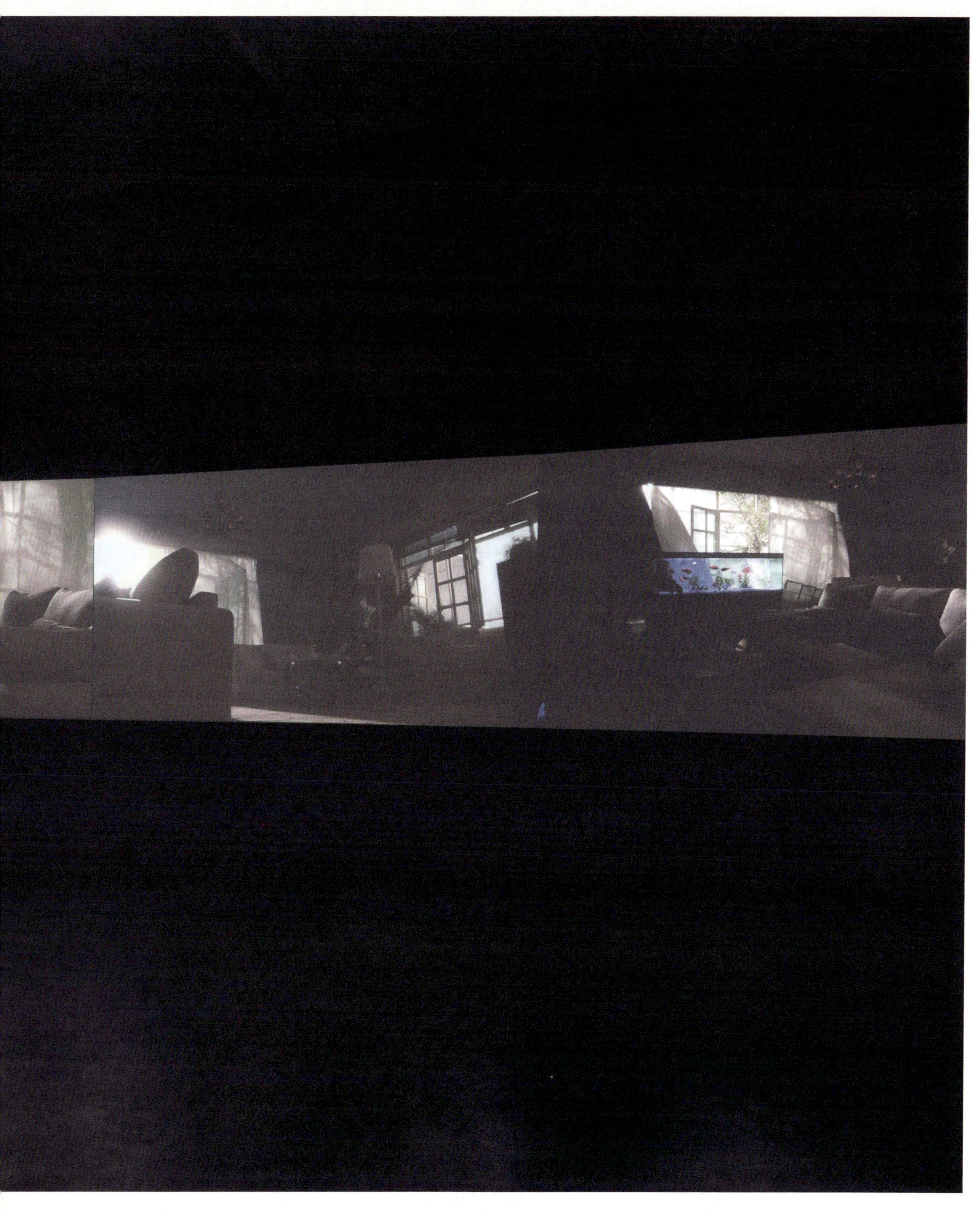

Public program

23 May 2014	*Hans van Dijk: 5000 Names*. Curator's Lecture With: Marianne Brouwer, Zhang Li UCCA
20 July 2014	*Owning an Image*. Academic Lecture With: Zhang Hai'er, Zhang Li UCCA
3 September 2014	*The Great Departure. Contemporary Art in China in the 1980's and early 1990's and its representation in Europe during the exhibition China Avant-Garde* With: Andreas Schmid Witte de With Center for Contemporary Art
23 October 2014	*Digitizing for the Future: Hans van Dijk's Archive* With: Antony Yung (Senior Researcher, Asia Art Archive) Witte de With Center for Contemporary Art
27 November 2014	*The Social Botany Project* With: Xu Tan Witte de With Center for Contemporary Art

Hans van Dijk
Painting in China after the Cultural Revolution
Style Developments and Theoretical Debates
Part I: 1979–1985

Following the end of Mao Zedong's "Cultural Revolution" (1966–1976), China witnessed a period of relative liberalization under Deng Xiaoping's reforms. Initially, his new cultural policy seemed to be a turning point for the arts, as, after thirty years of ideological dogmatism and cultural isolation, it appeared that the socialist doctrine that art should be subservient to politics was going to be abandoned.

However, in this paper, it will be argued that Deng in fact intended the arts to continue to play their traditional role in legitimizing the nation-state, and in defining China's "national identity," albeit along different lines than in Mao's time. An important difference is that in Deng's program, the indigenous cultural heritage, which had been condemned under Mao's regime as "feudal" and "elitist," was rehabilitated in order to support the creation of a new national confidence. The fact that the Deng government continued to define a political role for the arts became increasingly clear when it was confronted with an unexpected result of the introduction of modern Western art in the 1980s: young artists gradually moved away from the officially sanctioned experiments in art toward an independent art movement.

This is the first of two articles in which I will discuss the developments in the contemporary Chinese art world. Part I covers the period 1979–1985, and deals with the various new currents, their style developments, the debates on the indigenous cultural heritage and Western art, important exhibitions, and the reaction of the authorities. Part II, following the same lines, discusses the period 1985–1989.

The Political Role of Art in Chinese Tradition

Under Deng Xiaoping's reforms, China has experienced the second large-scale introduction of (modern) Western art in the 20th century. The first one took place following the fall of the Qing Dynasty in 1911, which ushered in the end of the country's extreme cultural isolation. Thousands of Chinese artists went to study in Japan and Western-Europe for shorter or longer periods of time.

In the 1920s and 30s, a lively art world of rich diversity came into existence, in which experiments were undertaken, both within Eastern and Western artistic styles, and in combining the two. The Japanese invasion and the civil war endangered the development of the new art forms, and the final blow was administered by the establishment of the People's Republic in 1949, when cultural isolation was reinstated as well as the policy of making the arts subservient to political goals—although this time, it was maintained by force. China remained closed to foreign cultural influence except for the forceful and large-scale introduction of Russian socialist realism in the early 1950s, which continued to remain the only foreign stimulus until Deng Xiaoping's "Open Door" policy.

The Deng government gradually relieved the arts of the obligation of fulfilling merely propagandistic tasks, and attempted to revive the nation's traditional cultural heritage, for example by the rehabilitation of the Lingnan School of painting.[1] At the same time, the "Open Door" policy led to China's being exposed to modem Western culture, including Western philosophy and art, on an enormous and unprecedented scale. This sudden and massive confrontation could not but lead to great confusion and bewilderment.

The introduction of Western art into China was confrontational because traditionally, the arts were a major component of the Chinese cultural and political identity. The traditional ideal had always been to create a society in which the arts, the philosophical world-view, and the political order formed one indivisible whole. Particularly the art of painting—as it had developed from around 1000 A.D. onwards—had long been considered as one of the purest and most essential expressions of Chinese culture.

Already in the Song Dynasty, the scholar-painter Ouyang Xiu (1007–1072) held that politics unrelated to the arts is bound to become empty and corrupt, and, vice versa, art unrelated to politics will lose all contact with reality, and will degenerate into superficiality.[2] The view that the art of painting was especially important in this respect was reflected in the establishment, during the Northern Song Dynasty, of the Imperial Painting Academies. Previously, painting had been the responsibility of the Academy for Literature.[3]

1—See MS 1980, No. 12, p. 44. For historic studies of the School, see Ralph Crozier, *Art and Revolution in Modern China: The Lingnan (Cantonese) School of Painting*, 1906–1951, University of California Press, Berkeley 1988; Hans van der Meyden, "Over de oorsprong der Lingnan-school en haar invloed op de modern Chinese schilderkunst" ("On the Origins of the Lingnan School and its Influence on Modern Chinese Painting"), in *Aspecten van de moderne Chinese en Japanse kunst* (Aspects of Modern Chinese and Japanese Art), Department of East-Asian Art History, University of Amsterdam, 1983.

2—See Jacques Gernet, *A History of Chinese Civilization*, Cambridge U.P., 1989, p. 345.

3—See William Watson, *Art of Dynastic China*, London: Thames and Hudson, 1981, p. 268; and H.A. van Oort, *Chinese Kunst*, Baarn (The Netherlands): Het Wereldvenster, 1980, pp. 77, 81.

In 1942, Mao Zedong echoed the same view when he stated "What we demand is the unity of politics and art, the unity of content and form, the unity of revolutionary political content and the highest perfection of artistic form."[4] Significantly, during the "Anti-Rightist Campaign" (1957–1960), the old academies for traditional Chinese painting were re-established.[5] Probably in reaction to this, those artists who had adopted the Western technique of oil painting tried to justify their art by claiming that they were engaged in "creating oil painting with a national character" (*youhua yishu minzuhua*).

Deng Xiaoping's cultural policy was based on the idea that, in the field of science and technology, China should make use of Western knowledge and experience in order to modernize, while in the field of culture, the traditional Chinese heritage could play the role of a binding element in establishing a new self-confidence in the nation, which was in a state of crisis due to the havoc of the Cultural Revolution.[6] In regard to the arts, this policy echoed the 19th-century motto "Chinese learning for the essence, Western learning for practical purposes" (*Zhongxue wei ti, Xixue wei yong*).[7]

The more traditionally oriented artists did indeed use the new cultural freedom to try to restore the long-neglected cultural heritage. But at the same time, and this was an effect unintended by the government, many younger artists interpreted the new cultural policy as an official legitimation for increasing their interest in Western art and culture. Moreover, they embarked on a critical reflection both on recent history, and on the value of the Chinese cultural heritage in comparison with that of the West.

Artists and writers formulated criticisms on the "Cultural Revolution" which went much further than the official repudiation of this period. In their works, they started to address the problems of both the individual, and society at large, often using art styles derived from modern Western art. Far from enthusiastically eulogizing Deng's "Four Modernizations," they increasingly dissociated themselves from the official conception of art as a binding nationalistic element in society. At the end of the 1970s, artists for the first time organized themselves into groups, in order to be able to operate outside official art circles. The authorities interpreted these developments as a form of "westernization" threatening to China's cultural and political order. Between 1979 and 1989, the dividing lines between the various movements within the Chinese art world were formed by the respective positions they adopted towards traditional Chinese art and culture on the one hand, and those of the West on the other. This situation was similar to that at the beginning of the twentieth century.

From 1979 onwards, the art world began to divide itself into an official and an unofficial camp. The former applied itself to traditional Chinese painting and woodcutting, as well as to oil painting as developed under the influence of Russian socialist realism. In unofficial art circles, the emphasis was on all kinds of experimental art forms, partly derived from modern Western art.

4—*Selected Works of Mao Zedong*, Vol. III: Yenan Forum on Literature and Art, Beijing: Foreign Languages Press, 1967, p. 90.

5—MS 1960, No. 4, p. 24; *Zhongguo Meishu Cidian*, Shanghai cishu chubanshe, 1987, p. 153; Laing 1988, p. 26.

6—Ying Ruocheng, Vice-Minister of Culture in the early 1980s, in an interview with E. Wright, BBC broadcast of September 1989. Paul S. Ropp has pointed out the similarities between Chinese art policies around 1960, post-1976, and during the Qing Dynasty, stating that in these periods, the government tried to demonstrate its allegiance to traditional Chinese culture by implementing a conservative art policy. See Paul S. Ropp, *Dissent in Early Modern China*, University of Michigan Press, 1981, p. 37.

7—This motto was first formulated by Zhang Zhidong (1837–1909). See Immanuel C.Y. Hsu, *The Rise of Modern China*, Oxford 1990, p. 369. See also MS 1979, No. 12, p. 3, where a report is presented on the Third National Conference of the Art and Literature Association, held in Beijing in 1979. Artists were expected to support the socialist line, to accept the Party's rule, serve the people, and to contribute to the "Four Modernizations" policy.

Seeking New Directions

In February 1979, Jiang Feng, Chairman of the Chinese National Artists' Association, delivered the opening speech of the "New Spring Exhibition" (*Xinchun Huazhan*) in Beijing's Zhongshan Park. He argued in favor of greater pluriformity in the arts and called upon artists to organize themselves into groups.[8]

His summons did not go unheeded. In that same year, exhibitions were held in Beijing and other large cities, showing a wide array of art works ranging from post-impressionism, expressionism, abstract art and academically painted nudes, to experimental art executed in the traditional ink-wash technique.

The "New Spring Exhibition" had been organized by the artists themselves, who, thanks to Jiang Feng's support, had been relatively free to do what they wanted. In order to create similarly favorable circumstances for future exhibitions, the participants established an association called the "Beijing Oil Painting Research Association" (BOPRA, *Beijing Youhua Yanjiuhui*). Its membership consisted of around forty artists of all ages, i.a. Liu Haisu (1896), Wu Zuoren (1908), and Wu Guanzhong (1919), who belong to the generation who introduced modern Western art into China at the beginning of this century.[9]

8—See Zhang Qiang 1988, p. 119, appendix II. Jiang Feng (1910–1982) already raised the appeal to reject traditional Chinese painting in 1957, which won him the label "anti-nationalistic", subsequently leading to his persecution as a "Rightist". In 1978, Jiang was rehabilitated after twenty years, and immediately carried on his crusade where he had left off. For the effect of the "Hundred Flowers" campaign on painting, see Laing 1988, p. 28.

9—From Tao and Li 1988.

The second exhibition organized by BOPRA in 1979 not only included still life, landscapes, and portraits depicting the way of life of China's ethnic minorities, like the first exhibition, it also included abstract art and nudes. This was a daring act, as these subjects transgress both official policy and general Chinese conservative and puritan mores.
The exhibition toured a number of large cities, each time creating a major commotion among the public and the authorities. The art press warned against the effect of "alienation" which abstract art supposedly engenders among "the masses," and the "moral decadence" which is said to result from exposing the public to nude paintings.
Apart from BOPRA, a number of other associations were established by artists who organized group exhibitions of painting in various styles and techniques, as well as sculpture. Among those in Beijing who rapidly acquired fame were "The Nameless Painting Association" (*Wuming Huahui*), "Contemporaries" (*Tongdairen*)[10], and the "April Association" (*Siyue Yinghui*), which was an association of photographers. The artists of "The Nameless Painting Association," i.a. Zhao Wenliang and Yang Yushu, continued to produce still life and landscape paintings in the free style they had created in the 1960s. Their aim was to develop and expand the Chinese painting tradition by, among other things, using oil paint as a medium. A number of their "traditional" oil paintings were exhibited in Beihai Park in Beijing in 1979[11] Other groups worked in expressionistic styles, or in decorative styles inspired by folk art, for example "Expression" (*Shenshe*) in Yunnan Province, or "Wild Grass" (*Yecao*) in Sichuan Province.
An exhibition which caused much sensation was held in Shanghai entitled "Exhibition by Twelve Artists" (*Shi'er ren Huazhan*).[12] More than 150 works were exhibited by both professional and self-taught artists, i.a. impressionistic and cubistic oil paintings, historic subjects executed in traditional ink wash, and gouache. But also in inland Xi'an, experimental art of many kinds was shown at the "Modern Painting Exhibition" (*Xiandai Huihuazhan*), giving rise both to positive comments and negative reactions such as "monstrous", "ghostly," and "westernized".[13]
The authorities looked on and took no action, not even during the exhibition in the autumn of 1979 of the "Stars Group" (*Xingxing Huahui*), which displayed satirical sculptures of Mao and other political leaders, causing much commotion and a great deal of hilarity.

10—MS 1980, No. 8, p. 47.

11—From the manifest *Zhi you gudu er jianqiang de ren cai zuiqiu zhenli* (Only Those Who are Strong Because They Are Solitary Can Pursue Truth), published on the occasion of an exhibition in the Beijing Friendship Hotel in 1984.

12—MS 1979, No. 5, p. 13.

13—Tao and Li 1988, p. 11.

Wang Keping and the "Stars Group"

Wang Keping was born in Beijing in 1949, the son of the writer Wang Lin.[14] At the end of the 1970s, he was a scriptwriter for Beijing Central Television, writing scripts based on modern Western literature in which his employer never took any interest. He dissociated himself from his own past as a Red Guard, and developed a cynical view on politics. Without any higher art education, he embarked in 1978 on making wooden sculptures and relief work in a primitive style. Sometimes his natural, organic shapes evoke erotic associations, but there are also biting political caricatures of Mao and other top leaders. The sculpture "Blind and Silent" (1979) is a finely worked, cylindrical wooden head, representing the average Party cadre. One eye and the mouth are enclosed by a circle: a symbolic expression for the blindness and vacant words of Chinese officialdom. Its sober, primitive style endows the sculpture with a directly provocative power. Another fine example is "Wan wan sui!" (1978), a statuette representing Lin Biao, holding Mao's "little red book" in one hand, and a knife, symbolizing his later treason against Mao, in the other. Encouraged by the liberal atmosphere surrounding the "Wall of Democracy," Wang established the "Stars Group" in Beijing, together with, a.o., Qu Leilei, Huang Rui (b. 1952 in Beijing), Mao Lizi (b. 1950 in Shaanxi Province), and Ma Desheng (b. 1952 in Beijing). In November 1979, they exhibited 150 works by about 20 artists in Beihai Park in Beijing, including sculptures by Wang Keping, photographic-realist paintings by Mao Lizi, and expressionist and cubist paintings by Huang Rui. The exhibition lasted ten days and attracted around 30,000 astonished and enthusiastic visitors. From the visitors' book, Fox Butterfield quotes the following comment: "Have the Chinese people gone numb? No, I have seen that the Chinese people's spirit is still alive. This is the best art exhibit since Liberation".[15] Although the press did not devote a single word to the exhibition, the

14—Butterfield 1982, p. 435 ff. On the "Stars", see MS 1980, No. 9, p. 12; 1980, No. 12, pp. 13, 26, 33; Cohen 1987, p. 59; Zhang and Li 1986, p. 323.

15—Butterfield 1982, p. 438.

fame of the "Stars Group" was now firmly established. It became the very symbol of the demand for artistic freedom.

The "new spring" announced by Jiang Feng was followed by a cold winter. The "Wall of Democracy" was closed, and Wang Keping and the other participants in the Beihai Park exhibition were banned from exhibiting their works anywhere for an indefinite period. Like many other members of the "Stars Group," Wang left the country. Since 1984, he lives and works in Paris.

The political opposition to experimental art increased rapidly during 1979–1981, and was followed by the full-blown campaigns "Against Spiritual Pollution" and "Against Bourgeois Liberalism." In regard to art, these campaigns were specifically directed against Western influences, causing a rift between artists from the world of traditional Chinese painting and other artists, exactly as has happened previously during the "Anti-Rightist Campaign" (see above).

Both artists and cultural officials were in a state of uncertainty about how to interpret the official art policy—in some cities, abstract art could be exhibited, while it was not allowed in others.[16] The experimental art that continued to be produced in these years remained in the art studios, or circulated only within small circles.[17] In January 1983, however, reproductions of erotic works by the blacklisted Wang Keping appeared in the magazine *Meishu.*

16—Cohen 1987, p. 82 explains that the reason was, in some cases, the difference in ideological attitude of the responsible culture officials, and, in other cases, the slowness with which policy guidelines were transmitted from Beijing all the way down to the localities.

17 — This is extensively discussed in Cohen 1987, pp. 7, 25.

"Scar-Art"

The controversial exhibitions held around 1980 had, to a certain extent, dealt with the same subject matter as the "scar-literature" (*shanghen wenxue*) which emerged after the Cultural Revolution, and which dealt with the personal experiences of individuals during this period of upheaval, and their attempts to cope with them.

"Scar"-painting only lasted a few years. Using the realistic, and sometimes dramatic and romantic style until recently used for propaganda art, it produced paintings of fights between Red Guard factions, and of their primitive living conditions after Mao had sent them all off to the country-side in order to end the chaos he had himself created. Many of these works reflected the mood of the despair and disillusionment prevailing among these youths, who felt that Mao had abandoned and betrayed them.

Artist Mao Lizi used photographic-realism, such as *trompe-l'oeuil* effects, to depict crushed cigarette butts lying on a concrete floor as symbols of despair. Other "scar" artists were Cheng Conglin (b. 1955 in Sichuan Province), Zhang Hongnian (b. 1947 in Nanjing), Gao Yaguan, Su Gao'er, and others.[18] In the Chinese art press, the works in this genre (which often appear sentimental and melodramatic to the Western eye) were categorized as "art of reflection" (*fansi yishu*).[19]

18—Works by the said artists can be found in Tao and Li 1988, and in *Youhuaxuan* (Selected Oil Paintings), Hunan meishu chubanshe 1985.

19—Tao and Li 1988, p. 11.

Yuan Yunsheng and the Beijing Airport Wall Painting

An early *cause célèbre* in the Chinese art world illustrating the limits of the new "liberal" art policy was that of Yuan Yunsheng's 1979 wall painting for the new Beijing Airport.[20] He had painted a brightly colored scene depicting a Dai ethnic minority festival, in a rich, vibrant, and decorative style inspired by the Mexican socialist-realistic art of Diego Rivera (1886–1957), José Clemente Orozco (1883–1949) en Siqueiros (1896–1974). The work of these artists had been introduced into China in the 1960s, together with the propaganda art of Cuba, North-Korea and Vietnam.[21]

What the authorities found offensive was the fact that Yuan had included a number of nudes among the festive throng, which were subsequently removed in the following year. But by then, through reproductions in the magazine *Meishu*, the work had already acquired nation-wide fame for its dynamic vitality.[22]

20—Yuan Yunsheng (b. 1937 in Jiangsu Province) was a victim of the 1957 "Anti-Rightist Campaign", as a result of his criticism of the educational program at the Central Academy of Fine Arts in Beijing, which was exclusively devoted to socialistic realism. He was punished by being sent down to the countryside, where he stayed uninterruptedly (except during the years 1963 and 1964) until 1979, when he returned to Beijing. See Cohen 1987, pp. 42–44.

21—MS 1963, No. 6, 1964, No. 5.

22—Cohen 1987, pp. 39–40.

Chen Danqing and the Sichuan School

Simultaneous with "Scar-art" but much less controversial and appealing to a far greater number of artists working in all kinds of disciplines, was the interest in the depiction of life in the countryside and the cultures of China's ethnic minorities. This interest had been aroused in many young artists who, like many of their generation, had been sent to the country-side at the end of the Cultural Revolution, and had there acquired first-hand knowledge of the life of farmers, herdsmen, and ethnic minorities. After their return to the cities, they looked back to the plain and rugged life of this period with feelings of nostalgia, which was reinforced by their confrontation with the straitjacket of official art policy. They came to identify urban culture with the trammels of politics and ideology, and compared it unfavorably to the authenticity of life in the country-side.

In the field of pictorial art, these feelings were felt to be the most adequately expressed in the paintings of Tibetans made by Chen Danqing (b. 1948), a Sichuanese and member of the "Contemporaries" Group (*Tongdairen*).[23] The religion, dress, and pastoral way of life of the Tibetans stand in great contrast with the urban life of the Han-Chinese in the big cities, and Chen expressed this contrast in a series of seven paintings showing Tibetans paying a visit to a Han Chinese city. The sober grandeur in which he depicted the theme of alienation and confrontation immediately struck a sympathetic chord in the hearts of the post-Cultural Revolution Chinese urban south. The paintings took the public by storm, and also rapidly acquired international fame. Chen Danqing has been living and working in New York since 1982.

The great number of artists who work in a more or less similar style are categorized by the Chinese art press as "Sichuan School," which is said to comprise (from Sichuan Province): He Duoling (1948), Shang Yang (1942), Luo Zhongli (1948), Cheng Conglin (1955) and Long Quan (1956), as well as Ai Xuan (1947) from Zhejiang Province.[24] Especially He, Luo, Cheng and Ai devote much attention to the psychological expressiveness of their figures, following Chen Danqing's example. In reaction to the invariably positive hero models of the socialist-realist propaganda art of the 1960s, they have concentrated on depicting feelings of insecurity, bewilderment, and open-mindedness. Unfortunately, in some cases this is done with so much emphasis that the result is often more melodramatic, depressive, or sentimental than psychologically refined. They also devote much care and precision to the detailed depiction of the texture of clothes and objects, a tendency which is pushed to extremes in the still life paintings and portraits by other artists working in more academic styles.

Long Quan and Shang Yang have developed a free, expressive landscape-style showing a strong feeling of love and attachment towards nature. The work of Long Quan appears to be influenced by Fauvism and Cubism, while Shang Yang's early works are still clearly related to the relatively realistic, slightly dramatic Russian landscape painting. His later works, on the other hand, show expressionist influences.

Because the world depicted by "scar"-art and artists of the Sichuan School was in stark contrast with the prevalent ideal, some of their paintings were criticized as "anti-social" and even "anti-Chinese." One particularly controversial work was Luo Zhongli's "Father" (1980), a large photographic-realist portrait showing the cragged and weather-beaten face of an old farmer.[25] It was not accepted by the official "Second National Exhibition of Young Artists" (*Di'er ju quanguo qingnian meizhan*) held in 1981 in Beijing, until the artist added a ball-point sticking out from underneath the farmer's cap, to allay the selection committee's fears that the portrait would be interpreted as symbolizing the continued existence of backwardness and analphabetism in China. Eventually, the work was even awarded first prize at the exhibition, probably for its technical perfection of detail, which gave rise to a heated controversy in the art press that did not subside until 1985.

Opposition Against the "Sichuan School"

For some time, it seemed as if the "Sichuan School" had given rise to a successful new, national art movement, and this impression was reinforced by the School's international

23—An exhibition of the Group was held in Beijing in 1980, at the Central Academy of Arts (*Zhongyang meishu xueyuan*). When Chen's father became a victim of political accusations, he was refused access to any art education. However, in 1978, his exceptional talents were discovered and he was appointed a lecturer, under Wu Zuoren, at the most important national art academy, the Central Academy of Arts. For articles about him and examples of his work, see Tao and Li 1988, ill. 112 and 114; MS 1981, No. 1, pp. 28, 29, 42, 43; 1982, No. 1, p. 11; Cohen 1987, pp. 103, 104.

24—Works by said artists can be found in Tao and Li 1988, and in *Youhuaxuan*, Hunan meishu chubanshe 1985.

25—Reproduced on the cover of MS 1981, No. 1.

recognition. The discovery that pictorial art was capable of expressing a much greater range of emotions and ideas than had ever been displayed by socialist-realism, and could even be used as a means of expressing personal feelings and experiences, led to an explosion of "rural" works.

The art press distinguished sub-trends such as "the daily life current" (*shenghuo liu*), comprising scenes of the daily life of farmers and ethnic minorities; "native soil realism fever" (*xiangtu xieshi re*); and "landscape fever" (*fengjing re*). Honesty, sincerity, strength, and passion were the most cherished values of the movement, as opposed to the debility and corruption of urban propaganda art.

However, compared to Chen Danqing's original works, those who set out to follow his example often fell into commonplace romanticism and sentimental nostalgia, even if their paintings often exhibited great technical perfection. The government found it very easy to assimilate these works in its policy of establishing an image of social harmony. As the official media invariably hush up conflicts and confrontations with ethnic minorities and tend to de-emphasize major setbacks in rural development, cultural officials were greatly relieved to see that, although abandoning socialist realism, artists did not treat "rural" subjects in a way that was aimed at exposing the ills of contemporary Chinese politics and society, and were far from embarking *en masse* on direct provocation and confrontation, like the "Stars Group" had in 1979.

But already in 1983, opposition arose in artistic circles against the anecdotic and aesthetic character of what was seen as a new academism, on the basis of a more intellectual approach to art. This opposition originated in the increasing awareness of Western art which Chinese artists had been able to acquire since 1978. The continued influx of information on Western art movements, and the debates and controversies which it elicited, precluded, for the time being, any form of stabilization in the Chinese art world.

Western Art Exhibitions in China

The number of exhibitions of foreign art held in China increased rapidly from the mid-1970s onwards, introducing increasingly controversial and challenging works to the astonished Chinese public, and eventually leading to what the Chinese art press called "the collision with Western culture" (*Xifang wenhua chongtu*).[26] The beginnings were cautious enough, starting slowly with North-Korean and Yugoslavian propaganda-art, and Japanese traditional and modern works[27], and, in 1977, an exhibition of 19th and 20th-century Romanian art: the first one since the Cultural Revolution to deal with non-political Western art. [28]

Then, a complete sensation was caused in March 1978 by the first exhibition of Western-European art, held in Beijing and Shanghai.[29] It comprised about 80 works of 19th-century French landscape painting, including Courbet, Jules Bastien-Lepage, and representatives of the Barbizon School, i.a. Corot and Millet. For everyone then younger than 30, this was the very first confrontation with the precursors of modern Western-European art.[30] There were so many people sitting down to copy the works that no one could get through and the organizers had to send the copiers away.[31]

Until 1985, all Western art introduced into China, apart from two small exhibitions devoted respectively to Picasso and the Paris-based Chinese artist Zao Wou-ki (see below), was firmly from before the Second World War. For example, the public had the opportunity to see 19th and 20th century Swedish socialist-realist art[32], and the Armand Hammer collection (an American private collection comprising 110 works by Rubens, Rembrandt, Goya, Millet, Pissaro, Degas, Van Gogh, Picasso, and many others), which attracted an immense crowd of spectators.[33]

In 1982, there was an exhibition of Australian landscape artists, as well as a large exhibition of French painting from the period 1620–1870.[34] In 1983, Italian Renaissance art was introduced[35], together with works by Picasso[36], and Zao Wou-ki (Zhao Wuji), a Chinese artist who emigrated to Paris in the 1940s.[37] The latter exhibition was much publicized in the Chinese press, and the artist's lectures, delivered at Zhejiang Art Academy in Hangzhou, attracted a huge audience. In 1984, a number of exhibitions were held of pre-

26—The following selection of exhibitions was made by the author on the basis of conversations held, between 1986 and 1989, with artists, art students and teachers at Chinese art academies, as well as on information provided in Chinese art magazines. Exhibitions of foreign political propaganda art are not included. It should be noted that the introduction of foreign art through the art press was far more comprehensive than through actual exhibitions. However, due to lack of space, a discussion thereof cannot be attempted in this article.

27—MS 1978, No. 2, p. 44.

28—MS 1978, No. 3, p. 47; MS 1979, No. 11 for illustrations.

29—The French title of the exhibition was *Paysages paysans français 1820-1905*. See MS 1978, No. 3 and JH 1978, No. 4.

30—This generation had previously seen only works by the early Russian landscape and socialist-realist Russian artists, such as Vasili Ivanovich Surikov (1848–1916), Ilya Efemovich Repin (1844–1930). See Laing 1988, p. 21; Cohen 1987, p. 18; Zhang and Li 1986, p. 233.

31—Oral information obtained in 1988.

32—Exhibited in 1979 in Beijing, Changsha and Shanghai, comprising works by, i.a., Larsson, Zorn, and Liljeford, whose work was introduced into China in the 1930s by Lu Xun. See MS 1979, No. 3, p. 39.

33—For reproductions, see MS 1982, No. 4, p. 64; 1982, No. 5, pp. 36–40; 1982, No. 6, pp. 61-64.

34—Reproductions can be found in MS 1982, No. 11, pp. 64; 1982, No. 12, pp. 34, 35,40. The exhibition contained 78 paintings from the Louvre and the Palace of Versailles, produced by 61 artists, a.o. Renoir, Rodin, Millet, Ingres, Georges de La Tour, and Fragonard.

35—May/June 1983, in Beijing, Luoyang, Shanghai and Guangzhou. On display were originals and reproductions of 80 works, accompanied by documentation materials. See MS 1983, No. 6, p. 20.

36—In May 1983, Beijing National Gallery showed 15 oil paintings and 13 graphical works by Picasso. See MS 1983, No. 6, p. 51.

37—September 1983. On display were 39 post-1935 works, including oil and ink-wash paintings in an abstract expressionistic style. At the opening, a speech was delivered by Wu Zuoren, Vice-Chairman of the Chinese National Artists' Association. Zao Wou-ki had become famous in China because of his cooperation with architect I.M. Pei, which had, in 1981, resulted in a number of controversial wall paintings in a Beijing hotel. See MS 1983, No. 10, p. 15; JH 1985, No. 12, p. 35.

war German Expressionists, and modern Russian painting and sculpture.[38] The following year, there was an exhibition of French art from 1730 to the present, especially Impressionists and *Les Nabis*[39], and one devoted to Spanish 18th and 19th-century art, at which Goya's works in particular created a deep impression.[40]

38—ZMB 1985, No. 20, p. 4: October 1984.

39—ZMB 1985, No. 11, p. 1.

40—ZMB 1985, No. 21, p. 2.

But 1985 was also the year of the inevitable, shattering blow. It fell with full, unexpected force when in November, China was confronted with the work of Robert Rauschenberg, at the country's first large exhibition ever of post-war modern Western art. The event sent a veritable shock wave through the entire Chinese art world. Reactions varied widely, from enthusiasm about Rauschenberg's creative, natural way of using materials and the humor in his work, to rejections of his "superficiality and subjectivism"[41] The exhibition, which exploded like a bombshell in the Chinese art world, and, especially in the minds of the young generation, made at least one thing abundantly clear: the challenge of modern Western art was far greater than they could ever have imagined.

41—The exhibition was held in Beijing and afterwards in Lhasa. See ZMB 1985, No. 19, p. 2; 1985, No. 22, p. 2.

Huang Yongping: Chinese Thought and Western Art

In 1982, a number of young artists, from the first batch of art graduates since the Cultural Revolution, decided to dissociate themselves from the prevalent approach to Western art, which, in their view, largely consisted of mechanical copying and an exclusive concentration on technical aspects. They wanted to go deeper than the surface, and analyze the theoretical and philosophical backgrounds both of modern Western art and traditional Chinese culture. Prominent figures were Huang Yongping and Gu Wenda of the Zhejiang Art Academy in Hangzhou, who were later to play an important role in the unofficial art movement in 1984–85. Now living abroad, they exerted a great influence on the Chinese art world throughout the 1980s.

Huang Yongping (b. 1954 in Xiamen, Fujian Province) graduated in Oil Painting in 1982.[42] In the following year, he and some colleagues organized an exhibition in his native city, entitled "A Modern Art Exhibition of Five Artists" (*Wu ren xiandai huazhan*).[43] The local authorities had not given permission to open the exhibition to the general public, and only allowed entry to a number of selected persons. Among the exhibits were sculptures, relief works, and paintings in figurative, expressionist, and abstract styles, made from a variety of materials such as iron, electric cords, wood and plaster.

42—The works he had produced for his final examinations were executed with a spray gun machine, in a coachwork factory. He had chosen both the venue and the technique used because he aimed to create an art form which was closely related to modern daily life. For articles by and about Huang, and examples of his work, see MS 1983, No. 1, pp. 22 and 25; 1989, No. 3, p. 30; JH 1986, No. 2, pp. 34; 1988, No. 2, pp. 38; ZMB 1986, No. 38; MSSC 1985, No. 6, p. 2; 1986, No. 4, p. 1; 1987, No. 5, p. 35.

43—Held in May 1983.

One of Huang's works, "Haystack," caused a great sensation. It was a new version of his copy of a painting by one of his teachers at the Academy, which, in turn, had been a copy of "Les Foins," a work by the French artist Jules Bastien-Lepage (1848–1884), painted in 1878. This work had been part of the exhibition of 19th-century French landscape painting held at Beijing National Gallery in 1978. It was the first exhibition of Western art held after the Cultural Revolution, and caused tremendous excitement in the Chinese art world. "Les Foins," which shows a country couple tired from hard labor resting in the grass, was one of the most popular works which numerous visitors copied on the spot, and some of these copies were afterwards hung in the art academies to be copied by students. "Les Foins" was also used by a great number of Chinese artists as the basis for various free variations, such as "Spring has Arrived" (1980) by He Duoling, who replaced the French farmer's wife by a Chinese girl in local costume flanked by an ox.[44]

44—It is a rather sentimental work executed in the photographic-realist style of the 1960s by the American painter Andrew Wyeth.

Huang Yongping's remake was more in the style of Marcel Duchamp. On the face of the farmer's wife in his copy of his teacher's copy of "Les Foins," he had attached a plaster head, of the type normally used for copying purposes during drawing classes, and he had attached a wooden foot to her leg which actually protruded from the picture-frame.

In 1986, during an art manifestation in Xiamen, he stated in the manifesto accompanying the exhibition that studying the ideas behind works of modern art was far more important than mechanically copying them, and that "works of art are for artists what opium is for the people".[45]

45—"Xiamen Dada— yizhong houadandai?" (Xiamen Dada: A Kind of Postmodernism?), Xiamen 1986.

At the Academy in Hangzhou, the work of Marcel Duchamp, Yves Klein, and John Cage had created an absolute sensation, and Huang Yongping, among others, had been greatly inspired by the discovery that Taoist and Zen-Buddhist thought had played a considerable role in the development of modern Western art in the 1960s. The persistent denial and undermining of all systems, doctrines, and dogmas in Zen-Buddhism offered these artists an indigenous weapon against all forms of academism in artistic theory and practice. It also provided a basis for a kind of art which turned away from trivial and anecdotal subject matter, towards the expression of more comprehensive natural and cosmic processes. Since this particular current of Chinese thought had proven to be relevant and fertile in modern Western art, it also seemed to hold promises for modern Chinese art. Huang began to create works in which he explored the relationship of Taoism and Zen Buddhism with modern language philosophy, and later, during the "Art Groups Movement 1985," he organized a Dadaistic manifestation which established him as one of the most influential leaders of the movement to link modern art and the traditional Chinese heritage. In the Spring of 1989, Huang was invited to participate in the "Magiciens de la Terre" exhibition in Paris, France. The June 1989 massacre in Beijing made him decide to stay there.

Gu Wenda

Gu Wenda (b. 1955 in Shanghai) studied traditional Chinese painting, calligraphy, and seal-engraving.[46] In the early 1980s, he was appointed a lecturer at the Zhejiang Art Academy in Hangzhou. In this period, he experimented both with traditional Chinese ink-wash landscape painting and oils.

For example, he painted a landscape in ink-wash technique in which he deliberately used the traditional tripartite landscape composition in a cool manner devoid of any charm, as if to caricaturize the painting handbooks: reeds and water in the foreground, two angular rock formations in the middle, and an isolated mountain top at the back. However, he created a rich variation of texture and fluttering movement by an original, utterly unconventional use of the ink-wash technique, which softened the formality of the composition and endowed the work with a surrealist flavor.

Gu used both ink-wash and oil techniques for his calligraphic experiments. In some cases, he broke down characters representing concepts in Chinese art theory to their various constituents, enlarged these, and placed them in a landscape. Other works consist of characters which are incorrectly written, or written as mirror images, so that their meaning has become ambiguous and mysterious.

Like Huang Yongping, Gu Wenda documented his own development in notes and articles which were subsequently published by the art press. In many of his essays, he displayed an intellectual approach to the artistic profession, strongly opposing the primacy of self-expression which the "Stars Group" were still championing in the early 1980s, as well as the currents of "naive art" which had become increasingly popular.[47] Originally inspired by folk art and children's drawings, this latter genre later often declined into decorative mannerism and stereotyped quasi-naivety. Gu offered the following disparaging comment: "The similarity between peasant art, childrens' art, and expressionism is that they all consist of the direct expression of feelings. I believe that all great and superior artists have risen above these contaminations, since only after they had won this battle could their works display the inner victory which is impossible for peasant art, children's art, and expressionism to attain.[48]

Gu Wenda's works and writings were a source of inspiration to many young artists, and his controversial exhibitions of 1985 and 1986 won him immense fame. In the Spring of 1987, he emigrated to the USA, where he continues to work under the name Wenda Gu.

Disillusion: The Sixth National Art Exhibition

In 1984, the official Sixth National Art Exhibition was held, to which the Chinese art world had been looking forward with much enthusiasm. Expectations had been running very high, as the exhibition was expected to present an overview of the re-awakening of Chinese art after decades of lethargy and political exploitation".[49] The committee in charge of selecting the exhibits had been said to have acted in accordance with Deng Xiaoping's

46—For articles by and on Gu Wenda, and examples of his work, see MS 1986, No. 7, p. 37; 1987, No. 8, p. 24; 1989, No. 1, p. 64, 1990, No. 8; JH 1984, No. 6, p. 28; 1985, No. 2, pp. 29, 30, 32; MSSC 1987, No. 5, p. 20; XMS 1982, No. 1; 1983, No. 4; 1985, No. 4; 1986, No. 2; ZMB 1985, No. 9; 1986, No. 2; 1988, No. 2; Zhang Qiang 1988, pp. 52 and 76.

47—Good examples are the colorful naive paintings of rural scenes by Qiao Xiaogang (b. 1957 in Hebei Province) and Fei Zheng (b. 1938 in Heilongjiang Province), and "Clay Doll Salesman" by Fang Bingshan (b. 1940 in Jiangsu Province).

48—Gu Wenda "Yishu Biji, 1985-3-30' in Huejia, 1985, No. 1.

49—These official national exhibitions have been regularly organized since 1949 by the Ministry of Culture (the former Ministry of Propaganda) in cooperation with the Chinese National Artists Association (*Zhongguo meishujia xiehui*). They are organized on a mammoth scale, often comprising many thousands of works, which are put on display in a number of big cities, supposedly providing a representative and up-to-date overview of all facets of contemporary Chinese art. The selection of the exhibits takes place according to the art policy guidelines in force at that particular moment. See MS 1983, No. 12, pp. 62 and 64.

art policy of "Letting a hundred flowers bloom and a hundred schools contend".[50] After the exhibition was opened, however, it was clear that the committee had been influenced by the official warnings that year against "bourgeois liberalism," as there were almost no works on display by the provocative art groups which had been active around 1980.[51] Instead, the scene was dominated by works eulogizing the history of the Chinese Communist Party and the "Four Modernizations," which were interspersed by paintings depicting scenes of rural and urban daily life, and themes from the well-known classical novels (*Dream of the Red Chamber*, *History of the Three Kingdoms*, and *Journey to the West*). Almost all the works exhibited were executed in realistic styles, ranging from the decorative to the expressionist. Abstract works were conspicuously absent, and the techniques employed were also mostly conventional, often derived from traditional Chinese painting or socialist-realist propaganda art.[52]

50—MS, December 1983. The "Double Hundred" policy had originally been formulated by Mao Zedong in 1956, and initiated a short period of artistic and intellectual freedom which lasted less than a year. It was followed by a severe political backlash, the "Anti-Rightist Campaign", which, in fact, continued until 1976.

51—For an overview of reactions to the exhibition, see JH 1985, No. 1, p. 6, and JH 1988, No. 11, p. 16.

52—On display were a number of nostalgic and dreamily romantic landscapes and paintings of figures executed in these techniques. See the illustrations in MS 1985, No. 5 and JH 1984, No. 6.

The disappointment following this and other official exhibitions was especially acute as in these years, Chinese artists had become increasingly aware, through numerous exhibitions and a flood of publications, of recent art developments abroad. Their own works and cautious experiments suddenly looked unbearably boring and tedious in comparison, and seemed to lose all credibility altogether when they were confronted in 1985 with the work of a Robert Rauschenberg.

Again: Seeking New Directions

In the 1980s, the interest of young Chinese for foreign, especially Western, culture, soared to unprecedented heights. A flood of translations of Western literary and academic works was produced, ranging from 19th-century German philosophy to the reports issued by the Club of Rome. The works of Kant, Nietzsche, Kafka, Hesse, Sartre, and others attracted huge (although often temporary) attention. The inevitable result of this overwhelming torrent of new influences was confusion and chaos. Artists joined the general search for a new formula to provide answers to all questions, especially how art can fulfil an avant-garde role. In 1986, Gu Wenda declared in an interview that he had been strongly influenced by the philosophy of Nietzsche:

> "Unlike the philosophy of science and analytic philosophy, which operate on a level different from everyday life, the philosophy of Nietzsche is a battle with existence itself. That is the reason that my paintings possess an outwardly directed, expansive power. I also found Schopenhauer and Freud fascinating to read, but at bottom, I am not a scholar or theoretician, and I am interested in a wide range of subjects...."[53]

53—Interview by Fei Dawei with Gu Wenda, in MS 1986, No. 7, p. 53.

He conceded that the passive study of Western art was useful, but that, on the international level, it was not much more than walking on a beaten track. For this reason, he wanted to "engage in a battle against modernism," especially because he felt that many Chinese artists behaved like "spiritual slaves of modern Western art".[54] This attitude greatly contributed to his growing fame among young Chinese artists, who, during 1985 and 1986, had begun to reflect on how they could establish a modern art of their own. They had begun to feel that officially sanctioned contemporary Chinese art, such as it was taught at art academies, published in the official art press, and shown at official exhibitions, was below the artistic standards they had come to appreciate in modern Western art, and in the authentic old works of traditional Chinese painting they had rediscovered. At the same time, they found that their teachers, most of whom had been taught oil painting techniques in Moscow in the 1950s, or dealt exclusively with traditional Chinese art, not only possessed no significant knowledge of the theory and practice of contemporary Western art, but were also unable to point the way to an original modern Chinese art. As a result of all these factors, a great part of the young generation began to lose confidence in the entire official art scene, and, following up on the initiative of the first independent groups around 1980, now started to establish a fully-fledged art world of its own.

54—Ibidem.

1984–85: The Unofficial Art Movement

The new art movement of 1984–85 was unlike the one in 1979–80 in that it was initiated by the young generation of artists, and took place largely outside the official art circles. In 1985, the "Anti-Spiritual Pollution Campaign" seemed to show signs of abatement, and in the ensuing atmosphere of relative freedom, young artists all over the country seized the opportunity to establish groups and associations, in order to study Western art and literature and organize exhibitions of their own works.
They received support from a number of (mostly young) scholars who had retreated into the background following the closing of the "Wall of Democracy" in 1979. In 1985, a number of art historians and philosophers among them succeeded in establishing two new art magazines, *Zhongguo meishu bao* (Fine Arts in China) in Beijing, and *Meishu sichao* (The Trend of Art Thought) in Wuhan, with the aim of stimulating the development of independent art. At the same time, xeroxed and mimeographed documents produced with private funds came into circulation.
Zhongguo meishu bao was a weekly on newsprint paper, which appeared from July 1985 until late 1989. It became the most important source of information on the huge number of exhibitions which were held during that period. It also carried articles on foreign modern art, architecture, fashion, and design, and provided an outlet for the ideas and views of the unofficial art world. *Meishu Sichao* was a bi-monthly, also on newsprint paper, which appeared until late 1987, and published articles on the theoretical aspects of the new art movement.

Polemics in the Art Press

Until 1985, as we have seen, the Chinese authorities had denounced the first experiments on Chinese soil with critical-realism and abstract art as "bourgeois-liberalism," reversing earlier, more liberal official statements. In reaction, a number of artists and art-theorists opened a battle-front in the theoretical field, hoping that, among other things, a re-definition of terms in art theory would pave the way toward greater artistic freedom.
Until 1985, major debates were held about a number of issues, such as realistic versus nonrealistic art, the question of whether or not there were aesthetical norms involved in abstract art, the relationship between form and content, the acceptability of self-expression as the highest value in art, and more academic subjects, such as the methodology of art history, and the role of art criticism.[55]
Of all these issues, the claims that abstract art had a right to exist, and that self-expression was the most important thing in art, were the most controversial in political and ideological terms, as they went against the official view that art had to serve political goals, and so these claims were usually denounced as "westernized." It should be pointed out, however, that also among young artists, self-expression and individualism were debated issues. Some of them held that they could lead to the same isolated position of traditional literati-art *vis-a-vis* society, and that concern for social problems was a prerequisite for the development of credible modern Chinese art. This conviction led, after 1985, to a considerable widening of the range of themes under debate, as a great variety of both Chinese and Western theories and topics from the fields of culture, history, and philosophy were brought under discussion.

55—This is a selection from a list of subjects covered by the art press until early 1985, published in MSSC 1985, No. 4, p. 24.

Wu Guanzhong: The Contents of Art Cannot be Prescribed

In 1979 and 1980, the then 60-year old artist Wu Guanzhong published a number of articles in which he argued that art should not aim at providing a form for any political, historical, or literary content, as form is the substance of art, and the beauty of the form is independent of the subject depicted (if any). He held that the content of a work of art is decided by the form as it develops during the creative process.[56]

56—Wu Guanzhong, "Huihua de xingshimei" in MS 1979, No. 5, p. 33; and idem, "Guanyu chocudangmei", in MS 1980, No. 10, p. 37.

Official art critics (including Jiang Feng) immediately denounced Wu's views as "westernized" and "idealist," and as such opposed to Marxism, which, being a materialist philosophy, denies the existence of independent abstract qualities. Wu's conception of aesthetics was rejected because it could legitimize "decadent (meaning abstract) art". Other authors rushed to Wu's defense, arguing that also in Chinese calligraphy and traditional landscape painting, the aesthetic effects were not only created by the depiction of certain subject matter, but also by abstract qualities such as rhythm and composition.[57] On the other hand, there were also those who, while agreeing with Wu's demand for artistic freedom, nevertheless disagreed with his line of argument. They held that his overemphasis on aesthetic purity could easily give rise to the same aestheticism and social escapism which, or so they believed, had sapped the strength of traditional literati-painting.

57—Xu Shucheng, "Zai tan chouxiangmei he Zhongguohua", in MS 1984, No. 5, p. 50.

Qu Leilei: The Primacy of Self-Expression

Qu Leilei, a member of the "Stars Group," defended the view that art is, in essence, "the expression of the artist's inner world, "i.e. "his experiences and feelings of happiness and unhappines".[58]
An official critic subsequently launched a long, verbose attack on Qu, stating that his view was not in accordance with the theory of dynamic reflection of dialectic-materialism. He wrote that, according to this theory, one's view of reality is partly determined by the social circumstances, so that one may not uncritically use one's personal experiences as the basis of one's artistic work. Moreover, an artist exclusively dealing with his own impressions would alienate himself from the masses.[59] In the same vein, another critic stated that Qu's view, which was aimed at the undesirable effect of legitimizing unlimited freedom for artists, was based on an "anti-social attitude inspired by Existentialism".[60]
Until this moment, not many artists active in traditional Chinese painting had participated in the polemics, but this changed when, in 1985, their speciality was also dragged into the arena.

58—MSSC 1985, No. 4, p. 27.

59—Qian He in MS 1981, No. 6, p. 10.

60—Yang Chengyin in XMS 1982, No. 1, p. 100.

Li Xiaoshan: The End of Traditional Chinese Painting

The initiator of the debate was Li Xiaoshan (b. 1957), then a fourth-year student at Nanjing Arts Institute, who, in July 1985, published the first of three articles in which he launched an all-out attack on the post-1978 attempts to revive traditional Chinese painting.
This triggered a heated debate which lasted until 1988, producing a flood of almost 300 articles, almost invariably critical of Li's standpoint.
Official art policy since 1979 had rehabilitated traditional Chinese art in order to strengthen nationalistic feelings, and the government regarded any attempt to undermine "Chinese tradition", or to stimulate interest in Western art, culture, and philosophy, as a direct attack on its own legitimacy. Moreover, such attempts were also rejected by a great part of society as "anti-Chinese".
It was in this atmosphere that Li sent shock-waves through the Chinese art world, by stating that traditional Chinese painting had run its course, and had long arrived at the natural end of its development: "Traditional painting [...] was rooted in a completely closed, autocratic society [...] The history of Chinese art [...] shows a clearly discernible course of development in which the pictorial form shed an increasing number of elements, leading to an increasingly sober use of point, line, and color. These artistic means were thought to possess aesthetic meaning in themselves.
The reinforcing of this relationship between general aesthetic values and the use of brush and ink—a development which was strengthened by calligraphy—could not but result in a hermetic form idiom. When the technical mastery over artistic means had reached its zenith, the art of painting was reduced to the rigid application of abstract forms.
The most important reason for the conservatism in the final period of Chinese painting was, that artists no longer sought to expand their views on art, but lost themselves in the making of endless variations on a limited set of themes [...]

In spite of this, contemporary artists continue to plow and weed in the garden of traditional art, reaping but a very poor harvest [...]. The most acclaimed and lauded artists of today regard themselves as the talented and enlightened representatives of Chinese culture, and look down upon the innovative movement in art with disdain. In reality, they are neither enlightened nor talented, but foolish and bone lazy, playing the role of modern Don Quixotes and making themselves look like fools in the eyes of future generations[...].[61]

61—Li Xiaoshan, "Dangdai Zhongguohua zhi wo jian", in JH 1985, No. 7.

Li bitterly ridiculed what he regarded as the posturings of those who, backed by official policy, still attempted to revive what he deemed beyond revival:

> "When, under the motto 'art-renewal', essential elements of traditional art are pushed aside, then what this boils down to is not a 'renewal', but a complete abandonment of traditional art. [...] Artists, ignoring this fact, have carefully barricaded themselves in a limited world of thought, in order to maintain something 'characteristically Chinese' in their work. In reality, they neither develop traditional art nor create original modern art, but only put out a kind of half-hearted products. It may also lead to those affected styles, consisting of all kinds of eclectic elements, with folk art techniques being presented as 'traditional', or original materials and tools being replaced by new ones. All this is claimed to be a 'renewal'."[62]

62—Li Xiaoshan, "Zuowei chuantong baoliu huazhong de Zhongguohua", in JH 1986, No. 1. His third article was entitled "Zhongguohua cunzai de qianti", published in MSSC 1985, No. 7, p. 7.

"Then there are those who, although possessing original ideas and using materials in an original manner, proceed to present themselves, not only as creators of Chinese art, but also as thinkers effecting a breakthrough in the realm of thought, and as giants of modern art, inevitably making themselves look silly. [...] Many Chinese artists find it hard to accept that they will only gradually succeed in playing any role in modern art, and that, for some time to come, it will only be a supporting one. They cling to the simple belief that the millennia-old Chinese art cannot stagnate and possesses great powers of survival—an enormously tempting illusion leading many talented artists into wasting their time trying to 'develop the tradition' (*fazhan chuantong*)."[63]

63—Ibid.

One of the few who supported Li was Liu Haisu (b. 1896), a veteran artist who has been an advocate for a more liberal art policy since the beginning of his career:

> "[...] I have read Li Xiaoshan's article with much attention and satisfaction. It demonstrates that the young generation has courageous ideas, and knows how to formulate these in a frank and original manner. The article has created a commotion in the art theory circles, like a stone dropped into a quiet lake...."[64]

64—Interview with Liu Haisu by Ding Tao in JH 1986, No. 3.

The art historian Liu Ruli (1910–1988) of Nanjing Arts Institute, while agreeing with Li Xiaoshan that traditional Chinese painting had begun to suffer from an impoverishment in form, technique, and content, remained confident in the possibility of continuing the tradition: "[...] A tradition is formed during an accumulative process—it does not consist of a rigid, unchanging set of examples. In each phase, a selection process takes place in which the valuable is retained and the superfluous abandoned".[65]

65—Liu Ruli, "Huatan xunli", in JH 1986, No. 5.

He found it encouraging to note that so many artists, in continuation of the debates during the "May Fourth" period in the 1920s, were concerned about the future of Chinese art, and had embarked on new roads. Leaving aside the artistic value of the resulting works, he thought that traditional art had proved to possess the power of regeneration.

In contrast to Li Xiaoshan, the artist Fan Zeng (b. 1938), founder of the Traditional Painting Department at Tianjin Nankai University, held that Chinese cultural tradition possesses "eternal value" and "enormous strength," and that it is vastly superior to the "fossilized, unfeeling, and impoverished" art of the European Middle Ages. He noted that the Japanese, in spite of centuries of effort, had been unable to master the Chinese tradition, and that neither they nor the Western Europeans "with their hollow eyes and pointed noses" had been able to grasp its essence. He predicted that it would take the latter at least 14 or 15 centuries before they could match the artistic level of the Chinese.[66]

66—Fan Zeng, "Zhongguohua zongheng tan", in JH 1986, No. 7. Since 1989, Fan Zeng lives and works in Paris.

Other strongly personal reactions came from Shi Hu (b. 1942), an artist attached to the People's Art Press in Beijing, who addressed an *ad hominem* attack to Li Xiaoshan[67], and from artist Dong Xinbin (b. 1940), a member of the Jiangsu Academy for Traditional

67—Shi Hu, "Man meng", in MS 1986, No. 2.

Art, who quoted Marx in defense of Chinese painting, which, in his opinion, was "still able to provide enjoyment and a high artistic standard".[68]

68—Dong Xinbing, "Ye tan jiju wo jian", in JH 1985, No. 8.

Later, the debate no longer saw any individual authors taking individualistic stands. It developed into a discussion of more abstract and theoretical issues such as "the confrontation between Eastern and Western culture" often discussed in long-winded essays lacking the confrontational quality of Li Xiaoshan's original article.

Official Art Criticism Criticized

Pi Daojian (b. 1941), opened an important theoretical debate in 1982, by criticizing the method of Chinese art history. He held that in China, the development of a scientific analysis of art had been obstructed by the continued application of the classical system of artistic concepts, which was devoted to connecting art with the ancient texts on art theory, and neglected to view art in relation to its socio-historic setting.[69]

69—Pi Daojian, "Yingdang zhongshi meishushi yanjiu de fangfalun", in MS 1982, No. 9. Pi Daojian is Director of the Institute of Theoretical Research of the Hubei Province Art Academy in Wuhan (*Hubei Meishu Xueyuan Lilun Yanjiushi*). He was one of the people who, in 1985, founded the independent art magazine Meishu sichao.

Chinese art theory, as developed over 15 centuries, had become a hermetic discipline, completely isolated from social history, ignoring social, economic, and political influences on art. At the same time, it also ignored developments within the history of art itself. Its purpose, Pi stated, was not to contribute to an understanding of art itself, but to support the existing moral and social order, and he criticized contemporary art theory for continuing this traditional practice.

In 1983, he received support for his views from the art historian Deng Fuxing (b. 1945), who stated that the simplified views of contemporary Chinese art theory were a result of the fact that it was aimed, not at any academic goal, but at the political objective of confirming the truth of the theoretical foundations of Marxism.[70]

70—Deng Fuxing, "Meishu lilun yanjiu fangfa chuyi", in *Meishu shilun congkan*, 1983, No. 4. Deng is attached to the Chinese Art Research Institute in Beijing (*Zhongguo yishu yanjiuyuan meiyansuo*).

In 1985, Pi Daojian also made a stand against the art critics. He held that their method merely consisted of the mechanical application of a pre-established set of ideas to works of art, not only thereby paralyzing the aesthetic sensibility of the public and its capacity for artistic reception, but also making it psychologically dependent on obsolete views. He rejected their belief that art criticism should play a moral and political role by assessing the effect of every concrete work of art on society, and passing a judgement on its social value.[71]

71—Pi Daojian, "Wode pipingguan", in MSSC 1985, No. 2.

In 1986, the art historian Liang Jiang (b. 1952) pointed out that the dilemma facing the arts in China was, to a great extent, the result of the attempt since the beginning of this century to achieve a "synthesis" between "Chinese spirituality" and "Western material culture." He held that this attempt was based on the mistaken idea that the material elements of culture could be separated from its spiritual (moral) elements, and that the persistance of this fallacy was an impediment to progress.[72]

72—Liang Jiang, "Lishi de chongfu yu xiandai de zhijue, in MS 1986, No. 7, pp. 13–15. Liang is attached to the Institute for Art Research in Beijing.

Liang argued that the mindless use of slogans prevalent since the founding of the People's Republic had led to the failure to solve the problem of China's culture. For example, the slogan "renewal of the arts" (*yishu chuangxin*) creates the impression that art can be evaluated by using the concepts of "old" and "new" as criteria, while, according to Liang, the only criteria that can be applied in evaluating art are "beauty" vs. "ugliness," and "genuine" vs. "fake".

Moreover, he was surprised to observe that Chinese artists did not in any way oppose the revival of the idea, previously raised during the "Anti-Rightist Campaign&," that "oil painting should be made to reflect our national character" (*youhua minzuhua*). Liang declared that the whole concept of minzu was obsolete and isolationistic. He concluded that a credible new Chinese art could only be built on the basis of a "renewal of ideas," and the establishment of a "modern consciousness".

(End of Part I. To be continued.)

Hans van Dijk

Painting in China after the Cultural Revolution
Style Developments and Theoretical Debates
Part II: 1985–1991

As already described in the first part of this article, the years 1984–1985 saw the rise of a vigorous independent art movement in China. It was the result of the disillusionment, especially among young artists, with the official, politically controlled art scene. Among other things, they had concluded that although artistic freedom had markedly increased between 1978 and 1984, the results of the various experiments to create a genuine modern Chinese art were boring and utterly disappointing when compared with the work of contemporary Western artists such as Robert Rauschenberg. The exhibition of Rauschenberg's work in 1985 was the first time that the Chinese public was exposed to post-1945 Western art, and it sent a veritable shock-wave though the Chinese art world.[1] Artists believed that, if they were to continue to work within the narrow confines of officially sanctioned art, they would be reduced to playing a conservative role while tempestuous changes were taking place everywhere else in Chinese society, and would be forever unable to develop authentic modern Chinese art. This was an absolutely unbearable thought. As a result, there was a sudden, large-scale, countrywide explosion outside the official circuit of hundreds of exhibitions and manifestations, involving a huge number of artists. The dimensions of this so-called "1985 Art Groups Movement" (*1985 nian yishu qunti*) far exceeded anything that had occurred in 1979, although the basic aims were similar. Artists tried to break away from both the traditional Chinese conception of art, which views the individual artist primarily as a continuator of the tradition, and from socialist-realist art, which is supposed to serve political ends. They gave expression to this double objective by making statements emphasizing their individual status as artists, experimenting with new techniques, and by trying to develop new styles.

1—On exhibitions of Western art in China and the reaction to Rauschenberg, see Part I of this article, pp. 33–34.

Between 1985 and 1987, the pace of artistic activity, as well as the exchange of views and interpretations in the Chinese art press, was greatly accelerated, and reached feverish heights, with artists conducting countless experiments and travelling all over the country in order to participate in art shows, meetings, and conferences. It was during these get-togethers that, from 1986 onwards, plans were made for the big, trail-blazing exhibition, which was eventually to take place in Beijing, in February 1989, under the title: "China/Avant-Garde."

The 1985 Movement has been analyzed in detail by the art historian Zhang Qiang (b. 1940), according to whom the majority of the artists involved were students and teachers at art academies, and the art departments of other educational institutions. He has pointed out that a great many of the participants belonged to the first batch of art students to graduate after the "Cultural Revolution," in 1982, and that, as a result of their relatively young average age, the Movement possessed little or no knowledge of the art experiments which had been conducted between 1979 and 1981.[2] By the time the 1985 Movement took off, many prominent figures of the earlier movements, for example of the "Stars Group," had already emigrated to the West.[3]

2—MS 1987, No. 10, p. 6.

3—On the movements of the early 1980s, for example the "Stars Group", see Part I, pp. 27–32.

In this article, I will describe a number of the most conspicuous events, art groups, personalities, and debates, as well as how innovations of the early 1980s were continued. I will argue that the 1985 Movement, although it arose in an attempt to break out of the narrow confines of the official art world, nevertheless shared the same basic objectives, which was the establishment of a "modern art with Chinese characteristics," and to use art as a means of promoting the spiritual rejuvenation of the entire society.

Among other things, it was the failure to achieve these objectives, in combination with institutional constraints and political interference, which caused the Movement to peter out in 1987. Art did not seem to succeed in playing the avant-garde role in society, which it had been planned to fulfil. Moreover, instead of establishing "the national identity" of modern Chinese art, artists had moved in a multitude of different directions. The Movement was thrown into confusion by the enormous diversity in styles and theories which it had itself brought about. Pluriformity, which the avant-garde had craved so much, seemed to have become a liability instead of an asset. Having lost all artistic direction, the Movement finally ended in confusion and unease.

"A Direct Contact With the Audience": Happenings

The initial momentum of the Movement was enormous. In the first place, artists had wanted to change the relationship between art and the public. A number of groups arose which aimed at establishing an informal and spontaneous form of interaction with the audience. Some of them were, directly or indirectly, inspired by the Polish experimental dramatist Jerzy Grotowski, whose book *Towards a Poor Theatre* had been translated into Chinese.[4] Grotowski is known for his training methods, which aim at liberating the actor from all his inhibitions, in order to enable him to communicate freely and directly with his audience. In the 1960s, Grotowski's methods had led to the rise of "living theater" in Europe and the US, and his book directly inspired the establishment in 1986 of the Hangzhou art group, "The Pond Society" (Chishe), which will be described in the next section.

4—Jerzy Grotowski, *Towards A Poor Theatre*, London: Methuen & Co. Ltd. 1968. A copy of this work can be found in Beijing National Library.

The desire to create a form of spontaneous interaction with the audience formed the background of a number of art happenings in Beijing, Nanjing, Canton, and Hangzhou. In Nanjing, in the hot, late summer of 1986, an event was held in Xuanwuhu Park entitled "Drying in the Sun" (*Shai taiyang*), referring to the custom in Nanjing to expose books, clothing and furniture to the sun after the rainy season, in order to prevent mildew. The exhibition was more than a local affair, as both the participating artists and the hundreds of enthusiastic viewers were not only from Nanjing but also from far-away places. More than 500 works were on display, and there was a luxurious abundance of song, artistic theories, and manifestos. For example, a theory was proclaimed according to which the happening was the starting point of a "Metal Culture," the successor to the then current "Earth Culture," and the herald of the "Crystal Culture" of the future.[5]

5—Based on personal interviews with participants; Zhang Qiang 1988, p. 59; and ZMB 1986, No. 46.

A number of artists, writers, musicians and film makers founded the group "Salon" (*Shalong*) in Canton in 1985. In September 1986, they organized a form of total theater at Zhongshan University, at which electronic music, spectacular lighting effects, modern dance, and art works were combined in one room. The local press published an euphoric description of the event, saying that it was an intoxicating, uplifting experience in which audience, dancers, stage settings and art works completely fused into one.[6]

6—Zhang Qiang 1988, p. 52–55; ZMB 1986, Nos. 24, 40, 42.

The Pond Society

As stated above, Grotowski's theories had inspired the founding of the Hangzhou art group "The Pond Society" in May 1986. The founders were five artists from the Zhejiang Art Academy in Hangzhou, led by Zhang Peili (b. 1957) and Geng Jianyi (b. 1962).[7] Zhang Peili later explained, the origin of the group thus:

7—For articles by and on Zhang Peili and Geng Jianyi, and reproductions of their works, see Zhang Qiang 1988, p. 18; MS 1985, No. 9, pp. 35 and 44; 1986, No. 11; 1987, No. 2; 1987. No. 8, p. 24; ZMB 1986, No. 34, p. 4; 1987, No. 45; 1988, No. 22; 1988, No. 35, p. 1; ZMB 1989, No. 11, p. 1; XMS 1984, No. 4.

> "... At that time, *Towards A Poor Theater*, the book by the Polish dramatist Jerzy Grotowski, was an important source of inspiration for us. The book deals with the state of mind reached after a person has overcome his personal and worldly problems. It is a condition in which one is no longer governed by personal experiences and feelings, but rather acts in a state of intoxication in which one ceases both to conform to general rules, and to strive to attain any pre-established goals. In this state of mind, an actor does not act in a certain way 'because he thinks that he should, but because he cannot do otherwise'.
> Jerzy Grotowski advocates this condition, not because he wants to offer the artist a world of self-satisfied self-intoxication, but quite on the contrary, because he wants to attain a 'pure, real art' in protest against the increasingly strong trend of art to 'prostitute itself. He holds that artist and audience should engage in an honest, genuine dialogue from equal positions, instead of the usual situation in which the audience is limited to a passive appreciation of what is offered. Moreover, artistic activities should possess a serious and lofty character, and no longer serve the attempt to achieve decorative and literary refinement. The artist's technical competence is only important insofar as it assists him during the dialogue [with the audience]."[8]

8—MSSC 1987, No. 1, p. 19. Zhang Peili wrote this article under the penname Shi Jiu.

For one whole year, the group engaged in public happenings and manifestations aimed at establishing a dialogue with the audience. One of their projects consisted in putting up paper figures executing *Taijiquan* movements, as visual complements to the familiar scene of people taking their daily exercise in the streets.[9] However, their activities only met with apathy or derision, and they decided, greatly disappointed, to abandon the playful approach. They began to make more aggressive and provocative works which were aimed at eliciting "an enforced reaction".[10] For example, they published Zhang Peili's *Art Project II: Realizing a Dialogue and Peeping At It*, which was a book of eight chapters containing a total of about 200 paragraphs, laying down minute prescriptions for the behavior of the prospective participants in the projected dialogue—their functions, rights and duties, appointment procedures, required certificates and identity papers—as well as guidelines for the content of the dialogue.[11] The Kafkaesque world of bureaucratic formalities thus evoked was strongly reminiscent of both the Imperial examinations in ancient China and the practices of contemporary Communist officialdom. Zhang Peili called his project "conceptual art".

9—Unpublished report on the group's activities by Geng Jianyi, August 1987.

10—Ibidem.

11—*Zhang Peili's Art Project I* was an illustrated article in ZMB 1987, No. 45, describing the production and exhibition of a series of paintings, and laying down rules for visitors' behavior. The article, however, was not published under said title.

The work of Geng Jianyi is characterized by a sustained, very individual attempt to explore the ambivalent interrelationship between the artist, his work, and the audience. The paintings he produced for his examination in 1985 at the Zhejiang Art Academy were executed in a style at once sober and compelling. Each painting showed two human figures, who, placed in a symmetrical composition of evenly colored, stylized planes, coolly observed the viewer in a confrontational manner.

About a year later, he painted two series of giant portaits which were entitled *The Second State* (120 × 160 cm) and *Double Happiness* (200 × 145 cm). Both series depicted laughing heads covering the entire canvas, executed in a monochrome, photo-realistic style. The heads illustrated various types of laughter, from sobbing to completely hysterical, confounding the viewer, who found himself deprived of the possibility to consider them in the conventional, contemplative manner usually adopted vis-a-vis traditional Chinese painting and photo-realism.

In 1988, Geng Jianyi published a description of the experimental design of a project called *Waterworks*, illustrated with photographs.[12] The floor plan shows walls, two meters in height, placed in a double spiral forming two separate corridors leading towards the center of the hall. The walls have holes at head level, some of which are surrounded by picture-frames. Through these holes, the visitors are brought into confrontation with each other, and reduced to a state of great confusion and embarrassment. This effect is stronger on a Chinese than on a Western audience, as the former, more than the latter, are accustomed to strict rules for proper behavior, and more easily disturbed when they find themselves in an unfamiliar situation.

12—ZMB 1988, No. 22. A full-size model of the project was erected by Geng in 1988 in the school at which he teaches. A number of the school's students played the role of visitors. Photos of the event can be found in said article.

Geng's work *The Registration Form* also dates from 1988. He sent this form, which looked official, to the artists who had registered for the "China/Avant-Garde" exhibition to be held the following year. The selection of the works to be exhibited was to take place in October 1988.

The form asked detailed questions about the applicant's health, education, family situation, cultural orientation, social and professional status, class-background, police record, etc. At the end of the form, there was a reassuring statement stating that the information would not be included in the government's file on the applicant, but would be kept as a private record. Many artists believed the form to be genuine, and sent it back completed together with the requested photograph. During the October selection meeting, Geng presented the completed forms as his entry for the exhibition. He offered the artists a certificate in which they were thanked for their cooperation, and assured of a guaranteed place in art history.

Some of Geng's works, such as his 1986 giant portraits, are considered, both in China and abroad, as important contributions to "scar-art"—the art of the disillusioned generation brought up during the "Cultural Revolution".[13] However, seen as a whole, his work is also an expression of the disappearance of established roles, positions, and customs in a destabilized, transitional society. As his work does not possess any stylistical unity, and is not accompanied by statements on philosophy or Western art currents (two prerequisites for avant-garde art, at least according to the Chinese avant-garde art press), his works are simply categorized as "absurdistic".

13—For an account on "scar-art", see Part I, p. 30.

Wu Shanzhuan

The Zhejiang Art Academy also produced other artists and art groups who parodied Chinese customs and institutions, and the "Cultural Revolution". In addition to the "Pond Society", there were also, for example, Wu Shanzhuan (b. 1960) and his group "75% Red, 20% Black, 5% White".[14]

In 1986, Wu and six of his fellow-students organized an exhibition at the Academy. They filled the entire hall with slogans and banners executed in the "Cutural Revolution" propaganda style, but carrying texts such as "White Cabbage Six Cents Per Pound", "No Water Today", and "Rubbish". Other banners carried texts with incorrectly written characters which have no, or an ambiguous, meaning. Wu published an accompanying manifesto in the form of an exasperatingly long-winded academic treatise explaining the historic origin and aesthetic qualities of the Chinese script, and offering detailed prescriptions as to how the characters should be positioned on banners. Also in the following years, he continued to mock bureaucratic and traditional social practices. For example, he designed official-looking seals and used them to stamp objects, thus endowing them with the status of "art".

In February 1989, he participated in the "China/Avant-Garde" exhibition in Beijing by selling frozen shrimps from Zhoushan Island, where he lived at the time. The original batch weighed a few hundred kilos and was dispatched with all the required official documents, stamped by the cultural center to which he was attached. Nevertheless, in order to get permission to transport the batch through Shanghai, he had to hand over half of it, and when, on the first day of the Beijing exhibition, he stationed himself at the museum entrance and started to sell the remainder, he was ordered by plain-clothes men to follow them. When released a few hours later, he put up a sign on his stall saying "Closed For Stock-Taking". In 1990 Wu moved to Iceland, and since late 1991 he has been living in Hamburg, Germany.

14—For articles by and on Wu Shanzhuan, and reproductions of his works, see: MS 1986, No. 8; ZMB 1986, No. 38; 1987, No. 40, p. 1; 1989, No. 6, p. 4; 1989, No. 11, p. 2; MSSC 1987, No. 1, p. 22; and the back cover of 1987, No. 5.

Huang Yongping's Dada Manifestation

In September 1986, the prominent artist Huang Yongping, also a graduate from Zhejiang Art Academy, organized a manifestation in his native city of Xiamen, Fujian Province, entitled "Xiamen–Dada".[15] Huang gave an extensive explanation of the ideas underlying the event, both in a accompanying manifesto, and in the weekly *Zhongguo Meishu Bao*.[16] He stated that he was in favor of continuing the confusion in the Chinese art world, and expressed the hope that the Dada Manifestation would contribute to it. He wrote:

> "It is safe to presume that the Chinese art world will not yet produce any new and original art concepts, but what we can do is fill in the gaps in our knowledge of modern art. Until now, Dadaism has not yet received our attention, and as it is something exotic, it will surely arouse keen interest..."[17]

More than 14 artists participated, with works executed in a variety of unusual materials. Some aimed at achieving esthetic effects, others at demolishing conventional art practices and conceptions, in a satirical or provocative manner.

Huang's own interest in Dadaism was related to his desire to free himself of the academic art education he had received, and develop a less formal way of creating art. As he said after his graduation from the Academy in 1982: "It has taken me five years to study art, and I will need ten years to unlearn what I learned".[18] As the first step towards this goal, he attempted to eliminate all personal feeling and make room for the coincidental, in order to give rise to a more objective and natural result. The first result of this approach was a series of paintings in 1985 entitled *Feibiaoxiande huiliua* (Non-Expressive Art). It was an effective reaction against the primacy of "self-expression" in traditional Chinese literati-art, as well as against the academic style of oilpainting taught at the Academy. Huang had been inspired by John Cage, who, in the early 1950s, had aimed at composing "anti-cerebral" music on the basis of Taoism, Zen-Buddhism, and other anti-authoritarian

15—It was held in the New Xiamen Museum (*Xiamen xin yishuguan*). An account of Huang's earlier activities can be found in Part I, pp. 34–35.

16—ZMB 1986, No. 46.

17—Huang Yongping, in *Xiamen Dada – yi zhong houxiandai?* (Xiamen Dada – A Kind of Postmodernism?). pamphlet accompanying the manifestation, Xiamen, September 1986.

18—MSSC, 1987, No. 5, p. 35. The motto cited was the title of one of Huang's works on exhibition in 1986.

ideas. While in the West, Taoism and Zen-Buddhism are often appreciated for their mystical qualities, artists in post-Mao China used them provocatively to oppose established art dogma, following the examples of Duchamp, Manzoni, and Yves Klein.

In his Dada pamphlet, Huang had pointed out the relationship between Dadaism and the modern art of the 1960s and Taoism and Zen-Buddhism. In 1989, he published an article entitled "The Signifying, Which is Completely Empty: 'Dada' and 'Zen'". In this article, he linked Taoism and Zen Buddhism to the theories of French language philosophers such as Barthes and Saussure, stating that he had been most deeply impressed by Foucault. He concluded that language cannot claim to possess any authority in its description of reality, and that it, moreover, gives rise to continuous oppression:

> "... The only thing left by history is a great amount of words and writings. As history itself cannot speak, we thus find ourselves in the middle of a big rubbish heap, including culture—philosophy, religion, and art—which manipulates people. If you keep silent, it means that you don't exist. If we do not rise above this [...] rubbish heap (our history, thoughts, and culture), we will be suppressed by all kinds of doctrines, value concepts, and sermons."[19]

19—MS 1989, No. 3, pp. 30–32. A German translation by E.R. Schneider of Huang's article can be found in *Gebrochene Bilder, Junge Kunst aus China* (Broken Pictures: Young Art From China), Bad Honnef (Germany): Horlemann, 1991.

In order to mock the elevated position of art in society and the mystification of art objects, the Xiamen group undertook to burn a number of paintings at the end of the Dada Manifestation, which caused the local authorities to put an end to their public activities.[20] Having thus finished with conventional art itself, in the following year, Huang also put a symbolic end to art history. He displayed a lump of papier-maché on a plate of glass, and called it "*The History of Chinese Art*" and [Herbert Read's] "*A Concise History of Modern Art*" *After Two Minutes in the Washing Machine*, 1 December 1987. The work, apart from being provocative in its deliberate destruction of renowned reference books, also presented a rigorous answer to the century-old problem in the Chinese art world of how to combine the Eastern and Western cultural traditions. Huang's solution was as drastic as the result was amorphous.

20—From Huang Yongping, *1983–1988 Huodong Jianli*. was a hand-written report illustrated with photographs, which was xeroxed for all those interested. For articles by and about Huang and his work, see Part I, note 42 on p. 34.

Views on East and West in China's North and South

In contrast, the "*Beifang yishu qunti*" (The Northern Art Group) was far more optimistic about the possibility of combining Eastern and Western art. The group consisted of a number of artists from the three provinces north of Beijing, who were united by the desire to establish a new world culture, whose coming they prophesied in difficult theoretical tracts full of quotations from a host of 19th-century German philosophers.

Having purportedly made a comparison of the Oriental and Occidental civilizations of the past 5000 years, the group concluded that both civilizations were past their zenith and currently in decline. However, they predicted that, since in both East and West, the cultural center of gravity had, over the centuries, been moving from South to North (respectively from India through South-China toward Beijing, and from Egypt through Greece toward central and western Europe), the two traditions would eventually merge in the far North, and usher in an era of a new world culture.

As a participant in this epochal movement, the international significance and avant-garde character of the group was of course beyond any dispute—at least, the Chinese art press launched enthusiastic reports suggesting that the group had reached a milestone in the history of art. However, their works did not quite match their theoretical prowess. They produced somewhat awkward paintings inspired by the Pre-Raphaelites and the surrealism of Delvaux and Magritte.[21]

In contrast, the claims of their southern counterpart, the "*Xinan yishu qunti*" (The Southwestern Art Group), were much more modest. This was an umbrella organization established in 1985 by Ye Yongqing, Zhang Xiaogang, and Xu Zhongmin, and consisted of various art groups from Sichuan, Yunnan, and Zhejiang Provinces, as well as a number of individual artists from Shanghai and Nanjing.

21—Articles on thc group and their works can be found in ZMB, 1985, No. 18; ibid. 1986, No. 36; MSSC 1987, No. 1, p. 21; and MS 1988, No. 3, p. 53.

They were in favor of a passionate, primitivistic art, and felt that they had to draw on the best that both East and West had to offer in this field. As Ye Yongqing stated:

> "... After many millennia of cultural development, we now have two cultural heritages at our disposal. They are both valuable, and fully deserve to be used and combined by us, and we may abandon them again afterwards. To combine is to create."[22]

22—From a privately sponsored publication by Ye Yongqing, August 1986, p. 11.

The group organized a number of exhibitions in 1985 and 1986. Although all the affiliated artists work realistically, they use a variety of styles, from the mystical and introvert to the expressive and sensual, and from the semi-surrealist to the narrative. The paintings are sometimes reminiscent of Indian and other non-Chinese art. None of them have any similarity to the historic, dramatic work of the North.

Experiments Based on Traditional Chinese Art

Other artists began to experiment with traditional Chinese themes and techniques. They developed in various directions, some of them in abstract-expressionism, others, like Wang Luyan in Beijing, moving further toward an increasingly free and expressive form of calligraphy. Artists like Zhang Qinghui (b. 1964) from Nanjing, and Xie Xiangli (b. 1963) from Hangzhou, experimented with landscape painting by abandoning realism and introducing innovative color use.

Still others continued the search initiated by Gu Wenda[23] for new ways to treat classical Taoist and Zen-Buddhist themes. Some, like Ni Haifeng (b. 1964), who was attached to a cultural center on Zhoushan Island, became fascinated by the expressive power of early Buddhist art. He produces collages covering entire walls, on which mythical fish and birds are combined with Chinese characters, Arabic numbers, and algebraic symbols.[24] In 1987, he owned a house on Zhoushan Island south-east of the city. His paintings cover the entire house, both inside and out, proliferating like weeds not only over floors and walls, but over objects in the rooms, and over the wall stretching between the house and the sea.

23—For Gu Wenda and his work, see Part I, pp. 35–36.

24—For illustrations, see JH 1990, No. 8, pp. 21–23.

Next to serious attempts to produce genuinely innovative Chinese painting, artists increasingly tend to engage in mass production for foreign markets, where the demand for "real Chinese," "underground", and "avant-garde" is booming. As early as 1979, the then Chairman of the Chinese National Artists' Association, Jiang Feng, complained that some artists produced, in addition to their normal work, "ten or twenty pieces of 'Chinese art' per day" for foreign buyers.[25] After a life-long struggle for pluriformity and against the dominant position of traditional painting, Jiang bitterly observed that the first effect of the liberalization of the arts had been that "the preference of foreigners is going to determine the preference of the Chinese".

25—MS 1979, No. 12, p. 11.

The Inspiration from China's Ethnic Minorities

Especially popular with foreign buyers is the depiction of China's ethnic minorities. The founding father of the genre is Chen Danqing, who is famous for his sober, realistic oil paintings of Tibetans seemingly lost in the bustling Chinese urban environment.[26] The genre is now practiced by a multitude of artists, partly attracted by its popularity on the foreign market, but most of them have become bogged down in technical overrefinement, repetitiveness, or sentimentality.

26—For Chen Danqing and the "Sichuan School", see Part I, pp. 31–32.

One of the few who match Chen's originality and authenticity is Zhou Yunxia (b. 1960), who works in Nanjing. Like Chen, he is self-taught and, as a result of his experiences during the "Cultural Revolution," seeks his subject matter outside official Han-Chinese culture. A worker himself, he depicts the urban underdog (whether Han or non-Han) in his anonymous every-day existence, using a somewhat primitivistic allegorical or narrative style. His individualistic stance and outlook on life has set him apart from the intellectualistic avant-garde circles, who show no interest in his work.

While Chen Danqing has brought the western Tibetans within the horizon of the Chinese art world, its interest in the southern minorities of the Miao, Yi and Dai, in fact, dates from the late 1930s. It was then, during the war, that the painter Pang Xunqin (1906–1985), having fled from Beijing to the south-west, made a series of water-colour drawings of the customs, dress, and natural environment of the Miao in Guizhou Province. In cooperation with the Beijing Academia Sinica, he also started a large collection of local costumes and embroideries.[27]

The interest in China's southern peoples continues up to the present day, and their influence is combined with various Western expressive and rcalistic styles. Since the 1970s, the Guizhou artist Dong Kejun (b. 1939) has been producing large-size woodblock prints, both in multicolor and black-and-white, depicting local festivals, rituals, dances, and mythical figures.[28]

Of a totally different nature is the work of Pan Dehai (b. 1957) from Kunming, whose dark, brown-black paintings depict ominous, legendary figures, almost completely submerged in the nondescript attributes and architectural elements in the background.

There are two teachers at the Sichuan Art Academy (*Sichuan meishu yuan*) in Chongqing who also work in this genre: Zhang Xiaogang and Ye Yongqing (both born in 1958). Zhang makes naive-realistic gouaches in which he combines elements from primitive folk art with memories of his childhood.[29] Ye works in a lyrical expressionistic style, and fills his flat, almost decorative compositions with a colorful variety of incongruous objects, such as birds, plants, flowers, trains, buildings, and human figures.[30]

27—Michael Sullivan, *Chinese Art in the Twentieth Century*, London: Faber and Faber 1959, pp. 54–57. Pang Xunqin studied in Paris and was active in art groups in Shanghai and Beijing which, early this century, introduced Western art styles into China. In 1956, he was appointed Director of the new Central Academy of Arts and Crafts (*Zhongyang gongyi meishu xueyuan*) in Beijing. A few years later, as a result of his interest in popular art, he was accused of "unpatriotic behavior" and dismissed from his post. See Laing 1988, p. 28.

28—*Chinese Literature and Art*, Summer 1989, pp. 93–97; MS 1985, No. 8, p. 22; ZMB 1988, No. 26, p. 1.

29—For works by Zhang Xiaogang, see Zhang Qiang 1988, illustration 37; Tao & Li 1988, ill. 125; MS 1982, No. 1, and 1989, No. 3, centerfold; the cover of JH 1987, No. 10; MSSC 1987, No. 1 inside cover; ZMB 1986, No. 51, p. 1, and 1988, No. 13, p. 1.

30—Publications by and on Ye Yongqing can be found in JH 1985, No. 6, p. 31, and 1990, No. 9, p. 46 ff; ZMB 1986, No. 51, and 1988, No. 13, p. 1.

Zhao Jianren, Outsider

The Chinese art world also has its outsiders, who deliberately stay outside the established circles, whether "traditional" or "avant-garde." An example is Zhao Jianren (b. 1960), who graduated in Graphic Arts from the Zhejiang Art Academy in 1986. For his graduation, he had made a series of lithographs depicting the daily life of miners. They are not shown as heroes of manual labor, as in socialist-realist art, but at lunch or between shifts, caught during private moments of tiredness, silent contemplation, and resignation. Since graduation, he has been experimenting with both figurative and abstract forms, seeking new ways of expressing tension, constriction, and release. Since 1987 he has, at the same time, been producing a flood of works in various styles, which present the object depicted in a more distant and objective manner. During an interview in July 1990, he said:

> "I draw everyday things, very vulgar and also somewhat malicious. It's a way of being concerned with the way we live."

At the Academy, Zhao learned to master a wide range of techniques which enable him to express in a multitude of ways the impressions he receives from his daily environment in Shanghai—a big metropolis where the confrontation with Western culture is dramatic. Some of his paintings point out the isolated position, which Western consumer articles, such as Coca Cola cans and cigarette packages, take on in Chinese society. They are treated as *Fremdkörper*, which are made innocuous by depicting them in isolation, in a damaged state, or in an artificially traditional setting. His 1988 work *Houzhe ju shang* (Late Starters Get On Top) is an acrimonious illustration of the official policy to use "Chinese learning for the essence, and Western learning for practical use," and has caused indignation in various quarters. More playful are his tableaux which visualize everyday phenomena such as the role of food in our lives, or which illustrate Chinese jokes and puns. Zhao's work does not receive much attention from the Chinese art world. For conservative tastes, it lacks the grandeur of traditional art, or is simply blasphemous. More progressive circles regard it as lacking revolutionary zest and avant-garde quality, and dispose of it as "pop-art." It was on the basis of this argument that Zhao was excluded from participation in the big 1989 "China/Avant-Garde" exhibition.

The Chinese Art Press on the 1985 Movement

From the very beginning, the progressive art press played a leading role in the "1985 Art Groups Movement." Especially *Zhongguo meishu bao* (Fine Arts in China) and *Meishu* (Art), both from Beijing, and *Meishu sichao* (The Trend of Art Thought) from Wuhan exerted a considerable influence with their programmatic calls to artists, and interpretations of the new developments.[31]

31—For the rise of the progressive art press, see Part I, p. 38.

The majority of the most active and influential theorists were of the "Cultural Revolution" generation, who combined a lack of formal education with a strong sense of intellectual independence. The artists and critics of the older generations either dissociated themselves from the commotion, or were simply ignored. Adding to this the tremendous energy with which the young theorists devoted themselves to the movement, it is easy to understand why they came to dominate the entire modern art scene.

They had a marked tendency to interpret the revival of the arts from a broad historical, philosophical, or social psychological viewpoint, but without producing any real professional art criticism to accompany the huge quantities of art works, which were then being produced, in an enormous variety of styles. One could not see the wood for the trees, and the theorists were unable to make clear what was happening, or to provide any concrete criteria to help one separate the wheat from the chaff.

The numerous programmatic mottos appearing in the above-mentioned magazines were of little practical value to artists, especially since the programs contradicted each other. For example, there were calls to aim at individuality and originality next to calls to emphasize national cultural characteristics, in order to establish a special niche for Chinese art in the modern international art scene. The lack of clarity and direction was all the more acutely felt around 1987, when the 1985 Movement had spent its initial momentum. People started to doubt the quality of the output of the previous years, and were uncertain about the future direction.

A summary of much-heard criticisms concerning the Movement was presented in an article by Gao Minglu, editor of *Meishu*, accompanied by his own counter-arguments.[32] There were the usual political-ideological criticisms, as well as the accusation that the Movement deliberately tried to mislead the public, by using its massive scale to pretend that it was an official campaign. Gao denied this, saying that the Movement should be regarded as a revival of the arts in the "May Fourth" tradition of the 1920s.[33] Other critics conceded as much, but held that the 1985 Movement was qualitatively inferior to the "May Fourth" art revival, and that its "provocative" character was greater than its artistic value. Gao, however, argued that the intellectual backgrounds of the two movements was different, since, in the 1920s, people had sought to synthesize Western and Eastern art, while nowadays, they also tried to emphasize the differences. While some critics attacked the 1985 Movement for being "even more Westernized than Taiwanese art," Gao was among those who defended Westernization as an inevitable stage in the process of artistic development.

32—ZMB 1986, No. 47.

33—MSSC 1987, No. 1, pp. 40–48.

"Rationalistic" vs. "Intuitionistic" Art

Already in an early stage of the Movement, a distinction was made in the art press between "rationalistic" and "intuitionistic" painting, although the precise meaning of these terms was never defined. Initially, the term "rationalistic painting" (*lixing huihua*) was linked to the art of the "North-East," taken to mean the area around Beijing, Shanghai, and Hangzhou. It was opposed to the "intuitionistic painting" (*zhijue huihua*) of southern provinces such as Yunnan and Sichuan. Both "schools" had their own champions, who confronted each other in ferocious polemics.

The defenders of "rationalistic painting" argued that this school distinguished itself by its openness toward the West, its historical and social commitment, and programmatic action. Sometimes, it was also stated that it was anti-traditionalist. Its opponents, on the other hand, dismissed it as "Westernized," and stated that "art is not philosophy," and that "rationalistic art is un-artistic." They themselves were in favor of "intuitionistic" painting because it emphasized self-expression, and appreciated the value of both Han-Chinese culture and the culture of China's ethnic minorities.

Their opponents, in turn, accused the "intuitionists" of having returned to "ivory tower art," and of being "unmodern, superficial, decorative, and commercialized." This last accusation was based on the fact that, in the early 1980s, a number of artists from Chongqing, Chengdu, and Kunming received the opportunity to exhibit their works in foreign embassies in Beijing. Since that time, Beijing artists, feeling passed over, deride them for being "embassy artists" (*dashiguan huajia*).

In subsequent years, the term "rationalistic" was used depreciatingly for those artists and theorists who were regarded as opposing the primacy of self-expression in art. Such widely divergent groups as the "Pond Society" with its experiments based on Grotowsky's ideas, and the "Northern Art Group" with its surrealist art, were all categorized as "rationalistic." Many artists who regarded themselves as "rationalistic" also called their art "religious" or "transcendent," in order to distinguish it from anecdotal, naive, or realistic art.

Gu Wenda, for example, declared: "Religious feelings (zongjiaogan) are the source of my artistic work."[34]

Gao Minglu, in an article describing the socio-psychological background to the 1985 Movement, pointed out that those artists who championed religion were not so much believers in any specific religious doctrine, as defenders of the right to use religious feelings as a source of artistic inspiration. They desired to have certain psychological experiences, which, according to Gao, they found not only in Zen-Buddhism and the thought of the Taoist philosopher Zhuangzi, but also in the writings of Sartre, Nietzsche, and Freud. This desire, he wrote, originated in an idealistic consciousness converting to the infinite, eternal sphere of the religious."[35] Artists regarded religion, and the art created under the influence of "religious feelings," as a force of social and cultural change, echoing the views of Cai Yuanpei in the 1920s, who called upon art to "replace religion."[36]

34—Interview by Fei Dawei with Gu Wenda, in MS 1986, No. 7, p. 53. The critic Peng De, however, is of the opinion that Gu Wenda's work is aimed at unmasking sexual taboos in China, for example by his calligraphic pieces in which the personal pronouns "he" and "she" are deliberately incorrectly written. See Peng De, "*Gu Wenda de su jie*", in MSSC 1987, No. 5, pp. 20–21.

35—MSSC 1987, No. 1, p. 46.

36—Cai Yuanpei was Dean of Beijing University, and a great champion of educational reform and cultural change in China. He based his ideas on the writings of the German philosopher Immanuel Kant, and exerted a great influence on artists like Liu Haisu, Lin Fengmian, and Xu Beihong, who laid the foundation for China's modern art education system. On Cai Yuanpei, see e.g. Michael Sullivan, *Chinese Art in the Twentieth Century*, London: Faber and Faber 1959, p. 22; and Rita Chang Yuan-chien in the catalogue *China Paris*, Taipei Fine Arts Museum: 1988, p. 50.

1987: The Movement Dissolves

The militant desire to make socially relevant art was reflected by the use of the term *qianwei* (a military expression meaning "advance guard" instead of the more common term *xianfeng*, for translating the word "avant-garde." This desire was characteristic of the "rationalist" camp, but it was also the expression of a more commonly felt need, namely to establish, once again, general standards and universal guidelines in order to put an end to what was viewed as the "chaotic" result of the immensely increased artistic pluriformity. Although pluriformity had been craved by all innovation-minded artists, the reality of a pluriform art world, once realized, did not seem satisfying as an end in itself. The attempt undertaken since 1986 by the art press to clarify the situation by making a broad distinction between "Eastern" and "Western" culture failed, as this distinction was clearly artificial. In the enormous diversity of artistic output, it is no longer possible to find a consistent set of similarities, whether on the basis of content or style, in the work of Chinese artists, which would set "Chinese" apart from "Western" art. People no longer understood what the Movement was all about.

In 1987, the various art groups established since 1985 began to dissolve. Many artists felt that the art revival had spent its force, and that they were moving in a vacuum. Apart from a lack of artistic orientation, the stagnation was also caused by institutional and political factors, such as the absence of independent art galleries, the fact that the art journals remained small in number and continued to be controlled by the Party, the lack of professional art critics, and active government interference.

The government strenghtened the position of traditional art in art education, by adjusting its entrance requirements and appointment policies. For example, in the 1988 written entrance examinations, the candidates were asked to explain their standpoint in regard to "the anti-traditionalism of recent years."[37]

Moreover, the authorities began to put pressure on the art magazines. They put an end to *Meishu sichao* in late 1987, and launched an official art magazine, entitled *Dazhong meishu bao* (Art of the Masses), which looked almost exactly like the influential *Zhongguo*

37—From the art education study catalogue *Quanguo meishuyuanxiao baokao zhinan*, Beijing: Renmin meishu chubanshe 1988, p. 159.

meishu bao. It was also printed on newsprint paper, and deliberately imitated its format and lay-out. Mailings and advertisements were sent to its subscribers in order to lead them to believe that their magazine had encountered political difficulties, and that *Dazhong meishu bao* was its successor.

The editors of *Zhongguo meishu bao* then brought the case before the court, and were judged to be in the right. *Dazhong meishu bao* had to retract its statements.[38] In spite of this victory, however, the distribution and sales of *Zhongguo meishu bao* became irregular in 1988, while *Dazhong meishu bao* was widely available, calling for the restoration of "a healthy Chinese art with national characteristics." In late 1989, publication of *Zhongguo meishu bao* stopped.

38—ZMB 1988, No. 25.

Thus, while the wave of activities in establishing "a genuine modern Chinese art" came to a halt, the need to define this concept as such became more urgent than ever, as a result of the growing knowledge about Western art, and the increased exposure to it. Shortly before the 1989 massacre and the subsequent political backlash, a major contribution to this end was made by the big retrospective exhibition of Chinese modern art of the period 1985–1989, entitled "China/Avant-Garde" (*Zhongguo xiandai yishu zhan*).

The Ideas Behind China/Avant-Garde 1989

The exhibition took place in early 1989, although preparations had already started in 1986. The fact that such an event could take place at all meant an enormous victory for the independent art circles over the official art world. About 300 works were exhibited, providing an overview of the Art Groups Movement of 1985–1987, although only works by artists between about 25 and 35 years of age were shown.

Some artists added lustre to the occasion by engaging in symbolic activities illustrating their views on art and society, which were not always appreciated by the authorities. Apart from Wu Shanzhuan's shrimp stall, there were also two participants who put the finishing touch to their works by firing a couple of revolver shots at them, as a result of which the exhibition was closed for a number of days.

The most active organizers of the exhibition were Gao Minglu, Peng De, and Li Xianting, who were also prolific writers and had come forward as "opinion leaders" of the avant-garde art world. Gao Minglu, as already stated, was editor of *Meishu*. Peng De (b. 1946) is Vice-Chairman of the Research Institute of the Hubei Province Chinese Artists' Association (*Hubeisheng wenlian lilun yanjiushi*), and co-founder and editor of the art journal *Meishu Sichao*. Li Xianting (b. 1950) is attached to the Chinese Art Research Institute in Beijing (*Zhongguo yishu yanjiuyuan meishu yanjiusuo*). He was editor of *Meishu* during the early 1980s, and co-founder and editor of *Zhongguo meishu bao* until its demise in 1989. He has published extensively in various art journals under different pen-names. In the Preface to the exhibition catalogue, Gao Minglu wrote:

> "The soul of modernism is modern consciousness, which is the self-awareness, and the new interpretation by modern man of his personal existence, his relation to the world, and the universe he lives in. This ideological revolution has led to the expansive techniques of modern art within culture: it has served as a matchmaker in bringing together many kinds of materials, and it has stimulated the fragmentary experiences in people's minds of society's culture and human history, into imagining and manufacturing fixed cultural images."[39]

39—"China/Avant-Garde" catalogue, Beijing: China Art Gallery 1989.

In 1988, Li Xianting had called upon artists to "follow the spirit of the times," instead of concentrating on esthetical or personal problems.[40] He did this in reaction to the rise in mid-1988 of a group in Hangzhou, calling itself "Academism" or "New Academism." This group opposed the tendency of the previous years to try to create art on the basis of philosophical programs, and favored renewed experiments with the artistic medium itself. Li rejected this proposal as a revival of "traditional isolationism."

40—ZMB 1988, No. 37, p. 1.

In his opinion, traditional landscape painting was the product of a passive, nostalgic mentality which fled from a confrontation with reality. The literati-painters, he stated, ignored

the confusion and unrest which had prevailed in Chinese society since the beginning of the century, and were not "honest" and "sincere" in their art.[41] Li stated that Chinese artists should develop a modern art of their own, by breaking away both from Western modern art, and traditional Chinese painting. Of the art in post-Mao China, he looked favorably upon the un-idealized landscape and figure paintings of the Sichuan School, and those paintings which showed the stark socio-psychological reality of contemporary Chinese society. He opined that art can only be important if it expresses the objectives of its time, and that the artist should "consider his own spirit as less important than the spirit of his time."
It seems that the organizers of "China/Avant-Garde" carefully chose the Chinese title of their exhibition ("Chinese modern art" instead of "modern Chinese art"), not only in order to forestall accusations of "Westernization," but also because some of them apparently felt that modern art in China should be viewed as an independent development next to international modern art, instead of being an integral part of it.
This attitude is, in fact, very widespread among Chinese artists and art critics. They generally seek for similarities in the works made by Chinese artists which can be called "typically Chinese," so that they can legitimately be said to occupy a special position in modern art.[42] Even many avant-garde artists feel the same nationalistic desire as the Chinese government to regard developments taking place in China as isolated from international trends. However, in the first two years following the 1989 Beijing massacre, they no longer had the possibility to conduct public debates and experiments going beyond the narrow official view on "Chinese art."

41—Similar criticisms of traditional Chinese painting were put forward by, e.g. the artist Zhang Jianjun, who stated that it was too yin, ("feminine, passive, yielding", as opposed to yang, the "male, active, outgoing" principle) to be able to convey emotions (Tao and Li 1988, p. 88); and by Ding Fang, editor of *Zhongguo meishu bao*, who wrote that, being ephemeral and graceful, it was unsuited to portray the tempestuous changes in contemporary China (from interviews with the author during 1987 and 1988).

42—Some Western art critics share this approach. See, for example, the catalogue accompanying the exhibition of modern Chinese art called *Art Chinois: Chine demain pour hier*, held in Pourriéres, France, in 1990, in which both French and Chinese art critics tried to demonstrate that modern art in China is essentially different from modern art elsewhere.

After the Massacre

Artists all over the country participated in the 1989 pro-democracy demonstrations. In Beijing, people marched under the banner of *Zhongguo meishu bao*, and the "no U-turn" traffic sign which was the symbol of the "China/Avant-Garde" exhibition held in February of that year. On 7 June, three days after the massacre, Zhang Peili and Geng Jianyi of the "Pond Society" displayed two enormous paintings of photographs showing victims killed by the army. The pictures measured 3×7 m each, and were placed on the Zhongan Qiao fly-over in the center of Hangzhou. In September, Zhang and Pei were interrogated by the police, but subsequently released.
After the massacre, innovative Chinese artists, if they did not move abroad, retired from the public arena for two years and continued to create art in the confinement of their studios.[43] There were no art exhibitions, and the art press cautiously maintained a low profile until late 1991. Following the closing down of *Meishu sichao* and the collapse of *Zhongguo meishu bao*, the remaining magazines *Meishu* and *Jiangsu huakan* ignored all art which could be associated with the pre-1989 innovations. This lasted for a year, until about mid-1990. Then, the art press started a large-scale attack on the 1985 Art Groups Movement which would also last for about a year, until mid-1991.
The magazine *Meishu* was filled with articles appealing to nationalistic sentiments and feelings of hurt national pride, including a number of vehement anti-Western tracts.
Wu Guanzhong, who had been an advocate of artistic liberalization ten years before, now stated that "China possesses the capacity and the artistic level to become the cultural center of the world."[44]
Ku Yuan, a teacher at the China Central Academy of Fine Arts, noting that the prices of Chinese paintings on the international art market were lower than those of Western paintings, wrote an article entitled "The People Are The Mother of The Cultural Workers," in which he suggested that there was "a deliberate attempt to humiliate our national art". At the end of the article, he pointed to the historic lesson of the Opium War, in order to call to mind the threat posed by the West to China's cultural and territorial integrity.[45]
In February 1991, *Meishu* published an article by Qian Haiyuan which denounced the 1985 Art Groups Movement on the basis of Mao Zedong's 1942 Yan'an speeches on art, and the motto of the post-1978 art policy, "Chinese learning for the essence, Western learning for practical use" (*Zhongxue wei ti, Xixue wei yong*, or *liang wei* for short).[46] Qian criticized the Movement on the following scores:

43—The following is based on my findings during my recent visits to China, in Winter 1991 and Spring 1992.

44—MS 1990, No. 9, p. 16.

45—MS 1990, No. 10, pp. 8/9.

46—For an extensive discussion of the relevant debates during the 1930s, see Petra Kolonko in "The Challenged National Identity. When Chinese Wanted to Become Westerners – The 'Debate on Total Westernization'", in *China 1934-1935*, No. 2 in the series East Asian Civilizations, Unkel/Rhein; Bad Honnef (Germany): Horlemann Verlag, 1983.

1. its anti-traditionalism, meaning the two-pronged reaction of the Movement against both traditional Chinese painting and socialist realism;
2. its tendency toward "total Westernization" (*quanpan xihua*), which was said to go against the government's *liang wei* policy[47];
3. its promotion of "bourgeois liberalism" by calling for "spiritual enlightenment," "the elevation of art above politics," as well as through its theory that there is a "generation gap" in the Chinese art world.

47—"Total Westernization" was a term coined by Hu Shi in the 1920s. For the subsequent debates on this radical approach and the more conservative liang wei compromise, see the source mentioned in the previous note.

Qian Haiyuan concluded that a detailed reassessment of the 1985 Art Groups Movement had to be made according to Marxist principles, in order to "return Chinese visual art to the right socialist track, and push it in the healthy *liang wei* direction".
However, attacks of this kind started to abate in mid-1991, and as of late 1991, the art magazines have again begun to allow themselves more latitude. New exhibitions have been organized, enabling artists to see each other's latest works. For example, the art historian Wang Liu from Chongqing organized an exhibition of photographs of the recent works of about 40 artists, entitled *Cailiao huazhan (*Exhibition of Materials), which traveled from Chongqing to Beijing and Nanjing in the second half of 1991. In Beijing and Shanghai, artists once again started to organize their own exhibitions. In July 1991, sixteen artists between 26 and 31 years of age displayed works showing various kinds of realism in the Beijing History Museum, under the title *Xin shengdai huazhan* (Exhibition of the New Generation).
Both exhibitions featured the kind of realistic works which are, in my opinion, typical for the post-1989 period. They reveal and sometimes caricaturize the stark reality of life in present-day China, often in reaction to the idealized images of official art. In this respect, they are reminiscent of earlier realist works, for example those of 1980, 1981 (Cheng Conglin et al.)[48], and 1985, 1986 (Zhang Peili and Geng Jianyi et al.). Both Zhang and Geng participated in the *Cheku zhanlan* (Garage Painting Exhibition) of November 1991 in Shanghai, together with about eight other artists. Generally speaking, the paintings on display there were of low quality, which was the main reason for the exhibition's failure. Another reason, in my opinion, was the fact that it fell back into the rhetorics of an earlier period, claiming that art could play a vanguard role in the transformation of society etc. Such high-sounding claims had already lost their credibility even before the massacre, and became even less credible afterwards.
Next to the revival of realism, there are new developments such as the work of Yu Youhan (b. 1943 in Shanghai), which caricaturizes the official political propaganda, and of Wang Guanyi (b. 1957 in Harbin), who makes paintings combining "Cultural Revolution" propaganda with Coca Cola and Nescafé advertisements. The 1989 massacre has, at least for the time being, put an end to the patriotic urge which pervaded the whole artistic atmosphere of the 1980s, to create a "Chinese modern art" which could contribute to the restoration of national self-confidence.

48—See Part I, pp. 31–32.

The Position of Modern Chinese Art

Apart from institutional and political factors, one of the impediments to its development throughout the 1980s has been the persistent idea, both on the part of Chinese and some Western critics, that Chinese modern art is a separate category outside the whole of international developments in modern art. It is still widely believed that "China and Chinese culture" is a closed, intact, and exotic entity standing quite apart from the rest of the world. As the late John K. Fairbank stated: "The unity of the Chinese world-within-a-world is like a religious faith".[49] As we have seen, writers such as Li Xiaoshan and Liang Jiang tried, in vain, to undermine this "faith" in 1985 and 1986.[50]
Michael Sullivan has described traditional Eastern culture as "an undifferentiated esthetic continuum," and traditional Western culture (with Europe as its historical center) as "a differentiated logical continuum."[51] By this, Sullivan means to say, in general although not absolute terms, that the Eastern mentality is intuitionistic and atheistic, and does not ascribe a special place to the human individual within the whole of nature and the

49—*The New York Times*, 24 November 1975, p. 35.

50—See Part I, pp. 40–43.

51—Michael Sullivan, *The Meeting of Eastern and Western Art*, revised edition, Berkeley/London: University of California Press 1989, p. 276.

cosmos, while the Western mentality is empiristic and theistic, and places the individual at the center of the world.

However, since the beginning of this century, the uniform "undifferentiated esthetic Continuum" no longer exists in China. It was put to an end by Chinese artists themselves. Admittedly, many Chinese artists still have common concerns, for example, in choosing subjects from their (increasingly incoherent) cultural environment, or in trying to define their own position in the "confrontation between East and West." However, in doing this, they take a critical and individualistic stance which was absent, or secondary, in Chinese art history up to the beginning of this century, and which places them squarely in the center of the modern art world.

Paradoxically, however, Chinese and Western art critics still try to locate their paintings within the frame-work of the "undifferentiated esthetical continuum of Eastern art" from which these artists have so successfully broken away. This is not only a paradox, but also denigrating toward the artist as a person: instead of evaluating his or her art as an individual achievement, it is regarded from the viewpoint of a collectivity, be it "nation" or "race." As we have seen, in the 1980s, even the most vocal representatives of the "avant-garde" held more or less nationalistic views in regard to modern art.

Both the practice of developing modern art, and its evaluation in the Chinese art press, have been bogged down by the, in my opinion, misdirected search for establishing "a national identity" in modern art. If the Chinese art world were to abandon this search, there would be more room for the Chinese artist to start developing her/his own individual artistic identity.[52] If the problem of "national identity" were to disappear from the artistic agenda, pluriformity would, moreover, no longer be a source of confusion and unease. Ironically, it seems that the isolated position of artists and theorists which followed the 1989 massacre and lasted about two years, has contributed to leading their attention away from narrow historical and ethnocentric concerns toward a more personal and individualistic artistic development. When the political pressure continues to decrease, it will be interesting to see whether the quest for a national artistic identity will be taken up again, or whether modern art in China will be able to break away from this narrow paradigm altogether.

52—Zhang Peili, for one, already stated in 1987 that he felt that he considered himself to be a modem artist in the first place, and only in the second place a Chinese citizen (personal interview). Reportedly, Gu Wenda, after five years in New York, now regards himself as an American citizen.

Bibliographical References Part I and II

Butterfield 1982: Fox Butterfield, *China Alive in the Bitter Sea*, New York: Bantam Books 1982

Cohen 1987: Joan Leopold Cohen, *The New Chinese Painting 1949–1986*, New York: Harry N. Abrams, Inc., 1987

Laing 1988: Ellen Johnston Laing, *The Winking Owl*, University of California Press, 1988

Tao and Li 1988: Tao Yongbai and Li Jianguo, *Zhongguo youhua 1700–1985* (Chinese Oil Painting 1700–1985), Nanjing: Jiangsu meishu chubanshe, 1988

Zhang Qiang 1988: Zhang Qiang, *Huihua xinchao* (New Tide of Painting), Nanjing: Jiangsu meishu chubanshe, 1988

Zhang and Li 1986: Zhang Shaoxia and Li Xiaoshan, *Zhongguo xiandai huihua shi*, Nanjing: Jiangsu meishu chubanshe, 1986

MS *Meishu* (monthly): Renmin meishu chubanshe, Beijing
JH *Jiangsu huakan* (monthly): Jiangsu meishu chubanshe, Nanjing
XMS *Xin meishu*, journal of the Zhejiang Academy of Fine Arts: Shanghai Renmin meishu chubanshe
MSSC *Meishu sichao*: Hubei meishu zhongxin, Wuhan
ZMB *Zhongguo meishubao*: Zhongguo yishu yanjiuyuan meishu yanjiusuo, Beijing

CHINA INFORMATION

Vol. VI, No. 4
(Spring 1992)

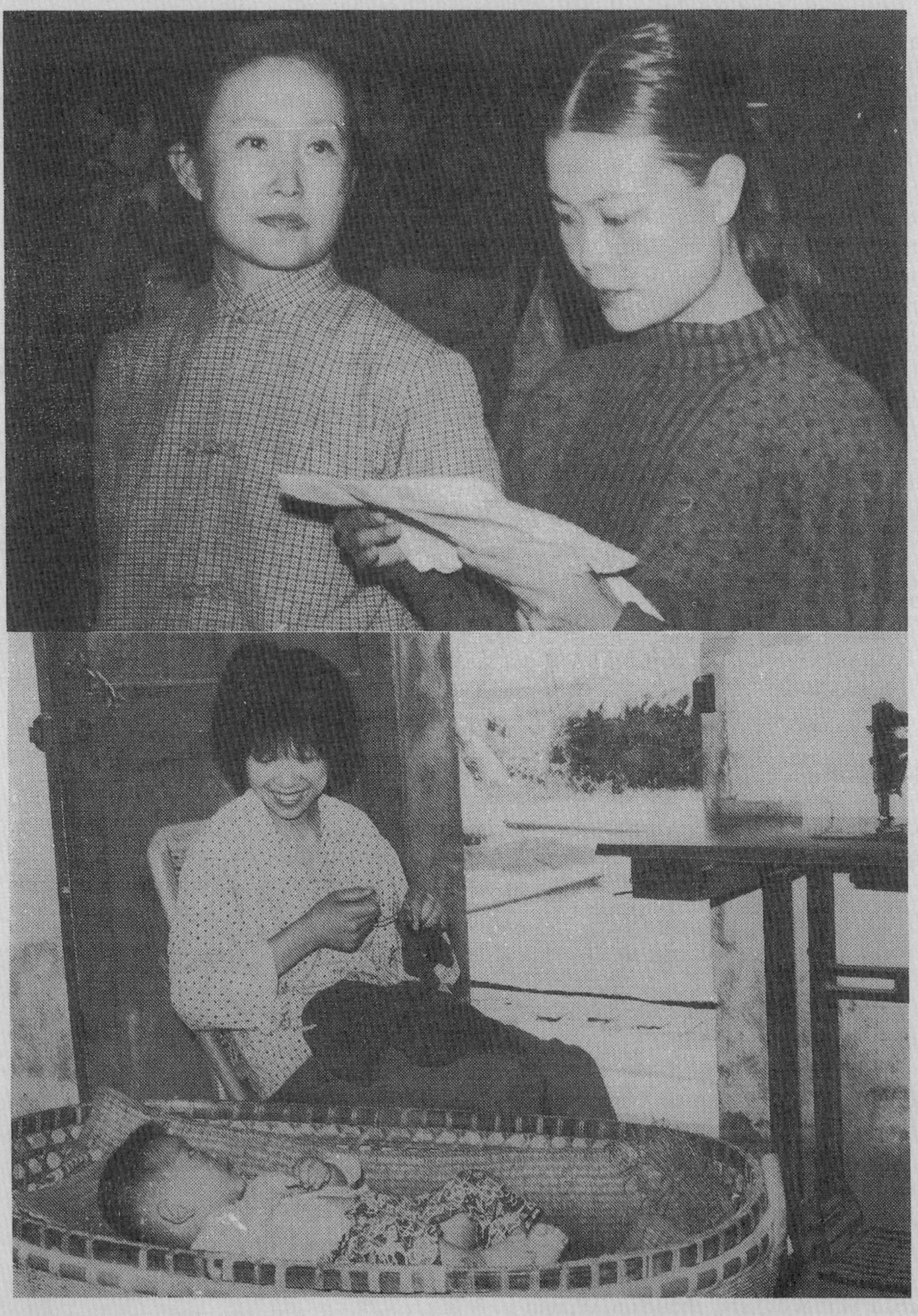

Published by:

The Documentation and Research Centre for Contemporary China, Leiden.

Opposite page: Cover of *China Information 6, no. 4 (Spring 1992)*, Leiden University, containing Hans van Dijk's *Painting in China after the Cultural Revolution: Style Developments and Theoretical Debates. Part II: 1985–1991*

Hans van Dijk
Projects 1993–2002

1993–1994
NAAC
Project overview:
- Organization of touring visits to the Chinese art world in Beijing, Shanghai, and Hangzhou for Jörg Immendorf (Hamburg), Günther Uecker (Düsseldorf), Andrew Solomon (*The New York Times*), Thomas Fuesser (*Der Stern*, Germany), 1993–94.
- Realization of the exhibition *Horst Janssen* in cooperation with the Goethe Institute, Beijing; Gallery of the International Cultural Palace, Wangfujing, Beijing, April 1994.
- *Zhao Bandi, Moonflight*, solo show, a contemporary art exhibition in cooperation with Hanmo Art Center, 26 June–26 July 1994, Hanmo Art Center, Beijing.
- Catalogue *Zhao Bandi, Moonflight*, published by NAAC, Beijing, 1994. Design: HvD. First use of the name NAAC, replacing the proposed "New Amsterdam Gallery" (NAG).
- Publ. Hans van Dijk, "Zhao Bandi's Lift-Off," in: *Hanmo Art Journal*, July 1994. Photo: Xu Zhiwei. Chin. translation: Zhang Li.
- Publication of the Ubu Roi Art Research Committee Report (URARC), NAAC, Beijing, August 1994.
- Selection of Chinese photographers in preparation for *Breda Fotografica*, a photo exhibition in the Netherlands, July–August 1994. Unrealized.
- Preparations for the dual exhibition of German artist Günther Uecker with the Chinese art group Xin Kedu (New Measurement Group), in cooperation with the Goethe Institute, Beijing, planned for 8 June–September 1994, at Hanmo Art Center, Beijing. Unrealized due to censorship. Seminars and lectures by Günther Uecker in cooperation with the art magazine *Jiangsu Art Monthly*, 17–30 September 1994. Press conference: poster design by HvD.
- Research and selection of artists for the *Metropolis Cultural Festival*, organized by the Goethe Institute, Beijing, fall 1994.
- Preparations for future exhibitions in cooperation with Hanmo Art Center and other locations in Beijing, including the *Series Installation* exhibitions of artists Li Yongbin, Gu Dexin, and Ni Haifeng. Unrealized.
- *Ding Yi, Abstract Art Exhibition*, Shanghai Art Museum, Shanghai, 13–17 October 1994. Catalogue: *Ding Yi*, publ. Shanghai Art Museum, New Amsterdam Art Consultancy, 1994.
- *Zhang Hai'er*, Song He Tang Pavilion, Ritan Park, Beijing, 7–18 December 1994. In cooperation with Red Gate Gallery, Beijing. Originally planned with the artists Zhang Yajie and Wang Yigang. Catalogue publ. NAAC and Red Gate Gallery, Beijing 1994.
- Las Meninas, an IT art project involving linking up China with the Netherlands and Belgium. With Bart Vanwalle, Ghent, Belgium, 1994–95, unrealized.

1995
NAAC
Project overview:
- Research and organizational work for *Förändring–Utveckling* (Change–Development), an exhibition dedicated to contemporary Chinese art, Konsthallen, Göteborg, Sweden, 31 January–12 March 1995; and Löns Museum, Jönköping, Sweden, June–August 1995. Artists: Ai Weiwei, Cai Jin, Ding Fang, Ding Yi, Hong Hao, Li Tianyuan, Liang Weizhong, Shi Cong, Sun Liang, Su Xinping, Yang Feiyun, Yu Youhan, Wei Dong, Zhang Enli, Zhang Hai'er, Zhao Shouqing, Zhou Jirong. Catalogue*: Bian Hua, 90-talskonst fran Beijing och Shanghai* (Change, artists from the 90s from Beijing and Shanghai), publ. Konsthallen Göteborg, 1995.
- *Xu Zhiwei, The Arts' Environment. Eighty photographs of artists in Beijing 1992–1994*, Ammonal Gallery, Beijing, planned 16–25 April 1995. Shut down by police on 15 April 1995.
- *Modern Chinese Art in the Goethe Institute*, Goethe Institute, Beijing, 21 May–21 July 1995. Artists: Ding Yi, Duan Jianyu, Li Tianyuan, Wu Xuefu, Zhang Hai'er, Zhao Bandi.

NAAC in cooperation with Neuer Berliner Kunstverein:
- *Brief an Peking/ Arbeit III* (Letter to Beijing/Work III); works by German installation artist Günther Uecker and the Chinese art group Xin Kedu (New Measurement Group), Neuer Berliner Kunstverein, Berlin, 2–16 July 1995.
- Catalogue: *Uecker – Brief an Peking. Gruppe Xin Kedu – Arbeit 3*, publ. Ostfildern, Cantz/ Neuer Berliner Kunstverein, 1995.
- Publication: *Die Arbeit III der Gruppe "Xin Kedu". Ein Dialog mit* Günther *Uecker, 23.6.–22.8. 1994* (the date is referring to the first planned exhibition in Beijing).
- *Geng Jianyi, Liu Anping, Action/ Solution*, an installa-

tion project at the Huashan Art School, Shanghai, summer 1995. Unrealized.

- Research and curatorial work for the exhibition *Configura 2 – Dialog der Kulturen* (Dialogue of cultures), Galerie am Fischmarkt and other locations in Erfurt, Germany, 17 June – 10 September 1995. Artists: Ai Weiwei, Duan Yingmei, Feng Mengbo, Geng Jianyi, Jiang Jie, Li Hongjun, Liu Wen, Liu Anping, Ni Haifeng, Wang Peng, Xin Kedu, Zhang Huan, Zhang Peili, Zhao Bandi. Catalogue: *Configura 2 – Dialog der Kulturen Erfurt 1995*, publ. the free state of Thüringen and the city of Erfurt, 1995, with texts by Jule Noth and Hans van Dijk. Xin Kedu, publication of their work: *Arbeit der Gruppe "Neuer Massstab" (4).*
- Hans van Dijk, publication of "The Myth of Art History" in *Jiangsu Art Monthly* 1995 no. 8, August, pp. 35–36.
- *Chen Yanyin & Jiang Jie*, Kvindemuseet Danmark (The Women's Museum in Denmark), Aarhus, 3 September – 2 October 1995. Catalogue: *Kvindelig Kinesisk Avantgarde* (Women of the Chinese Avant-Garde), *sculptures and installation by Chen Yanyin and Jiang Jie.* publ. the Women's Museum Denmark, Aarhus, 1995.
- Han Lei, *Alienation: 50 photographs by Han Lei*, Contemporary Art Gallery Beijing, 5–9 November 1995. Catalogue: foreword by Han Lei, design by HvD, publ. NAAC, Beijing, 1995.
- *Han Lei – Alienation, Fotografien aus China im Podewil,* 15 December 1995, Podewil, Berlin.
- Research and curatorial work for the exhibition *6. Triennale der Kleinplastik 1995. Europa – Ost Asien* (6th Triennial of small sculpture 1995, Europe – East Asia), Stuttgart Südwest LB Forum, Stuttgart, 14 October 1995 – 14 January 1996. Organized by the Institut für Auslandsbeziehungen (German Institute for Foreign Relations). Subsequently the exhibition traveled to Vienna, Taipei, Hong Kong, Seoul. Artists: Jiang Jie, Zhao Bandi, Gu Dexin, Ni Haifeng, Ai Weiwei.
- Catalogue: *6 Triennale Kleinplastik 1995, Europa – Ostasien*, publ. Trägerverein der 6. Triennale Stuttgart, Südwest-LB Forum, Cantz Verlag, 1995.
- *Xu Zhiwei, A New Light on Chinese Artists*, photographs of artists in Beijing by Xu Zhiwei, 9–13 December 1995, CIFA Gallery of the Central Academy of Fine Arts, Beijing. Postcard: design by HvD.

1996

NAAC
Project overview
CIFA Gallery

- Wang Xingwei, *The Dust of the Romantic History of Male Heroism*, 23–30 March 1996. Invitation card with photographs: design by HvD.
- *CanTonShangHai-BeiJing*, group exhibition, 2–16 April 1996. Participants: Zhang Hai'er, Hong Hao, Liu Ye, Ding Yi, Wu Xuefu, Duan Jianyu, Sun Kai. Invitation card: design by HvD. Expanded and prolonged until 24 April 1996. Announcement: design by HvD. Added artists: Han Lei, Lin Wen, Zhao Bandi, Jiang Jie, Li Yongbin.
- Zhou Tiehai, *Too Materilistic Too Spiritualized*, 26 April – 8 May 1996. Invitation card: design by HvD.
- Luo Yongjin, *Celebrations & Celebrities*, 10–22 May 1996. Invitation card: design by HvD.
- *CanTonShangHai-BeiJingHangZhou*, group exhibition, 24 May – 4 July 1996. Installations by Zhang Lei & Haiying, 6–9 July 1996. Invitation card: design by HvD.
- *CanTonShangHai-BeiJingHangZhou-LuoYang*, group exhibition, 11 July – 29 August 1996. Invitation card: design by HvD.
- Li Yongbin, *Video Art*, 30–31 August 1996. Invitation card: design by HvD.

Other projects
Overview

- *Xu Zhiwei, The Arts' Environment. Eighty photographs of artists in Beijing 1992–1994*, Agfa Gallery Hong Kong Art Center, 5–20 January 1996, sponsored by the Goethe Institute and NAAC. Catalogue: ed. Karen Smith, design HvD, publ. NAAC, Beijing, 1996.
- Research and organizational work for *Prospect 96. Photographie in der Gegenwartskunst* (Photography in Contemporary Art), Triennial of Contemporary Art, Kunsthalle Schirn, and Frankfurter Kunstverein, Frankfurt, 9 March – 12 May 1996. Artists: Liu Anping, Wang Youshen, Zhao Shaoruo. Catalogue: Schirn Kunsthalle Frankfurt, publ. Stemmler, Zürich, 1996.
- Assistance in realizing *3×3 On Paper, Three Generations of Flemish Artists*, Yan Huang Art Museum, Beijing, 31 May – 16 June 1996, in cooperation with Las Meninas.

Artists: Fred Bervoets, Leo Copers, Jan Cox, Karel Dierickx, René Heyvart, Roger Raveel, Philippe Vandenberg, Philip van Isacker, Dan van Severen. Patronage Frank Uytterhaegen. Catalogue. Invitation card: design HvD.
- Hans van Dijk, publication of "Art Theory is no Art" in *Jiangsu Art Monthly* 1996 no. 7, July.
- *China: Aktuelles aus 15 Ateliers* (China: News from 15 Studios), 14 June–21 July 1996, Reithalle/Alte Kaserne, Munich, in cooperation with Hahn Produktion and Artcircolo, Munich. Artists: Cai Jin, Chen Haiyan, Geng Jianyi, Han Lei, Guo Wei, Hong Hao, Hu Zhiying, Lin Yilin, Shen Xiaotong, Wang Gongyi, Wang Jin, Wang Xingwei, Xing Danwen, Xu Tan, Zeng Hao, Zhang Hai'er, Zhang Huan, Zhang Peili, Zhao Bandi. Catalogue: *China: Aktuelles aus 15 Ateliers*, publ. Hahn Produktion, Munich, 1996, with texts by Jule Noth and Hans van Dijk. When the exhibition ends, a selection of the works is shown at Littmann Kulturprojekte, Basel, and at Parco Square and Kirin Art Space, Tokyo, 1997.

1997

NAAC
Project overview
- *Face to Face*, a three-part exhibition series pairing German and Chinese artists, curated by Claudia Albrecht of the Siemens Kulturprogramm and Hans van Dijk. Part 1: *Face to Face, Luo Yongjin & Thomas Struth – Photography*, Art Gallery of the Beijing International Art Palace, Holiday Inn, Crowne Plaza, Beijing, 22 February–3 March 1997. Invitation card with photos Part 2, featuring *Ding Yi & Katharina Grosse*, and Part 3 featuring *Zhang Peili*, remain unrealized.
- Research for exhibitions of contemporary Chinese art at *ASIAN ART NOW!*, Asian Fine Arts Factory, Berlin. Artists: Ding Yi, Ji Wenyu, Li Hongjun, Li Jiwei.
- Research and organizational work for the exhibition *Zeitgenössische Fotokunst aus der Volksrepublik China* (Contemporary Art Photography from the People's Republic of China), Neuer Berliner Kunstverein, Berlin, 27 September–9 November 1997; Städtische Kunstsammlungen, Chemnitz, 17 January–8 March 1998; and Kunsthalle Darmstadt, 15 March–19 April 1998. Curated by Andreas Schmid. Artists: An Hong, Geng Jianyi, Gu Dexin, Liu Zheng, Lu Yuanmin, Mo Yi, Qiu Zhijie, So Hing Keung, Wong Wai-hung, Yang Zhenzhong, Zhang Hai'er, Zhao Liang, Zhao Shaoruo, Zheng Guogu, Zhuang Hui. Catalogue: publ. NBK, Berlin, and Edition Brauss, Heidelberg, 1997.
- *New Art Works from China*, Flanders Contemporary Art, Minnesota, USA, 1997, with Ding Yi.

1998

NAAC
Project overview
- Ding Yi dual exhibition: *Ding Yi: Crosses '89–'97*, Beijing International Art Palace, 11–14 January 1998. In cooperation with ShanghART Gallery. The latter organizes *Ding Yi Crosses '97* at the Shanghai Art Museum in 1997. Catalogue and twin invitation cards: design by HvD.
- *Mondrian in China – A Documentary Exhibition with Chinese Originals*, Beijing International Art Palace, 14–29 March 1998; New Library in Shanghai, 23 April–2 May 1998; Guangdong Museum of Art, Guangzhou, 16–24 May 1998. Curated by Hans van Dijk. In cooperation with the Royal Netherlands Embassy and the China International Exhibition Agency. Artists: Ding Yi, Liu Ye, Luo Qi, Mai Zhixiong, Yi Ling. Catalogue: *Mondrian in China – A Documentary Exhibition with Chinese Originals*, ed. Hu Fang and Zhang Wei, design Chen Tong and HvD, publ. the Dutch Ministry of Foreign Affairs no. 118. Invitation cards, exhibition leaflet: design by HvD.
- Zheng Guogu, *Sixteen of the Ten Thousand Customers and Other Works*, Beijing Photo Gallery, Beijing, 4–12 July 1998. Invitation card designed by the artist.
- Preparations and assistance for *Permeke, the famous artist from Flanders*, National Art Museum of China, Beijing, 25 November–15 December 1998; the Guan Shanyue Art Gallery, Shenzhen, 5–30 January 1999; Shanghai Museum, 25 February–28 March 1999. Organized by the China International Exhibition Agency and the Organizing Committee of the China Permeke Exhibition.
- Preparations for *Different Worlds – Photography from the People's Republic of China*, Provincial Museum for Modern Art (PMMK), Oostende, Belgium,

21 November 1998–10 January 1999. Artists: Li Guanyang, Wang Shilong, Wang Wenlan, Yang Limen, Yu Zhao, Yuan Ling, Zhang Qijun, Zhang Shenming, Feng Lei, Han Lei, Lu Nan, Zhang Hai'er, Zheng Nong, An Hong, Geng Jianyi, Gu Dexin, Hong Lei, Qiu Zhijie, Wang Jinsong, Wang Xingwei, Xu Ruotao, Zhang Dali, Zhao Bandi, Zhao Shaoruo, Zheng Guogu, Zhuang Hui. Unrealized.

1999

CAAW
Longzhaoshu, south Beijing and elsewhere
Project overview

- *Innovations Part I*, group exhibition, CAAW, south Beijing, 27 February–21 March 1999. Artists: Ding Yi, Wang Xingwei, Xie Nanxing, Zheng Guogu, Sun Kai, Zhang Hai'er, Ai Weiwei, Zhao Bandi, Mai Zhixiong, Hong Lei.
- Research and assistance for *Transformations: Painters Examine Change in China – Chen Weimin, Liu Yang, Su Xinping, Zhang Bin, Zhang Yizhi, and Posters from the Gu Zhenqing Collection*, Carleton College Art Gallery, Northfield, Minnesota, 5 April–9 May 1999. Catalogue.
- *Innovations Part II*, group exhibition, CAAW, south Beijing, 24 April–2 June 1999. Artists: Sui Jianguo, Lu Qing, Gu Dexin, Xu Hongming.
- *Concepts, Colors and Passions*, group exhibition, CAAW, south Beijing, 3 July–15 August 1999. Artists: Chen Shaoxiong, Zhao Bandi, Xie Nanxing, Ding Yi, Ai Weiwei, Meng Huang, Zheng Guogu.
- Assistance with *Hsin, a Visible Spirit: Contemporary Photography from the People's Republic of China*, Cypress College Gallery, Cypress, California, and BC Space Gallery, Laguna Beach, California, 23 August–24 September 1999. Artists: An Hong, Fang Zhong, Han Lei, Li Yuxiang, Lu Zhirong (RongRong), Sun Hongbin, Tang Xiaomei, Wang Mei, Wang Qiang, Wang Xingwei, Xie Wenyue, Yuan Dongping, Zhang Chaoying, Zhang Dali, Zhang Hai'er, Zhang Ou, Zheng Guogu. Booklet.
- Assistance with *Food for Thought: Chinese Contemporary Art*, De Witte Dame, Eindhoven, 21 November–20 December 1999. Curated by Martijn Kielstra and Nina Simone Bakker. Artists: An Hong, Feng Zhengjie, Feng Mengbo, Hu Xiangdong, Lin Tianmiao, Ni Haifeng, Ellen Pau, Qiu Zhijie, Shi Qing, Shi Yong, Xu Tan, Xu Zhen, Zhang Dali, Zhang Peili.
- *Duan Jianyu & Li Tianyuan – Recent Works*, CAAW, south Beijing, 30 October–26 December 1999.

2000

CAAW
Longzhaoshu, south Beijing and elsewhere
Project overview

- *Lost Paradise – Recent Works by Meng Huang*, CAAW, south Beijing, 8 January–8 March 2000.
- *Caught & Arranged, Photography*, 25 March–23 April 2000. Artists: Feng Qianyu, Han Lei, Hong Hao, Lu Qing, Yang Yong.
- *Arranged & Caught, Photography*, CAAW, south Beijing, 29 April–5 June 2000. Artists: Liu Xia, Wang Yiwu, Xu Xiaoyu, Zhao Hang, Zhou Meijun. Single invitation: design by HvD.
- Assistance with the realisation of *Beijing Shanghai Shenzhen: Cities of the 21st Century*, Bauhaus Dessau, Dessau, 20 May–23 July 2000. Artists: Han Lei, Zheng Guogu, and others. Book, Siemens Kulturprogramm & Bauhaus Dessau Foundation.
- Assistance with the realization of the "Thematic Area" of *EXPO 2000 Hannover*, Hannover, Germany, 1 June–31 October 2000. Artists: Lin Yilin, Chen Qingqing, Wang Jinsong, Wang Jin.
- Assistance with *The Sun Rises in the East: The Current Artistic Scene in Asia*, Rencontres internationales de la Photographie, Arles, France, 4 July–20 August 2000. Artists: Zheng Guogu, Zhou Meijun, Hong Lei, Gao Bo, and others.
- *Zheng Guogu: More Dimensional*, CAAW, south Beijing, 10 June–30 July 2000; and BizArt, Shanghai, 13 September–10 October 2000. In collaboration with BizArt Art Center. Invitation: design by HvD.
- *Short Report – New Works from Seven Young Artists*, CAAW, south Beijing, 5 August–10 September 2000. No data on the artists.
- *Ding Yi: Fluorescent Paint on Tartan*, CAAW, south Beijing, 17 September–29 October 2000.
- *Hsieh Tehching – One Year Performance*, CAAW, south Beijing, 20 November 2000. In collaboration with Davide Quadrio, BizArt Art Center, Shanghai.
- *Interim*, CAAW, south Beijing, 1–28 December 2000. Artists: Ding Yi, Li Tianyuan, Lu Qing, Wang Xingwei, Xu Xiaoyu, Zhang Hai'er, Zheng Guogu.

1999–2000
MCAF
Frank Uytterhaegen, Pascale Geulleaume, Hans van Dijk (curator)
Project overview
- *Modern Chinese Art Foundation Collection*, painting, sculpture, print work and photography, Caermersklooster, Provincial Center for Art and Culture, Ghent, Belgium, 12 November–5 December 1999. Curated by Hans van Dijk. Artists: Zhang Hai'er, Ai Weiwei, Zhou Yunxia, Hong Lei, Guo Wei, Gu Dexin, Geng Jianyi, Ding Yi, Zhang Yajie, Zhuang Hui, Zeng Hao, Zhao Bandi, Liu Anping, Hong Hao, Liu Wei, Wei Dong, Wang Xingwei, Zheng Guogu. Catalogue: *Modern Chinese Art Foundation*, ed. HvD, publ. Provincial Management East Flanders, Ghent 1999.
- *Portraits, Figures, Couples and Groups*, MCAF at BizArt, Shanghai, 8 November–4 December 2000. Curated by Hans van Dijk. Artists: Ai Weiwei, An Hong, Cang Xin, Chen Shaoxiong, Chen Xi, Guo Wei, Hai Bo, He Yunchang, Hong Hao, Huang Yan, Li Dafang, Li Zhanyang, Liu Anping, Liu Wei, Liu Xiaodong, Lu Zhirong (RongRong), Luo Brothers, Qi Zhilong, Qiu Zhijie, Shi Yong, Song Dong, Wang Jin, Wang Keping, Wang Qingsong, Wang Shilong, Wang Xingwei, Wang Yuping, Wei Dong, Xu Zhiwei, Xue Jiahui, Yang Shaobin, Yang Zhenzhong, Zhang Hai'er, Zhang Qijun, Zhang Yajie, Zhao Bandi, Zheng Guogu, Zhou Tiehai, Zhu Fadong, Zhuang Hui, Zhou Yunxia. Catalogue: *Portraits, Figures, Couples, Groups from the Collection of the Modern Chinese Art Foundation*, 2001, ed. HvD, publ. MCAF, Ghent, design: e-tion graphic design, Shanghai.

2001
CAAW
Caochangdi, Beijing
Project overview:
- *Inaugural Exhibition of the New Gallery*, CAAW, Caochangdi, Beijing, 1 January–17 February 2001. Artists: Lu Qing, Wang Xingwei, Xu Xiaoyu, Sun Kai, Xu Hongming, Meng Huang, Liu Ding, Cheng Li, Hong Lei, Zhang Enli, Zheng Guogu.
- *Yan Lei – International Scenery*, CAAW, Caochangdi, Beijing, 17 March–28 April 2001. 8 Postcards: design by HvD.
- *Human Scenery Four Views*, CAAW, Caochangdi, Beijing, 13 May–24 June 2001. Artists: Feng Feng, Ma Tiange, Wei Qingji, Duan Jianyu.
- *Wang Yin Recent Oil Paintings*, CAAW, Caochangdi, Beijing, 8 July–19 August 2001.
- *Visibility*, CAAW, Caochangdi, Beijing, 1–23 September 2001. Curated by Zhang Li. Artists: Bai Yiluo, Zhao Liang, He Yunchang, Xu Ruotao, Ma Han, Peng Donghui, Zhu Hongling.
- *Still Paint – Chen Danqing & Wang Xingwei*, CAAW, Caochangdi, Beijing, 28 September–28 October 2001.
- *Winter Show – The Four Seasons*, CAAW, Caochangdi, Beijing, 10 November 2001–March 2002 (dates unknown).

2002
CAAW
Caochangdi, Beijing,
Project overview:
- *Xu Hongming Works (1998–2001)*, CAAW, Caochangdi, Beijing, 10 March–14 April 2002. Curated by Hans van Dijk.
- *WXY*, CAAW, Caochangdi, Beijing, 27 April–14 May 2002. Curated by Ai Weiwei. Artists: Wang Yin, Wang Yonggang, Xiao Yu, Yang Maoyuan.
- *Sculptural Dialogue*, CAAW, Caochangdi, Beijing, 5 May–5 June 2002. Artists: Kristian Blystad, Bard Breivik, Sigurdur Gudmundsson, Li Gang, Shi Zhongyin, Wang Shugang.
- *Facing Reality*, location and date unknown. Artists: Wang Shilong, Han Lei, Zhang Hai'er.
- *Chinese Texture of the Soul – Hong Lei's Paintings, Photos and Installations*, CAAW, Caochangdi, Beijing, 20 July–20 August 2002. Curated by Liu Ding.
- *CUT IN*, CAAW, Caochangdi, Beijing. Curated by Ai Weiwei. Artists: He Yunchang, Yang Zhichao, Zhu Ming.
- *Meaningful Life*, CAAW, Caochangdi, Beijing, 28 September–15 October 2002. Curated by Ai Weiwei. Artists: Xu Yihui, Xu Ruotao, Yu Bogong.
- *Self-Talking*, TOM COM Art Channel, Photo Show Nominees, CAAW, Beijing, 19 October–5 November 2002. Curated by Wu Hong. Artists: Bai Yiluo, Jiang Zhi, Meng Jin, Sun Hongbin, Wang Xinyi, Weng Fen, Yang Qiang, Yang Yong, Yi De'er, Zheng Hongsheng, Zhu Handong, Zhu Jiangbo, Yan Jun.
- *Hai Bo Photography Exhibition*, CAAW, Caochangdi, Beijing, 9 November–5 December 2002.

Acknowledgements

UCCA, Witte de With, and Marianne Brouwer would like to express their gratitude toward the following persons and institutions whose contributions to the project were invaluable:

Ai Weiwei
An Hong
Cang Xin
Chen Shaoxiong
Chen Shaoping
Ding Yi
Duan Jianyu
Feng Mengbo
Thomas Fuesser
Geng Jianyi
Gu Dexin
Hai Bo
Han Lei
Hong Hao
Hong Lei
Huang Yong Ping
Li Yongbin
Liang Juhui & Yu Guoqing
Lin Yilin
Liu Anping
Liu Ding
Liu Ye
Luo Yongjin
Meng Huang
Mai Zhixiong & Zhao Lelin
Ni Haifeng
Qiu Zhijie
RongRong
Shi Yong
Sun Kai
Tang Song
Wang Guangyi
Wang Jinsong
Wang Luyan
Wang Xingwei
Wang Yin
Wu Shanzhuan
Wang Shilong
Xu Tan
Xu Hongming
Xu Zhiwei
Yan Lei
Yu Youhan
Zhang Enli
Zhang Hai'er
Zhang Peili
Zhao Bandi
Zhao Liang
Zhao Shaoruo & Annie Cui
Zheng Guogu
Zhou Tiehai
Zhu Fadong
Zhuang Hui

Robert Bernell
Ria van Boekholt
Waling Boers
Josien Brenneker
Chen Tong
Jean-Marc Decrop
Dong Shuo
Peter Cox
Monica Dematté
Jan van Dijk
Pieter van Dijk
Raven van Dijk
Ronald van Dijk & Effie Ferdinandus
Ernst Dinkla
Egbert Dommering
Britta Erickson
Albert Groot
Guan Yi
Fiona He
Lorenz Helbling
Cees Hendrikse
Victoria & Henk de Heus-Zomer
J.V.M Holthuis
Effy Iwen Hong
Claire Hsu
Hu Fang
Rose Jiang Wei
Jeannette ten Kate
Martijn Kielstra
Monique Kies
Erika Kiffl
Venus Lau
Joanna Lee
Leng Lin
Li Xianting
Carol Lu
Urs Meile
Annemarie Montulet
Henny van Nistelrooy
Magnus Nordenhaake
Jochen Noth
Jule Noth
Pan Yan
Robin Peckham
Pi Li
Davide Quadrio
Margo Renisio
Andreas Schmid
Rob Schröder
Karen Smith
Andrew Solomon
André Straatman
Su Wei
Sun Hongbin
Tang Di
Jérémie Thircuir
Laura Trombardi
Frank Uytterhaegen & Pascale Geulleaume
Jeroen Vinken
Xie Wenyue
Ian Yang
Pauline Yao
Anthony Yung
Zhang Li
Zhang Wei

Asia Art Archives
NAAC/CAAW Archives
Boers-Li Gallery
Canvas International Art
Collectie G+W Nederland
Collectie de Heus-Zomer
DSM Art Collection
East Asian Library—Leiden University Libraries
Embassy of the Kingdom of the Netherlands in Beijing
Groeninghe Foundation
okamoto deguchi & odd design beijing
ShanghART Gallery
Sinopia East Asia Fine Arts Collection
Vitamin Creative Space
Walker Art Center

And those who wish to remain anonymous

AMMODO
Mondriaan Fund

Colophon

This publication follows the exhibitions *Hans van Dijk: 5000 Names* (Ullens Center for Contemporary Art, Beijing, 24 May–10 August 2014) and *Dai Hanzhi: 5000 Artists* (Witte de With Center for Contemporary Art, Rotterdam, 4 September 2014–4 January 2015), both curated by Marianne Brouwer and developed together with Defne Ayas (Director, Witte de With, 2012–2017), Philip Tinari (Director, UCCA), and Samuel Saelemakers (Curator, Witte de With).

Author
  Marianne Brouwer
Editor
  Samuel Saelemakers
Associate Editor
  Patrick Rhine
Publication Coordinator
  Maria-Louiza Ouranou
Design
  Kristin Metho
Print
  Epopee
Publishers
  Witte de With Center for Contemporary Art, Rotterdam;
  Ullens Center for Contemporary Art, Beijing

Cover image: Thomas Fuesser, *Hans van Dijk (Beijing 1993)*, 1993
© Thomas Fuesser

Overleaf: Hans van Dijk, *Johnny Dai*, vignette of his own name, one of three, digital file, 2002, coll. van Dijk family

ISBN 978-94-91435-51-5

Supported by

A
O M
D M
O

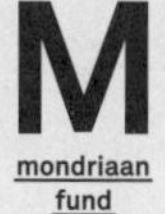

Witte de With Center for Contemporary Art is supported by the city of Rotterdam and the Ministry of Education, Culture and Science.

Distribution

This book is available at Witte de With, and via the following distributors:

Cornerhouse, Manchester
(UK and Ireland only)
Online catalogue:
www.cornerhouse.org
publications@cornerhouse.org
T +44 161 200 1503

Idea Books, Amsterdam
(The Netherlands and all other countries, except the Americas)
Online catalogue:
www.ideabooks.nl
idea@ideabooks.nl
T +31 (0)20 622 61 54

D.A.P., New York (U.S.A. only)
Online catalogue:
www.artbook.com
dap@dapinc.com
T +1 212 627 1999

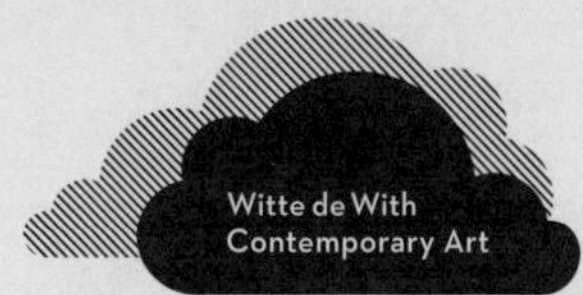

UCCA
Ullens Center for
Contemporary Art
尤伦斯当代艺术中心

戴志汉

J o h n n y

***D** a i*